INVESTING IN BANKRUPTCIES
AND TURNAROUNDS

INVESTING IN BANKRUPTCIES AND TURNAROUNDS

SPOTTING INVESTMENT VALUES
IN DISTRESSED BUSINESSES

SUMNER N. LEVINE
State University of New York
Stony Brook, NY

HarperBusiness

A Division of HarperCollins*Publishers*

International Standard Book Number: 0-88730-459-1

Library of Congress Catalog Card Number: 90–25047

Printed in the United States of America

Library of Congress Cataloging-in-Publication Data

Handbook of turnaround and bankruptcy investing / [edited] by Sumner
  Levine.
    p.   cm.
   Includes bibliographical references and index.
   ISBN 0-88730-459-1
   1. Bonds—United States.   2. Securities—United States.
3. Corporate debt—United States.   4. Bankruptcy—United States.
5. Corporations—United States—Finance.   6. Corporate turnarounds—
United States.   I. Levine, Sumner N.
HG4963.H36   1991
332.63'234–dc20   90–25047
                                         CIP

91 92 93 94 PS/HC 9 8 7 6 5 4 3 2 1

CONTENTS ═══════════════════════

PREFACE

This book is intended for both individual and institutional investors interested in exploring opportunities in distressed companies. The basic assumption underlying investor interest is that the security prices of such companies are near their lows, thereby providing the opportunity of realizing substantial gains if recovery or reorganization is successful. Typically, investors hope to achieve returns of 20 percent to 30 percent per year.

In organizing this book, an effort was made to provide readers with a fairly broad overview of the subject. Included are discussions of techniques for predicting bankruptcies and turnarounds, bond default rates, approaches for evaluating distressed credits and equities, and much more.

An understanding of the legal issues involved is important to investors in bankruptcies since returns will depend on the outcome of the chapter 11 bankruptcy process. Hence, a survey of the chapter 11 bankruptcy process is also included. This, along with several case studies included here, should provide investors with some appreciation of the relevant issues and risks associated with bankruptcy proceedings.

While most investors will probably assume a passive role, others may seek operational control of the distressed company. Several chapters have been included which address the interest of the latter investor.

Finally, I wish to express my gratitude to a superb group of contributors whose expertise and effort made this book possible. My special thanks are extended to my wife Caroline, without whose publishing experience and persistence this book would not have seen the light of day.

SUMNER N. LEVINE

CONTRIBUTORS

Jay Alix is the founder of Jay Alix Associates, Southfield, Michigan, specializing in turnaround management. He is a CPA and holds a Bachelors degree in Finance from the Wharton School, University of Pennsylvania, and an MBA from Rutgers University.

Edward I. Altman is the Max L. Heine Professor of Finance at the Stern School of Business, New York University. He is the recipient of several awards and the author of numerous books on bankruptcy and default rates.

Jeffrey Bagner is with Fried, Frank, Harris, Shriver, & Jacobson in New York. He is a graduate of New York University and holds a JD from the Columbia University Law School.

Richard Bookstaber is a principal at Morgan Stanley & Co. Prior to his current position, he was on the faculty of Brigham Young University. He received a BA from Brigham Young and a Ph.D. from MIT.

David J. Breazzano is President of the T. Rowe Price Recovery Fund. Prior to his present position, he was a Vice president at the First Investors Asset Management. He earned a BA from Union College and an MBA from Cornell University.

William A. Cornish, CFA, is President of Duff and Phelps Credit Rating Co., Chicago. Mr. Cornish received a BS from Yale and an MBA from Harvard.

Martin Fridson, CFA, is Managing Director of High Yield Research at Merrill Lynch Pierce Fenner & Smith, Inc. He is a graduate of the Harvard Business School.

Steven I. Hochberg is an Associate Director with Sigoloff & Associates and an Associate Director of the Turnaround Management Association. He is a graduate of the University of Michigan and holds an MBA from Harvard University.

David P. Jacob is Director of Research at J.P. Morgan Securities, Inc. He was previously affiliated with Morgan Stanley. He earned a BA from Queens College, City University of New York and an MBA from New York University Graduate School of Business Administration.

Peter S. Kaufman is a partner in the Gordian Group, a New York merchant bank specializing in troubled companies. He was a former Vice President of the First Boston Corporation. He holds a BA degree from Yale and JD from University of Virginia School of Law.

Robert Levine is currently a Vice President with Nomura Securities International, New York. Previously he was a Managing Director at Kidder

Peabody. He earned an MBA from the Wharton School of Finance and an undergraduate degree from City College of New York. He is also a CFA.

Sumner N. Levine has been on the Faculty of the State University of New York at Stony Brook. He has contributed and edited numerous publications on finance and allied subjects. He is also Director of Nortech Associates which specializes in the biomedical industries.

John Lonski is an Assistant Vice President and Senior Economist at Moody's Investors Service. Previously he was employed by the National Economic Research Association. He was awarded a BS from Rensselaer Polytechnic Institute and an MA from Michigan State University.

Douglas Lucas is with Moody's Structured Finance Group. He graduated from UCLA and received an MBA from the University of Chicago.

Thomas Moers Mayer is affiliated with Robinson, Silverman, Pearce, Aronsohn and Berman, New York. He is a graduate of Dartmouth College and the Harvard Law School.

William L. Norton, Jr. is managing partner in the law firm of Norton, Pennington in Atlanta. Previously he had served as Bankruptcy Judge for the Northern District of Georgia. He is author and editor of *Norton Bankruptcy Law and Practice,* among other publications. He is president of the American Bankruptcy Institute.

John R. O'Neill is a Tax Partner in the New York office of Arthur Andersen & Co.

David B. Post is currently with Arthur Anderson & Co., Altanta, Georgia. He was previously Executive Director of the Turnaround Management Association. He is a CPA, received a BS in Business Administration from the University of North Carolina and a JD from Duke University Law School.

George Putnam, III is Editor and Publisher of the *Bankruptcy Data Source* and the *Turnaround Letter.* Previously he was a member of the law firm of Dechert, Price, & Rhoads. He graduated from the joint JD-MBA programs at Harvard University.

Ronald G. Quintero, CFA, is a principal in R.G. Quintero & Co., New York, specializing in turnaround bankruptcies. Previously he was with the Financial Restructuring Group of Bear Stearns & Co. He is a graduate of Lafayette College and earned in MS an Accounting at the New York University Graduate School of Business Administration. He is also a CPA.

William J. Rochelle III is with Fulbright Jaworski & Reavis McGrath (New York), where he specializes in bankruptcy and corporate reorganizations. He received his BA and JD from Columbia University.

Paul F. Sheahan is a Tax Manager with the New York office of Arthur Andersen & Co.

Robert H. Siegler is with Ladenburg, Thalmann & Co., Inc. Previously he was a Managing Director with Bear Stearns & Co. He has an MBA from the University of Chicago and a BA in Economics from the University of Rochester.

Mike Singer is President and Director of Research at R.D. Smith & Company (New York), a firm specializing in distressed companies. Prior to joining his current employer, he was Senior Vice President at Jefferies & Company, and Manager of Corporate Finance at First Boston. Mike has a BA from Columbia University and a BS in Chemical Engineering from University College London.

Rose H. Staples is with the law firm of Norton Pennington. Previously she was a partner in Staples and Staples. She is a graduate of the Emory University School of Law, and a member of the American Bankruptcy Institute.

Roger D. Timpson is a member of R.G. Quintero & Co. Prior to his present affiliation, he was Chief Financial Officer of Environmental Techtonics. He has a B.S. from Rennselaer Polytechnic Institute and an MBA from George Washington University.

Jeffrey I. Werbalowsky is with Houlihan, Lokey & Zukin Capital and is Managing Director of the Financial Restructuring Group. He was previously Chief Executive Officer of Cheviot Capital Corp. He earned a BA from the University of Virginia and a JD from the Columbia University Law School.

Martin J. Whitman, CFA, is a principal in the firm of Whitman, Heffernan and Rhein. He holds a Bachelors Degree from Syracuse University and a Masters Degree from Princeton.

Investing in Distressed Situations: An Overview

Sumner N. Levine
State University of New York

This chapter briefly reviews several common approaches to investing in distressed firms, specifically:

1. Investing in the securities of firms that are expected to avoid bankruptcy and all its uncertainties (prebankruptcy investing)
2. Investing in the debt of firms that are in chapter 11 bankruptcy and are expected to emerge reorganized
3. Purchasing a bankrupt firm with the intent of participating in the management

Needless to say, the time, effort, and risk are substantially greater for the third approach than for the two preceding ones.

Before proceeding, a word or two about the usage of the term "distressed security" in the present context: as employed here, the term refers to securities (equities or debt) of firms that either are in chapter 11 bankruptcy or are experiencing problems that are threatening to force them into bankruptcy or liquidation. Usually the problems are operationally or financially related. Some firms, such as Manville or Texaco, have filed for chapter 11 bankruptcy as a legal maneuver, but these are exceptions.

Returns from Distressed Securities

Customarily, equity investors have focused on growth situations or profitable companies deemed to be undervalued. Bond buyers have traditionally been insistent on the financial soundness of the issuer. Why, then, this interest in floundering, often debt-ridden, companies? The answer

1

Table 1.1. Annualized Returns of Firms after Chapter 11 Filing, 1979–83

Firm	Stock Return (%)	Mutual Shares* (%)	Holding Period (Months)
Advent (R)	-76.6	-13.0	13
Airlift International	-24.0	4.4	30
Allied Technology (R)	-19.3	10.7	18
American International	82.8	10.8	29
Arctic Enterprises (R)	348.0	7.2	10
Autotrain (L)	-41.1	0.4	29
Bobbie Brooks (R)	30.5	12.0	13
Colonial Commercial (R)	72.0	3.4	25
Combustion Equipment (R)	-25.0	4.1	47
Computer Communication (R)	-10.2	0.7	33
Data Dimension (R)	120.0	8.7	22
Empire Oil (L)	-100.0	34.0	12
Fashion Two-Twenty (R)	-44.0	-17.3	9
FSC	19.9	6.5	26
Gamex (R)	111.3	26.7	18
Goldblatt Brothers (R)	48.8	8.3	29
Good L. S. (R)	-37.5	2.6	32
HRT	48.9	15.7	13
Inforex (R)	-5.5	15.3	11
Itel (R)	254.6	8.7	33
Keydata (R)	-12.5	-8.5	24
Lafayette Radio (R)	-8.7	3.3	18
Lawhorn (R)	-30.0	-8.0	12
Lionel	32.0	19.4	21
Lynnwear (R)	-6.5	1.0	24
Manville	30.0	2.5	22
Mays (R)	39.8	16.9	23
McLouth Steel (R)	-38.1	3.7	16
Med Pak (L)	-50.0	3.5	24
National Shoes	69.3	3.3	36
NuCorp	-40.2	25.4	17
Penn Dixie (R)	0.0	6.3	21
Revere Ware	12.0	17.1	14
Richton International (R)	3.0	3.0	20
Rusco (R)	120.0	25.6	15
SBE (R)	20.0	14.0	12
Sam Solomon (R)	177.5	2.7	24
Sambos	81.5	5.5	9
Saxon	-12.0	14.9	21
Scatrain	14.6	4.4	33

(*continued*)

Table 1.1.   (cont.)

Firm	Stock Return (%)	Mutual Shares* (%)	Holding Period (Months)
Shelter Resources	-13.6	20.8	15
Stevcoknit (R)	131.3	5.7	17
South Atlantic	73.6	21.6	15
Tenna (L)	-33.3	-0.3	36
Topps and Trowsers (R)	70.4	14.4	15
Unishelter	-80.8	-7.2	15
UNR	105.9	-14.0	17
Upson	2.3	-3.7	42
Van Wyck (R)	57.1	10.3	29
Wickes	29.1	-22.1	19
Average	28.0	8.5	21.5
Average Annualized S&P 500		15.8	

Note: (R) indicates that a firm was reorganized, while (L) indicates that the firm's assets were liquidated. Twenty seven firms were reorganized as of December 31, 1983. Some firms had not finished reorganization by December 31, 1983. Their holding period returns were calculated as of December 31, 1983.

* Returns over same holding period as stock; for comparability, returns have been annualized.

SOURCE: S. E. Moeller, *AAII Journal* (American Association of Individual Investors, Chicago, IL 60611) April 1986, pp. 9–12.

seems to be the feeling that greater returns can be achieved (presumably for the risk undertaken) with relatively neglected distressed issues than in the more visible and more efficient segments of the financial market. Whatever the reason, it is certainly true that astonishing returns have been realized.

Chrysler, which was on the verge of bankruptcy (but which never filed), had its stock appreciate from under $3 a share in 1982 to a high of $48 in 1987, corresponding to an annual compounded rate of return of about 74 percent. Toys 'R' Us, which emerged from the bankruptcy of Interstate Stores with the stock selling at only a few cents a share, experienced an appreciation to $48 a share. Holders of junk bonds (low rated bonds) have also fared well, receiving an average compounded annual return of 25–30 percent in recent years.

Table 1.1 shows the return realized for stocks purchased after chapter 11 bankruptcy and held until the companies were reorganized, acquired, or liquidated. Also shown, as a basis of comparison, are the corresponding transactions of Mutual shares, a well-known fund investing in distressed

Table 1.2.   Target and Minimum Rates of Return on Distressed Security Investing (based on 48 respondents)

Target Rate of Return	Respondents Number	Percent	Minimum Rate of Return	Respondents Number	Percent
<20%	0	0%	<20%	2	4%
20	4	8	20	15	31
25	11	23	25	16	33
30	16	33	30	10	20
35	5	10	35	4	8
40	9	18	40	2	4
>40	4	8	>40	0	0
Total	49	100%	49	47	100

SOURCE: Edward I. Atman "Investing In Distressed Securities," Stern School Business, New York University (1990).

situations. The results show that holding a portfolio over the indicated period resulted in gains greater than the S&P and Mutual Shares. Figure 3 shows that, after bankruptcy, returns tend to be greater for the larger companies traded on the New York Stock Exchange.

However, as a glance at Table 1.1 also shows, investors can experience substantial losses with distressed securities. This is not an area for the naive investor. Success in this area requires substantial financial skills and, for those venturing into bankruptcy situations, an understanding of the processes and risks involved with chapter 11. Patience is another trait essential for investors in distressed securities. As shown in Table 1.1, the average chapter 11 proceeding takes 21.5 months, but specific situations may take much longer. Toys 'R' Us took four years to emerge from bankruptcy. Penn Central, another very successful investment, took eight years to emerge.

As compensation for the risks involved, the targeted range of return expected by investors falls mostly in the range of 25 to 30 percent per annum, as shown in Table 1.2, based on the survey of 48 distressed security investors made by Altman. Risk reduction requires careful selection of securities and diversification among at least 10 different issues.

The Prebankruptcy Portfolio

Securities suitable for prebankruptcy portfolios are those of distressed companies that are judged to have a high probability of turning around. Intelligent selection requires an understanding of the causes of a firm's distress, the steps required to remedy the problems, and an estimate of the earnings potential of the restored company. The determinations to be made are as follows:

Nature of the Business

With the aid of annual reports, SEC filings, Moody's and S&P directories, and the like, a good deal of information can be readily assembled concerning the business of a publicly traded company. Items of interest include: the growth rate and competitive situation of the industry, earnings growth, return on equity, debt structure, ratio of cash flow to fixed charges, maturity date of major loans, and any pending major legal suits.

Nature of the Problem

With the above information assembled, the investor hopes to be able to diagnose the cause of the distress. Is the situation due to a nonviable core business, poor management, excessive debt, an isolated incident of bad luck, government regulations, a distressed economy, labor problems, or legal problems?

Salvageability of the Situation

The crucial issue before the prebankruptcy investor is the likelihood that the company's difficulty can be resolved and a turnaround achieved within the investor's time horizon. Until there are definite indications that the firm will be able to cope with the basic problems and turn the situation around, it is advisable for investors to hold back on any major commitment. All too frequently, firms flounder for a few years and then succumb. It is therefore essential to be alert to relevant developments. Are there signs that a burdensome debt is being reduced or refinanced? News of a new product, a joint venture? New management? A more favorable labor contract, an improvement in the economy? It is also helpful to monitor insider sales or purchases of stock for evidence of upcoming changes. An increase in stock prices accompanied by increased volume may be an early indicator that something is afoot.

Other helpful indicators of a potential turnaround, notably Altman's Z-score, are presented in Chapter 2. The insightful chapters by Quintero and Timpson (Chapter 13) and Putnam (Chapter 9) provide additional guidelines.

Expected Returns

It is worthwhile estimating whether the expected returns will meet the investor's target rate, assuming that a turnaround occurs. Space does not permit a detailed discussion, so only the essentials will be given. With equities, the market price of the stock can be estimated from the product of a representative industry P/E ratio and an earnings estimate based on examining predistress earnings performance or sales and profit margins. Using the current price of the stock, the projected price, and the holding period, the internal rate of return can be calculated by the usual methods.

With bonds, the internal rate can be estimated from the holding period, coupon rate, current price, and projected price. The latter can be estimated by assuming that the bond is upgraded on turnaround to provide a return equal to the next higher bond rating category (say, from B to BB) of bonds with similar characteristics.

Bankruptcy Investing

Readers unfamiliar with chapter 11 bankruptcy will find the discussion in Chapter 12 helpful. Essentially, companies can emerge from bankruptcy by reorganization, liquidation, or acquisition. Bankruptcy investors seek investments that will meet or exceed their target rate in companies that will be reorganized (thereby avoiding liquidation).

In a recent study of reorganization, Ramaswami and Moeller (1990) found that the probability increases with the size of the firm's unencumbered assets and the relative growth rate of the industry, but decreases with rising long-term interest rates that occur during the bankruptcy period. Also of interest are the data given in Table 1.3 which indicate the number of bankrupt firms returning more than Mutual Shares, one of the best managed mutual funds investing in distressed firms. As shown, most firms providing greater returns, before failing, traded on the NYSE and were of large size.

The investor in chapter 11 also has to consider the following issues:

1. The causes of the bankruptcy and the likelihood of reorganization
2. What securities are available (secured debt, unsecured debt, stock, etc.) and the level of risk exposure and return for each
3. When the investment should be made

A major consideration bearing on the type of investment is that of the claims priority discussed in chapter 11. Essentially, the claims priority determines the order in which security holders get paid off on reorganization, as shown in the following, with the claims of a given security taking precedence over those below:

1. Super priority claims (debt of lender to the bankrupt firm)
2. Secured debt
3. Priority claims (professional fees associated with the bankruptcy, trade debt, certain claims for wages, etc.)
4. Senior unsecured debt
5. Subordinated unsecured debt
6. Preferred stock
7. Common stock

As shown, the claims of the secured debt holders are met first, while those of the common stock holders are the last to be satisfied. Among the uncertainties of the bankruptcy process is the possibility that a secured claim filed within 90 days of bankruptcy may be deemed a preference (see glossary) and relegated to an unsecured claim.

Table 1.3. Characteristics of Firms Different from Mutual Shares

	Number of firms earning more than Mutual Shares	Number of firms earning less than Mutual Shares
Listing		
New York Stock Exchange	13	4
American Stock Exchange	5	7
Over-the-counter	7	14
Size		
Over $100 million	11	6
$25-$100 million	9	9
Under $25 million	5	10

SOURCE: S.E. Moeller, *AAII Journal*, April 1986.

Secured Debt Investments

Secured debt has a lien (or claim) on specific property such as real estate or inventories. The lien is retained even if the property is transferred to another corporation. This secured interest creates a first right to the proceeds derived from the sale of the specified property. If the face value of the secured loan (generally in the form of a bond) exceeds the payment from the sales of the secured property, the difference is considered an unsecured loan. Thus, if the bond has a face value of $100,000, but the sales proceeds are $80,000, then the remaining $20,000 is considered an unsecured loan. When the market value of the property securing the loan covers the amount of the loan, the loan is considered fully secured; otherwise, the loan is undersecured.

In addition to a degree of safety to principal provided by fully secured debt, such debt, unlike unsecured debt, is entitled to interest payments on the loan due during the bankruptcy process (post-petition interest).

Among the key issues the secured bond investor must address are the following:

1. Which assets secure the debt?
2. What is a realistic appraisal of the market value of the assets?
3. How long would it take to sell the assets?
4. Which protective covenants are provided in the bond?

Information pertaining to the above is available in the files of the bankruptcy court hearing the case and in SEC disclosures. Estimates of the market value of specific assets can be provided by commercial real estate agents and by business appraisers, a listing of which is available from the American Society of Appraisers (Washington, D.C.).

On reorganization, secured lenders are usually paid in cash for the full amount of the debt, though sometimes combinations of cash with some new debt and new equity are provided. It is worth noting that the most the secured debt holder can receive is the face value of the bond plus post-petition interest.

The return is usually greater when the investor takes a position early in bankruptcy. An investor may do so if he is confident of the value of the assets securing the debt and that the outcome will be reorganization rather than liquidation. Often when assets are liquidated under duress, they receive substantially less than originally estimated.

Unsecured Debt Investments

Unsecured debt is not backed by collateral and consists largely of long- and medium-term notes and debentures (unsecured bonds). Unsecured notes are categorized as senior and subordinated (junior) with the claims of the latter taking a position after the former on liquidation or reorganization.

The return to the unsecured debt holder is much less certain than that to the secured debt holder. Generally, on reorganization, the unsecured debt receives a combination of new notes, equity, and possibly some cash. Often the unsecured debt holders receive enough stock to become the major stock holders. On liquidation, the unsecured holder may receive next to nothing. Because of the uncertainties as to what will be awarded on reorganization, the prudent course for the unsecured investor is to wait until the shape of the proposed reorganization begins to emerge and more information becomes available.

Stock Investments in Bankruptcies

Common stocks are on the lowest rung of the priority ladder and as such usually receive nothing on liquidation. On reorganization, the original stock (old stock) is often substantially diluted (known as a reverse split) by an issuance of new stock in the reorganized company. Dilution may consist, for example, of an exchange of one share of new stock in the reorganized company for 20 shares of old stock. When Sambo's reorganized, old stock holders had to exchange 125 shares of stock for each share of new stock.

Investors who purchase old stock of a company in distress before the company files for bankruptcy and who hold the stock during bankruptcy are vulnerable to substantial losses. Assume that the old stock is purchased at $2.00 a share and that the approved reorganization plan calls for 20 old shares to be exchanged for one new share. The new stock would have to appreciate to $40.00 a share for the investor to just break even. This may take years—if it's ever realized. If the old shares were acquired at 40 cents during chapter 11, then the new stock would have to appreciate to only $8.00 to break even. Of course, in practice, investors don't know what the dilution will be until a plan of reorganization is approved. They know much less as to how the new stock will subsequently fare. Because of these substantial uncertainties, it's probably best to hold off purchasing stock until a plan of reorganization is approved or at least is close to approval. Even then, it is wise to examine the company's past earnings, performance, and the current industry situation to determine whether or not earnings will support a target price, assuming a conservative P/E ratio. For example, in the case of the $8.00 break even price mentioned above, earnings would have to be $1.00 per share of new common stock, assuming a P/E ratio of 8.

Purchasing the Company

For those who are disposed to take an active role in their investments, attractive opportunities may arise during the actual purchase of bankrupt companies. However, the amount of time, effort, and resources required to turn the situation around is often substantial. It is difficult enough to successfully operate a profitable acquisition—even successful businesses have problems. Most companies in bankruptcy have serious problems and are beyond salvaging. A considerable amount of screening is usually necessary to identify situations that meet the investor's acquisition criteria. After a suitable company has been identified, the investor then faces the task of selling his plan to the debtor-in-charge, creditors, and banks. A detailed discussion of the issues associated with acquisitions is beyond the scope of this discussion, and the reader is referred to the references at the end of the chapter for further details. In what follows, we briefly consider the two activities mentioned above—finding and screening candidates.

Where to Find Acquisition Opportunities

Candidates for acquisition opportunities may be found among the following:

- The files of the clerk's office of the regional U.S. bankruptcy courts. These are open to the public. An example of the information available can be appreciated by examining some of the filing forms given in the appendix to this book. Caution is necessary, since the financial statements are not required to be audited.
- Bankruptcy attorneys. A helpful organization for making contacts is the American Bankruptcy Institute (Washington, DC).
- Turnaround consultants. Contacts can be made through the Turnaround Management Association (Cary, North Carolina).
- Workout departments of major commercial banks.
- Organizations that sponsor relevant meetings, seminars, and workshops helpful in building a network of contacts, including

American Bankers Association
Association of Insolvency Accountants
National Association of Bankruptcy Accountants

• Newsletters (listed below) and the financial press often provide leads.

Screening Acquisition Prospects

The next step is to screen prospects. Factors that favor an acquisition candidate are

1. Availability of competent management
2. A good product line, preferably in an expanding industry
3. Manageable acquisition price
4. Availability of adequate financing to accomplish a turnaround
5. Availability of a good sales organization
6. Little competition
7. Favorable government policies and programs.

Factors that militate against an acquisition are:

1. Investor's lack of familiarity with the industry
2. Lack of competent management
3. Poor products
4. Acquisition or turnaround costs too high
5. Poor marketing organization
6. Highly competitive industry
7. Contracting industry
8. Survival of the firm dependent upon the development of new product lines
9. Unfavorable government regulations
10. High degree of exposure to product liability or pollution problems
11. Better opportunities elsewhere.

Information Sources

Newsletters

1. *Defaulted Bonds Newsletter*
   Bond Investors Association, Inc.
   P.O. Box 4427
   Miami Lakes, Florida 33014

2. *Junk Bond Reporter*
   Junk Bond Reporter
   P.O. Box 30240
   Bethesda, Maryland 20824
   Gives new items and developments about
   junk bonds. Published weekly.

3. *Turnaround Letter*
   New Generations Investments
   225 Friend Street
   Boston, Massachusetts 02114
   Provides specific investment recommendations. Published monthly.

4. *Turnaround and Workouts*
   Beard Group Inc.
   P.O. Box 9867
   Washington, D.C. 20016

Semimonthly publication. Covers news and developments in bankruptcies and turnarounds.

In-depth Reports

A number of brokerage houses and investment banks issue in-depth reports on specific situations, including Merril Lynch, Kidder Peabody, Salomon Brothers, and First Boston. Special services include

1. *Bankruptcy Data Source*
   New Generation Investments Inc.
   225 Friend Street
   Boston, Massachusetts 02114
   Follows all publicly traded companies that are in bankruptcy.

2. *Distressed Securities Service*
   130 Research Services
   Southeast Executive Drive
   Brewster, New York 10509
   Provides comprehensive reports on specific situations.

3. *High Yield Credit Critique*
   McCarthy, Crisanti, Maffei, Inc.
   71 Broadway
   New York, New York 10006
   Issues in-depth reports on specific situations. Also issues *High Yield Credit Comments*, reporting news and updates.

Compendia and Listings

1. *Moody's Bond Record*—a comprehensive monthly guide to thousands of fixed income issues.
   Moody's Bond Survey—weekly news publication on fixed income securities.
   Moody's Investor Service
   99 Church Street
   New York, New York 10007

2. *High Yield Hand Book*—an annual review of all nonconvertible high yield public debt with tables.
   CS First Boston
   Park Avenue Plaza
   New York, New York 10055

3. *S & P Bond Guide*—statistical data on thousands of U.S. and Canadian corporate bonds issued monthly.

   S & P Credit Week—news and events about fixed income securities.
   S & P High Yield Quarterly—comprehensive ratings and news for high yield bonds.
   Standard and Poor's Corporation
   25 Broadway
   New York, New York 10004

4. *Companies Filing Under Chapter 11 Petitions*—quarterly listing of all public companies filing under Chapter 11 includes district, assets, liabilities, equity, and debt.
   Securities and Exchange Commission
   450 Fifth Street N.W.
   Washington, D.C. 20549

International Bond Ratings

1. *Financial Times Credit Rating International*—summarizes credit ratings of leading credit services throughout the world.
   Financial Times
   Tower House
   Southhampton Street
   London WC2E 7HA, England

2. *Credit Week International and International Rating Guide*—news and ratings of international debts.
   Standard and Poor's Corporation
   25 Broadway
   New York, New York 10004

On-line Services

Bloomberg Financial Markets—On-line service offering a broad range of fixed income information and computations.
Bloomberg LP

499 Park Avenue
New York, New York 10022

Legal Developments

Bankruptcy Reporter—cases, news, and information covering the broad range of bankruptcy law.
West Publication

50 W. Kellog Boulevard
P.O. Box 64526
St. Paul, Minnesota 55164

References and Further Reading

Altman, E. I. *Corporate Financial Distress*, John Wiley, New York. (1983).

Bibeault, E. B. *Corporate Turnaround*, McGraw-Hill, New York. (1982).

Fridson, M. S. *High Yield Bonds*, Probus, Chicago. (1989).

Goodman, S. J. *How to Manage a Turnaround*, Free Press, New York. (1982).

Howe, J. T. *Junk Bonds*, Probus, Chicago. (1989).

Levine, S. N. *The Acquisition Manual*, New York Institute Finance, New York. (1989).

Ramaswami, M., and S. E. Moeller. *Investing in Financially Distressed Companies*, Quorum Book, Westport, Conn. (1990).

Scharf, L. A., E. A. Shea, and G. C. Beck. *Acquisitions, Buyouts, Sales, Buyouts and Takeovers*, Prentice Hall, Englewod Cliffs, N.J. (1985).

2

Techniques for Predicting Bankruptcy and Their Use in a Financial Turnaround

Edward I. Altman
Stern School of Business
New York University

Introduction to Bankruptcy

During the last twenty years in the United States, the emphasis on corporate bankruptcy has been transformed from the small, undercapitalized firm or fraud-related occurrence, to one that typically involves large firms with complex capital structures. Indeed, at least 26 companies have filed for bankruptcy protection with over $1 billion in liabilities at the time of filing in the last two decades (Table 2.1). To put it simply, bankruptcy is big business these days, with continuous monitoring by the legal and accounting professions, institutional investors, and turnaround and restructuring specialists.

Of critical importance to most of the interested parties in a distressed firm situation is the early identification of an impending crisis and the possibility of avoiding a further deterioration and eventual bankruptcy. The relevant parties who can make use of an accurate bankruptcy prediction tool are listed in Table 2.2. The obvious ones are lenders, investors, and managers, with serious interest also shown by regulators, attorneys, and accountants. The application to lenders, investors, and others is beyond the scope of this chapter, and the reader is referred to Altman (1983 and

Source: Edward I. Altman, *Corporate Financial Distress*, Chapter 4, John Wiley & Sons, 1983. Dr. Altman is Max L. Heine Professor of Finance, Stern School of Business, New York University.

Table 2.1.   Largest U.S. Bankruptcies (as of May 1990)

Company	Liabilities ($ Millions)	Bankruptcy Date
Texaco, Inc. (incl. capital subs.)	21603	Apr-87
Campeau Corp. (Allied & Federated)	9947	Jan-90
Lomas Financial Corp.	6127	Sep-89
LTV Corp. (incl. LTV Int'l NV)	4700	Jul-86
Penn Central Transportation Co.	3300	Jun-70
Eastern Airlines	3196	Mar-89
Drexel Burnham Lambert	3000	Feb-90
Wickes	2000	Apr-82
Global Marine Inc.	1800	Jan-86
ITEL	1700	Jan-81
Public Service, New Hampshire	1700	Jan-88
Baldwin-United	1600	Sep-83
Integrated Resources	1600	Feb-90
Revco Corp.	1500	Jul-88
Placid Oil	1488	Apr-85
Ames Department Stores Inc.	1440	Apr-90
McLean Industries	1270	Nov-86
Hillsborough Holdings (Jim Walter)	1204	Dec-89
Bell National	1203	Aug-85
GHR Energy Corp.	1200	Jan-83
L. J. Hooker	1200	Aug-89
Manville Corp.	1116	Aug-82
Braniff Airlines (1)	1100	May-82
Continental Airlines	1100	Sep-83
Circle K	1100	May-90
W.T. Grant	1000	Oct-75
Charter Co.	976	Apr-85
Allegheny International	845	Feb-88
North American Car Corp.	841	Dec-84
Seatrain Lines	785	Feb-81
A.H. Robins	775	Aug-85
Penrod Drilling	764	Apr-85
Storage Technologies	695	Oct-84
General Development	695	Apr-90
Coral Petroleum	682	May-83
Nucorp Energy	615	Jul-82
Continental Mortgage Investors	607	Mar-76
Evans	600	Mar-85
Allis Chalmers	570	Jun-87
United Merchants & Manufacturing	552	Jul-77
Coleco Corp.	536	Jul-88
Maxicare Health Plans	535	Mar-89
AM International	510	Apr-82

(continued)

Table 2.1.   (cont.)

Company	Liabilities ($ Millions)	Bankruptcy Date
OPM Leasing	505	Mar-81
Bevill Bresler Schullman	498	Apr-85
Smith International Inc.	484	Mar-86
Saxon Industries	461	Apr-82
Commonwealth Oil Refining Co.	421	Mar-78
W. Judd Kassuba	420	Dec-73
Erie Lackawanna Railroad	404	Jun-72
White Motor Corp.	399	Sep-80
Sambo's Restaurants	370	Jun-81
Investors Funding Corp.	370	Oct-74
Todd Shipyards	350	Aug-87
AMAREX	348	Dec-82
Food Fair Corp.	347	Oct-78
Buttes Oil & Gas	337	Nov-85
Great American Mortgage & Trust	326	Mar-77
McLouth Steel	323	Dec-81
World of Wonder	312	Dec-87
MGF Oil	304	Dec-84
U.S. Financial Services	300	Jul-73
Hunt International	295	Apr-85
Radice Corp.	291	Feb-88
Chase Manhattan Mort. & Realty Trust	290	Feb-79
Doskocil Co.	265	Mar-90
Daylin, Inc.	250	Feb-75
Guardian Mortgage Investors	247	Mar-78
Waterman Steamship Corp.	242	Dec-83
Revere Copper & Brass	237	Oct-82
Air Florida System	221	Jul-84
Chicago, Rock Island & Pacific	221	Mar-75
Hellenic Lines, Ltd.	216	Dec-83
Wilson Foods	213	Apr-83
Lion Capital Group	212	Apr-84
KDT Industries	203	Aug-82
Equity Funding Corp. Of America	200	Apr-73
De Laurentis Entertainment	198	Aug-88
Triad America Corporation	198	Jan-87
Interstate Stores, Inc.	190	May-74
Fidelity Mortgage Investors	187	Jan-75
HRT Industries	183	Nov-82
Technical Equities Corp.	180	Feb-85
Braniff Airlines (2)	178	Sep-89
Terex Corp.	176	Mar-83
Lionel Corp.	175	Feb-82

(*continued*)

Table 2.1.   (cont.)

Company	Liabilities ($ Millions)	Bankruptcy Date
Omega, Alpha Corp.	175	Sep-74
Marion Corp.	175	Mar-83
Michigan General	170	Apr-87
Dart Drug Stores	169	Aug-89
U.N.R. Industries	165	Jul-82
Thatcher Glass	165	Dec-84
Towner Petroleum	163	Sep-84
Otasco Inc.	163	Nov-88
Dreco Energy	161	Jun-82
Reading Railroad	158	Nov-71
Anglo Energy	155	Nov-83
Boston & Maine Railroad	148	Dec-75
Westgate-California	144	Feb-74
Pizza Time Theatre	143	Mar-84
Cook United, Inc.	143	Oct-84
Colwell Mortgage & Trust	142	Feb-78

1990) for a more complete discussion. At the end of the chapter, we will discuss one application for utilizing a distressed firm prediction model in a financial turnaround situation.

The primary purpose of this chapter is to present a number of techniques for the early detection of financial distress and bankruptcy of corporations. These techniques were developed by this writer and others, based on a combination of traditional financial statement analysis methods and relatively sophisticated statistical techniques. The essential idea was to enhance the information content of financial ratios in order to screen firms as to whether or not they have a financial profile similar to past bankrupts. In

Table 2.2.   Financial Distress Prediction Users

- Lenders
- Investors
- Security Analysis
- Regulators
- Auditors
- Managers of troubled companies
- Bond raters and credit scoring firms
- Advisors—turnaround and restructuring
- Government officials
- Researchers
- Mergers and acquisitions analysts
- Purchasers from suppliers

X_4 = market value of equity (preferred + common)
  divided by book value of total liabilities
X_5 = sales divided by total assets

Each of these financial ratios is defined in Appendix A, where the information content of the ratio and its insertion into the formula is described.

If ratios calculated from a company's financial statements and stock market results are inserted into the formula, a single number will result, which typically has a range from −2 to +10. Scores above 10 are possible, however, primarily if the firm's market value of equity is high combined with relatively small amounts of total liabilities. The range of Z-scores achieved by firms in my original sample of 33 bankrupt and 33 carefully matched healthy firms showed that all firms scoring below 1.8 were classified as bankrupt and did actually go bankrupt. Those scoring above 3.0 were classified as healthy and survived. Scores between 1.8 and 3.0 are classified into a gray area, which indicated less clearly the firm's ultimate fate. In all cases, the higher the Z-score, the healthier the firm and the lower the probability of failure.

The beauty of this analysis, if deemed accurate and helpful, is that it can easily be applied in about 15 minutes by a nonstatistician using only a firm's balance sheet and income statement, a current stock price, and a handheld calculator.

Initial Sample (Group 1)

The initial sample of 33 manufacturing firms in each of the two groups is examined using data compiled one financial statement prior to bankruptcy.

Table 2.3. Classification Results, Original Sample

	Number Correct	Percent Correct	Percent Error	n	Actual	Predicted Group 1	Group 2
			One Year Prior Results				
					Group 1	31	2
					Group 2	1	32
Type I	31	94%	6%	33			
Type II	32	97	3	33			
Total	63	95	5	66			
			Two Year Prior Results				
					Group 1	23	9
					Group 2	2	31
Type I	23	72%	28%	32			
Type II	31	94	6	33			
Total	54	83	17	65			

Since the discriminant coefficients and the group distributions are derived from this sample, a high degree of successful classification is expected. This should occur because the firms are classified using a discriminant function that, in fact, is based upon the individual measurements of these same firms. The classification accuracies for the original sample are shown in Table 2.3.

The model is extremely accurate in classifying 95 percent of the total sample correctly. The Type I error (classifying a bankrupt firm as healthy) proved to be only 6 percent, while the Type II error (classifying a healthy firm as bankrupt) was even better at 3 percent. The results were encouraging, but the obvious upward bias should be kept in mind, and further validation techniques are appropriate.

Results Two Statements Prior to Bankruptcy

The second test observes the discriminating ability of the model for firms using data compiled two statements prior to bankruptcy. The two-year period is an approximation, since the actual time prior to failure for the correctly classified firms was approximately 20 months, with two firms having a 13-month lead. The results are also shown in Table 2.3. The reduction in accuracy is understandable because impending bankruptcy is more remote and the indicators are less clear. Nevertheless, 72 percent correct assignment is evidence that bankruptcy can be predicted two years prior to the event. The Type II error is slightly larger (6 percent in this test, compared to 3 percent in the original test), but it is still extremely accurate.

Secondary Sample of Bankrupt Firms

In order to test the model rigorously for both bankrupt and nonbankrupt firms, two new samples are introduced. The first contains a new sample of 25 bankrupt firms whose asset size range is similar to that of the initial bankrupt group. On the basis of the parameters established in the discriminant model to classify firms in the secondary sample, the predictive accuracy for this sample as of one statement prior to bankruptcy is described in Table 2.4.

The results here are surprising because one would not usually expect a secondary sample's results to be superior to the initial discriminant sample

Table 2.4.   Classification Results, Secondary Sample
of Bankrupt Firms

| | | Bankrupt Group | | |
	Number of Firms	Number Correct	Percent Correct	Percent Error
Type I	25	24	96%	4%

(96 vs. 94 percent). The possible reasons are that the upward bias normally present in the initial sample tests is not manifested in this investigation and/or that the model is not optimal. The results on a secondary sample of nonbankrupt firms were also impressive.

The results of extending the Z-score model to more than two years prior to bankruptcy, however, were not very accurate, and one would have to conclude that the original model essentially had a two-year prediction potential.

The Proof of the Pudding

The results of any model are only as good as its prediction accuracy on observations that take place after the model has been built. In our case, we have tested the model on a number of bankrupt firm samples from the 1970s and 1980s. In all cases, the one-year prior accuracy was well over 80 percent, indicating a fairly robust model and one that is still applicable today.

Figures 2.1 and 2.2 illustrate the use of the Z-score model on actual firms. LTV is a large steel producer that experienced problems in the 1970s and 1980s but was not considered a prime bankruptcy candidate when it finally did file in July 1986. The Z-score model, however, showed a steady deterioration with its score falling into the bankrupt zone (below 1.81) as

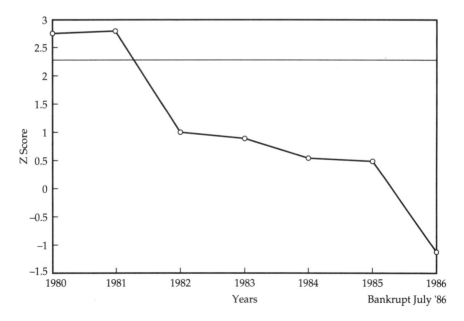

Figure 2.1.   Z-Score Trend—LTV Corp

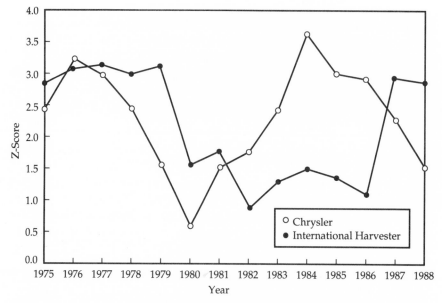

Figure 2.2. Z-Score Analysis—International Harvester (Navistar) and Chrysler

early as 1982 and steady deterioration thereafter. We are confident that this firm's bankruptcy was a "surprise" because LTV's outstanding public debt was trading in the low 80s the day before the filing. Most distressed firms' debt sells in the 40–60 range just prior to a formal bankruptcy petition and then lower immediately after the filing. LTV's debt sold in the 30s just after!

Figure 2.2 illustrates how a model can be technically wrong on a prediction. International Harvester and Chrysler Corporation demonstrated clear signs of distress with the Z-score model indicating as much or worse in 1980–1982 (Harvester) and 1980 (Chrysler). In each case, however, the firm did not file because it was rescued—Harvester by its bankers, and Chrysler by the federal government. In essence, these examples show that in reality, bankruptcy is not an economic-financial event, but a behavioral one. As long as a firm can still obtain credit or guarantees, it will not be forced into bankruptcy. So, in one sense we are trying to predict the behavior of creditors in our bankruptcy specifications. As long as the model is consistent with creditor assessments and decisions, it will be very accurate.

The Statistical Road to Bankruptcy

The empirical results indicate that the Z-score approach is an accurate forecaster up to two years prior to bankruptcy. In order to investigate the possible reasons underlying these findings, the trend in the five predictive

Table 2.5. Average Ratios of Bankrupt Group prior to Failure—Original Sample

Ratio	Fifth Year		Fourth Year		Third Year		Second Year		First Year	
	Ratio	Change[a]	Ratio	Change[a]	Ratio	Change[a]	Ratio	Change[a]	Ratio	Change[a]
Working capital/total assets (%) (X_1)	19.5		23.2	+3.6	17.6	−5.6	1.6	−16.0	(6.1)	−7.7
Retained earnings/total assets (%) (X_2)	4.0		(0.8)	−4.8	(7.0)	−6.2	(30.1)	−23.1	(62.6)	−32.5
EBIT/total assets (%) (X_3)	7.2		4.0	−3.2	(5.8)	−9.8	(20.7)	−14.9[b]	131.81	−16.1
Market value equity/total debt liabilities (%) (X_4)	180.0		147.6	−32.4	142.3	−4.4	74.2	69.0[b]	40.1	34.1
Sales/total assets (%) (X_5)	200.0		200.0	0.0	166.0	−34.0[b]	150.0	−16.0	150.0	0.0
Current ratio (%)	180.0		187.0	+7.0	162.0	−25.0	131.0	−31.0[b]	133.0	+2.0
Years of negative profits	0.8		0.9	+0.1	1.2	+0.3	2.0	+0.8[b]	2.5	+0.5
Total debt/total assets (%)	54.2		60.9	+6.7	61.2	+0.3	77.0	+15.8	96.4	+19.4
Net worth/total debt (%)	123.2		75.2	−28.0	112.6	+17.4	70.5	−42.1[b]	49.4	−21.1

[a] Change from previous year.
[b] Largest yearly change in the ratio.

variables is traced on a univariate basis for five years preceding bankruptcy. The ratios of four other important but less significant ratios are also listed in Table 2.5.

The two most important conclusions of this trend analysis are (1) that all of the observed ratios show a deteriorating trend as bankruptcy approaches and (2) that the most serious change in the majority of these ratios occurred between two and three years prior to bankruptcy. The degree of seriousness is measured by the yearly change in the ratio values. The latter observation is extremely significant as it provides evidence consistent with conclusions derived from the discriminant model. Therefore, the important information inherent in the individual ratio measurement trends takes on deserved significance when integrated with the more analytical discriminant analysis findings.

Aggregate Firm Applications—Assessing Distress in 1990

One application of a distressed firm classification model is to assess an aggregated sample of companies in order to analyze trends in the economy. For example, one might apply a model like Z-score to an entire industry so as to compare individual firm profiles with its industry peer group. Another is to take an even larger sample, like the S&P 400 industrials, and examine the overall vulnerability of this large firm sample over time.

Figure 2.3 presents the proportion of the S&P 400 (actually 382 firms qualified with the requisite data) that show signs of financial distress. The chart clearly shows that the overall financial health of the S&P 400 and, by association, of smaller firms in the economy has steadily deteriorated since 1980. A decade ago, only 3 percent of the firms had Z-scores below 1.81, while about 10 percent were showing signs of distress in 1989. Nine percent had low Z-scores during the recession of 1973–1975.

Surprisingly, the Z-score's indication of increasing distress potential among our largest firms is not due to the so-called leveraging of America caused by the vast increase in highly leveraged restructurings that occurred in the late 1980s. Indeed, if one measures the equity/liabilities ratio in terms of the market value of equity, as we do in the fourth Z-score variable, the ratio actually increased (more equity per dollar of debt) from 1980 to 1989 (Figure 2.4). Of course, the book value of equity/total liabilities ratio fell over this same period rather dramatically—a 40 percent decline. The main reasons for the Z-score decline appears to be lower liquidity (X_1) and asset productivity (X_5). Profitability before interest and taxes (X_3) has actually improved somewhat.

Figure 2.5 shows the distribution of Z-scores in 1989, with the vast majority in the 3–5 range. Incidentally, a high Z-score, while indicating a lower distress potential, does not necessarily portend a higher return to owner's equity in the future. It simply means that the firm's distress potential is low.

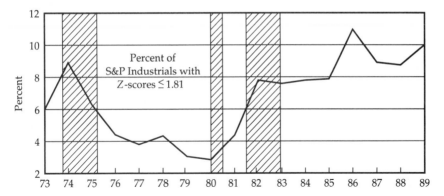

Figure 2.3. Chance of Bankruptcy within S&P Industrials. Shaded areas are NBER recession periods. (*) 1989 data are latest four quarters.
SOURCE: ML Quantitative Analysis, Compustat.

Finally, it should be noted that we do not expect anywhere near a 10 percent default rate of large companies in the next few years—as one might conclude from the Z-scores. There is always a relatively large percentage of distressed firms who either do not deteriorate further or who are merged with stronger entities or whose profiles are less applicable to precise interpretation by a standardized, general Z-score approach. For instance, many of the S&P 400 industrials are not strictly manufacturers,

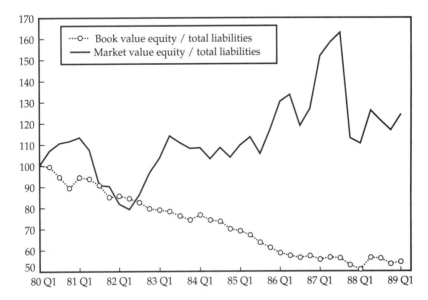

Figure 2.4. "X_4" Using Varying Measures of Equity. Book value equity/total liabilities—market value equity/total liabilities.

Percent
of Sample

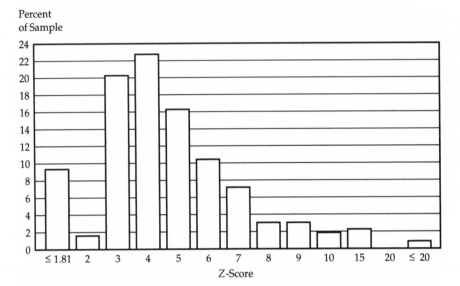

Figure 2.5. Distribution of S&P Industrials Z-Scores (as of March 1989).
Source: ML Quantitative Analysis, Compustat.

and therefore one should not interpret the scores and their proximity to the lower bound cutoff (1.81) as a precise indication of distress. In the next section we will explore one attempt to modify the Z-score model to accommodate nonmanufacturers. Also, the Zeta approach, to be discussed soon, is definitely applicable to a broad cross section of industrial groupings.

Adaptation For Private Firms' Application

Perhaps the most frequent inquiry that I have received from those interested in using the Z-score model is, "What should we do to apply the model to firms in the private sector?" Credit analysts, private placement dealers, accounting auditors, and firms themselves are concerned that the original model is only applicable to publicly traded entities (since X_4 requires stock price data). And, to be perfectly correct, the Z-score model is a publicly traded firm model and *ad hoc* adjustments are not scientifically valid. For example, the most obvious modification is to substitute the book value of equity for the market value. With the original 1968 model, analysts had little choice but to follow this procedure, since valid alternatives were not available.

A Revised Z-Score Model

Rather than simply using a proxy variable and inserting it into an existing model to calculate Z-scores, I advocate a complete reestimation of the

Table 2.6. Revised Z-Score Model Format: Private Firm Applicaton

Variable	Mean Bankrupt	Mean Nonbankrupt	Univariate F	Stepwise Order	Percent of Discriminatory Power (Scaled Vector)
$X_1 = \dfrac{\text{working capital}}{\text{total assets}}$	−0.061	0.414	32.6	5	0.067
$X_2 = \dfrac{\text{retained earnings}}{\text{total assets}}$	−0.626	0.353	58.8	1	0.121
$X_3 = \dfrac{\text{EBIT}}{\text{total assets}}$	−0.318	0.153	26.6	4	0.318
$X_4 = \dfrac{\text{N.W. (book value)}}{\text{total liabilities}}$	0.494	2.684	25.8	2	0.203
$X_5 = \dfrac{\text{sales}}{\text{total assets}}$	1.503	1.939	2.8	3	0.291

Note: Multivariate $F = 20.33; F_{(5,60)} = 7.00(0.01\text{level})$.
xpNote: $Z = 0.717(X_1) + 0.847(X_2) + 3.107(X_3) + 0.420(X_4) + 0.998(X_5)$.

model, substituting the book value of equity for the market value in X_4. One expects that all of the coefficients will change (not only the new variable's parameter) and that the classification criterion and related cutoff scores would also change. That is exactly what happens.

Table 2.6 lists the results of our new Z-score model with a modified X_4 variable. The equation looks different than the earlier model; note, for instance, the coefficients for X_1 (0.717 vs. 1.210) and so on. The actual variable that was modified, X_4, showed a coefficient change to 0.420 from 0.600; that is, it now has less of an impact on the Z-score. X_3 and X_5 coefficients were virtually unchanged.

The Type I accuracy is only slightly less impressive than the model utilizing market value of equity (91 percent vs. 94 percent) and the Type II accuracy is identical (97 percent). Note that the nonbankrupt group's mean Z'-score is lower than that of the original model (4.14 vs. 5.02). Therefore, the distribution of scores is now tighter with larger group overlap. The gray area (or ignorance zone) is wider, however, since the lower boundary is now 1.23 as opposed to 1.81 for the original Z-score model. All of this indicates that the revised model is probably less reliable than the original, but only slightly less. Due to lack of a private firm data base, we have not tested this model extensively on secondary sample bankrupt and nonbankrupt entities. We await tests by practitioners on this relevant alternative.

A Further Revision—Eliminating Sales/Assets

Our final Z-score modification analyzes the characteristics and accuracy of a model without X_5—sales/total assets. We do this in order to minimize the potential industry effect that is more likely when such an industry-sensitive variable as asset turnover is included. The book value of equity was used for X_4 in this case. This model would seem to be more generally applicable across many industrial sectors, not just for manufacturers.

The classification results are identical to the revised five-variable model (Z-score). Of course, all of the coefficients for variables X_1 through X_4 are changed, as are the group means and cutoff scores (Table 2.7). This particular model is also useful within an industry where the type of financing of assets differs greatly among firms and important adjustments, such as lease capitalization, are not made.

The Second Generation ZETA Model

While the Z-score remains an accurate and popular tool for early identification of corporate distress situations, it is not as accurate or robust as the next generation Zeta approach. Built and first published in 1977 (Altman, Haldeman, and Narayanan, 1977), the ZETA® approach is now an established credit scoring service (ZETA Services, Inc., Hoboken, N.J.),

Table 2.7. Revised Z-Score Model—Four Variables; Univariate and Multivariate Tests

Variable	Mean Bankrupt	Mean Nonbankrupt	Univariate F	Stepwise Order	Percent of Discriminatory Power (Scaled Vector)
$X_1 = \dfrac{\text{working capital}}{\text{total assets}}$	-0.061	0.414	32.6	4	0.267
$X_2 = \dfrac{\text{retained earnings}}{\text{total assets}}$	-0.626	0.353	58.8	1	0.205
$X_3 = \dfrac{\text{EBIT}}{\text{total assets}}$	-0.318	0153	26.6	3	0.304
$X_4 = \dfrac{\text{N.W. (book value)}}{\text{total liabilities}}$	0.494	2.684	25.8	2	0.224

Note: Multivariate $F = 19.01; F_{4.61} = 7.00(0.01\text{level})$.

$Z'' = 6.56(X_1) + 3.26(X_2) + 6.72(X_3) + 1.05(X_4)$.

Table 2.8. ZETA Score Model: Variable Descriptions

V_1 Overall profitability (return on assets-EBIT/total assets)
V_2 Size (based on tangible assets)
V_3 Debt service (interest coverage)
V_4 Liquidity (current ratio)
V_5 Cumulative profitability (retained earnings/total assets)
V_6 Capitalization (based on a 5-year average market value of common stock)
V_7 Stability of earnings over a 10-year period; standard error of estimate of 10-year regression of EBIT/total assets)

utilized by a wide variety of financial and industrial institutions as well as by regulatory bodies (for example, the National Association of Insurance Commissioners).

The Zeta approach is similar to Z-score in that it also entails a discriminant analysis statistical model involving seven financial indicators (Table 2.8). Note that several variables are identical or similar to Z-score (V_1, V_4, V_5 and V_6) with a few new ones. In particular, Zeta introduces a firm size measure (Tangible Assets, V_2), a debt service measure (EBIT/interest, V_3), and a stability of earnings measure (standard error of EBIT/Total Assets around a 10-year trend). The market value of equity variable (V_6) is based on a 5-year average of the variables rather than the point estimate in Z-score.

One of Zeta's major attributes is its adjustment for important accounting reporting changes over time, for example, lease capitalization, introduced in 1980. And Zeta is applicable to all industrial firms, not just to manufacturers. A private firm model is also available from the Zeta Services, Inc. Zeta's major drawback for the individual user is the unavailability of the model's coefficients. While institutions can subscribe to the service, the reader of this chapter cannot apply it directly from this written text.

An example of the Zeta system is, again, the LTV case, which shows unmistakable distress as early as 1982 and extreme distress in 1985. Zeta scores below −3 are very poor, with the Zeta equivalent at that point equal to the lowest nondefault bond rating (Caa or CCC). Table 2.9 shows the average Zeta scores on bankrupt firms from 1984–1988 at various points prior to filing. The −3.63 average one year prior is quite indicative of a sound early warning indicator. Another distinction of Zeta is its 70 percent accuracy as much as five years prior (original sample accuracy), which seems to have held up over time. So Zeta demonstrates a "longer" early warning signal than any other model that I know. Still, a relatively large number of publicly traded companies now have negative Zeta scores (the model's cutoff point), showing a fairly high degree of corporate vulnerability.

Table 2.9. Average ZETA® Credit Scores for Bankrupt Companies (1984–1988)

Years Prior to Bankruptcy	All Bankruptcies All Years	Nonfraud, Nonlegal Bankruptcies						
		All Years	1988	1987	1986	1985	1984
0	-6.44	-6.90	-8.48	-5.84	-6.98	-6.07	-5.38
1	-3.63	-4.11	-5.60	-3.81	-2.97	-3.61	-3.72
2	-2.15	-2.50	-3.56	-2.23	-1.86	-2.20	-2.10
3	-0.96	-1.38	-2.46	-1.51	-1.10	-0.52	-0.81
4	-0.62	-1.03	-1.85	-0.58	-0.82	-0.67	-0.65
5	-0.24	-0.71	-1.00	1.06	-0.76	-1.75	-0.24

Other Statistical Models

A number of authors have attempted to build and test models similar to Z and Zeta. Many of these models are described in Appendix 2.2. While the list is not exhaustive, it does give a fairly complete picture of the topic's popularity and importance. For more details on the techniques and their empirical findings, the reader is referred to the actual articles or books describing the approaches.

A number of related statistical approaches have been utilized, including (1) linear and quadratic discriminant analysis, (2) logit and probit regression analysis, (3) gamblers ruin analysis, (4) principal components and factor analysis, and (5) recursive partitioning algorithms. All of these techniques demonstrate acceptable to extremely accurate tests.

This does not mean that the interested distress prediction observer should simply use the objective "black box" output resulting from the models. The results are essentially a first pass screen, and low Z or Zeta scores or their equivalents should lead to an in-depth analysis of other factors and indicators.

An Overall Evaluation (Scott)

Scott (1981) compared several of the leading empirical models, that is, Beaver (1967), Altman (1968), Wilcox (1971), Deakin (1972), and Altman et. al. (1977) in terms of their observed accuracies and of their coherence to Scott's own conceptual bankruptcy framework. Scott's model includes assumptions about firms with (1) imperfect access and (2) perfect access to external capital markets. He concluded that "though the models are not based on explicit theory their success suggests the existence of a strong underlying regularity" (p. 324). While he found it hard to determine which model discriminated best, due to different data and different procedures, he felt that the best multivariate models outperformed the best single variable models, although not every multidimensional model behaved in this way.

Scott concluded that

> Of the multidimensional models, the ZETA model is perhaps most convincing. It has high discriminatory power, is reasonably parsimonious, and includes accounting and stock market data as well as earnings and debt variables. Further, it is being used in practice by over thirty financial institutions (pp. 324–325).

Qualitative Factors—Management

In addition to the quantitative, objective, but strictly historical data-based predictive approaches discussed above, nonquantifiable factors can also be immensely helpful in making a final decision on the expected performance of a firm. Many of these variables are related to one's assessment of the quality and availability of management.

One type of qualitative investigation would be to observe the turnover of top and middle-to-upper management, that is, just below the top level. Indeed, a *high* degree of turnover just below the CEO and a low turnover at the very top seem to be typical of distressed companies. Bibeault (1982) has done some work in this area, as well as on the question of corporate turnaround.

A model that combines some of these qualitative factors with the more objective quantitative measures was promoted by Argenti (1976). His A-score system is represented in Table 2.10. Argenti's approach is interesting in that it attempts to quantify the relative importance of qualitative and quantitative factors. While one can agree with most of the variables indicated and the direction of their influence, it is hard to justify the subjective, *ad hoc* weights given to each factor. For example, a firm with an autocratic chief executive, poor response to change, and high leverage will fail Argenti's test. A number of other combinations of negative factors will also lead to the "at risk" conclusion. While I cannot endorse this unscientific approach to weighting, the variables presented are very helpful in several of the qualitative areas.

Caveats of a Successful Turnaround

Before we discuss the application of early warning systems as an **active, dynamic** tool to manage a financial turnaround of a distressed firm, a few comments about management's role in a turnaround are in order. There is no question that management is the key to a successful turnaround. More than anything else, the right management style and talent is critical to effecting change. A few caveats are in order at this point:

Table 2.10. Argenti's (A-Score) System

	Weight	
Defects in Management	8	The chief executive is an autocrat.
	4	He is also the chairman.
	2	Passive board of directors.
	2	Unbalanced board, i.e., too many engineers.
	2	Weak finance director.
	1	Poor management depth.
Defects in Accountancy	3	No budgets or budgetary controls.
	3	No cash flow plans, or not updated.
	3	No costing system.
	15	Poor response to change; old-fashioned product; obsolete factory; old directors.
Total defects	43	
Mistakes	15	High-leverage firm could get into trouble by stroke of bad luck.
	15	Overtrading. Company expanding faster than its funding.
	15	Big project gone wrong.
Total mistakes	45	
Other symptoms	4	Financial signs, such as Z score.
	4	Creative accounting. Chief executive is the first to see signs of failure and attempts to hide it from creditors and the banks.
	3	Nonfinancial signs, such as untidy offices, frozen salaries, chief executive "ill," high staff turnover, low morale, rumors.
	1	Terminal signs.
Total symptoms	12	
Total possible score	100	

Summary of Results

Score	Prognosis
0–10	No worry (high pass)
0–25	Pass
10–18	Cause for anxiety (pass)
18–35	Grey zone—warning signal
>35	Company is "at risk"

1. Usually a new senior management team is necessary to guide a successful turnaround—and that new management team must be in control, i.e., have full power to make the requisite changes. This is especially true if the old management team was responsible for the distress situation. It is almost impossible for a manager to fire workers whom he hired and to sell assets that he bought—measures that are usually necessary in a turnaround.
2. Giving the new management team control means that they report directly to the board, where the chairman of the board is also the CEO. Incentives for accomplishing savings must be provided. As long as the old chairman stays in place, true control will not shift to the new managers.
3. Management must have as its goal the protection and enhancement of the owners' investment.
4. The first thing to do after assuming control of a distressed situation is usually to stop the cash bleeding of the firm. No matter how brilliant a turnaround strategy is being planned, there will not be a patient to save unless the negative cash outflow is stanched. There are exceptions, of course, such as the need to negotiate a new agreement with creditors, but even here the objective is to eliminate or reduce cash interest payments—at least in the near term.
5. After the cash flow is stabilized, the patient (firm) can have its bones mended (e.g., cost reductions), followed by rehabilitative action (e.g., sale of assets and investment in more profitable activities).

Early Warning Indicators and a Successful Turnaround

The key to any successful turnaround, just as the key to curing serious illness, is the early identification of the true magnitude of the problem. Too often we are myopic about our own faults, and realization comes too late. We will now explore how a technique, like Z-score, can provide an active, dynamic tool for managing a financial turnaround.

Active versus Passive Use of Financial Models*

Statistically verified predictive models have long been used in the study of business. Generally, these models are developed by scientists and tested by "observers" who do not interact with or influence the measurements of the model. Consequently, the models, when valid, have predicted events with satisfactory accuracy, and business analysts may regard them with a reasonable degree of confidence. This "passive" use of predictive models, for

*Much of the material in this section is derived from E. Altman and J. La Fleur, "Managing a Return to Financial Health," *Journal of Business Strategy*, Summer 1981.

example, for credit analysis, investor analysis, and so forth, overlooks the possibility of using them actively. In the "active" use of a predictive model, the role of the observer is shifted to that of a "participant." For example, a manager may use a predictive model that relates to the business affairs of a company by deliberately attempting to influence the model's measurements. The manager, acting as a participant rather than as an observer, makes decisions suggested by the parameters of the model in order to "control" its prediction.

In the specific case we will discuss, the Z-score bankruptcy predictor model was used *actively* to manage the financial turnaround. Management decisions were made over a period of five years to foil the model's prediction of bankruptcy. These decisions, many of which were specifically motivated by considering their effect on the financial ratios in the model, led directly to the recovery of the company and to the establishment of a firm financial base.

I did not indicate earlier what management could do with the results of the model when it became clear that a firm was headed toward bankruptcy—in other words, when its overall financial profile was consistent with that of other firms that had gone bankrupt in the past. It took GTI Corp., and specifically the management strategy formulated and implemented by Jim La Fleur, to turn the model "inside out" and show its ability to help shape business strategy and avert bankruptcy.

What the Z-Score Told GTI

When Jim La Fleur took charge of the company, GTI had experienced the following changes during the first six months of 1975:

Working capital decreased by $6 million
Retained earnings decreased by $2 million
A $2 million loss incurred
Net worth decreased from $6.207 million to $4.370 million
Market value of equity decreased by 50 percent
Sales decreased by 50 percent

Noticing an article in *Boardroom Report* about the Z-score, La Fleur saw the potential application of the bankruptcy predictor to the problem at hand. Plugging in the preliminary numbers for the five ratios, La Fleur put the Z-score to work for GTI. The resulting Z-score was 0.7. At that level the predictor forecast severe distress and possible bankruptcy. When more accurate numbers were inserted into the Z-score formula, it fell even lower, to 0.38, about half the earlier calculation. The prognosis was grave.

A Tool for Recovery

Despite its portent of doom, the Z-score was also seen as a management tool for recovery. Clearly, the predictor's five financial ratios were the key to the Z-score movement, either up or down. While the previous management had inadvertently followed a strategy that had decreased the ratios and caused the Z-score to fall, GTI's new management decided to reverse the plunge by deliberately increasing the ratios.

Inherent in the Z-score predictor was the message that *underutilized assets* could be a major contributor to the deterioration of a company's financial condition. Such deterioration had taken place at GTI over several years. The company's total assets had grown out of proportion to other financial factors. I have found this to be the case of many business failures, particularly larger ones.

By using retrospective analysis, La Fleur concluded that the Z-score could have predicted GTI's turn toward financial distress. For example, historical data showed that GTI's Z-score started to dive precipitously two years earlier, in 1973. The retrospective Z-score slide became even steeper in 1974, as GTI dropped at year-end to $0.19 in earnings per share. Thus, GTI's Z-score had been falling for several years, as shown in Figure 2.6, even during periods when the company's profits were rising. That was further proof of the predictor's validity and suggested its ability to help set strategy to guide the company's recovery.

The Effects of Growth Fever

For more than two years previously, as a member of the board of directors, La Fleur had cautioned against what appeared to be overaggressive policies of debt and expansion by GTI's operating management. The warnings, unfortunately, had little effect.

Along with most of the industry, GTI had succumbed throughout the 1960s to a highly competitive growth fever. During those years, many managers focused almost entirely on their P&L statements. They were willing to borrow whatever was necessary to increase sales and profits. With stock values rising, they expected to obtain very favorable equity funding in the future to pay off the accumulated debt. That strategy served well until economic downturns of 1969 and 1972. Then, with profits falling, many companies had trouble servicing the debt, which had seemed so easy to handle a few years earlier. (Sounds familiar in 1989 and 1990 as well.) But GTI, like many others, continued pursuing the same strategy, despite changing economic conditions. That worked for a while.

But early in 1975, GTI started losing money. Before that profit slide could be stopped, GTI's 1975 net loss increased to more than $2.6 million on sales of $12 million, a loss of $1.27 per share.

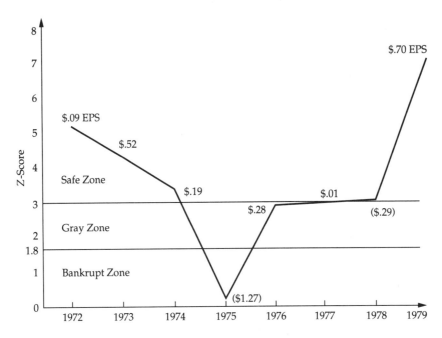

Figure 2.6.   GTI's 1972–1979 Z-Score Curve with Annual EPS Notations

Taking Quick Action

During the month of May, a member of the audit committee discovered information indicating that the figures reported for the first quarter of 1975 were incorrect. As the evidence developed during the ensuing audit meetings, it was obvious that the company's problems were serious. GTI's auditing firm began a thorough reexamination of the company's first quarter activities. The auditors quickly confirmed that there was, indeed, a material discrepancy in the figures, and they set to work revising first-quarter figures.

At that point, GTI's board of directors chose a new executive team, asking La Fleur, a fellow board member, to take over as chairman and chief executive officer. Having observed GTI going into debt to finance its operations for several years, even with record sales and profits on paper, La Fleur was determined to find the underlying problems. It didn't take long.

Inventory, out of control, revealed itself as a major contributor to the company's ballooning assets. In many instances, returned goods had been set aside and not properly accounted for. Adding to that difficulty, work-in-progress was grossly out of proportion to sales. Again, these symptoms seem to be common among crisis corporations.

Genesis of Strategy

From this new evidence of excess assets, a recovery strategy emerged to find ways to decrease GTI's total assets without seriously reducing the other factors in the numerators of the Z-score's ratios: working capital, retained earnings, earnings before interest and taxes, market value of equity and sales. GTI started looking for assets that were not being employed effectively—that is, not earning money. When identified, such assets were sold and the proceeds used to reduce the company's debt. The effect was a decrease in the denominators of all five Z ratios simultaneously. It is not enough simply to sell assets—the proceeds had to be utilized as soon as possible. GTI's Z-score rose accordingly. Having evolved the strategy, La Fleur began to implement the action to eliminate GTI's excess assets. Excess inventory was sold as quickly as possible, even at scrap value in some cases.

While the bankruptcy predictor was originally designed for an observer's analysis of a company's condition, GTI used it as an aid to managing company affairs. The predictor actually became an element of active strategy to avoid GTI's impending bankruptcy.

Stopping the Cash Bleed

In quick order, GTI's cash bleed was stanched. The staffs at two unprofitable West Coast plants were reduced to a skeleton crew within 10 days, and the corporate staff at headquarters was pared from 32 to 6. A year earlier, with company profits at $1.5 million, the corporate staff expense had been over $1 million! All capital programs were frozen. Only the most critical production needs, repairs, and maintenance were authorized. GTI asked its creditors for additional short-term credit, then pushed strenuously ahead on its collections. Inventories were placed under strict control. Taking effect, these measures got cash and expenses under control and improved debt service capability.

Reducing costs further took more analysis. A management function/location matrix and a "job-versus-cost" grid, was constructed for each of GTI's plants. The grid showed each executive's job, what work he performed, and how much that job cost the company. When overlaps or duplications were found, jobs were consolidated. Where the revenues from different locations did not cover the identifiable cost, it was clear that a problem existed.

Finding Lost Profits—Employee Assistance

Employees were also involved in the turnaround. A simple questionnaire was handed out to the 250 employees of GTI's largest plant in Saegertown, Pennsylvania, asking them why they thought the plant was no longer profitable. The implied question, of course, was about the underutilized assets that had depressed GTI's Z-score. The employees knew what was wrong. They were specific about how to improve the use of their machines. Many of the suggestions were implemented, and productivity improved. Eventually, however, this plant was sold and product lines moved elsewhere.

Several weeks later, similar questions were asked at GTI's plant in Hadley, Pennsylvania. The employee responses resulted in changing the plant's organization from functional to product line, another move that more effectively employed the company's assets. Because they participated in the changes, the plant's employees really worked to make the reorganization succeed. After a few weeks, the plant began to turn a profit. In fact, profitable product lines were moved form Saegertown to Hadley.

Those profits were the forerunner of profits that would be produced in other parts of the company as time went on. Although it did not jump as a result of the increased profits, the Z-score did begin to react. By mid-1976, after slanting down for three years, the Z-score bottomed out and started up. GTI began turning the corner.

Selling Off a Product Line

Though cost reduction and increased profits had eased the problems, GTI needed stronger recovery actions. The function/location matrix analysis was extended to include products and was used to rate product profitability throughout the company. Plans were made to eliminate the losers and strengthen the winners. As a result, late in 1976, GTI sold one of its major underutilized assets. GTI's crystal base product line had appeared fairly strong, but the product matrix analysis presented a different view. Crystal bases were not complementary to GTI's other products, and although the line had been marginally profitable in the past, demand for its products was likely to decrease. The line also appeared to need a great deal of capital to be competitive in the future.

The cash generated by the sale of the crystal base product line was used to reduce debt. The consequent decrease of both total assets and debt produced a dramatic effect. The Z-score leaped from under 1.0 to 2.95. In one transaction, GTI zoomed almost all the way into the Z-score predictor's safe zone.

Although to outside observers the company did not appear to turn around for another year and a half, La Fleur felt the firm was on the road to recovery with the sale of the crystal base product line. The company had come from almost certain bankruptcy to the stage where it could begin contemplating new products. In less than 18 months, the Z-score had climbed from 0.38 in the near-death bankrupt zone almost all the way to the Z-score's safe zone (see Chart 2.6).

With heightened confidence in the model, GTI started working to put the Z-score firmly in the safe zone. Since the company's improving stability and profitability were corroborating the Z-score approach, GTI's headquarters staff began figuring how a proposed new product or financial transaction would affect the Z-score. Further, GTI extended the product evaluation matrix from simple profit and loss to multiyear projections of return on assets. This involved taking a hard look at projected working capital and capital expenditure requirements, product by product. This analysis established what costs would be if the company attempted to expand within its current markets.

Progress in Operations

While doing this planning, GTI continued to make progress on the operations side, finishing 1976 with $0.28 earnings per share and an increasing Z-score as well. In 1977, earnings sagged to $0.01 per share but with an improving overall financial condition, GTI's Z-score continued gradually to rise. The company even bought out a competitor's glass seal product line with notes secured by the acquired assets—with negligible adverse impact on the Z-score.

Then in 1978, GTI boosted its Z-score again by shutting down an entire division, which made ceramic capacitors, and selling its assets. That transaction, again based on the strategy of selling underutilized assets to pay off debt, occurred later than it should have. This was a case of emotion interfering with a rational, proven strategy. La Fleur had been swayed toward saving this technically interesting product line, though the Z-score strategy consistently suggested disposal. Though delayed, the difficult disposal decision was made.

As a result of the closing of the capacitor division and the sale of its assets, GTI's 1978 bottom line sustained a $0.29 per share loss, but the Z-score increased automatically as the company paid off more debt. As anticipated, operating profits continued to gain throughout the year, paving the way for a strong 1979. Once again, the asset-reduction strategy had worked.

Into the Safe Zone

GTI's Z-Score continued climbing, rising through the Z-score's safe zone, as 1979 pretax profits reached $1.9 million and $0.70 per share on sales of $21 million. From a balance sheet viewpoint, GTI's strategy, in five years, had decreased the debt to equity ratio from 128 to 30 percent and increased stockholder's equity from $3.5 million to $4.7 million. The debt to equity (market equity) improved even more in 1981, to just under 10 percent.

Conclusion to the GTI Story

We believe that certain predictive models offer opportunities to be used as management tools. Supporting that view, GTI's employment of the Z-score bankruptcy predictor has been described as a specific illustration of how an ordinary passive model can be used actively with substantial success.

With emphasis made on prudent selection and use, managers are encouraged to search out and review predictive models that relate to their company's activities. Improved business strategies could very well result. It is quite conceivable that a large number of firms presently in a distressed situation can learn from, and perhaps be put on the road to recovery by, the strategies used by GTI.

An Alternative Use of Z–score–Chapter 11 Planning

One final suggestion on the use of an effective credit scoring tool is to simulate various reorganization strategies while in chapter 11. Firms can analyze the feasibility of a plan "in the laboratory" instead of guessing and hoping that a plan will be feasible and acceptable to creditors. The successful bankruptcy reorganization of Storage Technologies Corp. utilized the Z-score approach in its financial rehabilitation plan.

References and Further Reading

Altman, E. I. "Financial Ratios, Disciminant Analysis and the Prediction of Corporate Bankruptcy," *Journal of Finance* (September 1968).

— "Bankruptcy Identification: Virtue or Necessity?" *Journal of Portfolio Management* (Spring 1977).

— "Commercial Bank Lending: Process, Credit Scoring and Costs of Error in Lending," *Journal of Financial and Quantitative Analysis* (November 1980).

— *Corporate Financial Distress*, John Wiley, New York (1983).

— *Investing in Distressed Securities*, Foothill Group, Los Angeles (1990).

Altman, E. I., R. Haldeman, and P. Narayanan. "ZETA Analysis: A New Model to Identify Bankruptcy Risk of Corporations," *Journal of Banking and Finance* (June 1977).

Altman, E. I., and J. La Fleur. "Managing a Return to Financial Health," *Journal of Business Strategy* (Summer 1981).

Argenti, J. *Corporate Collapse*, McGraw-Hill, New York (1976).

Ball, M. "Z-Factor: Rescue by the Numbers," *Inc. Magazine* (December 1980).

Beaver, W. "Financial Ratios as Predictors of Failure," in *Empirical Research in Accounting, Selected Studies, 1966, Journal of Accounting Research* (January 1967).

— "Alternative Accounting Measures as Predictors of Failures," *Accounting Review* (January 1968).

Bibeault, D. *Corporate Turnaround*, McGraw-Hill, New York (1982).

Blum, Mark P. "Failing Company Discriminant Analysis," *Journal of Accounting Research*, vol. 12, no. 1 (Spring 1974).

Deakin, E. B. "A Discriminant Analysis of Predictor of Business Failure," *Journal of Accounting Research* (March 1972).

Dun and Bradstreet. *The Failure Record*, New York (1976).

Edmister, R. O. "Financial Ratios and Credit Scoring for Small Business Loans," *Journal of Commercial Bank Lending* (September 1971).

Eisenbeis, R. A. "Pitfalls in the Application of Discriminant Analysis in Business, Finance and Economics," *Journal of Finance* (September 1977).

Frydman, H., E. Altman, and D. L. Kao. "Introducing Recursive Partitioning for Financial Classification: The Case of Financial Distress," *Journal of Finance* (March 1985).

Libby, R. "Accounting Ratios and the Prediction of Failure: Some Behavioral Evidence," *Journal of Accounting Research* (March 1975).

Martin, D. "Early Warning of Bank Failure: A Logit Regression Approach," *Journal of Banking and Finance* (November 1979).

Neter, J. "Discussion of Financial Ratios as Predictors of Failure," *Empirical Research in Accounting: Selected Studies 1966, Journal of Accounting Research*, Supplement to Volume 4 (1967).

Scott, J. "The Probability of Bankruptcy: A Comparison of Empirical Predictions and Theoretical Models," *Journal of Banking and Finance* (September 1981).

Sinkey, J. "A Multivariate Statistical Analysis of the Characteristics of Problem Banks," *Journal of Finance* (March 1975).

Taffler, R. "Finding Those Firms in Danger," *Accountancy Age* (July 16, 1976).

Wilcox, J. W. "A Gambler's Ruin Prediction of Business Failure Using Accounting Data," *Sloan Management Review*, vol. 12 (September 1971).

Wilcox, J. "The Gambler's Ruin Approach to Business Risk," *Sloan Management Review* (March 1976).

Appendix 1   Z-Score Model Description

Variable	Discussion
$X_1 = \dfrac{\text{Working Capital}}{\text{Total Assets}}$	Frequently found in studies of corporate problems, this is a measure of the net liquid assets of the firm relative to the total capitalization. Working capital is defined as the difference between current assets and current liabilities. Liquidity and size characteristics are explicitly considered. Ordinarily, a firm experiencing constant operating losses will have shrinking current assets in relation to total assets.
$X_2 = \dfrac{\text{Retained Earnings}}{\text{Total Assets}}$	This is a measure of cumulative profitability over time, and the balance sheet figure is used. The age of a firm is implicitly considered in this ratio. For example, a relatively young firm will probably show a low RE/TA ratio because it has not had time to build up its cumulative profits. Therefore, it may be argued that the young firm is somewhat discriminated against in this analysis, and its chance of being classified as bankrupt is relatively higher than an older firm. But this is precisely the situation in the real world. The incidence of failure is much higher in a firm's earlier years; over 50 percent of firms that fail do so in the first five years of existence. It should be noted that the retained-earnings account is subject to manipulation via corporate quasi reorganizations and stock dividend

---

(continued)

Appendix 1   (cont.)

Variable	Discussion
$X_3 = \dfrac{\text{Earnings Before Interest \& Taxes}}{\text{Total Assets}}$	declarations. It is conceivable that a bias would be created by a substantial reorganization or stock dividend. This ratio is calculated by dividing the total assets of a firm into its earnings before interest and tax reductions. In essence, it is a measure of the true productivity of the firm's assets, abstracting from any tax or leverage factors. Since a firm's ultimate existence is based on the earning power of its assets, this ratio appears to be particularly appropriate for studies dealing with corporate failure. Furthermore, insolvency in a bankruptcy sense occurs when the total liabilities exceed a fair valuation of the firm's assets with value determined by the earning power of the assets.
$X_4 = \dfrac{\text{Market Value of Equity}}{\text{Book Value of Total Liabilities}}$	Equity is measured by the combined market value of all shares of stock, preferred and common, while liabilities include both current and long-term. Book values of preferred and common stockholders equity may be substituted for market values when the latter is not available. The substitution of book values, especially for the common stock component, should be recognized as proxy without statistical verification, since the model was built using market values (price times shares outstanding). The measure shows how much the firm's assets can decline in value (measured by market value of equity plus debt) before the liabilities exceed the assets and the firm becomes insolvent. For example, a company with a market value of its equity of $1,000 and debt of $500 could experience a two-thirds drop in asset value before insolvency. However, the same firm with $250 in equity will be insolvent if its drop is only one third in value.
$X_5 = \dfrac{\text{Sales}}{\text{Total Assets}}$	The capital-turnover ratio is a standard financial ratio illustrating the sales-generating ability of the firm's assets. It is one measure of management's capability in dealing with competitive conditions.

It should be noted that variables X_1, X_2, X_3, and X_4 should be inserted into the model as *decimal fractions*; for example, a working capital/total assets of 20 percent should be written as 0.20. The variable X_5, however, is usually a ratio *greater than unity*; for example, where sales are twice as large as assets, the ratio is written as 2.0.

Appendix 2 Summary of Major Studies Using Statistical Classification Techniques for Predicting the Failure of Nonfinancial Firms.

Purpose and Sample Characteristics	Statistical Method and Important Variables	Contribution and Critique
1. *W. Beaver (1967)*. To test the usefulness of ratio analysis in the context of failure prediction. Analyzes 79 firms that "failed" from 1954 to 1964 and a paired sample of nonfailed firms. Matching characteristics: industry classification code and asset size.	Does *not* use a multivariable approach. Empirical tests focus upon comparison of means, dichotomuous classification tests and analysis of likelihood ratios. Of 80 ratios tested, cash flow to total debt is key variable.	One of the first and most extensive failure-prediction studies. Concludes that accounting data (i.e., financial ratios) can predict failure at least five years in advance. Cautions against using ratio analysis indiscriminately because different ratios have different predictive abilities and because it is easier to predict nonfailure than failure. Major shortcomings: definition of failure and lack of multiple-variable analysis.
2. *E. Altman (1968)*. To assess the quality of ratio analysis as an analytical technique using the prediction of corporate bankruptcy as an example. Thirty-three failed manufacturing firms from the period 1946 to 1965 and a paired sample of nonfailed firms are analyzed. Pairings made on the basis of industry and asset size.	Uses multiple discriminant analysis to analyze 22 variables. Develops a five-variable *linear* model consisting of (1) working capital/total assets, (2) retained earnings/total assets, (3) earnings before interest and taxes/total assets, (4) market value of equity/book value of total debt, (5) sales/total assets.	Reconfirms usefulness of ratio analysis and demonstrates importance of multiple-variable analysis. To date, most widely referenced failure prediction model. Shortcomings: model doesn't have predictave ability beyond two years prior to failure; doesn't develop a theoretical framework for failure prediction; fails to avoid several potential MDA pitfalls.
3. *E. Deakin (1972)*. To develop an alternative to the Beaver and Altman models. Analyzes 32 firms that fail between 1964 and 1970 and a paired sample of nonfailed firms matched by industry classification. asset size, and year of data.	Uses *linear* multiple discriminant analysis and 14 of Beaver's ratios to find combination of variables with greatest predictive accuracy. Ratio of cash flow-to-total debt is an important variable.	Model predicts failure as far as 3 years in advance with fairly high accuracy. Only minor extension of Beaver and Altman. Shortcomings: small-sample problems; doesn't attempt to find a subset of 14-variable set; pitfalls in application of MDA not avoided.

(continued)

4. *R. Edmister (1972)*. To test the usefulness of financial ratio analysis for predicting *small* business failure. Works with two different samples of loss and nonloss SBA borrowers. Each sample contains an equal number of loss and nonloss cases (42 and 562). The large sample only has data for one year prior to loss (failure); the small sample has three years of data.

Uses stepwise, zero–one, linear, multiple regression analysis. Nineteen ratios are tested and a seven-variable regression equation developed. The independent variables (regressors) are transformed to dichotomous zero–one variables.

First failure-prediction model for small businesses. Finds that at least three consecutive financial statements are required for accurate discrimination between loss and nonloss borrowers. Shortcomings: transformation of independent variables to zero–one form gives up information and is arbitrary; selection of "less than .31" as the correlation-coefficient cutoff point for an included regression variable (in the stepwise procedure of the regression) may exclude important variables and also is arbitrary.

5. *M. Blum (1974)*. To aid in assessing the probability of business failure, where failure is defined in accordance with the meaning the courts have given it in the context of antitrust defense (i.e., Failing Company Doctrine). Paired sample of 115 failed firms (1954–1968) and 115 nonfailed firms. Matching characteristics: industry, sales, employees, and fiscal year.

Uses *linear* multiple-discriminant analysis. A 12-variable model with emphasis upon liquidity, profitability, and variability is developed. One year before, failure model is 93–95 percent accurate, 80 percent two years before, and 70 percent thereafter up to five years before.

Application of MDA using accounting and financial market data to Failing Company Doctrine. Stresses the importance of a failure-prediction model to have theoretical justification and sound validation procedures. Shortcoming: doesn't test for equality of group dispersion matrices.

6. *R. Libby (1975)*. To jointly evaluate (1) the predictive power of ratio information and (2) the ability of loan officers to evaluate ratio information in a failure-prediction framework. Employs Deakin's (1972) sample.

Uses principle-components analysis to identify five independent sources of variation in the Beaver-Deakin 14-variable set and MDA to test classification accuracy. The five dimensions are labeled (1) profitability, (2) activity, (3) liquidity, (4) asset balance, and (5) cash position. The 5-variable set is only slightly less accurate than the 14-variable set.

Illustrates the usefulness of principal-components analysis in reducing the dimensionality of a data set and shows that accounting ratios enable bankers to make highly accurate and reliable predictions of business failures.

(continued)

7. *R. Elam (1975)*. To determine if capitalization of nonpurchase leases enables financial-statement users to predict bankruptcy more accurately than without such an adjustment. Analyzes 48 bankrupt firms (1966-1972) with reported lease information and a matched sample of nonbankrupt firms. Matching characteristics: data year, industry, sales, and reported leases.	Uses MDA to test a set of 28 ratios. Single-ratio and multiratio predictions are made. Models with lease data are not more accurate than ones without lease data.	First researcher to incorporate and test the effect of lease data on the accuracy of bankruptcy predictions. Rejects hypothesis that lease data enhances ability to predict bankruptcy. Shortcomings: doesn't attempt to find "best" model; simply tests 25-variable model; several misconceptions about theory and application of MDA. Altman (1976) concludes that the effect of leasing on failure prediction is not yet resolved.
8. *J. Wilcox (1976)*. To show how to usefully quantify the risk of financial failure through the gambler's ruin approach. Uses matched samples of 52 bankrupt firms and 52 nonbankrupt firms from Wilcox (1973).	Uses gambler's ruin model to discriminate between bankrupt and nonbankrupt firms. Important variables are net liquidation value, average adjusted cash flow, and the concept of "size of bet." Model's accuracy is comparable to other failure-prediction studies.	Develops a strong conceptual framework with implications for the management process and prevention of bankruptcy. Seems to be overly concerned about "evils" of statistical searching. Extreme probability estimates.
9. *E. Deakin (1977)*. To assess the impact, frequency, and nature of bankruptcy *misclassification* using his 1972 model as modified by Libby (1975). A sample of 63 bankrupt firms (1966–1971) and a *nonmatched* sample of 80 nonfailing companies are analyzed. Data are from the period 1964 to 1969.	Uses both linear and quadratic MDA. The five ratios from Libby (1975) are (1) net income/total assets, (2) current assets/total assets, (3) cash/total assets, (4) current assets/current liabilities, and (5) sales/current assets.	Focuses upon the concepts of *failing* and *nonfailing* rather than failed and nonfailed to emphasize that a company may enter the failing state and still avoid the failed state. Adopts a unique classification rule based upon both linear and quadratic equations. Compares model's predictions with auditor's opinions. Shortcomings: doesn't attempt to measure costs of misclassification; overly concerned about size of Type-II error; to reduce costs of the Type-I error, the firms in the "investigate-further" group could be classified as failing.

(continued)

Appendix 2 (cont.)

10. *E. Altman, R. Haldeman, and P. Narayanan (1977).* To construct, analyze, and test a new bankruptcy classification model that explicitly considers recent developments with respect to business failures. A sample of 53 bankrupt firms (1969–1975) and a matched sample of non-bankrupt firms are analyzed.

Both linear and quadratic classification equations are employed. The "ZETA" model is a seven-variable one consisting of (1) return of assets, (2) stability of earnings, (3) debt service, (4) cumulative profitability, (5) liquidity, (6) capitalization, and (7) size, ZETA model outperforms Altman's 1968 model.

Most sophisticated and up-to-date MDA model of corporate bankruptcy. Employs linear and quadratic equations; tests for model efficiency; explicitly considers cost of misclassification and *a priori* probabilities, among others.

11. *H. Frydman, D. K. Kao and E. Altman (1985).* To combine recursive partitioning analysis (RPA) with MDA to assess distress of industrial corporations. Samples of 58 bankrupt manufacturing and retailing firms (1971–1981) and 142 non-bankrupt firms are analyzed.

RPA was found to be extremely accurate. Technique is nonparametric and does not rely on many restrictive assumptions. RPA has attributes of both classical univariate analysis and multivariate procedures. Cash flow/debt, cash/sales, debt/assets, interest coverage, market value equity/total capital and quick assets/assets used in RPA model.

MDA complements the RPA technique by providing a scoring system for trend analysis; confirmation requires prior probabilities and misclassification costs.

SOURCE: *Corporate Financial Distress*, Edwards I. Altman, ©1983, John Wiley & Sons, Inc., Reprinted by permission of John Wiley & Sons, Inc.

3

Allocating Value in Restructuring Transactions

Jeffrey I. Werbalowsky
Houlihan, Lokey, Howard and Zukin Capital

Introduction

Balancing the need to preserve contractual expectations with the social costs of business failure has been an issue that society has addressed since the beginning of commerce. From dealing with default by killing, imprisoning, enslaving, and impoverishing the debtor (techniques that some frustrated creditors contend would work well today), modern American society has evolved elaborate mechanisms to provide a legal and financial structure in which a debtor may attempt to renegotiate unfulfilled contractual commitments. This renegotiation is intended to allow the parties to mitigate the damages caused by the debtor's default, while enabling the debtor to continue to employ its assets in an economically productive manner.

Understanding the financial aspects of this restructuring process is especially useful for business owners, investors, lenders and their professional advisors in coping with the leveraged corporate aftermath of the eighties. A comprehensive analysis of restructuring options for overleveraged enterprises requires a truly interdisciplinary evaluation of legal, financial, operational, tax, and accounting factors. This chapter admittedly lacks such grandiose scope and may disappoint professionals in each of the foregoing disciplines by oversimplifying important aspects of the restructuring process in an attempt to provide a basic, broadly usable restructuring framework.

This framework is based on a series of six financial analyses that should be made by the parties in interest to foster intelligent restructuring negotiations. The first step requires that the constituent parties understand the basic causes of the problem before attempting a solution. The business should then be valued on some articulated basis. Next, the parties must determine their respective economic positions—the value of their current stakes in, or claims against, the debtor. The fourth step involves determining a new capital structure for the business in light of current and anticipated future operations. The fifth step values this hypothetically restructured business. The final step allocates, through negotiation, the value of the restructured enterprise to the parties of interest.

Utilizing this basic approach, with the necessary refinements, modifications, and additions inevitably required to address a particular situation, may enable the participants to consensually allocate value in restructuring distressed transactions more efficiently. The utilization of a fairly simple framework to organize and evaluate complex restructuring issues will hopefully reduce the time and expense necessary to reach a satisfactory result. Focusing the parties on some common analytical framework may hopefully eliminate some of the angst which often impedes negotiations. Finally, this approach may allow more input in restructuring transactions from those who best understand the problem, rather than from those who best understand the process.

Identifying the Problem

The first step in designing an effective restructuring solution is understanding the basic cause or causes of the firm's economic problems—why the company is unable to fulfill its contractual obligations. The two general categories of corporate distress are operational and financial.

Operational Distress

Operational distress encompasses the traditional elements of business failure: mismanagement, product inadequacy, manufacturing and marketing inefficiency, industry downturn, and so on. Operational distress hits the slide rule company faced with competition from electronic calculators, the small contractor whose aggressive pricing yields negative margins, and the strike-plagued manufacturer. From a broad perspective of income versus outflow, the company's failure is linked to the inability to generate an appropriate level of income.

Financial Distress

Financial distress stems from the relative amount of debt the company employs to finance its operations. Debt is an attractive means of obtaining capital for two basic reasons. Firstly, our tax code provides a strong incentive to finance companies with debt, rather than equity, since dividend payments to shareholders are not deductible, while interest payments are.[1]

Secondly, a company need only pay for its use of debt with a predetermined interest rate unrelated to the company's success. This is in contrast to equity capital,[2] which is generally entitled to an allocable share of all residual profit generated by the business. Optimistic financiers of companies understand that increasing the relative amount of leverage—debt in the capital structure—enables equityholders to realize greater potential returns as a percentage of their investment.

However, the concomitant burden that comes with increased return is increased risk. Because a corporation's fixed obligations increase with increased debt, its residual cash flows exhibit greater variability. This can provide equity owners with substantial returns on positive results, or quickly produce insolvency with a shortfall in performance.[3] Many of the leveraged corporations of the eighties are finding that poor and even average performances with an equity-based balance sheet may create defaults with a leveraged one. Although a sufficiently elevated profit level can theoretically satisfy the most leveraged corporation's cash needs,[4] from a broad-based perspective of income versus outflow, overleverage represents an excess outflow problem.

Effective restructuring solutions first require a diagnosis of the nature of the corporation's financial problem—Does it stem primarily from operational or financial distress? In general, problems of operational distress need to be addressed before a permanent solution to financial distress is implemented. Otherwise, although clever securities can be devised and brilliant tax attribute preservation schemes implemented, the constituents will not be able to make informed judgments on capital structure and value allocation. This may result in a flawed capital structure for the reorganized enterprise, ensuring a future repetition of the restructuring exercise.

Although corporate default often involves elements of both types of distress,[5] an increasing percentage of restructuring transactions involve operationally healthy companies. If the corporate distress stems from leverage or can be substantially confined to this element (i.e., once the operational problems have been identified and addressed), the parties in interest can employ a series of analyses to evaluate renegotiation of the distressed enterprise's capital structure and reallocation of its value.

Determining Value

The first step in allocating value in a restructuring transaction is quantifying it—How much is the company worth? This analysis assesses asset value, ignoring for the moment prioritization of the various claims and interests entitled to that value. There are a variety of methods to ascertain value,[6] foremost among them market-based comparable and discounted cash-flow approaches. The latter method, although useful and often utilized, relies on operating projections, a predictive exercise fraught with particular uncertainty and suspicion in distressed situations. A liquidation analysis might be employed where operational viability is in doubt. Whatever methodology is ultimately employed, and whatever valuation basis is presumed,[7] the goal of this analysis is to credibly establish the current value of the company.

Determining Current Value Allocation

After establishing the company's present value, the participants can ascertain the current value of their present economic interests in or claims against the debtor. Only when each class recognizes the value of its current position can it intelligently negotiate a maintenance or enhancement of that value in a restructuring transaction. One of the most important (and most neglected) valuation exercises in the restructuring process is assessing the value of the equity component of the distressed business.

Valuing Equity

In many distressed transactions, the troubled business is insolvent from a fair market value of assets versus liabilities as well as a book value perspective. However, Accounting 101 notwithstanding, controlling equity most definitely has a positive value in even the most troubled transaction unless and until equityholders are finally divested, voluntarily or involuntarily, of their rights in the business.[8] The ability to control the enterprise's assets, to direct the restructuring process, and to capture the surplus value of the business in the event of a "turnaround" or successful restructuring all represent material benefits[9] that are often overlooked by creditors, while being implicitly overvalued by equityholders.[10] This is in large part due to the subjective nature of these elements of value and the difficulty in their precise quantification.

There are various techniques for measuring the value of equity in a distressed situation, the most straightforward being to open up a copy of the *Wall Street Journal* and check yesterday's closing stock price. In the relatively unusual situation where there is an active, reasonably efficient market for the stock, this may provide a good value indication. But even so, the public market reflects a minority trading value, not the control value that represents a progressively larger component of equity value as the degree of distress increases. Thus, a "control premium" must be applied to the minority trading values to properly value the equity tranch of a distressed company. Determining an appropriate control premium may involve a comparison with other similar change of control restructuring transactions that have occurred in the market.[11] In the likely absence of truly comparable distressed transactions, analysis of a variety of subjective factors may be necessary, as discussed below.

Other approaches must be employed in situations where equity is privately held or trading results are not considered meaningful. In certain situations where volatile asset values may eventually produce solvency, through market fluctuation or operational turnaround over time, option pricing techniques viewing the equity as an "out of the money" call option may be used. A Black Scholes or other option pricing formula may be utilized, using the current company value as the current market price, total liabilities and preferred stock (depending on its terms) as the strike price,[12] and the length of time equity can prolong the restructuring process or "hold off" creditors as the term of the option.[13]

In certain situations, the control or nuisance value of equity may be the element of greatest worth. Creditors may be willing to pay some portion of their present discounted cost of judicially divesting equity of its ownership rights for a prompt voluntary asset turnover. Bankruptcy lawyers are well aware of the chapter 11 settlement dynamic that often requires "throwing a bone to equity" in palpably insolvent situations to avoid the costs (which the creditors invariably bear) of additional delay or a contested cramdown plan confirmation hearing.[14]

Where management owns the equity, substantial practical and logistical problems may arise if creditors attempt to force a nonconsensual resolution of a restructuring transaction. In such a case, the increased negotiating leverage developed by the threat that equity/management may desert the company creates enhanced equity value, *ceteris paribus*.

Other methods are being developed by restructuring professionals who utilize linear regression and other multivariate analyses to determine equity value in distressed situations. These methods attempt to predict a likely outcome of the restructuring process based upon an analysis of other restructuring transactions.[15] Factors in such a formula used by the author's firm include, among others, secured and unsecured leverage ratios, amount of stock owned by management, nature of the company's assets, transaction size, complexity of capital structure, default date, general creditor temperament, restructuring method, and even the relative proficiency of the respective parties' professional advisors.

Valuing Debt

Techniques similar to the foregoing can be used to determine values for creditor positions. Market trading values can be employed for bond positions if available, although the lack of an efficient, active bond market has been especially evident in many recent distressed situations. Market comparable yield to maturity and similar calculations can be made if instruments are not yet in default, while a liquidation analysis and absolute priority allocation projection may be more appropriate for certain operationally distressed situations.

Care should be taken to consider the true costs and risks involved in reaching some final allocation in privately valuing creditor positions. If a creditor is fully secured with abundant collateral at a market interest rate but faces a material risk of a fraudulent conveyance attack, its claim cannot properly be valued at 100 percent of face amount. The particular economic effects of chapter 11, including, for example, the general nonaccrual of interest on unsecured or undersecured obligations, the possible susceptibility of a claim to diminution or avoidance,[16] and the potential treatment of the claim under the "cramdown" provisions[17] of the Bankruptcy Code all must be factored into the pricing analysis. These issues often come under consideration even outside a bankruptcy, as the parties compare their respective out-of-court treatment with what would be provided under chapter 11. This comparative exercise involves a new variable after the LTV decision,[18] which creates certain material risks for bondholders who participate in out-of-court exchange offers prior to a bankruptcy filing.

Much more could be written regarding valuation methodology, while not doing justice to this complex and challenging area. Suffice it to say that a principled restructuring approach requires the parties to reach some understanding of their current respective economic positions prior to considering a modification of those positions, through allocation of the value of the restructured enterprise.

Developing A New Capital Structure

Financial distress implies that the corporation cannot satisfy the obligations embodied in its current capital structure. A new capital structure that satisfies the company's operational requirements must therefore be devised and then reconciled with the parties' allocational desires.

The analysis does not end there, however, as the tax factors mentioned above may still compel the inclusion of additional debt in the new capital structure.[19] In cases where prolonged losses have created net operating loss carryforwards and other potential tax benefits, however, the tax shield of debt may not be immediately required if these benefits can be preserved.

Tax attribute preservation requires a chapter by itself to provide even a basic understanding of the Byzantine rules and regulations governing this area. Many of these tax-restructuring strategies involve reducing cancellation of indebtedness income, avoiding a "change of ownership," and minimizing the tax damage should a change of ownership occur.[20] Once the operational and tax issues have been considered in formulating a rational capital structure, the process of valuing the restructured enterprise and allocating that value to the parties can proceed. In practice, the three last steps of the framework discussed here—developing the new capital structure, valuing the restructured company, and allocating that value—prove to be an interactive exercise, as the desires of the parties almost inevitably compel deviation from an operationally optimal capital structure. This stems in large part from the fact that creditors (for regulatory, risk preference, and a host of other reasons) generally prefer holding debt rather than equity. Therefore, the focus of many restructuring transactions is placed, ironically enough, on the maximum level of debt that the restructured company can bear. This requires a continual assessment of the viability of the revamped capital structure and the balancing of creditor desires with the restructured company's financial stability.

Valuing the Restructured Company

Once the financial distress is removed or reduced from an overleveraged enterprise through rationalization of its capital structure, enterprise value should be reassessed. Although some valuation theorists may argue that in a world of perfect information and no taxes or transaction costs, enterprise value is wholly independent from capital structure,[21] practice suggests otherwise.

Two general sets of factors tend to reduce the enterprise value of an overleveraged company. First, overleverage creates a variety of operational problems that can cause a direct decrease in earnings or cash flow. Reduction of trade credit, for example, compels a company to replace this interest-free source of funds with bank borrowings or other capital with a higher cost.[22] Borrowing costs are increased as lenders perceive greater repayment risk and raise interest rates to compensate for that risk. Customers are hesitant to provide the company with long-term orders, and suppliers refuse to make long-term commitments. All of these factors can be shown to have a negative effect on profitability with a corresponding decrease in enterprise value.[23]

The second set of factors reducing value involves the risk, time, expense, and difficulty that potential buyers and investors associate with a financially distressed situation. Since a valuation depends on assessing the price of a hypothetical transaction between a willing buyer and willing seller, these buyer impediments tend to reduce this hypothetical price. This does not mean buyers or investors will not become involved in a distressed situation, merely that they will demand a higher rate of return on their invested funds, which again translates to a lower price. This phenomenon can be empirically demonstrated by observing the rise in market-derived values for companies that publicly announce a successful restructuring in or out of court. Although there may be a decrease in the price of some component of the capital structure, adding up the prices of each element of the capital structure will demonstrate the increase in total value and illustrate the speculative discount placed on a financially distressed company.

The elimination of these two value detriments increases the value of the deleveraged enterprise. Immediate quantification of this increase may be difficult and may depend upon uncertain assessments of future benefits. Notwithstanding this difficulty, some determination of the value of the restructured enterprise enables the parties to collectively evaluate the benefits available from a restructuring.

Allocating Value in the Restructured Company

Once armed with the foregoing analyses, informed negotiation allocating the value of the restructured company can occur. Recognizing the present value of the company and the respective economic positions of the creditors and equity, as well as the increase in value available upon a restructuring, the parties are in a position to seek some portion of that increase to enhance their present positions.

It is worth noting that the obvious allocational scheme of the senior creditors being paid in full first, then intermediate creditors, and so on down the priority hierarchy with the residual paid to equity is not rigidly applied in the context of a consensual restructuring. Although this absolute priority rule is the basic legal allocational framework, consensual restructuring transactions often deviate from this procedure both in and out of bankruptcy.[24] Senior classes often perceive the benefits of a restructuring to be sufficiently great for them to voluntarily give up some value to junior classes in order to obtain their cooperation.[25] Where senior classes will clearly be paid in full in a timely manner even absent a restructuring, this "give up" dynamic is less likely to occur.

This aspect of the restructuring analysis focuses on the issues of how much value is allocated to each class and the form that value is given. What is sought is an acceptable allocation, not a "fair" one. Outside of a bankruptcy court, an objectively fair allocation that is unacceptable to one or more key constituencies doesn't do the financially distressed company a bit of good.[26]

How Much Value?

The question of how much value each constituency should be allocated in the restructuring is not susceptible to precise analysis. In game theory parlance, the restructuring negotiation dynamic represents a multiparty, positive sum cooperative game with a broad set of possible settlement points. Each party is ultimately faced with the choice of acceding to the restructuring or holding out. A common negotiating strategy is to allocate value in a manner that provides a debt or equity class with better treatment under a successful outcome than a failed restructuring, giving each class an incentive to cooperate.[27]

Even though a class believes its treatment under a restructuring plan is superior to its present prospects, it may still feel entitled to a greater share of the benefits of a restructuring and threaten the entire deal in a game of "economic chicken." Convincing the parties that the economic "pain" and restructuring benefits are being shared in appropriate measure is one of the collective challenges of the negotiation process.

Form of Value

Intertwined with the issue of allocation is the question of the form that allocation (usually through cash and/or securities) will take. While it is relatively simple to decide that a creditor class will receive $45 million of value, it is decidedly more difficult to choose the types of securities that represent that value.

A basic framework for the process is that the total securities distributed or retained by all parties in interest should represent the capital structure determined by the parties (as discussed in "Developing a New Capital Structure," above). The demands by creditors for particular securities often compel modifying the target capital structure, sometimes with a seriously depressing effect on value. The parties must be careful not to win the allocational battle and lose the restructuring war, by devising an infeasible capital structure acceptable to everyone. Creativity can be brought to bear in addressing the allocational desires of the parties as long as securities are designed within the company's cash flow and leverage constraints. An acceptable allocation combined with an appropriate capital structure are the hallmarks of a successful restructuring.

Conclusion

The difficulties in defining and then achieving a successful restructuring transaction provide a series of challenges to those seeking a solution to corporate overleveraging. Sequential analysis of the key restructuring issues provides a logical frame of reference for constituencies faced with confusing and potentially combative situations. By fostering a collective understanding of the major financial issues through use of the analytical framework provided in this chapter, the restructuring participants will hopefully overcome the difficulties inherent in the restructuring process.

Notes

1. To illustrate, consider the artificial choice of an all equity or all debt capitalization for a California corporation in a combined federal and state marginal tax bracket of 40 percent, with projected annual operating profits of $100,000 and initial capitalization needs of $1,000,000. Financiers could provide the $1,000,000 in required capital through debt and have the corporation pay out its entire $100,000 profit per year through a 10 percent interest rate (leaving the corporation with no income tax liability). An equity financing would produce only $60,000 of net profit to be paid out to the financiers, after the corporation's $40,000 of corporate tax payments. Avoiding this double taxation on dividend distributions—once at the corporate level and then again at the recipient level—provides a strong incentive to employ maximum leverage.
2. Specifically, common stock. Preferred stock, depending on its terms, may be similar to a debt instrument with a fixed return.
3. Note, however, the attraction for an equity financier of a risky, leveraged corporation; his "upside" is unlimited, but his downside is confined to his original investment because of the limited liability of shareholders operating behind the corporate veil.
4. Even this does not hold true in practice because some leveraged corporations with escalating earnings can simply outrun their working capital and suffer chronic cash flow problems that lead to default.
5. Financial distress can cause operational distress through inadequate capital investment, insufficient research and development efforts, and curtailment or cessation of projects that do not produce an immediate return. Moreover, deterioration of employee morale, defection of key personnel, and management distraction from operations all have a deleterious effect on profitability.

Conversely, prolonged operational distress often creates losses that are financed by borrowings, leading to an overleveraged capital structure. It is therefore not surprising to see both elements of distress as a factor in many major corporate defaults.

6. See generally, J. Zukin, *Financial Valuation: Business and Business Interests* (Prentice Hall Law and Business, Englewood Cliffs, N.J., 1990).

7. Will the business be liquidated? Prepared for immediate sale? Down-sized and then operated on a reduced basis? Establishing the basis of the valuation again suggests the need for addressing major operational issues before embarking upon the financial restructuring process.

8. Until the appeal period terminates on a decision confirming a creditor's chapter 11 plan of reorganization or validating a foreclosure that "wipes out" equity, for example.

9. The preservation of valuable tax attributes may require equity to maintain ownership and control, avoiding a "change of ownership" per Section 382 of the Internal Revenue Code, providing another benefit of equity ownership in an insolvent corporation. See generally, Jacobs, "The Chapter 11 Corporate Tax Survival Kit, or How to Succeed as *Guardian ad Litem* of a Corporate Debtor's NOLs," *Tax Lawyer* 42 (1988): 3 [hereinafter *Jacobs*].

10. This situation is respectively manifest by the oft-heard creditor comment, "There's no value at all left for shareholders here," and the equity counterpoint, "This is still *our* company."

11. See, for example, Franks and Torous, "An Empirical Investigation of U.S. Firms in Reorganization," *Journal of Finance* (1989) 747; Gilson, John, and Long, "Troubled Debt Restructurings—An Empirical Study of Private Reorganization of Firms in Default" (unpublished manuscript, 1990).

12. If applicable, the analysis should take into account that this strike price may rise over time to the extent that interest and/or dividends are accruing on these amounts.

13. See n. 8 *supra*. For a full discussion of the theories of option pricing, see R. Jarrow and A. Rudd, *Option Pricing* (Richard D. Irwin, Homewood, IL, 1983).

14. The bankruptcy process in many ways provides equity, through the chapter 11 debtor in possession, with extraordinary bargaining leverage unavailable outside a bankruptcy court. The exclusivity period within which only the debtor in possession has the right to propose a reorganization plan and the relative ease with which it is traditionally extended in large cases, *but* compare *In re Public Service Co. of New Hampshire*, 99 BR 155 (Bkrtcy. D.N.H. 1989) (refusal to grant second extension of exclusivity in multi-billion dollar case), produces the peculiar situation of the party least economically entitled to retain value (the equity) possessing the exclusive means to provide or withhold value (at least temporarily) from senior claimants. This is the basic settlement dynamic of chapter 11. See generally Broude, "Cramdown and Chapter 11 of the Bankruptcy Code: The Settlement Imperative," *Business Lawyer* 39 (1984): 442.

15. See n. 11 *supra*.

16. See 11 USC Sections 544 *et seq*.

17. See 11 USC Section 1129(b).

18. *In re Chateaugay Corporation, Reomar, Inc., LTV Corporation, et al.*, 109 B.R. 51 (Bkrtcy. S.D.N.Y. 1990) (disallowing a portion of the claim of bondholders who

participated in a prebankruptcy exchange offer as unmatured interest pursuant to 11 USC Section 502(b)(2)).

19. See n. 1 *supra*.

20. The bankruptcy process provides substantially greater flexibility in dealing with each of these three issues, which may affect the parties' selection of a restructuring environment. See, for example, Internal Revenue Code Sections 108(a)(1)(A) (no discharge of indebtedness income recognized in bankruptcy), 382(L)(5) (bankruptcy exception to change of ownership rules), 382(L)(6) (bankruptcy option for potential increase in tax attribute utilization). See generally *Jacobs*. Additionally, the recent passage of the Revenue Reconciliation Act of 1990 has created a host of new concerns in this area, particularly in connection with "debt for debt" exchange offers.

21. See Modigliani, Miller, "The Cost of Capital, Corporation Finance and the Theory of Investment," *American Economic Review* 48 (1958): 261.

22. Consider the simple case of an overleveraged corporation unable to obtain its historical trade credit level of $10 million. It is producing and shipping $20 million of goods every month, paying its vendors cash for the $10 million in goods and services every month it requires to operate, and collecting $20 million in accounts receivable every month, which represents payment on last month's shipments. Assume it produces annual cash flow of X, and it is sold to a well-regarded investor for the industry standard price of six times cash flow, or 6X. Upon closing, the trade creditors are reassured of the company's financial stability and agree to immediately restore the $10 million of trade credit. The first month after closing, the investor finds that instead of paying cash for the $10 million of services and supplies delivered to the company, vendors extend trade credit so that no cash is expended. At the end of that first month, the investor finds an extra $10 million in the company's bank account because of the extension of $10 million in trade credit. The company is still generating annual cash flow of X, and the investor therefore feels the company is worth 6X, plus the $10 million of surplus cash. The elimination of the taint of financial distress appears to have created $10 million in additional value.

23. See also n. 5 *supra*.

24. See n. 11 *supra*.

25. See n. 14 *supra*.

26. The Bankruptcy Code does provide certain objective standards for the allocational "fairness" of the treatment of dissenting classes (through the "fair and equitable" provisions of Section 1129(b)) and the treatment of dissenting claimants within an accepting class (through the "best interests of creditors" provisions of Section 1129(a)(1)).

27. Utilizing such a strategy does raise the familiar "free rider" problem of holders having a collective cooperation motive but an individual holdout incentive. Section 1126 of the Bankruptcy Code addresses this problem by binding minority holdouts to a class acceptance of the requisite magnitude.

Corporate Bond Defaults and Default Rates

Douglas J. Lucas
Moody's Investors Service

John G. Lonski
Moody's Investors Service

Various readings of credit quality bear out the need to be vigilant about the future of lower-rated bonds. According to the ratings distribution of speculative-grade bonds, the junk bond market is riskier now than it was in the past. The record shows that the lower the rating, the higher the rate of default. During the past 20 years, the average one-year default rate for the less risky Ba-rated company was 1.66 percent, one quarter of the 7.00 percent default rate of the riskier B-rated junk category. Meanwhile, the ratings distribution of junk bonds has become skewed toward lower ratings and thus a higher rate of default. From year-end 1987 to the end of 1990's third quarter, Ba-rated bonds fell from 38 percent of the face value of debt designated as speculative-grade by Moody's to 27.6 percent.

Over the same two-year period, the total face value of B3- and Caa-rated bonds, which are most susceptible to either a force exchange or outright default, climbed from 19 to 30.6 percent of bonds graded speculative by Moody's. Furthermore, the amount of Caa-rated bonds, which are closest to default, swelled from year-end 1987's $7.2 billion, or 4.9 percent of total rated junk outstanding, to $26.5 billion, or 12.3 percent of total junk, by the end of 1990's third-quarter. As the risk profile of the junk bond universe grows, so too should the incidence of default.

This decline in ratings is reflected in data from the federal government, which show a significant deterioration in aggregate measures of credit quality during the 1980s (see Figure 4.1). For nonfinancial corporations, net interest expense as a percentage of earnings before interest and taxes (EBIT) rose from 18.2 percent in 1979 to 36.0 percent by year-end

SOURCE: Moody's Investors Service

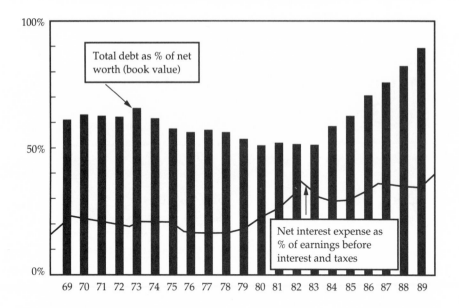

Figure 4.1.   Trends in Leverage and Interest Coverage—U.S. Nonfinancial Corporations

Source: Federal Reserve Board of Governors, U.S. Department of Commerce, Moody's estimates.

1989. Similarly, net cash flow fell from 25.5 percent of total debt in 1979 to 18.2 percent in fourth quarter 1989. Finally, total debt soared from 53.6 percent of net worth at year-end 1979 to 90.5 percent by year-end 1989. On average, leverage has increased and the protection of interest and principal has declined.

When appraising the prospective impact of a recession on the fate of speculative-grade bonds, the steeper risk profile of high-yield bonds should be considered. Compared with the 42 percent before the 1982 recession, less risky Ba-rated bonds now account for only 27.6 percent of outstanding junk bonds. In addition, all aggregate approximations of credit quality were much sounder at the time of the 1982 downturn than they are today. Before the 1982 downturn, the net interest expense of nonfinancial corporations was 27 percent of EBIT (compared with the latest 36 percent), net cash flow was 26 percent of total debt (compared with the latest 18 percent), while total debt was 52 percent of net worth (compared with today's near 90 percent). Consequently, the 1990-1991 economic slowdown should trigger something more severe than the 1982 recession's relatively mild incidence of default.

While not all issues downgraded to Caa will default, the frequency of such rating reductions may help reveal the future direction of the default rate. Indeed, the greater number of Caa downgrades was consistent with 1990's higher default rate compared with 1989. From January through October 1990 there were 72 downgrades to Caa, affecting about $19.2 billion of bonds. Both the number and the amount affected were well above 1989's 52 Caa downgrades, which affected roughly $16.8 billion of bonds. Thus far in 1990, these low-end downgrades have been skewed toward the industrial sector; they accounted for 90 percent of rating actions, affecting 93 percent of the dollar amount. By contrast, in 1989, industrials accounted for 68 percent (34) of the Caa downgrades and 74 percent ($12.5 billion) of the dollar amount affected.

During the early 1990s, defaults may increase because of the recent emergence of new speculative-grade bonds that either delay the payment of cash interest or promise to compensate the bondholder with a higher coupon if the bond's credit standing subsequently declines. Payment-in-kind (PIK) notes, deferred-interest (zero coupon) junk bonds, and extendible reset notes have been issued, generally by companies with uncertain or inadequate cash flow protection. Often, the intention of issuing companies has been to meet payments through faster cash flow growth and asset liquidation. Because their repayment presupposes improved financial performance, or the sale of targeted assets at a satisfactory price, these securities are beset with considerable uncertainty.

For most delayed-cash and adjustable-coupon issues, the shallowness of existing debt protection implies that there is little or no room for error. Near-perfect execution of strategy has now become critical in view of the growing aversion on the part of investors to supply new funds to trouble speculative-grade debtors. With limited access to stopgap funding, a misstep could quickly lead to financial distress. For deferred interest securities whose future cash payment obligations compound relentlessly and for coupon reset provisions that could burden the issuer with prohibitively expensive borrowing costs, either an unexpected drop in cash flow or inadequate bids for offered assets may seriously jeopardize the issuer's ability to fully meet the terms of repayment.

As we move into the early 1990s, a growing number of deferred- interest securities are scheduled to switch to cash payment. Also, sinking fund requirements and maturation will add to the cash demands placed on speculative-grade issuers. Finally, for some outstanding junk issuers, as shorter-term bank loans and bridge loans that helped finance acquisitions come due, liquidity needs will rise.

Unfortunately, the present time may not be the best of times for the more speculative credits to tap the credit market. Although some higher-risk issuers may manage to raise cash either through earnings, asset sales, or new equity investment, others will discover that borrowed funds may be available only at prohibitive costs. Stricter bank capital requirements, more severe assessments of bank loan quality by regulators, federal stipulations that thrifts rid their portfolios of junk bonds, and possible tighter regulation of insurance and pension fund investment in speculative-grade securities have reinforced a growing aversion toward investment in steeply leveraged companies.

Furthermore, help from a more vibrant economy may not be forthcoming. The Fed appears likely to adhere to a relatively tight monetary policy, a position that promises to limit the growth of both revenues and cash flow. Interest-sensitive companies may be especially vulnerable. Equally important, a restrictive Fed policy will curb liquidity. The emergence of the large-scale issuance of high-yield bonds was fueled in part by the upsurge in liquidity that stemmed from very rapid monetary growth in 1985 and 1986.

Although the economy may avoid a downturn, the consensus forecast by the Blue-Chip Economic indicators of 1.9 percent real GNP growth for 1990 hardly portends a widespread rebound in earnings. Indeed, that same consensus foresees a 2.4 percent slide in pretax profits for 1990, while the growth rates of capital spending and personal disposable income are expected to fall by more than a percentage point from their 1989 pace. Slower personal income growth would likewise imply sluggish household spending. Furthermore, consumer confidence might wilt in response to a weaker labor market and regional declines in real estate values.

Methodology

Moody's Rating Database

Moody's drew on a proprietary database of public debt ratings and defaults covering U.S. and non-U.S. industrial companies, utilities, financial institutions, sovereign issuers, and structured finance entities that issued long-term debt rated by Moody's. Municipal debt issuers were excluded, as were issuers with short-term debt ratings only. In total, our database includes more than 4,000 issuers that met the criteria during the 20-year period studied. At year-end 1989, the database contained rating histories of 3,042 companies. These issuers account for almost the total dollar amount of long-term corporate debt in the U.S. public market. The database also tracks defaults and distressed exchanges.

Figure 4.2 illustrates the steady growth of rated issuers since 1970; the number of rated issuers is broken out by implied senior unsecured rating in Figure 4.3.

In analyzing the relationship between default and credit rating, the most useful unit of study is the individual issuer, a departure from other studies that base statistics on the par amount of debt. Since we are assessing the likelihood that an individual issuer will default, a weighting by par amount would be misleading for the purposes of this study. For example, the assignment of a rating to a $25 million issue or to a $100 million issue involves a single credit judgment; issue size is irrelevant to the relationship between rating and likelihood of default. Rating statistics

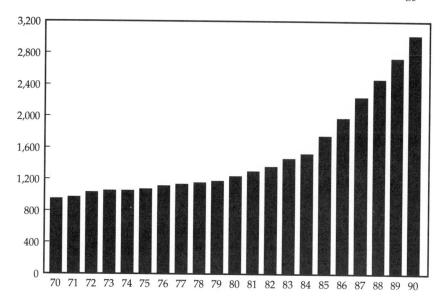

Figure 4.2. Number of Rated Issuers, 1970–1990

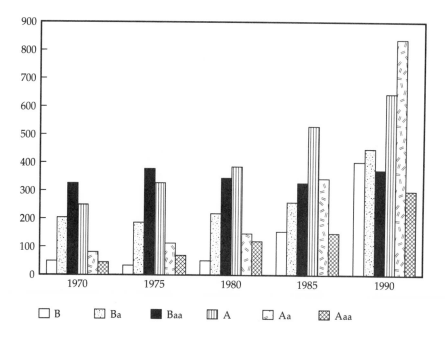

Figure 4.3. Number of Rated Issuers, 1970–1990

are limited to one observation for each legal entity. To tabulate multiple debt issues by a single issuer separately would bias the results toward the default characteristics of issuers with multiple issues. However, different issuers within an affiliated group of companies were measured separately because not all subsidiaries have cross-default provisions, nor are affiliated companies always rated the same. For example, 30 legal entities affiliated with Penn Central issued rated debt. Moody's tabulated the history of each one individually.

To compare default likelihood for issuers with different types of debt (e.g., secured, senior unsecured, subordinate), Moody's categorized all issuers by their actual or implied senior unsecured debt rating, the reason being that Moody's ratings assess both probability of loss and anticipated severity of loss. For example, although there is usually equal probability of default for the subordinated and senior debt of an issuer, the subordinated debt will generally carry a lower rating to reflect higher anticipated losses. To isolate the prediction of default frequency from recovery considerations, we used an issuer's senior unsecured rating or equivalent. Fifty-six percent of observations in this study were based directly on senior unsecured ratings and therefore required no modification. Twenty-six percent were implied from subordinated ratings by assuming a rating one letter grade above the subordinate rating or, following the introduction of numerical rating modifiers in 1982, one numerical notch above for investment grade and two numerical notches above for speculative grades. The last 18 percent of observations were implied from secured ratings by dropping one letter grade below the secured rating or, following the introduction of numerical rating modifiers, one numerical rating notch below the secured rating.

Definition of Default

Moody's defines default as any missed or delayed disbursement of interest and/or principal. Although this definition includes companies that make a delayed payment within the grace period provided in the transaction, there is only one such instance included in these statistics. Cannon Group, which habitually paid interest on the last day of its 30-day grace period. We also include distressed exchanges where (i) the issuer offered bondholders a new security or package of securities containing a diminished financial obligation (such as preferred or common stock or debt with a lower coupon or par amount) and (ii) the exchange had the apparent purpose of helping the borrower avoid default. The date of default used in the study was the earliest of an announcement of intent to default, distribution of a distressed exchange offer, failure to pay interest or principal when due, or a filing for bankruptcy.

Moody's compiled the default histories used in this study from a variety of sources, including our own library of financial reports, press releases, press clippings, internal memoranda, and records of analyst contact with rated issuers. Moody's also examined documents from the Securities and Exchange Commission, Dun & Bradstreet, the New York Stock Exchange, and the American Stock Exchange.

Corporate Default Rates

Rating Histories of Defaulting Issuers

Of the 274 rated issuers that defaulted from 1970 through year-end 1989, only one company defaulted on investment-grade debt. That company was Manville Corporation, which voluntarily entered bankruptcy as a result of asbestos litigation in 1982 when its senior debt was rated A. There were no defaults by Aaa- or Aa-rated issuers. As expected, the number of defaulting companies that once had investment-grade ratings increases as their rating histories are traced from 1 year to 30 years prior to default. For example, as shown in Table 4.1, 17 bond issuers had investment-grade ratings at the start of the calendar year in which they defaulted (second column), and 30 issuers held investment-grade status as of January 1 of the second year preceding default (third column). Table 4.1 presents the rating out to 30 years prior to default, when 6 of 31 defaulting companies had ratings in the investment-grade category. The ratings of three defaulting companies were withdrawn before they defaulted.

The company with Aaa-rated debt on the fourth January 1 prior to default is Getty Oil, a subsidiary of Texaco. On the fifth January 1 before their respective defaults, both Getty and Texaco Inc. were rated Aaa. Texaco is the sole company with a Aaa rating between 6 and 20 years prior to default. DFC Financial (Overseas) and DFC Overseas Investment

Table 4.1. Rating History of 274 Defaulting Issuers

	Rating at Default	Rating Calendar Years Prior to Default									
		1	2	3	4	5	10	15	20	25	30
Aaa					1	2	1	1	1		
Aa		2	1	2	5	4		1	1	1	1
A	1	1	5	12	8	6	9	3	4	3	2
Baa		14	24	27	29	25	23	18	9	7	3
Ba	33	82	110	95	81	81	40	24	23	17	15
B	154	142	96	72	49	37	18	17	7	8	7
Caa	65	21	6	5	5	4	2	5	1	1	2
Ca	16	8	7	5	5	5	5	2	2	1	1
C	2										
NR	3	4	25	56	91	110	176	203	226	236	243

NR = Not Rated

were rated Aa3 on review for downgrade on the first January 1 before default, and DFC Financial was rated Aa3 on the second January 1 before default. The two entities with Aa-rated debt on the third January 1 before default are MCorp and First Republicbank. Four years before default, the Aa category also included Manville, Texaco, and Texaco Capital. Manville is the sole A-rated legal entity at time of default and at January 1 before default. During the second year before default, the A category also included First City Bancorporation, Lomas Financial Corp, Mission Insurance, and Smith International. The Baa ratings during the first year before default include Arlan's Department Store, Equitable Lomas Leasing, Leaseway Transportation, Lomas Financial Corp., Parkview-Gem, United Merchants, Revere Copper, Smith Industries, a Penn Central subsidiary, two Storage Technology subsidiaries, and three Kaneb Service subsidiaries.

Average Default Rates by Rating Category

To assess rating-specific default experience in recent years, Moody's calculated default rates in a variety of ways. The methods used include the following:

- *One-year default rates by letter-rating category, 1970–1989* (Tables 4.6 and 4.7). One-year default rates are the percentage of issuers in each rating category on January first of a given year that defaulted on or before December 31 of the same year.
- *One-year default rates by alphanumeric-rating category, 1983–1989* (Tables 4.8 and 4.9). The time period for these data is shorter because numerical rating gradations were not introduced until 1982.
- *One- to 20-year default rates by rating category for cohorts, 1970–1989* (Table 4.10). These are calculated similarly to one-year default rates, except that issuers are followed over a longer period. For example, issuers in each rating category on January 1, 1970, were followed through to December 31, 1989. The rates are cumulative in that each year's default rate includes the defaults of previous years.
- *Average default rates for cohorts, 1970–1989* (Tables 4.11 and 4.12). These are averages of the default rates contained in Table 4.10, covering 1 to 20 years. For each year in succession, we calculated the incremental increase in cumulative default rates of all cohorts. These incremental increases were averaged, weighting by the number of issuers in the cohort, and the average increase was then added to the previous year's average cumulative default rate.

The complete year-to-year results of that analysis are presented at the end of this report. Following is a discussion of the average default rates derived from each of the methods of calculation described previously.

Results

The study confirms earlier research that found an inverse relationship between default rates and rating classification. In other words, progressively lower-rated companies are much more likely to default on their obligations to bondholders. That relationship was found to hold, on average, throughout the 20-year study period. In fact, 66 percent of the 209 cohort cumulative default rankings shown in Table 4.10 maintain a strict inverse relationship between default rates and rating classification. Of the remainder, there is usually only one default rate out of sequence.

The markedly higher default rates for lower rating classes show up clearly in one-year default rates by letter-rating category (illustrated in Figure 4.4 and derived from Table 4.6). On average, in the 20-year study period, 3.6 percent of speculative-grade issuers defaulted within one year, compared with 0.07 percent of investment-grade issuers. The same relationship shows up distinctly within the speculative-grade categories, increasing from a 1.7 percent one-year default rate for Ba-rated issuers to 7.0 percent for B-rated credits.

The pattern also holds generally for issuers ranked by numerical-rating category during 1983 through 1989 (illustrated in Figure 4.5 and derived from Table 4.8). Investment-grade issuers defaulted at the rate of 0.09 percent per year during that period, while the one-year default rate for speculative-grade issuers was 4.25 percent. Default rates rise sharply from

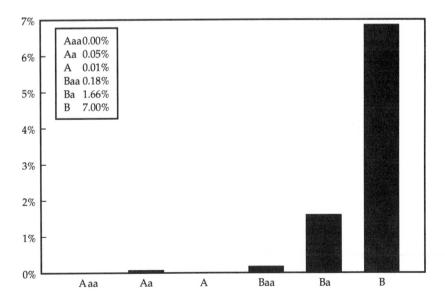

Figure 4.4. Average One-year Default Rates 1970–1990

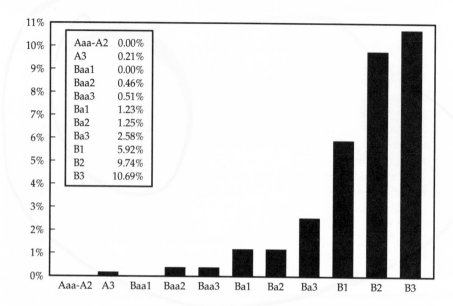

Aaa-A2	0.00%
A3	0.21%
Baa1	0.00%
Baa2	0.46%
Baa3	0.51%
Ba1	1.23%
Ba2	1.25%
Ba3	2.58%
B1	5.92%
B2	9.74%
B3	10.69%

Figure 4.5.   Average One-Year Default Rates 1983–1990

the 1.2 percent for Ba1- and Ba2-rated issuers to more than 10 percent for B3 issuers.

Finally, the higher default risk for lower-rating categories holds up when defaults by rated issuers are traced over periods of up to 20 years. For example, over five years, 13 percent of speculative-grade issuers defaulted on average, while the default rate for investment-grade issuers over the same time period was only 0.9 percent. The propensity to default within five years also rose sharply by letter-rating category from 0.2 percent for Aaa-rated issuers to a 21.1 percent default rate for issuers rated B. See Figures 4.6, 4.7 and 4.8 for illustrations of 5- , 10- , and 15-year default rates. Complete 1-year to 20-year average default rates are presented in Table 4.11.

Throughout the study period, there was a sharp distinction between companies in the investment-grade Baa category and companies in the upper-speculative-grade Ba category. In the past 20 years, Ba companies have been two to nine times more prone to default than Baa-rated companies over any time period. B-rated companies have been up to four times more prone to default than Ba-rated companies.

The data on multiple-year default rates also show that over time the riskier credits that survive tend to become stronger. For B-grade companies, the cumulative default rate rises quickly to 16 percent in three years, but then default rate only increases by another 12 percent, as shown in Figure 4.9. Investment-grade issuers, on the other hand, have a fairly steady default rate, as also shown in Figure 4.9.

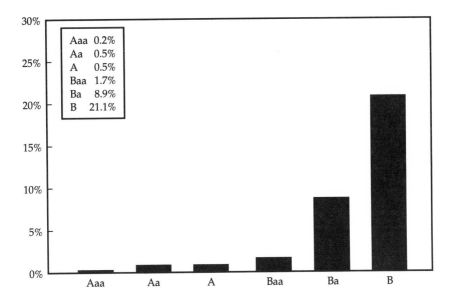

Figure 4.6. Average Five-Year Default Rates

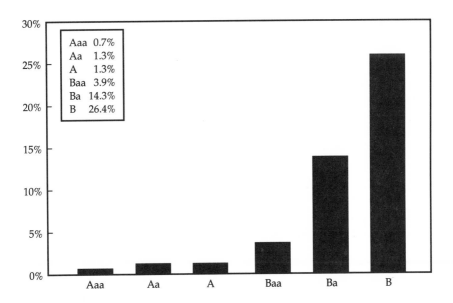

Figure 4.7. Average Ten-Year Default Rates

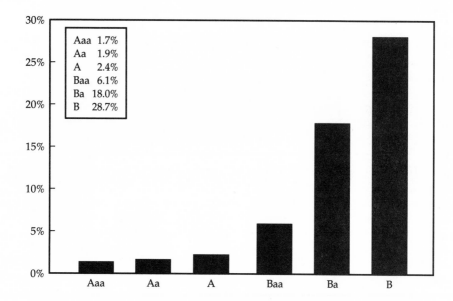

Figure 4.8.   Average Fifteen-Year Default Rates

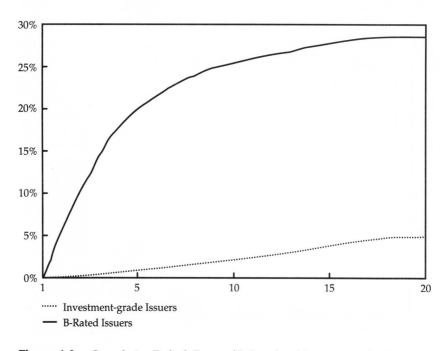

Figure 4.9.   Cumulative Default Rates of B-Rated and Investment-Grade Issuers

Default Rates Excluding Special Events

To show default rates caused by fundamental credit factors. Moody's also calculated default rates excluding the 24 defaults during the study period that were precipitated wholly or in part by "special events." Special events are defined as rapid changes in a company's prospects or financial position that (a) result in a sudden shift in credit quality but (b) the precise timing and nature of which could not have been predicted by the normal tools of fundamental credit analysis. Examples include mergers, acquisitions, takeovers, divestitures, capital restructurings (many due to leveraged buyouts), and filing for bankruptcy protection as a defense against litigation. Although Moody's considers susceptibility to takeover-related special events into ratings on individual companies, by definition the full implications for ultimate default experience of individual companies cannot be predicted in advance. (See "Special Event Risk in the U.S. and Eurobond Markets, 1984–1988," Moody's Special Report, May 1989.)

Complete year-by-year listings of default rates by rating category, excluding special-event–related defaults, appear in Tables 4.7, 4.9, and 4.12.

As shown in Figures 4.10, 4.11, and 4.12, special events had their greatest impact on default rates of higher-rated companies. Since the only defaulting company ever rated Aaa anytime prior to default experienced a special event, the default rates for Aaa companies fall to zero when

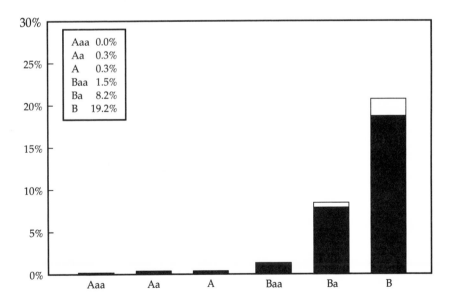

Figure 4.10. Average Five-Year Default Rates without Special Events

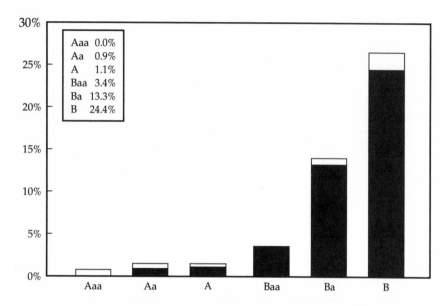

Figure 4.11.   Average Ten-Year Default Rates without Special Events

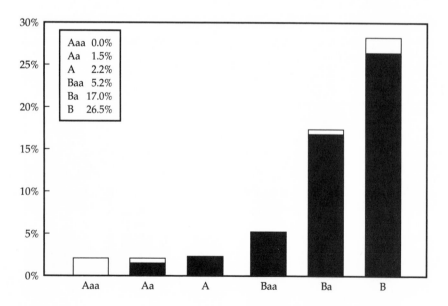

Figure 4.12.   Average Fifteen-Year Default Rates without Special Events

special events are excluded. In contrast, special events account for only 8 percent of defaults within 10 years of a B rating. Essentially the same pattern appears for average 5-year and 15-year default rates when special events are excluded.

The importance of special events on default rates for investment-grade companies is largely attributable to only two special-event defaults. Manville, the only issuer to default while rated investment grade, sought bankruptcy protection in 1982 as a defense against asbestos liability while rated A. Texaco and one subsidiary were rated Aaa until four years before seeking bankruptcy protection in 1987, as a result of litigation with Pennzoil over the purchase of Getty. The severity of the Texaco defaults was limited to a delay in interest payments, which were eventually made up, along with accrued interest. Texaco has since returned to investment-grade status.

Default Rate Volatility by Rating Category

As shown in Figure 4.13, derived from Table 4.6, the one-year default rate for speculative-rated companies varied from a high of 10.9 percent in 1970 to 0.4 percent in 1979. To assess the consistency of each rating category's one-year default rate over the 20 years of the study, Moody's calculated their standard deviation. The same calculation was made for the 5- and 10-year default rates of cohorts formed in 1970 through 1980, and 1970 through 1985, respectively.

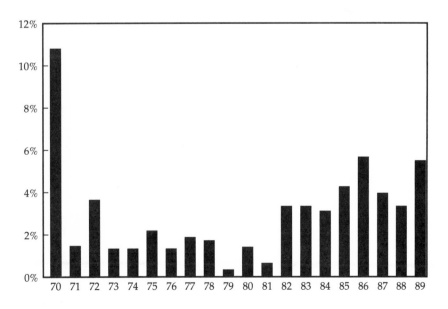

Figure 4.13. One-Year Speculative-Grade Default Rate

In addition to much higher default rates at lower rating categories, the study found significantly higher volatility in default rates by companies at the lower end of the rating spectrum.

As shown in Figure 4.14, the standard deviations for one-year default rates during the study period range from zero to 0.3 percent in the investment-grade categories. The Ba standard deviation rises to 1.8 percent and the B standard deviation is 4.9 percent.

A look at standard deviations of default rates over longer bond holding periods shows that volatility does not diminish over time. As illustrated in Figures 4.15 and 4.16, the standard deviation of 5- and 10-year default rates of investment-grade issuers was below 0.7 percent. Default rates of speculative-grade issuers, by contrast, were seven to eight times more volatile than those of investment-grade issuers.

These results may help to explain the higher-than-expected risk premiums that market observers have noted for speculative-grade bonds. Note that the standard deviations were calculated on the entire universe of Moody's-rated issuers and are not the product of a small sample of firms. While investors can mitigate exposure to default risk of any one company through portfolio diversification, the variation in default rates from one investment period to another cannot be eliminated. Its likely cause is broad economic conditions, which vary from period to period. The yield on a poorer quality bond must compensate not only for the higher likelihood of default but also for the greater uncertainty concerning what the actual default rate will be in any particular holding period.

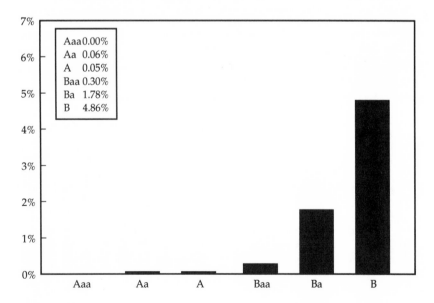

Figure 4.14.   Standard Deviation of One-Year Default Rates

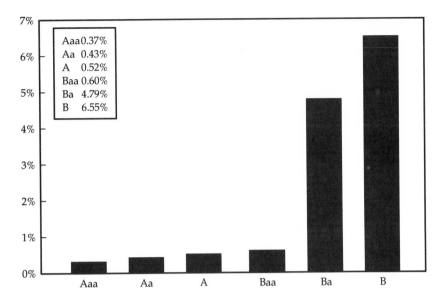

Figure 4.15. Standard Deviation of Five-Year Default Rates

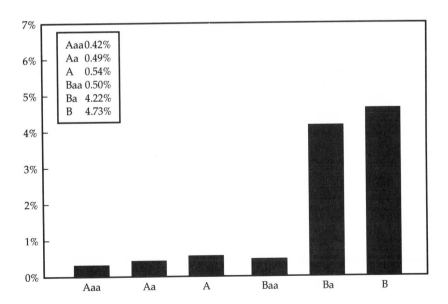

Figure 4.16. Standard Deviation of Ten-Year Default Rates

Comparison with Previous Default Studies

Hickman, 1958

A number of earlier studies have examined the relationship between credit ratings and default rates. The first was conducted by W. Braddock Hickman in *Corporate Bond Quality* and *Investor Experience*, 1958. One of Hickman's analyses compares investment-grade and speculative-grade bond defaults over four-year periods. Moody's four-year cumulative results (Table 4.2) are markedly lower. However, the studies differ in several important respects. For instance, Hickman's numbers are based on the par amount of fixed-rate, single-maturity bonds, while Moody's are based on the number of issuers and their actual or implied senior unsecured rating; also, Hickman studied four-year periods from 1912 through 1943, while Moody's studied four-year periods from 1970 through 1989. The higher default rates in Hickman's study may be attributable in part to his sampling of years surrounding the Great Depression.

Altman and Nammacher, 1985

Default Rate Experience on High-Yield Corporate Debt," *Financial Analysts Journal* (July-August 1985) and subsequent updates. They show par-weighted yearly default rates, not including distressed exchanges., for nonconvertible speculative-grade debt. The important differences between the study and Moody's are that Altman and Nammacher do not include distressed exchanges and they weight their default statistics by the par value of rated debt, whereas Moody's assigns equal weight to each issuer. Although the correlation between the two sets of data at 0.87 is close, Moody's one-year default rates for speculative issuers are higher, on average, perhaps due to the inclusion of distressed exchanges (see Table 4.3).

Altman, 1988

In "Measuring Corporate Bond Mortality and Performance" (February 1988) and subsequent updates, Edward Altman reports average 10-year cumulative default rates for S&P-rated debt issued from 1971 to 1989. The methodology is similar to that of Moody's analysis presented in Table 4.11, except that default rates are weighted by par amount and only initial ratings on new issues are considered. Defaults, but not distressed exchanges, were

Table 4.2.	Four-Year Default Rates	
	Hickman 1912–42	Moody's 1970–89
Investment Grade	3.0%	0.7%
Speculative Grade	26.8%	11.0%

Table 4.3. One-Year Speculative-Grade Default Rate

	Altman	Moody's
1970	11.4%	10.9%
1971	1.2	1.6
1972	2.7	3.7
1973	0.6	1.4
1974	1.1	1.4
1975	2.6	2.3
1976	0.4	1.4
1977	4.5	1.9
1978	1.3	1.8
1979	0.2	0.4
1980	1.5	1.5
1981	0.2	0.7
1982	3.1	3.4
1983	1.1	3.4
1984	0.8	3.2
1985	1.7	4.4
1986	3.4	5.7
1987	5.5	4.0
1988	2.5	3.4
1989	4.0	5.6
Average of Years	2.5%	3.0%
Weighted Average	3.2%	3.6%

tracked through 1989. By comparison, Moody's statistics are based on the number of issuers and on their senior unsecured ratings. Moody's results are compared with Altman's findings in Table 4.4.

Asquith et al. 1989

Paul Asquith, David W. Mullins, Jr., and Eric D. Wolff's "Original Issue High Yield Bonds: Aging Analyses of Defaults, Exchanges, and Calls")

Table 4.4. Ten-Year Cumulative Default Rates

Rating	Altman 1971–89	Moody's 1970–89
Aaa/AAA	0.2%	0.7%
Aa/AA	2.1	1.3
A	1.1	1.3
Baa/BBB	4.1	3.9
Ba/BB	15.0	14.3
B	32.9	26.4

(the "Harvard Study") was released in June 1989. The Harvard Study bases cumulative default rates on new speculative-grade debt issues. A cohort is formed of all new issues brought to market each year from 1977 through 1986. For each cohort, distressed exchanges and defaults are tracked through 1988—the same general methodology used by Moody's in Table 4.10, except that Moody's cohorts are formed according to the rating of issuers on January 1 of each year from 1970 through 1988. In Table 4.5, Harvard statistics, based on number of new issues, and Moody's statistics for Ba and B issuers, are default rates for the cohort of the period indicated. Also shown in Table 4.5 is the average default experience of Ba and B issuers using the averaging technique of Table 4.11.

Besides the difference between basing statistics on the number of new issues, compared with the number of issuers, the two studies look at dissimilar segments of the market. Cohorts in the Harvard study include 24 to 200 new issues, compared with 208 to 845 new and existing B and Ba issuers in Moody's study. Neither set of statistics reporting individual cohorts displays a smooth increase in default rate with the age of the cohort, another indication of the variability of default rates. Rather than examine the experience of specific cohorts, it seems more informative to average the experience of many cohorts, as in Table 4.11.

Table 4.5.   Cumulative Percentage Defaults through 1988

Period	Years	Harvard Speculative New Issues Cohorts	Moody's B & Ba Issuers Cohorts	Moody's Avg. Default Rates for B and Ba Issuers
1970–88	19	NA	23.6%	23.0%
1971–88	18	NA	14.2	22.7
1972–88	17	NA	14.7	22.5
1973–88	16	NA	13.5	21.9
1974–88	15	NA	13.9	21.1
1975–88	14	NA	14.8	20.4
1976–88	13	NA	13.4	19.5
1977–88	12	23.1%	13.1	18.5
1978–88	11	33.3	15.3	17.6
1979–88	10	29.3	17.4	16.6
1980–88	9	32.4	19.0	15.7
1981–88	8	16.7	19.4	14.6
1982–88	7	26.8	18.6	13.3
1983–88	6	21.6	19.6	12.4
1984–88	5	14.7	19.5	11.0
1985–88	4	6.9	16.0	9.3
1986–88	3	8.5	12.0	7.5
1987–88	2	NA	7.1	5.4
1988–88	1	NA	3.3	2.9

Table 4.6. One-Year Default Rates by Year and Rating, 1970–1989

	1970	1971	1972	1973	1974	1975	1976	1977	1978	1979	1980	1981	1982	1983	1984	1985	1986	1987	1988	1989	AVG.
Aaa																					0.00%
Aa																				0.3%	0.05%
A																					0.00%
Baa	0.3%			0.5%				0.3%					0.3%		0.6%		0.8%		0.5%	0.5%	0.17%
Ba	8.4%	1.5%	0.5%	0.5%		1.6%	1.1%	0.6%	1.1%	0.5%			2.6%	1.0%	0.5%	2.0%	1.2%	1.4%	1.5%	2.2%	1.47%
B	21.6%		11.8%	3.4%	6.9%	3.0%		8.8%	5.3%		4.4%	4.1%	2.2%	6.0%	6.5%	8.7%	11.6%	4.6%	3.9%	7.3%	6.41%
All Investment Grades	0.1%			0.2%				0.1%					0.1%		0.2%		0.2%			0.2%	0.06%
All Speculative Grades	10.9%	1.6%	3.7%	1.4%	1.4%	2.3%	1.4%	1.9%	1.8%	0.4%	1.5%	0.7%	3.4%	3.4%	3.2%	4.4%	5.3%	3.0%	2.7%	4.8%	3.26%

Table 4.7. One-Year Default Rates by Year and Rating, 1970–1989, without Special-Event Defaults

	1970	1971	1972	1973	1974	1975	1976	1977	1978	1979	1980	1981	1982	1983	1984	1985	1986	1987	1988	1989	AVG.
Aaa																					0.00%
Aa																				0.3%	0.05%
A													0.2%								0.01%
Baa	0.3%			0.5%				0.3%				0.3%	0.6%		0.6%		0.6%		0.5%	0.5%	0.18%
Ba	8.4%	1.5%	0.5%	0.5%		1.6%	1.1%	0.6%	1.1%	0.5%			2.6%	1.0%	0.5%	2.0%	1.9%	2.6%	1.5%	2.7%	1.66%
B	21.6%		11.8%	3.4%	6.9%	3.0%		8.8%	5.3%		4.4%	4.1%	2.2%	6.0%	6.5%	8.7%	11.6%	5.3%	5.7%	8.4%	7.00%
All Investment Grades	0.1%			0.2%				0.1%				0.2%	0.2%		0.2%		0.2%			0.2%	0.07%
All Speculative Grades	10.9%	1.6%	3.7%	1.4%	1.4%	2.3%	1.4%	1.9%	1.8%	0.4%	1.5%	0.7%	3.4%	3.4%	3.2%	4.4%	5.7%	4.0%	3.4%	5.6%	3.57%

Table 4.8.   One-Year Default Rates By Year and Modified Ratings, 1983–1989

	1983	1984	1985	1986	1987	1988	1989	Average
Aaa-Aa2								0.00%
Aa3							1.1%	0.21%
Baa1								0.00%
Baa2				2.5%			0.7%	0.46%
Baa3		1.8%		0.9%			0.9%	0.51%
Ba1				1.2%	5.1%		1.0%	1.23%
Ba2		1.5%	4.6%	1.1%	0.8%		1.7%	1.25%
Ba3	2.4%		1.8%	2.6%	2.4%	2.9%	3.8%	2.58%
B1	1.3%	8.3%	4.4%	9.8%	4.2%	5.0%	7.3%	5.92%
B2	18.5%	3.7%	17.9%	7.0%	6.8%	7.0%	11.7%	9.74%
B3	11.1%		5.0%	26.9%	8.7%	8.3%	5.9%	10.69%

Table 4.9.   One-Year Default Rates By Year and Modified Ratings, 1983–1989, without Special-Event Defaults

	1983	1984	1985	1986	1987	1988	1989	Average
Aaa-Aa2								0.00%
Aa3							1.1%	0.21%
Baa1								0.00%
Baa2				2.5%			0.7%	0.46%
Baa3		1.8%					0.9%	0.38%
Ba1				1.2%	4.0%		1.0%	1.05%
Ba2		1.5%	4.6%		0.8%		1.7%	1.10%
Ba3	2.4%		1.8%	2.0%	2.4%	2.9%	3.8%	2.49%
B1	1.3%	8.3%	4.4%	9.8%	4.2%	4.5%	7.3%	5.82%
B2	18.5%	3.7%	17.9%	7.0%	5.4%	5.8%	11.7%	9.23%
B3	11.1%		5.0%	26.9%	8.7%	8.3%	5.9%	10.69%

Table 4.10. Cumulative Default Rates for Cohorts Formed 1970 through 1989

Years:	1	2	3	4	5	6	7	8	9	10
Cohort Formed January 1, 1970										
Aaa	0.0%	0.0%	0.0%	0.0%	0.0%	0.0%	0.0%	0.0%	0.0%	0.0%
Aa	0.0%	0.0%	0.0%	0.0%	0.0%	0.0%	0.0%	0.0%	0.0%	0.0%
A	0.0%	0.0%	0.0%	0.0%	0.0%	0.4%	0.4%	0.4%	0.4%	0.4%
Baa	0.3%	0.3%	0.6%	1.2%	1.5%	1.5%	1.8%	2.4%	2.7%	2.7%
Ba	8.4%	9.9%	10.3%	11.3%	11.8%	12.8%	13.3%	13.8%	15.3%	15.3%
B	21.6%	21.6%	27.5%	27.5%	29.4%	29.4%	29.4%	33.3%	33.3%	33.3%
Cohort Formed January 1, 1971										
Aaa	0.0%	0.0%	0.0%	0.0%	0.0%	0.0%	0.0%	0.0%	0.0%	0.0%
Aa	0.0%	0.0%	0.0%	0.0%	0.0%	0.0%	0.0%	0.0%	0.0%	0.0%
A	0.0%	0.0%	0.0%	0.0%	0.4%	0.4%	0.4%	0.4%	0.4%	0.7%
Baa	0.0%	0.3%	0.9%	1.1%	1.1%	1.4%	2.0%	2.6%	2.6%	2.8%
Ba	1.5%	2.0%	3.0%	3.6%	5.1%	5.8%	6.1%	7.1%	7.1%	7.1%
B	0.0%	8.3%	8.3%	11.1%	11.1%	11.1%	16.7%	16.7%	16.7%	16.7%
Cohort Formed January 1, 1972										
Aaa	0.0%	0.0%	0.0%	0.0%	0.0%	0.0%	0.0%	0.0%	0.0%	0.0%
Aa	0.0%	0.0%	0.0%	0.0%	0.0%	0.0%	0.0%	0.0%	0.0%	0.0%
A	0.0%	0.0%	0.0%	0.3%	0.3%	0.3%	0.3%	0.3%	0.3%	0.3%
Baa	0.0%	0.5%	0.8%	0.8%	1.1%	1.6%	2.2%	2.2%	2.7%	2.7%
Ba	0.5%	1.5%	2.0%	3.5%	4.0%	4.5%	5.6%	5.6%	5.6%	6.6%
B	11.8%	11.8%	14.7%	14.7%	14.7%	20.6%	20.6%	20.6%	20.6%	20.6%
Cohort Formed January 1, 1973										
Aaa	0.0%	0.0%	0.0%	0.0%	0.0%	0.0%	0.0%	0.0%	0.0%	0.0%
Aa	0.0%	0.0%	0.0%	0.0%	0.0%	0.0%	0.0%	0.0%	0.0%	0.0%
A	0.0%	0.0%	0.3%	0.3%	0.3%	0.3%	0.3%	0.3%	0.3%	0.6%
Baa	0.5%	0.8%	1.0%	1.3%	1.8%	2.3%	2.3%	2.8%	2.8%	3.3%
Ba	0.5%	1.1%	2.2%	2.7%	3.2%	4.3%	4.3%	4.3%	5.4%	7.0%
B	3.4%	6.9%	6.9%	6.9%	13.8%	13.8%	13.8%	13.8%	13.8%	20.7%
Cohort Formed January 1, 1974										
Aaa	0.0%	0.0%	0.0%	0.0%	0.0%	0.0%	0.0%	0.0%	0.0%	0.0%
Aa	0.0%	0.0%	0.0%	0.0%	0.0%	0.0%	0.0%	0.0%	1.1%	1.1%
A	0.0%	0.0%	0.0%	0.0%	0.0%	0.0%	0.0%	0.0%	0.3%	0.6%
Baa	0.0%	0.5%	0.8%	1.3%	1.8%	1.8%	2.3%	2.3%	2.8%	3.3%
Ba	0.0%	1.1%	1.7%	2.2%	3.4%	3.4%	3.4%	3.9%	5.6%	6.1%
B	6.9%	6.9%	6.9%	13.8%	13.8%	13.8%	13.8%	17.2%	24.1%	24.1%
Cohort Formed January 1, 1975										
Aaa	0.0%	0.0%	0.0%	0.0%	0.0%	0.0%	0.0%	0.0%	0.0%	0.0%
Aa	0.0%	0.0%	0.0%	0.0%	0.0%	0.0%	0.0%	0.9%	0.9%	0.9%
A	0.0%	0.0%	0.0%	0.0%	0.0%	0.0%	0.0%	0.0%	0.3%	0.3%
Baa	0.0%	0.0%	0.3%	0.8%	0.8%	1.3%	1.3%	2.1%	2.6%	3.2%
Ba	1.6%	2.7%	3.8%	4.4%	4.4%	4.4%	4.9%	6.6%	7.1%	7.1%
B	3.0%	3.0%	9.1%	12.1%	12.1%	12.1%	15.2%	21.2%	21.2%	21.2%

(continued)

Table 4.10.   (cont.)

Years:	11	12	13	14	15	16	17	18	19	20
Cohort Formed January 1, 1970										
Aaa	0.0%	0.0%	0.0%	0.0%	0.0%	0.0%	0.0%	2.2%	2.2%	2.2%
Aa	0.0%	0.0%	0.0%	1.3%	1.3%	1.3%	1.3%	1.3%	1.3%	1.3%
A	0.8%	0.8%	0.8%	0.8%	0.8%	0.8%	1.2%	1.2%	1.6%	1.6%
Baa	3.0%	3.0%	3.9%	4.2%	4.5%	5.2%	6.1%	7.0%	7.3%	7.6%
Ba	15.3 %	16.3%	16.7%	17.2%	17.2%	17.7%	19.7%	19.7%	19.7%	20.2%
B	33.3%	33.3%	37.3%	37.3%	37.3%	39.2%	39.2%	39.2%	39.2%	39.2%
Cohort Formed January 1, 1971										
Aaa	0.0%	0.0%	0.0%	0.0%	0.0%	0.0%	2.1%	2.1%	2.1%	
Aa	0.0%	0.0%	0.0%	0.0%	0.0%	0.0%	0.0%	0.0%	0.0%	
A	0.7%	1.1%	1.4%	1.4%	1.4%	1.8%	1.8%	2.5%	2.5%	
Baa	2.8%	3.7%	4.0%	4.3%	4.8%	5.7%	6.6%	6.8%	7.1%	
Ba	8.1%	8.6%	9.1%	9.1%	9.6%	12.2%	12.2%	12.2%	12.7%	
B	16.7%	22.2 %	22.2%	22.2%	25.0%	25.0%	25.0%	25.0%	25.0%	
Cohort Formed January 1, 1972										
Aaa	0.0%	0.0%	0.0%	0.0%	0.0%	1.9%	1.9%	1.9%		
Aa	0.0%	0.0%	0.0%	0.0%	0.0%	0.0%	0.0%	0.0%		
A	0.6%	1.0%	1.0%	1.0%	1.3%	1.3%	1.9%	1.9%		
Baa	3.3%	3.5%	3.8%	4.3%	5.1%	6.0%	6.2%	6.8%		
Ba	7.6%	8.1%	8.6%	9.6%	12.1%	12.1%	12.1%	12.6%		
B	26.5%	26.5%	26.5%	29.4%	29.4%	29.4%	29.4%	29.4%		
Cohort Formed January 1, 1973										
Aaa	0.0%	0.0%	0.0%	0.0%	1.9%	1.9%	1.9%			
Aa	0.0%	0.0%	0.0%	0.0%	0.0%	0.0%	0.0%			
A	0.9%	0.9%	0.9%	1.3%	1.3%	1.9%	1.9%			
Baa	3.8%	4.3%	4.8%	5.6%	6.3%	6.6%	7.1%			
Ba	7.5%	7.5%	8.6%	11.3%	11.8%	12.4%				
B	20.7%	20.7%	24.1%	24.1%	24.1%	24.1%	24.1%			
Cohort Formed January 1, 1974										
Aaa	0.0%	0.0%	0.0%	1.8%	1.8%	1.8%				
Aa	1.1%	1.1%	1.1%	1.1%	1.1%	1.1%				
A	0.6%	0.6%	1.0%	1.0%	1.6%	1.6%				
Baa	3.8%	4.3%	4.6%	5.3%	5.6%	6.1%				
Ba	6.1%	7.8%	11.7%	12.3%	12.3%	12.8%				
B	24.1%	24.1%	24.1%	24.1%	24.1%	24.1%				
Cohort Formed January 1, 1975										
Aaa	0.0%	0.0%	1.5%	1.5%	1.5%					
Aa	0.9%	0.9%	0.9%	1.9%	1.9%					
A	0.3%	0.6%	0.6%	1.2%	1.2%					
Baa	3.7%	4.0%	4.5%	4.7%	5.3%					
Ba	8.7%	12.6%	13.7%	13.7%	14.2%					
B	21.2%	21.2%	21.2%	21.2%	21.2%					

(continued)

Table 4.10.   (cont.)

Years:	1	2	3	4	5	6	7	8
Cohort Formed January 1, 1976								
Aaa	0.0%	0.0%	0.0%	0.0%	0.0%	0.0%	0.0%	0.0%
Aa	0.0%	0.0%	0.0%	0.0%	0.0%	0.0%	0.8%	0.8%
A	0.0%	0.0%	0.0%	0.0%	0.0%	0.0%	0.0%	0.3%
Baa	0.0%	0.3%	0.6%	0.6%	0.9%	0.9%	2.0%	2.6%
Ba	1.1%	2.2%	3.2%	3.2%	3.8%	4.3%	5.4%	5.9%
B	0.0%	6.3%	9.4%	9.4%	9.4%	12.5%	18.8%	18.8%
Cohort Formed January 1, 1977								
Aaa	0.0%	0.0%	0.0%	0.0%	0.0%	0.0%	0.0%	0.0%
Aa	0.0%	0.0%	0.0%	0.0%	0.0%	0.8%	0.8%	0.8%
A	0.0%	0.0%	0.0%	0.0%	0.0%	0.0%	0.3%	0.3%
Baa	0.3%	0.6%	0.6%	0.6%	0.6%	1.8%	2.3%	2.9%
Ba	0.6%	1.7%	1.7%	2.2%	2.8%	3.9%	4.4%	4.4%
B	8.8%	11.8%	11.8%	14.7%	17.6%	23.5%	23.5%	23.5%
Cohort Formed January 1, 1978								
Aaa	0.0%	0.0%	0.0%	0.0%	0.0%	0.0%	0.0%	0.0%
Aa	0.0%	0.0%	0.0%	0.0%	0.7%	0.7%	0.7%	0.7%
A	0.0%	0.0%	0.0%	0.0%	0.0%	0.3%	0.3%	0.3%
Baa	0.0%	0.0%	0.0%	0.0%	1.2%	1.5%	2.1%	2.9%
Ba	1.1%	1.1%	1.1%	1.7%	2.8%	3.9%	3.9%	6.7%
B	5.3%	5.3%	10.5%	13.2%	18.4%	18.4%	21.1%	21.1%
Cohort Formed January 1, 1979								
Aaa	0.0%	0.0%	0.0%	0.0%	0.0%	0.0%	0.0%	0.0%
Aa	0.0%	0.0%	0.0%	0.7%	0.7%	0.7%	0.7%	0.7%
A	0.0%	0.0%	0.0%	0.0%	0.3%	0.3%	0.3%	0.8%
Baa	0.0%	0.3%	0.3%	1.5%	1.8%	2.1%	2.9%	2.9%
Ba	0.5%	0.5%	1.0%	2.0%	4.0%	6.6%	9.6%	14.6%
B	0.0%	5.3%	7.9%	13.2%	13.2%	15.8%	18.4%	23.7%
Cohort Formed January 1, 1980								
Aaa	0.0%	0.0%	0.0%	0.0%	0.0%	0.0%	0.0%	0.9%
Aa	0.0%	0.0%	0.0%	0.0%	0.0%	0.0%	0.0%	0.0%
A	0.0%	0.0%	0.3%	0.5%	0.5%	0.5%	1.3%	1.6%
Baa	0.0%	0.0%	0.9%	1.2%	1.5%	2.6%	2.6%	2.9%
Ba	0.0%	0.5%	2.8%	3.8%	6.6%	9.9%	14.6%	16.0%
B	4.4%	6.7%	13.3%	17.8%	22.2%	24.4%	31.1%	31.1%
Cohort Formed January 1, 1981								
Aaa	0.0%	0.0%	0.0%	0.0%	0.0%	0.0%	0.8%	0.8%
Aa	0.0%	0.0%	0.0%	0.0%	0.0%	0.0%	0.0%	1.3%
A	0.0%	0.3%	0.3%	0.3%	0.3%	1.0%	1.3%	1.8%
Baa	0.0%	0.6%	1.1%	1.4%	2.2%	2.2%	2.5%	3.1%
Ba	0.0%	2.9%	4.1%	6.1%	9.8%	15.5%	16.7%	17.1%
B	4.1%	10.2%	14.3%	20.4%	22.4%	30.6%	30.6%	30.6%

(continued)

Table 4.10.   (cont.)

Years:	9	10	11	12	13	14
Cohort Formed January 1, 1976						
Aaa	0.0%	0.0%	0.0%	1.2%	1.2%	1.2%
Aa	0.8%	0.8%	0.8%	0.8%	1.7%	1.7%
A	0.3%	0.3%	0.8%	0.8%	1.6%	1.6%
Baa	3.2%	3.8%	4.1%	4.6%	4.6%	5.2%
Ba	5.9%	7.6%	11.4%	12.4%	12.4%	13.0%
B	18.8%	18.8 %	18.8%	18.8%	18.8%	18.8%
Cohort Formed January 1, 1977						
Aaa	0.0%	0.0%	1.1%	1.1%	1.1%	
Aa	0.8%	0.8%	0.8%	1.6%	1.6%	
A	0.3%	0.8%	0.8%	2.1%	2.1%	
Baa	3.5%	3.8%	4.4%	4.4%	5.0%	
Ba	6.1%	10.0%	11.1%	11.1%	11.7%	
B	23.5%	23.5%	23.5%	23.5%	23.5%	
Cohort Formed January 1, 1978						
Aaa	0.0%	1.0%	1.0%	1.0%		
Aa	0.7%	0.7%	1.5%	1.5%		
A	0.8%	0.8%	1.9%	1.9%		
Baa	2.9%	3.5%	3.8%	4.4%		
Ba	11.8%	13.5%	13.5%	14.0%		
B	23.7%	23.7%	23.7%	23.7%		
Cohort Formed January 1, 1979						
Aaa	1.0%	1.0%	1.0%			
Aa	0.7%	1.4%	1.4%			
A	0.8%	1.9%	1.9%			
Baa	3.5%	3.8%	4.4%			
Ba	16.2%	16.2%	16.7%			
B	23.7%	23.7%	23.7%			
Cohort Formed January 1, 1980						
Aaa	0.9%	0.9%				
Aa	0.7%	0.7%				
A	2.3%	2.3%				
Baa	3.5%	4.4%				
Ba	16.4%	17.8%				
B	31.1%	31.1%				
Cohort Formed January 1, 1981						
Aaa	0.8%					
Aa	1.3%					
A	1.8%					
Baa	4.2%					
Ba	18.4%					
B	30.6%					

(continued)

Table 4.10. (cont.)

Years:	1	2	3	4	5	6	7	8
Cohort Formed January 1, 1982								
Aaa	0.0%	0.0%	0.0%	0.0%	0.0%	0.8%	0.8%	0.8%
Aa	0.0%	0.0%	0.0%	0.0%	0.0%	0.0%	1.2%	1.2%
A	0.2%	0.2%	0.2%	0.2%	1.0%	1.0%	1.5%	1.5%
Baa	0.3%	0.3%	1.2%	2.1%	2.4%	3.0%	3.6%	4.7%
Ba	2.6%	4.8%	6.6%	10.6%	16.1%	17.2%	17.6%	18.4%
B	2.2%	8.9%	13.3%	15.6%	24.4%	24.4%	24.4%	24.4%
Cohort Formed January 1, 1983								
Aaa	0.0%	0.0%	0.0%	0.0%	1.4%	1.4%	1.4%	
Aa	0.0%	0.0%	0.0%	0.0%	0.4%	1.7%	1.7%	
A	0.0%	0.0%	0.0%	0.2%	0.2%	0.7%	0.7%	
Baa	0.0%	0.9%	1.3%	2.2%	2.5%	2.8%	3.8%	
Ba	1.0%	2.6%	6.1%	11.7%	12.8%	14.3%	15.8%	
B	6.0%	10.3%	17.2%	25.0%	26.7%	28.4%	29.3%	
Cohort Formed January 1, 1984								
Aaa	0.0%	0.0%	0.0%	0.8%	0.8%	0.8%		
Aa	0.0%	0.0%	0.0%	0.8%	1.5%	1.5%		
A	0.0%	0.2%	0.4%	0.6%	1.3%	1.3%		
Baa	0.6%	0.6%	0.6%	0.9%	1.2%	2.2%		
Ba	0.5%	3.7%	11.1%	12.5%	14.8%	17.1%		
B	6.5%	14.6%	22.0%	24.4%	27.6%	31.7%		
Cohort Formed January 1, 1985								
Aaa	0.0%	0.0%	0.0%	0.0%	0.0%			
Aa	0.0%	0.0%	0.0%	0.6%	0.6%			
A	0.0%	0.2%	1.1%	1.9%	1.9%			
Baa	0.0%	1.2%	1.2%	1.5%	2.5%			
Ba	2.0%	6.3%	8.2%	10.9%	14.8%			
B	8.7%	17.3%	21.3%	24.7%	28.0%			
Cohort Formed January 1, 1986								
Aaa	0.0%	0.0%	0.0%	0.0%				
Aa	0.0%	0.0%	0.6%	0.6%				
A	0.0%	0.2%	0.7%	0.8%				
Baa	1.1%	1.1%	2.3%	3.4%				
Ba	1.9%	5.6%	7.8%	11.2%				
B	11.6%	15.5%	19.3%	22.7%				
Cohort Formed January 1, 1987								
Aaa	0.0%	0.0%	0.0%					
Aa	0.0%	0.0%	0.0%					
A	0.0%	0.0%	0.2%					
Baa	0.0%	0.8%	1.8%					
Ba	2.6%	4.5%	8.2%					
B	5.3%	11.4%	17.1%					

(continued)

Table 4.10. (cont.)

Years:	1	2
Cohort Formed January 1, 1988		
Aaa	0.0%	0.0%
Aa	0.0%	0.2%
A	0.0%	0.2%
Baa	0.0%	0.3%
Ba	1.5%	6.4%
B	5.7%	11.4%
Cohort Formed January 1, 1989		
Aaa	0.0%	
Aa	0.3%	
A	0.0%	
Baa	0.5%	
Ba	2.7%	
B	8.4%	

Table 4.11. Average Cumulative Default Rates 1 to 20 Years

	1	2	3	4	5	6	7	8	9	10
Aaa	0.0%	0.0%	0.0%	0.1%	0.2%	0.3%	0.4%	0.4%	0.6%	0.7%
Aa	0.0%	0.1%	0.1%	0.3%	0.5%	0.7%	0.9%	1.1%	1.2%	1.3%
A	0.0%	0.1%	0.2%	0.4%	0.5%	0.6%	0.8%	0.9%	1.1%	1.3%
Baa	0.2%	0.5%	0.9%	1.3%	1.7%	2.2%	2.6%	3.1%	3.5%	3.9%
Ba	1.7%	3.7%	5.5%	7.2%	8.9%	10.4%	11.4%	12.4%	13.4%	14.3%
B	7.0%	11.8%	15.9%	18.9%	21.1%	23.0%	24.4%	25.5%	26.0%	26.4%
Investment Grade										
	0.1%	0.2%	0.4%	0.7%	0.9%	1.1%	1.4%	1.7%	2.0%	2.2%
Speculative Grade										
	3.6%	6.5%	9.0%	11.0%	12.8%	14.4%	15.4%	16.4%	17.3%	18.1%

	11	12	13	14	15	16	17	18	19	20
Aaa	0.8%	1.0%	1.2%	1.4%	1.7%	2.1%	2.8%	3.3%	3.3%	3.3%
Aa	1.4%	1.5%	1.6%	1.9%	1.9%	1.9%	1.9%	1.9%	1.9%	1.9%
A	1.6%	1.9%	2.1%	2.2%	2.4%	2.6%	2.8%	3.0%	3.2%	3.2%
Baa	4.3%	4.7%	5.1%	5.6%	6.1%	6.7%	7.3%	7.8%	8.1%	8.3%
Ba	15.2%	16.0%	16.8%	17.5%	18.0%	18.6%	19.2%	19.3%	19.5%	19.9%
B	26.8%	27.2%	28.0%	28.3%	28.7%	29.1%	29.1%	29.1%	29.1%	29.1%
Investment Grade										
	2.5%	2.8%	3.1%	3.4%	3.7%	4.1%	4.5%	4.9%	5.1%	5.2%
Speculative Grade										
	18.8%	19.6%	20.4%	20.9%	21.4%	21.9%	22.3%	22.4%	22.6%	22.9%

Table 4.12. Average Cumulative Default Rates 1 to 20 without Years Special-Event Defaults

	1	2	3	4	5	6	7	8	9	10
Aaa	0.0%	0.0%	0.0%	0.0%	0.0%	0.0%	0.0%	0.0%	0.0%	0.0%
Aa	0.0%	0.1%	0.1%	0.2%	0.3%	0.5%	0.6%	0.7%	0.8%	0.9%
A	0.0%	0.0%	0.1%	0.2%	0.3%	0.5%	0.6%	0.7%	0.9%	1.1%
Baa	0.2%	0.5%	0.8%	1.2%	1.5%	1.9%	2.3%	2.7%	3.1%	3.4%
Ba	1.5%	3.3%	5.0%	6.5%	8.2%	9.6%	10.5%	11.5%	12.5%	13.3%
B	6.4%	10.8%	14.6%	17.2%	19.2%	21.0%	22.4%	23.5%	24.0%	24.4%

Investment Grade

	1	2	3	4	5	6	7	8	9	10
	0.1%	0.2%	0.3%	0.5%	0.7%	0.9%	1.2%	1.4%	1.6%	1.8%

Speculative Grade

	1	2	3	4	5	6	7	8	9	10
	3.3%	5.9%	8.3%	10.1%	11.8%	13.3%	14.3%	15.2%	16.1%	16.8%

	11	12	13	14	15	16	17	18	19	20
Aaa	0.0%	0.0%	0.0%	0.0%	0.0%	0.0%	0.0%	0.0%	0.0%	0.0%
Aa	1.0%	1.1%	1.2%	1.5%	1.5%	1.5%	1.5%	1.5%	1.5%	1.5%
A	1.4%	1.7%	1.9%	2.0%	2.2%	2.4%	2.6%	2.8%	3.0%	3.0%
Baa	3.7%	4.1%	4.4%	4.8%	5.2%	5.7%	6.1%	6.4%	6.6%	6.6%
Ba	14.2%	15.0%	15.8%	16.5%	17.0%	17.6%	18.2%	18.3%	18.5%	18.9%
B	24.8%	25.2%	26.0%	26.3%	26.6%	27.0%	27.0%	27.0%	27.0%	27.0%

Investment Grade

	11	12	13	14	15	16	17	18	19	20
	2.1%	2.3%	2.6%	2.8%	3.1%	3.4%	3.7%	3.9%	4.1%	4.1%

Speculative Grade

	11	12	13	14	15	16	17	18	19	20
	17.6%	18.3%	19.1%	19.6%	20.1%	20.7%	21.1%	21.2%	21.3%	21.6%

Investing in Debt Instruments of Distressed Companies

Michael C. Singer
R. D. Smith & Company, Incorporated

In recent years there has been a sizable increase in the opportunities for investing in the debt instruments of distressed companies. While the supply of securities of financially troubled companies has increased sharply, so has the amount of funds attracted to this area. Perhaps contrary to general perception, the types of investments available are numerous, ranging from low-risk secured instruments to very speculative investments.

This chapter attempts to summarize the investment analysis of distressed debt—from the early warning signals indicating a possible reorganization to allocating estate value among the claims and interests in a bankruptcy. While many of the rudiments of reorganization and bankruptcy procedure are by now well established, there is still a good portion in a state of flux and evolution. Each reorganization has its own unique characteristics, and therefore the summary presented herein is by no means comprehensive. It should, however, give the potential investor a good sense as to the methodology involved and many of the factors to consider.

Defining the Market for Distressed Debt Instruments

One might define a distressed debt instrument as one that carries with it a reasonable degree of probability that it will be involved in a restructuring due to troubled financial circumstances. In the public securities market

The author thanks his colleagues at R. D. Smith & Company and Smith Management for their input in the preparation of this Chapter. In particular, the contributions by Craig Davis, Kevin McCabe and Ned Elton are much appreciated. The information herein has been obtained from sources which we believe to be reliable, but we do not guarantee its accuracy or completeness.

this risk will start to manifest itself when the fixed income paper of the company involved starts to trade at higher-than-normal yields. At this point a more in-depth analysis is warranted to see whether the higher yield is an aberration, and there exists a good opportunity to lock in that yield or whether the securities are on their way to even higher nominal yields (and possibly to a restructuring).

Of course, distressed debt investing need not be confined to the public markets. Claims and interests throughout the right-hand side of the balance sheet can present opportunities, including the bank debt, trade claims, and private placements, as well as such off–balance sheet items as executory contracts and other claims.

The size of the market in the debt instruments of financially troubled companies has increased considerably in recent years. While the 1980s saw the enormous growth of leveraged buyouts and the related high-yield debt market, the fastest growing area in fixed income securities at the beginning of the 1990s must be the distressed credit area. To put this in perspective, one estimate is that in 1985 there were about $2 billion of publicly traded securities that were in default. By 1987, that number had increased to over $10 billion, and as 1990 draws to a close, the amount of securities in default is estimated at over $30 billion, with the prospect of substantial defaults to come.

Perhaps the most interesting point to note in this recent growth of distressed companies is that there has been a distinct change in the type of large credits going into default. It used to be that fairly well capitalized companies got into some kind of operating or legal problem and, as a result, defaulted—Manville, Texaco, LTV, Public Service Company of New Hampshire, and so on. Most recently, however, it is the debt that was never particularly well structured in the first place that is defaulting, simply because of excessive corporate leverage and overly optimistic projections.

Early Warning Signals

In the chronology of analyzing a credit, predicting distress before it occurs is the first consideration when looking for investment opportunities in debt instruments of distressed companies. While most of this chapter is aimed at evaluating situations from a securities *purchase* point of view, it is inherently logical that good returns can be made in the distressed credit area with appropriately timed short sales of securities.

There are certain factors to look out for that might indicate an early stage of financial distress at a company. These factors are often quite discernible when the debt securities of the company are still trading at fairly "healthy" levels. This stage of the analysis is not only of import to the potential short seller, but is, of course, also key to the holder of the securities, who needs to monitor and regularly review the credit for early signs of problems.

Early warning signals, in this context, are those factors that point to a company's future inability to service debt using cash resources—in the short-term and into the future.

While smaller operating margins and larger operating losses may eventually lead to distress, often a well-designed, highly leveraged capital structure will be able to weather "normal" or even extended losses, provided there has not been a fundamental adverse change in the profitability of the business in the long term.

What is more likely to signal financial distress in the short-to-medium term are certain "trigger" events. These are events that, in conjunction with poor or unanticipated operating performance, suddenly and substantially increase the risk of investment in a corporate security. This is manifested by lifting the desired return for a debt issue from a high-yield return to an equity-type rate of return.

The potential occurrence of these trigger events, and the ability to predict that they are more likely to occur, is the basis for the early warning system. The trigger events below are discussed in no particular order and are not meant to be all-inclusive or, for that matter, mutually exclusive in predicting or precipitating distress. They are illustrative, however, of the more common factors.

Violation of Debt Covenants

Clearly a thorough understanding of the terms and conditions of the securities is essential to gauge the sensitivity of a debt instrument and therefore the capital structure to changes in operating performance. Debt covenants can often be regarded as simply strict guidelines within which lenders request that borrowers operate. When a borrower defaults on nonmonetary covenants, as long as there is a good reason and perhaps in exchange for some additional financial consideration to the lenders, waivers or amendments are usually forthcoming. What are more critical are "exploding" covenants, usually involving accelerated principal and/or increasing interest payments, where a compromise may not be forthcoming.

Shown in Table 5.1 is a summary of certain terms of publicly traded debt issues of the Circle K Corporation and Hillsborough Holdings Corp. These issues were chosen for no other reason than that they contain a number of the trigger events we look for and will be referred to herein. For purposes of this discussion, we are ignoring subsequent events at these two companies.

The Circle K Debenture issue contains a good example of an "exploding" debt covenant, if violated. Under the Maintenance of Net Worth covenant, Circle K is required to maintain a minimum net worth. If this is violated for two consecutive quarters, the company must redeem 10 percent of the issue.

It is likely that Circle K would already be in a deteriorating financial condition if its net worth fell below the level specified and stayed below for two quarters. The requirement to redeem 10 percent of the issue under

Table 5.1. Summary of Certain Terms of Publicly Traded Debt Issues of the Circle K Corporation and Hillsborough Holdings Corp.

Issuer	Circle K Corporation	Jim Walter Homes, Inc. and United States Pipe and Foundry Company.
Date of Issue	October 30, 1986	January 1, 1988
Principal Amount	$150,000,000	$443,046,487
Maturity	November 1, 2006	January 1, 1990, unless extended by the issuers, but not beyond January 1, 1995.
Description	Convertible Subordinated Debentures	Senior subordinated extendible reset notes.
Interest	7-1/4%	16-5/8%, subject to reset; payment-in-kind option until January 1, 1993.
Reset Provisions	None	If the maturity date is extended, the interest rate will be reset to a rate necessary so that the notes have a bid value of 101 percent of the principal amount as of a date 30 days to such maturity date. The new rate will be determined by Drexel Burnham and by one other nationally recognized investment banking firm (as defined). The new rate will not be lower than the old interest rate then in effect.
Payment-in-Kind Provisions	None	Until January 1, 1993, the issuers may elect to pay interest in notes and may be required to do so by the terms of the bank credit agreement. After January 1, 1993, interest will be payable in cash only.
Conversion	Convertible into common stock at $22.50 per share, subject to adjustment under certain conditions at any time.	None

(continued)

Table 5.1. (cont.)

Optional Redemption	May be redeemed at any time after November 15, 1991 at certain specified prices; may be redeemed before if the common stock price equals or exceeds 140 percent of the conversion price for any 20 trading days within a period of 30 consecutive trading days.	None
Put Option	Holders of the debentures have the right to cause the company to redeem the debentures on November 1, 1991, at 107.57 percent of the principal amount plus accrued interest.	Holders of the notes have the right to require the issuers to repurchase the notes at 101 percent of the principal amount, plus accrued interest, prior to January 1, 1991, in the event of a change of control (as defined) of Hillsborough Holdings (the holding company guarantor).
Mandatory Redemption	Annual payments, commencing November 1, 1996, sufficient to retire 75 percent of the debentures prior to maturity.	None
Subordination	Subordinated to all existing and future senior indebtedness.	Subordinated to all existing and future senior debt.
Restrictions on Additional Indebtedness	None	No further indebtedness allowed unless certain specified ratios of cash flow to interest expense are met at the time of incurrence.
Maintenance of Net Worth	If the Company's net worth at the end of each of any two consecutive quarters is $150 million or less, then the company shall make an offer to all holders to acquire on the last day of the next quarter 10 percent of the aggregate principal	None

(continued)

Table 5.1. (cont.)

Maintenance of Net Worth (cont.)	amount of debentures originally issued at a purchase price of 100 percent of principal amount plus accrued interest. The company may credit against any such payments the principal amount of debentures acquired by the company.

those conditions could be "explosive," exacerbating any cash drain at the company. This covenant is not uncommon in the debt issues of a number of the more highly leveraged companies financed in recent years. Two recent examples of companies where the covenant has been triggered and has substantially influenced financial viability are Northern Pacific and the LVI Group.

The above are brief summaries of the principal features of the debentures and notes indicated. The descriptions are not complete and have been included for the sole purpose of providing illustrative examples of trigger events mentioned in the accompanying text.

Both the debentures and the notes described above contain various other covenants; only the above-mentioned terms and conditions have been mentioned for the purposes of discussion.

Future Cash Payments on Split Coupon Debt Issues or on Pay-in-Kind Debt Issues

In the last few years it has become increasingly common for leveraged buyouts to be financed in part by securities having an initial zero coupon before switching to a more typical high-yield coupon when the expected growth materializes. Similar in concept to the split coupon is the pay-in-kind debt instrument that later converts to a cash payer. The coupon will generally be the same (or a slight premium) during the pay-in-kind period as when the debt becomes cash paying.

Typically, the zero coupon or pay-in-kind feature lasts for the first five years before converting to cash payments. A number of those securities issued several years ago are now becoming, or are soon to become, cash payers. Where the companies have been unable to realize the previously expected growth, one can expect restructuring.

The Jim Walter notes (see Table 5.1) contain a payment-in-kind provision that allows—and under certain conditions mandates—the company to make coupon payments only in the form of additional notes for the first five years from the date of issuance. Starting in the sixth year, interest would be payable in cash only. If the company's cash flow has not grown sufficiently by then, this event would trigger a restructuring.

Future Resets of Coupon

While on the subject of changes in coupon as a trigger event, mention must be made of resets. The Jim Walter notes contain a reset provision that, if the maturity date of the notes is extended, the interest rate will be reset to a rate necessary so that the notes have a bid value of 101 percent of the principal amount. Also, in this case, the new rate will not be reset to lower than the old interest rate then in effect. This coupon can only increase. Note that there is no maximum coupon feature. Again, this is a potentially exacerbating term: if operating cash flow is deteriorating and the company's financial condition is declining, it is highly likely that the coupon rate will have to be reset at higher levels to reflect the higher risk, further aggravating the decline. Without a maximum, the coupon rate could become indeterminate, necessitating a restructuring.

The reset feature of debt instruments has proven to be more troublesome than originally envisaged. In addition to the Jim Walter reset, other large companies that were recently forced to restructure as a result of tough-to-negotiate resets include Western Union and SCI Television.

Puts, Sinkers, Maturities Coming Due

An eye must be kept on the vulnerability of a company to maturities coming due. This is particularly the case when large payments become due at a time when the company can least afford it. Circle K's debentures have a stated maturity of November 1, 2006. However, as indicated in Table 5.1, holders of the debentures have the right to put the debentures in full to the company as early as November 1, 1991, and at a price of 107.57 percent plus accrued interest. Unless the company is doing well enough so that its stock is trading close to or above the conversion price specified in the debentures on November 1, 1991, the debentures will be trading at a discount, and it is likely that debentureholders will exercise their right to put at that date. As in our previous examples, the requirement to come up with cash, to fund the redemption of the debentures, would come at a time when the company is not doing that well, further exacerbating the financial situation and possibly triggering a restructuring.

Perhaps the most extreme example of a company's vulnerability to maturities coming due—and certainly the most sudden—is when the company has a large amount of commercial paper outstanding and there is a liquidity crisis. The demise of Penn Central was a classic example of this. More recently, Integrated Resources' reorganization was set off, and Drexel Burnham's bankruptcy precipitated, by their inability to roll over commercial paper coming due.

In addition to financial trigger events, mention should be made of other corporate developments that should be monitored in the event they signal financial distress.

"Band-Aid" Cash Generation Decisions

There are situations when a company is experiencing a deterioration in cash flow and, as a consequence, takes actions—such as selling a core asset—to increase cash and "band-aid" the problem. However, if the action involves the sale of a good cash-generating asset, for example, the decision to raise cash in this fashion could put the long-term viability of the company in an even more precarious position. In the meantime, the cash infusion gives the appearance of health, whereas in reality the core problem has not been addressed and a restructuring, while delayed, is even more certain.

Some recent examples of situations where companies sold, or attempted to sell, key assets to raise cash include AP Industries (sale of its automotive parts business—its main source of operating cash flow), Federated Department Stores (attempted sale of Bloomingdale's), United Merchants & Manufacturing (sale of several profitable subsidiaries), and Southland (sale of its interest in Citgo). In each case the sales provided temporary sources of cash without solving the long-term ongoing cash generation requirement to service debt.

Other "band-aid" decisions to look out for include the repurchase of high-yield debt, sale and leaseback transactions, factoring, and capital transactions between related parties.

Mounting Litigation

Increasingly in recent years, companies have reorganized in chapter 11 in order to be able to handle onerous litigation. In the cases of Manville and A. H. Robins, this litigation built up steadily and involved so many cases that their resolution could only be arrived at with the company operating on a different basis. Litigation as an early warning signal is more difficult to monitor, but it is a non–balance sheet item that should be watched, particularly the relationship of potential claims to the capital of the company.

Decisions by Regulators

Investors in distressed savings and loans, banks, insurance companies, utilities, and even healthcare companies need little reminder of trigger events, caused by government agencies, that have hastened the demise of some of these entities. From the imposition of Diagnostic Related Group fees that put many large healthcare companies at risk, to the recent wipe-outs of subordinated debt by regulators at many distressed savings and loans, the risk of a regulated entity suddenly defaulting has to be that much greater than a nonregulated company. This is, of course, particularly true in a highly leveraged entity. Government action tends to be less predictable, and it may be too late, in many instances, to avoid the effect of such actions.

Recession, Poor Management, and Fraud

Last but not least, mention should be made of three staples that could lead to reorganizations. The United States is fortunate not to have experienced a general extended recession for almost the entire decade of the 1980s. At the same time, the leveraged buyout industry has bloomed. In most cases the continuing economic growth that the leveraged buyouts needed to be successful has, in fact, transpired. While industry-specific recessions have caused distress and bankruptcies (most notably in the oil service, real estate, and steel industries), some of the highly leveraged companies are still not tested as to what the effects will be of an overall economic recession.

With hindsight it is often easy to blame poor management. However, signs of trouble can often be discovered, say, by knowledge of internal rivalry leading to poor decisions or self-dealing by management (e.g., fees for transactions, sale of stocks), thereby lowering their longer-term incentive.

Fraud is possibly the most devastating cause of insolvency and perhaps the hardest to discern and predict at an early stage. As seen from companies such as Wedtech and ZZZ Best, management fraud can wipe out virtually all creditors. Probing analysis of managers or professional consultants who had worked for the company may be the only way to ferret out the possibility of fraud.

Valuing the Estate

With a good knowledge of the terms and conditions underlying the debt of a company and a thorough understanding of the factors causing its distress, it is appropriate to turn to valuing the estate available for creditors and other interested parties.

The objective of the bankruptcy process is to maximize values available for, and for allocation among, the various claimants and interests. The valuation of the enterprise may therefore be performed in two ways: (a) liquidation of assets through the sale of individual assets and/or business units, with perhaps sensitivities as to "fire sale" vs. orderly liquidation values; and (b) a "going concern" scenario, which may carry with it sensitivity analyses of worst, expected, and optimistic cases.

Which path the bankruptcy takes will generally be the one that maximizes value for the estate and, in fact, is typically a combination of liquidation of certain assets and the maintenance of a core business as a going concern.

At this stage the reader may wonder why one looks at the bankruptcy process when considering valuation methodology. Surely, a distressed credit can reorganize successfully outside bankruptcy. Of course, companies can, and often do, reorganize outside of bankruptcy. However, the negotiations between the debtor and the creditors are usually carried out with the *threat of bankruptcy* as the backdrop to the negotiations. An understanding of the values in bankruptcy and their possible allocation among claimants is therefore key to understanding the probable direction of the restructuring (in or out of bankruptcy) and its impact on securities values.

The methods for calculating going concern and liquidation values are standard, as in any credit analysis, and thus are not discussed in detail here. Rather, to illustrate the different ways in which bankruptcy estate values may be set, three recent bankruptcies have been selected:

Going Concern: The Western Company of North America

The Western Company of North America ("Western") filed for bankruptcy protection in February 1988, after extensive negotiations with creditors failed.

Western has two core businesses. Western Petroleum Services provides pressure pumping services for new and existing wells to major and independent oil and gas companies primarily in the southern United States. Western Oceanic provides offshore contract drilling services internationally to major independent producers and foreign governments. Western Oceanic has a rig fleet of twelve jack-ups and one semisubmersible rig of average "commodity-type" quality.

At the time of filing for bankruptcy, both the onshore and offshore segments of Western suffered from chronic oversupply of usable equipment. This supply/demand imbalance was expected to continue for several years, barring any unforeseen political event that might influence future oil prices significantly.

Other than a small amount of real estate, Western's main asset was its usable equipment. Given the glut of this equipment in the marketplace, a liquidation of assets would have yielded little more than scrap value. A sale as a going concern would also have generated little value due to the outright malaise in the oil service industry; in fact, a buyer would pay little more than scrap value even when purchasing on a "going concern" basis. The liquidation value of Western shortly after the bankruptcy filing was therefore estimated at about $150 million.

In order to maximize value, it seemed appropriate to reorganize the capital structure, substituting equity for a good portion of the debt and thereby creating a more viable concern. If the oil service industry remained stagnant, Western could muddle through its debt service payments; if things improved, creditors would see the value of their interest increase as the value of the equity increased. Rather than focusing on the existing depressed going concern value, creditors could look to a future value of the enterprise based on reasonable projections of future cash flow. Clearly it was incumbent on the debtor to convince the creditors that its projections were realistic and that an increasing estate value was likely. If not, the liquidation path would be more appropriate.

Based on projections provided by Western, it was expected that Western's value could increase to $500 million by 1995 using a reasonable multiple of cash flow in that year. Value comparisons were also run against selected publicly traded companies in the oil services industry to make sure that the value of a restructured Western (historically an average performer in its industry) would fall within the context of typical value criteria of its peers (e.g., market value to cash flow, to book value, to revenues).

Creditors agreed to the plan of reorganization put forward by Western, and the company emerged from bankruptcy in May 1989. A firming of oil prices in the latter half of 1989 and a renewed interest in investment in oil service companies propelled the value of new Western common stock, so that the market capitalization of Western was over $350 million, less than one year after emerging from bankruptcy and just over two years from when the company had originally filed for bankruptcy protection.

Liquidation: MCorp

MCorp, at one time one of the largest commercial banks in Texas, filed for bankruptcy in the spring of 1989, following the seizure of 20 of its 25 bank subsidiaries. The bank had been under severe financial pressure as a result of continued softness in the real estate and energy sectors of the economy in the southwestern United States.

After the FDIC seized most of its bank subsidiaries, MCorp was left as a holding company with a number of relatively liquid assets and the stock of five banks subsidiaries. It therefore appeared that the way to maximize estate value was to liquidate these assets. This involved taking each asset and assigning a real value to it—that is, a price at which it could be sold. In some instances (for example, where many of the assets are illiquid), it is useful to build in a sensitivity to the analysis so that forced sale values, as well as orderly liquidation values, can be used. Assets that may not be reflected in book assets but that are marketable and have real value (for example, gates and departure/landing "slots" at airlines, undervalued lease arrangements, overfunded pension liabilities, etc.), should be incorporated in liquidation value. Also, any expenses involved in liquidation should be deducted. Perhaps the most frequently ignored or miscalculated number in assessing an estate value is the amount of cash/asset buildup or deterioration as a result of ongoing operations during the liquidation period, particularly if the bankruptcy and time to realize value is a lengthy process. The analysis should therefore include a well thought out adjustment for estate values based on an evaluation of the impact of bankruptcy on the operating cash flow and on asset values.

In the case of MCorp, the adjustment of book value to estimated realizable value was relatively straightforward. An exit from bankruptcy was assumed at December 31, 1991, and the following adjustments were made:

MCORP

Combined Parent Company
Balance Sheet Valuation

As of October 31, 1989
(all figures in thousands)

	As per schedule (1) Oct. 31, 1989	Adjust- ments (2)	Adjusted value on Dec. 31, 1991
Cash and negotiable instruments	$ 18,649		$ 18,649
Prepaid expenses	(841)	841	0
3.12 mill. Shares of GME common	140,175	26,825	167,000
$35.5 mill. Lomas 8% sr. notes	30,510		30,510
1.44 mill. Shares of Lomas common	3,060	(1,710)	1,350
Other	26		26
Total marketable securities	173,771	25,115	198,886
360,000 Shares of Lomas preferred	22,140	(17,640)	4,500
Other	25,922		25,922
Total nonmarketable securities	48,062	(17,640)	30,422
Other current assets	1,987		1,987
Total current assets	241,628	8,316	249,944
Net property	259		259
Loans, net of allowances	88,196	(70,750)	17,446
Investment in bank subsidiaries	71,986	(11,986)	60,000
Nonbank subsidiaries (3)	(46,462)	166,462	120,000
Misc. receivables	2,274		2,274
Investments in partnerships	12,092	(6,046)	6,046
Other assets	11,068		11,068
Total assets	$381,041	$85,996	$467,037
Pension overfunding	-		15,000
Cash buildup	-		33,248
Total value of the estate	$381,041		$515,285

(1) The preceding table is a summary of the balance sheet support for MCorp's monthly operating statements filed with the bankruptcy court.

(2) Reflects the sale of MVestment for $105 million in cash and a $15 million note, the net cash received by MCorp from the sale of the GME stock in late November 1989, the value of the Lomas common stock at market value and the Lomas preferred stock at 10 percent of liquidation value. Also haircuts investments in partnerships by 50 percent.

(3) The negative $46,462 is a contra to the equity account primarily related to the acquisition of the trust operations from the subsidiaries. It is not a true liability. The $120 million offset represents the full value of the sale of MVestment.

Thus, rather than a book value of assets of $381 million shortly after the bankruptcy filing, MCorp was expected to have an estate value of around $515 million by the time it emerged from bankruptcy, assuming that date to be December 31, 1991.

Going Concern and Liquidation: Todd Shipyards

Often the reorganization will involve both a liquidation of certain assets and the restructuring around a core business as the going concern.

Todd Shipyards filed for bankruptcy in August 1987. Todd was primarily involved in shipbuilding and repair and, through a subsidiary, ARO Corporation, in the manufacture of air-powered equipment and certain other products. ARO was not part of the bankruptcy petition.

Todd's bankrupt operations were limited to shipbuilding and repair activities at four shipyards, and most of this activity was for the U.S. government. The company's severe liquidity problem was brought about by substantial cost overruns on certain fixed price contracts, as well as the inability of the government and Todd to resolve differences on certain issues with respect to work performed by Todd.

For purposes of valuing Todd's estate, it was assumed that the non-bankrupt ARO could be valued as a going concern and was a saleable asset — its value to be included as a net cash number in Todd's asset valuation. The shipyards, on the other hand, had a negative operating cash flow and might have to be liquidated in order to maximize the value retained by the estate.

In terms of off–balance sheet items, it was noted that Todd's pension plan was overfunded by about $40 million, that Todd had certain claims against the government, and that there was the possibility that certain net operating loss carryforwards (NOL) would be available for income tax purposes. The realization of any of these items had its risks, and therefore a range of values was used. The value of the NOL was believed to be small and was therefore assumed to be zero.

Assuming a two-year bankruptcy, the estate value of Todd was estimated as seen on the following page.

The estimated value of the estate — assuming the sale of ARO, the liquidation of the shipbuilding operations, and a two-year bankruptcy — was therefore expected to be in the $200–290 million range. Clearly there are a number of assumptions imbedded in the valuation, but, in terms of an approximation of ultimate value, the analysis should be appropriate. Of course, the more precise the liquidation value, the better. The "haircuts" used are simply estimations of how the book values of the the assets would have to be discounted in order to be sold. In this case the most sensitive number is that used for the shipyards. As an extremely depressed industry with virtually no interested buyers, the value of the yards is discounted severely (by 70 percent) so that the value used is probably close to the price at which the real estate alone could be sold, with little or no value

Todd Shipyards
Balance Sheet Valuation

As of September 27, 1987
(All Figures in Millions)

	Book value	Adjustment for sale of ARO[a]	Net book value	Liquidation "haircut"	Estimated value
Cash	$11.0	$105.0	$116.0	-	$116.0
Accounts receivable					
U.S. government	65.7	-	65.7	40%	39.4
Other	46.6	(25.0)	21.6	25%	16.2
Unbilled costs and estimated profits on incomplete contracts	26.1	-	26.1	50%	13.1
Inventories	29.7	(22.0)	7.7	25%	5.8
Other assets	8.3	(5.1)	3.2	50%	1.6
Property for resale, at net realizable value	2.8	-	2.8	50%	1.2
Total current assets	190.2	52.9	243.1		193.3
Note receivable from customers	5.0	-	5.0	25%	3.8
Land	2.8	-	2.8	25%	2.1
Plant, drydocks and equipment, net	201.5	(30.7)	170.8	70%	51.2
Other assets	6.2	(5.6)	0.6	50%	0.3
Total assets	$405.7	$16.6	$422.3		$250.7
Pension overfunding				$ 20 - 40	
Cash deterioration (2 years)				$(70) - 0	

[a] Assumes sale of ARO for $110 million, and $5 million of cash retained by ARO.

for the facilities and equipment. To the extent any of the shipyards could be maintained as profitable going concerns, the values could be improved substantially.

The other important factor is the operating cash drain during the reorganization. It is assumed that, based on historical performance, it could be as much as $70 million, with an optimistic case that the cash drain can be stopped at the shipyards and a breakeven cash flow attained.

In general, the discount on receivables reflects a value that a factor would pay for them, say, 20 to 25 percent below face value. In this case, because of disputed items with the government, a greater discount rate was used for those receivables. Todd's inventories were small and were probably relatively marketable raw materials and therefore discounted by only 25 percent. In certain bankruptcies, such as toy manufacturers, the book value of inventory can be significant and of relatively little realizable value.

At the time of this writing, Todd is about to emerge from bankruptcy, about three years after filing. ARO has continued to grow and, as part of the reorganization, is being sold for substantially more than originally anticipated. Negotiations with the government have apparently proceeded well: the company was able to stem the cash drain on an operating basis at the shipyards. Two of the four shipyards have been closed, and the company will emerge reorganized, based on the two remaining shipyards operating as a going concern.

One final general consideration in appraising estate value is the availability of net operating tax loss carryforwards (NOLs). While recent rulings have made the transfer of NOLs to new investors more restrictive, the value of the available ongoing NOL should be taken into account in assessing the value of the estate, particularly if there is little other value left for creditors.

Having determined the likely value of the estate, it is now possible to estimate what the fundamental value of each of the claims and interests in the enterprise may be worth at the time a bankruptcy is consummated.

Needless to say, the first step is to determine what the claims and interests are—the amount of each and how they rank. One might divide this task into balance sheet items and off–balance sheet items.

Balance Sheet Items

Every company has its own unique capital structure. However, a general classification of prepetition claims may be ranked within the following categories:

Tax claims
Secured debt
Senior unsecured debt
Trade claims
Senior subordinated debt
Subordinated debt
Junior subordinated debt
Preferred stock
Common stock

Within this general scheme of things will be many other considerations:

• The treatment of claims at a subsidiary level versus those at a holding company

- The amount of collateral available for secured debt. Is the debt over-collateralized so that it may accrue postpetition interest? Is the debt undercollateralized so that only a portion of the debt will be treated as secured and the remainder as senior unsecured?
- Where do trade claims rank? Are there terms in the various debt layers that affect the trade's rank?
- Where a company has several public debt issues, what are the terms in each indenture that may affect ranking?
- Was any of the debt issued with an original issue discount, either as a direct financing or as the result of an exchange offer?

In other words, in order to accurately rank claims, a thorough review and understanding of the documents underlying the claims is required. Also essential is a knowledge of the treatment of certain claims under the bankruptcy code.

This may be an appropriate point to note that the bankruptcy process is an open, "cleansing" process. All claims—financial, contractual, suits—must be filed with the Bankruptcy Court or else they are automatically dismissed. The bankruptcy code outlines how each of these claims is then to be handled. During the process, a stream of information is filed regularly with the court, so that there is often better financial disclosure on a company in bankruptcy than there is for a company filing just with the Securities and Exchange Commission. Once a company emerges from bankruptcy as an operating entity, it is "clean" of unknown liabilities and operations have been trimmed of excess overhead.

The bankruptcy process, then, will assist in determining the second part of the claims analysis:

Off–Balance Sheet Items

The recent spate of defaults and bankruptcies in the leverage buyout market can be understood from the financial statements of the companies involved—without going too far into the footnotes or assessing contingencies. Growth of operating cash flow simply was too slow to meet increasing debt service. However, in the past, many of the larger bankruptcies were precipitated by off–balance sheet items such as product liability claims and unfavorable outcomes in litigation. Also, the ultimate values received by creditors were substantially influenced by the resolution of certain sizable off–balance sheet items.

Some of the more common items to assess in this regard are as follows:

1. Product liability: the Manville and A. H. Robins bankruptcies were precipitated by these companies' product liability claims; their settlement was key to the timing of the reorganization and the amount received by creditors and interests.

2. Pension obligations: whether a company's pension fund is overfunded or underfunded can have a substantial impact on values. The LTV Corporation bankruptcy has been centered around negotiations with the Pension Benefit Guarantee Corporation.
3. Health benefits: certain companies, such as those involved in coal mining and steel, may have substantial obligations to maintain health benefits for existing and retired employees. This was a significant factor in the Kaiser Steel bankruptcy.
4. Executory contracts: damages resulting from the rejection of executory contracts (such as supply agreements, royalties, etc.) will result in additional general unsecured claims with the amount based on the terms of the contract and the general law of contracts.
5. Unexpired leases: similarly, unexpired leases on real property that are rejected will generate unsecured claims; however, the lessor may only claim an amount equal to the greater of the rent reserved for one year or 15 percent of the term remaining, not to exceed three years' rent.
6. Environmental claims: increasingly, companies have been the subject of claims by local and federal authorities and others as a result of the environmental harm caused by products or processes.
7. Other litigation: the need to assess potential settlements in other litigated matters is also essential; the largest U.S. bankruptcy to date was primarily determined by a settlement between Texaco and Pennzoil.

Certain Other Considerations Affecting Value of Claims

1. *Avoidance of Transfers.* The bankruptcy code gives the trustee the right to avoid transfer of assets under certain situations, and such actions could seriously impact the value of claims. Most commonly these avoidance actions are classified under preferential prepetition transfers (or "preference payments") and fraudulent transfers (or "fraudulent conveyances").

   • *Preference Payments.* The Code outlines in detail which transfers may be avoided because they are preferential. Broadly speaking, any payments, outside the ordinary course of business, that were made to any third party within 90 days prior to the bankruptcy filing, or to an insider within one year prior to the filing, should be reviewed to see if they might be deemed preferential.
   • *Fraudulent Conveyances.* In simple terms, a fraudulent conveyance occurs when, within one year before filing, a transfer of assets was made for less than fair value and the debtor was insolvent or became insolvent as a result of the transfer. Alternatively, if the transfer was made with the intent to defraud any entity to whom the debtor was or became indebted, it could be avoided. Remedies in these cases call for "avoiding" the transaction that

can result in taking collateral away from the fraudulent lenders or even subordinating their claim to existing creditors.

2. *Equitable Subordination.* In the event that a creditor engages in misconduct directed at other creditors, the court may impose the remedy of equitable subordination. In this case the court may subordinate, for purposes of distribution, all or part of a claim to all or part of another similar type of claim (i.e., debt claims can be subordinated to other debt claims, not to equity claims). Claims by those closely related to the debtors, such as "insiders" or affiliated corporations, typically will be studied carefully to see if equitable subordination is justified.

3. *Substantive Consolidation.* When a company and all its operating subsidiaries file for bankruptcy, it is possible that separate plans of reorganization will result for each of the subsidiaries, with different distributions to the creditors of each. Alternatively, the Bankruptcy Court has the power to substantively consolidate the bankruptcy proceedings of interrelated debtors. In a substantive consolidation, all of the assets and liabilities of the debtors are combined and all intercompany claims and guarantees eliminated. The court looks to a variety of factors to justify substantive consolidation: in general, the more interrelated the finances, management, assets, ownership, and so forth of the separate subsidiaries, the more likely there will be substantive consolidation.

Needless to say, regular consultation with the code and, where appropriate, knowledgeable bankruptcy counsel, is important in making a proper determination as to claim priority. Rights to setoffs and the treatment of various forms of taxation usually need to be considered. The ongoing costs of the bankruptcy—lawyers, advisors, and so forth—are priority items and can impact an estate's value, particularly if the estate does not generate positive cash flow during the bankruptcy.

The Negotiated Plan of Reorganization

Once ranking, priority, and size of claims has been established, how much each will receive in the chapter 11 bankruptcy is a negotiated process, so that a consensual plan agreed to by all creditors and interests can be arrived at.

Because the process is a negotiated one, there is no defined outcome of how an estate will be allocated among the claims and interests. Some of the factors to be considered include

- Size of the estate relative to aggregate claims
- Size of creditor class relative to other classes
- Nature of participants in creditor class
- Amount claims would get using a strict priority distribution

Table 5.2. Relative Distributions of Value in Selected Bankruptcies

Company	Class of claim	Total claim ($ millions)	Estimated value to be distributed per $100 of claim	% of value distributed of class above	Comments
Global Marine	Secured debt	$606.3	77.5%	-	Subordinate debt was forced to receive only 2.8 cents of value or else face a potential cramdown.
	Unsecured debt	155.1	39.3	50.7%	
	Subordinate debt	402.0	2.8	7.1	
Grant Broadcasting	Secured first lien	$ 30.0	90.0%	-	Trade creditors (programmers) threatened to stop supply and thereby negotiated a higher payout.
	Second lien	81.0	15.0	16.7%	
	Third lien	59.0	1.0	6.7	
	Trade claims	200.0	25.0	-	
Maxicare	Senior unsecured debt	$150.0	32.0%	-	A quick bankruptcy was perceived to be the only way to preserve value in Maxicare. Therefore, the subordinated creditors were treated relatively well to minimize any delays in confirmation.
	Senior subordinate debt	145.0	12.9	40.2%	
	Subordinate debt	155.0	5.2	40.6	
Republic Health	Secured debt	$172.0	100.0%	-	The company filed an 1126(b) bankruptcy agreed to by at least two thirds of each creditor class prior to filing.
	Secured second lien	247.4	80.8	80.8	
	Unsecured debt	50.0	46.0	56.9	
	Subordinate debt	260.0	19.0	41.3	
Western Company of North America	Senior unsecured debt	$550.0	36.9%	-	Although the junior securities received a small piece of the total distribution, they were able to receive relatively high percentage payments due to their ability to hold up the plan. In addition, the size of their claims was much smaller than the senior claims.
	Senior subordinate debt	27.0	28.5	77.3%	
	Subordinated debt	31.0	21.6	75.8	

Additional Comments Regarding Relative Distributions of Value

Global Marine   Senior creditors received new notes and 60 percent of the new equity. Remaining creditors received equity; with common stockholders receiving a token payout in order to prevent a cramdown in a nonconcensual plan.
Grant Broadcasting   In addition to receiving 50 percent of the equity, bondholders were reinstated, but interest and principal were payable only from cashflow. The remaining equity went to creditors whose claims arose from programming they had provided to Grant.
Maxicare   Senior unsecured debt's payout consisted mostly of cash and new notes, as well as 16 percent of the new equity. Senior subordinate and subordinate creditors received 33 percent of the new equity. Trade creditors were left with almost 50 percent of the new equity.
Republic Health   Bondholders received substantially all of the equity (85 percent, with the remainder going to preferred and common equity holders).
Western Co. of North America   Senior creditors received value in the form of cash, new notes, equity (70 percent of the restructured company), and some real estate interests. The remaining creditors received only equity.

- Possibility of a cramdown
- Business need for cooperation of creditor class
- Threats of litigation between classes

In order to make a first estimate of what one class of claims would get versus another, one might use a rule of thumb approach of distributing to the next junior class: 60 percent of value distributed to the immediately senior class. All things being equal (which they hardly ever are), this may turn out to be a useful estimate of estate value allocation. Table 5.2 presents five bankruptcies that had three or more classes of claims and shows how one class of claims fared versus another, with some brief comment as to rationale.

Timing to Realize Value

A very important component of return on investment on a distressed security will be the expected time it will take to restructure the company and implement a reorganization plan. While the availability of markets makes it possible to trade in most of the instruments that are involved in the restructuring—and therefore it is not necessary to wait until the end of the bankruptcy to realize at least some value—the level at which they trade will depend on the time taken to realize the expected value when the company exits bankruptcy. Timing of a reorganization can be quite difficult to determine, particularly if a bankruptcy is involved and if no negotiations between the different groups have occurred prior to the bankruptcy filing. Some factors to consider in attempting to assess timing are as follows:

- Level of harmony between the creditor groups
- Whether an approved plan has been predetermined prior to filing for bankruptcy
- Number and complexity of litigious issues between creditors
- Complexity of the debtor's capital structure: for example, single debtor entities versus holding company and subsidiary debtors
- Amount and complexity of litigation with third parties
- Value of the estate and maintenance of such value over the period of reorganization
- Resolve of different claimants

Table 5.3 shows the time taken to reorganize companies through a bankruptcy process for several recently consummated plans involving sizable debtors. A brief comment relating to the time taken to complete each plan is given. It is interesting to note that the average time taken to reorganize through the bankruptcy process using our sample of 12

Table 5.3. Time Taken to Reorganize Through Bankruptcy

Company	Months in Reorganization	Comments as to Timing
American Healthcare	26	Delays were caused by disputes between creditor's groups. The bank group faced potential lender liability claims and the nature of their security came into question. In addition, the company received a bid to be acquired that never went through. These situations combined to created a protracted bankruptcy.
Coleco	20	The core business was sold shortly after the Chapter 11 filing and creditors were left with a pile of cash. Most of the secured debt in the capital structure had traded hands at discounted values and holders were willing to except a reduced payout. The equity was not organized into a strong group and failed to have a significant voice in the proceedings. An uncomplicated capital structure and relatively passive creditor group combined for a quick bankruptcy.
Crystal Oil	3	The company entered bankruptcy with a pre-approved plan and was able to avoid a drawn out battle. Creditors included banks, trade claims and subordinate bondholders. The company was able to satisfy the banks and trade creditors while subordinate bondholders were faced with a wipeout. Without any power to negotiate, the bondholders consented to the plan in order to receive some value.
Evans Products	20	The judge in this case declined to extend the companies exclusivity period and creditors submitted their own plan. Old management was removed and creditors were satisfied with the values they received.

(continued)

Table 5.3. (cont.)

Company	Months in Reorganization	Comments as to Timing
Global Marine	37	This company went through an extended bankruptcy for three main reasons. It had a complicated capital structure that created subordination questions. The creditor's group had divergent interests and often disagreed among themselves. The company was operating in a severely depressed market and had no incentive to come out of bankruptcy quickly.
Grant Broadcasting	18	Grant was a relatively small bankruptcy with a limited number of creditors and legal issues. As such, its reorganization was uncluttered and quick.
Hecks	31	The plan of reorganization was contingent on financing from a third party. As a result, the plan was delayed until an agreement with the guarantor of the new financing could be structured. Until this agreement was in place the form of any possible plan was uncertain.
Manville	74	This bankruptcy involved litigation over contingent liabilities due to asbestos health claims. The first plan the company submitted lumped the asbestos health claimants with the other creditors. This was viewed as unexceptable and a new plan included separate trusts for asbestos health claims. The bankruptcy proceedings involved lengthy and repeated appeals which continually delayed the confirmation of a plan.
Smith International	21	The company went into bankruptcy as a result of litigation involving another company. The lawsuit was settled and Smith was able to confirm a plan quickly.

(continued)

Table 5.3. (cont.)

Company	Months in Reorganization	Comments as to Timing
Storage Technology	33	This case involved a large IRS tax claim that required extended negotiation. In addition, the business was difficult to stabilize in bankruptcy. As a result, creditors were unsure about the value of the estate.
Texaco	12	Filed for bankruptcy in order to avoid seizure of assets due to $10 billion lawsuit. After the lawsuit was settled for $3.5 billion, creditors were reinstated.
Western Co. of North America	15	The company was anxious to get out of bankruptcy and presented a plan to the bank group that satisfied their desire to begin receiving interest again. The bankruptcy proceedings were not held up by combative outside advisors and the company was able to negotiate their own plan.

debtors came to just over two years. However, there is a substantial divergence in timing. Crystal Oil entered bankruptcy with a plan previously approved by creditors (as defined in Section 1126(b) of the bankruptcy code) and emerged three months later. At the other extreme, Manville Corporation was involved with contingent liabilities due to thousands of asbestos health claims, and the complex bankruptcy proceedings involved lengthy and repeated appeals that delayed the confirmation of a plan to more than six years after the company filed.

Investment Strategies

An analysis of a distressed company will often give rise to a broad range of investment opportunities. Given an accurate analysis of the value of the business and a reasonable estimate of securities values, generally greater returns can be obtained—at greater risk—through investments lower down the capital structure. Looking at this another way, one can identify three major types of investment strategies in the financially troubled securities marketplace: very high yields, capital appreciation, and bankruptcy arbitrage.

Very High Yields

One would define this investment as the purchase of a security with a current yield or yield to maturity well in excess of what an equivalent security not involved in a restructuring would yield. For example, a company in reorganization may have fully secured debt where payments will be made or will accrue even in bankruptcy and there is little or no risk to principal loss. Depending on liquidity, these investments may yield in the 15–20 percent area in the current environment compared with 9–11 percent yields more typical in the "healthy" collateralized securities area. Such high income investments are generally the most conservative in the distressed securities investment spectrum, having the lowest risk/reward relationship.

Capital Appreciation

Far more common are those investments looking for capital appreciation. These would be found in debt or equity securities trading at substantial discounts from fundamental values. For example, if one's analysis showed a debt security to be worth at least 80 cents on the dollar at the end of a reorganization and if the expected time to reach that stage from the date of investment were three years, then an investor looking for at least a 25 percent annual compounded rate of return would be prepared to pay no more than 40 cents on the dollar in purchasing the security. The expected rates of return in these types of investments typically will be similar to those expected from equity-type investments. Also, the more junior the securities, the greater the risk and, consequently, the greater the required return.

Conversely, short sellers will implement an investment strategy when a security is selling substantially in excess of fundamental values. If trigger events loom, as discussed previously under "Early Warning Signals," an investor believing a restructuring is likely may be able to sell a security while it is still fully valued and bet on the amount of time it will take for the market to sense the need for a restructuring and for the reorganization to take hold. The amount of upside loss potential, particularly in the case of a debt security trading close to par, may be very limited in this investment strategy. If a security of a company already involved in a reorganization is still trading well above its fundamental value, a short sale may be justified to generate a capital gain.

Bankruptcy Arbitrage

Once a plan of reorganization has been announced, one can evaluate the new securities to be received and then estimate the probability of success and the time it will take to complete the reorganization. Investing at this stage, known as bankruptcy arbitrage, is analogous to risk arbitrage in pending mergers: one estimates the deal risk, values the new package of securities, assuming the deal goes through, and finally, if the deal falls apart, evaluates the downside risk and fundamental value.

The risk of this type of investment can be quite low in cases where the deal risk is low and the new package of securities consists primarily of cash or good quality debt securities. Alternatively, the risk can be high where deal risk is considerable and the new securities to be received are mostly equity, which may have a less certain value.

The above investment strategies can all be performed on a "passive" basis. Other strategies, based on a more active role by the investor (to gain control of a class of securities or to gain control of the entire company) will involve additional refinements. For example, in order to gain control of an entity, one's analysis will have to identify which class of securities will be the controlling class in a reorganization. This may well be the class that, in a distribution of new equity of the surviving concern, receives a controlling position of the new equity. When considering the acquisition of a control investment situation, factors in addition to fundamental analysis come into play. These include the nature and distribution of the various holders of the relevant class of securities, the ability to accumulate a control position, and the price that will have to be paid to gain control. With the increasing number of leveraged buyouts that are failing, one would expect that active investment strategies, through the purchase of distressed debt securities, will become increasingly common.

Investment Characteristics

Investment opportunities in debt instruments of distressed companies cover a broad range. Contrary to a tendency to categorize financially distressed securities as a whole as high-risk securities, the investment opportunities and risk range from low risk/lower return to high risk/higher return.

In many respects bankruptcy investing can be regarded as conservative and risk-averse. After all, investments are generally made only after many, if not all, adverse events have occurred, securities are trading at lower, if not their lowest, levels, and high discount rates are used in calculating fundamental values.

Most debt securities of financially troubled companies can be treated as if they were equity or quasi-equity securities. As mentioned under "Investment Strategies," many bankruptcy debt securities are likely to receive a significant amount of equity upon emergence from bankruptcy. Current income and yield are usually not important (with the exception of very high yield investments).

As discussed earlier, the supply of financially troubled securities substantially exceeds demand. This creates a trading imbalance and an inefficient market: the analysis is more complex than the "standard" security investment; the "Street" usually drops coverage of the company; investors often sell for psychological reasons or, indeed, because in some cases they are not allowed to hold defaulted securities. In addition, the market for the debt instruments can be illiquid, and this is particularly the case for non–publicly registered debt, such as bank debt and private placements.

All of these factors give rise to opportunities for the investor prepared to understand the fundamental values underlying the debt instruments of a distressed company. By having the flexibility to go short as well as long, by setting desired rates of return according to investment risk, by allowing the investment time to realize reorganization goals, and, perhaps most important, by having a diversified portfolio of debt securities, the prudent investor will have the framework for generating good returns from debt instruments of financially troubled companies.

6

Analyzing and Evaluating Distressed Credits

Robert H. Siegler
Ladenburg, Thalmann & Co., Inc.

Martin S. Fridson
Merrill Lynch, Pierce, Fenner & Smith, Inc.

Introduction

Bankruptcies and restructurings have achieved a prominence in the fixed income market that is unprecedented in the post–World War II era. Edward I. Altman has estimated that as of the beginning of 1990, $75 billion of public, noninvestment-grade corporate debt was either bankrupt or distressed.[1] (Altman defines "distressed" bonds as those that are priced to yield 1,000 basis points or more above the prevailing rate on U.S. Treasury obligations.) Considering also the much larger amount of private debt in default or in distress, the total market measures some $300 billion, by Altman's reckoning. The partially overlapping high-yield market (defined as public, corporate debt that is nonconvertible and noninvestment grade) is only about two-thirds as large.

In view of the dramatic deterioration of both real and perceived credit quality that has occasioned the expansion of the universe of distressed securities, successful investing in the corporate bond sector requires skilled and detailed financial analysis. Whether investors enter the distressed market of their own volition or find themselves involuntary holders of defaulted debt, they must apply a systematic and rigorous analytical model that dynamically adjusts to the specific facts of each restructuring. Correctly using a well-designed model will yield insights into the critical elements driving the restructuring in each instance. Failure to follow a systematic model will produce disappointing returns, but the proper approach can generate long-term performance that exceeds every fixed income and equity benchmark.

The opportunity to capture superior returns arises in part because the broad majority of capital market participants do not feel comfortable assessing the complex situations presented by bankruptcies and restructurings. Financial distress provides multiple opportunities for investors to anticipate major price dislocations, but doing so requires expertise in valuing assets and a willingness to take risk. A comparatively limited group of astute investors—including Max Heine, Sam Zell, Carl Lindner, Charles Allen, and Warren Buffett—has earned large profits over the years by mastering the special challenges of distressed securities.

Our objective in the following pages is to describe techniques that enable investors to establish their own successful records in the distressed sector. We have divided the discussion into three sections.

First, we present an analytical framework, or model, that is frequently employed by bankruptcy/restructuring specialists. The model's components are asset valuation, liability analysis, and analysis of reorganization catalysts. A special strength of the model is its flexibility, which permits it to be used throughout the entire life cycle of a restructuring.

The second section of our discussion examines the phases of a restructuring and provides illustrative examples of the nature of the opportunities that arise during different phases. We have identified four "windows" in the restructuring process during which capital commitments may be appropriate.

1. Deterioration—the period preceding bankruptcy or restructuring
2. Postbankruptcy filing—a period of disorder and continued deterioration
3. Plan formulation—the time of consensus building
4. Plan implementation

The characteristics of an investment opportunity are affected not only by timing, as represented by these windows, but also by the attributes of the security under consideration; an unsecured obligation, for example, differs fundamentally from a secured piece of paper.

Finally, it should be noted that two emerging trends have become increasingly important in the distressed/restructuring marketplace. The first is the escalation of investment activity in private debt, which has exceeded the growth—phenomenal in its own right—in the public segment. Five years ago, the number of financial institutions and other entities capable of purchasing nonpublic debt could be counted on one hand; today, this market has come into its own and has already begun to display signs of maturation. The second new trend is represented by a growing segment of distressed/ restructuring investors who seek more than a passive financial interest. Instead, they are attempting to acquire, or negotiate for, control of reorganizing companies.

One last note, before we describe our model: in our discussion we use the terms "defaulted," "distressed," "bankruptcy," and "restructuring" more or less interchangeably. In the broadest sense, the sector of the capital markets with which we are concerned is the universe of credits that are going through major balance sheet reconfigurations. Of only secondary concern is the question of whether the adjustment is to assets (as in restructuring) or to liabilities (as in bankruptcy). More pertinent are the dislocations in pricing of the issuers' stocks and bonds that arise from the balance sheet overhauls.

We emphasize this point because we believe that some investors miss excellent opportunities to exploit their analytical skills by restricting their activities to bankruptcies. Typically, they justify their narrow focus on grounds of the expanded volume of information and the ability to achieve greater accuracy in quantifying liabilities ordinarily associated with a bankruptcy. These points have merit, but other situations within the broad universe of restructurings provide investment opportunities, on both the long and the short side, comparable to those available in bankrupt securities. Nonbankruptcy opportunities include many instances in which a company's management has voluntarily restructured or liquidated a line of business, simply as a means of extracting greater value for shareholders, rather than in response to external pressures.

Analytical Model

Asset Valuation

Whether a company is bankrupt or merely attempting to restructure, asset valuation is a critical step in the investor's decision-making process. The value of new securities offered in an exchange or reorganization plan ultimately depends on the asset value available—either in liquidation or on an ongoing-concern basis—for the class of claims that the investor holds. Therefore, placing a value on the company is essential when deciding between accepting an offer, holding out for a bigger payment, or pushing the company into bankruptcy or liquidation.

A distressed company's total value is important to all participants, but the implications can vary significantly according to where an investor's claim resides in the capital structure. For example, the value of an equity, or residual, interest is affected by the values of all of a company's assets and liabilities, both on– and off–balance sheet. In contrast to the comprehensive analysis required to value an equity, a more focused analysis of a specific collateral pool and the strengths and weaknesses of the indenture or loan agreements may suffice to value a secured debt obligation. (That is, the secured debt's value has only limited sensitivity to the amount of asset value supporting liabilities that rank junior to it.)

Corporate structure likewise has significant implications for the eventual distribution of value to claimholders. A prime example involves the differences in treatment in bankruptcy that arise between a company engaged in one basic business activity (albeit through a number of distinct subsidiaries) and a holding company that has subsidiaries engaged in a variety of disparate businesses.

Although the behavior of a court depends heavily on the specific facts of a bankruptcy, the single-business type of structure is generally more likely than the holding company structure to result in *substantive consolidation*. If a bankrupt corporation is substantively consolidated, then all unsecured claims of similar standing are treated identically, even if they were originally assertable against different entities. In this event, the creditors of strong subsidiaries are disadvantaged vis-à-vis weak subsidiaries' creditors. Substantive consolidation is less likely in the case of a holding company with subsidiaries that are separately managed, have nonidentical boards of directors, and, by virtue of their unrelated businesses, display no intertwining of operating assets. Valuation of individual subsidiaries becomes more critical when the creditors of all subsidiaries are not thrown into a single class.

In most cases where liabilities are restructured within the confines of the individual subsidiaries (i.e., where substantive consolidation does not occur), creditors are much better off if they hold obligations of operating subsidiaries, rather than equivalently structured obligations of holding companies or of financing subsidiaries. (By the latter term, we refer to entities that are strictly conduits for raising capital—with or without cross-guarantees involving affiliates—rather than captive finance subsidiaries that purchase accounts receivable generated by related operating companies. Financing conduits are common in the casino and transportation industry, while captive finance subsidiaries are frequently found in the retailing and capital goods segments.) The fundamental advantage of being an operating company lender lies in having a direct claim on productive assets, rather than the residual claim represented by a holding company's assets, which consist primarily of equity interests in subsidiaries. Several bankruptcies of recent years affirm this point and, more generally, underscore the importance of the placement of a claim within the capital structure. Examples include Allegheny International, Allied and Federated Department Stores, Itel, Leaseway Transportation, LTV, McLean Industries, and Wickes Companies.

Once the analyst has determined which assets are available to satisfy the claim in question, the next step is to value the relevant assets by one or more standard methods. Three commonly employed methods are

- Multiple (of cash flow or earnings)
- Liquidation value
- Private (or acquisition) value

Even though the three methods use fundamentally different starting points, they often produce similar, overlapping ranges of estimated values. The bankruptcy investor's objective, it should be noted, is to establish an ownership interest at a significant discount to the long-term, noncyclical value assigned by these methods to a group of assets.

The first valuation method, applying a multiple to cash flow or earnings, focuses on the ability of the company's core operations to generate earnings and other cash flows, as well as the funds needed to sustain those flows. An analyst should begin by examining a basic cash flow, normalized for cyclical fluctuations and stripped of unusual, nonrecurring gains or losses. (Such adjustments require analytical judgment and are not, for example, a function of the formal accounting standards that determine whether an item can lawfully be labeled "extraordinary.") Next, the analyst should run a broad array of hypothetical pro forma scenarios and identify opportunities to increase cash flow. For example, there may be cost-cutting potential in the form of structural or operational streamlining. The company may be uneconomically attempting to service excessively dispersed geographical regions or habitually reinvesting in product lines that generate rates of return below the company's cost of capital. Identifying assets and business units that produce no net cash flow—or worse, that require substantial capital injections—can point to candidates for divestment, joint venture arrangements, or new business development.

In conjunction with a close examination of possibilities for enhancing a distressed company's cash flow, a review of broader industry trends is appropriate. Industry cyclicality, as well as the company's competitive position and market share trend within the industry, will all contribute to modeling the pro forma earnings capacity and cash flow.

Investment implications of the earnings or cash flow multiple method are most pronounced when prevailing multiples are outside their normal, historical ranges. Successful bankruptcy investors have historically resisted the temptation to apply bull market multiples that embodied aggressive growth assumptions. Instead, they have turned cautious when other investors have grown increasingly euphoric, as in the late 1980s, when cash flow multiples of 10 times or higher were not uncommon in sales of companies with unspectacular growth prospects. Cooler-headed bankruptcy players have either upgraded their holdings to the more senior tiers of distressed companies' capital structures or—to be even more conservative—have let their cash balances build. By the same token, multiples sometimes become unrealistically low. As the 1990s began, investors could choose from a growing number of distressed (or perceived to be so) credits trading at a mere 2.5 to 3.5 times cash flow. We believe that a diversified portfolio of credits acquired at such exceptionally low multiples (either prior to bankruptcy or in liquidation) will substantially outperform the standard debt and equity indexes over the long run.

A specific illustration of overshooting on the downside involves Amphenol, a worldwide leader in the manufacture of electronic connectors. Growth in sales of connectors, particularly of the electronic variety, has outpaced Gross National Product growth for the past 30 years and is expected to continue to do so for the foreseeable future.[2] Amphenol's operating margins have historically been in the 17 to 20 percent range and operating cash flow, $66 million in 1989, was perceived to be stable as of April 1990. Nevertheless, Amphenol's outstanding public debt was trading at that time at an aggregate value of just $75 million, a steep discount from its face value of more than $200 million. Taking into account as well the company's $160 million of senior bank debt, the market was effectively capitalizing Amphenol at $235 million, a mere 3.5 times cash flow. Other connector companies were concurrently capitalized at cash flow multiples of 7 to 10. Admittedly, perceived bankruptcy risk was a depressing influence on the trading values of Amphenol's debt. Nevertheless, the market was permitting the long-term, value-oriented investor to acquire, for all intents and purposes, an equity interest in an attractive business at an exceptionally low multiple. If restructuring were ultimately required, investors stood to be overcompensated for participating in the process.

To determine whether prevailing cash flow multiples are inside or outside the normal range, a good rule of thumb is the reciprocal of 1.5 to 2 times the yield on long-term government bonds. For example, when long governments are yielding 9 percent, a normal multiple falls in the range of $[1 \div (9\% \times 2)]$ to $[1 \div (9\% \times 1.5)]$, or approximately 5.5 to 7.5 times. Applying a higher multiple in a particular instance requires a high level of certainty that either the liquidation or the acquisition method represents the more appropriate valuation method.

The liquidation method of valuation assumes a sale of all of the distressed company's assets and distribution of the proceeds (net liabilities) to creditors. Applying the technique requires an assessment of the market for each of a company's assets or business units. An orderly sell-off will preserve the value of a manufacturer's work-in-process inventory, while a "fire sale" auction will generate proceeds well below stated values.

Fortunately, there are willing buyers—at a price—for many types of corporate assets. Ready markets exist for real estate, used industrial equipment, transportation equipment, oil and gas reserves, tax loss carryforwards, and retailing franchises. In addition, in each of these categories there are well-developed fraternities of specialized, professional brokers and investors. Offshore entities frequently display interest in assets that come onto the block, seeking through acquisition to gain entry into the large and politically stable U.S. market.

Other kinds of cross-border considerations influence liquidation values as well. Currency fluctuations may be a factor, along with foreign companies' needs for materials or products that cannot be sourced outside the U.S. Accordingly, while the sale price of an asset is ultimately tied to its cash-generating potential, there are several reasons why simply applying a multiple to current cash flow may not be the best valuation method in all instances. Management mistakes, which are frequently the underlying causes of bankruptcies, can likewise cause intrinsic value to diverge from a cash flow multiple valuation, since a mismanaged company's reported cash flow may be well below the potential that better operators could unlock.

Another alternative to valuation by an earnings or cash flow multiple, as noted above, is to estimate the private value of the business as a whole. In contrast to the liquidation method, which assumes a piecemeal sale of the company's assets, the private value method assumes sale of the entire entity to a well-capitalized investor who recognizes the magnitude of the opportunities that frequently arise in bankruptcy reorganizations.

Private value is most appropriate as a standard when a unique property comes onto the market, but in practice there is rarely a bankruptcy in which an attempt is not made to sell the whole business and thereby create determinable values (usually cash) for distribution. In some cases the debtors themselves orchestrate the auction process (Saxon Industries); in other cases third parties independently attempt to induce a transaction (Allegheny International, Revco); in still other instances a transfer of ownership is best described as opportunistic (Anglo Energy, Braniff Airlines, Dart Drug Stores).

Because pure monopolies rarely become available lock, stock, and barrel, their auctions typically produce aggressive bidding. The sale of Public Service of New Hampshire, for example, comfortably achieved the higher end of its expected value range.

Summarizing the valuation process to this point, we find that assigning an earnings or cash flow multiple establishes a floor, with the liquidation and private value methods potentially justifying some upward adjustment. In addition, some adjustment may be warranted by certain cost advantages enjoyed by bankrupt companies. These advantages produce higher cash flows than similar assets would generate outside of chapter 11 reorganization proceedings.

The economic benefits of bankruptcy fall into three categories. First and most important, while a company is in bankruptcy, it is not required to pay the principal or interest on its unsecured debt, and in many cases, a bankrupt company is excused from servicing its secured debt as well, provided it can establish that the holders are adequately secured. A second economic benefit of bankruptcy is the ability, under certain circumstances, to cancel onerous supply or labor contracts. In a related area, some bankrupt major steel companies have attempted to reduce their operating cost structures by shifting the burden of their retirement benefit programs to the Pension Benefit Guaranty Corporation. Finally, a onetime benefit typically arises from disruption of the normal receivables/payables cycle. A purchaser of raw materials or goods acquired for resale is not required to pay prepetition invoices while in bankruptcy. The debtor-in-possession, however, retains the purchased items and can capture their full value through further processing or sale. In a typical case, then, the bankrupt company receives 100 cents of revenue today, but repays the vendor several years later with a sum that is reduced from the original invoice amount by both the time value of money and the general settlement of prepetition debts at less than face value.

Liability Analysis

Having described the various methods of evaluating a distressed company's assets, we now turn our attention to the right side of the balance sheet, that is, the liability structure. Liability analysis is essential to determining the value of a claim in bankruptcy, which depends in part on the size of other claims that rank ahead or pari passu.

Parenthetically, the analyst must be careful not to overlook off–balance-sheet liabilities. Several of the largest bankruptcies, including Manville, Texaco, and A. H. Robbins, have resulted directly from litigation, including massive tort claims, either manifest or projected. In this connection, it is worthwhile to remember the dynamic nature of the bankruptcy/restructuring process—in this case as it affects and is affected by the progress of ongoing litigation. One's analysis must be equally dynamic if it is to capture the full scope of influences imbedded in a security's price.

Liabilities that arise subsequent to a bankruptcy filing inject a similarly dynamic element into the bankruptcy process. In the process of evaluating its businesses in an effort to restructure itself, it is not uncommon for a company to decide to scale back or divest certain operating units. The disengagement process translates into laid-off workers, canceled leases, rejection of supply contracts, and refusal or inability to act on previous commitments to deliver goods or services. All of these actions tend to generate damage or contract rejection claims.

Generally speaking, off–balance-sheet contingent liabilities that arise in this manner following a bankruptcy are treated as unsecured claims. Exceptions, however, include pension, tax, and environmental claims, which typically acquire priority status and transcend ownership boundaries. (In other words, such claimants cannot necessarily be isolated in one part of a corporation and precluded from going after the assets of other affiliates.)

After quantifying, to the extent possible, the scope and size of assertable claims, the next step is to rank the company's various claims in order of priority. The key dividing line is between secured and unsecured creditors.

Judging the probable status of secured debt requires a thorough assessment of, among other factors, the following:

- Structure of the collateral agreements
- Perfection of lienhold interest
- Relationship between amount of secured debt outstanding and value of collateral (which provides insights into the likelihood that post-petition interest will be paid)
- Contractual agreements and governing state statutes regarding payment of interest on the interest that has defaulted

- Background history of the creation of the lien
- Whether any unique relationship exists or previously existed between the lender and the borrower
- Governing debtor-in-possession (DIP) financing arrangements
- Potentially competing lienhold interests

A special analytical issue that arises in connection with properly (or overly) secured debt involves continued accrual of interest during bankruptcy. The bankruptcy code provides that a secured debtholder's claim will continue to accrue, and therefore increase, at the contract rate until the aggregate claim achieves the level of the collateral value. Rarely, however, is there a convenient means of determining a value for the collateral that is satisfactory to the potentially competing interests of the borrower and the lender. If determining value becomes a substantive issue, it usually gets resolved through negotiation. If the parties prove unable to find a negotiated solution, a valuation hearing may be required.

Continued accrual of postpetition interest results in a building claim and, ultimately, building recovery levels. To the extent that a secured claim is purchased at a discount to its total accreted value, the purchaser can, in the venerable phrase, "buy dollars at a discount." Years ago, the discount was often extraordinarily steep, with secured railroad bonds commonly trading at 15 cents on the dollar. Over the past five years, though, pricing of oversecured, fully accruing public debt has dropped expected annualized returns to the respectable but not spectacular 18 to 25 percent range. Potential returns of 30 to 100 percent remain available in the private marketplace.

Unsecured claims of bankrupt companies (and, for that matter, secured claims with questionable collateral value) are more often than not best evaluated as de facto equity instruments. Holders of unsecured debt are entitled to residual values, if any, available after satisfying the mortgage interests attached to individual assets or business units or to the entire enterprise. As a function of price, the unsecured tier may be a very attractive place to have a capital commitment. Not to be overlooked, however, are the major problems that originally drove the company into bankruptcy. Unless the problems have been corrected, the "de facto equity," like the actual common equity, may have no real value. Several transportation bankruptcies (Branch Trucking, McLean Industries, Seatrain, White Motor) have completed the reorganization process with little or no value distributed to unsecured creditors. Similar outcomes are probable in the growing population of financial services and bank holding company bankruptcies. To determine whether they are likely to wind up in such an unfortunate position, unsecured creditors must evaluate the pricing of their instruments in light of their residual interest. The analysis is analogous to the comparison made by secured creditors between their instruments and the value of underlying collateral.

Reorganization Catalysts

The third critical element needed to determine the expected return imbedded in the price of a distressed security, after evaluating the company's assets as well as its liabilities, is to estimate the lengthiness of the reorganization proceedings. Due to the time value of money, the rate of return to securities holders declines as the period to receipt of reorganization proceeds lengthens.

Factors to consider in predicting the time required for a company to emerge from reorganization proceedings include, but are not limited to, the following:

- Novelty of legal issues framing the reorganization process
- Viability of company's basic business activities
- Jurisdiction (i.e., the record of the court and of the judge assigned to the case)
- Capability of professionals engaged by the debtor and other parties in interest
- Negotiating strategies employed
- Level of sophistication of interested parties
- Complexity of capital structure
- Nature and quantifiability of unsecured claims pool
- Extent to which a financial reorganization is dependent upon a reorganization of the underlying business
- Economic motivation of interested parties (including extent to which claimants are original holders at 100 percent of face amount versus later buyers at deep discounts)
- Management's ability to administer the affairs of the debtor-in-possession
- Involvement of regulatory agencies
- Composition of the creditors' committee

In general, factors that add complexity or conflict tend to lengthen the reorganization process.

Windows of Opportunity

Armed with the general analytical model we have described, the investor can approach a particular opportunity with the objective of maximizing returns. Critical to success in any given instance will be the choice of when to become involved.

The attractiveness of an investment opportunity at a point in time is a function of both the nature and attributes of the security and the status of the issuing firm's restructuring. An unsecured debt fundamentally differs from a secured obligation. An asbestos bankruptcy within a year of the chapter 11 filing is structurally different from the same entity after plan confirmation, since the reorganization plan will quantify what previously had been an indeterminate liability. Likewise, bankruptcies due to excessive leverage differ from those caused by business declines because the issue of fraudulent conveyance can impair the liens of secured leveraged buyout debt.

For illustration purposes, we have identified four phases, or "windows," in the restructuring process during which investment opportunities are most likely to be present:

1. Deterioration: prebankruptcy and/or restructuring
2. Postbankruptcy filing: chaos and continued deterioration
3. Plan formulation: building a consensus
4. Plan implementation

Deterioration

The deterioration phase generally is marked by declining cash flows as business prospects diminish and asset sales either are delayed or generate proceeds far below expectations. Companies in this phase often have narrowing profit margins, troubled supplier relations, diminishing working capital, and debt covenant violations. These problems are usually underscored by a lack of sufficient cash to meet near-term debt repayment obligations.

While debt service problems can be triggered by unexpected events such as massive judgment claims or the discovery of fraudulent accounting techniques, in most cases, companies' debt service problems follow substantive declines in cash flows relative to cash debt service requirements. Thus, depending on one's position, a large cash flow decline should stimulate either a search for short sale opportunities or a review of current holdings.

An illustration in point is Southmark, a diversified real estate holding company with insurance, brokerage, and banking activities. For several years, Southmark financed growth and acquisitions with debt. At the same time, various keep-well and equity maintenance agreements with the government required Southmark to inject hundreds of millions of dollars into its San Jacinto Savings and Loan subsidiary. Despite a severe debt amortization schedule at the holding company level, Southmark transferred $326 million down into its subsidiaries, affiliates, and partnerships during fiscal 1986. By way of comparison, Southmark's 1987 earnings before interest and taxes (EBIT) totaled $241 million.

In fiscal 1988, EBIT dropped to $131 million, reflecting Southmark's problems with southwestern U.S. real estate investments and a sharp downturn in the real estate syndication market following tax law changes. Meanwhile, interest expense increased as the parent borrowed money to support unprofitable subsidiaries such as San Jacinto.

In early 1989, Southmark found itself up against a wall as cash flow continued to decline and the company faced significant debt maturities, particularly the $125 million of 10 7/8 percent notes due November 1, 1989. Management was removed, advisors were hired, and a business plan of rehabilitation was proposed to creditors. The plan's cornerstone consisted of rebuilding around San Jacinto. When Southmark had not managed to turn itself around by May 1989, the sale of its securities was appropriate, and indeed, as Figure 6.1 shows, the 11 7/8 percent notes of 1993 peaked in early 1989, then retreated to a fraction of their previous value.

Although Southmark's financial state had been declining since 1987, many investors were slow to appreciate the magnitude of the deterioration. The company changed its method of accounting in 1988, reformating its balance sheet, income and cash flow statements so that only consolidated numbers were presented. Its assets at book levels, in retrospect, proved to overstate their value.

Postbankruptcy Filing

Bankruptcy restructurings historically have provided one of the greatest opportunities to buy a dollar at a discount. Following a bankruptcy filing, many investors will unload bonds either to clear out nonperforming assets or because they are discouraged by a postfiling disruption in the firm's business. Often this distressed selling will fuel a precipitous price decline, creating a buying opportunity for investors able to properly analyze this type of situation. Secured debt instruments that are overcollateralized can be particularly attractive at this point because they often produce expected

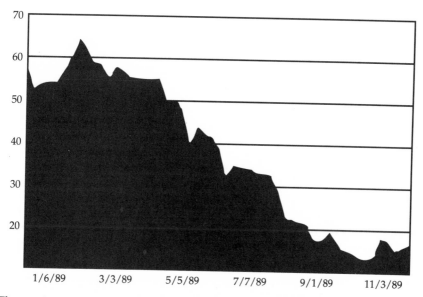

Figure 6.1. Southmark 11.875% Notes '93 Price Performance

rates of return exceeding those available in equity or other debt instruments with substantially less risk.

Public Service of New Hampshire (PSNH) third mortgage bonds are one such example. Shortly after PSNH filed for chapter 11 in January 1988, the bonds traded in the low 80s as many investors liquidated their holdings of this now nonperforming debt. However, the mortgage bonds not only had a par principal claim, but they also had 6.15 points of accrued prepetition interest and an assertable right for postpetition interest since the non-Seabrook assets of PSNH securing the bonds were worth over $1.3 billion, and the aggregate mortgage debt, including the third mortgage, was only $765 million. Thus, an investor could purchase a 106.15 claim for 80 (75 cents on the dollar) and accrue an additional claim at a 13.75 percent rate on principal (17.2 percent on the purchase price). At the time of the chapter 11 filing, the expected annualized rate of return on these mortgage bonds was 33.5 percent, based on a two-year reorganization period, or 28.1 percent, assuming a three-year reorganization. Given the security's overcollateralization and the substantially diminished likelihood of capital loss, the mortgage bonds were a compelling investment opportunity (Figure 6.2).

Plan Formulation

As the bankruptcy or restructuring progresses and a reorganization plan is formulated, negotiated, and finally settled upon, the process of evaluating an investment opportunity becomes substantially more precise. Assets,

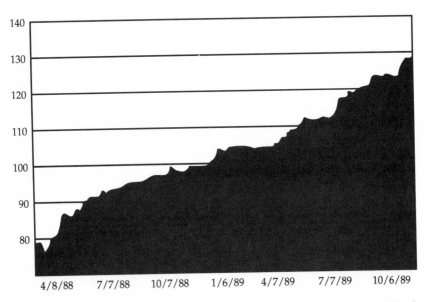

Figure 6.2. Public Service of New Hampshire 13.75% 3rd Mortgage Bonds '96 Price Performance

liabilities, and timing are definable with greater accuracy, and events once unimaginable in the collective consciousness of the marketplace come to pass.

In the case of Public Service of New Hampshire, the investment prospects for the unsecured bonds became much more clearly defined in the fall of 1989 when the State of New Hampshire agreed to provide rate relief. That development had two important repercussions for investors:

1. Since rates would be raised whether or not the controversial Seabrook nuclear plant operated, it became possible to estimate a ranges values for PSNH without knowing whether Seabrook would be fully licensed.
2. PSNH was now likely to emerge from bankruptcy in the near future, a fact that made it far more attractive to potential buyers.

Since opportunities to buy utilities are rare, investors could anticipate that PSNH would command a price high enough to return substantial value to unsecured debtholders and to pay postpetition interest to boot.

That scenario played out as several bidders emerged, and PSNH was essentially auctioned off by the bankruptcy court. While each successive bid placed a higher value on the company, the price of PSNH's unsecured debentures lagged, creating multiple purchasing opportunities for investors (Figure 6.3).

Plan Implementation

Even when a plan of reorganization has been approved by the bankruptcy court, multiple investment opportunities may exist. Often the debt and

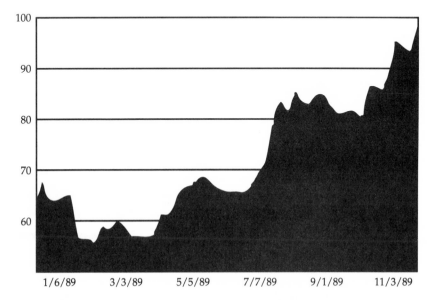

Figure 6.3. Public Service of New Hampshire 17.5% Unsecured Debs '04 Price Performance

equity securities of a rehabilitated company are undervalued because bankruptcy players already have garnered significant profits and are uninterested in holding what will become plain vanilla securities. Meanwhile, mainstream investors may still be put off by the bankruptcy stigma.

In the case of Texaco, for example, even after the company's reorganization plan had been submitted and had received the support of the major interested parties in early 1988, bonds could be purchased at prices that offered in excess of a 10 percent return over a two-month period (or a 75 percent annualized rate), since the plan called for the debt (subsequently rated BBB) to be reinstated with all back interest paid by the end of April.

Conclusion

Conceptually, the identification of investment opportunities in distressed securities is a simple process. The investor estimates the amount of assets that will ultimately be available to settle all claims, subtracts the value of liabilities that rank ahead of or pari passu with a specific claim, then judges how long it will take for the reorganization proceedings to be completed. From these facts, it is a straightforward matter to assign a price that produces a satisfactory rate of return in light of the associated risk.

In practice, however, quantifying the key variables requires exhaustive fact gathering and a fair amount of subjective judgment. Moreover, the financial and operating condition of a company in or near bankruptcy is typically quite fluid. A dynamic analysis is therefore essential.

The positive message here is that, despite the increased investor interest in distressed securities that has accompanied the sector's growth, exploitable inefficiencies in pricing remain. Given the magnitude of assumptions that must be built into any evaluation of a financially troubled company, a wide range of opinions can emerge even if all investors are thorough in their analysis.

This is not to say, however, that everybody's opinion is equally correct. At the point at which the company emerges from reorganization proceedings or completes its restructuring, it will be apparent that in retrospect some investors paid too dearly for their holdings, while others missed an excellent opportunity by being too conservative in their valuations. Still other investors will prove to have gained or lost by virtue of good or bad timing in their commitment of capital. In short, the distressed securities sector represents one of the toughest tests of analytical skills that can be found in the capital markets. Those who accept the challenge stand to reap vast rewards if they can consistently make top grades.

Notes

1. Edward I. Altman, "Investing in Distressed Securities: The Anatomy of Defaulted Debt and Equities," The Foothill Group, (April 1990).

2. See Jerry H. Labowitz, Stanley L. Rubin and Donna G. Takeda, "Highlights of 10th Annual Connector Industry Conference," Merrill Lynch Capital Markets, (November 1989).

Appendix

Case Study: Farley Inc.

Comment on Speculative-Grade Securities *

Issues	Amount ($MM)	Maturity	Rating MY/S&P	Earliest Call	Price	Recent Price
14⅝% Sr. sub. ext. reset nts.	250.0	02/15/91	Caa/CCC	02/15/91	105.00	28
15⅝% Sub. reset nts.	250.0	02/15/96	Caa/CCC	02/15/93	106.94	13

Note: The company can extend the maturity of the sr. sub. nts. for three or five years. The interest rate must be reset so that the bonds trade at 102 with a maximum coupon increase of 300 bp. If the maturity is not extended, the company must retire the notes at 105.
The interest on the sub nts. must be reset so that the bonds trade at 102 with a maximum coupon increase of 100 bp.

Investment Recommendation

Although Farley, Inc. is in dire financial condition, we believe the bonds are an attractive investment at current prices. Under a worst case scenario, we value the 14⅝ percent senior subordinated notes at 30 and the 15⅝ percent subordinated notes at 15. Additionally, we expect that the company will propose a debt restructuring because it does not currently generate any cash flow with which to service its debt, has a $150 million bank loan that comes due this April, and has been unable to complete its acquisition of West Point Pepperell. Separately, we believe that the Fruit of the Loom's public bonds are vulnerable should an intercompany transaction occur and that Farley Inc. will propose an exchange offer at West Point Pepperell that will negatively impact that company's increasing rate notes and preferred and common stock.

Description

Farley, Inc. (Farley) is 76.4 percent owned by William Farley and is the product of several successive leveraged acquisitions. The company

*In our opinion, the securities discussed herein should only be considered for inclusion in accounts qualified for speculative investment.

currently consists of (1) four metals businesses (Farley Metals), (2) Acme Boot Company, Inc. (Acme Boot), (3) 12 million shares of Fruit of the Loom, Inc. (FTL) Class B common stock, (4) common and preferred stock in West Point Pepperell, Inc. (WPM), and (5) cash and marketable securities. The bonds were issued in 1988 as a "blind pool financing" with $300 million of the proceeds allocated for the acquisition of other businesses and the balance used to retire existing debt.

The Company

Farley Metals.   Farley Metals was acquired from NL Industries in 1982 for $124 million. It comprises four distinct metals businesses that primarily produce parts for the automotive industry (85 percent of its 1989 sales were to OEMs, mainly Ford and General Motors). Doehler-Jarvis (80 percent of sales) manufactures aluminum die castings; Tool and Engineering produces body-part prototype dies; Southern Fastening manufactures and distributes metal fasteners; and Magnus produces bearings.

In 1989, results were essentially flat versus 1988 despite a sharp decline in the second half of the year. The weakness was mainly due to softening demand in the automotive market. We estimate that Farley Metals generated $18.6 million in operating earnings in 1989, but spent $34 million on upgrading and refurbishing equipment ($15 million estimated maintenance level) and $15 million on management fees to Farley Industries, Inc., which is 100 percent owned by William Farley. This resulted in a free cash flow deficit of $15.4 million. In 1990, we project operating income of $31 million and a free cash flow deficit of $7 million (see Table 6.1).

Farley previously announced its intention to divest these businesses. Management has asserted for some time that the sale of Doehler-Jarvis will be completed imminently (the reported asking price is $125 to $150 million). Based on a nine times projected cash flow multiple (adjusted for normalized capital expenditures and management fees), we would value

Table 6.1.   Farley Metals Financial Projections ($ Millions) FYE 12/31

	Projected 1990	%Sales	Estimated 1989	%Sales	1988	%Sales
Net sales	$365.0		$380.1		$378.2	
EBIT	15.0	4.1	18.6	4.9	18.5	4.9
EBITDA	31.0	8.5	33.6	8.8	31.6	8.4
Capital expenditures	23.0	6.3	34.0	8.9	27.3	7.2
Management fees	15.0		15.0		14.7	
Free cash flow (deficit)	($7.0)		($15.4)		($10.4)	

Doehler-Jarvis at $100 to $125 million and all four companies at $125 to $150 million. Additionally, Farley is fully drawn down on a $150 million short-term credit agreement that is secured by the operating assets of Farley Metals and expires in April 1990. The loan was essentially a bridge for the sale of Doehler-Jarvis.

Acme Boot. Acme Boot produces men's and women's boots and shoes under the Acme, Dan Post, Dingo, and Lucchese brand names. It operates 37 retail outlets (10 percent of sales) and maintains over 9,000 accounts. During the last few years, Acme has been suffering from a decline in the westernwear fad and poor economic conditions in its primary markets (energy and farm sectors). In 1989, we estimate that the unit generated free cash flow of $4 million versus $2.4 million in 1988 due to higher selling prices and a more favorable product mix. We project 1990 free cash flow to be $4.5 million (see Table 6.2). Farley has advanced funds to Acme in the past and recently paid off the outstanding balance on Acme's $20 million revolving credit facility. We estimate the unit's value to be less than $25 million.

Table 6.2. Acme Boot Company Inc. Financial Projections ($ Millions) FYE 12/31

	Projected 1990	%Sales	Estimated 1989	%Sales	1988	%Sales
Net sales	$158.0		$147.0		$133.7	
EBIT	4.5	2.8	4.0	2.7	1.7	1.3
EBITDA	5.5	3.5	5.0	3.4	3.2	2.4
Capital expenditures	1.0	0.6	1.0	0.7	0.7	0.5
Free cash flow	$ 4.5		$ 4.0		$ 2.5	

Fruit of the Loom

Public Debt Issues	Amount ($MM)	Maturity	Rating (Mdy/S&P)	Recent Price	First Call Date	First Call Price	YTM%	CY%
7% Debentures	125.0	03/15/11	B2/B-	58.25	Anytime	100.0	12.75	12.01
10¾% Sr. sub. notes	250.0	07/15/95	B2/CCC	82.50	07/15/90	108.00	15.71	13.03
12⅜% Sub. debs.	100.0	06/01/03	B3/CCC	82.00	06/01/90	106.12	15.63	15.09

Farley acquired Northwest Industries for $1.4 billion in 1985. After the buyout, Farley sold off Northwest's nonapparel businesses and kept Union Underwear (now Fruit of the Loom). In 1987, FTL underwent a restructuring that included an initial public offering of common stock and a refinancing of its acquisition debt. FTL produces men's and boy's underwear (43 percent of sales), activewear for the imprinted market (48 percent of sales), branded women's and girl's underwear (5 percent of sales), and family socks (4 percent of sales). Its brand names include Fruit of the Loom, BVD, and Screen Stars. The company is a fully integrated manufacturer and performs its own spinning, knitting, cutting, and sewing functions.

FTL has enjoyed substantial growth in revenues and profits over the past few years. This was the result of Farley's heavy investment in the company since its acquisition, primarily in its basic businesses and product line extensions such as activewear. We believe that FTL also benefits from brand recognition, strong management, low-cost production, dominant market share, and relationships with mass merchants. In 1989, FTL generated $289.2 million in operating income and $282.2 million in cash flow after capital expenditures versus $200.6 million and $184 million, respectively, in 1988. This was largely the result of rapid growth in its activewear division and underwear lines (see Table 6.3).

Farley owns 12 million shares of Fruit of the Loom Class B common stock. This represents a 19.5 percent economic interest, but, because B shares carry five times voting rights of A shares, this also constitutes 49 percent voting control. While B stock is clearly worth more than A stock to Farley because of its voting privileges, it automatically converts to Class A stock if it is sold. Therefore, we currently value this stock at $156 million (12 million shares @ $13 per share). However, while Farley cannot monetize its control premium by selling its shares, the company could receive a higher price for its stock if it were able to arrange the sale of the entire company at a premium. In addition, William Farley personally owns 3.2 million shares of Class B stock (which he received as dividends in connection with the offering of the Farley securities), as well as 1.8 million shares of Class A stock.

Farley does not have direct access to the cash flow of FTL. FTL has over $400 million in bank debt, which prohibits dividends unless shareholder equity is $450 million (it was $305 million as of 9/30/89) and limits payments to 30 percent of net income. FTL's 10¾ percent senior subordinated notes limit dividends to 50 percent of net income. Also, A shares are entitled to receive the first dollar of dividends before B shares can be paid (there are 46.4 million A shares outstanding). Based on this, we do not believe that Farley Inc. will receive any dividends from its stock for several years. Separately, FTL's public bonds have further downside potential because debt covenants do not appear to restrict the company from purchasing an asset from WPM or Farley or from making an intercompany loan. (FTL currently has $218 million of borrowing capacity under various lines of credit—$105 million of which is available for any purpose—and the bank loan agreements contain the only additional restrictions on future indebtedness.) While Farley or WPM would benefit from such a transaction, the market's negative perception could jeopardize Farley's investment in FTL.

Table 6.3.   Fruit of the Loom, Inc. Financial Projections
($ Millions) FYE 12/31

	1989	%Sales	1988	%Sales
Net sales	$1,320.9		$1,004.7	
EBIT	289.2	21.9	200.6	20.0
EBITDA	367.2	27.8	266.5	26.5
Capital expenditures	85.0	6.4	82.5	8.2
Free cash flow	282.2		184.0	
Interest expense	124.7		104.6	
EBITDA/interest	2.95x		2.55x	
EBITDA—Cap-X/interest	2.26x		1.76x	

West Point Pepperell.   In April 1989, Farley acquired 95 percent of WPM through West Point Acquisition (WPA) at $58 per share for roughly $2.9 billion. WPM is a major diversified apparel and textile company that was founded in 1880 and consists of five divisions: Household Fabrics (47 percent of sales) produces bed linens and bath towels; Apparel Fabrics (12 percent of sales) manufactures and sells knitted and woven fabrics; Sanderson (4 percent of sales) produces home furnishing fabrics; Cluett Peabody (31 percent of sales) manufactures and markets apparel, primarily men's shirts, suits, and hosiery; and Industrial Fabrics (6 percent of sales) produces a variety of fabrics mostly for industrial uses. In October, the company agreed to sell Cluett Peabody for $600 million. This price was renegotiated, and it has been reported that this sale will be completed soon at $360 million plus $65 million of seller paper.

In fiscal 1989, Household Fabrics performed well mainly by reducing SG&A expenses and continuing to integrate the acquired assets of J. P. Stevens into its operations. We believe that the division benefits from its dominant market share (#1 in sheets and #2 in towels) in markets that have shown strong and consistent growth. WPM's other businesses are generally well run and have strong brand names. However, they have not performed well recently, particularly Cluett Peabody and Apparel Fabrics, which have been negatively impacted by sluggish consumer retail demand combined with very cautious reordering by many retailers. We believe this trend will continue well into 1990, and it will be difficult for the company to sell its remaining divisions at acceptable prices.

We estimate that WPM generated operating earnings of $227.2 million and cash flow after capital expenditures of $283 million in FYE 9/30/89 versus $189.5 million and $150.2 million, respectively, in FYE 9/30/88. This cash flow was sufficient to cover interest expense at WPM in fiscal 1989 by $146 million. However, if the interest and dividends on WPA's debt and preferred stock were included, this would result in a deficit of $107.4 million. We project that fiscal 1990 operating earnings and cash flow after

Table 6.4.   West Point Pepperell, Inc. Financial Projections ($ Millions) FYE 9/24[1]

	Projected[2] 1990	%Sales	Estimated 1989	%Sales	Proforma[3] 1988	%Sales
Net Sales:						
Household fabrics	$1,328.0		$1,265.2		$1,183.3	
Other	530.0		1,302.5		1,298.2	
Total net sales	$1,858.0		$2,567.7		$2,481.5	
EBIT:						
Household fabrics	$154.0	11.6	$137.8	10.9	$102.9	8.7
Other	57.0	10.8	89.4	6.9	86.6	6.7
Total EBIT	$211.0	11.4	$227.2	8.8	$189.5	7.6
EBITD:						
Household fabrics	$252.0	19.0	$230.3	18.2	$176.6	14.9
Other	88.0	16.6	134.9	10.4	122.9	9.5
Total EBITD	340.0	18.3	365.2	14.2	299.5	12.1
Capital expenditures	(85.0)	4.6	(82.2)	3.2	(149.3)	6.0
Total EBITD - Cap-X	255.0	13.7	283.0	11.0	150.2	6.1
WPM interest expense	(86.8)		(137.0)		(126.2)	
Net cash flow	168.2		146.0		24.0	
WPA interest expense	(214.1)		(186.5)		(183.3)	
WPA preferred dividends	(75.2)		(66.9)		(66.9)	
Free cash flow	($121.1)		($107.4)		($226.2)	

1. The company is currently changing its fiscal year end to 12/31.

2. Proforma to reflect the sale of Cluett Peabody and the subsequent paydown of the new bridge loan agreement.

3. Assumes that the transaction took place at the beginning of the fiscal year.

Note: Figures represent our best estimates of operating results but may not reflect all adjustments relating to the J. P. Stevens acquisition or the company's other accounting adjustments.

expenditures (excluding Cluett Peabody) will be $211 million and $255 million, respectively (see Tables 6.4 and 6.5).

WPA financed the acquisition of its WPM stock with a $688 million bank tender offer facility, $705 million of increasing rate notes, $200 million of increasing rate preferred stock, and a $172.9 million investment by Farley consisting of $220 face amount of junior PIK preferred stock and $10 million of common stock. In addition, banks provided a $1.035 billion bridge facility to WPM in order to retire existing debt. On March 14, 1990, WPM announced that it had negotiated an amended bridge facility consisting of a $550 million term loan and a $650 million revolving credit agreement, both of which mature on December 31, 1994. The original loan was due to mature on March 31, 1990. The new agreement continues to prohibit WPM from upstreaming its cash flow in order to service the debt at WPA until the merger is completed (WPA has depleted the $110 million that was in escrow at the time of the acquisition to finance interim interest and dividends). Additionally, WPA's bank tender offer facility expires on March 31, 1990.

We believe that the proceeds from the anticipated sale of Cluett Peabody will be used to reduce the outstanding balance on WPM's new revolving credit facility. Despite this, we feel that it is unlikely that the merger can be completed unless Farley can complete additional asset sales or negotiate an exchange offer that permanently reduces WPA's debt. This is because WPM's bridge facility is overcollateralized (the estimated $650 million outstanding is secured by the assets of WPM, which we value at $1.8 to $2.0 billion—seven to eight times our fiscal 1990 EBITD after capital expenditures projection) and the bank lenders are unlikely to approve a merger that creates an overleveraged nonviable entity. Additionally, a default at WPA would not trigger a default at WPM under the terms of the new bridge agreement.

We believe that WPA's bank lenders have significant leverage over the increasing rate note and preferred stockholders in an exchange offer negotiation because the WPA tender offer bank facility is currently overcollateralized (the $733 million loan is secured by WPA's stock in WPM, which we value at $1.3 billion—28 million shares @ $47 share).

WPM is extremely difficult to value because it is so dependent on a restructuring. Farley paid $2.9 billion for the company. Although operations have improved since the buyout and the Cluett Peabody sale is near completion, we believe that Farley's investment has little to no value; we estimate that WPM is currently worth $1.8 to $2.0 billion but has $2.3 billion of consolidated debt and senior preferred stock outstanding. Also, a restructuring at WPA will be extremely difficult to accomplish because only $317 to $517 million of value is available for the $705 million of increasing rate notes and $200 preferred stock ($1.8 to $2.0 billion minus $1.48 billion of consolidated debt). Additionally, even though WPA is required to purchase the remaining 5 percent of WPM's common stock at $58

Table 6.5.   West Point Pepperell, Inc. Projected Capitalization ($ Millions) FYE 9/24[1]

	Projected[2] 1990	Estimated 1989	Proforma[3] 1988
West Point Pepperell debt			
Bridge financing[4]			
Term loan	$550.0	$960.0	$960.0
Revolver	100.0	75.0	0.0
Assumed debt	100.0	110.0	110.0
Total	$750.0	$1,145.0	$1,070.0
West Point acquisition debt			
Tender offer facility[4]	$919.5	$733.0	$688.0
15¼% Sr. sub. incr. rt. nts.[5]	388.6	388.6	388.6
16¼% Sub. incr. rt. nts.[5]	244.6	244.6	244.6
15⅜% Bridge nts.[5]	71.9	71.9	71.9
Total	1,624.6	1,438.0	1,393.0
Total Debt	$2,374.6	$2,583.0	$2,463.0
Tender offer preferred stock			
17.5% Series A preferred[5]	$41.9	$41.9	$41.9
17.5% Series B preferred[5]	49.4	49.4	49.4
15⅞% Bridge preferred[5]	108.8	108.8	108.8
Junior PIK preferred (Farley)	220.0	220.0	220.0
Total	420.1	420.0	420.0
Total debt + preferred stock	2,794.7	3,003.0	2,883.0
Common stock (Farley)	10.0	10.0	10.0
Total capitalization	$2,804.7	$3,013.0	$2,893.0

1. The company is currently changing its fiscal year end to 12/31.

2. Reflects the sale of Cluett Peabody and the subsequent paydown of the revolving credit facility of the new bridge loan agreement ($650 million available/$500 million outstanding minus $400 million of sale proceeds).

3. Assumes that the transaction took place at the beginning of the fiscal year.

4. Wells Fargo Bank and Bankers Trust are the agents for both loans, but the lending groups are slightly different. Total borrowing capacity under the WPM revolver is $75 million, and the WPA tender offer facility is $796 million.

5. Coupon and dividends reflect current rates on 9/24/89; they increase by 50 basis points quarterly until April 1990 and 25 basis points per quarter thereafter. IRN coupons are PIK above 18 percent.

6. Dividend increases monthly.

per share, we would expect these shares to trade closer to the company's fundamental value of roughly $35 to $42 per share ($1.8 to $2.0 billion minus $750 million of WPM debt divided by 30 million shares), reflecting the uncertainty and timing of the merger.

Cash and Marketable Securities. Prior to its February 15, 1990 coupon payment, Farley had $110 million of VF Corp. common stock (3.48 million shares @ $31.5 per share). Assuming that this stock was sold to pay the coupon, roughly $72 million in cash or marketable securities would remain. Although we believe that this position is currently $60 million, Farley was recently granted a waiver from its bank lenders to purchase its bonds in the open market with a portion of its cash.

Analysis

Farley's $500 million of public debt produces annual interest expense of about $76 million, and its $150 million bank credit line has annual interest expense of roughly $17 million. The company's next semiannual bond coupon payment of $37.9 million is due August 15, 1990. These payments will likely increase to the maximum reset amount of $42.8 million beginning February 15, 1991. The company also faces an April 1990 final maturity date on its bank credit agreement. Unfortunately, Farley cannot meet these requirements because it receives no dividends from its investment in FTL or WPM and the combined businesses of Farley Metals and Acme Boot do not generate any cash flow after capital expenditures and management fees.

Farley can avoid a default for 12 to 18 months by funding its interest payments with the sale of securities in its investment portfolio (the company paid its February 15, 1990 coupon by selling its VF Corp. common stock holdings), provided that it can also extend the maturity on its bank loan agreement or sell Farley Metals in order to repay this debt. We believe, however, that Farley's only realistic alternative is to attempt to eliminate its cash interest expense and permanently reduce debt by offering bondholders an exchange offer package consisting of a reduced amount of new deferred interest securities and an equity interest in the company (we estimate that Farley's equity value is currently a deficit of $200 million to $284 million). In the meantime, we believe that management is increasing value by using the company's cash balances to buy some of its bonds in the open market at their currently discounted price levels. We do not believe that the company will either sell or borrow against its FTL common stock in order to retire the remaining bonds, even at a premium, without first completing an exchange offer. This is because the FTL stock is Farley's only tangible asset and the company would need to offer bondholders either all of the sale proceeds or the stock's full collateral value backing a loan (up to the face amount of the bonds) in order for bondholders to agree to a tender offer. FTL, however, could acquire an asset from Farley or WPM or provide an intercompany loan to either entity. Separately, we believe that Farley's investment in WPM has little or no value and that the merger will not be completed unless the holders of WPA increasing rate notes and preferred stock agree to an exchange offer, which will be extremely difficult to accomplish.

Valuation

We believe that Farley will attempt to restructure its debt. We estimate that the company's value is currently at least $216 million. This is a minimum valuation because the only two assets to which we have ascribed any value are publicly traded common stock and cash (see Table 6.6). Based on a worst case scenario of a bankruptcy where a distribution to bondholders does not occur for three years, the company would be currently worth approximately $111 million (if discounted back at 25 percent). This represents 22 percent of face value in aggregate, or an equitable distribution of roughly 30 for the 14⅝ percent senior subordinated notes and 15 for the 15⅝ percent subordinated notes. We believe that these estimates will be increased as the company uses its cash to buy bonds at their currently discounted levels. Additionally, if a debt restructuring can be accomplished in less than three years or if Farley sells its FTL common stock to repay debt, then bondholder distributions could be significantly greater.

Table 6.6.   Farley, Inc. Estimated Asset Values ($ Millions)

		Low	High
Farley Metals and Acme Boot	$150		
Secured bank debt	150		
Net equity		$ 0	$ 0
Fruit of the Loom stock		156	240
West Point Pepperell		0	50
Cash and securities		60	60
Total assets		$216	$350
Total bonds outstanding		$500	$500

---

issuer(s). MLPF&S, its affiliates, directors, officers, employees and employee benefit programs may have a long or short position in any securities or options of this issuer(s).

The bonds of the company are traded over-the-counter. Retail sales and/or distribution of this report may be made only in states where these securities are exempt from registration or have been qualified for sale. MLPF&S usually makes a market in the bonds of this company.

Unique Factors in the Credit Analysis of High-Yield Bonds

William A. Cornish, CFA
Duff and Phelps, Inc.

The credit analysis of high-yield bonds is based on the same in-depth, fundamental research on which the credit analysis of investment-grade bonds is based. The goal is to determine the amount of business risk associated with the operating characteristics of the company and the amount of financial risk associated with the balance sheet, the maturity schedule, and the interest burden associated with the debt structure. Once the credit rating has been determined, it must be monitored on a regular basis to detect any changes in the credit worthiness of the company.

The High-Yield Deal Structure

The unique factors in the credit analysis of high-yield bonds typically relate to financial risk, reflecting what is called "financial engineering." Over the past 10 years, there has been tremendous creativity in the shape of these transactions. It is evident that there have been some compromises that have created tensions in the structures. The cause of the tensions is the difference in the objectives of the various participants in high-yield transactions. Thus, analytical clues are provided by understanding these disparate goals.

- Commercial banks seek returns above what they receive from the conventional banking business and protection against loss.
- The leveraged-buyout (LBO) organizations are willing to take significant risk for extraordinary returns—typically in the neighborhood of a

SOURCE: From *High-Yield Bonds: Analysis and Risk Assessment*, by permission of the Association for Investment Management and Reasearch, Charlottesville, Virginia, 1990, pp. 28-33.

50 percent return over a four- to seven-year period. This provides the necessary cushion against loss on some of the deals.

- The company's management wants two things: to survive and to participate in the equity gains.
- Investors want to get paid in accordance with the terms of the issue they own. Ironically, fixed-income investors typically supply most of the capital for a highly leveraged corporations, but they probably have less to say about the structure than the rest of the participants.
- The investment banker is interested in fees. To earn fees, the investment banker must make the deal go through, and consequently, the investment banker wants to strike the necessary balance between what the banks want, what the LBO organization wants, and what the management and investors want.

How Claims Affect Credit Worthiness

Some typical types of claims against the assets of a firm are listed in Table 7.1. This is not a comprehensive list, but it illustrates the diversity of these instruments. The tensions and compromises inherent in the different objectives drive the structure. To understand how these different claims affect the credit worthiness of a company, one must understand the characteristics of each claim.

Banks almost always have a senior claim, which is typically a secured position (either by assets or the stock of operating subsidiaries). Bank debt has relatively short maturities, typically two years or less, and is almost always variable rate. Thus, a credit analyst must consider both economic risk with respect to the company's operations and what is likely to happen

---

Table 7.1.   Opportunities for Investors

High-Yield Structure: Typical Types of Securities

Bank debt
Broker loans
Reset notes
Senior debt
Senior subordinated debt
Subordinated debt (Payment-in-kind)
Junior subordinated debt (Payment-in-kind)
Preferred
Preferred (Payment-in-kind)
Common equity (if any)

SOURCE: *High-Yield Bonds: Analysis and Risk Assessment,* (1990) pp. 28–33) by permission of the Association for Investment Management and Research, Charlottesville, Va.

in the financial markets, because rising interest rates could squeeze cash flow significantly. The payoff to banks is accomplished through a combination of three sources: asset sales, refinancing, and repayment out of operating cash flow. The risk is that the bank debt cannot be repaid on schedule. If the debt is to be repaid through the proceeds of sales of assets, one must determine the likelihood, price, and timing of those asset sales. Also, one must evaluate whether the assets to be sold are essential for the operation of the business; are these the really profitable components of the firm (the "crown jewels"), and what is the diversification effect of selling these assets?

If the debt is to be repaid through refinancing, one must determine the availability as well as the rate required to refinance. The company must be able to refinance at a reasonable price relative to its structure, and that will be dependent on the operating performance of the business, the general condition of financial markets, and what people feel about the sector of the market. For example, currently the high-yield market is in disfavor, resulting in historically wide yield spreads over Treasuries for those companies that are able to obtain financing, and many companies in the present environment simply cannot find lenders.

Nonbank shorter-maturity claims must be analyzed carefully. Typically, this is the portion of the short-term debt that the banks will not provide because there is not enough cushion in the asset valuations. There are two primary sources of short-term nonbank financing: broker loans ("bridge" loans) and reset notes. Investment banks make broker loans to help make a deal possible and to earn spread income. Reset notes are a particular concern to credit analysts because they imply escalating interest rates. When interest reset is about to occur, companies try to sell assets or refinance to avoid the higher rates. Essentially, reset notes are a flawed claim. The problem is that companies able to afford the escalating interest rates are also able to refinance or sell assets; those in trouble cannot, and they may be forced into bankruptcy.

Long-term debt securities sold to investors are always subordinate. In a takeover situation, there will usually be some previously outstanding senior debt, but the new securities will typically be subordinate—in spite of their names. These securities are divided into two categories: current pay and deferred pay. The current-pay securities pay the cash interest on a predetermined schedule. Deferred-pay instruments, usually payment-in-kind securities (PIKs), were developed to provide companies flexibility in meeting cash flows in the early years of a highly leveraged structure. In most of these deals, the projections are for negative coverage during the early years when the bank debt is being paid back. During this period, deferred-pay securities forgo payments. As a result of the early-year deferrals, they require an explosion of payments in later years, which can cause a deterioration in the quantitative measures of liquidity. Although such securities provide extra flexibility in the early years, there is a heavy cost in the subsequent years. In many structures, these securities prevent any improvement in credit quality over the forecast period. In select cases, these deferred-payment securities are a good investment because companies that are able to do so try to retire these securities early.

In summary, the makeup of the capital structure is critical in terms of appraising credit quality. It is important to know the absolute level of debt, the amount and timing of the interest expense, and the maturity schedule, as well as the priorities for the alternative debt instruments.

Cash-Flow Forecasts

Cash-flow forecasts are critical to the analysis of debt structures. They are the basis for putting debt structures together—banks, rating agencies, and investors review the cash flows. In addition, they may be included in prospectuses. As such, they are part of the due diligence process.

Company officials and their investment banker will often say that management forecasts of cash flows are conservative. In general, however, they prove to be just the reverse. Management forecasts are characterized by all the good things in life—namely, increasing profit margins, improvements in working-capital turnover, and modest expenditures on plant and equipment, all of which occurs during years of steadily rising revenues. An analyst should use management forecasts as one, and *only* one, input for making independent forecasts. Many analysts use only crude approximations to adjust forecasts—for example, cutting forecasts by 10 or 20 percent across the board. Clearly, there is room for greater sophistication in the development of cash-flow forecasts by both management and credit analysts.

Forecasts tend to be fairly accurate in the first year. After that, the accuracy often deteriorates. Management has a relatively good feel for what is going on in the near future, but as the time horizon increases, its accuracy diminishes. Therefore, it is important for analysts to identify stress points as well as critical variables and monitor them carefully and often.

There are three key stress points: asset sale target dates, reset note repricing dates, and the date deferred-pay securities start paying. As an example, in our analysts, we might ask the following questions: Are you meeting your asset sales target dates? What is going to happen to the existing interest rates when the reset notes are repriced? What will happen to the required cash flows when the deferred securities start paying?

Then we look at the three critical variables: economic sensitivity, pricing and volume considerations, and technological change. It is important to incorporate what is happening in the economic environment into an analysis of the credit worthiness of a highly leveraged company. It is also important to determine how sensitive the business is to volume and pricing changes, i.e., what is the competitive environment in the industry? One must also look at the company's vulnerability to technological change. Finally, I should mention the sensitivity to interest-rate change because of the importance of variable-rate debt to many of these companies.

Corporate Structure

The corporate structure is an important consideration in the credit analysis of high-yield bonds. It is critical to look at how cash passes between subsidiaries and the parent and between subsidiaries. The structures can be quite complex and often confusing: Table 7.2 shows an example of such a structure. At this writing, Farley, Inc. has three primary operating subsidiaries: Fruit of the Loom (20 percent owned), Acme Boot (100 percent owned), and West Point Pepperell (95 percent owned). The question is, Where is the parent company, Farley, going to get the cash to meet its debt-repayment obligations? In the current environment, none of these units can provide any cash to the parent. The metals division has its own senior subordinate debt, subordinate notes, junior subordinate debts, and preferred stock. Given these requirements, its cash flow is insufficient to contribute to the parent's debt service coverage.

Farley has a fee collector—a related but independent organization that provides services to the Farley companies. I do not know whether it could be attached in bankruptcy; it is not owned by Farley. It enters into a contractual agreement with each of the subsidiaries to receive fees for corporate services.

Both Fruit of the Loom and Acme Boot have bank borrowings secured by receivables and inventories and a restriction against the payment of dividends. In addition, Fruit of the Loom is not allowed to make intercompany loans; Acme Boot can make intercompany loans, but there are some restrictions on these loans. Farley has put some cash into Acme soot. West Point Pepperell has limits on its bridge loan related to asset sales, dividends, and financial ratio requirements. In addition, negotiations

Table 7.2. Complex Capital Structure: Farley, Inc.

Fruit of the Loom 20 percent owned	Acme Boot 100 percent owned	West Point Pepperell 95 percent owned	Farley, Inc. metals division
Bank borrowings	Bank borrowings	Bridge loan limits • Asset sales • Dividends • Financial ratio requirements	Senior subordinated debt
Secured by inventories/ receivables	Secured by inventories/ receivables		
Dividend restrictions (none paid)	Dividend restrictions (none paid)	Merger debt being negotiated	Subordinated notes
No intercompany loans	Restricted intercompany loans		Junior subordinated debt
	Farley has put in cash		Preferred stock

are underway regarding its merger debt. Under such conditions, the question the analyst must address is, Where (if any place) is the cash to service the parent's debt going to come from?

Debt Covenants

It is important to analyze the debt covenants as part of the credit analysis of high-yield bonds. The emphasis should be on any restrictions on cash flows. The most restrictive covenants are typically in bank loan agreements. Event-risk covenants are a more recent consideration. The language in these covenants is still weak, but they are attracting more attention and could become significant if people start looking more closely at them.

Ability to Negotiate

The company's ability to negotiate when in trouble is another consideration. Banks and private placements are more likely to do so. It is more difficult to negotiate with public debt issues because of the large number of parties involved. Clearly, the difficulty of renegotiating public bond issues is a cause for concern in evaluating the credit of high-yield bonds. On the other hand, banks and private placement holders are often willing to extend credit terms for higher yields. In my opinion, we are going to see considerable refinancing activity to lower interest rates and improve the structure in the next several years. You could even see some equity or common stock financing from these structures to improve the balance sheets.

Conclusion

The developments in the high-yield bond area are evidence of a fascinating new world where the overall level of financial leverage and risk has increased. In this high-financial-risk type of world, superior credit analysis will pay off in terms of spotting credits that may be improving and will be upgraded, and also being able to avoid trouble situations. This market is here to stay for some time to come.

Some Frequently Asked Questions

Question: Do you feel there has been a change in the quality of bonds in given rating categories over time?

Author: In the 1950s, Harris Trust had a rule that no bonds went into any trust accounts unless you could assure them that there was going to be double-digit coverage (10 times or above). Since then, there has clearly been deterioration in the quantitative protection measures. There has also been a major decrease in the number and proportion of industrial companies that have been given an Aaa rating. In many instances the qualitative factors remain the same. Recently, however, we at Duff and Phelps, Inc., added IBM to our watch list for possible downgrading. As few as five years ago, no one would have considered this.

Question: Do you agree with the observation that banks are too willing to push a company into bankruptcy to protect their investment?

Author: Banks have that reputation, and I suspect that trend will continue. Banks are under a lot of pressure to maintain their credit status. Obviously, it is a weakening industry. So if they cannot see their way out and they think they are going to have to put assets on a nonperforming basis, they will be more likely to push a company into bankruptcy to recover their assets. It is necessary from their perspective.

Question: How important is the quality of management in a credit analysis?

Author: Management is almost always the key ingredient. In fact, management and qualitative factors are much more important than statistics. Unfortunately, management is also the most difficult factor to evaluate. Some industries are driven by the economics of the situation; it is very difficult to move away from it. Management is hired to do a job within an economic and industry environment. There are always problems, but management is supposed to solve the problems, so they become a critical aspect of any analysis.

Question: Do you think the current high interest rates on junk bonds imply more defaults because of an inability to restructure or refinance?

Author: The default rate is related in part to the economy. There is certainly a recession under way in certain industries, such as automobiles and some metals. Also, earnings in the chemical industry are starting to turn down—and that used to be a characteristic of a recession. Our economy has become more complex, which is probably why the government has not declared a recession yet. In this particular environment, where it is much more difficult for firms to increase sales and earnings, more companies are being pushed to the edge. I don't know when we will see an upturn.

Question: Do you see the public junk bond market dissipating in coming years in favor of a private market, given the private market's confidentiality and ability to negotiate? Do you see a trend in the mix between these two sectors?

Author: I don't know which way it will go. My remarks concentrated on the disadvantages of the public market, but there definitely are some advantages to this sector. The public sector broadens the size and scope of the market because public funds are available through mutual funds and individual investors. Also, there is a degree of liquidity in the fact that an investor may change his securities to try to maximize returns. The big problem with insurance company private placements is that, although some of them are marketable, they generally cannot be easily sold if you change your strategy and want to do something differently. So I think the public markets are still going to be very important sources of capital and liquidity for companies and investors interested in the high-yield market.

Question: Will banks share the content of bank loan agreements with individual investors?

Author: Analysts should always ask for bank loan agreements—we always do. We are in a position to obtain them, but I do not know the extent to which banks are willing to share that information with the general public.

Question: What kind of rating differential do you give for current-pay versus PIK securities?

Author: The differential depends on the nature of the individual credit. There is always at least a one-step differentiation, but it may be two or three steps, depending on how we feel about that particular credit and how large the senior debt ahead of it is. It is an individual case-by-case decision.

Question: Why don't credit analysts use replacement cost in adjusting operating cash flows?

Author: I don't know. Replacement cost accounting in an inflationary environment was supposed to be a huge advance. In reality, it is a very artificial system, so interest in it has faded. What analysts are really doing is asking questions such as, If this is what you think your volume is going to be, how much do you have in the way of capacity restraints? What sort of modernization work is required? They are looking at what is required to carry forward the business, rather than saying, "Well, you have to recapture all the capital." This is more pragmatic than the theoretical approach of replacement cost.

Question: Do you think the junk bond market has reached its bottom yet in terms of the spreads? How do you feel about investing in quality high-yield bonds, considering these spreads?

Author: We at Duff and Phelps think the spreads are attractive at this point. In fact, through our money management company, our firm recently did a collateralized bond obligation (CBO).

8

The Composite Hedge: Controlling the Credit Risk of High-Yield Bonds

Richard Bookstaber
Morgan Stanley & Co., Inc.

David P. Jacob
J. P. Morgan and Co., Inc.

The correlation between long-term corporate bonds and Treasury bond yields drops as bond quality drops. Their low correlation with Treasuries has led some to conclude that low-quality bonds have too great a residual basis risk to be hedgeable. But the correlation coefficient between the bonds and equity of a firm increases as bond quality drops. This suggests a composite hedging strategy that consists of positions in government bonds or bond futures and positions in stock.

For bonds of the highest quality, the composite hedge is the same as a conventional interest rate hedge—it calls for a full position in Treasuries. As bond quality decreases, however, the composite hedge calls for a larger investment in the equity of the underlying firm. The exact allocations will depend on the firm's debt-to-equity ratio, the volatility of its value, and the length of time to the bond's maturity.

For lower-quality issues, the composite hedge significantly outperforms a conventional interest rate hedge. Furthermore, a composite hedge preserves any mispricing in the underlying bonds. It thus offers a valuable tool for credit conversion: if the high-yield bond sector is undervalued, the investor can retain differentially higher returns by investing in this sector while relying on the hedge to reduce the investment's risk to acceptable levels.

Bond hedges typically focus on controlling the interest rate risk associated with a bond position. While this focus may be appropriate for hedging positions in government or high-quality corporate bonds, it is

SOURCE: Reprinted with permission from the "Financial Analysts Journal," March/April (1986).

insufficient for lower-quality corporate issues, which are affected by factors other than interest rates. In particular, the possibility that the firm will be unable to make the payments on its debt obligations clearly influences the price of these bonds. A successful hedge in these bonds must thus consider, in addition to interest rate risk, a credit component to control the price changes induced by changes in credit quality.

This article presents a hedging strategy that addresses both the credit risk and the interest rate risk by employing a composite hedge consisting of positions in government bonds or bond futures and positions in stock. For very high quality corporate bonds, the optimum hedge constitutes a position in government bonds because these bonds are essentially free of credit risk. For bonds close to default, the optimum hedge involves positions in the stock of the underlying firm and only a small position in government bonds. The rationale for using the stock position is based on the likelihood that the bondholders will become owners of the firm's assets, hence subject to the same considerations that affect current equityholders. Changes in the interest rate environment, however, will have little effect on these bondholders, because they are unlikely to receive the promised stream of debt payments.

Interest Rates and Bond Quality

Table 8.1 shows how the effectiveness of an interest rate hedge drops as bond quality declines. The first column shows the correlation coefficient between long-term corporate bond and Treasury bond yields. This is 0.86 for higher-quality issues (those rated Aaa to A) but drops significantly as quality declines, down to 0.77 for bonds rated Baa to Ba and to 0.51 for bonds rated B to Caa. The low correlation between Treasuries and low-quality bonds explains why hedges derived from traditional interest rate hedging models are largely ineffective for low-quality issues.

In fact, this low correlation has led some to conclude that low-quality bonds have too great a residual basis risk to be hedgeable. But note that the declining correlation between Treasuries and corporate bonds as bond quality declines is offset by an increase in the correlation between the firm's equity and its bonds.

There is virtually no correlation between equity and the performance of high-quality bonds. High-quality bonds behave very much like pure

Table 8.1. Corporate Bond Correlations

Rating	Correlation with Treasury bonds	Correlation with equity
Aaa- A	0.86	0.09
Baa-Ba	0.77	0.25
B-Caa	0.51	0.28

interest rate instruments; events important to the firm have only a slight impact on bond price. For lower-quality bonds, however, the equity component becomes more significant. The correlation coefficient rises to 0.25 for bonds rated Baa to Ba and to 0.28 for the lowest-quality group. Paying more attention to the equity component will lead to better hedges, particularly as bond quality diminishes.[1]

Equity Claims and Debt Claims

The value of all corporate securities is contingent on the value of the underlying firm. Equity, for example, represents a residual claim on the earnings of the firm, after all other claims are paid. If the firm cannot meet these obligations and goes into default, equityholders receive nothing. The payoff to equityholders is thus the greater of either the value of the firm in excess of its debt obligations or zero.

The debtholders' contingent claim on the firm differs from that of the equityholders. If the firm cannot satisfy its debt obligations and goes into default, debtholders receive ownership of the firm. Because the firm will default when its value falls below the value of its debt obligations, the payoff to debtholders is the smaller of either the debt payment or the value of the firm.

To see the contingent nature of these securities more clearly, consider the following simplified corporate financing structure. A firm has one zero coupon bond outstanding and must make a payment of $100 million in one year to pay off this obligation. If the payment is not made, ownership of the firm will revert to the debtholders.

Figure 8.1 shows the payoff to equity and debt at the end of the year as a function of the firm's value. The value of the debt equals the value of the firm as long as the firm's value is below the $100 million due the

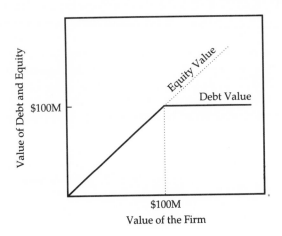

Figure 8.1. Equity and Debt Components of Firm Value

bondholders; it is worth $100 million for any firm value above that point. The equity has no value until the firm reaches the $100 million mark; it then gains one-to-one with firm value after that point.

The payoff to equity is similar to the payoff of a call option, with the underlying asset being the value of the firm and the call option exercise price being the payment due the debtholders. The payoff to equity is the maximum of zero or the firm value minus $100 million. The payoff to debt can also be expressed as an option on the value of the firm, although the specifications of the option payoff as usual. The debt is an option that pays off the minimum of $100 million or the value of the firm.

Because we can express the debt and equity of the firm as options, we can apply option pricing methods to price them. More importantly, from the standpoint of being able to hedge the debt, we can express their functional relationship to one another and to the value of the firm. In practice, of course, the payoff to the debtholder is more complex than the simple zero coupon bond used in this example; beside the coupon payments and call features, a firm may have a number of different debt instruments outstanding, each with a competing claim on the firm. However, the same principle applies to each: all corporate bonds can be analyzed as contingent claims on the firm and can be analyzed as options.[2]

A Composite Bond Hedge

The key principle of option pricing theory is that any option can be replicated by a dynamic hedging position in the underlying asset and risk-free borrowing or lending. The market price of any option must equal the cost of forming the replicating portfolio.[3]

If we think of a corporate bond as an option on the value of the firm, then the relationship between the bond and the value of the firm may be written in the following form:

$$P = F_v V + F_f E \tag{1}$$

Here V represents the market value of the firm, and E represents the "exercise price" of the debt—the amount that must be paid to debtholders if the firm is to remain solvent. The weights given to V and E represent the proportions of firm value and risk-free bond necessary to replicate the debt claim. The debt is comprised of proportion F_v of the underlying firm and proportion F_f of a risk-free bond.

Because the value of the firm, V, is both unobservable and nontradable, we need to find a suitable proxy to implement the model; we may use the firm's equity as the proxy. Specifying the relation with a slightly different functional form, Equation (1) becomes

$$P = D_K S + D_f E \tag{2}$$

where S is the market value of the firm's equity and D_s, is the corresponding equity weight used to create the bond. Because equity is itself an option on the value of the firm, D_s will have a functional relationship to V.

The proportions D_s and D_f are not constants, but variables, dependent on a number of factors and with a functional form that is quite complex, particularly for a coupon-paying bond with a call provision. Three factors are critical, however, in determining the composition of the bond — (1) the debt-asset ratio of the firm, (2) the volatility of the firm's value, and (3) the time to maturity of the debt.

The Debt-Asset Ratio

The larger the ratio of the present value of the debt to the asset value of the firm, the more likely the firm will fail to meet its debt payments. If the debt-asset ratio becomes much greater than one, there is a high likelihood that the debtholders will become owners of the firm's assets. The debtholders' implicit option will behave more like the equity of the firm than like a pure interest rate instrument.

Consider, for example, the price behavior of very low-rated debt. Bonds of firms near default exhibit price volatility and sensitivity to new information in much the same way equity issues do. Such bonds respond modestly to interest rate movements (i.e., they have low duration), because there is little chance their holders will receive the scheduled flow of payments.

Debt behaves more and more like equity, the greater the likelihood the firm will default. Thus the weight of the equity used to determine the current value of the debt will be greater, the greater the debt-asset ratio. Conversely, as Figure 8.2 shows, the proportion of default-free debt held in the replicating portfolio for the corporate debt, D_f, will be a decreasing function of the debt-asset ratio.

Volatility of Firm Value

The volatility of the value of the firm will affect the values of the firm's debt and equity. The greater the volatility, the greater the likelihood an in-

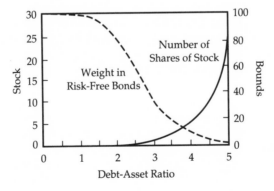

Figure 8.2. Hedge Positions as a Function of the Debt-Asset Ratio

the-money option will move out of the money, or vice versa. We typically think of volatility as being bad for firm equity. In the case of a firm facing imminent default, however, the value of the equity, like that of any out-of-the-money call option, will increase with increasing volatility.

Because equity has no value if firm value does not exceed the bond payment, it is in the equityholders' interests to move the firm into higher-risk areas. Equityholders are in essence gambling with someone else's money. This explains why some troubled companies run after high-risk, high-return projects.

For the debtholder, an increase in volatility is never good. Unlike the equityholder, the debtholder faces a ceiling on his return; higher volatility can only lead to a drop in the value of the debtholder's claim. Inasmuch as the equity component of a bond increases as the firm's debt-asset ratio increases, it is natural to expect it also to increase with the riskiness of the debt.

Time to Maturity

The effect of time to maturity on a composite hedge is best considered by looking at the simplified case of a firm with one zero coupon bond as its obligation. The effect of time to maturity on the chances for default in this case depends on the initial quality of the bond. For a high-quality bond, the longer the time to maturity, the longer the time for a possible deterioration in quality to occur. As with the team that is ahead in a basketball game, a longer time to the final buzzer can only turn a victory into a loss.

Conversely, as with a team trying to play catch-up ball, a longer time to maturity can only improve the chances of payment for a firm that can-not now meet its obligations. For such a firm, a current maturity would lead the debtholders to become owners of the firm. The appropriate hedge would accordingly be all equity. If the payment is several years away, how-ever, there remains some chance that the firm will recover; the replicating portfolio would in this case include some position in default-free bonds as well.

For a low-quality bond, a longer time to maturity means a greater chance of moving out of the default level by the time the obligation is due. Thus less equity is needed in the composite hedge, the longer the time to maturity.[4]

An Illustration

The sensitivity of a bond's price to the default-free interest rate and the equity value of the firm will not be static. It will change with changes in the value of the firm, the debt-asset ratio of the firm, the volatility of the firm, and other factors as well.[5]

Figure 8.3 shows the variations in the sizes of the equity and inter-est rate hedge components for one sample bond. The chart at the top presents the price histories of equity, corporate debt, and government bonds. The chart at the bottom traces the sizes of the equity hedge, D_s, and

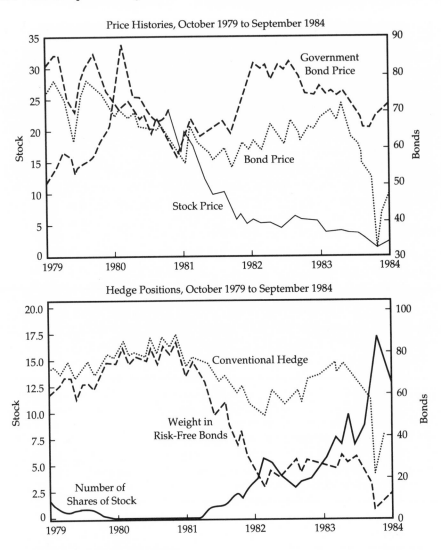

Figure 8.3.   Dynamic Hedging

the interest rate hedge, D_f, that result from the composite hedging method. For purposes of comparison, it also shows the hedge ratio based on a more conventional, duration-based hedging approach.

In the early part of the period depicted in Figure 8.3, the composite hedge closely matches the duration-based hedge: the equity hedge is negligible, and the bond component is high. A look at the equity price during this two-year period shows why: it is still relatively high—between $11 and $33—and the firm is not yet an inferior credit. The bond's price over this period closely parallels the government bond price, so the choice of a high interest rate component in the hedge is evidently a good one. The hedging mix over these two years illustrates that, for higher-quality bonds, the composite hedge closely matches a conventional hedge.

Midway through the time period, the behavior of the bond changes dramatically. While Treasury prices rise, the bond remains fixed; the spread widens. Equity drops below $5. At this point, other factors beside the interest rate enter the picture.

The effect of credit considerations is reflected in the composition of the hedge. The proportion of Treasury bonds held drops dramatically—from about 80 to 20 percent—while the equity position rises steeply. In contrast, the duration-based hedge remains about 60 percent in Treasuries; it does not respond to the changing character of the bond. The composite hedge is particularly sensitive to stock price changes below the $3 level. At this point, the company's default becomes a real possibility, and the proportions of equity and Treasury bonds in the hedge respond accordingly.

Figure 8.3 suggests that no static position can be effective. A dynamic hedging strategy is needed to unbundle the complex, dynamic price behavior of high-yield bonds.

The Potential of High-Yield Hedges

The potential of composite hedging depends on whether it performs significantly better than the simpler, alternative interest rate hedge. To answer this question, we performed two sets of tests on 82 high-yield bonds of 63 different companies.[6] We used monthly data on each bond from 1979 to 1983—a five-year period of historically frequent and dramatic changes in credit quality.[7]

A Negative Report

The pure interest rate hedge is the most widely used form of bond hedging.[8] If bonds are viewed as pure interest rate instruments, differing from Treasury bonds only in having fixed yield spreads, then an interest rate hedge will be effective. As we have noted, however, more than interest rates are involved in making bond prices move. For lower-quality bonds, shifts in firm value, as reflected in changes in equity value, have a significant impact on bond price. As a result, the conventional interest rate hedge may be ineffective and may actually increase the risk of a bond position.

An unhedged bond position has an observable variance of changes in its market price. The objective of a hedge is to reduce this variance— ideally, to zero. Hedging effectiveness can thus be measured as the reduction in the variance of the change in the bond price. Figure 8.4 shows the hedging effectiveness of a duration-based interest rate hedge.

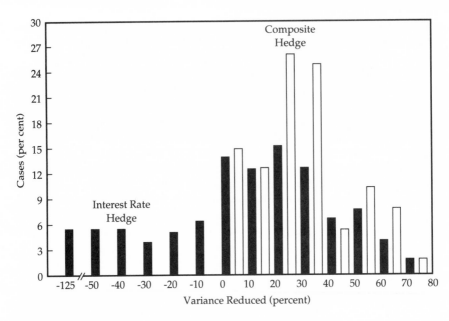

Figure 8.4.   Distribution of Percentage Variance Reduced

A perfect hedge will reduce variance 100 percent; a completely ineffective hedge, having no impact on variance, will reduce it not at all. As
Figure 8.4 shows, the interest rate hedge reduced variance between 80
and −121 percent. That is, in some cases the hedge actually increased
variance, because the bond price movement had so little relation to interest rate movements. In two cases (Ames Department Stores' 10 percent of
1995 and Welded Tube of America's 10 percent of 1995), a concentration
solely on interest rate risk more than doubled the variance of the position.

This illustrates the problem of trying to hedge high-yield bonds with
interest rate vehicles alone.

A Composite Hedge: Uniform Improvement

Figure 8.4 also shows the reduction in variance offered by a composite
hedge using the firm's equity as a proxy for the value of the firm and
Treasury bonds as the risk-free rate.[9] For this hedge, a greater amount
of equity was shorted against a long bond position, the higher the value
of the firm. The greater the interest rate component, the larger the short
position in Treasury instruments. The composite hedge clearly performed
better than the interest rate hedge in reducing the variance of the bond.

The superiority of the composite hedge is even more evident on a
bond-by-bond basis. In the case of all 82 bonds, the variance reduction
from the composite hedge equaled or exceeded that of the interest rate

hedge; in a number of cases, the composite hedge proved vastly superior. As would be expected, the value added by the composite hedge was higher, the greater the debt-asset ratio or credit risk of the bond.

For some of the higher-quality issues, the performances of the two approaches were nearly the same. This is not surprising; the interest rate hedge is, after all, a special case of the composite hedge. With high-quality issues, the composite hedge will put little weight on the equity component and will behave much like a pure interest rate hedge.[10] As credit risk increases, however, the composite hedge proved many times more effective in reducing price risk, even though in some cases the improvement meant only an ineffective hedge versus a disastrous one.

The composite hedge was most effective with the lower-quality issues, particularly with those that had severe credit deterioration. That is, the hedge is most effective where it is most critical—in protecting against catastrophic drops in value. The hedge is not as effective in protecting against small variations in price. Indeed, the bulk of the variance remaining after a composite hedge stems from the basis risk that remains in tracking the smaller errors.

A Case Study

Early 1982 saw a softening in oil prices, which presaged a downturn in contract drilling. Recognizing the vulnerability of its onshore drilling contracts, Kenai Corporation sought to reduce its exposure to this part of its business. With the glut of oil rigs on the market, prices dropped rapidly, however, and Kenai found it could not sell off drilling operations at anything greater than fire-sale prices.

Faced with a drop in revenue from the oil price decline, Kenai turned to other business areas to reduce expenditures. In mid-1982, it cut back personnel, closed several field offices, and sold some oil and gas properties. In late 1982, Kenai restated a bank loan agreement with new collateral terms and deferred payments, leading Standard & Poor's to lower the rating of Kenai's subordinated debt to B from B+. With further deterioration in 1983, Kenai sold off more oil and gas properties and, in September 1983, announced it was getting out of the exploration and production segment of the business to concentrate on oil services—the reconditioning and manufacture of oil field equipment and tools.

By late 1983, with no recovery in sight for its drilling operations, Kenai wrote down the value of its drilling rigs and remaining oil and gas properties. This coincided with a violation of bank loan covenants and a downgrading in Moody's rating from B2 to B3. The spring of 1984 saw a severe deterioration in the fortunes of the company. Unable to sell off oil rigs, Kenai was forced to eliminate an area of business with higher potential— exploration and production. Then, in June, a lawsuit threatened the area Kenai had targeted for growth—oil services.

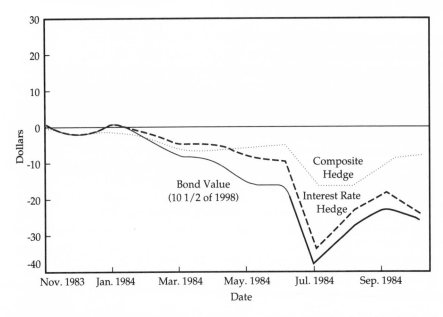

Figure 8.5. Kenai Corporation—Cumulative Value of Hedged and Unhedged Positions

Ironically, the one area of business that remained intact was the area it had tried to abandon two years earlier—onshore oil drilling contracts. As this was the worst performing area in the oil and gas business, it left Kenai with few prospects for a return to profitability. In July 1984, Kenai completed the sale of its oil and gas properties. In August, it defaulted on interest payments. Its S&P rating dropped from CCC to CC. An unsuccessful bank restructuring began in September and led to a decline to a D rating the following month.

Figure 8.5 traces the effect of these events on the value of one of Kenai's subordinated debentures—the 10.50 percent bond due 1998. The solid line depicting the bond price shows a gradual decline from the benchmark value set in November 1983. The most notable drop occurred between April 1984—when the auditors qualified the fiscal-year 1984 results and S&P reduced the bond rating from B to CCC—and July, the month before default.[11] The bond price actually improved after the default, indicating an overly pessimistic market expectation for the imminent default.

An investor who bought this bond in October 1983 would have experienced a capital loss of $38 by July of 1984, and a loss of $25 by October 1984. Given the October 1983 bond price of $70, this means a capital loss of 54 percent by July and 35 percent by October. Figure 8.5 shows how a composite hedge and an interest rate hedge would have affected this loss.

The interest rate hedge would have been ineffective; the value of this hedged position would have moved down virtually in parallel with the bond itself. Since Kenai's difficulties had little to do with the interest rate environment, this result is not surprising.

The protection offered by the composite hedge is evident. Although it would not have given perfect protection, it would have limited the maximum loss to just $15 by July (compared with the $38 for the unhedged position) and to $6 by October (versus the $25 loss for the unhedged position). The mechanism affording this protection—the increasing size of the short position in the hedged stock and interest rate vehicles—is illustrated by the top line in the figure. The total value of the hedged position is equal to the value of the bond plus the value of this hedge.

Figure 8.5 may actually understate the effectiveness of the composite hedge in at least one respect. Because monthly data were used to generate this example, the hedge could only be adjusted monthly. As with any dynamic hedge, infrequent adjustments reduce effectiveness. Even better results might be expected in an actual application, with the hedge being reevaluated on a daily basis.

The Alchemy of Credit Conversion

A composite hedge can be applied to reduce the credit risk of an entire portfolio. A portfolio of high-yield bonds contains residual equity risk that, after the effects of diversification, is closely correlated with the systematic risk of the equity market. Composite hedge technology can reduce this equity-market risk. The result is a portfolio of lower-grade bonds that tracks, from a risk standpoint, like a higher-grade portfolio.

The reduction in risk will not come, of course, without a proportionate reduction in expected yield. If the underlying bond portfolio is mispriced, however, that mispricing will survive the hedge; any mispricing in the high-yield bonds will not be undone by hedging with fairly priced instruments. Thus if the high-yield bond sector is undervalued, the investor can retain the differentially higher return, while relying on the hedge to reduce portfolio risk to high-quality bond levels.

Diversification Results

Figure 8.6 illustrates the impact of diversification on bond price risk. The figure plots the average monthly returns and standard deviations of return on unhedged positions in 82 medium to low-grade bonds over a five-year period. The unhedged bonds have an average monthly return of 1.16 percent—a 13.07 percent average compound annual return. The standard deviation of return for the bonds averages just over 5 percent—over four times the mean return. Furthermore, the returns vary dramatically from one bond to the next. Indeed, the pattern could easily be mistaken as belonging to equity returns. The returns range from a high of 2.42 percent to a low of 0.43 percent, while the standard deviations are as high as 9.03 percent and as low as 2.75 percent.

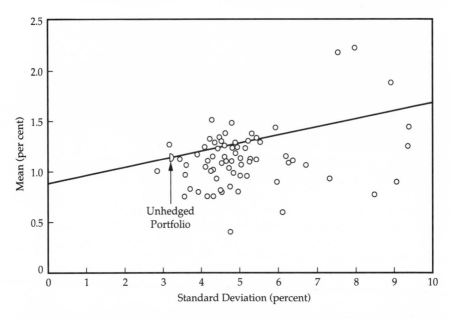

Figure 8.6. Effect of Diversification on Means and Standard Deviations of Monthly Returns (82-bond sample, 10/1978–10/1984)

Point D in the figure represents the diversified portfolio constructed by investing equal dollar amounts in each of the 82 issues. It has an average monthly return of 1.07 percent and a standard deviation of 3.09 percent. The diversified portfolio offers a return close to the average of the individual issues, and it does so with a standard deviation that is roughly three-fifths that of the average issue. Only two of the issues have a lower standard deviation than the diversified portfolio, and 46 have lower average returns.

The line drawn through portfolio D's return, connecting it with the return on the risk-free rate (as measured by the 90-day Treasury bill rate), expresses a linear risk-return tradeoff for the portfolio in mean-standard deviation terms. It can be interpreted as a Capital Market Line. We term it a "quasi-capital market line," because it will conform to the actual Capital Market Line only if the bonds upon which it is based are fairly priced relative to other securities.

Most of the bonds in the sample lie below this line. Diversification obviously offers efficiencies in risk control. If the bond were of higher quality, diversification would have been less effective and the portfolio would have fallen toward the center of the cluster of individual returns.

Hedging Results: Preserving Return

Figure 8.7 illustrates the results of using the composite hedge to hedge the price risk of each of the 82 bonds. The overall leftward shift of the points

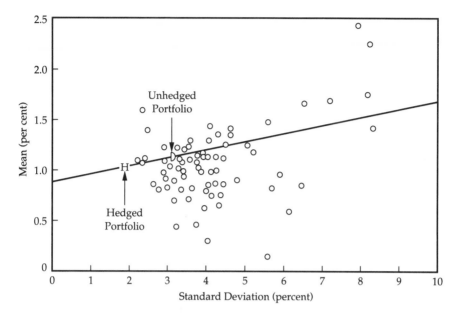

Figure 8.7. Effect of Hedging on Means and Standard Deviations of Monthly Returns (82-bond sample, 10/1978–10/1984)

indicates that the hedge lowers risk. This result is not surprising, since we have already established that the hedge is effective as a risk-reduction instrument.

What is noteworthy is the preservation of returns. The quasi-capital market line in this figure, based on the risk-return tradeoff of the hedged bonds, is virtually identical to that of Figure 8.6, which is based on the unhedged bonds.

This leads to a point of critical importance for the application of these risk-control tools in active management: hedging a portfolio of mispriced bonds will retain this mispricing. If a portfolio has a superior risk-reward tradeoff, and therefore lies above the Capital Market Line, then it will continue to lie above that line after it is hedged. This result is a natural consequence of conservation of value in finance: when a mispriced security is hedged with instruments that are fairly priced, the mispricing is retained.

While hedging reduces risk uniformly, its effect on return depends on the path of the bond price. If the bond price is at its low point when the hedge is initiated, the return will be better without the hedge. Overall, the average return from a hedged portfolio is lower than that of an unhedged portfolio—1.09 percent, compared with 1.16 percent. The standard deviation is also lower, however—4.15 percent, compared with 5.01 percent. As the quasi-capital market line shows, the reduction in return is commensurate with the reduction in standard deviation. The effect on hedging is essentially to lower the leverage of the bond position.

Combining diversification with hedging leads to the lowest-risk portfolio—point H in Figure 8.7. This position is consistently priced from a risk-return standpoint, as indicated by its position on the quasi-capital market line. It is the lowest risk position, with a standard deviation of 1.83 percent—less than two-thirds the risk of the unhedged portfolio, and less than two-fifths that of the average individual unhedged bond position.

Turning Junk Bonds into Gold

The objective of the hedge is to convert a low-credit portfolio into a portfolio with higher credit quality, hence the term "credit conversion." The motivation for the credit conversion is to allow risk-averse investors to take advantage of any mispricing in the high-yield sector without changing their risk profile.

Because the bulk of institutional investors are risk-averse, particularly in their bond positions, an incremental risk premium has come to be associated with higher-yielding bonds. These bonds offer an extraordinary yield differential to entice investors to take on the additional risk. The difficulty for many investors is finding a way to take advantage of this mispriced sector of the bond market, to engage actively in the high-yield market without increasing their risk profile.

The mispricing in the high-yield bond sector may be likened to finding a defective roulette wheel in Las Vegas that favors the player over the house. Playing that wheel over a period of time is likely to generate higher returns than the available alternatives. However, the potential for high payoffs is not without risk. Suppose you gather up your life savings of $100,000 and head off to take advantage of this money machine, only to discover that the roulette wheel is in the high-stakes section of the casino, and the minimum bet is $50,000. Although the odds are attractive, the risk-return tradeoff may still be undesirable. Hedging the risk of the mispriced high-yield bond sector is similar to transforming the one $50,000 bet into a thousand $50 bets. The risk can be pared down to a comfortable level.

The credit conversion allows the investor to do this. Investors may buy the mispriced issues and manage the risk by hedging the credit risk down to the desired level.[12] If the issues *are* mispriced, that mispricing will remain even after the portfolio has been hedged.

Implications

Composite hedging technology opens the door to a broad range of trading strategies. One obvious extension is to default insurance.[13]

A hedge is costly insurance: in protecting against loss, it cuts off potential profits as well. A more attractive strategy might be a put option that gives the bondholder the right to sell the bond at a prespecified exercise price. Such an option amounts to an insurance contract that guarantees against any loss exceeding the exercise price of the option. Because the greatest risk with high-yield bonds is a catastrophic drop in prices induced by default, such protection could be given by a far out-of-the-money option. The further out of the money the option is, the less costly the insurance protection.

An option-type payoff can be generated through an appropriate strategy of hedging between the underlying instrument (in this case, the high-yield bond) and a risk-free asset. Because the high-yield bond is itself an option on the value of the firm, the composite hedge technology is implemented as an intermediate step in forming the desired option payoff. Rather than following a strategy that completely counteracts the underlying bond position, the coverage from the composite hedge is adjusted to meet the dynamic hedging conditions dictated by the option to be created. The result is a compound option strategy—an option is created on an instrument that is itself treated as an option.

The composite hedge can be decomposed into its interest rate and credit risk components, and a hedge can be constructed to address just one of these two risks. An investor interested in protection against only the credit risk component of bond price risk can establish a hedge based on a spread off Treasuries, rather than hedging the bond price itself. If the bond price change is due exclusively to interest rate changes, then the spread will not change appreciably, and the hedge will leave the position largely unaffected. If the spread changes dramatically as the result of a change in credit risk, however, the hedge will protect the position against the resulting change in bond values.

The opportunities the composite hedge offers for altering the return distribution of high-yield bonds will undoubtedly make high-yield bond issues more attractive. Investors who have been uncomfortable with the risk characteristics of this sector of the bond market can now mold the risk-return tradeoffs to meet their investment objectives.

Notes

1. This relation is verified in a portfolio context by R. Ibbotson and R. Sinquefield, *Stocks, Bonds, Bills and Inflation: The Past and the Future* (Charlottesville, Va.: Financial Analysts Research Foundation, 1982). They find a correlation between a common stock index and a long-term corporate bond index of 0.16, compared with a correlation between the stock index and long-term government bond index of only 0.02. Because the long-term corporate bond index did not differentiate between issue quality, it does not represent the ideal sample for verifying our results.

2. There is a large body of theoretical literature on applying option pricing methods to the pricing of corporate claims. Two early papers that treat the debtholder's claim to the firm in detail are R. Merton, "On the Option Pricing of Corporate Debt: The Risk Structure of Interest Rates," *Journal of Finance* 29 (1974), pp. 449–70, and D. Galai and R. Masulis, "The Option Pricing Model and the Risk Factor of Stock," *Journal of Financial Economics* 3 (1976), pp. 54–81. A more complete treatment of the actual development of this method is presented in R. Geske, "The Valuation of Corporate Liabilities as Compound Options," *Journal of Financial and Quantitative Analysis*, 1977, pp. 541–52.

3. This is the method underlying the first major papers on option pricing—F. Black and M. Scholes, "The Pricing of Options and Corporate Liabilities," *Journal of Political Economy* 81 (1973), pp. 637–54, and R. Merton, "Theory of Rational Option Pricing," *Bell Journal of Economics and Management Science* 4 (1974), pp. 449–70. A simplified exposition of this approach and its application to portfolio strategies is presented in R. Bookstaber, *Option Pricing and Strategies in Investing* (Reading, Mass.: Addison-Wesley, 1981) and Bookstaber, "The Use of Options in Performance Structuring: Molding Returns to Meet Investment Objectives," *Journal of Portfolio Management* (Summer 1985): 36–50.

4. The effect of time to maturity—or, more specifically, time to crisis—on the probability of default is treated in R. Johnson, "Term Structures of Corporate Bond Yields as a Function of Risk of Default," *Journal of Finance* 22 (1967), pp. 313–45. His empirical study notes the same points that come out of our option-related model.

5. The volatility of the firm and the debt-asset ratio of the firm have long been known through empirical work to be important determinants of yield spreads. L. Fisher ("Determinants of Risk Premiums on Corporate Bonds," *Journal of Political Economy* 67 (1959), pp. 217–37) showed the risk of default to be a function of "the coefficient of variation of the firm's net income" and "the ratio of the market value of the equity in the firm to the par value of the firm's debt." These two factors are similar to the volatility in firm value and the debt-asset ratio in our model. Virtually all later literature on default risk relies on these two variables as well.

6. A complete list of the bonds is found in R. Bookstaber and D. Jacob, *The Composite Hedge: Controlling the Credit Risk of High Yield Bonds* (Morgan Stanley Fixed Income Research, 1985).

7. The selected sample is actually biased to some degree against demonstrating the full effectiveness of the hedge; in picking a five-year period for the tests, we excluded companies in default because in many cases they did not have bond or equity price data over the five-year period. All deviations from a perfect hedge increase the variance of a hedged position. A large number of minor deviations in tracking, which arise as the inevitable result of basis risk, can have as much of an effect on variance reduction as one failure to track during a significant drop in price. In most hedging applications, the cost of the second failure is far greater than the first. This is particularly true when hedging high-yield bonds, where catastrophe protection is the overriding concern.

A more accurate representation of hedging effectiveness requires giving more weight to the protection against large price movements than to the minor relative price changes induced by basis risk. Most of the variance that remains in the composite hedge is due to the large degree of tracking failure and basis risk from small, uneventful vibrations in the bond and equity prices. Casual empirical study shows that, on a day-by-day basis, the bond and equity of even a lower-quality firm will not correlate closely. Indeed, frequently the bond and equity will move in opposite directions. However, during substantial movements, the two conform much more closely to the model relation.

8. The methods of hedging interest rate risk are presented in A. Toevs and D. Jacob, *Interest Rate Futures: A Comparison of Alternative Hedge Ratio Methodologies* (Morgan Stanley Fixed Income Research, 1984). That study compares the regression-based and duration-based approaches to hedging interest rate risk, and indicates that both approaches give similar results. In practice, the duration-based hedge is preferable because of its computational simplicity.

9. The bond used in the interest rate hedge is the U.S. Treasury bond 8-¾ of 8/15/2000.

10. It is notable that our sample did not include any leveraged buyouts. These usually lead to increases in the equity value and a drop in the bond value, and would therefore be poor candidates for the composite hedge proposed here.

11. Kenai was not the only firm in the oil industry to suffer setbacks in 1984. While the entire industry felt the impact of oil prices in this period, the most highly leveraged firms, such as Kenai, were the most penalized.

12. If the high-yield bond market is relatively mispriced, changing the risk of the portfolio by borrowing funds or by putting a portion of the funds in the risk-free asset will not give the same results as using the composite hedge a the risk control instrument. The mispricing will be enjoyed only to the extent the actual bonds are held. The composite hedge can be thought of as a means of locking in the mispricing while selling off the fairly priced components of the portfolio.

13. An intuitive understanding of default insurance comes by looking at the payoff to a high-yield bond from a slightly different perspective than that used in the text. Consider a high-yield bond as giving a payoff consisting of a risk-free bond and a put option written on the value of the firm. For example, if the bond has a promised payment of $100 million in one year, then the high-yield bond can be expressed as a bond giving the $100 million payoff with no risk of default plus a short position in a put option (i.e., a written put option) paying the maximum of zero or the difference between the value of the firm and a $100 million exercise price in one year.

It turns out this payoff is identical to that used in the text example, because B-Max (O,B -V) = Min (V,B). However, expressing the payoff in terms of a put option helps us to represent the credit risk of the bond more clearly. If the bond defaults, the loss to the bondholder is equal to the loss to the put option writer; it is the difference between the firm value and the bond's promised payment. The bondholder receives a premium for writing this put option. This premium is reflected in the differential expected return above the risk-free rate that the high-yield bondholder enjoys.

The bondholder can eliminate the credit risk of the bond, then, by buying back the put option that he has implicitly written. That is, the bondholder needs to buy a put option that will pay off the difference between the bond's promised payment and the value of the firm if this difference is positive. Naturally, if the market is pricing the bond efficiently, the cost of buying or creating this option should equal the differential return of the bond over the risk-free rate, and eliminating the credit risk should lead to a yield comparable to Treasuries. However, if the high-yield bond is underpriced by the market, the result should be a positive yield differential. The investor need not fully insure the position. Buying out-of-the-money put option protection will allow a measure of protection while retaining some of the high yield.

CHAPTER

9

Trading in the Distressed Market

David J. Breazzano
Fidelity Management &
Research Co.

Peter S. Kaufman
Gordian Group, L.P.

Introduction

No adequate phrase describes the market that this chapter addresses. "Bankrupt" is applicable, but not to the entire relevant market, since workouts can take place not only "in court" under the protection of federal bankruptcy laws, but also "out of court," such as a restructuring or exchange offer before a company is under the jurisdiction of a bankruptcy court. "Troubled" and "broken" begin to speak to the issue more accurately, although not precisely; in point of fact, it is more by default, if you will, than by design that "distressed" has become the generic label of choice.

Of course, there is one logical genesis for the word "distressed" in conjunction with the types of investments we shall discuss here: distressed is the only possible outcome for an investor who enters this particular fray without being fully armed in terms of knowledge, analysis, and trading acumen. Trading in distressed securities is not for the faint of heart. It is arguably one of the most difficult, sophisticated types of investing, with rewards—and risks—commensurate with its difficulty. It demands technical skills, but it is hardly a science. It requires patience, logic, stamina, guts, and years of experience to develop the appropriate judgments necessary to be successful. Financial analysis, legal acumen and horsetrading sense are all prerequisites for simply keeping one's head above water in this field. With this in mind, we will present a framework for trading in the distressed marketplace.

More troubling than the provenance of the name of the market is the question of when to label a security or claim "distressed." Again, there are pointers, but no guidelines that apply absolutely. For instance, if the issuer has declared bankruptcy, then it is safe to include its obligations in this market. But what if the issuer has not declared bankruptcy? One pointer is to determine the yield; if it starts to get 700–800 basis points over Treasuries, then it is beginning to be eligible for the distressed market. Has the price dropped below 75 cents on the dollar? That is often a bright line test, as the next stop below 75 may well be 40 or worse. Is it beginning to trade on dollar prices and therefore on underlying asset value, an equity-like characteristic (as opposed to trading on a yield basis, like a healthy fixed income security)? Has the market's time horizon changed, in other words, from a focus on calls/maturities to a potential restructuring event?

We posit that there is no rigid formula, nothing quantifiable that will apply in every case; rather, identifying the contents of this particular market is not unlike the famous Supreme Court pronouncement about pornography: it is difficult to define but one knows it when one sees it.

Similarly, the size of the market defies precise parameters, but an estimate is useful in establishing a context for our discussion. The market consists of both public securities and private claims, and the latter actually constitutes a larger portion. In 1990 the size of the distressed market totals between $200 and $300 billion in face amount (with, of course, a much lower market value). Historically, the market has grown dramatically, and we see no reason why this growth should not continue.

The types of investment vehicles found in this market are varied (the one generalization that can be made is that most distressed investing focuses on debt instruments). In fact, we submit that any instrument can be deemed part and parcel of the distressed market so long as one has a claim or, in the case of in-court proceedings, one is able to file a proof of claim (or proof of interest if it is an equity) under the Bankruptcy Code, in respect of any such obligation. Included in this market are bonds, notes, debentures, and stock (both common and preferred) issued by corporations, partnerships, or individuals, as well as loans made by banks to such entities and claims of trade suppliers, governmental agencies, and tort plaintiffs against such entities. This list is illustrative in nature and is not meant to be a complete compilation of all of the types of investments available in this market.

With the general background of size and composition of the market in mind, the next order of business is to begin the process that will lead to a particular investment.

Philosophy of Approach to Distressed Investing

At the outset, we note that there are two primary groups of holders of distressed market securities and claims—the willing and the unwilling.

The former purchases at distressed price levels, while the latter owns at appreciably higher, predistressed levels. This portion of the chapter addresses the willing purchasers of distressed claims.

While all the professionals in this field agree that the goals and risks in the distressed market vary greatly from other more traditional forms of fixed income and equity investing, there are different approaches to investments in the distressed market. Perhaps the most critical distinguishing characteristic among the players in this field is the required hurdle rate, or rate of return on investment (in other words, the internal rate of return, including capital appreciation and any additional forms of income that may accrue to the holder during the period of time that one holds the investment). The spectrum ranges from those who need a 20 percent annual return to those who require a 50 percent or higher return. Professional investors determine these minimum goals based on a combination of factors that include the cost of their capital, the risks that they are willing to take and the profile of their own clientele.

Another distinguishing factor among these professionals is their penchant for investing at varying times along the life cycle of a company's visit to the realm of distress. Some participants are traders, some are longer-term investors, some like to participate in out-of-court restructurings and some will only purchase claims of companies in bankruptcy. (Actually, while most of these participants invest in the distressed market by purchasing a position, or "going long," a growing number will "sell short" distressed securities that they believe are overvalued by the market). The common thread binding all of these professionals, however, is that each will proclaim that any investment is attractive to them in this market "at the right price."

Distressed market players can be active participants or passive investors. The latter do an analysis and determine whether they have found an undervalued situation (or an overvalued situation, in the case of a short seller) that will, in their view, improve in price either by the passage of time or as a result of intervention by other participants. At that point they will consider investing.

Active players, on the other hand, determine whether an outside catalyst is required to speed price appreciation or, as likely, to create additional value. Active players seek membership on creditors' committees or acquire substantial positions that will enable them to influence a reorganization. The extreme example of an active player is someone who purchases claims with the goal of ultimately acquiring, or controlling, the entity and its underlying assets.

As an aside, it is important to note that the returns on distressed investments have a low correlation with more traditional forms of investing. Therefore, in addition to seeking high returns on the distressed investments, the fund manager also is able to achieve more effective overall portfolio diversification.

Composition of the Market

Before turning to the actual investment analysis that underpins activity in this market, it is important to understand how the product and the willing investor actually find each other. The mother lode of corporate product in the distressed market is the now-notorious high-yield market. The usual facilitator of product placement with a willing investor is the broker-dealer, and there are specialty trading desks that have emerged in the distressed market. The end user of the product is usually an institution (such as a fund whose mandate includes the pursuit of investments in the distressed market) or, in certain cases, "high net worth" individuals. It is the inter-relationship and dynamics between these three groups—the product (and, of course, the seller of such product), the dealer, and the end user—that will ultimately determine the specifics of any transaction.

With respect to end users, there are several types of institutional characteristics that one finds in this area. First, there are funds dedicated solely to investments in this generic area (sometimes referred to in the vernacular as "vulture funds"). Then there are funds within institutions that use such investments to augment other investment objectives (such as hedge funds or arbitrageurs). Broker-dealers themselves will position such investments in order to support trading activities as well as to invest for their own account. Finally, there are funds that primarily invest in the equity or new-issue high-yield markets but feel the need to participate to some degree as a willing investor in the distressed market, possibly to offset their losses in troubled situations where they might be unwilling participants.

The firms still in existence with strong specialty trading desks in this area include Oppenheimer, First Boston, R. D. Smith, Delaware Bay, Seidler Amdec, Merrill Lynch, Goldman Sachs, Salomon Bros., Kidder Peabody, Shearson Lehman, and Bear Stearns. These firms have developed a network of participants, and, in simplistic but time-honored terms, they essentially bring together willing sellers and buyers. The "value added" that the good specialty desks bring to the transaction takes the form of available product, execution, research capability and a feel for the pricing of what can often be relatively illiquid paper.

The sellers include unwilling high-yield holders as well as banks and trade creditors looking to liquify their claims today, thereby shifting to a buyer the risk of collecting a bigger payday tomorrow. The buyers, of course, are the investors discussed above.

The demise of major markets and certain of its primary participants often has upside potential for other constituencies. In the case of the high-yield market, reports of its death as the 1990s began were greatly exaggerated; the high-yield market was not dying so much as evolving. As the credit quality and price of securities of particular high-yield issuers decline, vulture funds and other willing buyers have replaced the more traditional high-yield purchasers.

An interesting "offline" aspect to the primary relationships in this market is the perspective brought by noninvestment professionals in the bankruptcy/workout world such as attorneys, financial advisors, and turnaround managers. These individuals are well-connected in the field and hence are often sources of excellent investment ideas. Professional investors welcome this not only because they always seek fresh opportunities, but also because any idea that does not involve a broker-dealer often enables the investor to go to the original source of the product and therefore circumvent trades with the broker-dealer and the attendant markup accompanying such trades. Moreover, there will usually be less competition, and hence a lower price, if one is able to discreetly go directly to the source.

Investment Analysis

The key to success in the distressed market, not unlike many other forms of investment, is to determine the appropriate price of a particular claim or security. Thus, when faced with a barrage of potential investment ideas from the various sources available, the investor needs to have a methodology for making such a determination. It is that process—the investment analysis peculiar to distressed investing—that is the subject of this section.

Parenthetically, we might note that many investment opportunities in this area involve leveraged buyouts that have failed or are failing. In fact, the whole reorganization process might be deemed a reverse LBO, insofar as it deleverages those companies that have been overleveraged. What is often attractive to distressed players is that the underlying businesses may be basically healthy, the same trait that attracted the LBO sponsor to the company in the first place. Thus, for example, if one can purchase all of the debt at 20–30 cents on the dollar, one is, effectively, purchasing the assets at less than one-fifth to one-third of what was paid, in most cases very recently, for the same business.

Asset Valuation: The Left Side of the Balance Sheet

Chapter 11 of the U.S. Bankruptcy Code (the "Code") provides for the reorganization of a debtor, but an entity can only be reorganized if it is determined that the creditors would thereby receive more than they would under a liquidation scenario. Chapter 7 of the Code, on the other hand, calls for liquidation. Therefore, a terminal value analysis is a necessary preliminary step in a workout or bankruptcy analysis. For our purposes, we will ignore the "true" liquidation process, such as selling the actual tracks of a railroad for scrap value. If the core underlying business is viable and has the requisite cash flow to survive the workout period, in all likelihood the entity will be successfully reorganized as an ongoing business, perhaps in some altered form, because bankruptcy courts have a strong bias toward encouraging reorganization (as opposed to liquidation).

Although a much greater number of companies file under, or are converted to, chapter 7 liquidations than are reorganized under chapter 11, the vast majority of large companies (with assets in excess of $50 million) are successfully reorganized under chapter 11. The preponderance of chapter 7 cases reflects, among other things, the substantial amount of administrative costs (such as legal expenses) associated with chapter 11; smaller companies (which represent most bankruptcy filings) typically do not have the cash flow or asset values to fund such costs. Larger companies, once debt service requirements are stayed by the proceeding, typically are able to pay such expenses. For purposes of this discussion, we will focus only on larger companies because the majority of distressed investors ignore small workouts and bankruptcies.

An ongoing business enterprise typically commands higher value than the piecemeal liquidation of its assets. Therefore, if possible, it makes economic sense to attempt a reorganization, either out-of-court or through chapter 11. If a reorganization is not feasible, assets and whole companies always can be liquidated under chapter 11, giving the debtor more maneuverability than under chapter 7.

In any event, the threshold analysis is to fix the terminal value of the entity. To do so, one must consider the assets on a deconsolidated, or individual asset, basis. In other words, the investor concentrates on the left-hand side of the balance sheet.

For our purposes, terminal value is defined either as (a) what one could reasonably expect to derive from an orderly sale of each particular business segment or asset or (b) the enterprise value that would result from the appropriate financial restructuring of a "going concern." The terminal value includes the estimated value of the business at the end of the reorganization period, as well as any cash that might build in the estate during the proceeding. Business values generally are calculated based on multiples of earnings, cash flow, or other operating measures, compared to those of similar companies in the public or merger markets.

Cash often accumulates during a bankruptcy as the debtor stops making interest and principal payments (other than on certain types of adequately collateralized debt) and rejects uneconomic contracts. Cash also can be generated from asset sales during the proceedings. Such additional cash is net of the administrative and other expenses that are inherent to the process (legal fees, financial advisory fees, etc.); such expenses can be substantial, exceeding $1 to $2 million per month in large cases. The investor then discounts the terminal value at an appropriate rate to derive the net present value of the assets.

For example, assume XYZ Division of the Acme Company, at the end of an estimated two-year workout period, will have a value of $83 million for its ongoing business operations. Moreover, XYZ Division will also have generated $10 million in free cash flow during each of those two years, or an additional $20 million, less estimated reorganization expenses of $5 million, for a total cash buildup of $15 million. This results in a terminal value of $98 million. If the appropriate discount rate is 30 percent, the net present value of the assets of XYZ Division is approximately $58 million. Therefore, $58 million is the maximum price the investor should be willing to pay either for these assets or for the aggregate claims against these assets.

Part of the investor's analysis is to gain an understanding of how and why the company became troubled. Economic conditions, commodity cycles, mismanagement, overleverage, operational deficiencies and tort liabilities are only a few causal factors. It is incumbent upon the investor to be fully aware of exactly what went wrong and whether the problems are soluble. Too often analysts confuse operating distress with financial overextension. Operating problems with the underlying business often are much more difficult (and sometimes impossible) to solve than correcting an inappropriate capital structure.

Approaches for assessing value vary, but among them are to determine:

a. Where the particular asset would trade if it were capitalized by 100 percent equity and no debt (again, to ignore the right side of the balance sheet for now);
b. What a strategic buyer might pay for these assets;
c. What debt levels such an asset could reasonably support;
d. What the market value of the assets would be with an optimal debt/equity capital structure;
e. What the value might be of any "extraneous" assets, such as real estate holdings, that are not integral parts of the company's primary business operations.

For example, under (a), one might affix a multiple to operating earnings or cash flow, or use a discounted cash flow model, depending upon what is appropriate to the particular industry or comparable public companies. Under (b), the relevant analysis includes consideration of the synergies (i.e., franchises, trademarks, customer base, economies of scale, etc.) that could be achieved with existing assets of the potential purchaser and the value of those synergies to such purchaser (perhaps measured by comparable recent mergers and acquisitions).

One approach for (c) and (d) is to determine a realistic "free cash flow" going forward (EBITD less maintenance capital expenditures and working capital requirements) and discount it by the estimated total cost of capital to the company or segment. For example, if the XYZ Division generates annual free cash flow of $10 million, and its estimated weighted average cost of capital is 12 percent, then it could have a value roughly of 10/.12, or about $83 million. Therefore, XYZ Division could service up to $83 million of 12 percent debt, although it would have no cash flow available for debt amortization. A lesser amount of debt, perhaps at a lower interest rate, with the balance in equity, may be more financeable and would help optimize the market value of XYZ Division. Finally, (d) would involve a thorough review and valuation of all noncore assets of the distressed entity.

The investor, when doing the analysis, also takes into account that, under chapter 11, a debtor can reject uneconomic leases and executory contracts. This advantage both enhances the viability of the debtor going forward and creates claims for damages (cancelled leases or contracts do not simply go away, but instead give rise to general unsecured claims, which the vulture might wish to purchase at some steep discount). Moreover, the bankruptcy court has the ability to create value for the estate by overriding certain contractual provisions, such as onerous restrictions on assignability of leases.

The next step is to estimate the time necessary to realize those values identified in the foregoing analysis. This brings into play nonquantifiable judgments that require experience and familiarity with the process in order to estimate a reasonable length of time of the workout, reorganization, or proceedings.

Issues that will come into play when making these judgments include:

a. Problems with the underlying business and the length of the business cycle (since creditors often place a premium on cash and debt securities, as opposed to being converted to equity holders, it is preferable to many creditors to reorganize in an "up" cycle when the company is better able to handle higher leverage and has more cash and cash flows);
b. Litigation such as product liability, pension, and environmental;
c. Whether fraudulent transfer claims exist;
d. Whether blocking positions have been established in any tranches of the securities;
e. Public policy issues, etc.

Rules of thumb are difficult, but it is a certainty that no one ever became wealthy in this business by underestimating the amount of time the workout process will take.

It is also very important for investors to ascertain who the other large holders in a particular situation are and what their individual agendas may be. For example, certain institutions, such as some insurance companies, S&Ls (or the RTC), and occasional mutual funds, are reluctant to accept a reduction in the principal amount of their debt as part of a restructuring. This can result in the reorganized company remaining overleveraged, thereby impairing the reorganization value if the market believes the company retains a significant amount of default risk going forward. The presence of such institutions in any given restructuring dramatically reduces the likelihood that a successful deal will be achieved within a reasonable amount of time unless creative new securities can be designed that (a) satisfy such institutions' need for cosmetic par recoveries and (b) do not overly burden the company's ability to service its new debt load.

Finally, there is also a small group of distressed investors who pursue "scorched earth" tactics such as filing involuntary chapter 7 petitions and seeking the appointment of operating trustees, in an effort to gain leverage for themselves, perhaps to the detriment of other creditors. These various types of holders can cause significant delays in the restructuring process and, as a result, can impair the realization or creation of value.

Liabilities: The Right Side of the Balance Sheet

Having established the asset values, the investor then allocates to the liabilityholders the estimated value to which each is entitled both under the law and in the likely actual outcome. Capital structures can be complex and consist of many different tranches of debt. Preferred stock is often present, followed by the common equityholders at the bottom of the pecking order.

The "absolute priority rule" of the Bankruptcy Code (no class receives any value unless each class senior to it has received its claim in full) is seldom applied, but it remains a good benchmark to begin this particular analysis. A cramdown occurs when the absolute priority rule is strictly applied, effectively giving no recovery to any class junior to an impaired class. Under the Code, a junior class that is being threatened with a cramdown has an extensive arsenal of legal weapons available to delay reorganization (such as seeking court-appointed examiners to review relevant transactions) and to lessen recovery to senior classes (legal expenses of committees representing junior creditors are paid by the estate and therefore effectively come out of the pocket of senior creditors).

With time value of money so important to creditors, "buying off" junior creditors in order to achieve a consensual plan (one that is approved by the requisite majority of all creditor classes) often raises the net present value of recovery to senior classes. Therefore, a successful cramdown is rarely executed. This means that having done the requisite financial analysis, the investor then needs to make subjective judgments to determine what value must be given up to junior classes, including old equity, in order to achieve a consensual reorganization plan.

One also has to be mindful of actual and potential off–balance sheet liabilities that, under law, may rank *pari passu* or be entitled to priority over other creditor classes. For example, claims of the PBGC, EPA, and IRS may not appear in an entity's schedule of liabilities when an investor begins analysis. Perhaps more significantly, certain guarantees by the company may not appear on the balance sheet, but they have the potential to be veritable black holes for companies such as Southmark. Such off–balance sheet claims may have a substantial impact upon the recovery of other classes of creditors at the conclusion of the reorganization as well as delay the proceedings while these claims are resolved.

Another peculiar, albeit infrequent, land mine is the potential of having a claim reinstated by a debtor. Reinstatement occurs when the company, as a part of the plan of reorganization or out-of-court restructuring, cures all past defaults and agrees to honor the debt contract going forward. In a reorganization, if a debt class is unimpaired, as is the case upon reinstatement, no vote by that class is required, and owners of such securities are effectively disenfranchised from the reorganization process. Typically, reinstatement is viewed positively by creditors since they receive all to which they were otherwise entitled. However, in some instances, especially where the reorganized entity still retains significant credit risk, reinstatement may not be viewed positively. Reinstatement occurs most typically with respect to low-coupon, long-maturity debt securities. For example, such a security may trade in the marketplace at a steep discount post-reorganization, so that the investor in effect does not receive value in the full amount of the claim, even though that claim absent reinstatement might be entitled to 100 percent recovery.

Reinstatement risk, therefore, places a ceiling on recoveries; it contributed to the difference in trading prices of the Eastern Airlines convertible debentures during the summer of 1989 prior to the collapse of Eastern's proposed "100 cents" plan. Among other instruments, Eastern had outstanding a 5 percent debenture due in 1992 and a 4¾ percent debenture due in 1993. Because of the lower coupon and longer maturity, the 4¾ percent traded at almost a 10-point discount to the 5 percent, and both traded substantially below par, even though both were in the same class and were to receive 100 percent recoveries. As a result of this risk, some investors seek to buy into what they believe to be the senior-most class that will be impaired in order to have substantial leverage in the reorganization.

It is also important here to be mindful of the corporate structure—is the claim made against a holding company or against an operating subsidiary? This is but one of the many issues that arise in perusing through the bond indentures, bank loan agreements and other corporate documents when the investor is trying to categorize and define the tranches of claims. Another critical aspect of the analysis is a thorough understanding of the subordination clauses in each relevant instrument.

For example, in the Revco bankruptcy case, the capital structure includes senior secured bank debt and public bonds, senior unsecured notes, senior subordinated, subordinated and junior subordinated debentures as well as general unsecured trade claims. Partly as a result of the complexity of the capital structure (in addition to business problems at the operating level), the reorganization process is likely to last several years, longer than most analysts had originally predicted. In addition, the fraudulent conveyance issue in the Revco case has yet to come to the fore as of this writing, and resolution of that issue could further stretch out the process.

This is an appropriate juncture at which to examine some of the legal issues that are found in many bankruptcies and workouts and that influence the investor's judgments about value, price and timing.

Legal Issues

The legal issues relating directly to the claims against entities play a prominent role in reorganizations. Among them are fraudulent conveyance, equitable subordination, lender liability and original issue discount.

Fraudulent conveyance occurs if a debtor made a transfer or incurred a debt (a) with actual intent to defraud creditors or, more likely, (b) for less than "reasonably equivalent value", *and*

1. The debtor was or became insolvent as result thereof, or
2. The debtor retained unreasonably small capital as a result thereof, or
3. The debtor incurred debts beyond its ability to repay them.

The consequences of such a finding can include elimination of security interest and subordination of the claim of a creditor who participated in the underlying fraudulent transfer.

With respect to equitable subordination and lender liability, if a lender (typically, but not necessarily, a bank) is found to have overreached or engaged in activities that harmed the debtor or other creditors, its claims could be subordinated to those of other creditors. Significantly, as with fraudulent transfer liabilities, anyone who purchases a claim may end up purchasing the liabilities appurtenant thereto unless explicitly excluded in the contract of sale.

One also has to be cognizant of the original issue discount (OID) that may exist on any particular security. Simply put, OID comes into existence when a company issues a debt security with a face amount greater than the amount of proceeds that it receives from issuance of such security. For example, if Acme Corp. issues an 8 percent $1,000 principal amount bond, but only receives $800 on issuance (resulting in an implicitly higher yield than 8 percent), then there is $200 of OID that will accrete over the life of the bond. Under the Code, should Acme ever file under chapter 11, a holder of the security would only have a claim equal to the accreted value of the bond (plus any accrued but unpaid interest at the coupon rate of 8 percent) at the time of filing, since the Code does not permit claims for "unmatured interest," which is what the Code deems OID to be.

OID is a topic that the LTV bankruptcy case brought to the fore, and unless overruled on appeal it will have a deleterious effect on many out-of-court restructurings. The LTV decision stands for the proposition that if a security holder has a debenture with a face amount of $100 with no OID and a market value today of $30, and if the security holder exchanges that debenture for a new security with the same face amount of $100, then in the event of a bankruptcy filing postexchange, the holder's claim in a chapter 11 proceeding will be $30, which was the market value at the time of the exchange offer, plus any accretion up to the date of the chapter 11 filing. Holdouts on the exchange, however, would have a 100 cent claim in a bankruptcy proceeding, since no OID would be deemed to exist on the original instrument. The court, in other words, imputes OID to the new instrument based on market value at the time of the exchange. Such ruling effectively ensures that few exchange offers involving new debt securities will be completed unless security holders are quite certain that no bankruptcy filing post-exchange is on the horizon.

With these legal issues so important in the process, investors need to be cognizant of the history behind each claim and security, as well as that of the underlying entity, in order to be fully apprised of the risks entailed so that the price one pays for those obligations will appropriately reflect such risks. And, because workouts often are a zero sum game, what could be lost by one class of creditors might be a windfall to another group.

Summary of Investment Analysis

In short, one values the assets (the left-hand side of the balance sheet) and determines how those values will be distributed among the claimants (the right-hand side of the balance sheet). Expectations as to the recovery, tempered by nonquantifiable factors such as legal issues, motivations of other players in the particular situation and how much time the reorganization process will take, must determine what one is willing to pay (or sell short, as the case may be) for the various claims and securities.

Trading in the Distressed Market

After the analytical work is completed and judgments are made, the investor turns to the next step in the investment process: purchasing the security in the public market or the claim in the private market.

The Public Market

In broad terms, securities begin to trade down as the investing public becomes aware of weaknesses in the underlying creditworthiness of the issuer. And, while the investor may have a definite price in mind, he must also be aware of the trading patterns as a whole that are exhibited in this market. Often, when a financial problem surfaces, the existing holders want to deny the existence of any such difficulties, which presents an opportunity for the short seller.

However, as the underlying problems become more acute and more widely acknowledged, selling pressure begins to build. Contrary to conventional wisdom, we believe that lower prices bring sellers, not buyers; conversely, rising prices bring buyers. Put another way, the best way for a broker-dealer trading desk to arouse "buy" interest in a security is to have none for sale, and the best way to cause a lowering of price is to offer a bond widely.

Mechanically, the trading process works as follows. The trading desk, each morning, receives a list of securities and prices (the "daily run") from specialist firms known as "street brokers," such as Mabon Nugent.

The street brokers communicate only with broker-dealer trading desks; should a trading desk ever discover that the street broker is in direct contact with institutional investors, then the trading desk might "pull the wire" from the street broker (which means to cease doing business with that particular street broker). The role of the street broker is to aggregate the markets provided by the various trading desks and to transact trades between the desks. The trading desk takes the daily run, determines what markets it wishes to make and then begins phoning its institutional accounts.

For example, in the morning run Mabon Nugent might tell First Boston that on Acme 11.5% they have "22-5 for a million." This means that in the street market, Acme 11.5% bonds can be purchased for $.25 or sold at $.22, in an amount up to a million dollars face amount. First Boston, armed with this knowledge, might then contact Fidelity Investments and "make a market" of $21\frac{3}{4} = 25\frac{1}{4}$. This means that First Boston is willing either to sell Fidelity Acme bonds at $.25\frac{1}{4}$ or buy Acme bonds from Fidelity at $.21\frac{3}{4}$. First Boston knows that it can then turn around on either side of that trade and either buy or sell in the street market and earn $\frac{1}{4}$ point spread. Trading desks, of course, can also hold bonds themselves or buy from one account and sell into another account (avoiding the street broker and the associated mark-up); this example is simply illustrative of how the process can work.

Certain signals that alert the marketplace to problems about a particular bond include yields approaching a spread of 700–800 basis points or higher over Treasuries, covenant violations/bank renegotiations, sudden asset sales, dividend suspensions, margin deteriorations, upcoming reset dates, or PIKs and zero coupon bonds scheduled to convert to cash-pay in the near future.

Leaseway Transportation provides a good illustration of how trading patterns in distressed securities can develop. In 1989, concerns about the financial viability of this trucking company began to surface among the distressed cogniscenti, but there was little trading activity in the bonds. For a period of perhaps four months, a small number of Leaseway bonds were offered at 60 (the last reported trade had been at 70) with no bids. Suddenly, and for no apparent reason, a transaction took place at 20. This trade both opened the floodgates to other Leaseway trades at distressed levels and signaled the onset of major and immediate restructuring problems for the issuer.

The Leaseway example also points up some of the dynamics in this market that pertain to sellers who may be unwilling holders. For instance, if the holder is a mutual fund that must "mark to market" on a daily basis (as opposed to many insurance companies who are able to book bonds at original cost irrespective of current market value), the portfolio manager may be inclined to sell at depressed levels regardless of the fundamental value of the security because of concern that the price will continue to fall, hurting that fund's performance. In the case of Leaseway, so long as there was no trading activity while the bonds were offered at 60, there was plenty of room for "creative" marking to market, a common occurrence with illiquid and not easily valued securities. But when there was an actual trade at 20, the market value was redefined, and marking at 60 or 70 (again, the last reported trade before the trade at 20) was no longer possible.

Another lesson to be learned here is that the distressed market can be very thin, or "illiquid." As a consequence, as few as one or two participants can drive the market in either direction—up in the case of voracious buyers, and down if there are determined sellers.

Human emotional factors also become very important. As a security drops precipitously in price, holders begin to doubt their own analysis of the issuer, suspecting that the market "knows something" that they may have overlooked. Sometimes, in order to avoid the embarrassment of holding a security that subsequently defaults, holders will sell either when they fear a default is imminent or shortly after an actual default, further driving down the price. This is consistent with our belief that "the market always moves in the direction of maximum pain."

Technical issues and internal policies also influence sellers. For instance, normally a purchaser of a bond that has not defaulted must pay the seller not only for the bond itself but also for whatever interest has accrued up to settlement date. However, when a security defaults and then trades "flat," that is, trades without any accrued interest, certain high-yield mutual funds are inclined to sell such securities and redeploy the proceeds into "earning" assets so that they can maintain the fund's dividend. In addition, insurance companies that are able to mark assets at cost, as opposed to market value, often are forced to carry a large reserve for defaulted securities or to mark those securities to depressed market prices once a default occurs.

Another dynamic is the calendar year-end selling pressure that comes from certain holders' desire to take tax losses and/or eradicate portfolios of losers before having to report to fund shareholders.

All of these factors can combine to create "overselling"—securities trading significantly below their intrinsic worth, based on investment analysis, because of the foregoing, often noneconomic, reasons. Because it is impossible to know when a security has bottomed in price, owing to those nonquantifiable factors that influence trading patterns of distressed securities, an approach is to purchase incremental positions over time at appropriate levels that, taken as a whole, will allow the investor to achieve the desired hurdle rate—in other words, "average into" an overall position in the target securities, as opposed to attempting to "time" the absolute bottom of the market.

The charts in Figure 9.1 illustrate the trading pattern of two debentures after the issuers filed chapter 11 petitions. Investors that purchased A M International and Charter Co. debt securities several months following the

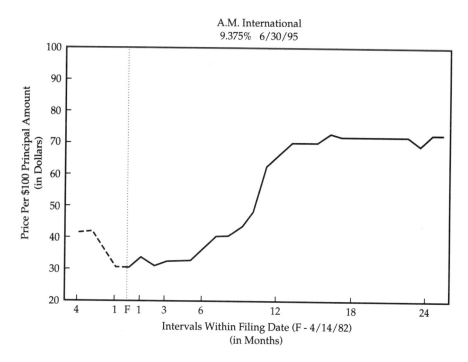

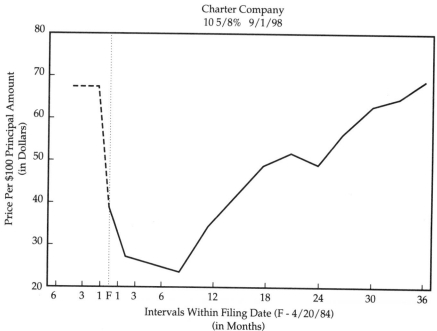

Figure 9.1. A M International 9.375% 6/30/95
Charter Company 10⅞% 09/01/98
SOURCE: T. Rowe Price Associates, Inc.

filings and sold them one or two years later when the companies emerged from chapter 11 realized substantial returns.

Of course, even if a bond trades down dramatically, it may not be oversold; rather, it may simply be reaching its appropriate pricing level. Vultures, for all of their acumen, are hardly infallible (in truth, quite the opposite over the past several years), and they may buy before the security is appropriately priced for them. LTV provides a good example, with the trading pattern of one of its debentures illustrated in Figure 9.2. After more than three years in bankruptcy, LTV's 13⅞ percent debentures were trading near their all-time lows as of this writing.

Recently, securities have traded up on news of a chapter 11 filing, in large part because participants have historically observed substantial returns obtained by buying at such times. Unfortunately, when the market becomes aware of such a phenomenon, the phenomenon changes, and today there is no substitute for disciplined analytical homework and disciplined trading. As the trading pattern of Eastern Airlines debentures in Figure 9.3 illustrates, the Eastern debentures traded up shortly after the chapter 11 filing. But when the company announced that its 100 cent plan was not feasible, the debentures plummeted. The investor has to be patient; if the security cannot be purchased at a level that analysis dictates, he must be ready to walk away from the situation. Many have fallen in love with an investment idea (having put much time and effort into conducting their due diligence) only to end up overpaying when their emotions led them to purchase at too high a price.

The Private Market

While established procedures exist for transferring publicly traded securities, the methods for transferring private claims are much less well defined. This is an evolving area, both in legal and financial terms, and as such is replete with pitfalls that investors cannot afford to overlook.

One very attractive aspect of private claims, such as bank debt and trade claims, is that they can often be acquired at substantial discounts to comparable public bonds. This discount reflects, in part, the difficulties in transferring claims and the illiquidity inherent in these claims. Because of the relative dearth of investors interested in (or, by charter, capable of) purchasing private claims, prices tend to be lower than in the more competitive public market. On the other hand, once such an investment is made, the purchaser may find it difficult (if not impossible) to sell the claims should his view of the situation, or his need for liquidity, change. Therefore, investors in private claims must be confident in their analysis and able to carry positions for a long period of time. The investor may have to wait until the conclusion of the chapter 11 proceeding, at which time he may receive cash and/or new securities. Fortunately, securities issued pursuant to a plan of reorganization may be publicly traded because the Code provides an exemption from registration with the SEC. (The

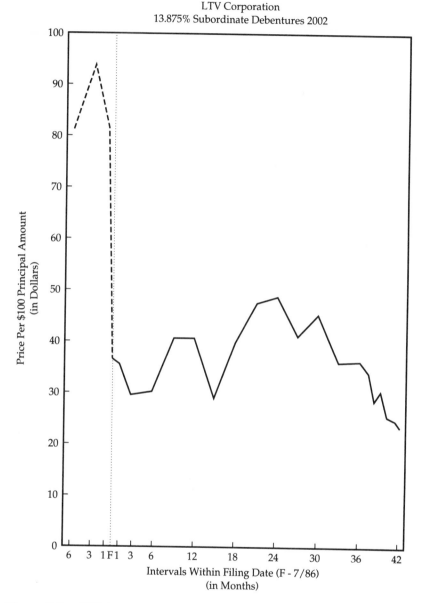

Figure 9.2. LTV Corporation 13.875% Subordinate Debentures 2002
SOURCE: T. Rowe Price Associates, Inc.

bankruptcy disclosure statement often provides more information than does a prospectus relating to a public offering.)

Unlike the public bond market, the types of transactions vary greatly insofar as an investor may buy a single claim, or investor groups may organize (as syndicates, consortiums, or partnerships) to purchase a large

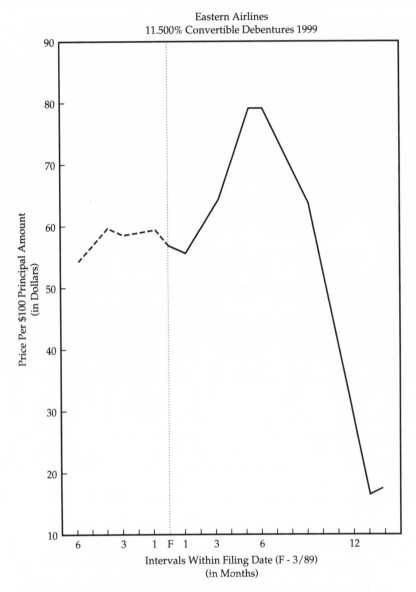

Figure 9.3.   Eastern Airlines 11.500% Convertible Debentures 1999
SOURCE: T. Rowe Price Associates, Inc.

claim or a block of multiple claims. The wholesale purchase of all or substantially all bank or trade claims against a particular debtor is not unheard of, and the transactions can be structured to obtain a premium in the form of passive or active control of the particular business or enterprise.

Extensive documentation is required when purchasing private claims, insofar as investors seek a claim whose face amount is fixed and not vulnerable to contingencies, defenses, or defects asserted by the target company or others, unless the purchase price is discounted enough to justify the risks of such contingencies. Accordingly, investors attempt to structure a transaction such that the only risks are the amount of recovery ultimately received for the claim and the timing of such recovery; both of these issues are determined by the workout process and plan of reorganization.

The sellers of private claims include creditors who (a) are in need of either liquidity or a tax loss or, in some cases, (b) who are compelled (by regulators, for example) to sell or write down their claims. It is important to note that trade creditors may be more willing to sell their claims at a substantial discount because of the nature of the claims' origination. Typically, a trade claim results from the sale of goods or services to the debtor, presumably at a substantial markup that provides a profit for the vendor on the transaction. Therefore, although a trade creditor may have a 100 cent claim, the cost to him of the goods or services may have been substantially less (that is, 66 cents, assuming a 50 percent markup). Accordingly, if the creditor were to receive more than 66 cents, he would not have suffered a loss. Thus, while bondholders and trade creditors are often at a *pari passu* priority level, the bondholder who purchased at 100 cents and the trader creditor who provided goods at 66 cents will have rather different points of view about a recovery of, say, 80 cents.

Trade creditors who have relatively small positions (that is, less than $100,000) often find it uneconomical to retain counsel to pursue their rights in a bankruptcy proceeding. Such a creditor might therefore be inclined to sell the claim at a substantial discount and get back to the business of being a supplier, not a bankruptcy creditor. For the vulture fund, it can make economic sense to aggregate a substantial amount of these claims at attractive prices and take appropriate action to enforce the rights of such claims.

Banks and other institutions with large troubled loan portfolios are sometimes motivated to sell in order to reduce nonperforming loans in their portfolios, to take tax losses or to reduce the burden on their probably overworked workout departments. It is important to remember that a bank's primary business is to lend money and receive timely principal and interest payments, not to be a quasi-equityholder facing a two- to five-year workout period.

Sourcing the product are the specialized trading desks mentioned before and certain end purchasers who seek to avoid the dealer middleman. These participants go to the claims docket, on file with the bankruptcy court, which is often a computer-generated printout of the creditors that the debtor has scheduled as well as entities that have filed proofs of claim. Such claims are often listed as disputed or undisputed, and the investor must decide if it is worth the risk to purchase a claim falling in the former category.

The mechanics of a private claims transaction are far more complex and unwieldy than the relatively simple commercial securities trades. In private transactions, the terms of sale are usually negotiated directly between buyer and seller, and, for bank debt deals, there is usually a lengthy purchase and sale agreement (a formal contract) negotiated between the parties. The seller might give the buyer certain representations and warranties, as well as indemnities against prior actions by the seller. Alternatively, the deal may be "as is," with no seller representations; the price will reflect how much comfort and protection the buyer will ultimately receive. The buyer generally is willing to accept the risk that the claims may be uncollectible, but not that they will be disallowed, subordinated, or impaired in some fashion.

Dealers tend to make these transactions on an agency basis (as opposed to acting as principal, the norm in the public market). Certain dealers that specialize in this market will buy for their own account, but they often elect to spread the risk by passing a portion of purchased claims to customers and other dealers. Alternatively, it is possible to sell participations in large claims, allowing the dealer to maintain control and spread the risk without a large commitment of capital.

Again, unlike public securities, the Bankruptcy Court must sign an order pursuant to Bankruptcy Rule 3001 to transfer private claims (after proofs of claim have been filed). Price and terms of such transactions are often disclosed as a matter of public policy.

Risks abound in the private claims market. For example, a passive purchaser of a private claim should not be held affirmatively liable for the intentional acts of the seller of the claim. However, lender liability issues can impact the enforceability of that lender's claim and/or the timing of a recovery on said claim even after the claim has been transferred. Moreover, transfer of claims under certain circumstances may be construed as effecting an ownership change that might have a deleterious effect on NOLs.

There are many other risks associated with buying private claims that are of much less concern to investors in public securities. One of these is the "preference" issue—did the original claimholder benefit from a preference, such as the receipt of a payment during the 90-day period prior to the chapter 11 filing? Under the Code, reorganization plan distributions from the debtor with respect to such a claim may be held up until a preference review has been completed and resolved. Other risks associated with private claims include the following:

- Is the claim genuine? (There is no title or ownership document, such as a bond certificate, for trade claims.)
- Is the amount of the claim correct? (Debtors often dispute the dollar amount of claims.)
- Was the claim previously sold, fraudulently, to another investor? (There is no registrar or transfer agent associated with trade claims.)

- Was the seller of the claim adequately informed about the bankruptcy proceedings? (Some bankruptcy judges have offered recission rights to uninformed sellers.)
- Was an accurate proof of claim filed prior to the bar date (the date set by the court after which new claims asserted against the debtor are forever barred)?
- Was proper notice given and an order entered transferring the claim pursuant to Bankruptcy Rule 3001?
- Was the seller of the claim an insider or a fiduciary? (In some instances, recovery on such a tainted claim could be limited to the purchase price).
- Has the seller indemnified the buyer in the event that the claim is subject to issues of lender liability, preference, fraudulent conveyance, subordination, reduction, and so forth? And even if the buyer is so indemnified, does the seller have the financial wherewithal to honor such indemnification?

These risks should be addressed in the purchase and sale documents.

Purchasing private claims is often a lengthy and tedious process, involving frustrating negotiations that as often as not fall through. If appropriate representations and warranties and indemnities are not forthcoming, one must be prepared to walk away from the transaction. But, if one has the patience and stamina to persevere in the private market, the ultimate returns can be quite rewarding.

Investment Strategies for the Active Player in the Distressed Market

There are multiple strategies employed by active investors in the distressed market, limited only by one's capital, risk profile, hurdle rate, intestinal fortitude and imagination. These strategies can best be understood in the context of in-court and out-of-court situations.

In the out-of-court scenario, the clock starts ticking when the company becomes unwilling or unable to meet its debt obligations on a timely basis. The real action, however, begins as soon as the company either defaults or proposes an out-of-court restructuring plan. Typically, these plans embody the carrot and the stick—debtholders are offered a new package of securities designed to have a market value higher than the current market value of the existing debt (a carrot), but the holders are also warned that should they not accept such a package, either a deal will go through without their approval and their allegedly protective covenants will be eliminated or the company could file for bankruptcy protection (a stick).

Carrots can also consist of the elevation of certain bondholders to a senior and/or secured position, thereby leaping over recalcitrant holdouts.

In return, however, the leapfrogging bondholders are asked to accept reduction in principal and/or interest with the view towards deleveraging the company. Cash is the ultimate carrot; the adage that "cash is King" still holds true in the 1990s. A partial cash payment or a cash tender offer (even at a discount) can be a sufficient inducement for a successful out-of-court restructuring to occur. Some companies may even undertake activities that contribute to the further decline in the market price of their securities, such as announcing a very pessimistic outlook for the company's prospects, thereby making the carrot look even more attractive.

Sticks commonly employ a mechanism whereby tendering bondholders must consent to an emasculation of the existing indenture. This is termed an exit consent, and it effectively eliminates all covenants except that which is mandated by the Trust Indenture Act—namely, the requirement to pay interest and principal.

The concept here, from the issuer's perspective, is to create an expectation that should the company fail several years or even months later, nontendering holdouts will find themselves completely disadvantaged vis-à-vis the bondholders who accepted the deal. Nevertheless, small holders (or large holders who "hold back" a small portion of their holdings) may be willing to take this risk by not tendering their bonds in return for continuing cash interest payments and the reasonable prospect of a successful and viable recapitalized company. Dart Drug Stores (a miscalculation) and SCI-TV (too early to know) are two restructurings in which a small number of holders elected to hold back.

From the perspective of the distressed investor who has been scrutinizing this scenario from afar, exchange offers present a window of opportunity. Uncertainty breeds volatile markets, and as we have already discussed, prices can fall precipitously. Thus, the putative bargain hunter might be able to buy into the game (or average into a previously existing position) at this time, with the expectation of playing a lead role in the ensuing negotiations with the company and perhaps improving the deal, thereby creating value for himself. In creating such value, the bargain hunter believes he also benefits his fellow bondholders, including our old friend, the shrewd passive investor, who has been counting on such a white knight to ride along and take charge of the situation.

In theory, any recapitalization that can be accomplished through a chapter 11 proceeding can occur out of court more quickly and less expensively, as long as all constituencies cooperate. In practice, however, that theory is more honored in the breach. Often the market value of a troubled enterprise is lower than that of an enterprise with similar operations but with a better capital structure. This reflects, in large measure, the discount that is ascribed to debt (and equity) securities of a troubled situation, and it is our belief that much of the value that a restructuring "creates" is simply a freeing up of the existing value that has been suffocating under the morass of an untenable capital structure.

To illustrate, let us return to the XYZ Division, which has become the latest victim of an ill-advised LBO, but still has $10 million in annual free cash flow after maintenance capital expenditures. Assume that part of the price of its freedom from Acme was issuing $100 million principal amount of discount debentures with the coupon now stepping-up to 15 percent, and that it is now unable to meet its current $15 million annual interest expense. Such debentures may be trading around 45 cents on the dollar because of the pending default and anticipated restructuring and because of the market's expectation of the adverse impact upon XYZ's business prospects that would result from a contentious bankruptcy filing; in any case, the total market capitalization of the debt is about $45 million. XYZ's equity is trading at minimum value because of the impending insolvency.

Should XYZ be successful in (a) compromising the principal amount to, say, $60 million from $100 million, and (b) reducing the coupon to 12 percent, there would now be 1.4× (up from 0.66×) coverage of interest expense by free cash flow. To convince bondholders to forgive $40 million of principal and reduce the interest rate, XYZ would offer bondholders a 75 percent equity position in the company. Assuming a market environment that existed as of this writing, the new 12 percent debentures might trade around 85 cents on the dollar. Because the interest expense was reduced to $7.2 million annually, XYZ would generate $2.8 million of free pretax cash flow available to the equityholders. If depreciation were assumed to equal capital expenditures, then pretax income will approximate $2.8 million, or $1.7 million of aftertax net income (assuming a 40 percent corporate tax rate and no available NOL).

At an 8× market multiple (price/earnings multiple), implying a $13.6 million total market value to the equity, the bondholders' new equity stake would be worth over $10 million, for a total package worth approximately $60 million (a $10 million equity stake and $50 million of new bond market value), or a 33 percent premium to the market value of the old bonds. The old equityholders would retain 25 percent of equity going forward, which today would be worth over $3 million, a significant premium to the minimal pre-restructuring equity value. Such a hypothetical restructuring points out how value could actually be "created," or, more accurately, freed up through the out-of-court restructuring process.

A militant distressed investor may take a large position in the bonds, or join forces with similar-minded investors, in order to control enough securities to prevent the company from reaching its minimum tender figure, thus effectively blocking any out-of-court restructuring. Under such circumstances, the company may have to sweeten the deal to the satisfaction of the holdouts or else file for bankruptcy protection. It is, in fact, not much more than a sophisticated, high stakes game of chicken. However, such activity may extract more than 75 percent of the equity of XYZ to the bondholders in the preceding example.

Certain investors buy into the senior-most impaired class or a class that is being asked to make concessions at prices they believe to be below liquidation net present terminal value in order to have downside protection. Others will invest in the most junior tranches, trading at very steep discounts because the class probably would be wiped out under a bankruptcy cramdown. Buying into the latter is the ultimate game of chicken, as the investor banks on the senior classes allowing a meaningful recovery to this class to avoid a bankruptcy filing.

Often holdouts use blocking positions not only to affect the exchange package itself, but also to influence policies of the company and, in some cases, to force a change in management of the company. This can be very difficult because it threatens management, and management may believe that the exclusivity period under chapter 11 will provide them a safe haven, allowing sufficient time to turn the company's operations around. Also, judges seem inclined, to some degree, to allow value to dissipate in order to save jobs and "preserve" business entities, such as in the Eastern Airlines and, arguably, the Dart Drug Stores chapter 11 cases.

Of course, the LTV decision with respect to OID discussed above certainly puts a crimp in generic exchange offers going forward. Likewise, as discussed earlier, there are instances where a very small number of holders, for whatever reason, elect to file involuntary petitions against companies. Such petitions certainly bring an abrupt halt to exchange offer discussions unless the company is able to convince a court to dismiss the involuntary petition because strong progress is being made toward an out-of-court restructuring. For example, the involuntary petitions against MGF Oil (even though it ultimately sought chapter 11 protection) and SCI-TV were dismissed by a bankruptcy court. MCorp, on the other hand, was unable to successfully combat the involuntary petitions.

There are, of course, many situations that cannot reasonably be resolved outside of chapter 11. One such example is Resorts International, in which fraudulent conveyance issues mandated a filing by the bondholders to preserve their rights under the relevant one-year limitation period provided by the Code.

Once a company submits to court supervision under chapter 11, a different set of dynamics comes into play. The in-court reorganization is a structured process governed by the Code and Rules thereunder. Early in a proceeding, a creditors' committee is appointed by the court. Such a group enjoys broad powers and usually has a major impact on the outcome of a case. Under the Code, committees should consist of the seven largest creditors willing to serve; however, the U.S. Trustee appointed to the case is empowered to appoint greater or fewer than seven. If large holders wish to remain passive and do not serve, the process may end up driven by small holders with different agendas. Such a circumstance may eventually turn a large passive holder into an active participant if he does not see a holder with similar goals step into the fray.

Serving on creditors' committees can be unappealing for certain legal reasons. Under the law, committee members are fiduciaries to the creditor class that the committee represents, and fiduciaries who acquire claims may be limited to recover only their cost upon reorganization, eliminating any possibility of a profit. Also, members frequently have access to material, nonpublic information. As a result of these and other factors, attorneys usually advise committee members not to trade in the claims and securities of the debtor. Because of these trading restrictions, many investors opt either not to serve on committees, or to acquire "full" positions early in a proceeding and then seek membership.

In order for a company to emerge from chapter 11, a plan of reorganization must be approved by 50 percent in number as well as two-thirds principal amount of those creditors who actually vote in each impaired class. Thus, if one acquires one-third of any particular class, such an investor may well hold a blocking position.

A creditor class that is not impaired by a plan of reorganization (such as through reinstatement) does not need to consent to the plan. In some cases, as discussed earlier, reinstatement may limit recovery to something less than 100 cents, but there are creditors who are quite happy to be reinstated. Creditors fortunate enough to be in this position may refuse to consent to any plan other than one that reinstates them or repays them in full.

Secured creditors often have a special status under the Code. Adequately secured creditors (where the value of the collateral exceeds the amount of such claims) are entitled to postpetition interest, paid either upon consummation of the plan, as with Public Service of New Hampshire ("PSNH") third mortgage bonds, or on a current basis during the proceedings, as with PSNH first and second mortgage bonds. Certain investors believe that purchasing these types of claims is a low-risk means of earning a good return, insofar as the bankrupt company is paying interest under court supervision.

Typically, however, the market discounts these claims because of the uncertainties surrounding bankruptcy. For example, as of this writing, Revco was paying interest on a current basis on its bank debt. However, the bank debt could come under attack on fraudulent transfer grounds, stopping future interest payments or even causing past interest payments to be returned to the estate. Moreover, secured creditors with inadequate collateral coverage may not be entitled to postpetition interest. If it is determined that creditors who received postpetition interest were in fact "undersecured," such interest payment may have to be refunded.

Under certain circumstances, such as when the debtor is determined to be solvent (the value of the company's assets exceeds all liabilities), unsecured and undersecured creditors are entitled to postpetition interest. This was the case in the Texaco bankruptcy in which Texaco reinstated all its debts.

Once a plan is approved by the court, all creditors are bound, even if they did not vote in favor of the plan; that is, in-court restructurings extinguish all dissenting interests. Because of the ability to bind a class of creditors in a confirmed plan of reorganization, when the holdout problem in out-of-court restructurings becomes insurmountable, the company and bondholders who have reached an accord in general may consider a "prepackaged" chapter 11 as a way to bind recalcitrant holdouts without letting the chapter 11 take on an uncontrollable life of its own.

A prepackaged chapter 11 is a process by which the company takes its proposed out-of-court restructuring plan, retools it into a plan of reorganization and then submits that plan at the same time that it files for chapter 11 or shortly thereafter. In reality, the restructuring process can still get out of control, and to date there have been very few successful prepackaged plans.

Because it is difficult to grasp the dynamics and strategies of distressed investing fully in the abstract, it is helpful to look at two case studies for illustrative purposes.

Case Study: Resorts International

At the end of 1988, entertainer Merv Griffin purchased control of Resorts International from Donald Trump in a highly leveraged transaction. Resorts was unable to service its debt, and within one year it defaulted on its obligations. The vultures quickly swooped in and purchased substantial blocks of its publicly traded securities. These included Griffin Resorts 13½ percent and 13⅞ percent bonds, secured by first liens on the Paradise Island facilities and the Atlantic City casino, respectively. Other securities included Resorts's unsecured 16⅝ percent, 11⅜ percent, and two different 10 percent issues.

Interestingly, when Hurricane Hugo was bearing down on Paradise Island, one trading desk executed what it called the "Hugo Trade," swapping an investor out of the 13½ percent and into the 13⅞ percent at a time when not everyone was aware of the differences in security underlying the two bonds. Moreover, the 13⅞ percent benefited from a $10 million letter of credit designed to make good any missed interest payments. This LOC resulted in a 5 point payment per 13⅞ percent bond at the end of 1989. But because at this time the market as a whole was generally unaware of either the underlying collateral differential or the LOC existence, the 13⅞ percent and the 13½ percent traded at roughly the same levels following the default announcement, thereby providing the astute investor with a windfall profit opportunity.

When the company defaulted, the *unsecured* debentures traded down, reflecting the expectation of substantially diminishing values, especially since most of the company's assets were securing the Griffin 13½ percent and 13⅞ percent bonds, leaving questionable value for the unsecureds. However, some of those familiar with the deal recognized that the Griffin bonds might be vulnerable to a fraudulent conveyance lawsuit, since such a suit, if successful, might void their security interests.

The theory was that because proceeds from the issuance of the Griffin bonds had been used to finance the Merv Griffin buyout, then if it could be successfully argued that the company had been rendered insolvent in the transaction, the Griffin bonds might be stripped of their collateral as a result of their "wrongdoer" status as participants in the "fraudulent transfer."

If one believed that this theory had merit, one would be interested in the unsecured debentures, since stripping the Griffin bonds of their collateral would "create" value for the unsecureds. Conversely, if one did not give credence to the fraudulent transfer notion, the Griffin bonds could represent a good investment.

However, there was a third way to trade in the Resorts/Griffin securities. Since both the Griffin bonds and the unsecureds were trading as if each could lose the legal argument, a viable hedge was to purchase both securities and offset industry valuation risk by shorting securities of another Atlantic City casino operator. To understand this better, it is helpful to set forth some of the underlying Resorts information as of late 1989:

	Face amount	Market price	Total market value
Unsecureds	$595MM	26	$155MM
Griffins	325	50	163
Total			$318MM

Thus, if one believed that within a 12 month period the total value of the estate that would accrue to the securityholders would be approximately $400 million, a belief to which many professionals did subscribe, then an attractive investment could be achieved by purchasing a weighted amount of both of the above classes. For example, if the market value of these securities did reach $400 million, this would represent a 25 percent appreciation from the $318 million market value above. Significantly, such returns would be locked in with this strategy, irrespective of the results of the fraudulent conveyance litigation. The risks in this strategy revolve around the length of time needed to resolve the relevant issues and the actual terminal value of the estate at the end of the process.

In order to hedge the latter risk, one could sell short the Trump Taj Mahal bonds which were trading near par at the time. The market, therefore was attributing a value of almost $700 million to the Taj. If this valuation was justified, it would support a $400 million value of the Resorts estate as Resorts' Atlantic City facility was located adjacent to the Taj. If, however,

Atlantic City casino values declined, surely the Taj bonds would drop in price. Further, proceeds from the Taj bond short sale could be used to "go long" Resorts bonds, increasing the potential returns on invested cash.

Because the unsecured holders in Resorts felt it was important to preserve their remedies with respect to fraudulent conveyance issues under the Bankruptcy Code before the relevant limitations period lapsed, a chapter 11 filing was inevitable. However, most of the constituents embraced the concept of a controlled, quasi-prepackaged chapter 11. Accordingly, the broad parameters of a reorganization plan were accepted by many of the relevant parties, and the company then consented to a chapter 11 filing. Within a few months after the filing, the company submitted its official plan of reorganization to the bankruptcy court, and at the time of this writing, it is in the process of attempting to emerge from chapter 11.

Case Study: Liquor Barn

The Liquor Barn case demonstrates some other dynamics that can come into play in distressed investing. Liquor Barn is a California-based liquor retailer (the largest such retailer in the United States) and was formerly a division of Safeway stores. After the Safeway leveraged buyout, Liquor Barn itself was sold in a leveraged transaction in 1987. Within one year, the company had materially missed its original projections, defaulted on most of its financial obligations and developed a cash crisis. The company filed under chapter 11 in late 1988.

Discussion of the capital structure is relevant here. The company's operating subsidiaries owed about $20 million to trade creditors. The holding company had about $65 million of bank debt, which was guaranteed on a secured basis by the operating subsidiaries. A potential argument was that the secured guarantees could be voided in conjunction with a possible fraudulent conveyance lawsuit. In such an event, the trade creditors would have received 100 cents on the dollar for their claims.

Investor interest centered on the trade claims. One investor's plan was to purchase at least one-third of the claims at a substantial discount (less than 30 cents on the dollar), and pursue the fraudulent conveyance litigation while maintaining the ability to block any plan. On the other hand, existing trade creditors were reluctant to pursue litigation, both because of the expense involved and the fear that a successful litigation would result in a Pyrrhic victory—100 cents recovery, but the possible destruction of Liquor Barn, a major customer for most of the trade creditors. Time ran out for the vulture buyer; before he could accumulate a one-third position in the trade claims, the remaining trade creditors reached a compromise with the banks that resulted in the sale of all operating assets as a going concern for cash in excess of $40 million. The trade and the banks agreed to share the proceeds (after paying administrative expenses) with each ultimately receiving cash distributions of approximately 35–40 cents on the dollar.

Although the return on the Liquor Barn trade claim investment was reasonable, the return could have been dramatically higher had the vulture investor been successful in his purchase program. This case illustrates the different agendas that can exist in the private claims sector.

Conclusion

Trading in distressed securities is enormously complex, risky, and fun. The investment environment is not static because bankruptcy law, investment techniques and trading patterns are constantly evolving. Distressed investing has become the "hot" area towards which capital and bodies have gravitated in 1990, and, accordingly we foresee a shake-out in this discipline at some point soon. The principles and tenets touched on in this chapter do not guarantee success if adhered to; rather it is the hope of the authors that this chapter has shed some light on the players, the process, and the dynamics of this most fascinating and rewarding aspect of the investment world.

10

Investment Opportunities in Distressed Equities

George Putnam, III
New Generation Investments, Inc.

The equity securities of troubled companies offer tremendous opportunities for investors, but not without substantial risks. Every year, several of the largest gainers in the stock market are companies that pull back from the brink of bankruptcy and return to profitability. Because these stocks drop to very low prices when the companies are in distress—sometimes as low as a dollar or less per share—there is significant price leverage when the companies begin to recover.

One reason these stocks drop so low is because the market for distressed securities is inefficient. Many professional investors will not go near the stock of a troubled company because it would "look bad" in their portfolio. An investment manager is not likely to lose his or her job as a result of buying IBM, but a lesser known stock that goes into bankruptcy could be hazardous to one's employment at many firms. Most brokerage houses will not follow, much less recommend, troubled stocks for similar reasons.

Another reason for the unpopularity of distressed stocks is the difficulty in analyzing them. When a company has been losing money for a while, traditional measures such as earnings per share and book value are not very useful. In fact, if the company is going through a significant restructuring, its historical financial statements may not shed any light at all on its future prospects.

Finally, these stocks do have a high degree of risk. If the company is not able to turn around, the stock can end up being nearly worthless. Many people look at a $2 stock and think, "How much lower can it go?" On a percentage basis, at least, the answer is "a lot!" When a stock goes to zero, your percentage loss is just as great whether you bought at 2 or at 50. The rest of this chapter discusses how to pick stocks that are on the road to recovery and avoid those that will become worthless.

Bankruptcy vs. Prebankruptcy Stocks

Many investors do not distinguish between stocks of companies that have filed for bankruptcy and those that are in distress but have not actually filed. On the cocktail party circuit the stories about "killings" made in the past in Toys "R" Us and Penn Central (both of which went through chapter 11) are usually indistinguishable from the stories about Chrysler and International Harvester (both of which managed to avoid bankruptcy). However, whether or not a company files for bankruptcy should have a significant effect on an equity investor's strategy.

While bankruptcy stocks are discussed in more detail below, it is important to recognize from the outset that the common stocks of companies in bankruptcy today almost never do well over the long term. Once a company goes into chapter 11, its creditors take control of the situation and they rarely leave much for the stockholders. Therefore, most equity investors will want to look for troubled companies that are either likely to stay out of bankruptcy or that have already emerged from chapter 11.

What to Look for in Turnarounds

As mentioned above, it is very difficult to value the stock of a distressed company by traditional financial analysis. Most popular multiples and ratios are not very helpful when some of the components are negative. Instead, it is usually necessary to look for broad indications of potential value rather than to try to use numerical formulas. The following sections discuss some of the key indicators to look for.

Core Business

The most important characteristic to look for in a troubled company is a solid core business. If a company is going to turn around, it must have at least one line of business that will provide both immediate cash flow and the opportunity for future growth.

The company's chance for survival may be further enhanced if it has some assets that can be sold off to raise cash without destroying the core business. These assets may be whole lines of business or just assets that are not essential to the core business. The cash raised can be used to pay off creditors and to bolster the company's core business.

This ability to sell assets or ancillary businesses favors large, multiline companies, and historically they have fared best in both bankruptcy and out-of-court restructurings. Smaller single-business companies have nothing to fall back on or sell when they get into trouble. Unless they can solve the problems in their main line of business, they are likely to end up in liquidation with no return to the stockholders.

An example of a multibusiness company that was able to pull back from the brink of bankruptcy was International Harvester (now called Navistar International). In the early 1980s Harvester was a major manufacturer of both heavy trucks and farm equipment. When it ran into substantial financial difficulties, the company sold off its farm equipment business and used the proceeds to pay down debt and focus on the truck business.

Strong Products or Brands

A well-known product or brand name can be very valuable to a distressed company. If the company is going to turn around, it must be able to maintain a certain level of sales to provide cash flow. This can be difficult when the company's problems become public knowledge, particularly where servicing or some other form of postsale contact with the company is important. Most people are reluctant to buy from a company that may shortly disappear. However, a well-known product or brand may help to reassure customers and distributors.

For example, when Chrysler was on the verge of bankruptcy in the early 1980s, customer and dealer loyalty was crucial to its survival. People who had bought Chrysler cars for generations were willing to believe that the company would again produce a good product, and they did not immediately defect to Chevrolet or Honda when they heard bad news about Chrysler.

Strong brand names played a different role in the case of A. H. Robins. Robins was forced into bankruptcy in 1985 because of product liability litigation over its Dalkon Shield intrauterine device. The Robins bankruptcy looked like it might follow the precedent set by Manville a few years earlier. Manville's bankruptcy was long and complex, and its shareholders ended up losing most of their value.

In Robins's case, a number of other pharmaceutical companies were interested in acquiring its strong consumer brand names, which included Robitussin, Dimetapp, and Chap Stick. A bidding war developed, and Robins was sold to American Home Products for more than $30 per share. American Home also funded a trust to settle the product liability litigation and end the bankruptcy.

New Management

More often than not, the management team that led a company into trouble is not going to be able to lead the company back to health. Sometimes poor management has caused the problems. Sometimes old management has lost the confidence of the creditors. And sometimes special turnaround expertise is needed to get the company back on its feet. At any rate, a change in top management is usually desirable at a troubled company.

However, it is important to note that the hiring of a turnaround guru is not necessarily a signal to rush out and buy the company's stock. Even the best turnaround managers may take a long time to revive a company, and there may be more bad news to cone. Very often, after a few months on the job the turnaround manager will decide that it is necessary to file for bankruptcy in order to provide breathing space for making changes at the company.

Also, even the most experienced turnaround managers can underestimate the problems at a troubled company. Victor Palmieri, a veteran of Penn Central and Baldwin United, two of the largest bankruptcies ever, thought he could rescue Crazy Eddie, an electronics retailer, when it ran into trouble in 1987. Palmieri brought in a new management team and made a substantial cash investment in the company. But the problems (which included alleged fraud by the founder of the company) proved to be too great, and the company was liquidated about a year later.

Thus, a change in management may be a good sign, but it does not make the company an immediate "buy." Rather, it means that the company's chances may be improved, and investors should watch for other favorable signs in the future.

Ability to Satisfy Obligations

Most companies get into trouble because they are unable to generate enough cash to satisfy their financial obligations. Therefore, if a company is going to successfully reorganize, it must somehow get its cash inflows and outflows back into balance. It can either increase cash inflows or decrease its obligations.

Usually, by the time a company is in distress, it has exhausted its means of increasing revenues. This means that it must be able to reduce its operating costs or its financial costs. On the operating side, a troubled company will close facilities, lay off workers, and sometimes even reduce management salaries. On the financial side, the company can sell off assets and use the proceeds to pay down its debt. If it is unable to raise cash to pay creditors, the company must try to persuade its creditors to accept less than the full amount they are owed. This often means persuading debtholders to accept stock in lieu of debt.

Once a company has pared its obligations down to a level where they can be satisfied out of current cash flow, its survival is no longer threatened. Then it can ride out an industry downturn or take whatever other longer-term steps may be needed to return to profitability.

We saw this strategy pay off in the energy industry in the mid-1980s. Oil drillers and oilfield supply companies that were able to cut down on their financial obligations when energy prices plummeted are now prospering as the energy industry gradually recovers.

Simple Capital Structure

The ability of a company to restructure its obligations may be directly related to the complexity of its capital structure. The more different classes of creditors that a company has, the more difficult it will be to get them all to agree on a restructuring outside of bankruptcy.

Where a company has a large number of different classes of creditors—such as holders of bank debt, senior bonds, subordinated bonds, junior subordinated bonds, and preferred stock—negotiations are likely to be protracted and the chances of one class failing to agree to an out-of-court restructuring are greatly increased. Also, even if the creditors do reach agreement, the more classes of creditors there are to be satisfied, the less value is likely to be left over for the holders of common stock.

Company-specific Problems vs. Industrywide Distress

In evaluating a distressed company, it is important to determine the extent to which the causes of the distress are unique to the company or affect the entire industry. Where the problems go beyond the specific company, it may take changes in industry conditions, or even broad economic conditions, to bring the company back. Under those circumstances, the goal of the distressed company may be just to survive until the industry begins to rebound.

Industrywide problems usually take longer to resolve than company-specific problems. In a troubled industry, investors should avoid the most severely distressed companies and focus on those that are going to be able to ride out a prolonged downturn. When the industry as a whole begins to recover, you will get a second chance to look at the marginal companies and see which ones are still around.

Stock Ownership

It is often useful to look at who owns the stock of a troubled company. Where management holds a significant amount of stock, they have an extra incentive to turn the company around. Often a turnaround specialist will be compensated partly with stock or options, which will make him particularly anxious to create value for stockholders.

The presence of a holder of a big block of stock can also be a good sign. In any distressed situation the creditors will play a major role in the restructuring of the company. If the company's stock is widely dispersed, there will be no one to look out for the stockholders' interests. The reorganization will be shaped largely by management and creditors, with the result that stockholders may find their holdings substantially diluted. But if there are major stockholders, they are likely to take an active role in the reshaping of the company. And as they look out for their own interests, these big holders will also protect the interests of their fellow stockholders who may only own a few shares.

Exchange Listing

Historically, the fact that a stock is listed on the New York Stock Exchange has been a source of some comfort to investors in distressed companies, particularly if the company was in bankruptcy. In the past, the NYSE would automatically delist any company that went into bankruptcy unless the officials at the exchange felt that the company had good prospects for survival.

The NYSE has changed its policy and is now much more lenient about letting companies remain on the exchange throughout the chapter 11 process. Therefore, NYSE listing is no longer an indicator of stockholder value.

Exchange listing does improve the likelihood that information will be available about a troubled company. Many troubled companies fall behind on their SEC filings and reports to shareholders. While the NYSE appears to be willing to tolerate some delinquency in filings when a company is in distress, it does put pressure on listed companies to fulfill their reporting requirements.

The American Stock Exchange and the NASDAQ National Market System seem much more likely to drop a stock that has gone into bankruptcy. Once a stock has been delisted from an exchange or the NASDAQ system, it can be very difficult to obtain information about the company.

Recognizing the Bottom

One of the most difficult aspects of investing in distressed equities is identifying when a company has turned the corner and begun to rebound. Very often the stock of a troubled company will fall sharply and then level off for a while. Then more bad news will come out, and the stock will drop to a much lower level. This process may be repeated several times until the company eventually files for chapter 11.

It generally pays to wait until you are fairly sure that all the bad news is out. Usually this means waiting until there is at least a little good news coming from the company, such as losses narrowing, cash flow turning positive, or backlogs growing. You may miss the absolute bottom, but at least you will be less likely to get an unpleasant surprise.

One phenomenon to watch out for is the "death spiral." In these situations, one item of bad news causes a loss of confidence in the company, which leads to more bad news, which causes someone else to lose faith in the company, and so on. At each stage in the downward spiral, many investors figure that the stock has hit bottom, and they jump in just before the stock drops still further.

Death spirals are particularly common in the retailing industry. In a recent example, Ames Department Stores had difficulty in assimilating a number of new stores that it acquired from another retail chain. These problems caused the company's bankers to become nervous about extending more credit. Suppliers became edgy, and when computer problems delayed some payments, many suppliers refused to ship more merchandise. Without new merchandise on the shelves, cash flow dropped, the lenders refused to extend more credit, more suppliers refused to ship goods, and Ames was forced to file for chapter 11.

Another type of news to be wary of is any indication of fraud or misstatement of financial reports. Very often the first news release indicating that fraud has been found at a company will give few details and will downplay the significance of the event. Usually the initial indication of fraud is only the tip of the iceberg, and frequently the company will be forced into chapter 11 to straighten out its problems. In recent years, this has happened to a number of companies that seemed to have fairly strong franchises, including Regina (vacuum cleaners), Miniscribe (computer disk drives), and Crazy Eddie (consumer electronics stores). In each of these cases, the common stock became virtually worthless.

Thus, while many contrarians have succeeded by investing on bad news, it is critical to determine whether the bad news is an isolated event or the first of many negative reports that will eventually lead to a bankruptcy filing.

Other Equity Securities in Nonbankruptcies

If a company manages to avoid chapter 11, there can be substantial price appreciation in other equity securities beside the common stock. If the company has issued warrants, they are likely to be trading at a very low price and have tremendous price leverage. However, the warrants also have a very high level of risk because they will almost always be worthless if the company files for bankruptcy.

Preferred stocks can also provide substantial appreciation, particularly if they have omitted some dividends. Frequently when a company encounters financial problems, it will stop paying dividends on its preferred stock. Unlike missing an interest payment on a bond, skipping a dividend on a preferred stock will not drive a company into bankruptcy. Instead, the unpaid dividends (which are known as arrearages) accumulate and must be paid off in full before any dividends can be paid on the common stock.

When a company begins to recover, its preferred stock can move up very sharply as investors see the prospect of not only having the regular dividend restored but also receiving all of the accumulated dividend arrearages. For example, when International Harvester was in trouble in 1982, its Class C preferred dropped as low as 6¼. As the company recovered over the next few years, the preferred stock rose to over 60 before being redeemed by the company.

Bankruptcy Stocks

When a company files for bankruptcy, it is generally advisable for long-term investors to avoid the common stock. There may be short-term trading opportunities in bankruptcy stocks, but over the longer term, common stockholders almost always fare badly in chapter 11. While there have been some bankruptcies in the past where investors made spectacular profits in the common stock, changes in bankruptcy law coupled with growing sophistication among creditors make it increasingly likely that stockholders in a bankrupt company will end up with little or no value.

The basic reason for this is that, under corporate and bankruptcy law, stockholders have the lowest priority claim on a company's business and assets. At least in theory, all creditors must be paid in full before the stockholders receive anything. In actual fact, this rule of "absolute priority" is often not strictly observed. Senior creditors are frequently willing to compromise with junior creditors in order to expedite the proceedings.

In the past it was quite common for creditors in a chapter 11 reorganization to make fairly sizable concessions to common stockholders so that the stockholders would support the reorganization plan. In the public bankruptcies of the 1970s and early 1980s you often saw the old stockholders end up owning anywhere from 20 to 100 percent of the equity in the reorganized company.

The Bankruptcy Code that was adopted in 1978 made it easier for creditors to enforce the rule of absolute priority. As creditors learned how to operate under the 1978 Code, they realized that they did not have to give as much value to the stockholders as had been common in the past. Now stockholders often receive 5 percent or less of the equity in the reorganized company, and it is not uncommon to see them get nothing.

Special Situations

The only type of bankruptcy where stockholders have sometimes fared well is the case where a company went into chapter 11 to solve a special, nonfinancial problem. These special problems usually relate to litigation. The best known of these special cases are Manville (asbestos liability), A. H. Robins (Dalkon Shield product liability), Smith International (patent litigation), and Texaco (litigation with Pennzoil over the acquisition of Getty Oil). In all of these cases except Manville, you could have made money by buying the stock shortly after the bankruptcy filing.

The key to evaluating these special bankruptcies is to figure out how large the potential liability is compared to the equity value in the company. In Robins the value of the company (largely because of its valuable consumer brands) was considerably greater than the litigation claims against the company, and the excess value flowed through to the stockholders. In Texaco and Smith, the companies used bankruptcy to negotiate favorable settlements to their litigation, thereby leaving a lot of value for their shareholders. Only in Manville was the value of the claims against the company so large as to leave almost nothing for the holders of the common stock.

Short-term Trading Opportunities

While there is not likely to be much profit potential for long-term holders of the stock of bankrupt companies, there may be good opportunities for short-term traders. Many bankruptcy stocks follow similar trading patterns over the course of the chapter 11 proceedings, and astute traders may be able to take advantage of these patterns.

In the days immediately preceding a bankruptcy filing, a company's stock usually drops sharply. Then after the filing it may rebound somewhat, perhaps even quite sharply. For example, in the case of Ames Department Stores the stock dropped from 6 to 1½ in the month before the bankruptcy filing. Then it bounced back to 3¼ during the week after the filing.

Some of this postfiling rebound may be attributable to speculation by investors who do not understand the bankruptcy process. Or it may also be caused by short sellers who have sold the stock short as it approached bankruptcy and then covered their positions after the filing.

After this flurry of activity surrounding the bankruptcy filing, most stocks drift lower for the remainder of the calendar year. Late in the year there may be another sharp drop as tax-sensitive stockholders sell their stock to take tax losses. Also, institutions who have been holding the stock hoping for a rebound may decide to get rid of it so that it does not show up in their year-end reports.

This drop in December may be followed by a bounce in January as speculators once again move in. In some instances this year-end activity has been quite dramatic. For example, Baldwin United stock rose from a low of ⅝ in December 1984 to 2½ in January 1985; then it did the same thing the next year, going from 1 in December 1986 to 3½ in January 1987.

Aside from this year-end activity, the stock will usually continue to fall as investors realize that they are not likely to recover much. However, it will sometimes jump up again when news of the company's reorganization begins to appear. This last jump usually has nothing to do with ultimate value. For example, when it was announced that Manville was about to emerge from chapter 11, its common stock rose to 3½ even though the company's plan of reorganization made it clear that the stock was worth less than 1.

Beware of Dilution and Reverse Splits

One of the keys to evaluating bankruptcy stocks is knowing exactly how much of the equity in the reorganized company will go to the stockholders. Put another way, one share of common stock in the bankrupt company is frequently not equivalent to one share in the reorganized company.

A large number of companies in chapter 11 satisfy some or all of their creditors by giving them stock in the company. As a result, the interests of the old stockholders are diluted, often very substantially. It is not unusual for old stockholders to end up with only 5 percent of the stock in the reorganized company, with the rest going to creditors. This means that although you may own the same number of shares after the reorganization, you only own ½₀ of the amount of total equity that you owned before.

It is also not unusual for common stock to undergo a reverse split when it comes out of bankruptcy. In the Manville example referred to above, the common stock went through a 1-for-8 reverse split. Some investors who bought the stock just before the reorganization took effect apparently did not realize that there was going to be a reverse split. They thought they were buying a $7 stock for $3, when in reality (after accounting for the reverse split) they were paying $3 for about 90 cents worth of stock.

Other Equity Securities in Bankruptcy

Preferred stocks can sometimes provide large gains in bankruptcy, but they can also fare quite badly. If there is enough value in the company to satisfy all the creditors who come ahead of the preferred stock, preferred stockholders will get most of the residual value, up to the liquidation value of the preferred stock.

This was the case recently in Public Service of New Hampshire's bankruptcy. All PSNH bonds were paid off more or less in full. The preferred stock, which traded as low as 4 early in the bankruptcy, received new securities worth about 25. There wasn't enough value to flow through to the common stock, however, and it languished at around 3 for most of the bankruptcy.

Where creditors senior to the preferred stock are not paid in full, the preferred usually does not do very well. In many such cases, the preferred stock will be treated the same as the common, or it may receive only a modest premium over the common stock.

As mentioned above, when a company goes into chapter 11, its warrants usually end up being worthless. In the Public Service of New Hampshire case, warrant holders received a token payment of 10 cents per warrant, but in most other cases warrant holders receive nothing.

Using Equity to Gain Control in Chapter 11

From time to time there are reports of investors buying large positions in the common stock of a company in chapter 11, apparently in an attempt to gain control of the company. While it is true that someone can often buy a large percentage of the common stock for a relatively small amount of money, they probably are not buying much control over the company.

Unless the creditors get paid off in full, they are the ones who usually control the outcome of the chapter 11 proceedings, and equity holders ultimately have little say in the matter. Someone who wants to get control of a bankrupt company would be better off buying up bonds or other creditor claims or perhaps coming in late in the bankruptcy and offering to make an equity infusion in the company. Those techniques are discussed in other chapters.

Postbankruptcy Stocks

Although the stocks of companies in chapter 11 are generally quite unattractive, they can regain their appeal when the company emerges from bankruptcy. If the reorganization plan is properly designed, the company will be getting a fresh start, having been relieved of many of the burdens that forced it into bankruptcy.

The stock of the reorganized company will often be undervalued because it is still tainted in many people's minds by the bankruptcy. Also, creditors who receive stock in partial satisfaction of their claims will often sell their stock as soon as they can. This will depress the price of the stock and make it attractive.

Using Bonds to Buy Stock

When a company is about to emerge from bankruptcy, there may be a chance to get new stock at a bargain price by buying the old bonds or other securities that will be converted into new stock under the plan of reorganization. For example, when Western Company of North America (an oil drilling company) was about to emerge from chapter 11 in early 1989, its plan of reorganization called for its old bonds, preferred stock, and common stock all to be exchanged for new common stock at varying exchange ratios.

Given the exchange ratios and the prices of the Western securities just before the reorganization took effect, you would have paid about $5.50 per new common share if you bought the old bonds or preferred stock, but you would have paid over $19 per new share if you bought the old common stock. (This is another example of how overpriced a bankruptcy stock can be.) When the Western reorganization took effect, the new common stock began trading at 6¼, and it rose as high as 18 over the next year.

Postbankruptcy Problems

Not every postbankruptcy stock is a good buy. Quite often the company or its investment bankers will be too aggressive in valuing its new stock. The stock will begin trading after the reorganization at a level that is not supportable, and it will drop sharply in a short time.

Also, not every reorganization plan is well structured, and some companies continue to have problems after they emerge from bankruptcy. In recent years, at least three companies listed on the New York Stock Exchange—Cook United, New American Shoe (formerly known as Amfesco), and Towle Manufacturing—have been forced to go back into chapter 11 within a couple of years after they emerged. Needless to say, the stockholders in these companies did not fare well.

The risks in postbankruptcy stocks are well illustrated by Cook United, a discount store chain in the Midwest. It emerged from chapter 11 in September 1986, and its stock began trading at 7. Within a few weeks, the stock dropped to 2. The company's troubles continued to mount, and it went back into bankruptcy in April 1987. The company was eventually liquidated, and stockholders received nothing.

Thus, while a company emerging from bankruptcy may present an opportunity to buy into a refurbished business at a bargain price, it is not a sure thing. As with any stock, it is important to study the company's financial structure and business prospects before investing.

Two Final Keys to Investing in Distressed Equities

As you can see from this chapter, distressed equities can provide opportunities for substantial capital appreciation. However, there are two key elements that should be part of any such strategy for investing in these securities: diversification and patience.

Diversification is important because virtually every investment in a distressed stock is fraught with uncertainty. The vagaries that make the analysis of "normal" stocks challenging are compounded by the special characteristics of the workout/bankruptcy process. Even the most thorough analysis can be thwarted by a recalcitrant creditor, an unpredictable judge, or many other factors. The only defense against this uncertainty is diversification.

Also, the same factors that make turnarounds particularly uncertain also tend to make them particularly slow. This is especially true of bankruptcies. The American judicial system has many great characteristics, but speed is not one of them.

Despite these disadvantages of uncertainty and long duration—or perhaps because of them—distressed securities can be very profitable. But to achieve those profits, you must be willing to jump in where most investors fear to tread.

Investing in Distressed Securities: A Portfolio Point of View

Robert Levine
Nomura Securities International

Although many investors in distressed securities[1] may just look at their investments on a case-by-case basis, it might be of interest to use a top-down analysis in order to understand risk/return aspects of the entire portfolio. Table 11.1 presents the returns on hypothetical portfolios with different average prices and default rates. The results may provide insight into the management of a portfolio of non-bankrupt distressed securities by showing what returns can be expected for investments at different yield levels and different average default assumptions.

Recent events in the high-yield market have forced portfolio managers to reevaluate their strategies for investment in the high-yield sector. In the past, many investors purchased a portfolio of high-yield bonds, hoping to achieve a high rate of return by choosing good credits with an eye toward holding them to maturity and collecting high coupons along the way. The default rate for high yield was assumed to range from 2 to 4 percent, far smaller than the incremental return of high-yield over safer investments. As Figure 11.1 shows, however, starting in mid-September 1989, prices of high-yield bonds tumbled. The severe widening in the yield spread

The author would like to express his appreciation to Stephen Freidheim of Nomura Securities International, and David Reiss and Chris Suan of Kidder, Peabody & Co. Inc. for their invaluable assistance in drafting and providing analysis for this article.

Table 11.1. Rate of Return on Hypothetical Portfolio at Different Default Rates and Purchase Prices

Default rate	Purchase price						
	40	50	60	70	80	90	100
0.0%	35.82%	29.06%	24.32%	20.72%	17.86%	15.50%	13.50%
2.0%	34.29%	27.51%	22.74%	19.14%	16.27%	13.90%	11.90%
4.0%	32.79%	25.97%	21.19%	17.57%	14.69%	12.33%	10.32%
6.0%	31.31%	24.47%	19.66%	16.03%	13.15%	10.77%	8.76%
8.0%	29.87%	22.99%	18.16%	14.52%	11.62%	9.24%	7.23%
10.0%	28.46%	21.54%	16.70%	13.03%	10.13%	7.74%	5.72%
12.0%	27.08%	20.13%	15.26%	11.58%	8.67%	6.27%	4.24%
14.0%	25.74%	18.76%	13.86%	10.17%	7.24%	4.83%	2.80%
16.0%	24.44%	17.43%	12.50%	8.79%	5.84%	3.42%	1.38%
18.0%	23.18%	16.13%	11.18%	7.45%	4.48%	2.05%	−0.00%
20.0%	21.96%	14.88%	9.90%	6.14%	3.17%	0.72%	−1.34%
22.0%	20.79%	13.67%	8.67%	4.89%	1.89%	−0.57%	−2.65%
24.0%	19.66%	12.51%	7.48%	3.67%	0.65%	−1.83%	−3.91%
26.0%	18.57%	11.39%	6.33%	2.50%	−0.54%	−3.04%	−5.14%
28.0%	17.52%	10.32%	5.23%	1.37%	−1.69%	−4.21%	−6.32%
30.0%	16.52%	9.29%	4.17%	0.29%	−2.80%	−5.33%	−7.47%
32.0%	15.56%	8.31%	3.16%	−0.75%	−3.86%	−6.41%	−8.57%
34.0%	14.64%	7.36%	2.19%	−1.74%	−4.88%	−7.45%	−9.63%
36.0%	13.76%	6.47%	1.27%	−2.70%	−5.85%	−8.45%	−10.65%
38.0%	12.92%	5.61%	0.38%	−3.60%	−6.79%	−9.41%	−11.62%
40.0%	12.12%	4.79%	−0.46%	−4.47%	−7.68%	−10.32%	−12.56%
42.0%	11.35%	4.01%	−1.26%	−5.30%	−8.53%	−11.20%	−13.46%
44.0%	10.62%	3.26%	−2.03%	−6.09%	−9.35%	−12.04%	−14.32%
46.0%	9.91%	2.55%	−2.76%	−6.84%	−10.12%	−12.84%	−15.14%
48.0%	9.24%	1.87%	−3.46%	−7.56%	−10.86%	−13.60%	−15.93%
50.0%	8.60%	1.22%	−4.12%	−8.25%	−11.57%	−14.33%	−16.68%
52.0%	7.99%	0.61%	−4.76%	−8.90%	−12.25%	−15.03%	−17.40%
54.0%	7.40%	0.01%	−5.36%	−9.53%	−12.90%	−15.70%	−18.09%
56.0%	6.83%	−0.55%	−5.94%	−10.13%	−13.51%	−16.34%	−18.74%
58.0%	6.29%	−1.09%	−6.50%	−10.70%	−14.10%	−16.94%	−19.37%
60.0%	5.77%	−1.61%	−7.03%	−11.24%	−14.67%	−17.53%	−19.97%

Assumptions: 13.5% average coupon
10-year average maturity
25% recovery rate
3-year recovery period
Semiannual coupon

between the high-yield composite and the 10-year Treasury during this period is illustrated by Figure 11.2. (Figure 11.2 also shows milestones in the high-yield market that were partly responsible for its volatility.)

Portfolio managers who previously only purchased higher-quality high-yield bonds at or near par must now rethink their investment strategy.

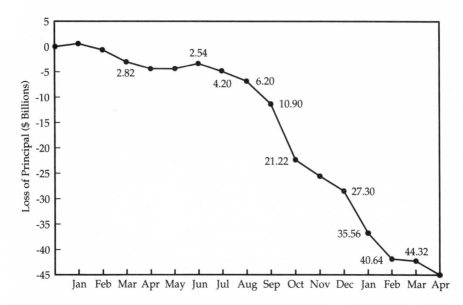

Figure 11.1.   High Yield Market Performance 1/89–4/90
Loss of Principal ($200 Billion Market)
From 1/1/89 through 4/30/90
SOURCE: Drexel Burnham Lambert and Salomon Brothers High-Yield Indices

Figure 11.2.   High Yield Composite Spread History
High-Yield Composite vs. 10-Year UST
SOURCE: Morgan Stanley

Although there is clearly a positive correlation between the yield on a bond and the probability of its default, no such relationship is yet clear between the yield on a bond and its total return. The popular wisdom of the 1980s was that the "safety" provided by current coupon bonds trading around par was more valuable than the higher yields of securities trading at distressed levels. As many of these "safer" companies have recently run into trouble, such wisdom is being questioned. Many portfolio managers have realized that the losses on bonds purchased at par can be much more devastating than those of bonds purchased at already distressed levels. As default rates have increased, many portfolio managers now look for investments with "upside" (that is, higher yielding investments) to offset the now increased "downside." The high coupons provided by speculative-grade bonds are now far less likely to be perceived as adequate compensation for the associated risks; investors now look for capital gain potential.

Investments at different quality levels in the high-yield market clearly require different types of analysis. Companies whose current coupon bonds trade above 80 (percent of par value) tend to be analyzed as going concerns, whereas those with bonds trading below 40 are generally differentiated based on the underlying asset values in a liquidation or restructuring. A bond that trades at distressed levels might be attractive if it returns just one coupon payment before the company is restructured. At the right price, such an investment may well provide a considerable total return. Companies whose bonds trade between 40 and 80 generally are at a turning point and will trade up or down significantly, based on the outcome of some event such as a good selling season for a retailer or the resolution of a strike for a company with labor problems.

The Distressed Security Sector

The distressed security sector has grown from a very small portion to a major segment of the high-yield market over a short period of time. As Figure 11.3 shows, at the beginning of 1988, about 5 percent of the then $160 billion high-yield market traded below 80. However, by March 31, 1990, 30 percent of all high-yield securities were trading somewhere below 80. More than a quarter of the market has fallen from over par to below 80. Furthermore, this sector continues to grow as more high-yield companies encounter difficulties relating to high leverage, poor operating performance, or other problems.

Default rates have ballooned. Recent high-yield default incidence suggests that previous studies, which looked at historical data, are not representative of the current high-yield market. Using historical default rates of 2–4 percent would appear to underestimate recent default experience. In all of 1989, close to $10 billion of high-yield bonds defaulted or underwent

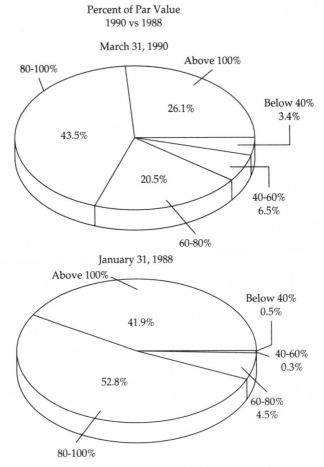

Figure 11.3.   Percent of Par Value 1990 vs. 1988
SOURCE: First Boston, 1st Quarter Review, April 1990

distressed exchanges. This represented about 5 percent of the market. Already, from January through May 1990, nearly $10 billion has defaulted or is undergoing a distressed exchange. (See Table 11.2 for a list of selected defaulted companies.)

Many funds that invest solely in the distressed sector have been started; however, it is not just dedicated funds that must understand the valuation of distressed securities. Because of the sheer volume of high-yield bonds descending into the distressed arena, it is important that all high-yield portfolio managers understand matters relating to investments in distressed securities.[2] Even issues that were at one time considered to be among the best high-yield securities are now trading at distressed levels. Charter Medical and Macy's are examples of credits that once were

Table 11.2.   Selected High-Yield Defaults and Distressed Exchanges since 1/1/89

Company	Amount of high-yield debt outstanding ($MM)	Company	Amount of high-yield debt outstanding ($MM)
1989:		Ponderosa	125.0
		Qintex Productions	42.0
After Six	20.0	Republic Health	557.4
Alpine Group	43.7	Resorts International	537.0
American Building	41.5	San Antonio Savings	24.0
American Capital	78.5	Santa Barbara S&L	50.0
American Continental	42.0	SCI Television	476.6
AP Industries	96.0	Seaman Furniture	86.2
Bastian Industries	42.3	Service Control	100.0
Benjamin Franklin Savings	32.1	Simplicity Holdings	61.0
Bond Brewing Holdings	685.0	Southmark	1,177.0
Bond Brewing Western		Vyquest	16.21
Australia	135.0	Webcraft Technologies	226.0
Circle Express	46.5	Western S&L	115.0
Columbia S&L of Colorado	40.0		9,958.01
Commonwealth S&L of Fl.	18.0		
Drum Financial Corp.	18.5	**1990:**	
Eastern Airlines	740.3	Allied-Federated	2,761.0
Erty Industries	14.3	Amdura	31.0
Fairfield Communities	35.0	Ames	200.0
Financial Corp. of America	23.1	ALC Communications	N/A
Financial Trustee Capital	110.0	Circle-K	448.4
First Texas Savings	65.0	Divi Hotels	110.0
FPA Corporation	50.5	Doskocil	92.5
Fruehauf	510.0	General Development	301.0
G-Acquisitions	45.0	Greyhound Lines	225.0
Gibralter Financial of		Insilco	427.0
California	25.0	Interco	900.0
Griffin Resorts	325.0	Lintner Textiles	200.0
Healthcare International	35.0	Miniscribe	90.0
Healthcare USA	20.0	Motor Wheel	
Integrated Resources	798.9	Corporation	100.0
Jim Walter (Hillsborough)	1,209.4	Service America	322.0
Kane Industries	70.0	Southland	1,832.0
Koor Industries	105.0	TGX	60.0
Leaseway Transportation	192.5	Univision	270.0
Lomas Financial	375.0	West Point Acquisition	700.0
Merabank, FSB	70.0	Western Union	912.0
Metropolitan Broadcasting	0.6		9,981.9
Miramar Marine	125.0		
Nelson Entertainment	57.5		
Olympia Broadcasting	23.4		

SOURCES: Moody's Investor Services, Kidder Peabody, and Drexel Burnham Lambert.

considered "core holdings" for many funds but that now trade at levels suggesting possible restructurings. Most high-yield portfolio managers have no choice but to become well versed in the techniques of analyzing distressed securities, as some of their higher-quality bonds deteriorate.

Proficiency in the lower-quality sector makes sense for high-yield managers to better understand distressed bonds currently owned and help guide future investment decisions. With a large selection of current coupon bonds available at low prices, investors who in the past only purchased bonds at or near par now give consideration to bonds trading at moderate to steep discounts. As they have seen many bonds drop 30 or more points in a matter of days, portfolio managers have become more cautious about buying higher-priced bonds because of their steep downside. Investors who in the past would only invest in premium bonds might now look to buy bonds trading at steep discounts in order to diversify the risk profile of the portfolio and create the opportunity for greater capital appreciation.

Distressed Securities: Portfolio Management

Distressed security investing in general focuses more on total returns than on yield because default rates are so significant. However, examining a group of distressed securities as a portfolio purchased at a particular average yield can provide insight into potential returns. Note that the ideas presented here merely provide a basis upon which investors can develop their own methodologies for managing their portfolios and making investment decisions. It is necessary to thoroughly research each potential investment to determine whether its return is appropriate.

The higher the average purchased yield of a portfolio, the higher the default rate that it can withstand. Table 11.1 illustrates this effect by showing the returns of a hypothetical high-yield portfolio at different average purchase prices and default rates.[3] Each entry in the table indicates the return on the portfolio, given the associated average purchase price and constant default rate. The returns assume a 13.5 percent average coupon, a three year bankruptcy (during which no interest is received), and a 25 percent recovery rate. The attractiveness of discount bonds is clear: a hypothetical portfolio purchased at 80 can withstand over a 4 percent higher default rate than one purchased at par, and it can still produce higher returns than the portfolio purchased at par. Of course, a portfolio of bonds purchased at 80 has a higher probability of experiencing defaults. But this risk/return decision must be made in accordance with the credit skills of the individual investor.

The maximum default rate sustainable to achieve a target total return is not a linear function of the average price of a portfolio. In Figure 11.4, we have plotted the default rates at which portfolios purchased at different levels achieve various returns. The choice of a return target depends on the level of return that is appropriate for each investor's objectives. It is

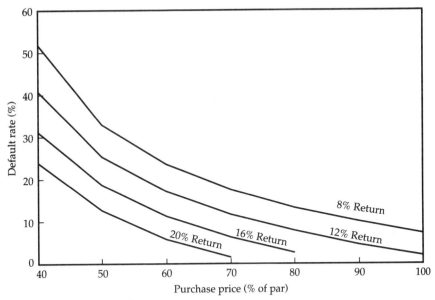

25% recovery rate assumed

Figure 11.4. Default Rates at Which Hypothetical Portfolio Achieves Various Target Returns. 25% recovery rate assumed

interesting to note that all else being equal, a portfolio purchased at 50 can withstand more than twice as high a default rate as one purchased at 70 and still achieve a 12 percent return (24.9 vs. 11.4 percent default rate). Similarly, a portfolio purchased at 70 can withstand more than twice as high a default rate as one purchased at 90 and still achieve a 12 percent return (11.4 vs. 4.4 percent default rate). We suggest that default risk/return curves at appropriate target levels be developed for each investor's risk preference.

The importance of proficient credit analysis and diversification is highlighted by Figure 11.4. For example, a current coupon portfolio purchased at 60, that is, a 40 percent discount from par, will have a 20 percent return with a 5.6 percent default rate, but only an 8 percent return with a 23.1 percent default rate. Clearly, the high current yield of high-yield portfolios can quickly be negated by defaults.

The lower the purchase price of the portfolio (and the higher the default rate), the larger the effect of the recovery rate and the greater the importance of liquidation analysis. Figure 11.5 illustrates the relative importance of recovery rates at different levels of default rates and purchase prices in achieving a desired return. The greater spread between the higher recovery assumptions shows that each additional recovered dollar allows the portfolio to withstand an increasingly higher default rate. The closeness of the curves toward the right of the figure (low default rates and

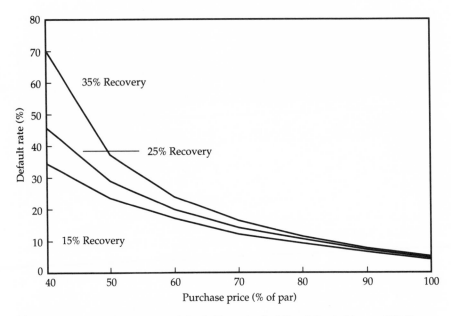

Figure 11.5.   Default Rate at Which Hypothetical Portfolio Achieves 10% Return. Using Different Recovery Rate Assumptions

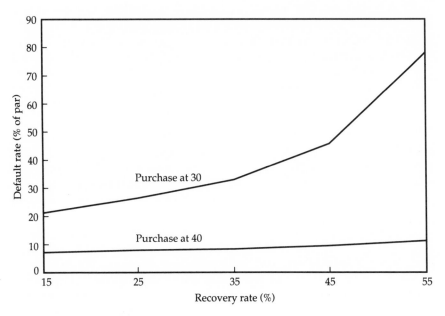

Figure 11.6.   Default Rates at Which Hypothetical Portfolio Achieves 30% Return. Average Purchase Price: 30 vs. 40

high prices) shows the relative insignificance of recovery rates at very low default rates to a 10 percent return portfolio. A sample portfolio purchased at par with a 10 percent target return and 15 percent recovery assumption can withstand a 4.0 percent default rate, whereas a similar portfolio with a 35 percent recovery assumption can withstand a 4.9 percent default rate. Obviously, the difference is much greater for more distressed bonds whose returns rely more on recovery of principal of defaulted bonds. A similar portfolio purchased at 60 achieves a 10 percent return at a 17.1 percent default rate using a 15 percent recovery assumption or a 23.7 percent default rate using a 35 percent recovery assumption.

Investors in distressed securities generally look for higher than average returns as compensation for the extremely risky nature of their investments. To achieve high returns, however, the purchase price level is crucial. To illustrate this we refer to a specific case, Figure 11.6, which shows the default rates at which the hypothetical portfolio achieves a specific, 30 percent return at various recovery rates. A portfolio purchased at 30 can withstand a far higher default rate than one purchased at 40. In Figure 11.6, the maximum default rate of the portfolio needed to achieve a portfolio rate of 30 percent that is purchased at 30 average price varies importantly with the recovery rate. The same portfolio purchased at 40 is much less dependent on the recovery rate (if a 30 percent rate of return is to be achieved). Although this effect is less conspicuous at lower target returns, it illustrates the growing importance of recovery rates to returns at lower prices.

This analysis does not suggest that it is prudent to randomly purchase a portfolio of distressed securities. Each investment is different, and investors must conduct thorough due diligence prior to the purchase of a security to determine its investment merits.

Valuing a Going Concern vs. Liquidation

Default risk may not be the only criteria necessary to evaluate an investment in a portfolio of distressed securities. Companies whose bonds are trading at distressed levels are generally not viewed as ongoing concerns but rather as a collection of assets to be divided among creditors (or, at best, as a company that will survive by taking measures such as selling assets and restructuring debt). An investor in distressed paper tries to value the assets of the company and determine the claim that each security in the capital structure has on those assets. An investment decision can then be made based on each security's value relative to its price and the estimated time until recovery.

By contrast, a company that is performing well is valued primarily by the cash flow it generates as an ongoing concern relative to the cash required to service its debt and meet its business obligations. Investors are interested in the potential growth and the stability of cash flow to meet interest payments on a timely basis. The analysis assesses the probability of cash flows to meet debt service requirements. If the analysis concludes that there is a good chance that debt service payments may be interrupted, an investment at par is unlikely to make much sense, regardless of the underlying asset value. For a company with sound performance whose bonds are trading around par, asset values are analyzed, but they are generally viewed as a second line of defense. In addition, as we indicate below, going concern asset value analysis often overestimates liquidation asset value analysis because a company's value is usually significantly impaired in bankruptcy.

Investing in Distressed Securities: Pitfalls

Investments in the distressed sector have many pitfalls not often encountered with other types of investments. First, good information is difficult to obtain; second, investor control over the company is diminished; and third (and perhaps most important), companies often lose value in bankruptcy.

Information

Information from management about the operations of a company in bankruptcy is difficult to obtain and is often suspect. If the company is in bankruptcy because its management was overly aggressive and took on too much debt, then there is little reason to believe that their overzealous thought process will metamorphose into a conservative approach. If the company is in, or on the brink of, bankruptcy as a result of dishonest or incompetent management, then it is likely that those tendencies also will persist.

Few securities dealers have enough analysts capable of providing meaningful sell-side research on distressed companies. In addition, equity analysts, a potential source of information on public companies, will generally terminate coverage of a company when it becomes distressed.

Control

A company in chapter 11 is under tight control by the bankruptcy court. The court approves or decides (1) how much value each security is entitled to, (2) how many creditor committees there can be, (3) how the company's cash flow can be spent, and (4) how the company will emerge from bankruptcy. These issues are all crucial to the value of distressed securities, yet are out of the control of investors and, in many cases, management.

Rival security holders in a bankruptcy tend to be more adversarial than those in a company that is performing well. In a bankruptcy, there is usually not enough value in the company to fulfill all claims, whereas in a sound company, all layers of investors can be satisfied. As a result, retrieving money from a bankruptcy can be anything between a negotiation and a battle, both of which require much time and effort.

Loss of Value in Bankruptcy

A company can lose considerable asset value as it goes into bankruptcy. For example, its reputation will most likely be damaged by the negative publicity surrounding its filing, reducing the value of its brand-name recognition. Very often, companies change their names as they exit bankruptcy. In addition, bankrupt companies can lose market share to competitors who claim in their advertising that the bankrupt company failed. Key employees often leave, hoping to move to a financially sound company. Such personnel may be difficult to replace, given the circumstances. Furthermore, asset erosion in bankruptcy can occur as the future growth of the company is constrained by restrictions imposed under the bankruptcy court—for example, limits on advertising budgets, key capital spending, or strategic acquisitions.

In summary, there are many factors to consider when investing in distressed securities. Potential investors must consider not only each credit but also the portfolio effect of investing in these highly risky instruments.

Appendix: Rate of Return Calculation

The internal rate of return calculation was used to calculate the return on the hypothetical portfolios. The cash flows used in the calculation were the sum of semiannual interest on the nondefaulted portion of the portfolio plus recovery of defaulted principal. It was assumed that defaulted principal was returned after three years. A 13.5 percent coupon and 10-year maturity were assumed in all cases.

Notes

1. The U.S. high-yield market has stratified into three distinct segments. We like to refer to them as the good, the bad, and the ugly. The good refers to the highest quality high-yield bonds. The bad refers to those securities that have been trading down in price because of severe credit problems. The ugly refers to companies already in bankruptcy or in the midst of a distressed exchange offer. For purposes of this chapter we refer to the overall distressed sector as including both the bad and ugly securities. Further reference is made to the non-bankrupt or bankrupt distressed sector when appropriate.
2. In fact, I would hazard to guess that even the best performing portfolio managers in the market have had to deal with distressed securities. This becomes

even clearer when one examines the published total return performance statistics of high-yield mutual funds.

3. This analysis assumes a constant default rate over time. In practice, bonds trading at higher yields would have not only a higher default rate but on average would most likely default sooner, thus reducing returns.

The Chapter 11 Process

Hon. William L. Norton, Jr.
Norton and Pennington

Rose H. Staples
Norton and Pennington

History of Business Bankruptcies

In a Supreme Court decision of the early 1930s, Justice Cardoza commented that a bankruptcy reorganization case involves a debtor who is a "financial wreck" with hope for survival and that a bankruptcy liquidation case involves a debtor who is "financially dead."

The present provisions in the United States Bankruptcy Code (Title 11 U.S. Code), which allow debtors to obtain relief from some, and frequently essentially all, of the prepetition debts of the debtors, are the most liberal provisions in favor of debtors and in compromising prepetition debts of any insolvency statute that any society has produced. The bias of congressional policy is in favor of continued employment and economic production by the rehabilitated business enterprise under a plan designed to pay the claims of the creditors.

Chapter 9 (municipalities), chapter 11 (businesses), and chapter 13 (individuals with regular income) are the relevant operating chapters of the Bankruptcy Code that allow reorganization and rehabilitation of the debtor as an alternative to the provisions of chapter 7, which allows only the liquidation of the debtor's assets. The American movement toward liberality in discharging debts for honest debtors and in the allowance of property exemptions to enable debtors to retain some equity in prepetition assets is rooted in the foundations of the American social-economic conscience. The evolution of the several United States bankruptcy statutes has moved away from the concept of severe punishment for debtors, which was their fate in many countries for centuries. Indeed until midway into the nineteenth century in many parts of the world, the treatment of debtors was akin to the treatment for criminal offenses. Liquidation of assets of individual and business debtors in Europe and Great Britain was the only type of bankruptcy relief in 1789, the year that the United States Constitution was enacted. Gaining a fresh start or getting back into any business after a bankruptcy is still very difficult in many European countries, where credit, job opportunities, and joint ventures are virtually unavailable to a bankrupt.

A provision in the Constitution provides that Congress has the exclusive authority to "enact uniform laws on the subject of bankruptcies." Thus, our bankruptcy system is a national law rather than state law. During the 1800s the four different bankruptcy statutes provided only for the liquidation of the assets of individuals and businesses. The Bankruptcy Act of 1898, which continued until the enactment of the Bankruptcy Reform Act of 1978, provided only for liquidations. The nearest thing to a business reorganization was the federal statute allowing equity receiverships, which permitted a business to continue under a federal court-appointed receiver. An action of reorganization and continuation of the business under an equity receivership plan essentially required a consensus of all the creditors. Naturally, unanimity among diverse creditors was difficult, and the equity receivership provision was unsatisfactory and inadequate to the needs of distressed business debtors and a working majority of creditors.

The disclosure of widespread frauds involving consensual plans of business reorganization, supervised by committees of creditors and private administrators outside the court system, demonstrated a need for bankruptcy laws different from the traditional liquidation process. Following the stock market crash of 1929 and the beginning of the Depression, Congress began investigations and hearings in 1932 concerning remedial legislation for financially distressed individuals and businesses.

Several statutes were enacted by Congress in the early 1930s to allow reorganization of railroads and corporations and to provide relief for homeowners, farmers, and individual debtors who were employed and had regular income. These statutes, individually enacted beginning in 1933, were ultimately included in the Chandler Act of 1938, which installed Chapter XIII for employed individuals with income and Chapters X, XI, and XII for business reorganizations in the Bankruptcy Act of 1898, as amended. After almost a decade of serious and intense congressional activity, in the fall of 1978 Congress enacted a comprehensive revised Bankruptcy Code to replace the Bankruptcy Act of 1892. The Bankruptcy Code of 1978 includes both the liquidation provisions and the reorganization provisions of chapter 11 of the Bankruptcy Code.

Business Bankruptcies under the 1978 Bankruptcy Code, as Amended

Chapter 11 Overview

The provisions of the Bankruptcy Code are based on a twofold goal:

1. To give the debtor a fresh start
2. To distribute assets equally among all creditors

The primary object of chapter 11 relief is to discharge a debtor from debts by confirmation of a plan of repayment or a plan of liquidation. Giving the honest debtor a fresh start is deemed to be in the national interest and good for the national economy. The debtor can then return to a productive role in society rather than remaining a constant drain on the economy.

The method set out in the Code to achieve this purpose is to allow the debtor to restructure claims and equity interests. Consequently, the Bankruptcy Code allows the debtor, within certain limits, to adjust debt structure and equity interests, to extend the time to pay secured and unsecured claims, and to satisfy liens based on the value of the collateral rather than on the face amount of the debt.

Also, rehabilitation under the Code allows the debtor to reinstate a debt that is accelerated by a contractual provision or a statute. Such reinstatement requires that the following steps are taken:

1. The default is cured.
2. The maturity date is reinstated as it existed before the default.
3. The holder is compensated for damages incurred as a result of reasonable reliance on the contract or statute that was the basis for acceleration.
4. No other legal, equitable, or contractual rights related to the claim are altered by the plan.

It is also the goal of the Code to provide for fair and equal treatment among creditors. Thus, for example, a creditor that receives a distribution of assets just prior to the date a chapter 11 petition is filed, under certain circumstances (called a "preference"), may have to return that distribution to the bankruptcy estate so that other creditors may also share in that distribution. Preferences are intended to discourage a "race to the courthouse" among like creditors. However, it is important for secured creditors to perfect their liens as soon as possible. Perfection of a lien within the 90-day preference period immediately preceding a bankruptcy petition is voidable. The classification requirements discussed below are another example of the Code provisions intended to promote equality of treatment among like creditors.

As to who can file a chapter 11 case, only a "person" is eligible for chapter 11 relief. "Person" is defined as an individual, a partnership, or a corporation. The definition, however, excludes stockbrokers, commodity brokers, and "governmental units."

In a bankruptcy case, "claim" and "debt" are defined in terms of a monetary obligation. Consequently, neither the protection nor the process of a bankruptcy case affects the regulatory or police action of a government against a debtor. However, the Bankruptcy Code contains a sovereign immunity waiver that applies in a chapter 11 case. Thus, the United States government, as well as any other government entity, generally speaking, stands in the same position as any other creditor.

Liquidation, Reorganization Plan.   A chapter 11 plan may be a plan of liquidation over a short term rather than a plan of reorganization providing for payments over for an extended period of time. A chapter 11 liquidation requires no mandatory trustee nor does it require the immediate cessation of the business. Therefore, it is generally less costly administratively than a chapter 7 liquidation would be. In addition, the owner's continued control of the business often results in a more profitable liquidation process. However, reorganization is generally preferred to liquidation.

Property.   A distinction exists as to property of the estate depending on the nature of the debtor. A corporate debtor's postpetition property constitutes property of the estate. On the other hand, an individual debtor's postpetition earnings from services are not property of the estate and thus may be used by the debtor in whatever manner the debtor chooses during and after a chapter 11 case. Realistically, however, an individual debtor's personal postpetition income is generally needed to support the plan of reorganization, unless, of course, this plan is a straight liquidation.

Compensation of Officers.   When the debtor is a corporation or a partnership, a question usually arises as to how the debtor's officers or principals will be compensated. Bankruptcy judges have been reluctant to exercise power over such compensation, and there is no statutory authorization for doing so. Some bankruptcy courts have viewed excessive salary as a ground for relief from the automatic stay or as a basis for the appointment of a trustee or an examiner. Other bankruptcy courts have begun to exercise some control over such compensation. Even the authorization granted under the U.S. Trustee Program adopted in 1986 does not extend to salaries of the debtor's principals. Consulting fee payments for present and former principals have been treated as preferences and have been recovered as fraudulent where the services were deemed worthless.

Trustee, Examiner.   Trustees and examiners have a role in chapter 11 cases. However, the appointment of a trustee in a chapter 11 case is an extraordinary occurrence. To justify such an appointment, the bankruptcy court must make a finding of "cause" as defined by the Code or a finding that the appointment is in the interest of creditors or shareholders. Generally speaking, a showing must be made with respect to some sort of fraud, abuse, or significant inadequacy on the part of management. The underlying premise of chapter 11 is to permit a debtor to operate its own business while reorganizing. Consequently, chapter 11 trustees and examiners are rarely appointed.

Party in Interest.   A chapter 11 case contemplates much more creditor involvement than the consumer chapters 7 and 13. Therefore, a "party in interest" has standing to be heard in a bankruptcy case on any issue in chapter 11 cases. A party in interest includes the debtor, the unsecured creditors' committee, a creditor, an equity security holder, and an indenture trustee, among others.

Disclaimer.   Our comments here are necessarily generalizations. An attorney specializing in bankruptcy law should be consulted with respect to specific fact situations.

Preconfirmation Matters

The bankruptcy process is started by the filing of a petition for relief under chapter 11 of the Bankruptcy Code. No other document filing is called a "petition." Not only does the filing date trigger deadlines for certain procedures, but it is also important in establishing rights and remedies available to the debtor and to interested parties.

To begin with, the filing date establishes the date for the determination of what constitutes the property of the estate. In addition, the "automatic stay" goes into effect instantaneously to protect the debtor from all creditor action to collect any debt from the debtor and to assert any claim or interest against the debtor's property, as well as to protect the property of the estate from all creditor action.

The concept of property of the estate is greatly expanded under the Bankruptcy Code. It includes every "equitable interest" as well as every "legal interest" that the debtor has in real and personal property. Property of the estate also includes prepetition property (previously property of the debtor) that can be regained and brought back into the bankruptcy estate through avoidable transfers. Certain prepetition transfers of property are deemed "preferences." Very generally speaking, these are transfers that occur within the 90 days preceding the filing date and that result in the transferee obtaining more through said transfer than it would have in a chapter 7 distribution.

Property may also be regained for the estate with respect to certain prepetition transfers that are deemed to be fraudulent conveyances under the state law. Such transfers, which occur within the state law statute of limitations, can be set aside in a bankruptcy case. In addition, under the Bankruptcy Code, a transfer that occurs within one year from the date the petition is filed can be set aside if the transfer was made with intent to defraud creditors or if the transfer was made for less than the "reasonably equivalent value" of the property. Whether the property was transferred by means of a foreclosure or a sale, some courts decide whether the transfer was for a "reasonably equivalent value" by applying the 70 percent test: a transfer for less than 70 percent of the current market value of the property can be avoided.

Property can also be brought back into the estate as a result of the "turnover" provisions of the Bankruptcy Code. Under those provisions, property in the possession or the control of an entity other than the debtor (including collateral in the hands of a secured creditor) can be brought back into the bankruptcy estate. When such property is in the hands of a secured creditor, the debtor must make provisions for "adequate protection" of the creditor's interest. Adequate protection, among other things, includes maintaining insurance in an amount sufficient to cover the value of collateral.

Automatic Stay.   The automatic stay is one of the most fundamental concepts of the Bankruptcy Code to protect the property of the estate for the benefit of the debtor and the collective body of claimants. It is often referred to as the "linchpin" of the Bankruptcy Code. As already noted, the automatic stay is self-operating and goes into effect the moment the chapter 11 petition is filed. Litigation regarding the automatic stay is a crucial factor if brought in early in the case. If the stay is terminated so as to allow foreclosure of significant property, the chapter 11 case may effectively thereby be over. As a rule, however, a lien holder should not move to terminate the stay in the first few weeks of the case. The bankruptcy judges prefer to give the debtor a "breathing spell," and motions to terminate the stay early in the case are often deemed premature. The rationale is that the debtor should be accorded a reasonable period of time free from the actions of creditors in order to devise and formulate a plan of reorganization.

Official or formal notice to the creditor is not required for the automatic stay to be effective against a creditor. Furthermore, the automatic stay imposes an affirmative duty on creditors to restore the status quo, as of the time the petition is filed; that is, the creditor must return property to the debtor after the filing and must dismiss suits and garnishments.

Taking action against the debtor or the debtor's property after the automatic stay is in effect is a violation of the stay. Such actions are void, whether or not the creditor had notice that the stay was in effect. Among the actions against the debtor's property that are prohibited by the stay is the postpetition perfection of a lien. Therefore, a creditor with a security interest in collateral that was not perfected at the time the bankruptcy petition was filed remains an unsecured creditor in the case.

The automatic stay prohibits action (1) against the debtor, (2) against the debtor's property, and (3) against the property of the estate. The stay continues in effect with regard to property of the estate as long as the property remains property of the estate, and this property is protected even as to postpetition creditors. This appears to be one of the main reasons there is a distinction between property of the estate and property of the debtor. The automatic stay continues in effect with respect to actions against the debtor and actions against the debtor's property until the debtor receives a discharge, or until the case is dismissed or closed. In the event the debtor receives a discharge, the discharge replaces the automatic stay as a permanent injunction.

The Bankruptcy Code provides for sanctions against parties violating the automatic stay. Many jurisdictions have held that the bankruptcy court has a general civil contempt power to enforce the automatic stay. In addition, the Code specifically provides that if an individual debtor is injured by "willful" violation of the stay, the bankruptcy court must award actual damages, costs, and attorney's fees to the debtor, and the court may award punitive damages under appropriate circumstances. The term "willful" essentially means that the party intended to commit the subject act. It does not mean malicious or felonious intent.

However, in a chapter 11 case, there is no co-debtor stay. Consequently, the automatic stay does not prohibit a creditor from pursuing a co-maker or a guarantor on a loan. Furthermore, it does not prohibit a creditor from seeking a remedy against an officer or a principal of a corporation when the corporation is the debtor. Nor does it prohibit a creditor from seeking redress from a partner where the debtor is the partnership.

The automatic stay may be lifted as to a specific property for "cause," shown by the plaintiff creditor, or because of a lack of "adequate protection" of the creditor's interest in the property. The following are some of the factors that are considered by the court in hearing a motion for relief from the stay:

1. Whether there is an equity cushion in the specific property
2. Whether there is cash flow to pay operating expenses
3. Whether there is a reasonable likelihood of a successful reorganization within a reasonable time

In a chapter 11 case, the lack of equity alone is often an insufficient reason to lift the automatic stay where the collateral is necessary for the successful reorganization of the debtor and where there is a reasonable likelihood of a successful reorganization within a reasonable time.

Petition, Statement of Affairs. Once the petition for relief is filed, the Code imposes certain obligations upon the debtor. Within 15 days of the date of filing, the debtor must file a statement of affairs relating to the history and financial affairs of the debtor, along with certain other schedules and documents, including a list of creditors and a list of assets of the debtor.

United States Trustee. The U.S. Trustee has certain supervisory powers in a chapter 11 case. Within 30 days of the date of filing, the debtor must submit to the U.S. Trustee (1) a physical inventory of the debtor's property, indicating the itemized values at cost, (2) a monthly report indicating the first month's income and expenses of the debtor, and (3) a business planning statement indicating how the debtor's affairs deteriorated so as to require the filing of a bankruptcy, and setting out the debtor's expectations regarding recovery or liquidation. The debtor is also required within that first 30-day period to file tax returns for all prepetition tax claims.

Executory Contracts. Within 60 days of the date of filing, the debtor must assume or reject every lease in which the debtor is a tenant of nonresidential real property. In most jurisdictions, this means that the debtor must file a motion to assume such lease or executory contract. Some jurisdictions, however, appear to require that an order authorizing the assumption of a lease be entered within the 60-day period.

In addition, sometime prior to the confirmation of a plan, the debtor must reject or assume all executory contracts and unexpired leases in the chapter 11 case. The right to reject permits a debtor to terminate contracts and leases having burdensome obligations. The rejection, however, constitutes a breach of contract. In determining the issues relating to the approval of an assumption or a rejection of contracts, the courts tend to uphold the debtor's "business judgment." If an executory contract is not assumed within the required time, the contract is deemed rejected.

A rejection claim becomes a prepetition claim. Consequently, burdensome contracts that would otherwise have to be performed after confirmation are converted into prepetition monetary claims that gain no priority over other prebankruptcy creditors.

With respect to personal property leases and residential leases, the debtor may assume or reject the contract at any time until confirmation of a plan, unless the court shortens the time.

Debtor in Possession.   Under the Code, a debtor has strong weapons to employ against creditors and other parties during the pendency of the case. In addition, a chapter 11 debtor is a debtor in possession and as such is given the operating powers of a trustee. Such operating powers cannot be terminated by the Court unless requested by a party in interest and then only after notice and hearing. Such requests are not granted frequently. The Bankruptcy Code encourages operation of the business by the debtor in possession.

The debtor in possession has the power (1) to use, sell, and lease property of the estate, (2) to borrow money postpetition, and (3) to assume or reject executory contracts as discussed above.

Sale of Property.   The debtor may not use, sell, or lease property of the estate without notice and a hearing. Estate property cannot be sold without court approval. A sale of a major asset cannot be ordered unless there is a good business reason other than creditor committee insistence on the sale. The decision to retain or to dispose of a major asset may shape the ultimate reorganization of the debtor.

Statutory authority provides a means for the debtor to sell property free and clear of any interest in the property, including interests in the nature of a lien as well as interests in the nature of co-ownership. Certain requirements must, however, be met. If the value of the lien or interest is more than the sales price, a sale is not permitted unless certain tests are met. Such a test would be whether the holder of the interest could be compelled to accept a money satisfaction of such interest in a legal or equitable proceeding. For example, some state court dockets may be so bogged down that it would take years to dissolve a partnership and sell partnership property for the payment of debts. An individual debtor, however, may be able to sell such co-owned property within months in a bankruptcy case and use the debtor's share to pay creditors. Some courts have held that the "test" would be met if the holder could be subjected to a "cramdown"; other courts reject the foregoing position.

Cash Collateral. The debtor's use of cash collateral is prohibited without the consent of those having an interest in the cash collateral or an affirmative authorization by order of a bankruptcy court. Without the foregoing, the use of cash collateral is a conversion. If the debtor uses cash collateral without court authorization, some courts grant a replacement lien to the injured party on other property of the debtor, or, particularly in the absence of unencumbered property, courts grant an administrative expense priority. Periodic cash payments may constitute adequate protection if the value of the collateral is not declining and is not likely to decline further.

The power to obtain postpetition financing in a chapter 11 case is crucial to the success of many chapter 11 reorganizations. Obtaining postpetition credit not in the ordinary course of business, however, requires court approval. A court order setting out the parameters of such postpetition financing is generally required. In such situations, super priority liens are often granted. The collateral securing a priority loan is not subjected to payment of chapter 11 expenses unless explicitly so provided in the court order. Often, the postpetition financing can be secured by the original first priority lien documents in cases where the relevant contract contains a future advance clause.

Avoiding Powers. The debtor also has what are called "avoiding powers." The debtor may "avoid" preferences and fraudulent conveyances. The debtor exercising avoiding powers under the Code, particularly the strong-arm powers, must do so, in compliance with the Bankruptcy Rules, by adversary proceedings to avoid liens, not by a provision in the plan of reorganization eliminating liens. If a debtor does not exercise those powers, an official committee of creditors may have standing to do so. The marshaling of assets is another tool available in a chapter 11 case. A debtor can marshal assets for the benefit of the estate, that is, require a creditor to foreclose outside collateral that is not property of the estate.

Committees. Important players in a chapter 11 case are committees of creditors and committees of equity security holders. A committee representing unsecured creditors may be appointed. It is usually comprised of the holders of the seven largest unsecured claims. A U.S. Trustee appoints such committees in virtually all districts. In unusual cases, additional committees may be formed and its members appointed by the U.S. Trustee or by the court. Equity committees (shareholders and bondholders) are generally appointed in large chapter 11 cases. Likewise, such committee is usually comprised of the holders of the seven largest equity interests. If a debtor does not exercise its powers, an official committee of creditors may have standing to do so.

Committees play a major role in negotiating the terms of the plan of reorganization with the debtor, and they take an active part in litigating controversies.

Dismissal, Conversion.   A chapter 11 case can be dismissed or converted to a chapter 7 case. The grounds for a dismissal or a conversion are generally the same. The nine grounds specifically set out in the Code are not inclusive. Lack of good faith is grounds for dismissal, but it is not specifically enumerated in the relevant Code section. The test for selecting whether a conversion or a dismissal is appropriate is "whichever is in the best interest of the creditors and the estate."

Dismissal is warranted if restoration of control to the debtor will not harm creditors. Conversion is warranted if court control and chapter 7 Trustee control of property of the estate is desirable. If dismissed, foreclosure can proceed because the estate is terminated; but if converted, the estate continues until a discharge is granted or the case is closed.

After notice and a hearing or on request of a party in interest, the court may convert to a chapter 7 or dismiss for cause. Continuing financial losses by the debtor would be included within cause. Courts are divided as to whether they may convert or dismiss a case on their own impetus when no party in interest requests such action.

Conversion or dismissal, however, is an extreme step that courts exercise only when the court is convinced that no other avenue remains. The moving party has the burden of proving there is a significant risk to creditors with no reasonable possibility of a plan being confirmed.

Some of the grounds for conversion or dismissal are as follows:

1. Continuing loss of diminution of the estate and absence of a reasonable likelihood of rehabilitation
2. Inability to effectuate a plan
3. Unreasonable delay by the debtor that is prejudicial to the creditors
4. Failure to propose a plan within any time fixed by the court
5. Denial of confirmation of every plan proposed and denial of a request made for additional time for filing another plan or a modification of a plan
6. Inability to effectuate consummation of a confirmed plan
7. Material default by the debtor with respect to a confirmed plan
8. Termination of a plan by reason of the occurrence of a condition specified in the plan
9. Lack of good faith in proposing a plan

Exceptions to Discharge.   The Code provision regarding exceptions to discharge applies in a chapter 11 case. A creditor that wishes to have its debt excluded from the discharge granted to the debtor has the burden of proving, by clear and convincing evidence, all of the elements relating to the particular grounds for excluding the debt from discharge.

Some of the obligations for which a debtor will not receive a discharge, providing the elements of the cause of action are established, are as follows:

1. A debt for money, property, or personal services, or the renewal of same which arose as a result of fraud or a false representation (if the false statement relates to the debtor's financial condition, said statement must be in writing to be nondischargeable)
2. The willful and malicious injury to property of another (this includes "conversion" of property)
3. Defalcation while acting in a fiduciary capacity (this requires an express, preexisting contract that creates a fiduciary relationship)
4. Alimony and child support
5. A debt resulting from a drunk-driving accident

The effect of a dismissal is that everything is returned to the status quo as though the bankruptcy case had never been filed. A dismissal does not prohibit a subsequent filing or a future discharge unless the order of dismissal specifically prohibits the same.

Confirmation Process

The Plan. As noted elsewhere herein, creditors play a larger role in chapter 11 than in chapter 7 and chapter 13 cases. A chapter 11 case is structured so as to promote a negotiated reorganization. This is evidenced in the Code sections governing the plan of reorganization. The proponent of a plan, within certain limits, is free to propose any method of treating the claims of creditors and the interests of equity security holders.

During the first 120 days after the date the petition is filed, the debtor has the exclusive right to file a plan ("exclusivity period"). A plan can be, but rarely is, filed with the petition. If the debtor has not filed a plan within the exclusivity period or if the debtor's plan has not been accepted within the 180-day period set out by the Code, a trustee, any committee, any creditor, any shareholder, or an indenture trustee may file a plan. If a plan is filed by someone other than the debtor and if the debtor's management is an obstacle, the other party (usually the unsecured creditors' committee) may prosecute and obtain confirmation without the assent of the debtor.

A chapter 11 plan may include certain optional provisions specifically identified in the Code and must contain certain mandatory provisions. The plan must segregate similar claims and designate classes of claims and interests other than administrative claims and tax claims. A plan may place a claim or an interest in a particular class only if such claim or interest is substantially similar to the other claims or interests of that class. Appropriate classification is required so as to treat creditors and security holders in a fair manner and so as to place similar interests together to obtain a representative class vote on the plan.

Claims or interests may be impaired by the plan or left unimpaired. A class of claims is impaired unless (a) the plan leaves the claimant's rights unaltered, (b) the plan cures any default that occurred on the obligation and reinstates the claim, or (c) the plan provides that the holder will receive cash equal to the allowed amount of the claim on the effective date of the plan.

A plan may deaccelerate a prepetition debt that has been accelerated either under a contractual right or under statutory authority. When a plan cures a default and deaccelerates the debt, the Code requires that the plan compensate the creditor "for any damages it incurred as a result of any reasonable reliance by such holder" on the contractual acceleration clause.

A plan may provide for the sale of the entire estate. If all or substantially all of the debtor's assets are going to be sold in a chapter 11 case, some bankruptcy judges require that such a sale must be conducted under the terms of the plan of reorganization rather than during the course of a case before a plan is confirmed. There have been recent changes in the Bankruptcy Rules which at minimum imply that the debtor can sell substantially all assets, pursuant to the appropriate motion, notice, and hearing, prior to the confirmation of a plan.

A plan may also provide for the assumption or rejection of executory contracts. However, waiting until the date of the confirmation hearing to assume contracts may risk forfeiting interest in executory contracts. See also the discussion above relating to assumption or rejection of contracts.

Although the proponent of a plan has great latitude in drafting the terms of a plan, the Code nevertheless sets out certain mandatory requirements for confirmation. The most notable of the mandatory provisions are:

1. The plan must segregate similar claims and designate classes of claims and interests other than administrative claims and tax claims.
2. The plan must specify which classes of claims are not impaired under the plan.
3. Unless a claim or interest holder agrees to different treatment, all members of a class must be treated equally.
4. The plan must be proposed in "good faith" and not by any means forbidden by law.
5. The plan must set out the means of carrying out the terms of the plan (e.g., sale of property, future income, substitute liens, influx of additional capital).
6. The plan must provide for the payment of all administrative expenses in cash in full at confirmation, unless the holder of the administrative claim agrees otherwise (includes fees for attorneys and others who deal with the debtor).

In classifying secured claims, generally every creditor must be in a separate class. Where secured creditors have different collateral, the nature of their claims will be so dissimilar as to require a separate classification. Ordinarily, secured creditors with liens in different properties may not be classified together because their legal rights are not substantially similar. The only possible exception to this rule is where the secured creditors have collateral that is in the same location, of the same age, and of equal value. If secured creditors have the same collateral but have different priorities against that collateral, the creditors' rights are different enough to require separate classification.

Courts have struggled with the issue of whether similar claims must be included within a single class. Of course, the issue most often arises in the classification of unsecured claims. As a general rule, the classification in a plan should not do substantial violence to any claimant's interest. The plan should not arbitrarily classify or discriminate against creditors. Being a court of equity, a bankruptcy court can permit discrimination when the facts of the case justify it. Courts frequently, for example, allow trade creditors to be put in a separate classification and treated better than other general unsecured creditors. The justification for that distinction is that continued transactions with trade creditors are necessary for the continued health of the debtor's business and may be necessary for the debtor's successful reorganization.

A significant line of cases permits the separate classification of similar claims if the separate classification is reasonable. A separate classification for co-maker debts is frequently allowed. Also, for administrative convenience, the Code expressly provides for a separate class of claims that are less than a specified dollar amount. Full payment in cash of small claims is common practice in reorganization cases.

The plan must specify classes of claims that are not impaired. If a class is impaired, the plan must specify how the impaired class is to be treated.

Unless a claim or interest holder agrees to less favorable treatment, all members of the same class must be treated equally.

The plan must state and set out the means for implementing the plan, including (a) the debtor's retention of all or part of the estate, (b) the sale of all or part of the property either free from or subject to all liens, or (c) the merger or consolidation of the debtor with other entities.

Disclosure Statement and Voting. Again, the premise underlying a chapter 11 case is that reorganization is best achieved through consensual workouts negotiated within the Code's framework. The essence of consensual reorganization is information. Only if adequate information is available will interested parties be able to make informed judgments as to the merits of a reorganization plan.

Adequate information as defined by the Code must be provided in a disclosure statement to all eligible voters (i.e., creditors and shareholders) to enable them to evaluate the proposed plan and make a reasonably informed business judgment. A court-approved disclosure statement is essential to the confirmation process. If a chapter 11 plan intends to bring about a change in the rights of particular creditors or shareholders, as it generally does, the disclosure statement must clearly put creditors and equity holders on notice that by voting for the plan, their rights will be altered. The hearing on the disclosure statement may be extensive. It frequently follows the filing of detailed written objections to the disclosure statement by the U.S. Trustee or by creditors.

Acceptances or rejections of a chapter 11 plan may not be solicited after the commencement of a case until a court-approved disclosure statement has been distributed to each holder of a claim or an interest. There may be concurrent solicitation with respect to two proposed plans.

The court, after notice and hearing, will approve a disclosure statement only if it contains "adequate information." "Adequate information" is determined on a case-by-case basis depending on the nature and sophistication of the creditors and interest holders in the particular case and on the nature and history of the debtor. It is that information which may practicably be disclosed and which is needed by a reasonable businessman with characteristics similar to the claim holders in the case. The bankruptcy court has great flexibility in making a determination as to the information in the disclosure statement.

A leading case relating to disclosure statements set out nineteen items of information that should be considered in order to adequately inform those entitled to vote about the proposed plan. Those items are

1. Discussion of the events leading to the filing of the bankruptcy petition
2. A description of the available assets and their value
3. A discussion of the anticipated future of the debtor
4. A disclosure of the source of information published in the statement
5. A disclaimer statement as to the validity of the information
6. A description of the present condition of the debtor
7. A summary of the scheduled claims
8. An estimate of the probable return to creditors in a chapter 7 liquidation
9. A description of the accounting method used to produce the financial information
10. A list of the future officers, directors, and insiders
11. A copy of the chapter 11 plan or a summary of the plan
12. An estimate of the administrative expenses to be incurred by the estate
13. A projection of the collectibility of accounts receivable
14. General financial information and data
15. Information relevant to the risks posed to creditors under the plan
16. An estimate of the likely recovery of property as a result of voidable transfers
17. Disclosure of litigation likely to arise in a nonbankruptcy contest

18. An estimate of the debtor's tax attributes
19. A discussion of the relationship of the debtor to any affiliates

Not all of the foregoing items of information are required in every case. In smaller cases, less information might be required, and in larger cases, more information might be required. The court, assisted by the comments of the U.S. Trustee, determines what information is required based on the size of the case and on the "hypothetical investor" whose relationship to the debtor is typical of the creditors in the particular case.

The disclosure statement must be submitted for court review on notice and hearing. A copy of the disclosure statement must be served on the U.S. Trustee for said Trustee's comments or objections. The hearing on the disclosure statement will be scheduled on 25 days notice after the statement and plan are filed with the court. Objections to the disclosure statement must be filed and served on the debtor, the Trustee, and all committees prior to the hearing or prior to a date set by the court. Untimely objections will be without effect.

Following court approval of the disclosure statement, the statement, with the plan or summary of the plan, and a notice of the hearing on confirmation of the plan must be mailed to all claim holders and equity interest holders. All persons entitled to vote on the plan must also be provided with a ballot for voting and a notice of the voting deadline. The mailing is ordinarily the responsibility of the proponent of the plan.

The Code designates the majority required for acceptance of the plan. The required vote for acceptance is two-thirds of the dollar amount, one-half of the number of the allowed claims that vote yes or no, and two-thirds of the shares that vote.

Confirmation Hearing. One of the requirements for confirmation of a plan is that each class of claims (creditors) and each class of equity interests (shareholders) must either affirmatively accept the plan or each such class must not be impaired by the plan.

As noted above, if a holder of either a claim or an equity interest has its rights altered (including extending the time of payment) or does not receive a full cash payment on the effective date of the plan, such claim or interest is impaired.

Assuming that the plan meets the other requirements discussed herein, a plan can be confirmed in only two ways. The first way is by obtaining a vote approving the plan by every impaired class. The second way of obtaining confirmation of a plan is referred to as the "cramdown." The cramdown method is used when one or more impaired classes vote against the plan.

The plan can be crammed down on an impaired class that does not accept the plan "on the request of the proponent of the plan." Neither the Bankruptcy Code nor the Bankruptcy Rules set out the manner in which such a request is to be made. Consequently, the request for a cramdown is usually made in the disclosure statement, in the plan, at the confirmation hearing, or in a combination of the foregoing. In any event, the request must be made no later than at the confirmation hearing.

Under the cramdown, a plan may be confirmed (1) if the plan does not discriminate unfairly against the dissenting class, and (2) if the plan is "fair and equitable" with respect to the dissenting class.

The discrimination issue arises generally with respect to the classification of unsecured claims, including deficiency claims. The discrimination test applies to claims having the same legal rights against the debtor, such as unsecured senior debt, unsecured junior debt, and unsecured trade debt. Generally, a plan does not unfairly discriminate among equal classes if the plan allocates value to the dissenting class in a manner consistent with the treatment afforded to other classes with similar legal claims. The foregoing discussion regarding classification of claims is also relevant here.

The "fair and equitable" test is both a general test and a specific test. As to the general test, the courts look at the entire plan in the context of the circumstances of the particular case before it and make a determination as to overall fairness. In addition, the code sets out certain specific requirements for the fair and equitable test based on whether the class comprises secured claims, unsecured claims, or equity interests.

With respect to secured claims, the fair and equitable provision of the Code requires that the holder of the claim (1) retain its lien and receive deferred payments to the extent of the allowed amount of the claim, or (2) receive the "indubitable equivalent" of the claim. The deferred payment provision requires payment in cash and not in any other kind of property. Generally, the allowed amount of a secured claim includes a certain market rate of interest over the term of the deferred payments.

The term "indubitable equivalent" is not defined in the Code. The bankruptcy courts uniformly agree that the return of the original collateral to the secured creditor provides the indubitable equivalent to said creditor. Beyond that, courts have varied opinions as to what constitutes indubitable equivalent. In many cases, the indubitable equivalent proposed by the plan is either a cash payment equal to the value of the claim or a lien in substitute collateral with value equal to the original collateral or the amount of the claim, whichever is less.

With respect to unsecured claims, the fair and equitable provision of the Code requires that (1) the holder receive "property" equal to the present value of the claim or that (2) a junior class receive or retain no property. In this case, the holder may be given "property" other than cash. Therefore, it would be possible, under some circumstances, to distribute stock or bonds to the unsecured creditors. If there are no junior classes, the second alternative is met. However, a class of equity interest holders is a junior class. Consequently, unsecured creditors must be paid their claims before any distribution can be made to equity interest holders. Furthermore, a distribution to equity interest holders of stock of no value is prohibited because the purpose of the fair and equitable test (sometimes called the absolute priority rule) is to preserve for creditors who are not being paid in full the potential future appreciation or profits of the debtor.

With respect to classes of equity interest holders, the fair and equitable provision of the Code requires that (1) the holders receive their liquidation preference or their redemption rights or that (2) a junior class receive or retain no property. An example of a plan that meets this test would be one that provides for a distribution to holders of preferred stock and cancels the common stock of the debtor.

The hearing on confirmation is an evidentiary hearing. However, if there is no objection to confirmation, the court may, without receiving evidence, find that the plan has been proposed "in good faith and not by any means forbidden by law." As to every other requirement for confirmation, the court must receive evidence as a basis for making its findings of fact and granting confirmation. At a confirmation hearing, the bankruptcy judge may rely upon prior testimony during the case.

Even absent an objection, the court has a duty to examine the plan to determine whether it conforms to the requirements of the Code (as set forth above). The court's decision at the confirmation hearing generally falls into one of the following categories: (1) granting confirmation of the plan, (2) affording the debtor an opportunity to modify the plan within a certain time limit, or (3) denying confirmation of the plan.

If the court confirms the plan, the order of confirmation constitutes a discharge of all the debts provided for in the plan and the order becomes the "new agreement" among the parties. If the court denies the plan, the case is dismissed and the parties are in the same position as if the chapter 11 case had never been filed.

The debtor must file a brief final report six months after the confirmation hearing, and the case is thereafter closed.

Appendix 1: Chronology of Chapter 11 Bankruptcy (prepared by Sumner Levine)

The usual sequence of events involved in chapter 11 is listed below. Because of different situations and complexities, the sequence may be somewhat different in a particular situation.

1. A bankruptcy petition is filed, either voluntarily or involuntarily, in a U.S. bankruptcy court.
2. The automatic stay becomes effective, prohibiting all collection action against the debtor. The debtor continues to run the business.
3. The clerk of the court notifies creditors of the bankruptcy.
4. A schedule of assets and liabilities is filed by the debtor.
5. A U.S. Trustee Office holds the first meeting of creditors.

6. Creditors file claims. All proof of claims must be filed before the bar date.
7. Creditor committees, and possible stockholder committees, hold a first meeting conducted by the U.S. Trustee.
8. Claims are allowed or disallowed by the court.
9. A disclosure statement is filed providing the background and summary of the reorganization plan.
10. A plan of reorganization is filed by the debtor during the first 120 days. Thereafter, any creditor may file a plan, although an extension period is sometimes granted the debtor.
11. The court approves or rejects the disclosure statement.
12. Creditors and stockholders vote on the plan of reorganization.
13. Court confirms or denies the reorganization plan.
14. Court closes the case.

Appendix 2: Outline of the Reorganization Plan (prepared by Sumner Levine)

The Bankruptcy Code specifies the contents of the reorganization plan that must be sent to all creditors. The Code requires that the following information be included:

1. Designate classes of claims. (Claims may be placed in a class if they are substantially similar to other claims in the class.)
2. State whether a claim or class is impaired (i.e., will not receive full payment) or unimpaired.
3. Provide for equal treatment for all claims of the same class. (A listing of claims priority is given in Chapter 1 of this book.)
4. Provide the means for plan implementation, such as given in Section 1123(a) of the Code quoted below:

   (a) (5) (A) retention by the debtor of all or any part of the property of the estate;

       (B) transfer of all or any part of the property of the estate to one or more entities, whether organized before or after the confirmation of such plan;

       (C) merger or consolidation of the debtor with one or more persons;

       (D) sale of all or any part of the property of the estate, either subject to or free of any lien, or the distribution of all or any part of the property of the estate among those having an interest in such property of the estate;

       (E) satisfaction or modification of any lien;

       (F) cancellation or modification of any indenture or similar instrument;

       (G) curing or waiving of any default;

      (H) extension of a maturity date or a change in an interest rate or other term of outstanding securities;

      (I) amendment of the debtor's charter; or

      (J) issuance of securities of the debtor, or of any entity referred to in subparagraph (B) or (C) of this paragraph, for cash, for property, for existing securities, or in exchange for claims or interests, or for any other appropriate purpose;

  (6) provide for the inclusion in the charter of the debtor, if the debtor is a corporation, or of any corporation referred to in paragraph (5)(B) or (5)(C) of this subsection, of a provision prohibiting the issuance of nonvoting equity securities, and providing, as to the several classes of securities possessing voting power, an appropriate distribution of such power among such classes, including, in the case of any class of equity securities having a preference over another class of equity securities with respect to dividends, adequate provisions for the election of directors representing such preferred class in the event of default in the payment of such dividends; and

  (7) contain only provisions that are consistent with the interests of creditors and equity security holders and with public policy with respect to the manner of selection of any officer, director, or trustee under the plan and any successor to such officer, director, or trustee.

(b) Subject to subsection (a) of this section a plan may—

  (1) impair or leave unimpaired any class of claims, secured or unsecured, or of interests;

  (2) subject to section 365 of this title, provide for the assumption, rejection, or assignment of any executory contract or unexpired lease of the debtor not previously rejected under such section;

  (3) provide for—

      (A) the settlement or adjustment of any claim or interest belonging to the debtor or to the estate; or

      (B) the retention and enforcement by the debtor, by the trustee, or by a representative of the estate appointed for such purpose, of any such claim or interest;

  (4) provide for the sale of all or substantially all of the property of the estate, and the distribution of the proceeds of such sale among holders of claims or interests; and

  (5) include any other appropriate provision not inconsistent with the applicable provisions of this title.

CHAPTER
13

Investing in Publicly Traded Debt Securities during Restructurings and Chapter 11 Reorganizations: A Comparison of Opportunities

Thomas Moers Mayer
Robinson Silverman Pearce
Aronsohn & Berman

The Game

The decade now ending has witnessed an explosion in bankruptcy and debt restructurings. More businesses have sought to reorganize in and out of bankruptcy court than in any decade since the Great Depression. The publicly traded debt and equity securities of such businesses have traditionally dropped to distress levels—in part because certain investors are legally prohibited (by "prudent man" statutes) or personally unwilling to invest in troubled companies. However, many of these businesses have successfully reorganized—in or out of court—and the securities' prices have rebounded.

Sometimes a business's turnaround is due to changes in its industry or in the general economy. Sometimes the turnaround is due to improved management. Often, however, a turnaround is due to advances in reorganization techniques. Advances in out-of-court restructurings probably derive from the successful restructuring of the Chrysler Corporation, since the subsequent workouts of Western Union Corporation, International Harvester, and the first two workouts of Allis Chalmers Corporation

SOURCE: *Investing in Troubled Companies*, Practicing Law Institute, New York, 1990.

were all documented as based on the Chrysler models. Advances in bankruptcy restructurings undoubtedly derive from the enactment in 1978 of the new chapter 11 as a reorganization chapter that kept management in control of the corporation. Compare Section 1104 of the Bankruptcy Code of 1978, 11 U.S.C. § 1104 and cases thereunder, in 5 *Collier on Bankruptcy* ¶ 1104.101[b] (L. King, 15th ed., 1985) with Section 156 of the Bankruptcy Act of 1898, 11 U.S.C. § 556 (1976) (the "Act"), repealed effective Oct. 1, 1979 (displacing management of every chapter X debtor with more than $250,000 in liabilities and installing a trustee). (All citations to the Bankruptcy Code, 11 U.S.C. §§ 101 *et seq.*, are hereinafter abbreviated as "Code § _____.")

If a restructuring can cure a business' insolvency and increase its value, the business' insolvency-depressed securities may be undervalued. A restructuring may also affect the value of debt securities quite apart from its effect on the value of the business through the acceleration of maturities. See H.R. Rep. No. 595, 95th Cong., 1st Sess. 353 (1977) and S. Rep. No. 989, 95th Cong., 2d Sess. 63 (1978), and the cessation of interest. See Code § 502(b)(2). See also Section V.D.I below. Understanding those consequences of a restructuring may help an investor spot undervalued and overvalued securities. Understanding how to block a restructuring out of bankruptcy may offer an investor opportunities for greenmail. Understanding the limitations on greenmail in bankruptcy can keep an investor out of jail.

However, not every restructuring succeeds, not every class of securities benefits from a successful restructuring, and, in some cases, a "successful" restructuring may not benefit *any* security holders. See Section V.D.3 below.

Moreover, an investor who correctly predicts the success of a restructuring and buys the right securities may still lose money by buying too early. Restructurings—especially in chapter 11—take time, and the investor often cannot cash in on its investment until the restructuring is completed.

In each case, the investor must consider at a minimum (a) what kind of restructuring is being sought and what kind of restructuring is required for the debtor in question, (b) how likely the restructuring is to succeed, and (c) when the restructuring is likely to succeed.

In each case the investor may have a choice between investments in secured, senior unsecured and subordinated debt securities. (The investor may also may have an opportunity to purchase claims held by banks, insurance companies, other lenders, trade creditors, or the government.)

Finally, each situation may present different opportunities to the investor. An investor may make a passive investment in the success (or failure) of a restructuring. An investor may make an active investment in the success of the restructuring as a participant in the restructuring, perhaps with a view towards obtaining a controlling interest in the debtor. Last, but not least, an investor may bet on the failure or modification of a restructuring by obtaining enough debt securities in a particular issue to block the restructuring.

This chapter examines various types of restructurings with a view to providing some guidance to those considering an investment in a troubled business.

Restructuring through a Sale of Assets

Sales Prior to Bankruptcy

The Company. Developmental Real Estate Corporation (DREC), a Delaware corporation whose stock is split equally between two shareholders, owns an office building subject to a first mortgage that secures (with recourse) $100 million in 20-year bonds issued in 1983 and due in 2003. In addition to the first mortgage on the office building, the indenture trustee holds as security from each of DREC's shareholders a personal demand note for $50 million. A declining real estate market has depressed DREC's asset values and business to the point where it is insolvent. One of DREC's shareholders wants to sell some of the company's assets—including the office building—to avoid chapter 11 proceedings at all cost. The other wants to file a bankruptcy petition and attempt to ride out the recession.

The bonds bear interest at a rate of 8 percent, which is less than the current market rate for new mortgages on office buildings. In the investor's judgment, the building is worth at least $80 million. (The demand notes are worth little because DREC's shareholders have few assets other than their DREC stock.) The bonds are trading at 50 cents on the dollar because their coupon is low and DREC is insolvent. The indenture requires the holders of 75 percent of the bonds to approve any sale or release of collateral. The bonds are not yet in default, but DREC does not have the cash to make the next interest payment on the bonds.

At $80 million, the office building constitutes 30 percent of DREC's assets. DREC recently hired several contractors to renovate the office building. However, the contractors exceeded the renovation budget and failed to meet contract specifications. They are engaged in a dispute with DREC, and several have filed mechanics' liens (ranking behind the mortgage bonds) to secure claims totaling $5 million.

Passive Investment. The simplest way to profit from a sales restructuring is to buy secured debt for less than the value of the collateral—in this case, at 50 cents given the 80 cents of collateral value. However, even an investment in secured claims that are underpriced relative to their collateral may not yield an acceptable profit if the sale is delayed or canceled—which could happen for several reasons:

Necessary Consents. The bond indenture requires the consent of holders of 75 percent of the bonds before the office building can be sold. Moreover, because the office building constitutes 30 percent of DREC's assets, the sale may require approval by a majority of DREC's shareholders entitled to vote on such a transaction. Del. Gen. Corp. L. § 271(a) (1989). If DREC were a publicly held corporation, the shareholder vote would require a proxy statement under Section 14 of the Securities Exchange Act of 1934, 15 U.S.C. § 78n (1988), which could further delay the sale. As it is, DREC may not be able to obtain shareholder approval because the shares are equally split between a holder who wants to sell and one who does not.

Clean Title. Because of the mechanics' liens filed against the office building, DREC may have difficulty delivering clean title to the purchaser in a timely fashion.

Transfer Taxes. The office building is real estate, and the sales, transfer, or recording taxes applicable to its transfer may reduce the proceeds of sale.

Income Taxes. The federal income tax consequences of a sale of assets may prove to be so great as to deter a troubled company from consummating the sale. Assuming DREC purchased the building recently for more than the sale price, taxes are not likely to be a major concern because the asset to be sold is real estate and depreciation is likely to be small. However, if the asset had been a collection of jet aircraft placed in trust five years ago to secure 10-year equipment trust certificates, the tax basis of the equipment today would probably be low and the capital gains tax substantial. Usually, but not always, a debtor has enough net operating losses (NOLs) to cover the capital gains tax. If the debtor does not have sufficient NOLs, the tax bill may force it to reconsider the sale. The tax position of a debtor in general and its tax basis in property in particular are generally not disclosed to the general public. However, where an asset has been pledged to secure indebtedness, the maturity of the indebtedness (together with reference to the asset's depreciable life under the Internal Revenue Code of 1986) will give some idea of the capital gains tax to be incurred in a sale of property.

Active Investment. As indicated above, the investor values DREC's office building at more than $80 million. However, there is no guarantee that the property will be sold for that price. One of the risks the passive investor takes is the possibility that an active investor will purchase the bonds with a view to controlling the disposition of the property in order to purchase the property at a low price—or for a consideration other than cash.

Prior to the 1934 adoption of Act § 77B—the first bankruptcy reorganization statute—debtors whose assets were subject to blanket mortgage liens often reorganized through the mechanism of foreclosure. This was one of the few nonbankruptcy reorganization techniques that bound nonaccepting creditors, and it worked as follows: The holders of a majority in amount of securities under a trust indenture were often authorized by the indenture to direct the indenture trustee in its exercise of remedies, including foreclosure. Those holders could direct the indenture trustee to foreclose on the trust estate and to accept cash or other property at the foreclosure sale from a new corporation previously formed to buy the business. The other property could even include the acquiring corporation's newly issued debt or equity securities, although that might present problems today under the securities laws. See Section 3(a)(9) of the Securities Act of 1933, 15 U.S.C. § 77c(a)(9) (1988). In theory, the minority holders would have no remedy other than to accept their pro rata share.

In practice, the minority holders would sue the indenture trustee, which is why no indenture trustee is likely to go forward with such a plan today without an indemnity from the majority holders.

Selling Property in Chapter 11

The Situation (continued).   DREC files a petition under chapter 11 and announces that it has an agreement to sell its office building for $80 million. The mechanics' lienors object to the sale. So does the Official Committee of Unsecured Creditors, representing approximately $50 million in unsecured debt.

Advantages of Chapter 11

Clearing Title.   As noted above, the mechanics' liens clouded DREC's title outside of bankruptcy. In a chapter 11 case, however, the bankruptcy court can give the purchaser clean title in an expeditious fashion by approving a sale during the case or under a plan of reorganization. See Code §§ 363(f) and 1123(a)(5)(D) and (b)(4). The ability to clear title expeditiously in a bankruptcy sale may make bankruptcy a creditors' remedy preferable to foreclosure. Although Texas allows mortgagees to foreclose in 30 days, foreclosure proceedings are much more protracted in many states. In Wisconsin, foreclosure apparently takes two years. See *In re Madison Hotel Assocs.*, 29 Bankr. 1003, 1008 n.3 (W.D. Wisc. 1983), *aff'd*, 749 F.2d 410 (7th Cir. 1984). In Minnesota, it takes 18 months (including the one-year period of redemption). See *In re Ahlers,* 794 F.2d 388, 398 and n.13 (8th Cir. 1986), *rev'd on other grounds,* 108 S. Ct. 963 (1988). In New York, a contested foreclosure generally takes at least six months. If the debtor will agree to sell the secured creditor's collateral, a bankruptcy sale under Code § 363(f)(5) may provide faster relief to a first lienor than foreclosure in state court against recalcitrant junior lienors.

Unfortunately, the debtor may not be able to sell the office building free and clear of all liens under Code § 363(f)(5). See Section II.B.3.(a), below.

Taxes.   If DREC were to sell the building and distribute its proceeds under a plan of reorganization, the proceeds might be exempt from recording taxes under Code § 1146(c):

> (c) The issuance, transfer, or exchange of a security, or the making or delivery of an instrument of transfer under a plan confirmed under Section 1129 of this title, may not be taxed under any law imposing a stamp tax or similar tax.

Although Code § 1146(c) seems primarily aimed at stock transfer taxes, several courts have held that the statute applies to real estate transfer taxes. See, for example, *In re Jacoby-Bender, Inc.*, 758 F.2d 840 (2d Cir. 1985); *In re Permar Provisions, Inc.*, 79 Bankr. 530 (Bankr. E.D.N.Y. 1987). Section 1146(c) protects both the debtor and the buyer from state real estate transfer taxes. *In re CCA Partnership*, 70 Bankr. 696 (Bankr. D. Del. 1987); *In re Permar Provisions, Inc.*, 79 Bankr. 530, 532 n.3 (Bankr. E.D.N.Y. 1987). Section 1146(c) shelters sales proceeds from real estate transfer taxes even if the property was sold pursuant to a *prepetition contract,* so long as the proceeds were vital to the plan of reorganization. *In re Smoss Enterprises Corp.*, 54 Bankr. 950 (E.D.N.Y. 1985).

An argument can be made that Code § 1146(c) also exempts sales under a plan from gains taxes. See *In re 995 Fifth Avenue Assocs., L.P.*, 116 Bankr. 384 (Bankr. S.D.N.Y. 1990) (§ 1146(c) exempts debtor from New York State Capital Gains Tax). But see *In re Jacoby-Bender*, 40 Bankr. 10, 15 (Bankr. E.D.N.Y. 1984) (§ 1146(e) does not exempt debtor from New York State Capital Gains Tax), *aff'd on other grounds*, 758 F.2d 840 (2d. Cir. 1985).

Attempts to stretch Code § 1146(c) may prove more difficult following the Supreme Court's decision in *California State Board of Equalization v. Sierra Summit, Inc.*, 109 S. Ct. 554 (1989). *Sierra Summit* concerned a long-standing Ninth Circuit rule providing that the constitutional doctrine of intergovernmental tax immunities prohibited a state from imposing a sales tax on a liquidation sale conducted by a bankruptcy receiver. The Supreme Court overturned the rule, holding (1) that a bankruptcy receiver is not an agency of the federal government and therefore is not shielded by the doctrine of intergovernmental tax immunities and (2) that Congress had not clearly legislated an exemption from state tax. *Sierra Summit* nowhere mentions Code § 1146(c), but its tone seems to press for a narrow interpretation of the statute.

Disposition of a Partial Interest. A debtor who has an interest in property as a tenant-in-common, a joint tenant, or a tenant by the entirety may sell the entire property, which is subject to its tenancy free and clear of the interests of the other tenants-in-common under Code § 363(h) if

- The property cannot be partitioned
- The debtor's interest, sold separately, would bring significantly less than the sale of the entire property free and clear of the other tenants' interests
- The benefit to the debtor's estate outweighs the detriment to the other tenants
- The property is not used to produce, transmit, distribute, or sell electrical power or synthetic or natural gas.

Where state law treats partners as joint tenants, a general partner who files a chapter 11 petition may have substantial leverage over other partners because Code § 363(h) may give the filing partner the ability to sell the property over the objections of the others. See *In re William R. Probasco*, 839 F.2d 1352, 1356-57 (9th Cir. 1988). But see *In re Normandin*, 106 Bankr. 14 (Bankr. D. Mass. 1989) (debtor cannot use § 363(h) to sell tenancy-in-partnership interest in property).

Problems with Bankruptcy Sales

Liens. Outside of bankruptcy, DREC could sell collateral free and clear of liens through a foreclosure sale, although that may take some time if the junior lienors oppose the foreclosure.

In a bankruptcy reorganization, the issue is more problematic. Because the price paid for the property is not sufficient to discharge the bonds and the mechanics' lien claims, DREC may not be able to sell the property free and clear of all liens.

Code § 363(f)(5) allows sales free and clear of "any interest in property of any entity other than the estate" if "such entity could be compelled, in a legal or equitable proceeding, to accept a money satisfaction of such interest." That would seem to cover most lienholders and would certainly include second mortgagees or DREC's mechanics' lienors. However, Code § 363(f)(3) specifically provides that collateral may be sold free and clear of all liens only if the price of the collateral is greater than the aggregate value of all liens on such property.

Those courts that have considered subsections (f)(3) and (f)(5) have held that the specific language of the former controls the latter, and therefore the debtor cannot, under Section 363(f), sell collateral where its price is less than the aggregate value of all liens on the property. See *In re Rouse*, 53 Bankr. 156, 157–58 (Bankr. W.D. Mo. 1985) (Stewart, B.J.); *In re Beker Indus. Corp.*, 64 Bankr. 900, 907–08 (Bankr. S.D.N.Y. 1986), *rev'd on other grounds*, 89 Bankr. 336 (S.D.N.Y. 1988); *In re Crutcher Resources Corp.*, 72 Bankr. 628 (Bankr. N.D. Texas 1987). The rule may be bent in an emergency, where the value of the property is dropping too fast to be sold pursuant to a plan. See *In re Rausch Mfg. Co., Inc.*, 59 Bankr. 501 (Bankr. D. Minn. 1985).

Property subject to multiple liens can clearly be sold free and clear of all liens pursuant to a plan of reorganization. Code §§ 1123(a)(5)(D) and (b)(4). However, confirming a plan takes time. See below, "Waiting for the plan."

Problems with Sales of Substantial Assets

Outside of chapter 11, DREC would have needed the consent of bondholders holding 75 percent of the bonds. DREC also might have needed shareholder approval for its sale of the office building. See Section II.A.2(a). By contrast, neither shareholder nor bondholder approval is required under Code § 363(b), which appears to authorize DREC to sell all or a substantial part of its assets after notice and a hearing. However, reduction of the estate to cash through the sale of its assets can constitute a liquidating plan of reorganization. Where the sale involves the distribution of non-cash proceeds to creditors as a compromise of their claims, the Fifth Circuit has held that the sale can be done only through a plan after circulation of a disclosure statement and a vote by creditors and shareholders: the bankruptcy equivalent of a meeting of shareholders. *In re Braniff Airways, Inc.*, 700 F.2d 935 (5th Cir. 1983).

Other courts have indicated that a debtor may sell a substantial part of its assets under § 363 without going through a plan as long as "sound business purpose dictates such action." *Stephens Industries, Inc. v. McClung*, 789 F.2d 386, 390 (6th Cir. 1986). See also *In re Lionel Corp.*, 755 F.2d 1063, 1070 (2d Cir. 1983) ("articulated business justification" is necessary). Sales of substantially all of the debtor's assets, without a plan or a vote by parties in interest, were also permitted under chapters X and XI of the Bankruptcy Act of 1898 if the assets' value was declining rapidly or was threatened by some emergency. See *In re Solar Mfg. Corp.*, 176 F.2d 493 (3rd Cir. 1949); *In re Pure Penn Petroleum Co.*, 188 F.2d 851 (2d Cir. 1951).

Waiting for the Plan.   Code § 1123(a)(5)(d) clearly indicates that DREC can sell all or any part of its property free and clear of all liens pursuant to a plan. If the court will not allow DREC to sell its office building prior to a plan, DREC will have to sell the building under the plan. However, that takes time. First, a plan and a disclosure statement must be drafted. Code § 1121(b) suggests that this can be done within 120 days by giving the debtor the exclusive right to file a plan during the first 120 days of the case. However, few sizable bankruptcies have a plan filed during that time period. Moreover, the debtor must file a disclosure statement with the plan. See Bankruptcy Rule 3016(c). The hearing on the disclosure statement is then held on 25 days notice. The Code and the Bankruptcy Rules leave to judicial discretion the amount of time granted for voting on a plan, but it is rarely less than 30 days. By extending the exclusivity period for 60 days after the debtor files its plan, Code § 1121(c)(3) suggests that 60 days is sufficient for the debtor to obtain approval of the disclosure statement and to solicit a vote on the plan. Finally, after the vote on the plan, the hearing on confirmation is held on 25 days notice.

Thus, if DREC had a plan and disclosure statement ready to file together with its chapter 11 petition, it would still take a minimum of 80 days to confirm a plan. If the debtor filed a plan and disclosure statement at the end of its 120-day exclusive period under Code § 1121(b), and finished soliciting votes on the plan 60 days later as contemplated by Code § 1121(c)(3), the plan could be confirmed no earlier than 205 days into the case.

Flies and Honey.   It is standard practice for debtors like DREC to sell their property first and distribute proceeds of the sale later. The property is sold free and clear of liens, and the liens on the property are transferred to the proceeds. See Code § 363(e). The proceeds are often distributed later after a subsequent hearing. Unfortunately for DREC's bondholders, the creation of a pot of proceeds and notice of its distribution will attract competing claimants like honey attracts flies. To the extent these claimants have prior liens, they are of course entitled to payment from the proceeds. However, the existence of a pot of money will lead claimants without liens to assert ingenious theories as to why they should be paid from the proceeds of the bondholders' collateral.

Certain claimants may be able to argue that their claim results from an extension of credit, provision of labor, or supply of materials that "benefited the bondholders." Those creditors may have a bona fide claim to be paid out of the proceeds pursuant to Code §§ 506(c) and 552(b). That issue is discussed below under Chapter 11 Reorganizations—Deductions for Expenses. Other claimants may surface with less meritorious claims, based on various theories of lender liability or unfair dealing. Unlikely as these claims may be when dealing with DREC's public bondholders, they may nevertheless delay the bondholders' receipt of the proceeds of their collateral.

The liquidation of W. T. Grant Co. provides one object lesson in the delays posed by the creation of a pot of money. In Grant, the secured bank creditors and the debtor reached a "global settlement" on July 20, 1978 that allowed an interim payment to the banks, but left behind a fund of $95,378,373 to be disputed by the debtor's subordinated debentureholders and the banks, whose claims constituted "senior indebtedness" under the debenture indenture. On January 26, 1983—four and a half years later—the second circuit approved the last of a series of settlements and compromises that permitted distribution of the fund, allocating less than one-fifth to the debentureholders. See *In re W. T. Grant Co.*, 699 F.2d 599 (2d Cir. 1983) (Friendly, J.).

Investing in Compositions

The Company

General American Glass (GAG) makes bottles and containers. Half of its business concerns the manufacture of standard containers for sale to wholesalers. The other half involves making special containers for particular customers, many of whom pay large sums in advance to fund GAG's creation of special molds for their product. GAG owes $10 million in unsecured debt to its suppliers and customers in addition to $5 million in bank debt that is fully secured by GAG's current assets. In addition, GAG owes $5 million (principal amount) under industrial development revenue bonds (IRBs), which GAG issued to finance its general bottling plant. Management holds 100 percent of GAG's stock.

In the last six months GAG's wholesale market has virtually disappeared because of a sudden switch by many dairies in GAG's area to nonglass containers. The general bottling plant is idle and virtually worthless. As a result, GAG is insolvent. With its bank credit fully drawn, GAG's accounts payable are now averaging more than 90 days in an industry where 30 days is customary. GAG's trade creditors are pushing for repayment. The IRBs have been in default for six months.

The Composition

GAG calls a meeting of its major trade creditors and major IRB holders and proposes to cash out all unsecured creditors and its IRBs at 50 cents on the dollar. The debtor's bank is prepared to lend the money necessary for the composition if 85 percent of the IRBs and trade debt accept. Management warns the trade creditors and IRB holders that GAG may not survive a chapter 11 filing.

Possible Investments

Passive Investment. GAG's offer constitutes a "composition of creditors." Typically, a composition constitutes an offer to pay creditors at less than 100 cents on the dollar. The offer becomes effective when creditors holding a minimum percentage of claims accept payment at a discount. The debtor may have accumulated the necessary cash, or it may raise the necessary cash by persuading new lenders or equity investors that its value more than justifies the new loan or investment once the accepting creditors' claims are discharged at the discount specified in the offer. The new lenders or investors condition their loan or investment on the acceptance of the offer. (The debtor can also issue notes instead of paying cash, but the Securities Act might apply to such a transaction—one reason why almost all compositions involving notes either predate 1933 or are done as exchange offers, discussed below.)

If the IRBs are for sale at less than 50 cents, an investor can make a passive investment in the success of GAG's composition. However, that investment requires a judgment that GAG's composition will succeed.

Reasons to Profit. GAG's creditors may accept such an offer for several reasons. If the creditors have held their claims against the debtor for a while, they may have written the claims down or off their books. Creditors have accountants who sometimes force writeoffs to reflect accounting rules rather than reality. All creditors (public or private) may have tax reasons to write off claims. GAG's IRBs may be held by regulated creditors such as banks, savings and loan associations, and insurance companies. Sometimes the regulators force writeoffs to reflect regulatory requirements rather than reality. If GAG has publicly held creditors, the management of such creditors may have forced writeoffs to increase reported losses in one fiscal period to make subsequent periods look more profitable by comparison.

If creditors have written their claims down to less than 50 cents, GAG's composition represents an unanticipated recovery and may succeed—

although creditors are likely to try to negotiate a higher price for their claims.

Finally, some claims may be held by creditors who simply cannot allow their debtor to file a chapter 11. Where the debtor is a franchise, its franchisee-creditors may be willing to compromise their claims. (Along similar lines, Chrysler dealers invested in new debt securities issued by the Chrysler Corporation when that company went through its restructuring.) In GAG's case, the trade creditors who have ordered specialized glass containers from GAG have the same stake in keeping GAG in business as the United States Department of Defense had in keeping Lockheed alive.

Risks.   There are certain factors that work against a composition. Compositions bind only those who accept them. They cannot bind those who do not accept. Unfortunately, compositions usually benefit the nonacceptors. If the holders of 85 percent of GAG's trade debt and IRBs accept the composition, the remaining 15 percent are likely to be paid in full. Every composition therefore provides an incentive for creditors not to accept its terms in the hope that other creditors, by accepting, will promote the value of the nonacceptors' claims.

COMMENT: The assent of 99 percent of all trade creditors to an out-of-court restructuring in no way binds the dissenting 1 percent. However, the dissenting 1 percent may not be able to force the company into bankruptcy if so many of their fellow creditors have accepted the restructuring. Under Code § 305(a)(1) a bankruptcy case may be dismissed or suspended if the court determines that

> an arrangement is being worked out by creditors and the debtor out of court, there is no prejudice to the rights of creditors in that arrangement and an involuntary case has been commenced by a few recalcitrant creditors to provide a basis for future threats to extract full payment.

H.R. Rep. No. 595, 95th Cong., 1st Sess. (1977). Section 305(a)(1) is discussed further below in the next section, under "Difficulty in obtaining necessary majorities."

Holdup Investment.   GAG's composition is conditioned upon acceptance by holders of 85 percent of the trade claims and IRBs. It follows that the holders of more than 15 percent of such indebtedness can block the composition. In particular, an investor who purchases more than $2,250,000 of the $5 million in IRBs has a blocking position. The debtor is always free to drop the percentage required for a composition, but any change in the terms of the composition releases those creditors who previously accepted its terms. See *Texas Belting & Mill Supply Co. v. C. R. Daniels, Inc.,* 401 S.W.2d. 157 (Tex. Civ. App. 1966).

An investor who acquires a blocking position at a price above the composition price is essentially playing a game of chicken with the debtor and its fellow creditors that may result in all players losing everything — especially if GAG's management is correct and GAG cannot survive a chapter 11 case. However, absent a peculiar provision of state law, the holder of a blocking position has no fiduciary (or other) duty to its fellow creditors or to the debtor.

However, the holdup investor should not expect to receive a preference — in this context, payments above or in addition to the composition price — in return for acceptance of the composition. A preference constitutes a fraud on the accepting creditors and renders the composition voidable at the election of any accepting creditor other than the recipient of the preference. See *White v. Kuntz*, 107 N.Y. 518, 525 (1887).

Active Investment. An investor can invest in a composition as its "Funder" — that is, by providing the cash needed to consummate the composition in return for a debt or equity investment in the debtor.

Such an investor will enhance the chances of successful restructuring by purchasing claims. In the standard composition, the debtor offers one cash discount to all creditors. The cash discount is presumably set at the margin — that is, it is high enough to attract acceptance from the last creditor needed to reach the required percentage of acceptances (the "Toughest Creditor"). However, there are always creditors who are prepared to accept a lower price. These creditors may have written off more of their claim than the Toughest Creditor — or they may have acquired their claim at a lower price. They may be under a greater compulsion to sell for cash. They may not know as much about the debtor as the Toughest Creditor. Or they may simply not be as aggressive as the Toughest Creditor.

In any event, a composition that pays all creditors the price demanded by the Toughest Creditor inevitably pays more than is necessary. In theory, the debtor can attempt to negotiate a separate discount with each creditor. However, the debtor may not have the cash necessary to fund the discounts. By contrast, the Funder has both the cash and the incentive to buy claims at a price below 50 cents on the dollar. Any Funder prepared to finance a 50-cent composition must believe that the debtor has sufficient value to pay creditors more than 50 cents on the dollar, so that a claim purchased at less than 50 cents should, in the Funder's calculations, be money good. A Funder who is not in control of the debtor is under no obligation to offer the same price to all creditors. See *Goldenbaugh v. Hoffman*, 69 N.Y. 322 (1877).

The second advantage to buying claims is the chance to influence creditors to accept the composition. An original creditor — one with a 100-cent basis in its claim — is often afraid of competing for the debtor's assets with a Funder who has acquired its claims for only 50 cents. The Funder can never compel the original creditor to accept a discount outside of a bankruptcy case, but the Funder may be able to compel the original creditor to accept an unacceptable discount under a chapter 11 plan — and the original creditor will know that.

Purchasing claims may not, however, be a technique available to share-holder/managers or their affiliates. State law generally condemns the purchase of claims against insolvent corporations by corporate insiders, and often prevents those insiders from enforcing purchased claims for more than the price paid for them plus interest on that price. See, for example, *Canton Roll & Machine Co. v. Rolling Mill Co. of America*, 138 F. 465 (4th Cir. 1909); *In re Jersey Materials Co.*, 50 F. Supp. 428, 430 (D.N.J. 1943); *Buckley v. Whitcomb*, 121 N.Y. 107, 24 N.E. 13 (1890).

It is even possible for an investor to conduct a hostile takeover of a corporation through purchasing claims in a composition, although the debtor always retains the ability to seek a friendly Funder and reorganize under a chapter 11 plan that gives the investor cash—and perhaps an inadequate amount of cash—and that gives the Funder the equity.

Section 14(e) of the Securities Exchange Act of 1934 (the "1934 Act") and the regulations promulgated thereunder, relating to tender offers for any securities, may also apply to the purchaser of debt securities such as the IRBs at issue here. That topic is covered elsewhere in these materials.

Investing in Exchange Offers

The Company

Youthful Exuberance Clothiers Holdings, Inc. (YECH) is a New York Stock Exchange-listed corporation owning a chain of retail clothing outlets across the United States. YECH has launched two major expansions in the last three years, financing each expansion with an issue of debentures:

- $100 million in 15-year 12 percent debentures (12s) issued in March 1986, with a 10 percent sinking fund in each of the issue's last 10 years that can be satisfied by YECH's deposit of debentures with the indenture trustee; and
- $50 million in 10-year 6 percent convertible debentures (6s) issued in July 1987. The 6s have no sinking fund.

Each indenture requires the affirmative vote of two-thirds of the outstanding debentures governed thereby for any amendment thereto.

Unfortunately for YECH, the recession of 1991 cuts retail sales and its cash flow to the point where its earnings before depreciation, interest, and taxes are less than $20 million per year—barely enough to meet the $15 million in interest payments on the 6s and 12s and not enough to meet the sinking fund payments on the 12s.

In short, YECH looks insolvent both in the "equity" or cash-flow sense of being unable to meet its debts as they mature. See Code § 303(h)(1), H.R. Rep. No. 595, 95th Cong., 1st Sess. 323 (1977) and S. Rep. No. 989, 95th Cong., 2d Sess. 34 (1978), and in the "bankruptcy" or balance-sheet sense of having assets whose fair salable value is less than the amount of its debts. See Code § 101(31), H.R. Rep. No. 595, 95th Cong., 1st Sess. 312 (1977); S. Rep. No. 989, 95th Cong., 2d Sess. 25 (1978).

Finally, both indentures prohibit YECH either from borrowing on a secured basis or discounting its receivables. In its present parlous state, YECH's only hope of raising essential cash to finance Christmas inventory is to borrow on a secured basis.

The Exchange Offer

YECH needs an exchange offer—a mechanism by which a troubled debtor reduces or postpones interest or principal payments, or waives honorous covenants, or pays debt with equity by swapping new securities for old ones. An exchange offer involving the exchange of new securities for old may not require the filing of a registration statement under the Securities Act of 1933 if no commission or other remuneration is paid or given directly or indirectly for soliciting such an exchange. Section 3(a)(9) of the Securities Act of 1933, 15 U.S.C. § 77c(9).

An exchange offer for debt securities is subject to Section 14(e) of the Securities Exchange Act of 1934, 15 U.S.C. § 78n(e) (1988) and Rules 14e-1 and 14e-3 promulgated thereunder. See *L.P. Acquisition Co. v. Tyson*, 772 F.2d 201 (6th Cir. 1985). The statute is merely an antifraud injunction similar to Section 10(b), and empowers the SEC to adopt the aforementioned rules. Rule 14e-1(a) requires YECH to keep its exchange offer open for at least 20 days from the date it is first published or given to security holders. Rule 14e-1(b) requires YECH to reopen the exchange offer for at least 10 days after any change in the percentage of the securities sought (although a 2 percent increase is deemed by the Rule not to be a change), or any change in the soliciting fee offered to dealers. Rule 14e-1(c) requires YECH to promptly pay the consideration offered in the exchange offer upon consummation thereof. Rule 14e-1(d) requires YECH to publicly announce any extension of the offer, together with the approximate amount of securities already tendered, no later than the next business day (or trading day for any exchange-listed security).

Rules 14e-2 and 14e-3 are aimed at above-market tender offers for equity securities and are not particularly relevant to YECH's exchange offer. Rule 14e-2 requires YECH to transmit its position on its own exchange offer. Rule 14e-3 prohibits trading on inside information—a lesser concern in this context than in a tender offer for a solvent company, and one not addressed further in this paper.

Exchange offers differ from ordinary compositions in several important ways. First, debt securities are issued pursuant to trust indentures. A trust indenture may be amended by a vote of a specified majority of indenture securities, except that no amendment may reduce or postpone principal payments or reduce interest payments in any indenture qualified under the Trust Indenture Act of 1939, 15 U.S.C. § 77aaa *et seq.* (1988). (The Trust Indenture Act applies to all issues of debt securities, with limited exceptions including certain exempted securities under the Securities Act of 1933 and issues of securities involving aggregate indebtedness of $10 million or less.) Section 316(b) of the Trust Indenture Act, 15 U.S.C. § 77ppp(b) (1988), does permit an indenture to provide that holders of 75 percent of the indenture securities may amend the indenture to postpone interest payments for up to three years, but few indentures have such a provision.

The concept of a trust indenture makes it possible for the requisite majority of indenture security holders to force the minority to accept changes in covenants such as the prohibitions on YECH's incurring any secured indebtedness. The indentures do not permit the reduction or postponement of principal or interest—but an exchange offer can effectively reduce the debt service burden on YECH in ways explained below.

The second difference between a composition and an exchange offer is that the latter generally applies to *publicly traded securities*. Because the debt securities trade in the market, their price generally declines as the issuer's prospects worsen. It is therefore possible for a troubled issuer to offer security holders new securities that, although not equal to the par value of the old securities, are nevertheless worth more than their current market price.

In YECH's case, the 12s are trading at 70. YECH offers to exchange for each $1,000 12 percent debenture

- $750 in new 10-year variable rate senior unsecured debentures (the "new debentures"); and
- 100 shares of YECH common stock

The new debentures are due in 2001 with 20 percent sinkers commencing in 1996. The new debentures give YECH the option to pay interest "in kind" by the issuance of additional new debentures for three years (that is, until 1994). The rate on the new debentures is set high enough to permit the new debentures to trade at par, with 100 shares of common stock, valued at $100 based on NYSE closing prices averaging approximately $1 per share over the last few weeks (assuming payment of $250 in debt with $100 in stock does not dilute the market's valuation of the equity), for a total payout of $850, or 85 cents on the dollar.

The 6s are trading at 50. YECH offers to issue in exchange for each $1,000 of the 6s

- $600 in new debentures
- 50 shares of YECH common stock

for a total payout of $650, or 65 cents on the dollar.

Those debentureholders accepting the exchange offer must also agree to indenture amendments that strip both the 6s and the 12s of almost all of their covenants, leaving YECH with the ability to borrow on any terms and to engage in other transactions (such as mergers, acquisitions, transferring assets to affiliates, etc.) that were formerly prohibited under the indentures.

Investment Opportunities

Passive Investment. As in the composition of GAG analyzed earlier under "Restructuring through a Sale of Assets," the YECH exchange offer allows an investor to buy debentures in the hope of making a profit when the exchange offer closes and securities worth more than the price of the debentures are distributed. Of course, if the exchange offer fails, the price of the debentures is likely to decrease and the investor will take a loss.

Reasons for Success. Like compositions, exchange offers cannot bind nonacceptors to reductions of principal or interest. However, an exchange offer contains certain inducements not present in a composition.

First, an exchange offer may extend the effective maturity of those securities. The YECH 12s' indenture provides for a 10 percent sinking fund payable with either cash or 12s in each of the issue's remaining 10 years. Therefore, although the 12s may mature in the year 2001, the 10 percent sinker makes the average life to maturity of the 12s approximately 5 years from 1991. If the exchange offer succeeds, the debentures tendered in the exchange will be used to satisfy the sinkers on the remaining debentures. That makes the remaining average life to maturity of the untendered debentures 10 years from 1991, not 5 — which may depress the market price of the remaining debentures.

Second, YECH's exchange offer may depress the price of untendered debentures by stripping them of their covenants. The new debentures may be more desirable because they contain some covenants. Exchange offers may even pressure hold-outs to accept by providing that accepting creditors will receive new securities which are secured, or which are issued by a subsidiary, and therefore are structurally senior to holdouts' old securities. In the Southland reorganization, the pre-bankruptcy exchange offer purported to *contractually subordinate* old non-accepting securities in favor of new securities issued to accepting security holders by having the acceptors vote in favor of an indenture amendment subordinating the old securities. As the exchange offer was followed by a chapter 11 reorganization, the legality of this procedure was not tested in court.

Risks of Success. If the exchange offer succeeds, holders of the 12s will exchange 100-cent claims for 75 cents in claims and 10 cents in stock, and holders of the 6s will exchange 100-cent claims for 60 cents in claims and 5 cents in stock. If YECH cannot avoid a chapter 11 case even with a successful exchange offer, the investor's stock will be close to worthless. The difference between the principal amount of the new debentures and the market price of the 6s and 12s exchanged therefore may be viewed as unmatured interest, and the claims under the new debentures may be reduced to reflect that difference. See *In re Allegheny International, Inc.*,

100 Bankr. 247, 249-51 (Bankr. W.D. Pa. 1989) and *In re Chateaugay Corp.*, 109 Bankr. 51 (Bankr. S.D.N.Y. 1990). In *Allegheny*, 10.4% debentures due in 2002 were issued in a 1984 exchange offer for outstanding preferred stock. The debentures traded at 65% of their face amount immediately after issuance. When Allegheny subsequently filed its chapter 11 petition in 1988, Judge Cossetti limited claims under the debentures to 65% of their face amount *plus* the amount of original issue discount which had accreted on the debentures from their issuance to the filing *plus* accrued but unpaid interest at the stated rate of 10.4%.

Chateaugay's analysis was even more draconian. In that case, LTV Corporation on May 16, 1986 offered one $1,000 15% senior note and 15 shares of stock in exchange for one $1,000 13-7/8% debenture. When LTV filed its chapter 11 petition *two months later*, Judge Lifland limited claims under the new 15% senior notes to the *trading price of the old 13-7/8% debentures*, minus the value of the common stock. Compare *In re Radio-Keith Orpheum Corporation*, 106 F.2d 22, 27 (2d Cir. 1939) (overruling shareholder's objection to allowance of debentures at par when they had been offered at $55).

Difficulty in Obtaining Necessary Majorities. Like most indentures, YECH's indentures can be amended only with the assent of a two-thirds majority of *all* securities issued under the indenture. Therefore, the failure of the debentureholders' vote can kill an exchange offer. For YECH, the seriousness of that problem depends on how widely the debentures are held. The problem may be exacerbated where the securities are bearer securities—such as Eurodollar bonds—so that no one knows who the holders are.

Instability. Like most exchange offers, YECH's is unstable. The announcement of YECH's exchange offer constitutes an admission by YECH that it is unable to pay its debts generally as they mature—which is one of two grounds for filing an involuntary bankruptcy petition. Code § 303(h)(1). Various creditors may have reason to file a petition. Indeed, the investor could be one of them, as explained below.

Arbitrage Investment

Interest-related Arbitrage. Prior to bankruptcy, the 6s and 12s traded at different prices and received different exchange offers reflecting their different interest rates maturities and amortization schedules. However, in a chapter 11 case all unsecured debt will be paid under a plan at the same time so that maturity and amortization are usually irrelevant. Moreover, in a chapter 11 case YECH's Debentures will not accrue postpetition interest, Code § 502(b)(2), so long as YECH is insolvent. As noted above, YECH is insolvent. In chapter 11, therefore, the 6s and the 12s *should trade at the same price*.

The equivalence of the debentures in bankruptcy and their divergent trading prices prior to bankruptcy sets up a natural arbitrage for an investor betting on the failure of the restructuring: the investor purchases the 6s at 50 and sells short the 12s at 70. Once YECH is in bankruptcy, the investor is guaranteed a profit because the debentures that traded at different prices prebankruptcy should trade at the same price postbankruptcy. This can be shown from analyzing the three possible scenarios for the value of plan distributions as compared to the price at which the investor shorted the 12s or purchased the 6s:

Scenario #1: Above the 12s' Price. Assume YECH's plan pays unsecured creditors 80 cents on the dollar, or 10 cents more than the 70-cent pre-bankruptcy trading price of the 12s. The arbitrageur has a 10-cent loss on its short position in the 12s. However, the 80-cent plan gives the arbitrageur a 30-cent gain over the 50-cent prebankruptcy trading price of the 6s. In this scenario, the arbitrageur will always make a profit because the gain on its long position in the cheap low-coupon debt will always exceed the loss on its short position in the expensive high-coupon debt.

Scenario #2: Below the 6s' Price. Assume YECH's plan pays unsecured creditors 40 cents on the dollar, or 10 cents less than the 50-cent pre-bankruptcy trading price of the 6s. The arbitrageur has a 10-cent loss on the 6s. However, the 40-cent plan gives the arbitrageur a 30-cent gain because it shorted the 12s at 70 cents. In this scenario, the arbitrageur will always make a profit because the gain on its short position in the expensive high-coupon debt will always exceed the loss on its long position in the cheap low-coupon debt.

Scenario #3: Between the 12s and the 6s. Assume YECH's plan pays unsecured creditors 60 cents on the dollar. The investor will realize both a 10-cent profit on the 6s it purchased at 50, and a 10-cent profit on the 12s it shorted at 70. When the plan distributions are between the prices paid for high- and low-coupon debt, the investor will always make money on both its short and its long positions.

The only risk to an arbitrage investment of this kind is that the exchange offer succeeds and the holders of 12s receive 85 cents in notes and stock (costing the investor 15 cents on its 70-cent short position) and the holders of 6s receive 65 cents in notes and stock (which provides a profit of only 15 cents)—yielding the investor no profit and probably a loss based on its cost of capital.

However, an arbitrage in debt securities of an insolvent issuer is not the same as an arbitrage position in equity securities because the holder of debt securities can take action: the arbitrageur has the ability to force YECH into chapter 11.

Blocking Position. The safest way for the arbitrageur to ensure the failure of YECH's exchange offer is to purchase more than one-third of the 6s—enough to block any amendment of the 6s' indenture. Because there are only $50 million in 6s and they are trading at 50 cents, the cost of a one-third blocking position is only $8,333,333—and 50 percent of that cost can be financed on margin. For a total cash investment of less than $4.2

million, an arbitrageur can block YECH's restructuring of $150 million in public indebtedness.

Involuntary Petitions.   The quickest way for the arbitrageur to ensure the failure of YECH's exchange offer is to join with two other debentureholders and file an involuntary bankruptcy petition against YECH. See, for example, *In re Midwest Processing Co.*, 41 Bankr. 90, 103–104 (Bankr. D.N.D. 1984) (major creditor who filed involuntary petition could induce two small creditors to join petition by indemnifying them against damages). Compare *In re Win-Sum Sports, Inc.*, 14 Bankr. 389, 392–93 (Bankr. D. Conn. 1981) (major shareholder's granting petitioning creditors an indemnity to induce involuntary filing did not preclude creditors from filing). As indicated above, YECH's announcement of its exchange offer is an admission of its inability to pay its debts as they mature and provides the grounds for a bankruptcy filing under Code § 303(h)(2).

However, an involuntary chapter 11 petition is not without its risks. A bankruptcy judge may dismiss a chapter 11 case if, *inter alia*, "the interest of creditors and the debtor would be better served by such dismissal or suspension." Code § 305(a)(1). The legislative history to this provision indicates that it could be used to deal with an investor who seeks to sabotage an exchange offer in order to profit from an arbitrage position:

> The court may dismiss or suspend under [paragraph (a)(1)], for example, if an arrangement is being worked out by creditors and the debtor out of court, there is no prejudice to the rights of creditors in that arrangement, and an involuntary case has been commenced by a few recalcitrant creditors to provide a basis for future threats to extract full payment.

H.R. Rep. No. 595, 95th Cong., 1st Sess. 325 (1977); S. Rep. No. 989, 95th Cong., 2d Sess. 35 (1978). See for example, *In re Rimpull Corp.*, 26 Bankr. 267, 272 (Bankr. W.D. Mo. 1982) (Stewart, B.J.) (dismissing chapter 11 case where out-of-court extension/composition of trade debt had been accepted by 67 percent of trade creditors holding 76 percent in amount of total trade debt). Indeed, even if no general out-of-court restructuring is imminent, the bankruptcy court may dismiss an involuntary petition where no other creditor has supported the three petitioners and where the debtor and nonpetitioning creditors appear to be negotiating individual settlements. *In re Investment Corp. of North America*, 39 Bankr. 758 (Bankr. S.D. Fla. 1984); *In re Luftek, Inc.*, 6 Bankr. 539, 547-48 (Bankr. E.D.N.Y. 1980). The motive of the petitioning creditors may also justify dismissal. *Investment Corp.*, 39 Bankr. at 759 (petitioners wanted control of debtor); *In re Win-Sum Sports, Inc.*, 14 Bankr. 389, 393-394 (Bankr. D. Conn. 1981) (same); *Luftek* 6 Bankr. at 548 (subsidiary of debtor's competitor joined in involuntary petition). However, the bankruptcy court must be convinced that an out-of-court restructuring will work. *In re Midwest Processing Co.*, 41 Bankr. 90, 104-05 (Bankr. D.N.D. 1984).

A decision by the bankruptcy court to dismiss (or not to dismiss) an involuntary petition is not reviewable "by appeal or otherwise," Code § 305(c), although there is a debate over whether such provision is constitutional after *Northern Pipeline Construction Co. v. Marathon Pipeline Co.*, 458 U.S. 40 (1982). Compare *In re Cash Currency Exchange, Inc.*, 762 F.2d 542, 555-56 (7th Cir.), *cert. denied*, 464 U.S. 904 (1986) (§ 305(c) clearly precludes review; however, decision was based on pre-*Marathon* case and never considers *Marathon*'s effect) with *In re Tri-County Farm Equipment Co.*, 87 Bankr. 667, 669-71 (D. Kan. 1988) (§ 305(c) cannot bar district court from reviewing decision). Compare *In re Colorado Industrial Bank of Loveland*, 85 Bankr. 855, 857 (D. Col. 1988) (proceedings under § 305(c) must, after *Marathon* and 1984 bankruptcy amendments, be viewed as "noncore," so that bankruptcy court order dismissing case would be vacated and the matter remanded to the bankruptcy court to issue proposed findings of fact and conclusions of law.)

It is also possible for the bankruptcy court to dismiss the investor's petition as filed in bad faith, in which case the investor may be subject to substantial penalties in the form of punitive damages under Code § 303(i)(2).

Chapter 11 Reorganizations

The Company

The Beneficial Uranium Processing Company of the United States (BUPCUS) processes uranium into plutonium for resale to major utilities. BUPCUS is foundering because of several adverse business developments. First, BUPCUS sells plutonium to utilities under long-term contracts that are substantially below market. Second, BUPCUS obtains its uranium under long-term supply contracts whose price is substantially above market. Third, BUPCUS's workers are beginning to develop health problems that they claim result from BUPCUS's reckless exposure of its workers to coal dust and uranium by-products. BUPCUS workers are filing law suits based on those health problems, which they assert will not be limited by workers' compensation statutes.

On December 31, 1988, BUPCUS had the following balance sheet:

Assets ($mm Book Values)	
Current Assets	
Cash and Marketable Securities	50
Accounts Receivable	150
Inventory (FIFO)	200
Total Current Assets	400

(continued)

Fixed Assets	
Processing Plant	1,000
Total Assets	1,400
Liabilities ($mm Book Values)	
Current Liabilities	
(trade payables; no portion long term debt is current)	200
Long-Term Obligations	
10% First Mortgage Bonds due 1999 secured by plant	500
Prime-rate unsecured Bank Revolver	100
14% Unsecured Eurodollar Notes due 1995	200
Total	800
Total Liabilities	1,000
Shareholders' Equity	400

Notwithstanding its nominally healthy balance sheet, BUPCUS's earnings before interest and taxes (EBIT) are only $100 million per year. (BUPCUS's depreciation is approximately equal to its capital expenditures.) BUPCUS's EBIT just barely covers its annual interest payments in large part because of the escalating costs of defending its workers' claims. Pressed by its workers' claims, BUPCUS files a chapter 11 petition on December 31, 1989.

The Postpetition Balance Sheet

After the petition is filed, BUPCUS's internal planning staff compiles a summary of BUPCUS's assets and liabilities, revaluing assets to their market values and classifying liabilities according to their secured and unsecured status:

Assets ($mm Market Values)	
Current Assets	
Cash & Marketable Securities	50
Accounts Receivable	140
Inventory (FIFO)	110
Total Current Assets	300

(*continued*)

Fixed Assets	
Processing Plant	500
Total Assets	800
Liabilities ($mm Allowed Amounts)	
Secured Claims	
First Mortgage Bonds	500
Unsecured Claims	
Prepetition Trade Claims	200
Prime Rate Bank Revolver	100
14% Eurodollar Notes	150
Total	450
Total Liabilities	950
Shareholders' Equity	(150)

Based on the above summary, unsecured creditors should be entitled to $300 million in value, based on BUPCUS's unencumbered assets, to satisfy $450 million in claims, for a return of 66 2/3 cents on the dollar. The bondholders are fully secured, but not oversecured. Under Code § 506(b), the bondholders are not entitled to accrue postpetition interest on their claims.

BUPCUS presents two different investment opportunities for purchasers of publicly traded debt securities: the 10 percent first mortgage bonds (10 percent bonds) and the 14 percent unsecured Eurodollar notes (14 percent Euros). Before purchasing either the 10 percent bonds or the 14 percent Euros, the investor should consider how BUPCUS's chapter 11 case will affect those securities.

First, chapter 11 proceedings will affect the value of the securities themselves, either by changing the asset values supporting the securities, or by changing the amount of claims that compete with the securities for those assets. Those effects are discussed below under "Investing in Secured Claims" and "Investing in Unsecured Claims." Second, the process of confirming a plan may threaten or enhance the value of the securities. Finally, a chapter 11 changes the role of management in ways that prospective investors in any BUPCUS securities must consider.

Investing in Secured Claims

Management and the Value of Collateral. A claim secured by collateral is actually two claims: a secured claim to the extent of the value of the collateral, and an unsecured claim for the balance. Code § 506(a); S. Rep. 989, 95th Cong., 2d Sess. 68, 118 (1978); see H.R. Rep. 595, 95th Cong.,

1st Sess. 356, 406 (1977). If the value of the collateral on the effective date of a chapter 11 plan exceeds the amount of the secured claim on the petition date, the petition-day amount of the secured claim may increase (to the extent of the excess) to include "postpetition interest[,] and reasonable fees, costs and charges provided for under the agreement under which such claim arose." Code § 506(b). (The bracketed, underlined comma is in the statute, and raises certain questions concerning the rate of interest applicable under Code § 506(b)—an issue examined further under "Interest" below.)

Clearly the investor must estimate how much the collateral is worth, but the investor should also make a judgment as to how management will want to value the collateral.

Sometimes that judgment is fairly obvious. In DREC's case, the bondholders' indenture trustee held both a lien on DREC's office building and management's personal notes as collateral. To escape or minimize personal liability, DREC management will probably place a high value on the office building to justify a 100-cent payment under a plan.

DREC management would not be alone. Lenders to many small debtors insist on personal guarantees from the shareholder/managers, and those guarantees often motivate management to make sure the lender is paid in full under a plan or in a liquidation. Management's presumed desire to discharge its personal liability by paying guaranteed creditors out of the debtor's assets is the primary reason why several courts have subjected such lenders to the one-year preference period applied to insiders under Code § 547(b)(4)(B). See, for example, *Levit v. Ingersoll Rand Financial Corp.*, 874 F.2d 1186 (7th Cir. 1989). It can also serve as an argument in favor of appointing a trustee under Code § 1104. Compare *In re Liberal Market, Inc.*, 11 Bankr. 742 (Bankr. S.D. Ohio 1981) (management's personal liability on guarantees, *inter alia*, justified appointing examiner with most of the powers of a trustee).

Where management has substantially all of its net worth tied up in the equity of the debtor, it will ascribe a high value to the debtor's business and hence a high value to collateral, for fear of increasing the degree to which the debtor is insolvent. The greater the insolvency of the debtor, the less value that will be allocated to the management/shareholders.

By contrast, managers with no meaningful equity may have an incentive to ascribe a low value to collateral so as to reduce the secured creditor's leverage under a plan.

Management plays the central role in the valuation of collateral first because the debtor-in-possession initiates objections to the allowance of claims. In some circuits, parties other than the debtor may object to claims only if the debtor-in-possession fails to do so without good cause. See *In re STN Enterprises*, 779 F.2d 901 (2d Cir. 1985). But see *In re Marin Motor Oil, Inc.*, 689 F.2d 445, 449-57 (3rd Cir. 1982), *cert. denied*, 459 U.S. 206 (1983) (creditors' committee has unfettered right to intervene in proceeding brought by debtor).

Operational Improvements. Management often uses chapter 11 to cut costs and to make improvements in the debtor's operations by rejecting burdensome executory contracts and abandoning burdensome property. (The standard definition of an "executory contract" is a contract that is sufficiently unperformed by both debtor and nondebtor parties that failure of performance by one will excuse performance by the other. See generally Countryman, *Executory Contracts in Bankruptcy*, Part I, 57 Minn. L. Rev. 439 (1973) and Part II, 58 Minn. L. Rev. 479 (1974); H.R. Rep. 595, 95th Cong., 1st Sess. 347 (1977); S. Rep. 989, 95th Cong., 2d Sess. 58 (1978).

Examples of burdensome executory contracts and leases that have been profitably rejected in recent major cases include pension plans (LTV Corporation, Wheeling-Pittsburgh Steel Corporation, Sharon Steel Corporation), collective bargaining agreements (Continental Airlines Corporation), raw material supply contracts (LTV, Wheeling-Pitt), and real estate leases (Allegheny International's lease of seven empty floors of a new building in Pittsburgh) to improve cash flow. In BUPCUS's case, there are two sets of burdensome executory contracts: BUPCUS's below-market sales contracts, which depress revenues, and BUPCUS's above-market supply contracts, which inflate costs.

The rejection of a burdensome contract or lease should decrease expenses and increase cash flow. Cash flow usually determines the going-concern value of the debtor. See Fortgang and Mayer, *Valuation in Bankruptcy*, 32 U.C.L.A. L. Rev. 1061, 1126–27 (1985). If cash flow is attributable to collateral, it may determine the going-concern value of that collateral. *Institutional Investors v. Chicago, Minneapolis, St. Paul & Pacific Railroad Co.*, 318 U.S. 802 (1943); *In re Wabash Valley Power Ass'n, Inc.*, 77 Bankr. 991 (Bankr. S.D. Ind. 1987); *In re Fibreglass Industries, Inc.*, 74 Bankr. 738, 742–46 (Bankr. N.D.N.Y. 1987); *In re Phoenix Steel Corp.*, 39 Bankr. 218, 231-33 (D. Del. 1984). If the rejection of burdensome contracts makes collateral more valuable, the increase inures to the benefit of the secured creditor. See *In re Jackson Brewing Co.*, 567 F.2d 618, 621 (5th Cir. 1978) (upholding rejection of low-priced prior purchase option on debtor's mortgaged property where the only effect of rejection was to enrich mortgagee). Compare *In re Minges*, 602 F.2d 38, 44 (2d Cir. 1979) (court noted but did not decide to challenge rejection of executory contract that benefited only secured creditor).

In BUPCUS's case, the rejection of the sales contracts boosts cash flow so much that the processing plant is worth $100 million more than it was at the commencement of the case. That allows the $500 million in first mortgage bonds to accrue 10 percent interest for two years during the chapter 11 case. The price for this improvement comes in the form of claims for damages arising out of the rejection of executory contracts. That facet of chapter 11 is examined below under "Dilution: Executory contract claims."

Deductions for Expenses. Just as operating improvements can add to the value of a secured creditor's collateral, so operating expenses can, in some circumstances, be a deduction from the value of collateral. If a secured creditor's collateral is sold, the creditor's lien attaches to the proceeds "except to any extent that the court, after notice and a hearing and based on the equities of the case, orders otherwise." Code § 552(b). The legislative history relevant to this language indicates that prepetition liens do not extend to proceeds of collateral

> to the extent that the estate acquired the proceeds to the prejudice of other creditors holding unsecured claims.... "Prejudice" is not intended to be a broad term here, but is designed to cover the situation where the estate expends funds that result in an increase in value of collateral. The exception is to cover the situation where raw materials, for example, are converted into inventory, or inventory into accounts, at some expense to the estate, thus depleting the fund available for general unsecured creditors.

H.R. Rep. No. 595, 95th Cong., 1st Sess. 376–77 (1977); S. Rep. No. 989, 95th Cong., 2d Sess. 91 (1978).

Section 552(b) and the above quoted legislative history have already been cited to justify deduction of operating costs from the proceeds of collateral. *In re J. Cotton Farms, Inc.*, 779 F.2d 1242, 1246-47 (7th Cir. 1985); *United Virginia Bank v. Slab Fork Coal Co.*, 784 F.2d 1188, 1191 (4th Cir.) *cert. denied*, 477 U.S. 905 (1986); *Smith v. Dairymen, Inc.*, 790 F.2d 1107, 1112-13 (4th Cir. 1986). See also *In re Delbridge*, 61 Bankr. 484, 486, 489, 490 (Bankr. E.D. Mich. 1986).

There is further authority to the effect that when a secured creditor seeks to liquidate its collateral, and the collateral is later sold at a going-concern value, the "equities of the case" prevent the creditor from receiving more than liquidation value out of the proceeds. *In re Vanas*, 50 Bankr. 988, 997–98 (Bankr. D. Mich. 1985).

The decisions on Code § 552(b)'s "equities of the case" language cannot be reconciled with the second and ninth circuit cases under Code § 506(c), which refuse to deduct operating expenses from collateral proceeds even if maintaining operations would preserve the going-concern value of the collateral. *In re Flagstaff Foodservice Corp.*, 762 F.2d 10, 12 (2d Cir. 1985) (before debtor could deduct "reasonable, necessary costs and expenses of preserving... collateral" under § 506(c), debtor had to show that expenses were incurred "primarily for the benefit of the creditor"). See also *In re Cascade Hydraulics and Utility Service*, 815 F.2d 546, 549 (9th Cir. 1986). But see *In re McKeesport Castings Co.*, 799 F.2d 91 (3d Cir. 1986) (utility bills incurred to keep business operating could be deducted from proceeds of collateral sold as a going concern under § 506(c) without any showing that expenses were incurred "primarily for the benefit of the creditor").

The equitable impulse behind Code § 552(b) is so strong that *Flagstaff* and its progeny are likely to be overruled or cut back by the first appellate court to consider Code §§ 552(b) and 506(c) in the same case. See Fortgang and Mayer, *1987 Interest and Costs for the Secured Creditor in Bankruptcy*, 13th Annual N.Y.U. Workshop on Bankruptcy and Business Reorganization 1401, 1485–1501 (1987).

COMMENT: *Flagstaff* and its progeny do not distinguish between the principal and interest components of a secured claim for purposes of deducting Code § 506(c) costs. Yet the statute itself makes a distinction. Section 506(b) provides that postpetition interest, fees, and expenses on oversecured claims is subject to Code § 506(c) deductions, but Code § 506(a) nowhere provides that the allowed amount of a secured claim on the petition date is subject to Code § 506(c) deductions.

Interest. Under the Bankruptcy Act of 1898, the courts were unanimous in holding that an oversecured creditor with a contract providing for the accrual of interest was entitled to accrued interest at the contract rate. See, for example, *Sexton v. Dreyfus*, 219 U.S. 339, 344 (1911); *Vanston Bondholders' Protective Committee v. Green*, 329 U.S. 156, 164 (1946). Cases under the Code have been nearly unanimous in holding that an oversecured creditor entitled to interest under its agreement with the debtor may accrue interest postpetition at the contract rate under Code § 506(b). See generally 3 Collier on Bankruptcy ¶ 506.05 at 506-39-40 & n.3 (L. King 15th ed. 1989). *In re Lift Service, Inc.*, 819 F.2d 546 (5th Cir. 1987) (*per curiam*); *In re Anderson*, 833 F.2d 834, 836 (9th Cir. 1987); *Grundy Nat'l Bank v. Tandem Mining Corp.*, 754 F.2d 1436, 1441 (4th Cir. 1985); *In re LHD Realty Corp.*, 726 F.2d 327, 333 (7th Cir. 1984). The only exceptions to the rule were a few scattered lower court cases. See *In re Anderson*, 28 Bankr. 682 (S.D. Ohio 1982), following *In re Marx*, 11 Bankr. 819, 820 (Bankr. S.D. Ohio 1981); *In re Minguey*, 10 Bankr. 806, 808 (W.D. Wisc. 1981).

But what if there were no contract rate? What if the oversecured creditor were the Internal Revenue Service or some other statutory lienor who did not have a contract, much less a contract rate? Would the statutory lienor be entitled to postpetition interest? Most courts under the Act held that it would not be. See, for example, Miles, *Determining the Limits of Postpetition Interest under Section 506(b) of the Bankruptcy Code: In re Ron Pair Enterprises*, 5 Bankr. Dev. J. 443 (1988); *United States v. Harrington*, 269 F.2d 719, 722 (4th Cir. 1949); *In re Boston & Maine Rwy. Co.*, 719 F.2d 493 (1st Cir. 1983), *cert. denied*, 466 U.S. 938 (1984), although the decisions rested somewhat flimsily on the Supreme Court's curious omission of postpetition interest as an entitlement of the oversecured statutory lienor in *New York v. Saper*, 336 U.S. 328 (1949). (The omission is curious because *Saper* did allow statutory lienors to accrue interest postpetition if the debtor was solvent. *Saper* also allowed the statutory lienor to accrue postpetition interest against any postpetition income generated by its collateral.)

In 1989, in a 5–4 decision the Supreme Court held that the IRS and other statutory lienors are entitled to postpetition interest to the extent they are oversecured. *United States v. Ron Pair Enterprises, Inc.*, 109 S. Ct. 1026 (1989). Unfortunately, *Ron Pair* rested not on a reinterpretation of *Saper* but on the placement of the underlined, bracketed comma in the below-quoted clause of Code § 506(b), which entitles the holder of an oversecured claim to

> interest on such claim [,] and reasonable fees, costs and charges provided for under the agreement under which such claim arose.

The five-justice majority held that the placement of the underlined and bracketed comma divorced "interest on such claim" from "provided for under the agreement under which such claim arose." They concluded from the comma that Congress had intended to change prior law and allow postpetition interest to oversecured statutory lienors.

Oversecured creditors with contract-based interest rates are not mentioned in *Ron Pair*, but the decision throws into question all prior decisions entitling such creditors to contract-based interest rates. The prior decisions were based on holdings that the crucial comma was irrelevant to the interpretation of the statute. See, for example, *In re Anderson*, 833 F.2d 834, 836 (9th Cir. 1987); *In re 268 Ltd.*, 789 F.2d 674, 676 (9th Cir. 1986); *In re W.S. Sheppley & Co.*, 62 Bankr. 271, 274 (Bankr. N.D. Iowa 1986) (Yacos, B.J., by designation); *In re Loveridge Mach. & Tool Co., Inc.*, 36 Bankr. 159, 161-65 (Bankr. D. Utah 1983) (Clark, B.J.). Compare *In re Small*, 65 Bankr. 686, 691 (Bankr. E.D. Pa. 1986); *In re Minick*, 63 Bankr. 440, 447 (Bankr. D.D.C. 1986) (*dicta* adopting Collier analysis in context of chapter 13 plan).

After *Ron Pair*, the comma matters. Those investors considering the purchase of high-coupon oversecured debt—and there is some on the market, most notably the Public Service of New Hampshire General Refunding Bonds Series D (17 percent) and E (18 percent)—should bear in mind that *Ron Pair* provides the debtor (and unsecured creditors) with at least an argument that the high-coupon rate should be replaced by some other, presumably lower, rate of interest.

Investing in Unsecured Claims

The investor in unsecured claims has no collateral to value. That investor has a general claim against those asset values that are not subject to the liens of secured creditors. Therefore, the value of the company as an enterprise assumes paramount importance to the investor in unsecured claims. Unlike the secured creditor, who can presumably run a lien search on its collateral, the investor in unsecured claims may not know how much unsecured debt will compete with its claims for the unencumbered value of the debtor. Certain factors affecting both questions—the value of the debtor and the claims against it—are examined below.

Cash Flow.   As indicated under "Investing in Exchange Offers—Arbitrage investments," the filing of a chapter 11 petition halts the accrual of interest on unsecured claims unless the debtor is solvent—which BUPCUS is not.

BUPCUS's interest costs accounted for approximately 82 percent of its $100 million in EBIT:

10% on $500mm Bonds:	$50,000,000
prime on $100mm bank line:	11,000,000
14% on $150mm Euros:	21,000,000
	$82,000,000

BUPCUS also does not have to contend with the cost of defending the lawsuits. Thus the filing of a chapter 11 petition allows BUPCUS to start accumulating cash at the rate of approximately $100 million per year. At that rate, based on BUPCUS's initial postpetition balance sheet, two year's accumulation of cash flow will make BUPCUS a solvent company.

The time BUPCUS will take to confirm a plan thus becomes a major factor in an investment decision. For the investor in the 10 percent bonds, time costs money because the 10 percent bonds do not accrue interest until BUPCUS becomes solvent or the collateral securing the bonds exceeds their principal amount. If the bonds are trading at or near par, therefore, the passage of time does not benefit the bond investor. If the Euros are selling at a discount, however, the passage of time brings increased accumulation of value towards 100 percent payment of the Euros and all other unsecured claims. Once BUPCUS becomes solvent, both the 10 percent bonds and the 14 percent Euros should accrue interest at their respective contract rates, although other rates have been advanced in cases under the Code. See "The solvent debtor: Interest on unsecured debt," below. Assume the Euros are selling at the asset coverage ratio for unsecured claims: 66 2/3 cents on the dollar. If BUPCUS emerges as a solvent debtor, a purchaser of the Euros will make money no matter when BUPCUS comes out of bankruptcy. A solvent BUPCUS will pay $140 in interest on a 14 percent Euro acquired for $666.67—an annual rate of return of 21 percent—in addition to paying $1,000 in principal on the Euro acquired for $666.67.

Such cash accumulation is one reason why investors try to acquire unsecured claims at a discount. Unfortunately for investors, however, recoveries on unsecured claims also depend on how much unsecured debt BUPCUS really has. As the amount of unsecured debt increases, the recovery of the investor is diluted. The dilution is often not known until the end of a chapter 11 case.

Dilution: Tort Claims. As Johns-Manville Corporation, UNR Industries, Inc., A. H. Robins Company, Inc., Emons Industries, Inc., and other debtors having massive tort claims have discovered, a chapter 11 case in general, and the setting of a bar date for the filing of claims in particular, will prompt hitherto unknown tort claimants to emerge with claims against the debtor. The same is true for BUPCUS. After BUPCUS establishes its bar date in the second year of the case, almost a billion dollars in claims are filed against BUPCUS by injured workers. BUPCUS's internal planning staff estimates the true amount of these claims at $350 million. Because BUPCUS has accumulated $200 million in cash during the two years following the chapter 11 petition, the internal planning staff's summary of assets and liabilities looks like this:

Assets ($MM Market Values)	
Current Assets	
Cash & Marketable Securities	
At Petition Date	50
2 Years' Accumulated Cash	200
Accounts Receivable	140
Inventory (FIFO)	110
Total Current Assets	500
Fixed Assets	
Processing Plant	500
Total Assets	1,000
Liabilities ($MM Allowed Amounts)	
Secured Claims	
First Mortgage Bonds	500
Unsecured Claims	
Pre-petition Trade Claims	200
Unsecured Bank Revolver	100
14% Debentures	150
Tort Claims	350
Total	800
Total Liabilities	1,300
Shareholders' Equity	(300)

After giving effect to both the massive tort claims filed against BUPCUS and its accumulations of two years of postpetition cash flow, unsecured creditors must look to $500 million in value from unencumbered current assets to satisfy $800 million in unsecured claims. Their prospective recovery has diminished from 66.67 cents on the dollar to 62.5 cents on the dollar.

Dilution: Executory Contract Claims. As the preceding section shows, the return on an unsecured claim can be diluted by tort claim filings. It can also be diluted by the rejection of executory contracts.

Laymen and nonbankruptcy lawyers often mistakenly interpret rejection of a contract as eliminating all claims and liabilities thereunder. This is not true. Code § 365(g)(1) provides that rejection is deemed to constitute "a breach of contract...immediately before the date of the filing of the petition." The nondebtor party to a rejected executory contract thus has a claim for damages for breach of contract, as of the filing date of the petition, calculated according to relevant nonbankruptcy law. See 3A *Collier on Bankruptcy* ¶ 63.33[2.4] at 1948 (J. Moore and L. King 14th ed. 1975).

The damage claims created by the rejection of executory contracts can dramatically increase the total amount of unsecured claims asserted against the debtor. Wheeling-Pittsburgh Steel Corporation's annual report for 1988 discloses allowed executory contract claims against that debtor in excess of $300 million—more than 25 percent of all prepetition liabilities.

Simple mathematics shows that rejection of an executory contract will in most cases enhance recoveries of unsecured creditors. The recovery of unsecured creditors is determined by the fraction

$$\frac{\text{Original Value}}{\text{Original Claims}}$$

which after rejection of executory contracts becomes the fraction

$$\frac{\text{Original Value} + \text{Value From Rejection Of Contracts}}{\text{Original Claims} + \text{Claims From Rejection Of Contracts}}$$

From this it can be seen that the fraction will increase (and recoveries of unsecured creditors will increase towards 100 cents on the dollar) as long as

$$\frac{\text{Original Value}}{\text{Original Claims}}$$

is less than

$$\frac{\text{Value From Rejection Of Contracts}}{\text{Claims From Rejection Of Contracts}}$$

To put numbers in the above equation, if unsecured creditors prior to the rejection of contracts will recover 50 cents on the dollar, so that the first fraction is 1/2, the rejection of contracts will benefit unsecured creditors as long as the additional value for the debtor is more than half the amount of the claims added to the unsecured claim pool.

There are, however, situations in which unsecured creditors will not benefit from the rejection of executory contracts. The first situation arises when

$$\text{Value From Rejection Of Contracts}$$

is applied to the payment of postpetition interest on secured claims by increasing the value of the collateral securing those claims. "Operational

---

Assets ($MM Market Values)

Current Assets

Cash & Marketable Securities	
At Petition Date	50
2 Years' Accumulated Cash	200
Accounts Receivable	140
Inventory (FIFO)	110
Total Current Assets	500

Fixed Assets

Original Plant Value	500
Increase from Sales Contract	
Rejections	100
Total Plant Value	600
Total Assets	1,100

Liabilities ($MM Allowed Amounts)

Secured Claims

First Mortgage Bonds	
principal	500
interest	100
	600

Unsecured Claims

Pre-petition Trade Claims	200
Unsecured Bank Revolver	100
14% Debentures	150
Tort Claims	350
Sales Contract Claims	100
Total	900
Total Liabilities	1,500
Shareholders' Equity	(400)

---

improvements," above, shows how BUPCUS's rejection of its long-term sales contracts benefited the 10 percent bonds by allowing them to accrue two years of postpetition interest. The summary of assets and liabilities after two years in chapter 11 shows the cost of that benefit: the filing of $100 million in claims by BUPCUS's customers.

Before BUPCUS rejected its sales contracts, unsecured creditors could look to $500 million in current assets to satisfy $800 million in unsecured claims for a recovery of 62.5 cents on the dollar. After BUPCUS rejected its sales contracts, unsecured creditors still had only $500 million in current assets to satisfy $950 million in claims for a recovery of 52.6 cents on the dollar.

The second situation arises when the method of calculating

Claims From Rejection Of Contracts

bears no relationship to

Value From Rejection Of Contracts

This can happen in several different ways. The rejection of a contract may entitle the nondebtor party to incidental or consequential damages that bear no relationship to the debtor's benefit from rejection. For example, if BUPCUS has a customer who literally cannot buy fuel elsewhere and goes out of business because of BUPCUS's contract termination, that customer may well have damages much greater than any increased value accrued to BUPCUS from selling the fuel elsewhere at the market price.

The steel company chapter 11 cases have shown how the "lost volume" theory of damages can create tremendous claims against a debtor under rejected supply contracts. Under that theory, a supplier cannot mitigate its damages because it has a practically unlimited supply of ore. A seller who has more ore than it can sell at the market price of $25 per ton, and who has a contract to sell ore at $35 per ton, arguably cannot sell the rejected ton *at all*. Its damages are not the $10 profit but the $35 sale. See U.C.C. § 2-709(1)(b). The debtor, of course, gains only the $10 difference. Thus, it is possible for contract rejection claims to balloon well in excess of the value received by the estate.

The following summary of assets and liabilities shows what happens when BUPCUS rejects its contracts to purchase uranium from its suppliers, thereby increasing its value by $100 million, and those suppliers file $300 million in claims based on "lost volume" theories:

Assets ($mm Market Values)

Current Assets

Cash and Marketable Securities	
At Petition Date	50
2 Years' Accumulated Cash	200
Accounts Receivable	140
Inventory (FIFO)	110
Total Current Assets	500

Fixed Assets

Original Plant Value	500
Increase from Sales Contract	
Rejections	100
Increase from Supply Contract	
Rejections	100

(continued)

Total Plant Value	700
Total Assets	1,200

Liabilities ($mm Allowed Amounts)

Secured Claims

First Mortgage Bonds		
principal		500
interest		100
		600

Unsecured Claims

Prepetition Trade Claims	200
Unsecured Bank Revolver	100
14% Debentures	150
Tort Claims	350
Sales Contract Claims	100
Supply Contract Claims	300
Total	1,200
Total Liabilities	1,800
Shareholders' Equity	(600)

After the supplier contracts are rejected, the value of the debtor's plant increases by an additional $100 million unencumbered equity which adds value to the claims of unsecured creditors, so long as the case ends before further interest can accrue on the bonds against such equity. However, total unsecured claims now total $1.2 billion. Unsecured creditors previously entitled to receive $500 million in value to pay $950 million in claims, for a return of 52.6 cents on the dollar, are now entitled to receive $600 million in value to pay $1.2 billion in claims, or 50 cents on the dollar.

There is some authority permitting unsecured creditors to object to the rejection of an executory contract where the benefit to the estate is disproportionately small and the damage claim from rejection is disproportionately large. See *In re H.M. Bowness, Inc.,* 89 Bankr. 238, 240 (Bankr. M.D. Fla. 1988) and *In re Sun City Investments, Inc.,* 89 Bankr. 245, 249 (Bankr. M.D. Fla. 1988) (court denied motion to reject executory contracts where rejections did not benefit estate but merely created large damage claims). (The rejection of unexpired leases of real property should almost never dilute creditor recoveries because the claim arising out of such rejection cannot exceed the sum of (a) rent for the three years following the earlier of the rejection or the lessor's retaking possession and (b) rent past due on the earlier of such dates.)

However, as a practical matter, the decision to reject executory contracts is made based on management's perception of cash flow savings from the rejection of contracts. The decision to reject is frequently made long before management has any idea what the claims for rejection will be.

It is therefore quite possible for the debtor to reject a contract even though the claims for rejection are so high that no creditor and no shareholder benefits from the rejection! Query: In that situation, who does management serve? See "The Powers and Temptations of Management," below.

The Solvent Debtor: Interest on Unsecured Debt. As stated several times above, unsecured claims accrue interest after a chapter 11 petition only if the debtor is solvent. Solvent debtors are presumed to be rare. See *United Savings Assoc. of Texas v. Timbers of Inwood Forest Assocs., Ltd.*, 108 S. Ct. 626, 634 (1988). However, Texaco, Inc., Johns-Manville Corporation, and A. H. Robins Company, Incorporated were all solvent debtors, as is Sunbeam Corporation. By accumulating $100 million in cash from operations each year, BUPCUS will eventually become solvent. The question of interest on unsecured debt has thus become more than academic.

Pre-Code case law unanimously required solvent debtors to pay unsecured creditors postpetition interest at their contract rates. See for example, *Sexton v. Dreyfus*, 219 U.S. 339, 344 (1911) (Holmes, J.); *American Iron & Steel Mfg. Co. v. Seaboard Air Line Rwy.*, 233 U.S. 261 (1914); *Vanston Bondholders' Protective Committee v. Green*, 329 U.S. 156, 164 (1946).

However, the Code ignored the issue of postpetition interest for solvent chapter 11 debtors. See Fortgang and King, *The 1978 Bankruptcy Code: Some Wrong Policy Decisions*, 56 N.Y.U. L. Rev. 1148, 1149–65 (1981). Code § 726(a)(5) does require liquidating debtors to pay interest at the "legal rate." Most cases under the Code have continued to apply pre-Code law and require solvent debtors to pay postpetition interest at applicable contract rates. See *In re Entz-White Lumber and Supply, Inc.*, 850 F.2d 1338 (9th Cir. 1988). Compare *In re Manville Forest Products Corporation*, 60 Bankr. 403 (S.D.N.Y. 1986) (to cure payment defaults under Code § 1124(3), solvent debtor had to pay interest on past due interest at the predefault contract rate). There is some authority to the contrary. See *In re Shaffer Furniture Co.*, 68 Bankr. 827, 829-31 (Bankr. E.D. Pa. 1987) (Pennsylvania statutory rate of 8 percent). Compare *United Savings Assoc. of Texas v. Timbers of Inwood Forest Assocs., Ltd.*, 108 S. Ct. 626, 634 (1988) (*dicta* noting that Code § 726(a)(5) requires solvent debtors to pay interest); *In re Turpin*, 26 Bankr. 987 (Bankr. S.D. Ohio 1983) (Code § 726(a)(5) applied to solvent chapter 13 debtor); *In re Hansberry*, 20 Bankr. 870, 872 (Bankr. S.D. Ohio 1982) (same).

The Process of Confirmation

Negotiated Plans. The primary function of the current chapter 11 is to encourage and facilitate the rehabilitation of a debtor's balance sheet through negotiations among the debtor and its various classes of creditors and shareholders. From that perspective, the UNR Industries, Inc.,

Johns-Manville Corporation, and A. H. Robins Company, Incorporated cases were not abuses of chapter 11. They were examples of its highest and best use because those debtors had absolutely no way to negotiate a global settlement of their mass tort liabilities outside of bankruptcy. The same is true of BUPCUS with respect to its workers' claims.

Chapter 11 encourages a negotiated restructuring in a number of ways. From the investor's perspective, the facilitation of negotiation is usually beneficial, because it leads to quicker confirmation and a quicker return on investment. However, the investor may find that it is the victim rather than the beneficiary of the negotiation.

Class Voting.   Code §§ 1123(a)(1)–(4) require a chapter 11 plan to divide claims and interests according to their respective rights and to deal with those claims and interests on a class-by-class basis. The plan is distributed with a disclosure statement to creditors pursuant to Code § 1125(a), and holders of claims in impaired classes thereafter vote their separately classified claims on the plan on a class-by-class basis pursuant to Code § 1126(c):

> (c) A class of claims has accepted a plan if such plan has been accepted by creditors, *other than any entity designated under subsection (e) of this section*, that hold at least two-thirds in amount *and one-half in number* of the allowed claims of such class held by creditors *other than any entity designated under subsection (e) of this section, that have accepted or rejected such plan.*

The italicized material is of special interest. Note the most important feature of chapter 11's class-by-class vote: when the requisite majorities of creditors accept treatment of their claims under the plan, they bind not only themselves but also those creditors who have not accepted the plan. Code §§ 1123(a)(4) and 1129(a)(8). The only exception to this rule is that the requisite majorities cannot bind other creditors in an impaired class to accept less than such creditors would receive in liquidation. Code § 1129(a)(7)(A)(ii).

In BUPCUS's case, the binding nature of the class vote is especially important because it makes possible a meaningful classwide settlement with BUPCUS's thousands of injured workers. No out-of-court restructuring can achieve such a settlement unless a class action is available. Personal injury lawsuits have generally been considered inappropriate for treatment through class actions, although U.S. District Judge Jack Weinstein in 1990 has tried to consolidate all asbestoses lawsuits against various defendants into one class.

The investor's perspective on class voting will change depending on whether the investor supports or opposes the proposed plan. An investor in an exchange offer can always retain its old securities, even though (as seen above) the covenants and other protections for those securities may change if the exchange offer is successful. However, the holder of a claim in a chapter 11 case will be forced to accept whatever plan treatment its fellow class members endorse, as long as the endorsement is by the requisite majorities and the holder receives more under the plan than it would upon liquidation.

Counting those Voting. Unlike all out-of-court restructurings that must obtain the requisite percentage of all claims in a class whether they vote or not, votes on a chapter 11 plan are counted like votes in a political election: the requisite majorities are determined from the pool of those voting—"that have accepted or rejected the plan"—and not from the pool of all those entitled to vote. Where the debtor seeks consents from classes of bearer debt securities, the difficulty of locating the holders may preclude any restructuring outside of chapter 11. This problem often arises with respect to Eurodollar securities such as the 14 percent Euros, which are typically in bearer form. By contrast, Code § 1126 counts only those bearer securities that vote.

Most investors should benefit from the principle that only those voting are counted because the investor is likely to be one of those voting.

Controlling the Vote: "One-half in Number". In an exchange offer, or any out-of-court restructuring requiring a majority of indenture security holders, the only relevant majority is the majority in amount. It matters not whether that majority is held by one holder or by many. That rule also held true for votes on plans of reorganization under chapter X of the Act. Act § 179, 11 U.S.C. § 579 and Rule 10-305(e) (1976). It is no longer true for votes on plans under the new chapter 11.

The majority-in-number provision is examined in greater detail elsewhere. See Fortgang and Mayer, *Trading Claims and Taking Control of Corporations in Chapter 11,* 12 Cardozo L. Rev. 1, 86-91 (1990). The majority-in-number requirement may make a chapter 11 plan more difficult to confirm than an out-of-court restructuring.

Suppose one institution held 75 percent of the BUPCUS 10 percent first mortgage bonds. That institution could bind other bondholders in an out-of-court restructuring to accept covenant amendments, a release of collateral, and (with the right indenture provisions) even a three-year deferral of interest. However, it cannot do so in chapter 11 if small bondholders constituting a majority of all bondholders vote against the plan.

With respect to the unsecured creditors of BUPCUS, the majority-in-number requirement may give worker claimants leverage they might not otherwise have—especially if the claimants are represented by a union. In the chapter 11 reorganization of Revere Copper and Brass, Inc., the United Steelworkers of America threatened to organize members into a blocking position based on the "majority in amount" requirement.

The "majority-in-number" test will probably not benefit investors. First, investors tend to be few in number compared with other creditors. Therefore, the majority-in-number test diminishes the leverage of the investor. Second, as noted above, the majority-in-number test magnifies the leverage of those creditors who may be opposed to the investor's interest in quick plan confirmation, such as an angry union seeking to disrupt a plan so as to magnify its leverage in collective bargaining. Third, those investors who seek to control a class may buy two-thirds in amount of the debt securities in the class only to find their control blocked by a myriad of small holders.

Disqualifying Voters: "Good Faith".   Not all votes that are cast are counted in the balloting. Votes cast by "any entity designated under subsection (e)" of Code § 1126 are not counted. Code § 1126(e) authorizes the court to designate, after notice and a hearing, any entity "whose acceptance or rejection of the plan was not in good faith."

Section 1126(e) has some specific applications of interest to investors seeking to control or influence the vote on a plan.

Conflict of Interest.   Return for a moment to YECH, discussed in the previous section. Assume that YECH files a chapter 11 petition and that both series of its debentures trade at 50 cents on the dollar. If the debentures can be cashed out at 50 cents on the dollar, there will be equity left for shareholders. Outside of bankruptcy, nothing would prevent a group of YECH's shareholders from buying the debentures at 50 cents on the dollar with a view to preserving their equity in YECH. See *Aladdin Hotel Co. v. Bloom*, 200 F.2d 627 (8th Cir. 1953) (bondholder could not object to amendment of indenture approved by requisite majority even though majority included bonds purchased by shareholders with the intent of furthering the amendment). If such shareholders acquired two-thirds of the YECH debentures, they could attempt to force the other debentureholders to accept a 50-cent plan that would leave the shareholders with their equity untouched and pay back their investment in the debentures. The entire scheme would cost the shareholders nothing more than the interest on the money spent to buy the debentures.

Code § 1126(e) provides the power to frustrate such a scheme. The House Report cites *Aladdin Hotel* as precisely the type of situation the Code was enacted to prevent. H.R. Rep. No. 595, 95th Cong., 1st Sess. 411 (1977). The subsequent legislative history to section 1126(e) indicates that Congress expected the courts to disqualify votes based on conflicts of interest. See Cong. Rec. H 11,103 (Sept. 28, 1978); S 17,420 (Oct. 6, 1978). The principle is clear: a creditor or shareholder with interests in two classes cannot vote its position in one class to benefit its interests in the other.

Blocking Positions.   Any out-of-court restructuring is vulnerable to opposition by a creditor (or shareholder) who holds enough claims or shares to prevent the accumulation of the requisite majorities in favor of the restructuring. The same is true with respect to a chapter 11 plan. However, the proponents of the plan may have a weapon against the holder of the blocking position in Section 1126(e).

The "bad faith" provisions of Code § 1126(e) are based on Act § 203, which was enacted specifically in response to the hotelier Conrad Hilton's accumulation of enough bonds to block a Section 77B reorganization in *Texas Hotel Securities Corp. v. Waco Development Co.*, 87 F.2d 395 (5th Cir. 1936). In the words of then-SEC Commissioner William O. Douglas, who helped to draft Act § 203,

> We envisage that "good faith" clause to enable the courts to affirm a plan over the opposition of a minority attempting to block the adoption of a plan merely for selfish purposes. The Waco case ... was such a situation. If my memory does not serve me wrong, it was a case where a minority group of security holders refused to vote in favor of the plan unless that group were given some particular preferential treatment, such as the management of the company. That is, there were ulterior reasons for their actions. According to the lower court, they said: "For a price you can have our vote." That is the type of situation that [Act § 203] is designed to meet ... where a fellow goes out and buys up securities at a default price and then sits back in a nuisance or strategic position and seeks to capitalize on that. It also covers the situation where he does not buy at a default price but nevertheless is working a "hold-up" scheme on those who are trying to get these securities in during reorganization.

Revision of the Bankruptcy Act: Hearings on H.R. 6439 before the House Comm. on the Judiciary, 75th Cong., 1st Sess. at 180, 183-84 (1937). See also *Young v. Higbee*, 324 U.S. 204, 211 n.10 (1945) (Act § 203 was enacted to overrule *Waco* and disqualify the votes of creditors who acquired their claims with the intention of preventing confirmation unless their demands were met, quoting Douglas's testimony.)

The cases on "good faith" under Act § 203 are anything but consistent. See Fortgang and Mayer, *Trading Claims and Taking Control of Corporations in Chapter 11*, 12 Carodozo L. Rev. 1, 91-99 (1990). However, two principles can be gleaned from both the cases and the legislative history. First, the holder of a blocking position cannot obtain "greenmail" — that is, special consideration for the holder different from the treatment to other members of its class. See, for example, *Young v. Higbee*, 324 U.S. 204 (1945) (preferred shareholders appealing on behalf of their class could not sell their appeal); *In re P-R Holding Corp.*, 147 F.2d 895 (2d Cir. 1945) (proponents of plan paying bondholders 50 cents in securities could not buy out objecting bondholders for 50 cents in cash); *In re Featherworks Corp.*, 25 Bankr. 634 (Bankr. E.D.N.Y. 1982) (secured creditor's change to acceptance of plan after receiving payment from debtor's principals was tantamount to accepting a bribe under 18 U.S.C. § 152 cl. 6). It also seems clear that a plan proponent cannot acquire claims to block a competing plan and monopolize a special profit through the confirmation of its own plan. See *In re Allegheny International, Inc.*, Ch. 11 Case No. 88-448 slip. op. (Bankr. W.D. Pa. July 12, 1990).

Finally, a creditor or shareholder who obtains a blocking position after a plan has been filed but before a disclosure statement has been approved with the intent of defeating the plan may have its votes disqualified under Code § 1126(e), because that subsection also applies to any vote that "was not solicited or procured in good faith or in accordance with the provisions of this title." The purchase of a claim or interest with a view to defeating a filed plan of reorganization is tantamount to the solicitation of a vote without a disclosure statement—prohibited under Code § 1125(b). Compare *First American Bank of New York v. Century Glove, Inc.*, 860 F.2d 94 (3rd Cir. 1988) (creditor could solicit votes against a plan after the plan and a court-approved disclosure statement were circulated by plan proponents).

Beyond Consent: Unimpairment. A plan need not be accepted by a class of claims or interests if the plan leaves the class "unimpaired" under Code § 1124. A class of claims is unimpaired if (1) its rights or interest are left unaltered by the plan, (2) all defaults (other than defaults related to bankruptcy or the financial condition of the debtor prior to the closing of the case) are cured, the class is compensated for reasonable reliance on such defaults, the maturity of claims or interests in the class is reinstated, and the rights of claims or interests in the class are otherwise left unaltered, or (3) such claims or interests are paid cash in full. As a practical matter, few debtors have the cash available to pay creditors in full pursuant to Code § 1124(3), and many are reluctant to spend money to cure defaults under Code § 1124(2).

In any event, from the investor's perspective unimpairment under Code § 1124 should be an unalloyed plus. No investor should ever purchase a security whose value will drop if its rights are restored. The only situations in which that might happen involve interest.

First, there is an argument (advanced by the debtor in the Sunbeam Corporation case) that any unsecured creditor paid the full amount of its prepetition claim in cash on the effective date of a plan has no right to postpetition interest even if the debtor is solvent. The Sunbeam creditors negotiated a compromise on that issue. If the argument were accepted by the court or the compromise reached by the creditors were low, the price of the securities might fall.

Second, the filing of a bankruptcy petition accelerates the maturities of all claims. See H.R. Rep. 595, 95th Cong., 2d Sess. 353 (1977). Therefore any debt security with a distant maturity and a below-market interest rate may actually gain value when a chapter 11 petition is filed because the securities are automatically allowed at par (assuming no original issue discount), even if they were trading at 70 cents. Section 1124(2) allows the debtor to regain the benefits of low-coupon debt by reinstating its maturity. In that case, securities prices that were buoyed by the acceleration of the debt will fall because of the deacceleration under Code § 1124(2).

Beyond Consent: Cramdown. If the requisite majorities in an impaired class do not vote for a plan, the plan may still be confirmed over the objection of the class as long as one impaired class has accepted the plan and the plan is "fair and equitable" with respect to each dissenting class. "Fair and equitable" is a term of art defined in Code § 1129(b)(2) as requiring minimum treatment of dissenting secured classes, dissenting unsecured classes, and dissenting equity classes.

Secured claims. A plan may be confirmed over the objection of a class of secured claims only if the plan provides that the holders of such claims

- retain their lien on collateral (or on the proceeds of the collateral) and receive cash payments whose present value equals the allowed amount of their claims, or
- receive the "indubitable equivalent" of their claims

Appellate courts have generally read the statutory language used in Code § 1129(b)(2)(A)(i)(II) and elsewhere as entitling secured creditors to receive payment over time with interest "at the market rate." See, for example, *In re Camino Real Landscape Maintenance Contractors, Inc.*, 818 F.2d 1503 (9th Cir. 1987); *United States v. Neal Pharmacal Co.*, 789 F.2d 1283 (8th Cir. 1986); *In re Southern States Motor Inns, Inc.*, 709 F.2d 647, 651–53 (11th Cir. 1983), *cert. denied*, 465 U.S. 1022 (1984); *Memphis Bank & Trust Co. v. Whitman*, 692 F.2d 427, 431 (6th Cir. 1982). But compare *In re Ahlers*, 794 F.2d 388 (8th Cir. 1986), *rev'd on other grounds*, 108 S. Ct. 963 (1988) (first and second farm mortgagees could be compelled to accept payment over 30 years at 12 percent).

Code § 1129(b)(2)(A) thus essentially requires money-good treatment of secured claims in cash. If a class of secured claims receives noncash consideration such as inferior securities—unsecured or subordinated notes, preferred or common equity—the holders are entitled to compensation for the surrender of their superior rights as secured creditors. See, for example, *In re Day & Meyer, Murray & Young, Inc.*, 93 F.2d 657, 658 (2d Cir. 1938). It follows that equity issued to satisfy secured claims must be conservatively valued. If the plan provides for the issuance of common stock whose value is estimated at $5 to $10 per share, the plan cannot compel a secured creditor to take stock for its secured claim under Code § 1129(b)(2)(A) unless the stock is valued at the lower end of the range— here, $5 per share. Otherwise, the secured creditor would not be receiving the "indubitable equivalent" of its claim.

This analysis provides an opportunity to investors who are prepared to buy a controlling position in a secured class, that is, to obtain two-thirds in amount of the claims in the class. But see "Counting those voting," above. That group would then be in a position to trade its secured claims for equity in the reorganized debtor on favorable terms, which could give the group a profit even if the secured claims had been acquired at par. Where the group has managed to acquire secured claims at a discount, the opportunity for profit is even greater.

Unsecured Claims.   Code § 1129(b)(2)(B) provides that a plan may be confirmed over the objection of an impaired class of unsecured creditors only if the plan

- provides that the holder of each unsecured claim receives property (not necessarily cash!) whose present discounted value as of the effective date of the plan equals the allowed amount of such claim; or
- provides no value to any class that is junior to such class.

Where the debtor is solvent, it is possible for a plan to pay unsecured creditors in full through the issuance of equity or debt securities and still leave value for equity classes. The more important aspect of Code § 1129(b)(2)(B), however, is the second option: wiping out the equityholders of the company. It is that second option that forms the background of most chapter 11 cases: the presumption that unsecured creditors of an insolvent debtor are entitled to receive all of the equity of the reorganized company. *In re Emons Industries, Inc.*, 50 Bankr. 692, 694 (Bankr. S.D.N.Y. 1985) (where the debtor is insolvent, any distributions to equity are "in the nature of a gift" from unsecured creditors).

From the perspective of an investor in BUPCUS, the cramdown provisions as applied to unsecured creditors can be a boon if the investor values BUPCUS's equity higher than the other holders of the 14 percent Euros. If those holders are unhappy with cramdown and the forced receipt of equity securities, their 14 percent Euros may be available for purchase at low values.

Moreover, an investor may be able to seek control of BUPCUS through the purchase of its unsecured claims. However, if the investor's purchases of unsecured debt securities constitute a "tender offer," the investor must comply with at least Section 14(e) and Rules 14e-1 through 14e-3 of the Securities Exchange Act.

Unsecured debt securities do not explicitly constitute "equity securities registered under section 12" of the Securities Exchange Act, so the hostile tender offer provisions of the Williams Act other than Section 14(e) would not seem to apply. However, at some point a debt security in a chapter 11 case may become entitled to receive an equity security, at which point it is an equity security. See section 3a(11) of the Securities Exchange Act, 15 U.S.C. § 78c(a)(11). At that point the investor in unsecured claims may have to comply with the Williams Act and the hostile tender offer rules promulgated under Sections 13(d) and 14(d). Where a chapter X plan had been confirmed but not consummated, and the equity securities to be distributed to unsecured creditors were trading on a when-issued basis, one court held that unsecured claims were "equity securities registered under Section 12," *SEC v. Texas International Co.*, 498 F. Supp. 1231 (N.D. Ill. 1980) (Marshall, J.), and one court held that such claims were not equity securities so registered. *Lipper v. Texas International Co.*, Fed. Sec. L. Rep. (CCH) ¶ 96,837 (W.D. Okla. April 6, 1979).

If the investor does not want equity securities, then the cramdown provisions can be quite dangerous. It would be quite possible, for example, for BUPCUS's management to use BUPCUS's accumulated cash to pay off the 10 percent bonds and to issue nothing but equity to BUPCUS's unsecured creditors. Once again, the value of an investment in BUPCUS securities depends on an analysis of management.

The Powers and Temptations of Management

Absent the appointment of a trustee under Code § 1104—unlikely without a showing of venality or fraud—management continues in control of a chapter 11 debtor. It is true that chapter 11 imposes on management certain annoying constraints not present outside of court. These include:

- meetings with, and investigation by, official creditor and shareholder committees, Code § 1103(c)(1) and (2)
- court approval of most borrowings, Code §§ 364(b) and (c). Although Code § 364(a) allows the debtor to incur credit in the ordinary course without court approval, lenders (other than trade creditors) will rarely extend credit without a court order
- court approval of the use of property "out of the ordinary course" of business. Code § 363(b)

These constraints are minor compared to the tremendous control given to management by the Code in a chapter 11 reorganization.

First, management runs the business. Code §§ 1107–08. Notwithstanding the requirement of court approval for the use of property, management can conduct most of the business of the debtor without judicial scrutiny, including transactions as momentous as the negotiation of a new collective bargaining agreement! See, for example, *In re DeLuca Distributing Co.*, 38 Bankr. 588 (Bankr. N.D. Ohio 1984); *In re IML Freight, Inc.*, 37 Bankr. 556 (Bankr. D. Utah 1984). Compare *In re Wil-Low Cafeterias*, 111 F.2d 429 (2d Cir. 1940) (chapter X trustee did not need order approving modification of collective bargaining agreement, given previous court order generally authorizing chapter X trustee to run business) with *Local Joint Executive Board v. Hotel Circle, Inc.*, 613 F.2d 210 (9th Cir. 1980) (chapter XI receiver lacked authority to make postpetition agreement without approval of bankruptcy court).

From the investor's perspective, the power to run the business is probably beneficial. An investor who does not like the management of the corporation usually will not invest in its debt securities.

Second, many decisions—such as the assumption or rejection of executory contracts and leases under Code § 365 and the abandonment of burdensome assets under Code § 554—are left to the "business judgment" of management. See *NLRB v. Bildisco and Bildisco*, 465 U.S. 513, 523 (1984); *Richmond Leasing Co. v. Capitol Bank, N.A.*, 762 F.2d 1303, 1309 (5th Cir. 1985) (*per curiam*); *Lubrizol Enterprises, Inc. v. Richmond Metal Finishers, Inc.*, 756 F.2d 1043, 1046–47 (4th Cir. 1985), *cert. denied*, 475 U.S. 1057 (1986). Rarely will a court overturn a debtor's business judgment.

From the investor's perspective, management's discretion in the rejection of contracts can be a boon—or a disaster. For the holders of BUPCUS's 10 percent bonds, management boosted the value of their bonds from 100 cents to 120 cents by rejecting BUPCUS's sales contracts. This increased the value of the bondholders' collateral to $600 million and allowed the accrual of two years of postpetition interest. The rejection of the supply contracts boosted the value of the collateral to $700 million and would have allowed another two years worth of postpetition interest.

For the holders of BUPCUS's 14 percent Euros, the decision to reject those contracts was a disaster, diminishing their recoveries from 62.5 cents to 52.6 cents even if the bonds accrued only two years' interests.

Third, the debtor exercises substantial control over the formulation and filing of a plan of reorganization and disclosure statement. As a legal matter, Code § 1121(b) precludes parties other than the debtor from filing a plan in the first 120 days of the case. That "exclusivity period" is routinely extended by courts. See, for example, 5 *Collier on Bankruptcy* ¶ 1121.04 at 1121–13 (L. King, 15th ed., 1985); *In re Texaco Inc.*, 76 Bankr. 322 (Bankr. S.D.N.Y. 1987). Compare *In re Public Service Co. of New Hampshire*, 88 Bankr. 521, 533–40 (Bankr. D.N.H. 1988) (debtor must show likelihood of successful reorganization in addition to complexity of case to justify extension). But compare *In re Timbers of Inwood Forest Assocs.*, 808 F.2d 363, 370–71 and nn. 12–13 (5th Cir. 1987) (*en banc*), *aff'd*, 108 S. Ct. 626 (1988) (courts should be mindful of the cost of delay to creditors and permit creditors to file plans of reorganization). As a practical matter, creditors who file a plan must also file a disclosure statement, Bankruptcy Rule 3016(a), which is often difficult or impossible because the information needed to compile a disclosure statement is controlled by management.

Where the debtor's management is committed to a quick exit from chapter 11, the exclusivity period does not represent a major threat to investors in either secured or unsecured debt securities. However, the exclusivity period can present a real problem if management wants to stay in chapter 11. Many bankruptcy courts will keep extending the period because, in the end, debtor's counsel enjoys natural advantages in front of many bankruptcy judges.

Debtor's counsel appears before the bankruptcy judge at almost every hearing and purports to represent all of the debtors' constituencies. By contrast, creditors' or shareholders' counsel—even counsel to an official committee—will appear less frequently and can represent only a particular creditor, shareholder, or class of creditors or shareholders. Many bankruptcy judges may therefore have a natural, if occasionally unfair, tilt toward the debtor and hence toward management.

In sum, management's extraordinary powers are primarily of interest to the investor. Those powers give management the ability to allocate value among its classes of claims and equity interests. There are few, if any, guidelines as to how management should exercise those powers.

14

Determining Whether a Company Is Really a Turnaround Candidate

Ronald G. Quintero
R. G. Quintero & Co.

Roger D. Timpson
R. G. Quintero & Co.

"Many men, seemingly impelled by fortune, hasten forward to meet misfortune halfway."
—Rousseau

In the seemingly genteel world of mergers and acquisitions, "turn-around candidate" is a term that is loosely applied to almost any company that is losing money. The spectrum of "turnaround candidates" ranges from viable companies that are experiencing a temporary downturn to corporate nightmares that are knocking on death's door. Distinguishing between the two can make the difference between a Toys "R" Us, where $1 invested in 1974 would be worth $1000 in 1989, and Crazy Eddy, where one of the most renowned turnaround artists of our time invested tens of millions of dollars in 1987, which became worthless within 12 months.

This chapter deals with several topics:

- Why companies get into trouble
- Characteristics of a turnaround candidate
- Analyzing the viability of a turnaround
- Characteristics of an unlikely turnaround candidate
- Balancing the risks and rewards

Why Companies Get into Trouble

"Troubles are exceedingly gregarious in their nature, and flying in flocks are apt to perch capriciously."

—Dickens

In order to decide whether there is a cure for the ailment, it is necessary to understand the symptoms and causes of the disease. Some are easily correctable. Others require sustained effort, with no assurance of success. Companies do not generally become ill suddenly. Problems tend to develop over a long period of time. They often require a comparable period of time to be resolved.

The Symptoms

The symptoms of financial distress are often confused with the causes of financial distress. The symptom is the external manifestation of financial distress. The symptom is a by-product or end result of the cause.

The most obvious symptoms of financial distress are mounting losses, insufficient cash flow to meet obligations as they become due, and bankruptcy. These symptoms are generally the end results of a series of contributory symptoms. These symptoms can be categorized as external symptoms, operational symptoms, financial symptoms, and miscellaneous symptoms. Examples of each category of symptoms are listed in Table 14.1.

Table 14.1.   Symptoms of Financial Distress

External Symptoms
- Competitors are known to be experiencing financial difficulties.
- Industry price structure has deteriorated.
- Industry cost structure has increased.
- Industry has surplus capacity.
- Customers are suffering from a downturn or industry slowdown.
- Legislative or regulatory developments threaten key products or may significantly increase the cost structure.
- Competition from new competitors or substitute products and
- services is being felt.
- Technological changes requiring significant product innovations or capital expenditures are necessary.
- Capital markets are restricting access to debt or equity funding.

Operational Symptoms
- Turnover of senior management has occurred.
- Members of the board of directors have resigned.
- Board members insist on improved directors' liability insurance coverage.
- Management information system fails to provide management information that is accurate, timely, and meaningful.
- Company has an inadequate planning process; business plans are not developed, meaningful, or executed.
- Management lacks credibility in the eyes of employees, customers, creditors, or vendors.
- The scope or scale of the business has changed as a result of rapid growth, acquisitions, new products, entry into new markets,
- or adoption of new production methods.

(continued)

Table 14.1. (cont.)

- Staff reductions, wage freezes, spending cuts, asset sales, product line eliminations, and other downsizing measures have been imposed.
- Labor unrest impedes productivity.
- Excessive overtime.
- Prices have been reduced to generate additional sales.
- Shipments are consistently late.
- A major customer has been lost.
- Company uses an unusually large number of vendors, perhaps to elicit additional credit, or because of poor vendor relations.
- Vendors demand C.O.D., payments in advance, deposits, cash payments, or simply refuse to ship under any terms.
- Creditors that are also customers are increasing purchases, possibly to offset outstanding balances due from the company.
- Key elements of the cost structure have increased significantly or are excessive in comparison to the level of revenue.

Financial Symptoms
- Company lacks certified financial statements.
- Auditor is late in completing the annual audit.
- Auditor has expanded the scope of the audit due to concerns over risk or the financial condition of the company.
- Auditor is unknown, poorly regarded, or inexperienced in the company's industry.
- A change of auditors has occurred, perhaps as a result of disputes over accounting or auditing issues.
- Accounting methods that maximize earnings are employed.
- Nontraditional financing methods, such as off–balance-sheet financing or offering unusual incentives for prompt paying, are being used.
- Indebtedness has increased.
- Company is shopping for new lenders or other sources of capital.
- Debt has been renegotiated at terms that are more onerous than those that were previously in place.
- Lenders have requested additional collateral, pledging of assets, equity infusions, and/or personal guarantees to keep loan in force.
- Bank is reluctant to engage in candid conversation about the company due to fear of lender liability.
- Lender has transferred the loan to the workout department.
- Company's financial projections are consistently inaccurate.
- Financial fraud has occurred.
- Owners have taken significant money out of the company.
- Personal guarantors have transferred personal assets to become judgement proof.
- Average days outstanding of accounts receivable have grown, suggesting possible customer dissatisfaction with products or services, or the failure of the company to recognize a writeoff.
- Returns and allowances have increased, suggesting a relaxing of quality control standards to generate sales more quickly or to reduce costs.

(continued)

Table 14.1.   (cont.)

- Inventory turnover has slowed, suggesting a possible accumulation of slow-moving or unsaleable goods.
- Accounts payable are being "stretched".
- Creditors have been asked to compromise their positions by extending the due date, converting current accounts to notes or equity, agreeing to a "haircut," or making other concessions.
- Security interests in assets are being granted to certain key creditors.
- Deposits in trust funds, such as payroll taxes, are delinquent.
- Discretionary expenditures such as capital expenditures, product development, advertising, and maintenance have been reduced.
- Dividends have been reduced or eliminated.
- Shareholders have made loans to the company or provided capital infusions.
- Legal costs have increased due to lawsuits or the cost of contesting creditor actions.
- Purchase commitments have been made at prices or terms in excess of those currently available.
- Long-term sale agreements are below current market prices.
- Company has a large unfunded pension liability.
- Company is liable for significant retiree medical costs.

Miscellaneous Symptoms
- Company is being "shopped" to several potential investors.
- Company representatives express a sense of urgency to close a transaction.
- Company representatives resist information requests or a thorough due diligence review.
- Judgements have been awarded against the company.
- Company has significant legal exposure as a result of environmental contamination, defective products, or other asserted or unasserted claims.
- Insurance coverage is insufficient to meet potential liabilities from pending litigation and unasserted claims.
- Company has engaged bankruptcy counsel and/or other insolvency professionals.

SOURCE: Adapted from Ronald G. Quintero, "Acquiring the Turnaround Candidate," in Sumner N. Levine, ed., *The Acquisitions Manual* (New York: New York Institute of Finance, 1989), pp. 384–87.

The Disease

Considerable effort and money can be devoted to diagnosing and treating the symptoms. However, the disease is the root cause of the symptoms. It is generally attributable to one or more of the following:

- Inadequate management
- Excessive leverage
- Undercapitalization

- Macroeconomic changes
- Legal or regulatory problems

Inadequate management most often takes the rap for all that befalls a company. More often than not, this is justified. Good management can navigate a company through treacherous shoals. Inadequate management can scuttle the best of companies, if given enough time.

History is an imperfect measure for judging management. Entrepreneurial management with the creativity, vision, and charisma required to build a company draws on different talents than the professional management required to run a larger and more complex organization. Management that functions well during good times often lacks the decisiveness to operate in a turnaround. Management must be well suited to the existing operating and financial environment of the company.

The leveraged buyout and financial restructuring frenzy of the 1980s sowed the seeds of the turnaround and workout candidates of the 1990s. Many companies employed so much leverage that they were ill equipped to adjust to any deviations from optimistic business plans. Financial inflexibility caused operating inflexibility. As a consequence, many of these companies failed to keep pace with competitors in product development, employee training, expansion, and employee remuneration. What began as a financial limitation evolved into an operational problem.

A companion of too much debt is insufficient equity. This may not be the result of excessive leverage. Many companies are operated with so little capital that they suffer financial distress as a result of their own success. Despite increasing sales and operating profits, they lack the cash to fund receivables and inventory. Some companies have reported their highest levels of sales and earnings just prior to going out of business.

An inability to adapt to macroeconomic change constitutes another cause of financial distress. The nature of these changes can include global, national, or regional developments affecting customers and markets, changes in the competitive environments, and other factors that are external to the company. Businesses compete in a dynamic environment. There is a continuous need to adapt to change. Since the environment will not stay still, neither can businesses. Change seldom kills business; rather, an inability to adapt to change can spell its demise.

A final category of turnaround candidates consists of those facing financial distress due to legal or regulatory problems. Texaco and A. H. Robins are examples of companies that were financially healthy, but potential legal claims caused them to seek relief via chapter 11. Less celebrated cases that are occurring with increasing frequency involve companies with environmental problems. The aggregate price tag for cleanups that will be mandated during the next decade is believed to be tens of billions of dollars. Many companies facing monumental liabilities are likely to face severe financial difficulties in complying with environmental regulations.

Characteristics of a Turnaround Candidate

"If you have better boards, or fatter pigs to sell, or if you build a better mousetrap, the world will beat a hard broad path to your door though you live in the woods."
—Anonymous

For a company to warrant being called a turnaround candidate, it must have reasonable prospects of being turned around. It must be worth saving. A workout banker we know once referred to one of the companies in his workout portfolio as a loan in search of a business. A turnaround candidate must have a viable core business and be capable of being fixed with the resources available to it. Some of the characteristics that make a turnaround candidate attractive are described below.

Capable Management. Capable management is the *sine qua non* of any turnaround. Without capable management, the best turnaround plan is doomed to fail because it will not be properly executed. A management team must be in place or promptly recruited. It is risky to invest in a company until the management team has been identified and put in place. Management should be motivated to remain with the company until the turnaround has been completed.

Employees. The cooperation and support of employees is required to execute a turnaround. A stable, turmoil-free work force is a critical ingredient to a turnaround. Their value to the company is at a premium if they are highly skilled, long-term employees and supportive of the company and management.

Cooperative Attitude. More often than not, turnarounds require a "sharing of the pain" among management, employees, lenders, and creditors. These are the "stakeholders" of the company. The support of government agencies may also be sought in the form of tax relief or debt guarantees. The rehabilitation of Chrysler stands as a shining example of a case where all constituencies cooperated to enable the rehabilitation of the company.

Business Plan That Makes Sense. There must be an identifiable series of achievable actions that can reasonably be expected to have a measurable impact upon the financial condition and performance of the company. The business plan should reflect several of the following actions:

- Reducing expenses
- Increasing revenues
- Developing a more profitable business mix
- Enhancing asset utilization
- Restructuring debt
- Raising capital

The business plan must be specific with respect to who is responsible for each action, how it will be implemented, the resources required to implement it, timing, and the operational and financial consequences.

Size. The larger that a company is, the greater the likelihood of a turnaround. A study of bankruptcy filings between 1979 and 1986 found that the confirmation rate on filings with asset values in excess of $1 million was five times as great as the rate of confirmations in filings below $100,000[1]. Large companies are more likely to be survivors than small companies because

- They have more stakeholders with more to lose if they go out of business.
- More often than not, they have better established business franchises than small companies.
- They have greater access to capital.
- They are better able to recruit capable management and professionals.
- They are more likely to have built up layers of fat that can be eliminated.

Return on Investment Requirements. In terms of initial expectations, there are generally two groups of investors in turnarounds: voluntary investors and involuntary investors. Involuntary investors generally become involved with the turnaround candidate before the onset of a financial crisis, without intending to invest in a turnaround. They include trade creditors, lenders, and long-term shareholders. Their main goal is to salvage whatever they can and to minimize any future erosion of their position. Voluntary investors are those who fund the turnaround. They seek rates of return in excess of the prime rate of interest on secured debt, above 20 percent on subordinated debt with equity kickers, and above 30 percent on equity or equity equivalents. These returns can be achieved through a combination of current income and appreciation in the value of equity and equity equivalents.

Positive Industry Fundamentals. Some companies defy the odds and languish in the midst of prosperity. The prospects for a turnaround are enhanced if the company's products are in demand, the industry is healthy, and customers are financially healthy.

Unrealized Opportunities. Turnarounds normally depend upon implementing change. A company may have unrealized opportunities to penetrate new markets, introduce new products, adopt a more profitable product mix, reduce expenses, or initiate other actions that can improve profitability and cash flow.

Significant Tangible Asset Value. Acquisitions of turnaround candidates are often based on asset values. The price paid is frequently a discount from the appraised value of the assets or the aggregate fair market value of the lines of business. Attention is focused on asset values, since there is often no cash flow or earnings upon which to base a capitalized value. Asset values provide a measure of downside protection in the investment.

Surplus Assets. Turnaround candidates are normally hungry for cash. The ability to raise cash by selling unused, underutilized,or unproductive assets is vital when buying time to stabilize the business. Obvious examples include real estate, equipment, lines of business, or subsidiaries. Less apparent sources of cash include improving inventory management practices and accounts receivable collections to reduce the required investment in these assets. Other cash sources may be slow-moving inventory that can be sold at reduced prices or aged receivables whose collection may be hastened by offering prompt payment incentives.

Unused Borrowing Capacity. Most companies that have experienced financial difficulty for some time have used up all of the borrowing capacity readily apparent to management. However, additional debt funding may be possible because (1) management is inexperienced in raising debt financing, (2) sources such as governmental programs or asset-based lenders have not been approached, (3) new equity has been invested in the company, (4) a credible business plan has been submitted to lenders, (5) new management or the company's advisers are able to persuade lenders to provide funding, or (6) investors guarantee debt. The trade may also be a source of borrowing capacity, either by "stretching" payments or obtaining a composition agreement, whereby they agree to receive payments over time or at a "haircut" from the balance outstanding.

Poor Management. In spite of what we said of the critical role of management in a turnaround, poor management can make a turnaround candidate enticing. Provided that poor management is not pervasive throughout all levels of a company, it can be a plus rather than a negative. Poor management can be bolstered or replaced.

It would be discouraging to learn that capable management seemed to make all the right decisions, and yet, despite that, the company was failing. It would lead you to the conclusion that the company was a hopeless case. On the other hand, if management is incompetent and the company has survived despite them, it would suggest that the company could thrive under good management.

Significant Market Share. The company should be a significant participant in its market, defined either in terms of its product, service, customers, or geographical location.

Barriers to Entry. Capital requirements, reputation, long-standing customer relationships, dependence on the company by key customers, proprietary technology, and regulatory restrictions all constitute barriers to entry that help to insulate the company from competition and make it more desirable.

Product or Service Uniqueness.   The more memorable the products or services of the company, the better. Factors that contribute to uniqueness include patent or copyright protection, brand name, trademarks, reputation for quality, trade secrets, customer loyalty, and proprietary or difficult-to-replicate technology. In retail and distribution businesses, service businesses, or real estate, location is an important attribute.

Enduring Demand.   Turnarounds do not generally occur overnight. The product or service must have an enduring demand so that there is an opportunity to reap the rewards after the turnaround is complete. Substitute products or services should be unfeasible or uneconomical.

Long-term Contracts.   Long-term purchase or sale contracts, as well as leases at desirable rates, can provide favorable price or cost advantages.

Limited Capital Requirements.   Turnarounds tend to be capital intensive at the onset. Like leveraged buyouts, they are more desirable if they do not require ongoing capital investments. Turnaround investors prefer to invest acumen rather than cash.

Manufacturing Advantages.   A company may be desirable in terms of manufacturing efficiency, proximity to customers or sources of supply, specialized production capabilities, or quality of plant layout and machinery.

Industry Consolidation.   Industries undergoing consolidation can provide excellent opportunities. Many such industries suffer from inadequate capitalization and lack of professional management. Turnaround investors with access to capital and management generally have the added advantage over competitors when picking up assets at a discount. They stand to cherrypick the most desirable companies, further hastening the demise of weaker participants.

Timing.   The time to invest in a cyclical industry or market is not at the sound of the first sputter. Turnaround investors are notorious "bottom fishers." They are also known as "gravedancers" who reap profits from doom. Although nobody knows the absolute bottom until after the fact, turnaround investing in a cyclical industry or market generally becomes desirable after significant carnage has already occurred.

Most turnarounds involve several phases. The deterioration that precedes the awareness of a need for a turnaround can occur over several months or even years. Deterioration may be tolerated until things reach a crisis stage, which may last 30 to 90 days. During the crisis stage, the ability of the company to survive outside of bankruptcy or on any terms may be in severe jeopardy. To abate the crisis, drastic measures are frequently taken to restore the company's credibility, eliminate cash drains, and raise capital. As the crisis subsides, a more deliberate surgical approach is adopted to effect the turnaround. The rebuilding phase can take anywhere from six months to two or three years. The best turnaround investment opportunities occur when cash is provided to alleviate the financial crisis or to fund the rebuilding phase.

Timing is also important in terms of the willingness of all parties involved to make the concessions needed to entice an investor to fund a turnaround. Often, at the early stages of financial distress, there is a failure on everybody's part to recognize the magnitude of the problem. There may be an unwillingness to make any concessions, stemming from a belief that the problem is temporary in nature. The realization of the possibility of a significant or total loss or of increasing exposure by shareholders on personal guarantees of indebtedness is a powerful incentive to forming modest expectations.

Synergies.   For a corporate buyer, a turnaround may be achievable because a company offers synergistic opportunities by

- Product line extensions
- Consolidating activities
- Upgrading the buyer's facilities
- Gaining key members of the target's management
- Absorbing some or all of the revenues of the turnaround candidate without requiring all of the expenses

The turnaround candidate may be subsumed into the buyer's company and relinquish its previous identity.

Bankruptcy Relief.   Bankruptcy is strong medicine that treats a symptom rather than offering a cure. It is expensive, disruptive, and often causes more harm than good. However, some companies can become attractive investments after being sanitized by bankruptcy. Examples of conditions that may be alleviated by chapter 11 include:

- Extensive financial exposure as a result of current litigation
- An excessive level of unsecured debt that cannot be compromised outside of bankruptcy
- Uneconomical long-term executory contracts that cannot be renegotiated, such as leases, purchase or sale agreements, or collective bargaining agreements
- Significant debt service obligations that cannot be met or deferred

Many of a company's financial ills may be temporarily stayed by a chapter 11 filing. The ability to limit, crunch down, or shed these liabilities depends upon the reorganization plan that is confirmed by the bankruptcy court. The reorganized entity may be a vastly more attractive investment and turnaround candidate than the company mired in its prebankruptcy sea of debt.

Endgame Strategy. The suitability of a turnaround investment opportunity to a particular investor depends upon his endgame strategy. The normal objectives in acquiring a turnaround candidate include

- Merging some or all of the business into an existing company
- Operating the company as an independent concern, with no planned timeframe for selling it
- Selling or liquidating the pieces
- Fixing up the company to sell to a third party or through a public offering

The latter two strategies, which are transactionally oriented, depend upon having a reasonable idea of the prospective value of the turnaround candidate and the nature of the prospective buyers. Some companies can be restored to health, but still tend to sell for little more than asset value. In an industry consolidation play, you may wind up building the largest and healthiest company in the industry, but you may also be restricted in buyers to other industry participants that are all too small or weak to acquire the company that you turned around and built up. The release valve to the public equity markets may not be achievable to some companies that lack the size or general appeal required to accommodate a public offering. A gain is never realized until cash has been received. Realizing cash depends upon the exit strategy.

Analyzing the Viability of a Turnaround

"Things are not always what they seem; first appearances deceive many."
—Phaedrus

There are three levels of analysis commonly applied to turnaround candidates to establish viability: financial analysis, operational analysis, and legal analysis. As compared to traditional acquisition due diligence, which is largely geared towards developing a detailed understanding of the acquisition target, the viability analysis seeks to establish whether the company is viable. Establishing viability based on legal considerations should be done by a lawyer. An example of financial and operation viability issues that could affect a manufacturing company is provided in Table 14.2.

A primary distinction between analyzing a financially distressed company and a profitable company is that there is less margin for error in the distressed company. The financially troubled company may be knocking on death's door. The objectives of the viability analyses are to enhance your understanding of the company and to identify the existence and magnitude of its current and prospective problems. The analyses provide the basis for developing a preliminary outline of a turnaround plan and determining whether a turnaround investment opportunity is worth pursuing.

Table 14.2.   Examples of Potential Viability Issues: Manufacturing Company

General
- What are the main reasons for the financial difficulties that the company is currently facing? How much is attributable to nonrecurring items? Uncontrollable events?
- How will developments in the overall economy affect the company? Regional economy? Developments affecting customers? Capital markets?
- What is likely to change to cause a hitherto unprofitable company to be restored to financial health?
- Is there enough time to reverse the downward spiral and effect a turnaround?
- If the company has public equity or debt securities, how do prices compare to prior levels?
- Has the company engaged bankruptcy counsel? Turnaround consultants? If so, are they capable?
- Can the company be sold? Is the company and/or its key assets marketable? Financeable? Is the business worth more in liquidation than as a going concern?

Products and sales
- What are the unique advantages and selling points of the company's products?
- Are market, competitor, or regulatory developments occurring that may make the company's product obsolete or uncompetitive?
- Are the company's products protected by patents? Trademarks? Industry reputation?
- Does the company hold any important patents that are about to expire?
- What is the general trend in sales? By product? Market?
- Have key customers switched to competitors?
- How are products priced in comparison to competition?
- Is there an opportunity to raise prices on a selective basis? In certain product or service categories? Across the board?
- Are custom orders, rush orders, or low-quantity products properly priced?
- How do gross margins vary among products? What is the explanation for variations? Is the management information system sufficiently reliable to draw conclusions?
- Can unprofitable products be eliminated? How would eliminating certain products impact the sales of others?
- Would the elimination of selected markets, customer categories, or individual customers improve profitability?
- Does the company have uneconomical long-term sales contracts? Can they be modified?
- How large is the sales backlog? Is it profitable?
- What is the status of new product development? Can it be accelerated? Should certain projects be aborted? What is the lead time required for new products to be profitable?
- Where are the opportunities to increase sales? What needs to be done to realize the opportunities?
- Would there be any benefit to hiring additional salesmen? Switching from salesmen to distributors in certain markets? Entering into joint sales and marketing joint ventures?

(continued)

Table 14.2. (cont.)

- Does the salesforce compensation system motivate the salesforce to generate sales? Open up new accounts? Promote profitable products?

Manufacturing and Distribution

- How do labor and manufacturing productivity levels compare to previous periods? To unit costs of production? What are the causes for changes?
- How does the company schedule and control manufacturing activities? Is scheduling based on a manufacturing and sales plan, machine throughput levels, and employee productivity levels?
- Is there excessive overtime? Are there constant setups for short production runs to fill rush orders?
- Do production facilities have an efficient layout?
- Would it be beneficial to increase the work force in order to avoid excessive overtime? To reduce the work force and pay more overtime, but be responsible for fewer people and lower fringe benefits, insurance, and taxes?
- Does the collective bargaining agreement give management the flexibility required to efficiently schedule and control production? Can counterproductive work rules be modified?
- How does the company's record for on-time deliveries compare to past history?
- Is there any change in the rate of product returns and allowances? Manufacturing defects? Scrap and rework levels? Why?
- Has there been a relaxing of quality controls? Maintenance? Reduced capital spending? Impact?
- How do the company's production methods compare to those of the competition? Machinery and equipment? Geographical location of manufacturing?
- Should the company subcontract or bring inhouse a larger proportion of manufacturing? Distribution?
- What are the breakeven levels of production for each facility? Product?
- Would it be beneficial to close certain manufacturing facilities? Warehouse facilities? Transfer production of certain products to other facilities?
- What is the company's production capacity? Is it suitable for near-term and long-term requirements?
- Is a regular maintenance program in place? How does machine downtime compare to historical levels?
- What near-term and long-term capital expenditures are required? Which capital expenditures could profoundly improve profitability? Is the cost justified? Financeable?
- What is the condition of the facilities and equipment? Housekeeping?
- What can be done to reduce the investment in inventory?
- Is the location of inventory clearly identified? Readily determinable?
- Are there problems with inventory control? Obsolescence? Physical security?
- Is inadequate inventory control impeding the ability to raise additional inventory financing?
- Have energy conservation methods been explored?

Purchasing

- Are materials and supplies being ordered and received on a timely basis?

(continued)

Table 14.2.   (cont.)

- Is there constant communication between purchasing and production to ensure that the right goods are purchased on a timely basis? Are shortages anticipated? Are vendors who are deficient in meeting delivery, schedules or quality standards weeded out?
- Are defective raw materials and purchased components harming production quality? If so, have alternative vendors been sought?
- Is the company taking full advantage of optimal vendor pricing, delivery, and payment terms? What checks are made to ensure that this is true?
- Are tests made to ensure that long-standing suppliers are providing products at competitive prices?
- Are products purchased in economical quantities? Excessive quantities resulting in cash being tied up in inventory?
- Are unreliable vendors being weeded out?
- Have vendors been evaluated in terms of delivery speed, with a view to minimizing the company's investment in inventory?
- What are the direct and indirect costs of each purchasing agreement?
- Does the company have uneconomical long-term purchase agreements? Can they be amended?
- Have any vendors stopped shipping to the company as a result of nonpayment? Are any of these vendors critical vendors?
- Is the company still enjoying normal credit terms from vendors?

Personnel
- What is the general attitude of the work force? Can a positive morale be restored?
- What porportion of the workforce is highly skilled or trained?
- Are employees properly trained for their jobs? Do they receive adequate supervision?
- Does the company have a lot of long-term employees?
- How does employee turnover compare to historical levels? Absenteeism?
- Is the work force willing to make the sacrifices necessary to turn the company around?
- Do employees believe that they are part of a turnaround program? Is information shared with them? Do they understand the severity of the problem? Do they know what is expected of them?
- When is the collective bargaining agreement up for renewal? Possible outcome?
- When did employees last receive raises? How does their total compensation and fringe benefit package compare to available alternatives in the local market? Compensation and fringe benefits paid competitors?
- Can employee compensation be reduced or adjusted according to the profitability of the company? Work rules amended? Overtime begin at 40 hours per week rather than 8 hours per day?
- Have all nonessential jobs been eliminated?

Management
- Can management turn the company around? Can new management be introduced in time to save the company?

(continued)

Table 14.2.   (cont.)

- Is management planning for the future or living in the past?
- Have irreplaceable members of management defected?
- Does the company have an experienced and properly trained tier of middle management?
- Does the company have a business plan? Is it reasonable? How was it prepared? Does the company have a history of successfully preparing and implementing its business plans?
- How long have key members of management been with the company? Are they experienced in the industry? Turnarounds?
- Why has management been ineffective in running the company?
- Is each member of management well suited to the tasks he/she faces?
- Is management committed to remaining with the company? Putting in the level of effort required for a turnaround? Taking a salary reduction?
- Are there any impediments to terminating members of management who are not working out?
- Does management effectively delegate authority?
- Does management communicate with each other? With employees? With shareholders? With creditors? With customers? Do they have credibility?
- Are management information systems adequate to run the business? Who receives the information? Is the information available on a timely basis? Is the information used? How?
- What kind of management reports are generated? Who receives them? How are they used?

Financial

- Does the company have the financial resources to survive? Fund a turnaround? Fund contingencies?
- Are audited financial statements available? How recent are they? Were they audited by a reputable accounting firm?
- How do financial ratios and operating results compare to historical levels? Competitors?
- Do financial statements and accounting policies provide a meaningful indication of the financial results and the financial condition of the company?
- What is the status if trade debt? Bank debt? Other obligations? Will creditors work with the company or are they seeking to put it into bankruptcy?
- Is the company actively attempting to raise capital? Restructure bank debt? Restructure trade debt? Raise new debt? Raise new equity? Status? Alternatives?
- Can better terms be obtained from an alternative lender?
- Has trade debt been "stretched" to the maximum?
- Can payments for items such as insurance be extended throughout the year without requiring large, up-front payments?
- Do the financial projections indicate that the company is self-supporting from operating cash flow? Are the projections realistic? What is the company's previous history in being able to reasonably project cash flow?
- Have all nonvital cash expenditures been eliminated? Has an analysis been performed to determine what is absolutely necessary for survival?

(continued)

Table 14.2.   (cont.)

- Can operating cash flow be increased to a level that will be sufficient to meet financial obligations?
- Can cash be realized by selling assets? Subsidiaries or lines of business? Sale/leaseback? Obtaining a refund of overpayments of income taxes? Refund of deposits and prepayments? Government subsidies or loans? Settling litigation where the company is the plaintiff? Product licensing or royalties? Leasing or subleasing property?
- Has financial fraud ocurred? Has it been stopped?
- Does the company have uneconomical leases? Can they be amended? Terminated? Sold or assigned?
- What has been happening to the average collection period of accounts receivable? Are collections being aggressively pursued? Are the collection personnel properly qualified, trained, and instructed?
- Can account receivable collections or cash flow be improved by modifying the terms of sale? Offering one-time prompt payment incentives? Cutting off delinquent customers?
- Are there one or a few major problem accounts? Background? Does it make sense to offset any liabilities due to these accounts against their outstanding balances?
- Is inventory saleable at full value within a reasonable time period? Test management assertions against agings, by item or inventory classification. Can all inventory be accounted for? Is some inventory being retained because to sell it would result in losses?
- Does the company have substantial unfunded liabilities for pensions? Retiree medical benefits? Warranty liabilities?
- Are reversion proceeds available by terminating an overfunded pension plan?

Survival

- Does the company's survival depend upon a series of favorable or uncontrollable developments?
- What motives do senior management have to ensure the survival of the company? Employees? Shareholders? Lenders? Vendors? Customers? Governmental entities?
- Are the banks about to call their loans? If so, can this action be forestalled? How long?
- Does the company have any operating permits or licenses that have been or are about to be terminated? Can they be reinstated?
- Does the company have any critical insurance such as property and casualty or workers' compensation insurance, or bonding that has been or is on the verge of being canceled? Can it be reinstated? Replaced?
- Are tax authorities about to padlock the company? Landlord? If so, what is the cost of remedying the situation?
- Is the company the target of any pending or potential lawsuits? Regulatory proceedings?
- Is vital equipment about to be reposessed by lessor or creditor? What is the cost of forestalling action?

(continued)

Table 14.2. (cont.)

- Does the company have significant financial exposure for environmental contamination? Uninsured or underinsured product liability claims?
- What would be the impact of bankruptcy on the company? Would it have any long-term benefits? Could the company be funded in bankruptcy? Could it eventually be reorganized?
- Does the company have adequate insurance or financial resources to deal with any large contingent expenditures or unforeseen events?

The viability analysis and general due diligence program should reveal a number of symptoms such as those listed in Table 14.1. The symptoms should be listed and accompanied by an indication of the appropriate remedial action for each symptom. This provides the basis for developing the framework for a turnaround plan. In designing the plan, it is important not to lose sight of treating the disease in addition to alleviating the symptoms.

Chapter 16 provides a detailed discussion of various types of turnaround and workout strategies. As we indicated previously, they consist primarily of (1) reducing expenses, (2) increasing revenues, (3) developing a more profitable business mix, (4) enhancing asset utilization, (5) restructuring debt, and (6) raising capital. After the means of accomplishing several of these tasks have been identified and quantified, they should be summarized within a financial framework to measure their aggregate impact. The potential results of a turnaround plan can be evaluated by reflecting their projected financial impact on the company's historical financial statements and then preparing a financial projection of the intended results.

Table 14.3 shows an example of the pro forma impact of a turnaround and restructuring plan on the historical cash flows of SOS, Ltd. The application of the intended plan and a description of each action are contained in Table 14.4. The pro forma impact of each action is separately indicated. For example, action #1 requires the turnaround investor to infuse $750,000 into the company. This amount is used to reduce bank debt and trade debt. Action #4 involves an across-the-board wage cut. This cut not only reduces expenses, but it will reduce the prospective investment in inventory and have various other balance sheet effects. The aggregate impact of all the items provides a pro forma "snapshot" impact of the turnaround program. This is an important starting point in determining whether a turnaround is even achievable. This analysis is often done on a back-of-the-envelope basis before a detailed business plan and financial projections are prepared. If the aggregate impact reveals the potential to create a profitable company with a somewhat decent balance sheet, then the turnaround plan has a chance of working. The pro forma impact of the turnaround program shown in Tables 14.3 and 14.4 is a company with a

Table 14.3. SOS, LTD. Pro Forma Impact of Turnaround and Restructuring Plan Based on Historical Cash Flow ($000)

	Actual					Turnaround and Restructuring Actions								(13) Pro Forma
		(1)	(2)	(3)	(4)	(5)	(6)	(7)	(8)	(9)	(10)	(11)	(12)	
Sales	$26,550	(6,200)				(725)								19,625
Cost of goods sold	(20,178)	4,650	142	550		979	139		160	90	193			(13,276)
Gross Profit	6,372	(1,550)	142	550		254	139		160	90	193			6,349
Selling, gen. & admin.	(6,903)	1,488	140	282				308	40	18				(4,627)
Operating profit	(531)	(62)	282	832		254	139	308	200	108	193			1,723
Interest	(1,991)	304	203										106	(1,379)
Income before taxes	(2,522)	242	485	832		254	139	308	200	108	193		106	344
Income taxes	833	(85)	(170)	(291)		(89)	(48)	(108)	(70)	(38)	(67)		(37)	(120)
Net income	($1,639)	157	315	541		165	90	200	130	70	125		69	223
Depreciation	990	(156)	(192)											642
Capital expenditures	(825)	130	160											(535)
Increase in long-term debt	500													500
Net investment in working capital:														
Accounts receivable	(354)	101												(253)
Inventory	(508)	129	6	25										(348)
Other	(13)	2	1											(10)
Bank debt	1,475	(225)												1,250
Payables and accruals	678	(219)	(5)	(18)										436
Net change in cash	$304	(82)	285	548		165	90	200	130	70	125		69	1,905

Note: See description of turnaround and restructuring actions in Table 14.4

300

Table 14.4. SOS, LTD. Pro Forma Impact of Turnaround and Restructuring Plan Based on Historical Cash Flow ($000)

	Actual	Turnaround and Restructuring Actions													Pro Forma
		(1)	(2)	(3)	(4)	(5)	(6)	(7)	(8)	(9)	(10)	(11)	(12)	(13)	
Assets															
Cash	$250			500											750
Accounts receivable	5,900		(1,550)			(181)							(625)			3,543
Inventory	6,350		(1,550)			(326)								(671)		3,803
Other current assets	425		(50)													375
Fixed assets, net	8,250		(1,300)	(1,600)												5,350
	$21,175		(4,450)	(1,100)		(508)										13,821
Liabilities															
Bank debt-current	6,750		(2,250)													4,500
Payables and accruals	5,650	(375)	(1,750)			(508)							(625)	(671)		1,721
Bank debt-long-term	8,000	(375)		(1,500)												6,125
	20,400	(750)	(4,000)	(1,500)		(508)										12,346
Stockholders' equity	775	750	(450)	400												1,475
	$21,175		(4,450)	(1,100)		(508)										13,821

(continued)

Table 14.4. (cont.)

(1) Sixty percent of the company is acquired for $750; proceeds are applied equally against bank debt and trade debt.

(2) The assets of a subsidiary will be sold for $2,250 plus the assumption of trade debt; proceeds will be used to retire bank debt.

(3) A manufacturing facility will be sold for $2,000; $500 will be retained, $1,500 will be used to retire bank debt.

(4) Imposition of a 10 percent wage reduction.

(5) Specifically identified unprofitable items will be eliminated from product line; netproceeds from reduction in recievables and inventory will be applied against payables.

(6) Certain raw materials will be resourced to vendors offering better pricing. Purchasing arrangements will be modified to result in lower prices.

(7) Administrative headcount reduction.

(8) An energy conservation program will be implemented.

(9) Workers compensation insurance will be placed with a new insurance carrier.

(10) Work rules will be amended to allow greater flexibility in the use of the production work force.

(11) Net reduction in accounts receivable as a result of hiring a new accounts receivable manager who will improve collection practices; proceeds from net reduction will be applied against payables.

(12) Net reduction in inventory as a result of improving MRP system, production scheduling, and improvements reflected in items (3) through (9), exclusive of items (5) and (6); proceeds from net reduction will be applied against payables.

(13) 1 percent reduction in interest rate on bank debt as a result of substantial paydown.

302

supportable level of trade debt and $1.7 million in operating profit to service $10.6 million in bank debt. At this point the company hardly looks like a gem, but it is sufficiently interesting to warrant additional investigation. By adding sales to the company, or doing things in addition to the cost cutting shown in the example, there is the possibility that the company can be an attractive turnaround buyout candidate. The pro forma analysis is useful because its starting point is to examine where the company has been and then assess what could be done differently.

Sometimes a pro forma analysis will reveal that even by making a series of improvements a turnaround of sufficient magnitude to attract new investors is not achievable. This doesn't mean that the company can't be turned around. It just means that it will have to be done with the resources of existing shareholders and creditors, rather than with funding from a new investor.

Since a turnaround does not occur in an instant, but over time, financial projections are indispensable tools for measuring the cost, timing, viability, and upside potential of a turnaround. These projections should reflect monthly cash flows for a least a 12-month period, and should provide quarterly, semiannual, or annual projections thereafter until the main impact of the turnaround has been realized. A complete set of projections should also include a balance sheet. Normally, that main impact of the turnaround will take two to three years to occur. An example of annual projections is provided in Table 14.5. In that example, the operating loss is reversed in year 19X1 as a result of the actions detailed in Table 14.4. The full annualized impact of these actions causes 19X2 to exhibit continuing marked improvement. Also, in 19X2 the elimination of the nonrecurring professional and related costs of initiating the turnaround causes selling, general, and administration expenses to decline. The pro forma analysis in Table 14.3 provides a check on the reasonableness of the financial projections. The sales levels, expense levels, and profit margins of the pro forma analysis resemble those projected for 19X2. It is useful to develop various financial projection scenarios reflecting a best case, worst case, and expected case in order to evaluate the possible outcomes of a turnaround program and their attendant costs.

The financial projections also provide a means of quantifying an exit strategy in order to determine whether the investment is worth the cost. Several different scenarios can be developed. Table 14.6 depicts the annual internal rate of return on the turnaround investment opportunity, based on the financial projections in Table 14.5. The resulting internal rate of return is 45.42 percent, assuming that the investment is sold after five years. By modifying the financial projection assumptions or the assumed length of time that the investment is held, the internal rate of return will change. To justify the risk, the projected returns on equity capital should be in the 30+ percent range. As is the case whenever projections are used

Table 14.5. SOS, Ltd. Cash Flow Projections for the Five Years Ended December 31, 19X5

	Actual	19X1	19X2	19X3	19X4	19X5
Sales	$26,550	20,018	21,219	22,704	24,293	25,994
Cost of goods sold	(20,178)	(14,141)	(14,690)	(15,568)	(16,583)	(17,694)
Gross profit	6,372	5,876	6,529	7,136	7,710	8,300
Selling, gen. & admin.	(6,903)	(5,043)	(4,741)	(4,978)	(5,226)	(5,488)
Operating profit	(531)	833	1,788	2,158	2,484	2,812
Interest	(1,991)	(1,594)	(1,429)	(1,390)	(1,322)	(1,226)
Income before taxes	(2,522)	(761)	359	769	1,162	1,586
Income taxes	883	266	(126)	(269)	(407)	(555)
Net income	(1,639)	(494)	233	500	755	1,031
Depreciation	990	642	674	708	743	780
Capital expenditures	(825)	(500)	(650)	(700)	(750)	(800)
Net divestiture proceeds	0	4,250	0	0	0	0
Equity investment in company	0	750	0	0	0	0
Net repayment of long-term debt	500	(1,875)	(250)	(500)	(750)	(1,000)
Net investment in working capital:						
Accounts receivable	(354)	842	(133)	(165)	(177)	(189)
Inventory	(508)	1,073	(69)	(110)	(127)	(139)
Other	(13)	(8)	(8)	(8)	(8)	(9)
Bank debt	1,475	(2,250)	128	170	187	202
Payables and accruals	678	(2,179)	141	192	212	229
Net change in cash	$304	252	67	87	86	106

Table 14.6. SOS, Ltd.
**Projected Internal Rate of Return on a
$750,000 Investment**

Description	Amount
Projected operating profit	$2,812
Capitalization multiple	×5
Gross value	$14,061
Less: projected debt	−8,812
Plus: projected cash	848
Projected net value	$6,097
Percent of SOS Ltd. purchased	80.0%
Share of net value	$4,878
Initial investment	$750
Internal rate of return	45.42%

Based on projections in Table 14.5. Amounts are
in thousands.

for decision making, the quality of the decision depends upon the quality
of the projections.

Characteristics of an Unlikely Turnaround Candidate

"All hope abandon, ye who enter here."
            —Dante

Some situations are simply not salvageable under any terms. Others are,
but the potential returns are insufficient to entice outsiders to commit
fresh capital. They depend upon those who are already involved with the
company to ante up. Realism, as always, must prevail. Any one of the
following can make an apparent opportunity a lost cause. A prospective
investor should have the self-discipline to know when to walk away from
a deal with the markings of a potential failure.

Lack of a Reasonable Business Plan.   A turnaround generally requires a substantial transformation of the operations and financial condition of the
company. To proceed without a detailed plan of how it is going to be
implemented and by whom is an invitation for disaster. Investing in a
turnaround candidate simply because it is cheap is pure speculation. The
absence of a business plan doesn't mean that a turnaround cannot be
achieved. However, significant funding should not be provided until
management can provide a detailed business plan that demonstrates that
funding is warranted.

Moribund Product.   Don't try to fight the market place. If a product is at the end of its life cycle, let it die.

Ineffective Leadership.   Implementing a turnaround is demanding. It requires the sustained effort of capable people to work under challenging circumstances. Management that has proved to be ineffective is unlikely to change. They presumably ran the company to the best of their ability and have a financial crisis to show for it. History has a way of repeating itself. More of the same tends to beget more of the same.

Liquidation Yields More Than a Turnaround.   If a liquidation yields more than the potential upside of a turnaround, then creditors and shareholders have little incentive to attempt a turnaround. The proceeds from a liquidation are more definable and imminent than the uncertain results of a turnaround. Where creditors can be made substantially whole through liquidation, they may be quick to pull the plug if a turnaround plan begins to falter.

Pervasive Fraud.   Where there has been pervasive fraud, there is the risk that (1) it may recur, (2) historical financial information is probably unreliable, (3) representations by the perpetrators of the fraud cannot be depended on, and (4) there may be undiscovered and unquantified problems. Even in instances where fraud has not been committed, you may be inviting disaster if you pursue a transaction where management has been untruthful in portraying the true financial condition of the company.

Excessive Optimism.   A turnaround should be predicated upon a reasonable set of assumptions. Prospective investors should be callously objective in evaluating the viability of a turnaround. It should not depend upon an interdependent series of events, all of which must have an optimal outcome in order for the turnaround to work. The underlying assumptions in such areas as prospective market share, sales growth rates, profit margins, expense structures, and so forth, should bear some reasonable relationship to the historical performance of the company. The timing and amount of projected cash proceeds from asset sales and divestitures should be reasonable. There needs to be margin for error. The turnaround should not depend upon technological breakthroughs, litigation windfalls, or new products or markets that the company has no track record for being able to deliver.

Lack of Creditor Support.   Most turnarounds require creditor concessions. In most financially distressed companies, creditors can

- Refuse to do business with the company
- Sue the company for payment
- Demand repayment of bank loans
- Force the company into bankruptcy

- Paralyze the company while it is in bankruptcy by refusing to grant credit, burdening it with numerous legal motions, or moving for the appointment of a trustee
- Seek the liquidation of the bankrupt company
- Complicate the confirmation of a reorganization plan to such an extent that a bankrupt company either never emerges from bankruptcy or else it emerges as a greatly weakened concern

Cost. The projected costs of implementing the turnaround may exceed the known financial resources available to the investor. Turnarounds are time and capital intensive. Unanticipated events arise that require the availability of cash. Turnaround candidates are usually stretched to their financial limit. Many turnarounds have failed, not because they were predicated upon a defective plan, but because they were insufficiently funded.

Lack of Employee Cooperation. Employees can make or break a company. If they are unwilling to make sacrifices for the company, insist on operating on a business-as-usual basis, or are antagonistic, the turnaround is doomed to failure.

Desertions. Departing key employees may be irreplaceable in the near term. Their loss to a direct competitor magnifies the impact of the desertion.

Customer Losses. Customer losses may be irreversible within a short enough time frame to save the company. Key customers may have switched to competitors or product substitutes. They may have left with malice because of late deliveries or quality problems that adversely affected their own operations. The company's reputation may have been irreversibly tainted. They also may be locked into long-term contracts or supply agreements with competitors.

Dependence on Uncontrollable Events. The prospects for a turnaround should be predicated on good work rather than on good luck. A question mark arises regarding any turnaround that depends upon uncontrollable events such as the demise of a competitor; unprecedented improvements in the price, cost structure, or product demand of an industry; or legislation that favors the company.

Litigation. Litigation can jeopardize the existence or prospective value of a turnaround candidate. Damage awards can prove to be debilitating. In some cases, awards have amounted to a multiple of the defendant's value. Legal costs and the disruptive effect of litigation can also be staggering.

Showstoppers. A company may lose the ability to operate as a result of

- Cancellation of required licenses, operating permits, or certifications
- Cancellation of insurance or bonding

- A demand for repayment of bank debt
- Foreclosure by a lender or lessor on facilities or on critical equipment
- Padlocking of the premises by the landlord, tax authorities, or law enforcement officers

Environmental Problems. Environmental liabilities constitute a contingent exposure of growing concern to many companies. Once environmental contamination is detected, the company is obliged by law to clean it up. The cost may be overwhelming. The company will normally be responsible for the cleanup even if the property is leased or the problem is attributable to a former occupant of the site. A prospective investor should obtain professional assistance in assessing the magnitude of any environmental problems that may exist and in determining the cost of rectifying them.

Unsuccessful Business Plan. Management's business plan to effect a turnaround may be well conceived, management may be well suited to the task, and they may have executed the plan masterfully. Large cash drains may have been eliminated, the cost structure reduced, and new management given a chance to turn the company around. Despite that, losses may persist. Variances and factors that emerged after the plan was formulated should be analyzed. Some companies simply cannot be turned around.

Irreversible Spiral. In some cases, no single element of a turnaround candidate represents an irreversible problem, but the collective impact of all the problems and the lack of strong redeeming merits militate against a turnaround. Some companies have lost money for so long that a complete overhaul of employees, attitudes, business practices, and many other facets of the business would be required to restore profitability.

Balancing the Risks and Rewards

"A strenuous soul hates cheap success."
—Fielding

The downside of an unsuccessful turnaround effort can be considerable. Not unlike any other investment, the principals' loss may include

- 100 percent of invested capital
- Liability for debt that is guaranteed personally or by controlled entities
- Personal liability for certain taxes and environmental liabilities of the business
- The time and effort of attempting the turnaround at the expense of other potential investments
- The damage to the investor's reputation for participating in a failure

At the same time, the greatest rewards are generally realized by those willing to undertake the most risk. On turnaround investments, most of

Table 14.7. Increases in Aggregate Common Equity Capitalization of Selected Well-Known Turnarounds

Company	Low Point	1 Year Later	2 Years Later	5 Years Later	10 Years Later
AM International	1982	933%	950%	8,370%	NA
Chrysler	1981	284%	1,209%	2,228%	NA
Itel	1981	825%	2,350%	12,043%	NA
Navistar	1982	322%	663%	1,512%	NA
Penn Central	1976	35%	4,332%	9,729%	24,931%
Toys "R" Us	1974	733%	2,567%	28,143%	331,161%
Wickes Companies	1982	200%	1,199%	2,583%	NA

SOURCE: Ronald G. Quintero, "Acquiring the Turnaround Candidate," in Sumner N. Levine, ed., *The Acquisitions Manual* (New York: New York Institute of Finance, 1989), p. 383.

the downside has already been realized by existing shareholders and creditors. Debt can normally be acquired at a discount from its face value. Equity is often available for little more than the cost of an equity infusion and the willingness to stand behind debt. The upside can be enormous in comparison to the capital investment. The increase in the aggregate market value of the equity of some better known turnarounds is shown in Table 14.7.

Not every company described as a turnaround candidate will, in fact, turn around. Even if it survives, it may remain marginal or provide an insufficient return to satisfy new investors. To make a proper evaluation of the suitability of the company as a turnaround investment requires an understand of (1) why the company got into trouble, (2) whether it possesses the characteristics of a turnaround candidate, (3) whether the company can be turned around, and (4) whether it has attributes that make a turnaround unlikely. Risk and hard work are the only guarantees provided by turnaround investments. The possibility exists, however, for tremendous personal, professional, and financial rewards.

Note

1. Edward M. Flynn, *Statistical Analysis of Chapter 11* (Washington: Administrative Office of the United States Courts, 1989), p. 34. Although the study did not determine the percent of confirmed cases that resulted in reorganizations (as opposed to liquidations), the principal compilers of the data observed that confirmed reorganization plans constituted between 70 and 80 percent of all confirmed cases.

15

Pitfalls in Acquiring Bankrupt Companies

Jay Alix
Jay Alix and Associates

General Overview of Insolvency

There are two basic types of insolvency:

a. *Financial or equity insolvency.* Insolvency in the equity sense refers to the inability of a debtor to pay obligations as they mature.
b. *Legal insolvency.* The bankruptcy definition of insolvency is a situation in which the liabilities of the debtor exceed the fair market valuation of its assets.

When a company becomes legally insolvent, there are several directions in which it may proceed:

a. Reorganization under chapter 11
b. Liquidation under chapter 11
c. Liquidation under chapter 7

Plan of Reorganization in Chapter 11

Generally, the plan divides creditors into various classes and priorities as defined in the Bankruptcy Code. All creditors in the same class are treated equally, but separate classes may be treated differently. The plan must designate the classes of claims that will receive treatment. It must specify any class of claims that is not impaired under the plan as well as the treatment of those classes that are impaired. Lastly, it must provide adequate means for the plan's implementation. Once confirmed, the plan limits the amounts and methods of repayment to creditors. Creditors are protected in that the plan must be confirmed by the court. It must be in the best interest of creditors, be feasible, be fair and equitable to any impaired, dissenting classes, and provide for priority claims.

A more detailed discussion of a plan of reorganization, its contents, and post-petition issues and opportunities will be discussed below.

Liquidating Plan in Chapter 11

This plan provides for the orderly liquidation of the debtor's assets and distribution of proceeds to the various classes of creditors. This plan differs from a plan of reorganization in that it does not provide for the continuation of the business, and it requires a minimal amount of financing during its implementation.

Opting for this plan versus converting to chapter 7 avoids the costs of a trustee and allows the people most familiar with the assets to dispose of them in an orderly fashion, which will most likely result in a higher liquidation value.

Chapter 7 Liquidation through a Trustee

A chapter 7 case requires that a trustee be appointed by the court. The trustee sells the assets as quickly as possible using Section 363 of the Bankruptcy Code. Once the estate is liquidated, the proceeds are distributed to the creditors. This type of liquidation generally results in a forced liquidation, which brings a lower value for the assets.

There is no creditors' committee, and the unsecured creditors usually receive only cents on the dollar. The equityholders generally receive no distribution, and because the company is liquidated, they have no further ownership interest.

Proxy Fights and Hostile Takeovers—Bankruptcy Style

During the chapter 11 proceeding and the process of preparing and confirming a plan of reorganization, proxy fights and hostile takeovers (bankruptcy style) may develop.

In addition to the debtor, there is the possibility that one or more additional plans may be filed by other parties of interest. This is where the real battles can begin.

General

In a normal, healthy company there is an annual ritual called the annual meeting of shareholders. At this meeting the shareholders vote for the members of the board of directors who will, in turn, determine the destiny of the company through their choice of officers to run the company.

Shareholders are usually allowed one vote per share of stock that they own. If the shareholders sign a proxy, however, they relinquish the right to cast their votes to the proxy holder. It is through this vehicle, in combination with actual ownership of stock, that a hostile takeover may occur. A person or group of people with a majority of the voting power can decide who will run the company.

In a bankruptcy situation, the fight for shareholder votes is generally not a factor. Creditor votes become the focal point of the takeover battle.

In a chapter 11 bankruptcy case the creditors in each class of creditors listed may vote to accept or reject a plan of reorganization. There are no proxies available for the votes of creditors. Votes are usually obtained, therefore, by convincing each creditor that this plan is in his or her best interest. The way someone votes for a plan is a matter of economic self-interest. The plan that best provides for a distribution will most likely be the plan for which the creditor votes.

However, an investor may buy claims from creditors, which would increase their voting power and, in turn, could enhance the likelihood of his plan being approved.

A class of claims has accepted a plan when it has gained a vote of at least two-thirds in amount and more than one-half in number of the allowed claims of such class held by creditors. This differs from the proxy fights in a healthy company, which requires a majority of the votes of shareholders.

Buying Claims

Although there is not much case law surrounding this issue, creditor claims may be sold to parties not otherwise affiliated with the debtor. An investor may purchase a claim with the idea of either ultimately receiving a distribution in excess of his investment or with the intention of participating in the formulation of a plan of reorganization. Buying a claim allows an investor who is familiar with the bankruptcy process to become a party of interest, which then allows him to participate in formulating a plan.

The creditor selling the claim may be strapped for cash or simply wish to avoid a long delay (which could take years) in receiving a portion of the distribution. The price the creditor is willing to accept, therefore, will be dependent on the anticipated distribution amount, the method of payment, and the timing of the payment.

An investor should be aware of the pitfalls of buying such claims. The purchased claim may have been miscalculated by the original creditor and may be objected to in court. In addition, the claim may be subject to defenses such as preferences, other avoidable transfers, and, in the case of secured claims, equitable subordination. The buyer may try to solicit warranties and representations from the seller for such defenses to the claim. The result of such attacks may leave the buyer with a reduced claim amount, a claim lower in priority than originally stated, or possibly a worthless claim.

Once agreement is reached to purchase an unsecured claim, the transaction must be approved by the court. The court's review of the sale ensures that the creditor has received full disclosure of the available information in the case and is making a decision based on the facts. For example, if there is a plan that is awaiting a vote that calls for a 50 percent distribution to unsecured creditors, and the creditor is informed of this proposed plan, he may not be willing to sell his claim for 20 percent of the face value.

An active investor may prepare and file a plan of reorganization independently or participate with a group in formulating a plan. The investor also may attempt to join the creditors' committee, on which he or she may already have served. This does not automatically give the investor a seat on the committee, however. The other committee members must vote to allow the investor a seat. The judge who originally approved the membership must also approve the admittance of a new member. If the investor is allowed to join, he or she may then participate in formulating the committee's reorganization plan and attempt to receive back more than was originally invested.

Plan of Reorganization

General

Confirmation of a plan of reorganization is the means by which the company is reorganized as a viable business that no longer will need the protection of the bankruptcy court.

After a chapter 11 has been filed and the debtor has contained costs and stabilized the business, the next step is to put together a plan of reorganization. Contractual relationships between the debtor and creditors are restated, thus allowing the debtor to operate outside bankruptcy while satisfying or discharging its obligations.

The plan can restructure the amount, nature, and maturities of claims against the debtor and provide for the orderly payment of these restructured claims.

Plan preparation and confirmation is the most significant event of a chapter 11 proceeding. A plan should be technically confirmable and structured to best serve the postconfirmation interests and goals of the company.

The driving concept behind a chapter 11 is that the active, ongoing company has greater value to the creditors than the various parts would have in a liquidation.

In most instances, a company would have experienced many difficulties prior to filing chapter 11. These difficulties may have been of a financial, management, or an operating nature, or a combination of these and many other factors. As a result, the plan may radically alter the company in any or a combination of the following ways:

- Management
- Ownership

- Debt structure
- Tax attributes
- Relationship with employees
- Litigation resolution
- Type of business

The debtor has the exclusive right to file a plan of reorganization in the first 120 days after the bankruptcy commences. The court can grant extensions. After this period has elapsed, any party of interest may file a plan of reorganization.

A party of interest may include the debtor, the trustee, a creditors' committee, an equity security holders' committee, a creditor, an equity security holder, or any indenture trustee.

Contents of a Plan of Reorganization

A plan of reorganization must

- Designate the classes of claims that will receive treatment
- Specify any class of claims or interest that is not impaired
- Specify the treatment of any class of claims that is impaired
- Provide the same treatment for each claim or interest of a particular class, unless an individual holder agrees to a less favorable treatment of his claim
- Provide adequate means for implementation

Disclosure Statement

Section 1125(b) of the Bankruptcy Code states that claimholders and creditors may not be solicited for either acceptance or rejection of the plan unless they first receive a copy or written summary of the plan and a court-approved disclosure statement.

The purpose of this statement is to inform equityholders and claimants, as fully as possible, about the probable financial results of acceptance or rejection of a proposed plan.

The disclosure statement should also include a debtor's statement of operations, value of the debtor's assets, and amounts of debt owing. In addition, the statement should explain what caused the financial difficulty and outline what the debtor has done or will do to remedy the problem. In an investor plan, it may not be possible to explain the causes of the financial difficulty.

Lack of feasibility is not an appropriate objection to a disclosure statement. Technically, feasibility is addressed at the confirmation hearing. Practically, however, feasibility concerns are best addressed before confirmation to avoid the "freight-train effect."

A potential investor's first opportunity to gain acceptance of his or her plan against a competing plan will come during the disclosure statement hearing. Should the court not approve the opposing disclosure statements, the latter would have to be revised, thus giving the creditors more time to review the investor's plan of reorganization. It is possible that an opposing plan proponent may rescind its plan and get out of the game.

Soliciting Creditors

Once the disclosure statement is approved, solicitation of creditors is allowed. The creditors must receive a copy or summary of the plan and a copy of the confirmed disclosure statement at the same time or prior to the solicitation. Parties other than the debtor may be involved in the solicitation. The power and duties of committees of creditors or equityholders include advising those they represent as to the feasibility of the plan and the collection and filing of acceptances.

It is at this point in the process that a potential investor gains a second opportunity to defeat a competing plan by attempting to obtain votes for his or her own plan. The investor highlights the most beneficial parts of this plan while showing its superiority over competing plans.

Feasibility of Plan

The bankruptcy judge must determine that the plan is feasible. Under Section 1129(a)(11) of the Bankruptcy Code, the court must find that confirmation of the plan "is not likely to be followed by . . . liquidation or the need for further reorganization . . . unless such liquidation is proposed in the plan." In other words, the court is required to scrutinize the plan to determine whether it offers a reasonable prospect of success and whether it is workable. If the evidence shows that a plan is not feasible, it cannot be confirmed by the court.

The process of determining feasibility provides the potential investor with a third opportunity to gain acceptance against competing plans.

Factors that the court must consider and that the investor may be able to use to attack competing plans include the following:

- Adequacy of capital
- Earning power of reorganized debtor and ability to generate positive cash flow
- General economic conditions and competitive environment in which the reorganized debtor will operate
- Ability of management
- The probability of the company's continuation
- Whether the reorganized debtor will be able to meet the debt service obligations
- Feasibility of planned property dispositions
- Impairment of ability to operate successfully because of the payments required under the "best interest of creditors" test
- Potential impact and provisions for contingent claims

- Whether the reorganized debtor will be able to obtain credit given the amount of other existing debt

The plan must be fair and must not discriminate.

Meeting Feasibility Requirements from a Financial Perspective

General. To establish that the plan is fair and does not discriminate, it is necessary that the plan be feasible within the meaning of the Bankruptcy Code. This requires that many matters of a financial nature be disclosed. In addition, the reorganization plan must meet several basic requirements before it can be confirmed. Accounting information and financial determination play a direct part in five of these requirements:

1. Payments made or promised for services must be disclosed and detailed
2. Regulatory rate changes provided in the plan must be approved
3. Plan must serve in the best interest of the creditors
4. Each class must grant approval when a "cramdown" is sought
5. Plan must be feasible

Items 1 and 2 are self-explanatory. The "best interest of the creditors" is determined by completing a liquidation analysis or liquidating balance sheet. All assets are converted into cash under liquidation assumptions, and the proceeds are allocated across the various classes of creditors in their rightful priority. The valuation of assets and liabilities is often the subject of dispute and expert financial testimony.

If the majority of creditors or stockholders in any given class have not approved the plan, it becomes important that the financial information is available to demonstrate that the amount provided in the plan for that particular class is at least equal to what they would have received had the debtor been liquidated under chapter 7. Having demonstrated this, the debtor may choose to exercise the cramdown election.

Regarding item 4, when there are dissenting creditors and acceptance of the plan is sought through the election of a cramdown, present value tables must be used to generate payments equal to the value of the collateral as well as the total amount of the claim in order to receive the "indubitable equivalent." The cramdown election is explained in detail in a later section.

It is necessary to include a projected statement of operations, a statement of cash flow, and a balance sheet. These statements will provide the basis for the feasibility determination.

Basis for Projected Financial Statements. The projected statement of operations should be prepared first. Sales and expenses should be developed from sales trends and historical comparative statements and then adjusted according to management's plans for changes, such as improvements and discontinued operations.

The projected statement of cash receipts and disbursements is the most important piece of financial information presented to the court and other parties. The projections must be based on objective facts regarding the timing of cash receipts and disbursements. The statement will serve as an indication as to whether the debtor will be able to meet payment obligations when they come due.

The cash budget represents the expected cash inflow and outflow for a period of time. The projection should include beginning and ending cash balances, receipts by source, and disbursements by purpose.

Lastly, a projected balance sheet should be prepared. Although the financial information included in the balance sheet is not as important for feasibility as that contained in the statements of operations and cash flow, it will assist the secured creditors in determining the financial position of the company as it emerges from chapter 11 and what their ongoing collateral coverage may be.

Sales forecasts and income statement projections are not valid as cash budgets. This is very important. A gross error commonly made in cash projections is adding depreciation back to projected income statements and then assuming it reflects the cash projection; it does not. The biggest differences between an income statement and a cash budget relate to the timing of cash flows and debt-related receipts and disbursements.

a. If sales are on an accounts receivable basis, the important point is when they will be collected (i.e., cash comes in after the sale is made).
b. If the debtor is currently on a C. O. D. basis with suppliers, then projections must assume that cash will be required coincident with the receipt of goods or services.
c. The treatment of accruals and prepaid items in the income statement rarely reflect the timing of actual cash flows.
d. A working capital line of credit has its own terms and formulas, which generally do not follow the same timing pattern of sales and expenses.

This all means that an accrual basis income statement projection often will substantially understate the debtor's current cash needs. Furthermore, the plan will require a source of financing. A bank will, in all likelihood, require and use these statements as its basis for loan decisions.

In addition, where the plan calls for installment payments to creditors, it will be necessary to prepare projected statements of operations, cash flow, and balance sheet. These projections will serve as a tool to demonstrate to creditors that funds will be available for payments in accordance with the plan. Again, the plan must be in the best interests of the creditors to be confirmed.

With respect to an impaired class of claims that has rejected the plan, the court may still confirm the plan. As of the effective date of the plan, creditors in the impaired class should receive or retain property of value that equals or exceeds the amount they would receive or retain if the debtor were liquidated under chapter 7. To support the "best interest of the creditors" test, a detailed liquidation analysis should be provided as part of the plan.

Liquidation Analysis

Liquidating Balance Sheet.   The balance sheet should

a. Serve in the best interest of the creditors, meaning that the amount is the same as would be received in a liquidation.
b. Utilize financial worksheets to isolate the answer required under (a).
c. Consider unrecorded liabilities and worthless assets:

   1. Additional claims
   2. Assets that have no value

   • Deposits
   • Refunds
   • Leasehold improvements

d. Prove solvency using book values versus fair market value. The Code states fair market value.

A liquidating balance sheet should be completed as soon as possible after filing. Several liquidation analyses can be prepared, changing the FMV assumptions:

• Chapter 11
• Chapter 7
• Complete raw material and work-in-process inventory
• Collect A/R

Liquidation Analysis Worksheets.   The first step in liquidation analysis is to determine the total amount that would be realized under *orderly* or *forced* liquidation conditions. The following worksheet format is suggested.

		Asset Valuation Worksheet		
Asset	Book Value	Fair Market Value	Estimated Realization Factor	Estimated Liquidation Value
(1)	(1)	(2)	(3)	(4)

List assets and their net book value. These can be found on the most recent balance sheet. The net book value is usually the historical cost of an asset less depreciation. Some assets, including inventory and long-term investments, are recorded at the lower of cost or market, making it important to determine the accounting methods used in preparing the statement. Any acquisition or disposition of an asset since the balance sheet date should be noted. An aging of accounts receivable and the age and category of inventory are useful for ascertaining current net book value.

Be aware that the selective application of accounting methods may give rise to asset values that do not properly indicate true physical and economic circumstances, such as

- Percentage of completion methods
- Capitalized nonrecoverable costs
- Immovable or special purpose assets

The fair market value is the price a willing buyer would pay a willing seller without time constraints. It is determined by the age, condition, and estimated useful life of the asset as well as market conditions. Recent appraisals are useful in determining this value.

The realization factor is an estimate of the percentage of fair market value that could be realized during an orderly liquidation through an auction sale with rights to name a floor price. Seasonal changes and market conditions can affect this factor. Forced liquidation through an auction sale without reserve, or without the rights to name a minimum price, will considerably lower this percentage.

The liquidation value is calculated by multiplying the fair market value (2) by the realization factor (3). The sum of the liquidation values equals the total projected amount that would be realized from the liquidation.

Secured Interest Worksheet
Estimated Liquidation

Creditor	Collateral	Debt	Value	Surplus	Deficit
(a)	(a)	(b)	(c)	(d)	(e)

Preparing the schedule of distributions (suggested format):

1. The priorities are classified as follows:
    a. Secured claims
    b. Administrative expenses
    c. Involuntary gap claims
    d. Wage claims
    e. Employee contribution claims
    f. Claims by grain producers and fishermen
    g. Consumer deposit claims
    h. Unsecured tax and custom claims
    i. General unsecured claims
    j. Tardily filed claims

(continued)

Secured Interest Worksheet (Cont.)

    k. Claims for fines, penalties, or forfeitures
    l. Interest claims
    m. Subordinated claims
    n. Shareholders
2. Evaluation of the estate–highlights of the liquidating balance sheet:
    a. Is the debtor involved in litigation?
    b. Is there potential for litigation from shareholders, franchises, customers, governmental entities?
    c. Have actions been taken by the tax authorities, or is there reason to suspect they might be?
    d. Are there any tax refunds due that can be offset against liabilities?
    e. Is the debtor a guarantor? Have assets been pledged?
    f. Are pension plan obligations up to date?
    g. Are any deposits nonrefundable?
    h. Are there any mechanic or trade liens?
    i. Is there a short-rate cancellation on prepaid insurance?
    j. Are accounts receivable subject to offset against liabilities?

Valuation Issues

General. In preparing a plan of reorganization, valuation issues play a leading role. The valuation of the creditor's collateral is a key issue in a bankruptcy proceeding.

There is no set standard of valuation in bankruptcy. Cases that have dealt with valuation point out that the going-concern method may not always be appropriate. The best rule of thumb is that the valuation should be in accordance with the proposed disposition of the collateral or in the context of commercial reasonableness.

The following are common types of collateral requiring valuation and acceptable ways in which this can be accomplished:

    a. Personal property—written appraisals, stated at public auction value, are a value indicator of the property.
    b. Residential real property—retail market value, as well as comparables of residential property, net of commission and selling costs, are appropriate.
    c. Income-producing commercial property should be valued on the going-concern basis based on an income approach.
    d. Generally, valuing undeveloped property at retail would not be appropriate. Most often a potential purchaser would be interested in a

bulk sale value or per acre value of similarly situated real estate obtained from a recognized expert.

In establishing any of the above values, it is important to engage an independent appraiser. In selecting an appraiser, it should be based on an appraiser's credentials and methodology that have been found to be acceptable to the bankruptcy court. Knowing the judge and his tendencies should also be considered when selecting an appraiser.

Valuation of an Entity. Valuations of assets and cash flows are wide open for dispute and attack because value can have many meanings and items can have many values depending on use. The valuation of an entity is influenced by the purpose of the valuation. There are specific valuation factors that can be considered in the valuation of a company:

- Capitalized earnings
- Dividend-paying capacity
- Net assets
- Market price of stock
- Present value of future cash flows

For companies whose worth is largely dependent upon its continuance as a going concern, potential earnings are generally the most important factor. For a company with substantial holdings of disposable assets, such as securities or real estate, overall valuation would usually be based on the fair market value of the assets.

In establishing the underlying credibility of the valuations and assumptions included in the plan, it is important that they be supported by a written valuation report prepared by a recognized expert.

Contents of Written Valuation Reports. A written valuation report should include

- Valuation considerations, scope, and limitations
- Valuation approach
- Review of the conditions of the economic and financial markets at and around the valuation date
- Overview of the industry

In the case of valuing an entire business or operating division, the report should include the above plus the following:

- Overview of the company
- Earnings capacity
- Dividend-paying capacity
- Net assets

- Market price valuation
- Present value of future cash flow
- The valuation of the company and considerations/assumptions taken

Confirmation of Plan

Confirmation of the plan binds all parties of interest to its terms. It is important that this plan gives each class of creditors enough value for their claim so that they will vote in its favor.

Many times, in order to gain acceptance, the plan must offer stock in exchange for the debt. It may offer common or preferred stock or a combination of both. The Bankruptcy Code requires that the stock issued must be voting stock.

Adequate financing is probably the most important ingredient in a plan that allows the company to be successfully reorganized. Without adequate financial resources, negotiations with creditors will falter, making approval nearly impossible to obtain. In addition, inadequate financing often leaves the postconfirmation company with such poor capitalization that liquidation would be almost inevitable.

As stated earlier, if more than one plan is confirmable, the court must choose only one to confirm. The court shall consider the desires of the creditors.

Cramdown

In the event that creditors have not accepted the plan, Section 1129(b) of the Bankruptcy Code permits the court to confirm the plan, provided the plan meets certain standards of fairness to the dissenting classes of creditors. This standard provided by the Bankruptcy Code is referred to as the cramdown provision.

The cramdown provisions are complex and provide three powerful options for dealing with a class of secured creditors:

1. The plan may provide that the dissenting secured creditor class retain its liens to the extent of its allowed secured claim and receive deferred cash payments totaling the amount of the claim. The payments must have a present value equal to the value of the collateral.
2. The plan may allow the dissenting creditor to realize the "indubitable equivalent" of its allowed claim. Under this option the debtor may abandon the collateral to the creditor or provide a replacement lien on similar collateral.
3. The plan may provide for the sale of the collateral with the secured's lien attaching to the proceeds of the sale. The claim then would be treated under one of the options previously mentioned.

With respect to a dissenting unsecured credit class, the cramdown option ensures that a junior class will be deemed to have accepted a plan of reorganization in which no class senior to it receives value worth more than 100 percent of the claims represented by such senior class and no class junior to it receives any value on account of its claims or interest, which center around the absolute priority rule.

Under the absolute priority rule, the equity interest is reduced to zero where all senior classes have not been paid 100 percent of their claims.

Although cramdown carries a connotation of being a powerful tool, in reality it would require a hearing to value the debtor's assets and the benefits received by the senior claimants to determine that no senior claimants received more than 100 percent of their claims. A valuation hearing can be very expensive and time-consuming and will most probably end up in prolonged litigation over the valuation of the estate. As a result, cramdown is more of a warning to the junior classes of creditors to accept the plan of reorganization. Also, it is an inducement to the debtor and senior claimants to make a reasonable proposal to the junior creditors in view of the difficulties encountered in the valuation hearing.

Voting on Plans of Reorganization and Confirmation Hearing

Section 1126 of the Bankruptcy Code covers this area. In short, a class of claims has accepted a plan that has gained a vote of at least two-thirds in amount and more than one-half in number of the allowed claims of such class held by creditors. In the class of stockholders, only two-thirds in amount is required. A class that is not impaired under a plan is conclusively presumed to have accepted the plan. A class is deemed not to have accepted a plan if such plan provides that the holders of claims or interests of such class do not receive or retain any property.

Creditors are allowed to vote in favor of more than one plan. First, a hearing will be held to determine whether the plans comply with the provisions of the Bankruptcy Code. Should more than one plan conform to the code, the court must decide which plan to confirm as the court may only confirm one plan. In this case the court shall consider the desires of creditors and equityholders.

The Self-Destructing Offer

Overview

In order to avoid costly delays and unwanted conditions in the purchase of assets either through a 363 sale or a plan of reorganization, it is wise for an investor to include in the offer or plan those conditions which must be met for the sale or plan to be consummated. These conditions are referred to as "self-destructing offers."

363 Sale

1. Minimum upset price. Get the debtor/trustee to agree that, at the hearing, all competing bids must be made at incremental levels from an original offer, for example, 10 percent over that offer.

2. Initial bidder compensation. Get the debtor/trustee to agree that, at the hearing and in the event that you are outbid, you will be compensated for your time and expenses for preparing the offer and attending the hearing.
3. Fee for due diligence.
4. Set terms and conditions of the sale.
5. Confidential offer.
6. Minimum notification period.
7. Conditional time offer (decreasing offer).

Plans of Reorganization

1. Obtain agreement from the debtor and approval by the court that the costs to develop a plan will be funded by the debtor.
2. Obtain an option to match a competing plan.
3. If filing a competing plan, get the creditors' committee to endorse the plan.
4. Obtain an agreement to the plan from the banks involved.
5. Obtain a contract with management for future services; in other words, get management to agree to the plan in order to maintain continuity of management.

Availability and Future Use of NOLs

Overview

In the past, decisions to purchase bankrupt companies were often based on the availability of net operating loss carryforwards and the ability of the purchaser to use them to offset future income taxes.

Gone are the days when a company could acquire another company with net operating losses and automatically benefit from future tax savings arising from the use of these net operating losses. The Tax Reform Act of 1986 made significant changes in the tax treatment of bankrupt and insolvent companies in regard to the discharge of debt and reorganization. The most significant changes affect the carryover of NOLs and who may use them. These changes make the future use of NOLs much more restrictive.

Most purchases, whether in bankruptcy or outside bankruptcy, involve a significant change in the ownership of the purchased company. It is those ownership changes that trigger the new rules of the Tax Reform Act of 1986.

The new rules generally pertain to ownership changes that occurred on or after January 1, 1987. These rules will not apply, however, to Title 11 companies that were filed with the court before August 14, 1986. For corporations filing before August 14, 1986, the rules under the pre-1986 Act amending the Internal Revenue Code will apply.

The Act has established new NOL limitations. It has brought about significant changes in the ability to carry forward NOLs by reorganized companies, whether outside bankruptcy or under the supervision of a court in Title 11 or similar proceeding.

The Act rewrote Section 382 of the Internal Revenue Code (IRC), establishing limitations that come into effect where there has been a purchase or reorganization of a corporation and there have been ownership changes of more than 50 percent of the loss corporation's stock within a specified period of time. The effects of Section 382 differ, however, depending on whether a corporation is in or outside bankruptcy.

Outside Bankruptcy

The Act enacted an amendment to Section 382 (IRC), which limits the use of NOLs. An ownership change during the three-year testing period will limit the availability to use carryforward NOLs by the surviving corporation. The testing period extends back three years from the day prior to the ownership change. If during this period there have been owner shifts accumulating to more than 50 percent, an ownership change will be deemed to have occurred. The Act provides that an ownership change must be determined where there have been "owner shifts" involving 5-percent shareholders. For this determination, all shareholders of less than 5 percent are grouped and classified as one 5-percent shareholder. If there should be a second ownership change in the future, the three-year testing period would start on the day after the first ownership change, assuming it is less than three years from the second ownership change.

If, in fact, it is determined that there has been an ownership change during the previous three years, the availability of NOL carryforwards will be reduced to an annual limitation. The annual limitation on the amount of NOL carryforwards that may be used to offset taxable income is limited to an amount equal to the absorption rate. The absorption rate is determined by multiplying the long-term federal rate, as determined by Section 1274 (IRC), by the value of the loss corporation at the time of change in ownership.

> An example: On the date of ownership change the value of the loss corporation is determine to be $2 million and the long-term federal rate is 8 percent. The annual amount available to offset taxable income would be $160,000. Any amount not absorbed in one year could be carried forward to future years.

Certain attribution rules apply in determining stock ownership for purposes of Code Section 382. Members of a "family" (an individual and his spouse, children, grandchildren, and parents, but not his siblings) are to be treated as one shareholder. Also, stock owned by entities such as corporations, partnerships, and trusts is generally deemed to be owned by the owners of that entity (e.g., shareholders, partners, and beneficiaries) rather than by the entity itself.

In addition to the above change in ownership rules, a two-year continuity of the business must be maintained from the date of the ownership change. If this condition is not met, the entire NOL will be disallowed. Continuity of business is considered met when a significant line of the historic business is continued or a significant portion of the acquired corporation's assets continue to be utilized.

In Bankruptcy

The limitations of Section 382 (IRC) will not apply if the corporation is in bankruptcy and the historic shareholders and creditors own at least 50 percent of the vote and value of the surviving corporation's stock immediately following the ownership change.

An ownership change would occur when there has been a more-than-50-percent owner shift of 5-percent shareholders. Those holding less than 5 percent would be grouped as one 5-percent shareholder.

An ownership change may also result in a consolidated return change in ownership (CRCO). If so, the CRCO limitation permits the use of those NOLs of the loss corporation's consolidated group, arising prior to the year of reorganization, to offset the future taxable income of only those companies that were members of the consolidated group on the first day of the taxable year in which the reorganization occurred. They would not be available to offset taxable income of corporations subsequently acquired, though future acquisitions may be structured to try to avoid this limitation.

If a corporation with available NOLs is acquired and becomes a member of another consolidated group, an additional set of restrictions may come into play. In general, the preacquisition NOLs of the acquired company may only be used against postacquisition income of that company. These rules are known as the separate return limitation year (SRLY) rules.

In general, debt discharged in a bankruptcy reorganization will reduce the loss corporation's NOLs. This rule may be avoided if stock is issued to the creditor. If the reorganization involves a more-than-50-percent ownership change and qualifies for the special Code Section 382 bankruptcy rule outlined above, NOLs are reduced by an amount equal to half of the difference between the debt exchanged and the fair market value of the stock issued. Any NOL generated in the year of the reorganization must first be reduced. Any amounts of debt forgiveness in excess of the current year's NOL are then used to reduce previous years' NOLs. In addition, NOL carryforwards must be recomputed and reduced by the amount of interest paid or accrued to creditors who exchanged debt for stock during the three taxable years preceding the year of reorganization and the portion of the taxable year of the reorganization prior to the ownership change.

Tax Avoidance

Acquisitions cannot be made for the purpose of avoiding the payment of taxes. Section 269 of the Internal Revenue Code provides the Service with an open-ended means of investigating transactions and challenging NOLs that have been acquired. Section 269 authorizes the Service to disallow credits for NOLs and other tax attributes where it is determined that the principal purpose of the acquisition was to avoid taxes.

Postconfirmation Issues and Opportunities

General

The purpose of chapter 11 generally is to develop a plan of reorganization that will be approved by the court. The effect of confirmation is to bind all parties of interest to the plan regardless of whether they are impaired or have accepted the plan.

Once the plan has been confirmed, the task of implementing the plan and meeting its terms comes about. Upon confirmation, the property of the estate is free of all claims of creditors and interestholders except those provided for in the plan. The confirmation will usually vest the property back to the reorganized company. However, there are variations to this:

- The claims that arose before bankruptcy are substituted by the terms of the plan.
- The reorganized debtor has the obligation to make all payments required by the plan.
- The confirmation essentially discharges all prebankruptcy unsecured claims not paid under the plan as long as the plan does not call for a liquidation of the business and the business will, in fact, go on.

The bankruptcy process can be a very exciting one for an investor hoping to buy a company at a great discount and reaping big returns in a turnaround situation. The court hearings, publicity, and winning the battles can be likened to watching a rodeo. But once the plan is confirmed and the rodeo is over, an investor may find that he has gotten more than he bargained for. Numerous issues and problems may occur postconfirmation for which the investor should be prepared prior to the formulation of the plan:

- Lack of cash for continuing operations
- Lack of credit for continuing operations
- Unforeseen taxes
- EPA problems
- Bad management
- Union contracts
- Bad public image
- Rejected leases
- Accounts receivable offsets
- Unprofitable production contracts
- Crises management

In purchasing a troubled company, a due diligence review should be made to determine the company's viability and actual condition, to afford the opportunity to evaluate management, and to rate the quality and quantity of information. A due diligence review would reduce the number of problem areas.

Postconfirmation Issues

Environmental hazards may have a significant impact on the reorganized company. Although the reorganized company will not be responsible for prepetition costs incurred for hazardous cleanup, it will be responsible for the ongoing cost of continuing cleanup to the extent that the environmental hazard represents continuing harm.

A default in the plan is another issue that may confront the reorganized company. If there is a default on the terms of a confirmed plan, the creditors have a number of options:

1. A party of interest may request a revocation of the order confirming the plan on the basis that the order was procured through fraud. The request for revocation must be made within 180 days of the confirmation date. An order can only be revoked if it was procured by fraud. An order revoking confirmation acts to revoke any debt discharge.
2. Dismissal or conversion to chapter 7.
3. Foreclosure on collateral.

The reorganized company also may find that it can no longer operate under the terms of the plan. In such cases, the company can convert to a chapter 7 liquidation, dismiss the case in its entirety, or proceed under the chapter 11, but with a modified plan. The requests for modification could be brought about by changes in the industry, in markets, or following acts of God. A modification also may result from an overly optimistic plan, created with the idea that a higher return to the creditors would ensure its confirmation. A modified plan would need to be confirmed by the court.

Another issue may be whether adequate postpetition financing exists.

Postconfirmation Opportunities

In most instances, the reorganized company is afforded the opportunity to continue its operations with the burden of servicing debt significantly reduced as a result of the debt forgiveness granted as of the confirmation date.

Additionally, the company has a renewed opportunity and higher probability of doing the following postconfirmation than it did prebankruptcy or during the chapter 11:

- Obtaining new trade credit
- Attracting new, competent management and employees
- Obtaining new financing
- Gaining customer confidence
- Making a profit

Turnarounds and Approaches to Managing Distressed Businesses*

David B. Post
Arthur Andersen & Co.

Steven I. Hochberg
Sigoloff & Associates

The well-publicized excesses of the 1980s have created a boom industry for a new breed of professionals known as turnaround specialists, or interim managers, who provide services and resources to troubled companies.[1]

This chapter will identify the characteristics of the increasing failure rate of businesses in the 1980s, discuss different business segments prone to failure, identify various warning signs, describe the issues that must be analyzed to determine whether or not a business can be turned around, and provide an approach to managing distressed businesses.

The Gathering Storm

The number of business failures increased to unprecedented levels during the 1980s. According to records maintained by Dun & Bradstreet, approximately 423,000 businesses failed in the 1980s, 4.5 times the 93,000 failures in the 1970s. Even in the 1930s, only 177,000 businesses failed.[2]

The rate of failure and the amount of money involved increased throughout the decade. In 1980, 11,000 businesses failed, involving $4.6 billion in debt, increasing in 1986 to a high of 62,000 failures, involving almost $45 billion in debt. By the end of the decade the number of failures had fallen to approximately 50,000 annually, but the amount of money involved remained steady at approximately $36 billion each year from 1987 through 1989.

More significant, perhaps, than absolute numbers is the failure rate per 10,000 listed concerns in the D & B statistical series. Not since the late 1920s and early 1930s has that rate exceeded 100 per 10,000 listed concerns.

*The authors wish to thank David S. Lindquist, an MBA student at Duke University, for his thorough review, his research assistance, and his input into the preparation of this chapter.

The range in the 1960s was from 37 to 64 per 10,000 listed concerns. By the end of the 1970s the failure rate had fallen to the mid to high 20s per 10,000 listed concerns. Following the recession in the early 1980s, however, the failure rate rose rapidly, hitting 110 in 1983. Although the economy recovered, the rate did not subside; it reached a high of 120 in 1986 and remained at or above 100 per 10,000 listed concerns for the remainder of the decade.

What is causing this alarming rate of failure? Several possible explanations exist. First, there appear to be an increased number of new business startups. Though few statistics are available for the number of startups before the mid-1980s, D & B statistics regarding the failure rate of businesses in each age category have remained relatively constant. The failure rate of 33 percent for businesses less than three years old has not varied significantly over the period of time that D & B has been maintaining those records. In addition, since records of startups were begun in the mid-1980s, the failure-to-start ratio has been approximately 25 percent. In other words, during the late 1980s, the number of startups numbered approximately 240,000 compared to approximately 60,000 failures. These statistics, therefore, seem to support the proposition that increased startups in the 1980s contributed significantly to the increased number of failures.

A second and equally likely explanation is that the venture capital boom of the early 1980s followed by the LBO explosion during the second half of the decade may have created an environment ripe for mass failures. Perhaps one of the more significant aspects of D & B's business failure records is its analysis of the causes of failure. Although the causes of business failure are addressed later in this chapter, it is generally accepted that most businesses fail as the result of internal, or management controlled, reasons. Although management is certainly responsible for the capital structure it creates and within which it must operate, it was not until 1983 that D & B first began to list "burdensome institutional debt" as a cause of failure, in other words, overleveraging. By 1988, this cause was attributable to approximately 9 percent of all business failures.

This statistic appears to mirror the LBO activity that accelerated in the mid-1980s. Venture Economics, Inc. tracked more than 1,000 LBOs between 1984 and 1989 involving more than $250 billion. Interestingly, the EBIT (earnings before interest and taxes) multiple increased as the size of the transaction increased. On average, between 1984 and 1989, leveraged buyouts of businesses for less than a $100 million acquisition price involved EBIT multiples of 8, while in the cases involving acquisition prices of more than $1 billion, apparently more aggressive postacquisition performance assumptions led to EBIT multiples of 12, indicating perhaps that larger companies have stronger core businesses that, in turn, are worth more.

Similarly, all indices portend that the failures are increasing in size. The size of chapter 11 filings is growing rapidly. The largest case in 1987 (excluding Texaco), Kaiser Steel with $706 million in assets, would not have been included among the 10 largest cases in 1989. Another view of the increasing size of chapter 11 cases is that the assets of the 10 largest cases in 1987 (again, excluding Texaco) totaled $2.4 billion compared to $27 billion for the 10 largest cases a mere two years later in 1989.

In response to these phenomena of more cases, larger cases, and highly leveraged cases, distressed security investment funds have grown rapidly in anticipation of the opportunities that await in the 1990s. In a research report jointly prepared by Turnaround Management Association and Venture Economics, Inc. in March 1990, more than $2 billion was committed for investment in turnaround funds or distressed securities by firms specializing in distressed situations. Several billion dollars more are being raised.

In short, the entrepreneurial spirit, the venture capital boom, and the leveraging of American business seem to have set in motion a phenomenon that may demand a "shakeout."

The significance of the overleveraging in the 1980s is that many businesses labeled as "troubled" or "failing" are, in fact, strong, viable businesses that are simply incapable of meeting the aggressive acquisition performance assumptions and are therefore unable to support the new debt loaded onto their balance sheets. Many of the LBOs of the late 1980s were based upon extremely aggressive forecasting of growth rates, cost cutting opportunities, asset and division sales, a continuing favorable economic climate, and other assumptions, all of which had to happen to generate the cash flow needed to service the debt and support the new capital structure. Much has been written and debated about whether the commitment of so much cash flow and other resources to debt service will ultimately affect R & D budgets and capital expenditure programs, thereby jeopardizing the strategic position of the businesses affected and the economy as a whole. This chapter will not attempt to address that issue; however, it is pointed out here so that the reader is aware that any factor that restricts a company's use of its available resources can ultimately affect its operations and its competitive viability.

Why Businesses Fail

Statistical studies and compilations indicate that the vast majority of business failures result from mismanagement. Academic studies, business professionals, and credit rating agency statistics, such as those maintained by Dun & Bradstreet, indicate that 80 percent or more of business failures are traceable to internal or management-controlled factors, such as

- Autocratic management evidenced by a reluctance to delegate authority or train new management
- Neglect of human resources
- Unclear lines of authority

- Uncontrolled or mismanaged growth
- Failure to respond to changes in the marketplace, including customers' expectations and competition
- Failure to adapt to new technologies
- Diversification into unfamiliar or noncore activities
- Outdated financial, operational, and marketing strategies
- Failure to plan, forecast, and budget
- Inadequate capital planning
- Excessive leverage

Even though numerous studies have shown these factors to be the primary causes of business decline, management is prone to blame the business's misfortune on external factors believed to be beyond their control, including:

- New legislation
- Government intervention, regulation, or deregulation
- Interest rate fluctuations
- Exchange rate fluctuations
- Labor unrest
- Unregulated international competition
- Litigation
- Fluctuations in raw materials or oil prices
- Recessions
- Changes in social mores and demographics
- Technological advancement

Some such changes certainly affect entire industries. For example, since the mid-1980s, oil price drops have halted virtually all drilling activities in the United States, and tax law changes have eliminated the viability of most passive tax shelters. However, where entire industries are not virtually eliminated, management must recognize that the rules have changed for all industry participants and that for a company to survive, management must adapt to a new competitive environment. For example, decreasing metal prices forced strategic changes for companies in those industries in the 1980s, including product mixes, vertical integration, and consolidation of capacity to become low-cost, supplier-independent, competitive producers.

That's not to say, however, that management is inept. But, to survive, management must maintain a constant vigil over its operations and its horizons. Capitalism breeds both success and failure. Darwin's theory of evolution can be applied in the marketplace: only the fittest survive. The marketplace is competitive, and even the strongest can either trip or be overtaken unsuspectingly—the now ubiquitous fax machine quietly and quickly eliminated the telegraph's *raison d'être*. And suddenly, Drexel

Burnham Lambert, the leading financier of the corporate takeovers in the 1980s, is no more.

Causes of Failure

With the exception of overleveraged buyouts, distress, regardless of cause, is typically evidenced by financial symptoms. Conversely, it must be recognized that financial problems are just that: symptoms, not causes. The root causes of the distress must be determined before a successful turnaround strategy can be implemented, and they must be examined on both macro and micro levels.

In light of the dramatic changes of the 1980s, the first issue that management or the turnaround specialist faces is whether the crisis is related to the business' viability or to its capital structure.

Although most companies in distress suffer from weak capital structures, there is a difference between companies that have declined because their products have been unable to satisfy a market need and companies that have been able to satisfy a market need but have declined because of a burdensome capital structure. The former generally have experienced successive periods of operating losses before interest, taxes, nonrecurring and extraordinary items, while the latter are likely to have positive net operating income but suffer strangulation by interest charges and debt retirement obligations. In the first situation, the financial distress is the symptom rather than the problem and requires an operational turnaround.

In the case of the highly leveraged company, the initial capital structure and projections, based upon optimistic assumptions, are deemed acceptable and are the problem. In other words, the company's operations and finances are not properly aligned with each other. Consequently, a financial restructuring is necessary. Though most companies in financial distress may assume that a restructuring will solve the problem, a careful analysis must be undertaken to determine that the business strategy and operations are, in fact, not the primary cause of the distress.

General market conditions are another macro issue to be considered. Is the entire industry facing distress, or is the distress specific to the company? If the industry is in distress, is a turnaround possible given general economic conditions and industry trends? If the distress is specific to the company, how can it regain a competitive position?

Companies Susceptible to Trouble

Given the market forces of capitalism, all businesses are as vulnerable to trouble as they are to the lure of success. We live in a world of rapidly changing technologies. A decade ago, the Macintosh was a juicy red apple available at grocery stores and fruit stands, not a computer technology. Today, not only is the best-selling car in the United States a foreign car, but so is the car recognized as having the highest customer satisfaction.

With the coming of the European Common Community in 1992, 250 million more consumers in a democratizing Eastern European bloc, and a McDonald's in Red Square, the world will continue to charge past even the futurists at blinding speeds. Given this climate of the unknown, business must adapt. New businesses will be born, others will die. Perhaps those with certain characteristics will be more susceptible than others.

The types of businesses susceptible to failure listed here are divided into two broad categories: those that face industry-wide problems and those that face company-specific problems. When entire industries suffer, many of the participants follow. The following are a description of certain industry types in which the participants are particularly susceptible to distress.

The fortunes of companies in *cyclical industries* often depend upon forces outside their control such as commodity prices or weather conditions. Those that are most likely to weather the effects of forces beyond their control are the ones that either sufficiently diversify without losing sight of their primary business or that are able to minimize fixed costs in unstable conditions. The ability to adapt is the ability to survive.

Companies in *newly deregulated industries* face the problem of having to learn to survive in a competitive environment without the legal protections previously enjoyed. This is usually a culture shock to both the industry and the individual businesses. Deregulation is generally accompanied by an anticipated shakeout of the weakest businesses as new competitive forces take hold in the marketplace. Management is forced to operate from an entirely different perspective.

As product acceptance and technology begin to take hold and as entrepreneurial companies survive the transition to professional management, *emerging industries* are born, intensifying competition and inviting foreign participants. The personal computer, originally seen as a sophisticated way to play video games, was not seen initially as a threat to the computer establishment. Within a decade, however, not only did IBM establish the standard, but some believe it lost the lead as the industry innovator to Compaq and other "Johnny-come-latelys." American entrepreneurs invented the semiconductor microchip, only to lose virtually the entire market to foreign competition in less than a decade. The same continues with the U.S. television industry. Japanese high-definition television technology is so threatening to the remaining American manufacturers that they are seeking government protection and R & D support to catch up.

Perhaps *declining industries* face the most difficult task of all. Declining industries are those in which the growth rate of total industry-wide unit shipments is declining. Maintaining market share involves shrinking. Maintaining volume involves increasing market share by taking business from competitors. By definition, some businesses must fail in a declining industry. Management that refuses to admit that the industry is declining or bets its future on the industry recovering is the most prone to failure. Evolution is an inevitable process. It has been reported that of the 100 largest companies at the beginning of the twentieth century, most have failed, some have merged, and those that remain have significantly repositioned themselves in the market. In military-related industries, declining defense budgets in the face of both national budget constraints and the warming of the Cold War may well force the defense contractors to revise their long-term market focus.

While some businesses are susceptible to trouble because of industry-wide conditions, others are susceptible to trouble regardless of the state of the industry. These companies must deal with company-specific problems.

Companies lacking a proprietary product, or "me-too" companies, are subject to attack from every direction. These companies, such as retail businesses and nonlicensed service sector businesses, generally encounter low entry barriers with respect to capital and expertise, face many existing competitors, command very small margins, and see an increasing number of competing companies steadily entering the market.

Single-product and *single-customer companies* must develop new products, attract new customers, or diversify to protect themselves from powerful competitors, customers, and changing trends. Few startups are able to maintain their initial success, but instead struggle to compete with both their past success and new market entrants. Reaching maturity takes several years during which time the company is vulnerable. Even Apple Computer, now more than 10 years old, continues to face a marketplace that questions whether it can ultimately survive as a company largely recognized for one product. Fads, such as the Pet Rock and the Cabbage Patch Doll, are the extreme; they can decline as quickly as they rose. The challenge for a business is to recognize that its product is a fad and to be prepared with a follow-up product. Even at maturity, single-customer companies must be prepared to reconsider their strategies. Otherwise, certain extinction is unavoidable.

Rapidly growing companies are often driven by entrepreneurial zeal and by an overwhelming emphasis on revenue growth. Often, inadequate attention is given to the effects of growth on the balance sheet. Huge revenue increases and significant investments into R & D can cause these companies to suddenly find themselves in a situation where the balance sheet simply cannot support the growth. Although rapidly growing companies are frequently in need of additional capital infusions to support the growth, new money often comes with a new set of disciplines including professional management. These companies, which generally concentrate on boosting revenues, frequently resist professional managers, believing that they will stifle creative thinking and growth and will try to implement what are perceived as unnecessary management control systems.

As the United States shifts from a primarily manufacturing economy, management of *service-oriented companies* must recognize that its most irreplaceable assets walk out the door every night. Effective management and retention of human resources have become a strategic imperative in the marketplace.

The 1990s promise to be the decade of dealing with *highly leveraged companies*. The LBOs of the 1980s were often based upon very aggressive cash flow assumptions where the business had to grow regardless of industry growth rates. In mature industries, such as the beleaguered world of retailing, where industrywide unit shipments are not growing, growth comes only at the expense of pushing competitors out of business—an optimistic assumption at best. And ironically, even if those LBOs are successful, their required growth creates another group of failing businesses. Since highly leveraged businesses require many factors to converge in order to be successful, they are highly susceptible to the external, uncontrollable causes of business failure, such as interest rate fluctuations or increased raw material costs.

Closely held businesses and *family-owned businesses*, by their nature, select leadership based not upon managerial talent but on family or personal relationships with the shareholders. Emotional ties can blind management to reality. More than in other businesses, owner/managers link their personal psyche to that of their business. To the owner/manager, business failure is usually perceived as a personal failing, almost a personality flaw. The owner/manager often believes that he is irreplaceable or is afraid to admit that he is. He wants to maintain control ad infinitum, failing to develop either a management team or a plan for management transition. Owner/managers are reluctant to acknowledge the early warning signs of failure and are also apt to ignore them. Recent studies have found that 70 percent of all family businesses do not successfully make the transition from the founder into the second generation.

Approximately 70 percent of *entrepreneurial* and *startup companies* fail within two years. Why did Compaq survive while dozens of other transportable and IBM clones failed? Presumably Compaq had better management, since everyone was producing the same product from the same parts. Founders do not necessarily come from managerial backgrounds. Entrepreneurs are like artists. They have visions of how to invent the better mousetrap. Their *modus operandi* is to capitalize on their headstart as a way to convert their vision to a profitable reality. Being a good entrepreneur, however, does not assure one of possessing the managerial skill to run the business. In fact, the same skills that keep an entrepreneur focused on an idea, regardless of obstacles, such as a refusal to delegate any significant authority, can make him a bad manager and oblivious to the competition or to new changes in the market. Ultimately, the market will evolve, forcing the entrepreneur to compete in a mature industry rather than in an emerging industry.

Early Warning Signs of Business Failure

What are the warning signs that a business is heading toward trouble? This is one of the questions most frequently asked of turnaround specialists.

A brief, admittedly nonconclusive, list includes the following, which should be understood to be merely *symptoms*, not the problem itself. Generally, the ultimate symptom of business distress is poor capitalization, or, stated another way, the company is unable to meet its trade or other debt obligations from its revenue stream and asset bases. Though poor capitalization is the symptom, the more relevant inquiry is to determine how it happened. The warning signs listed, particularly those indicated below under Declining Operating Performance, may provide both a barometer and some insight as to why the company is facing difficulty.

Declining Financial Performance

- Decrease in profits
- Decrease in sales
- Decrease in gross profit margins
- Decrease in net profit margins
- Increase in fixed costs relative to revenues
- Increase in interest expense as a percentage of revenues and cash flow
- Declining revenues per employee
- Changing accounting principles
- Nonoperational catastrophic losses such as embezzlement and legal judgments

Declining Asset Utilization

- A worsening cash position
- Reduced working capital
- Decrease in working capital ratio
- Decrease in quick asset ratio
- An increase in the debt:equity ratio
- A dwindling capital base
- Declining asset turnover rate
- Declining accounts receivable turnover rate
- Deteriorating accounts receivable aging
- Declining inventory turnover rate
- Deteriorating accounts payable aging
- Creeping loan balances, particularly asset-based debt levels, i.e., utilizing an increasing percentage of the collateral
- Circular borrowings and off-seasonal borrowings to pay down trade debt
- Failure to take purchase and other cash discounts
- Reduced capital expenditures
- Reduced R & D expenditures
- Financing the purchase of fixed assets out of working capital or asset-based loans secured by working capital
- Acquisitions of or expansion into noncore related businesses or into businesses that cut into or compete with the core business
- Overpaying for assets or business units

Declining Operating Performance

- Failure to have plans and projections; that is, no budgeting or forecasting techniques for either the short term or the long term
- Using last year as this year's budget: if a bad year becomes the measurement tool for the future, there's no benefit in "meeting budget"
- Failure to meet plans and projections
- Quality control problems
- Increased return of goods
- Increased scrap rates
- Increased customer complaints
- Late or slow delivery
- Increasing stress levels being felt by management
- Failure by management to take vacations
- Management turnover
- Employee turnover
- Employee layoffs
- General employee dissatisfaction and performance
- Trade credit difficulties and restrictions
- Delay in returning telephone calls
- Delay in preparing and submitting financial statements to banks, lenders, and credit suppliers
- Board of directors resignations
- Failure of board of directors to diligently exercise its oversight function
- Return of the "retired" founder to a visible management position

Again, these symptoms should not be analyzed as the problems. They are simply evidence that a problem exists, and it is the problem, rather than the symptom, that must be identified and remedied.

The Shadow of Chapter 11

Although the efficacy of chapter 11 may be questioned, it is the federal statutory scheme designed to provide a climate for a court-supervised turnaround. Federal bankruptcy laws have been promulgated in the face of depressions and recessions when business failures and job losses become so prominent. Policies underlying chapter 11 include preserving a business as an ongoing concern and maintaining employment stability.

In contrast to the laws in many countries, insolvency in the United States has always been treated as merely an economic problem rather than a matter of moral turpitude that exposes the debtor to jail and harsh punishment, as was the case in many European countries as recently as the nineteenth century. Bankruptcy laws were originally codified in the United States in 1898 and were rewritten in 1938, both times largely in response to depressions. The 1978 revision, which became operative in 1979, was motivated by the changing economic climate and created a new chapter 11 (replacing the old Chapters X and XI) as an option for any business in trouble.

Interestingly, chapter 11 does not require insolvency as a condition for filing for protection. In practice, chapter 11 leaves the debtor in possession of its business while providing it with legal protection from creditors so that it may reorganize its business operations and negotiate a consensual settlement with its creditors. In the process, the business survives, employment dislocation is minimized, and the nation's economy is served. To some extent, whether intended or not, chapter 11 acknowledged that the economy was dependent upon credit, that credit losses were to be anticipated, and that credit plays a part in pricing policies. However, the policy underlying chapter 11 also acknowledged that liquidation was not the only solution and that preserving the going-concern value of a company could be ultimately good for all stakeholders.

Much of the turnaround industry has emerged since the passage of the 1978 Code. This growth has often been attributed to the Code, since it provides a "shadow" in which troubled companies can judge what is likely to happen if the formality of legal process is sought. Not only have the ranks of practitioners expanded rapidly in the 12 years since chapter 11 became law, but many commercial banks have developed specialized work-out departments, some have established special departments for lending to companies in chapter 11, investment firms have enormous funds ready to purchase distressed companies, financial advisors now specialize in troubled businesses, consulting firms and accounting firms are training reorganization specialists, and some law firms are changing the names of their "bankruptcy" departments to "reorganization" departments.

With its roots in offering all stakeholders a forum in which to achieve a negotiated settlement and a policy not requiring unanimity, chapter 11 cast a predictable shadow for all businesses in distress. Any troubled business could ask itself and its creditors, "What is the likely outcome in chapter 11? If possible, let's spend our time and money solving the problem rather than entangling ourselves in the legal web." The theory is that if a company can analyze the probable results of a court-supervised settlement with creditors as part of a plan of reorganization, at least the same should be accomplished out of court, saving valuable time and scarce resources.

Whether the shadow of chapter 11 will actually reduce the number of filings remains to be seen. Unfortunately, the success rate has been extremely low. A 1989 study by the United States Administrative Office of the Courts indicated that only 7 percent of actual closed cases between 1979 and 1986 had resulted in confirmed plans with reorganized ongoing business operations. Taking into account the remaining open cases, that percentage is expected to rise to only 10–12 percent. That study also showed that the average case required almost two years to conclude. Experience has shown that the process is costly and expensive to all constituents.

Will more companies attempt to take advantage of the lessons learned from chapter 11 and reorganize without the legal protection of the court? Perhaps. It is probably safe to opine that all turnaround specialists would prefer to avoid the courtroom if reasonably possible. However, the 1980s also witnessed the increasing complexity of corporate capital structures, substantial foreign competition, growing global markets, new theories of litigation and increasing verdicts, rapidly changing technologies, environmental concerns, and changing government and industry regulation. Many, if not all, of these issues affect business success and failure as well as the need for the broad-ranging protection afforded by the expansive jurisdictional reach of chapter 11. Turnaround specialists, attorneys, financial institutions, the credit markets, bankruptcy courts, and the entire turnaround industry face substantial challenges ahead.

The Turnaround Specialist

Turnaround management involves many of the same activities as general day-to-day management. Don Bibeault noted that over 80 percent of the managers involved in successful turnarounds did not consider themselves to be turnaround specialists.[3] Nevertheless, few involved in the growing industry of turnaround management question that several factors distinguish the circumstances in which the turnaround specialist operates: first, a confined time frame in which to determine a direction and implement a plan; second, significantly restricted resources; third, exacerbated human resource problems, whether it be finger pointing, paralysis of the decision-making function (which these authors call "chapter 11 disease"), high turnover, or loss of management credibility; fourth, dysfunctional operations that must be remedied; fifth, the need to manage both the business and the trouble; and finally, an environment of stress.

The questions that the management of a troubled business must answer are often the most difficult it will ever face: is it capable of resolving the problem, or must turnaround specialists be employed? If turnaround specialists are employed, what particular skills, if any, are required to supplement existing management? Is existing management willing to transfer general management authority to the turnaround specialist?

If a turnaround specialist is hired, both the company and the specialist must be clear about who the client is. As obvious as this issue may appear at first glance, it can become blurred. In closely held businesses, often the owner/manager is as concerned about personal guarantees at risk as he is about the survival of the business. Or where a lender refers a specialist, is the specialist more concerned about his future relationship with his referral source than he is with his troubled client? Or where the shareholders are not involved in operations, is the client the management, the board of directors, or the shareholder?

Turnaround specialists generally fall into two broad categories: interim managers and crisis consultants. Interim managers generally accept key management positions such as CEOs, COOs, or CFOs to guide the company through troubled waters, with luck, to safety. Crisis consultants do not take operating roles with the company, but instead advise existing management. Although most specialists offer their services in both roles, most concentrate in one area or the other. Many troubled businesses have a tendency to lean toward a consultant initially, unwilling to turn over the operations to a newcomer. Though existing management's initial assessments may be correct, the troubled business must be willing to accept that an interim general manager may be required.

Another issue faced in selecting a specialist is whether to seek a generalist or an expert in a particular aspect of the business. Many troubled businesses believe their problem to be unique, requiring an industry-knowledgeable expert rather than an experienced general manager. Naturally, this determination must be made on a case-by-case basis, depending upon the particular company, industry, and problem involved.

Trouble requires its own management. This is where the turnaround specialist brings his or her art to the process. The turnaround specialist and the client have a doctor-patient relationship. To successfully recover, the business not only requires a capable doctor, but it must also be a patient willing to face its problems and accept the remedies.

The turnaround specialist not only brings a new perspective to the situation, but also has different priorities: first, the assignment is only temporary so that he will be moving on to the next job at the termination of the engagement; and second, his reputation within the creditor community, from where most of his work comes, is only as good as his performance on his last engagement.

The Turnaround Process

Although each turnaround situation is unique, the turnaround specialist generally follows a well-defined approach to recovery. Assuming that it has been determined that the business is viable and that it has a core around which it can reorganize or restructure, the turnaround process generally involves the following steps:

1. Analysis of Contextual Factors
   a. Symptom or problem
   b. Stage of decline
   c. Industry evolution: emerging or mature
   d. Company-specific or industrywide distress
2. Viability Analysis
   a. A core business
   b. Management credibility and cooperation
   c. Creditor cooperation
   d. Adequate financing

3. Analysis of Alternatives
    a. Turnaround or liquidate
    b. Turnaround: out-of-court or in-court
    c. Preparing for chapter 11
4. Turnaround Plan
    a. Controlling cash
    b. Sale or discontinuation of assets and/or segments
    c. Breakeven and cost reduction
    d. Managing human resources
    e. Managing creditors
    f. Turnaround financing
    g. Monitoring the Plan
5. Poststabilization: transition and strategies

Analysis of Contextual Factors

All turnaround situations have a starting point. How the business got into trouble is largely irrelevant. The turnaround specialist finds the company with certain problems at some stage of decline and must be prepared to confront the current situation and move the company forward. The company does not operate in a vacuum and must reckon with competitive forces. Therefore, the turnaround specialist must first understand the contextual factors that will influence the turnaround plan.

Symptom or Problem.   Before the root problem can be attacked, it must be properly identified, the critical factor being to distinguish between the symptom and the problem. Often, management cannot objectively identify its problems. Not only is existing management often blinded by its biases and unaware of the incremental decline, but honest self-assessment is very difficult. Consequently, management has a tendency to attack the symptoms of decline, and the results often resemble a patchwork quilt.

Deterioration of accounts receivable, for example, may indicate quality control problems on the production floor. Slower inventory turnover may be a signal that obsolete inventory has been hidden in a corner. Increased material usage variances in a manufacturing process may indicate that the purchasing department is buying cheaper products to enhance the appearance of its performance while increasing waste and scrap in the factory. Likewise, excessive management and employee turnover is a symptom, not a problem; the cause of the turnover is the problem. Compounding the real problem, a company in trouble often has an inadequate accounting system that may fail to provide either reliable or timely information.

Stages of Decline.   Although the lines between them tend to blur, the stages of decline determine the options and the courses of action available to a troubled business. In general, the severity of a company's liquidity problem determines its state of decline. Companies in the *early stage of decline* are generally characterized by a recent drop in sales or profits or both;

however, the survival of the business is not imminently threatened because the company's immediate liquidity is not threatened. The turnaround effort must determine the reason for the downward trends and implement a plan of corrective action. Unfortunately, current management often attributes early stage decline to external factors or to a nonrecurring aberration that, in their minds, has since been corrected.

Midterm decline is usually evidenced by several years of deteriorating sales or profits, causing a gradual erosion of the capital structure. This stage of decline is generally accompanied by a concern for impending trouble. Dramatic warning signs have become apparent and can no longer be ignored. Management often believes that external forces have caused problems that can only be solved if lenders are willing to provide further support. Likewise, concerned creditors begin to restrict additional credit, leading management to believe that it has no options without further credit support, thus creating a downward spiral. This may lead to "chapter 11 disease," or the paralysis of management's decision-making function.

If left unattended, midterm decline will develop into the *late stage of decline*, which is characterized by a crisis environment and a severe liquidity crisis. The late-stage company is near or in a bankruptcy proceeding. Its survival is threatened. Its resources are exhausted, creditors are very nervous and have lost confidence in management, and significant amounts of energy are being invested into worrying about the distress rather than about running the business.

Although troubled businesses tend to progress through the indicated stages, the speed with which the progression occurs can vary from several years to a mere matter of months. In some cases, such as with LBOs, companies can be financed into trouble without having experienced the gradual deterioration of its vital signs. The turnaround process will vary depending upon the stage of decline in which a troubled business finds itself and the nature of the company's problems.

Industry Life Cycle: Emerging or Mature.   All companies find themselves in a certain stage of an industry's life cycle. This stage can be a key factor in determining the appropriate turnaround strategy for renewing and sustaining profitability. Industry life cycles are generally categorized as either emerging or mature. Emerging industries are characterized by an expanding marketplace with the buildup of production, distribution, and management systems. Most definitions include newly formed or re-formed industries where increases in industry-wide unit shipments have resulted from technological innovations, shifts in relative cost relationships, the emergence of new consumer bases, or other economic and sociological changes that could allow a company to profitably produce the product or service demanded. Mature industries are characterized by a marketplace where industrywide unit shipments are either flat or declining. Consequently, industry participants are forced to maintain or scale down production, distribution, and management systems.

In emerging industries, the expanding market provides opportunities for increasing revenues; however, consumer demand is still evolving and not well defined. As a result, significant attention must be given to the company's ability to exploit these growth opportunities. Implementation can require substantial cash investment for product development, production facilities, distribution centers, management information systems, customer service, and the training and recruitment of management. The turnaround specialist needs to carefully prioritize each investment according to its cash impact on the business and its ability to quickly capture market share. The longer the lead time and the payback period, particularly when the company has a shortage of resources, the more difficult the turnaround will be.

In mature industries, a company can only grow at the expense of its competitors. While production, distribution, and management systems are usually in place, the turnaround specialist must choose between a defensive or offensive strategy. In short, defensive strategies involve digging in and protecting one's turf, while offensive strategies involve attempting to find and move into new and emerging markets. Defensive strategies attempt to develop or maintain competitive advantages in the existing industry by improving the product, process, or distribution system through investments in existing product or production technologies, horizontal combinations with competitors, or vertical expansion into earlier or later stages of the value chain. Offensive strategies are designed to quickly and effectively make the troubled company less dependent on existing products and customer mixes with the possibility of moving the core business into an emerging market niche or segment. This strategy can include a geographic expansion into less competitive markets, product line extensions using existing technologies, and the entrance into related industries utilizing the company's existing technologies.

Company-specific or Industry-wide Distress.   In addition, the turnaround specialist must determine whether the troubled business's problems are company-specific or industrywide. Where the industry is healthy but the company is in distress, the turnaround is not faced with the dual task of addressing both internally controllable and externally uncontrollable problems. However, where the company's situation is caused in part by industry-wide distress, the turnaround process must be planned accordingly. The oil patch problems of the 1980s and the growing distress in the real estate market during the early 1990s are examples where even many well-managed businesses have faced difficulty as the entire marketplace has suffered. Often the best that can be hoped for when facing industry-wide economic pressures is stabilization and survival until the entire industry recovers or until the shakeout reduces the number of competitors. This analysis is used by the turnaround specialist to determine a "best case" for the troubled business before initiating the engagement.

Viability Analysis

Among the very first issues that a turnaround specialist must confront is the cause of the distress and the viability of the distressed company. Viability generally turns upon several interrelated factors: the existence of a core business, the retention of capable and committed management, creditor cooperation, and adequate financial resources to fuel the company through the recovery.

A Core Business.   Although a core segment is characterized by many factors, the key issue is whether the segment can generate sufficient revenues both to fuel the company through the turnaround and to serve as a basis for operations once the company is stabilized. In identifying and analyzing core businesses, many fundamental questions must be addressed:

- What is the purpose of the business? Why does the business exist? For example, since the purpose of many closely held and family-owned businesses is often to provide employment for a select few, survival of the company may serve little purpose if the owners are near retirement and there is no heir apparent who wishes to run the company.
- Is the product or service still competitive or in demand? Changing demographics constantly shift consumer groups. As post-World War II "baby boomers" enter their 30s and 40s, their buying power and their tastes are causing wholesale changes in consumer products and their marketing. One example would be in the 1980s when the domestic auto industry failed to exploit the "yuppie" demand for BMWs and alike. Similarly today, department stores are having to rethink product and distribution strategies in light of the emergence of specialty retailing and the constantly changing multistore shopping concepts.
- Is the business' position along the value chain still needed? Is its market position sustainable? In some industries, manufacturers have created direct sales networks, eliminating the role of the wholesaler. In the case of the rapidly growing convenience store market, major oil companies are invading the market, muscling out the original operators who created it.
- Does the company have the infrastructure to compete? Are basic operations functional? Is the production facility capable, both in terms of quality and quantity, and is it in the best location? Has the company kept pace with product and process technology? Does the company have established distribution channels? Is the company's customer service department effective? Is management capable and committed?

Often the core segment is the company's original business. Troubled businesses are frequently characterized by diversification into new or related businesses, new product lines, or entrance into new markets that fail to be profitable. This usually inadvertent drift away from the core can drain resources, both financial and human, thereby jeopardizing the core itself.

The turnaround specialist often attempts to identify the core by analyzing the company's history to understand the changes that led to its decline. Another technique applied is Pareto's law, or the so-called 80:20 rule: 80 percent of the output is generated by 20 percent of the input. In other words, 80 percent of the revenues are attributed to 20 percent of the customers, and 20 percent of the product line is probably generating 80 percent of the profits and cash flow. Or 80 percent of the sales are probably being generated from 20 percent of the customer base by 20 percent of the sales force. Or, 80 percent of inventory is probably purchased from 20 percent of the suppliers. A detailed analysis of business segments, product lines, locations, customers, vendors, or whatever other criteria is applicable in a given situation provides valuable information about identifying the core and determining where cash can be quickly generated and which assets are presently needed. This analysis will also indicate the best utilization of all assets, including their possible liquidation. Those business segments, product lines, locations, customers, vendors, or other criteria are then ranked according to contribution to overall goals. Since a troubled company is faced with limited resources, those activities which provide no contribution should be eliminated, as should those where existing resources cannot support ongoing operating requirements.

In performing this analysis, it is important to note the admonition from many turnaround specialists: don't get burned by bad information, particularly by books and records that management has "cooked" to hide the bad news while hoping and praying for the recovery. In addition, a quick study of the industry, financial and production ratios, and existing conditions should be undertaken through available literature, trade associations, and analyst reports. Customer and market demographics must be identified along with a profile of competitors, including their relative strengths, weaknesses, and niches. Often, a fresh viewpoint from an uninitiated eye can be very beneficial.

Management Credibility and Cooperation.   Distressed businesses generally suffer from some loss of credibility with their creditors and a significant level of stress between their management and the stakeholders. Because a successful turnaround will require cooperation from all parties involved, the turnaround specialist must quickly move to eliminate or reduce whatever polarization exists.

The turnaround specialist must also determine whether existing management has the functional skills to execute a turnaround and whether the board of directors is willing to take whatever action is necessary to initiate and execute a turnaround plan. Though little empirical evidence exists, most turnaround specialists suggest, and the few studies that do exist indicate, that successful turnarounds are executed by new management.[4]

However, it is wrong to assume that elimination of the entire management team will resolve the primary problem. Several members of top management who are responsible for creating policy and overseeing execution may well have to go. However, middle management, which is involved in the daily execution of operating details, brings to the turnaround effort its many years of accumulated experience, its history of customer and vendor relationships, an understanding of the competition, ongoing contractual knowledge, and distribution and product development plans.

In closely held businesses where the board of directors and management are often the same individuals, personal agendas may prevent a successful turnaround from taking place. For example, preservation of private assets, or avoiding personal guarantees, may be a higher priority to those making the decisions than is maximizing repayment to creditors.

Successful turnaround specialists interview all significant stakeholder constituents to understand their agendas, their urgency, their willingness to support the turnaround process, and their anticipated level of cooperation. Given that so many CEOs also serve as directors, contemplating replacing them and obtaining the authority necessary to do so is a very sensitive issue that the turnaround specialist must address at the outset.

Creditor Cooperation. The turnaround specialist must negotiate with the different creditor constituents to achieve the concessions necessary to create both the "breathing room" the business needs to continue operations and the resources required for future operations. This task involves negotiating with trade creditors to ensure a continued supply of product, with secured and unsecured creditors to forebear during the turnaround effort, and with potential sources of *de novo* financing. The key ingredient to handling the right-hand side of the balance sheet is the credibility that the turnaround specialist brings to the negotiating table. This added credibility is particularly important if the current management's credibility has been damaged. Communicating accurate information to all parties is essential. Creditor constituents have been known to say, "To us, bad news is good news. We know we are being told the truth. And that makes it easier for us to assess the new starting point."

Adequate Financing. Given a viable core segment and a workable environment, liquidity, including all potential sources of cash, is needed to fuel the recovery. The turnaround requires money and time. The company must analyze every source of cash, both internal and external. Internal sources of cash include the liquidation af existing assets as well as the availability of the company's noncollateralized assets for the cash that they can generate. External sources include existing lenders, shareholders, *de novo* lenders, and new investors.

Analysis of Alternatives

Although a business may appear viable, a turnaround candidate and its stakeholders must address two fundamental questions: whether to attempt a turnaround or to liquidate, and whether to attempt an out-of-court turnaround or to file chapter 11.

Turnaround or Liquidate.   The primary consideration in choosing between the alternative courses of action is whether more value can be returned to the creditors and equityholders by ceasing operations and selling all of the company's assets or by attempting to increase the creditors' returns through continued involvement with an ongoing enterprise. In the former situation, creditors receive accelerated payment of a certain amount (presumably less than their original investment); in the latter, creditors may achieve a greater return by extending the terms of payment plus the possibility of investing further, thus increasing their risk.

As part of the turnaround specialist's initial analysis, the effects of liquidation must be determined. Each asset must be valued taking into account the appraisal values, disposition alternatives, and the time required to liquidate. Furthermore, hidden asset values not shown on balance sheets must be explored. For example, a favorable long-term lease may have significant value. After determining asset values, the relative priorities of the various creditors in the chain of distribution must be determined.

Many of the larger creditor constituencies will attempt their own analysis. More often than not, the analyses by the troubled company and the creditors will differ because each has access to different information. For example, turnaround specialists and certain creditor groups may have knowledge of or access to distribution channels unknown or otherwise unavailable to the troubled business. All parties should share their respective information to determine the highest possible valuation. Despite the valuation analysis, the most important factor in the creditors' minds is whether management has the credibility and capability to deliver more than liquidation values. In making this decision, each constituent faces a different decision matrix.

Secured lenders, though protected by collateral, may be required to provide additional funds to strengthen their collateral positions. One rule of thumb, though certainly not applicable in all situations, is that most banks are hesitant to consider providing new funds if more than 20 to 30 percent of the existing balance is needed.

In the case of syndicated loans where multiple banks may have participated in the loan, all participants must agree on the appropriate course of action. The difficulty, however, is that the level of sophistication and risk tolerance often varies greatly among the participants. Less sophisticated banks not only may be less comfortable with the workout process, but also may be more reluctant to provide additional money, even though the additional funds have been determined to be necessary to ultimately maximize recovery. Syndicated loans are particularly difficult because of the need to rearrange the participants' positions in the event that all of the participants do not take part in the new advance. Consequently, those participating in the new advance often expect and receive a more superior collateral position, increased fees, and possibly an equity position. A debtor anticipating new money must be prepared to provide a well-documented plan showing the lenders how and when they will be repaid.

Unsecured trade creditors have the least leverage and often the least information. Their primary leverage in the negotiation is that their goods and services are the lifeblood of the turnaround. Unsecured trade creditors must retain competent advice to analyze the secured creditors' loan documents, to determine whether security interests are perfected, to review grounds against the secured lender for potential lender liability, to identify fraudulent conveyances, and to evaluate equitable subordination. Although unsecured trade creditors know that liquidation will provide little relief on the old debt and will require substantial time to receive any payment, most do not want to lose the troubled company as an ongoing customer. Consequently, their support of a turnaround plan will be based upon the combination of ongoing revenues without further loss and the potential receipt of some or all of the antecedent debt.

Subordinated Debt Holders. Since the leveraged buyout explosion of the 1980s, subordinated debtholders have become a major constituent in the turnaround activities of the 1990s. While subordinated debt is classified as an unsecured debt, typically pari passu with prepetition trade creditor debt, subordinated debt is subject to a bond indenture providing contractual rights to protect bondholders through a variety of covenants. These debtholders have different concerns over impaired credits than secured creditors and trade creditors. On the one hand, they do not have to worry about extending additional credit. On the other hand, they tend to be the lowest creditor on the distribution list in the event of a bankruptcy. Because they can represent more dollars than the secured debtors or the trade creditors, they frequently must accept a conversion of part or all of their claim into equity as a means of recovering their investment.

Subordinated debt covenants are designed to set off early warning signs to protect the bondholders from incurring losses on their investment. These covenants consist of a variety of tests and restrictions, including debt incurrence tests, tangible net worth maintenance tests, restrictions on certain asset sales and use of proceeds, restrictions on corporate distributions, and negative pledge clauses. The covenants intend to control cash, but a default can occur even though the company has sufficient cash flow to fund its operations. Other potential alternatives available to bondholders when the value of their debt is unjustly impaired include legal claims against secured lenders and/or management for fraudulent conveyances, security fraud, constructive trusts, equitable liens, and inequitable conduct.

Upon default, the company is usually provided an opportunity to cure the default. Uncured defaults generally result in face-to-face negotiations between management, equityholders, and the bondholders, often leading to a restructuring of the debtenture if, as most indentures require, a two-thirds majority of the bondholders consent. Perhaps the most difficult aspect of the negotiation is addressing the different agendas of the individual bondholders. Those who invested at the original issue price—often par value—probably did so with an interest in securing fixed income payments over a long term. Since the best outcome for these investors is that the bonds will mature at par, these bondholders are more concerned with the business's long-term viability and the ultimate payout of the bond. In contrast, those bondholders who entered as investors, usually at a discounted price, are concerned with capital appreciation above their original cost and hope to do so in as short a holding period as possible without a preference as to the means. To them, bankruptcy or liquidation is usually quicker than a turnaround, and it is certainly quicker than waiting for their debt to mature.

Other Unsecured Creditors. Normally other types of unsecured creditors exist. Utility companies, communications companies, and insurance companies, for example, have unique requirements that can vary substantially from situation to situation. The special considerations and approaches required to work with these unsecured creditors must therefore be addressed on a case-by-case basis.

Other Considerations. In a liquidation, companies today have access to an increasing number of asset liquidators and brokers to maximize the recovery from assets. These professionals and their techniques have become much more sophisticated within the last few years. Investment bankers, barter agencies, and liquidators have established networks of interested buyers to maximize potential recovery. For instance, managing "going-out-of-business" sales, though generally subject to certain legal constraints, has become a highly professional business with targeted marketing, pricing, and timing techniques.

According to the findings in a recent study by the United States Administrative Office of the Courts, chapter 11 has, in fact, become a liquidation vehicle. Because chapter 7 has become synonymous with fire-sale prices and often only attracts bargain-hunting vultures, the so-called "liquidating 11" has become the preferred vehicle to increase the recovery. Although the result may appear to be the same, the psychological perception is different, and this difference assists the debtor in preserving maximum value for as long as possible.

In larger companies, the value of the parts may be greater than the whole; however, those parts each have some intrinsic value to someone. Therefore, the company may be sold or liquidated piecemeal. Some professionals in the turnaround industry suggest that true liquidations do not occur since assets do not disappear; instead, they simply attract new owners.

In the initial analysis, the turnaround specialist must identify which stakeholder has the greatest influence in determining the strategy to be undertaken. This includes assessing the preferences of those stakeholders who are affected by each of the alternatives as well as anticipating the residual action. The turnaround specialist also looks at the psychological profiles of all influential stakeholders. One outcome of this analysis could be that both equity- and debtholders prefer the speed and finality of liquidation rather than the cost, time, and trauma involved in a turnaround or a chapter 11 proceeding. On the other hand, the trauma to employees and communities of a shutdown and liquidation should be taken into consideration.

Turnaround: Out-of-Court or In-Court

If liquidation is ruled out as an alternative, the decision must be made as to whether the reorganization should be attempted with or without the protection and guidance of the Bankruptcy Court.[5] Because of the "shadow of chapter 11," a company in distress often follows a parallel track, developing both options, as negotiations advance, and as alternatives are explored. Chapter 11 can serve as a backdrop against which a reorganization plan can be judged. Because chapter 11 is a fallback option, if chosen, the out-of-court plan should project a better outcome.

The primary benefits of an out-of-court turnaround are derived from avoiding the many impediments associated with the bankruptcy process. First, though it must communicate frequently and fully with unofficial creditors' committees and other creditor constituents, management has more flexibility in an out-of-court environment than in a bankruptcy where official creditors' committees, attorneys, accountants, and other advisors are involved in much of the decision-making or approval process. The fishbowl effect of the chapter 11 process can obstruct daily operations and management decisions. Though chapter 11 specifically provides that the business may continue to operate "in the ordinary course of business," few attorneys will provide an opinion that a particular transaction qualifies. Consequently, creditors' committees must be provided notice and must approve activities that management previously believed to be in the ordinary course of business.

Second, chapter 11 carries a great deal of bureaucracy with it. The more complex the debtor, the more incumbent the need to allocate management personnel to deal specifically with the bankruptcy process. The complexity of the situation can be affected by the type and size of the business, the number and peculiarities of different locations, the number of business segments or legal entities, the number of contracts including leases, joint ventures, labor agreements, the number and sophistication of trade and other creditors, the number of customers, the capital structure configuration, and the number of employees. Each of the listed elements represents stakeholders interested in the outcome of the reorganization. Balancing the interests of each party coupled with the procedural requirements of bankruptcy demands the allocation of significant resources previously used to operate the business. Inherent delays and procedural requirements can actually interfere with optimal business decisions, which can ultimately impact the outcome of the reorganization itself.

Third, most observers suggest that chapter 11 should be used only as a last resort. The psychological concept of bankruptcy as an indication of failure rather than as a mode for reorganization can become a self-fulfilling prophecy. Filing can affect viability not only by scaring away suppliers, but also by scaring away customers to alternate suppliers and threatening revenue sources. This can occur when the customer is dependent on the debtor for the delivery of future goods and services, including long lead time products, warranties, proprietary maintenance, R & D, cooperative advertising, and rebate programs. For example, will homebuyers continue to contract with builders where the completion and delivery of the home and future warranty work is uncertain? Will travelers continue to patronize a troubled airline if their accumulation of frequent flier miles is in jeopardy? In addition, there is the risk that customers may not pay their bills if they are losing the opportunity to buy from the troubled business in the future or if they assume (probably correctly) that the debtor will exert little effort or have a difficult time collecting the account.

Filing chapter 11 will significantly affect trade supplier relationships. Regardless of the debtor's relationship with its institutional lenders, continued operation without trade support is impossible. The debtor should anticipate that vendors may assume a wait-and-see posture before determining whether or not to support the debtor's efforts to recover. That delay can bring the debtor's operations to an immediate halt. Lack of vendor support can hurt the business more quickly than any other problem.

Finally, chapter 11 is an extremely expensive process, usually more than anyone estimates at the time of filing. Everything costs more with more stringent terms. The costs mount in terms of dollars and in terms of the emotional impact upon the business, its employees, customers, and suppliers. Consequently, all parties must weigh the protection and control of the court against the costs that all will bear. The burden of chapter 11 appears to weigh most heavily on smaller companies, which have neither the financial resources nor the manpower to withstand a process that, as mentioned earlier, on average extends almost two years with only approximately 10 percent resulting in a confirmed plan of reorganization.[6] Regardless of this seemingly pessimistic view of chapter 11, approximately 15,000 businesses sought its protection each year during the 1980s.

Projecting the outcome of a turnaround is becoming more and more difficult as contingent claims play a more prominent role in the process. Potential liability for litigation claims, environmental issues, health and welfare, pension obligations, and warranties and guarantees are difficult to measure and even more difficult to build into a projection in determining a course of action. Five situations are generally recognized as reasons to file chapter 11.

1. If the debtor is in a freefall or is uncertain about the quality of its information, the filing provides both a new starting point and the time to gather information and to reestablish needed credibility with all constituencies. The automatic stay puts an immediate stop to all creditor action and ensures that all similarly situated creditors will be treated equally.

2. If the debtor faces factors largely beyond its control, such as litigation, product liability problems, environmental concerns, tax issues, or other contingent or unknown claims, the bankruptcy court provides worldwide jurisdiction and oversight.

3. If the debtor has a complex capital structure, the court can assist in managing the competing claims where consensus seems unattainable. The court is better equipped to resolve questions of adequate security, perfection of security, whether secured creditors are over- or undersecured, publicly held debt, the applicability of guarantees, cross guarantees, pledges and negative pledge covenants, and so forth. By virtue of the "cramdown" provisions, the court can bind dissenting classes as well as dissenting minorities within a class of creditors.

4. If the debtor faces a liquidity crisis, as most do, accompanied by a lack of creditor cooperation, chapter 11 can provide certain creditors who will provide liquidity with "super priority" status. The super priority safety net is occasionally considered the safest form of lending, not to mention a source for generating high fees for the lender. To the extent the debtor can show equity in the collateral, the available equity can also be utilized with an order of the court and without the consent of the secured creditor.

5. Chapter 11 also reduces interest charges claimed by unsecured creditors, penalty fees, and expenses accompanying default. Finally, the legal process can assist potential purchasers of assets by providing title free and clear of potential claims.

One of the primary advantages of Chapter 11 is the automatic stay, which halts all creditor action against the debtor. Chapter 11 serves as something of a "Chinese Wall" between the time prior to filing and the postfiling period. Nevertheless, when creditors' support can be marshaled, the automatic stay can be simulated in an out-of-court workout through consensual agreements or with the assistance of third parties such as the National Association of Credit Managers. Furthermore, Code Section 1126(b) provides for prepackaged reorganization plans wherein a plan is prepared, creditor support is solicited prior to filing the bankruptcy, the debtor files with the necessary number of votes already accumulated to confirm the plan, the court approves the plan, and the debtor emerges in a matter of weeks rather than in a matter of years.

Preparing for Chapter 11.   If a debtor is going to file, how should it prepare for the process?

Prepare Existing/Remaining Management.   Communication is the key to reducing the mystery of chapter 11. A weekend seminar away from the business conducted by some combination of the company's lawyers, accountants, and turnaround specialists will not only alleviate the fear of the unknown, but also serve as an opportunity to describe how the business will operate during the months ahead, to explain what can and cannot be said to customers, suppliers, creditors, and others, to introduce management to new players, and to answer questions in a nonthreatening environment.

Build up a War Chest of Cash, if Possible.   Albeit difficult, the company should attempt to stockpile cash at another bank that has no claims against the company. This cash will provide the funds necessary to meet payroll, purchase goods C.O.D., if necessary, make new deposits, provide retainers to professionals, and run the business through the initial stages while the creditors organize. If asset-based lenders have liens on receivables and/or inventory, creditors may seek court-supervised control over future cash receipts on the grounds that the company's cash receipts constitute the conversion of their collateral into cash. The inability to fund its operations can bring the business to a grinding halt.

Build up Inventory from Trade credit.   Inventory is the lifeblood of most debtors, and once a petition is filed, it may take time for suppliers to decide to ship new goods. Creditors have 10 days to reclaim goods if they file a written request seeking a return of the goods; however, the court can determine that the creditor is entitled to receive priority for payment rather than a return of the goods.

Arrange Debtor-in-Possession (DIP) Financing Prior to Filing.   Most companies entering chapter 11 must secure an adequate banking relationship in advance. Existing lenders are often unwilling to lend because the credibility of management is damaged and because a host of legal problems could complicate the lending relationship. Consequently, a new lender may prove to be more accommodating than the old lender in providing financing during a bankruptcy. Financing from a new bank reduces the control that the prepetition lender may attempt to exert through setoffs, sweeping cash accounts, and "bootstrapping" payment of the new loan onto payment of the existing loan.

A new genre of lending, known as DIP financing, has arisen in recent years. Recognizing the need that companies in chapter 11 have for a continued flow of financing, the bankruptcy court can provide the lender to a debtor-in-possession with what is called superpriority status, meaning that the lender is to be paid from the proceeds of its collateral before any other creditor. Furthermore, the DIP lender is provided adequate security with the blessing of the court and will be paid handsomely for its service.

In general, DIP loans are short-term, anticipating repayment within a year or at the outset, prior to the implementation of a plan of reorganization. Because of the perceived risk in financing a company involved in a bankruptcy, DIP lenders have been able to earn significant origination fees and charge interest rates somewhat above market rates. At the time of this writing, origination fees generally range between 1.5 to 3.5 percentage points of the amount committed, while interest rates on DIP loans range between 1.5 to 3.5 above prime. Because lenders engaged in DIP financing receive such attractive fees, the DIP facility has become a lucrative profit center to a growing number of lending institutions. Since the DIP loan is short-term with adequate collateral and court protection, the lender incurs little risk while having the opportunity to come to the rescue and to examine the borrower's operations closely in order to determine whether it wishes to pursue an ongoing banking relationship with the company or with any of its parts that emerge from the chapter 11.

Pay or Prepay Key Creditors.   When owners or mangers face personal liability, when employees are owed expense reimbursements, or when key suppliers are owed significant sums, payment may constitute a preference. However, the determination is not a preference until so ruled by the court. In the meantime, important constituents have been mollified and are in a more comfortable negotiating position. The constituents can then concentrate on their own business tasks rather than having to worry about their position as creditors.

Whether a turnaround is conducted in court or out of court, most distressed situations require additional financial resources, relief from some of the existing debt, or a combination of the two. Unless no other alternatives exist, creditors generally do not want their debt to be converted into equity in the troubled business, and the existing owners wish to maintain their ownership without dilution. When creditors are unwilling to provide further support through a composition and new lenders are not available, merging the business with, or being acquired by, an outside company may be the only other course of action. A discussion of those alternatives is beyond the scope of this chapter.

Certainly not all turnarounds involve decisions as drastic as having to choose between liquidation, chapter 11, and an out-of-court reorganization. Yet a turnaround can occur only when the company is viable and when management can convince creditors that the value of the business as a going concern exceeds the present value of liquidation. To avoid some loss to creditors, the problem must have been identified and attacked early enough to contain the loss of value. A complete turnaround requires perseverance, stakeholder cooperation, and sometimes luck.

Turnaround Plan

Business viability determination, core identification, and relevant contextual factors are critical issues that must be addressed at the outset of any turnaround effort. In addition, the in-court or out-of-court environment will likely affect the major assumptions built into the plan, including financing alternatives, timing considerations, human resources, and implementation approaches. Assuming that the viability analysis shows that the business has a sustainable core business, a turnaround plan must be prepared. Like all business plans, it should address the objectives and goals of the business, the means for accomplishing those goals, the costs and benefits to be derived by all parties, a long term strategic plan for the business and the time frame for accomplishing the plan. Since many of the tasks must be accomplished simultaneously, this discussion of the turnaround plan should not necessarily be construed to be sequential by nature. Each task must be managed, and often all must be managed simultaneously. The turnaround specialist must work closely with management, the various creditor constituencies, and shareholders to develop a plan that is reasonably achievable given both limited resources and limited time.

Controlling Cash. Turnaround specialists are often analogized as being business doctors. When they arrive on the scene, the patient is generally hemorrhaging cash. Therefore, the first operation is to control the cash, stop the bleeding, and transform the company from a consumer of cash into a generator of cash as quickly as possible. A failure to correct a negative cash flow will ultimately result in the patient's death. The stage of decline (early, midterm, or late) will dictate the time available for the company to eliminate its cash flow problems.

Cash management involves understanding both the sources and uses of cash and the timing of each. If a cash management system is not in place, one should be established immediately. A cash flow forecast should be prepared for as long a time horizon as possible. The master cash flow plan should then be broken down into its component parts beginning with weekly projections for one or two months followed by monthly projections for the subsequent two to three months. These projections should be rolled forward, comparing actuals to projections, and should be updated to the master plan as necessary.

The initial source of cash is the company's balance sheet. All existing cash accounts should be identified and perhaps consolidated. Accounts receivable aging schedules should be prepared, and collection and billing policies should be examined to provide a time and cash flow charting. Special attention should be given to past due accounts both as a source of cash and to determine the reason for nonpayment. Inventory must be analyzed to determine what goods are available for immediate production or sale, what must be purchased, and perhaps what can be returned for cash or credit. Prepaid expenses and payment policies can be a hidden source of cash. Refunds of prepayments can be sought and replaced with pay-as-you-go billing. Future prepayment obligations may likewise be converted to a monthly billing cycle. Inventory should be analyzed by product or segment rather than as a whole, with a view to what the turnover rates are and what they should be. Averages can be misleading, combining good performers with the bad. Property, plant, and equipment can often be a source of cash. Naturally, unused property or facilities can be sold or leased. Other strategies can include the sale-leaseback of existing equipment and facilities or the consolidation of facilities to reduce overhead. Often management is concerned about the accounting losses that may accrue upon the sale of fixed assets. Those considerations should be ignored. The initial workout is a cash game, not a P & L game.

Deferral of liability obligations is an obvious source of cash. The trade creditors are often the first to anticipate that a company may be approaching trouble because their payments are the first to be stretched. Nevertheless, the trade is the business' lifeline. The trade needs to be shown that the company is viable and that the business plan is reasonable and attainable. The mistake that many troubled businesses make is offering to pay a percentage of the old account along with the delivery and payment of new product. Instead, trade creditors must be convinced that a moratorium on existing balances is necessary until the cash flow situation is stabilized, that a flow of product is necessary to keep the company alive, and that the company can pay for the new goods. Examine the difference in the following example where a company owes trade suppliers $80, needs $50 for current shipments, and will incur $45 for selling, general, and administrative expenses.

Cash Impact from Alternative Trade Arrangements			
Cash Basis	Pay Old Balance	Pay New + 10%	Pay New Only
Revenue	$ 100	$ 100	$ 100
To trade	80	58	50
SG and A	45	45	45
Net Cash flow	($ 23)	($ 3)	$ 5

Trade creditors typically represent the largest number of creditors, each with its own individual concern of loss and with its own collection tactics. As the level of distress increases, the telephone rings more and more; if management avoids returning the calls, the situation is only exacerbated. The trade can generally be divided into two camps: those that are necessary as a future source of supply and those that are not. In addition, the 80:20 rule is particularly applicable to trade suppliers. Management must categorize the trade into significant groups according to the business's future needs and the trade support required. Critical suppliers must be identified, communicated with openly, and made part of the recovery process.

It is most important to establish a policy for each group and then stick to it, despite the threats and pressures from individual creditors.

Sale or Discontinuation of Assets and/or Segments.   Many turnaround plans require shrinking the company. Identifying the core business provides the turnaround specialist with a starting point for repositioning the company. The appearance of shrinking is actually the elimination of unprofitable, cash-consuming segments.

Assets or segments that are not critical to the recovery or that contribute little to the recovery of noncancellable fixed costs should be discontinued or sold. However, the decision to liquidate or to sell a segment or certain assets must be analyzed to determine the cash impact on the business, including not only the effects of the shutdown, but also such ancillary costs as employee severance and termination benefits, noncancellable fixed costs, environmental cleanup, other shutdown assessments, and tax implications. The effect of paring down the business to its core or to essential, though noncore, segments is that it will permit the company to increase its profitability by shrinking.

It is not unusual in the case of a troubled business to find unused or underutilized fixed assets, occasionally overlooked by management or assumed to be of no value. Instead of disposing of them, management may have decided to park them because of the negative impact that the paper loss on the disposition would have on the income statement despite the cash flow benefits. Although asset sales generate cash, care should be taken not to sell assets that will become necessary once the company has been stabilized. The sale-leaseback of fixed assets is an alternative method of generating cash from existing fixed assets that are needed on an ongoing basis. The sale of assets will require a legal checkup of loan documents to determine whether any liens exist, whether any covenants restrict asset sales, whether any notice requirements exist, and whether any secured creditors are entitled to any or all of the proceeds.

Breakeven and Cost Reduction.   Because negative cash flow is symptomatic of most troubled companies, it is critical to make the necessary operating changes to conserve and, when possible, generate cash. Expenses must be approached on a line-by-line basis. Whereas management may believe certain expenses to be sacred, the turnaround specialist must approach each expense from its inception. Instead of looking for ways to cut expenses, each expense item should be examined individually, asking whether it is necessary, how much is necessary, what contribution it ultimately makes to cash flow, and what alternative suppliers and/or services are available. For example, instead of determining that a certain number of dollars or people should be cut from salaries, a determination should be made as to what labor is needed, how much it will cost, and who can fill the positions. Naturally, human resource management is the most sensitive area and must be handled in such a manner to minimize disruption. The expense budget should then be used as a tool for implementation.

A breakeven analysis is designed to analyze the relationship between costs and revenues and to determine the sensitivity of anticipated changes and how much change is needed. It also serves as a tool for gaining control over all aspects of cash as quickly as possible. The "bleeding" must be stopped before the "patient" can be cured. Although the sale of assets and segments may generate much needed cash, the cash generated from those sources should not be included in the operating breakeven analysis. In other words, breakeven must be determined taking into account only operations that are to be continued.

Three levers are available for reaching and ultimately exceeding the company's breakeven point: increasing revenues, lowering variable costs, and reducing fixed costs. Although increasing revenues is usually the most difficult, companies in emerging industries have more opportunities than do companies in mature industries. The difficulty is that constrained resources may not enable the troubled company to increase revenues through otherwise basic revenue-enhancing strategies such as increasing prices, changing product mixes, adding new product lines, increasing advertising, and expanding into new markets.

Most variable costs are associated with the company's cost of goods sold, including raw material, labor, and variable overhead. Opportunities to reduce costs include lowering material costs; taking purchase discounts; improving production yields, quality, and efficiencies; improving quality of product design; and lowering labor costs. Since the turnaround process focuses on cash flow, these changes will show up more quickly on a cash basis than on the income statement because many of these costs are capitalized in inventory. By the same token, selling excess inventory, even if unprofitably, generates cash.

Though a difficult task, the costs easiest to control and cut in the short run are generally fixed costs such as facilities, research and development, marketing and sales, and general and administrative. The components making up these categories include payroll, rent, utilities, supplies, communications, travel, and entertainment. The turnaround specialist, however, must be cognizant of the company's need to be competitive on the other side of the turnaround, and therefore must be careful not to cut muscle while eliminating fat. The final component of the cost structure is interest expense. Controlling interest expense is a product of negotiating with existing lenders and arranging new financing alternatives, and it is an essential part of restructuring the right-hand side of the balance sheet.[7]

Attacking all components of revenue sources and the cost structure must be done for each product, division, or segment. Perhaps the most difficult aspect of cost reduction is identifying which costs are truly variable and which are indeed fixed. Many costs have components of both. Often, the marginal contribution of a product, division, or segment may be insufficient to cover fixed costs. However, its total elimination may actually accelerate losses and decrease cash in the short run. For example, assume that a business produces two products, A and B.

Product Line Contribution Analysis

	A	B	Total
Sales price per unit	$ 100	$ 98	
Variable cost per unit	70	78	
Contribution per unit	$ 30	$ 20	
Units produced and sold	1,000	900	
Total contribution	$30,000	$18,000	$48,000
Allocated fixed costs	$25,000	$25,000	$50,000
Net income (loss)	$ 5,000	($ 7,000)	($ 2,000)

At first glance, it may appear that the elimination of B would eliminate the loss, leaving a profitable operation producing only A. However, B is contributing $18,000 toward fixed costs. Elimination of B would increase the cash deficit from $7,000 to $20,000, that is, contribution of $30,000 from A less total fixed costs of $50,000. Again, each cost component, business, and product segment must be studied carefully.

Managing Human Resources.   The role of the turnaround specialist and his or her team is to bring about change. This requires quick identification of the problem, a clear articulation of the goals, and creation of the infrastructure to manage the process. To the extent that the company is unable to provide the infrastructure, the turnaround specialist must build it. Therefore, assessment of the production, marketing, sales, control, human resource, finance, accounting, and legal functions must be analyzed to determine where help must be sought.

Often middle management and the labor force "on the floor" are the key to the process. Although turnover, absenteeism, illness, and accidents are symptoms of unrest, employees have insights that top management seldom sees. By the same token, top management must often be replaced because its leadership has simply not been effective.

Regardless of circumstances, distress usually requires some reduction in the work force. Cutting employees is difficult for everyone. In a turnaround, onetime cuts are generally preferred over gradual cuts to minimize the disruption in the work force and to provide those remaining with a sense of security for future operations. However, quick reductions are often difficult to manage since time and experience are required to accumulate adequate information regarding the company's ongoing needs. In addition, hasty work force reductions can damage the intellectual infrastructure, which is the most difficult part of a company to replace. Often, a retention incentive program for employees should be implemented that includes incentives for both remaining with the company and for reaching certain performance goals. Both key employees and staff employees should be included in the process. The cost of the retention incentive for staff employees may at first glance seem high, but the cost of replacement and training can be even higher. On the other hand, if the learning curve is relatively short, new employees do not carry any emotional baggage from the period of decline and thus will not harbor any potential mistrust of management or of the turnaround specialist. In other words, history can prevent progress.

Family businesses create special considerations. Failure is an extremely emotional event. Since the owners are typically also the managers, replacement of management is an even more difficult process. The turnaround specialist must understand that the political forces at work are very powerful and that even within families, various powerbases exist. It's more difficult to tell a father that his child is incompetent than to tell a CEO that a vice president or manager is incompetent.

Dealing with organized labor is particularly difficult for the turnaround specialist who is inclined to make decisions quickly. The relationship between organized labor and management has usually developed over a long period of time; therefore, it is necessary to gain an understanding of the relationship including issues of credibility and trust. Often both sides harbor ingrained suspicions and preconceptions.

When a turnaround specialist is retained, he should make himself accessible to all levels of employees. Employees know when trouble is brewing and generally want to assist with the recovery process. Although some employee constituents may view the arrival of the turnaround manager with some trepidation, most welcome the person who can fix the company. The turnaround specialist, therefore, generally benefits by a honeymoon period. That time should be used to learn as much as possible as quickly as possible, to rejuvenate the work force, and to instill a sense of confidence in the future with realistic expectations.

The bottom line is that frequent and forthright communication is critical to all human resource management. Employees often have the most at stake in the outcome, yet are frequently excluded from the process. Both management and the turnaround specialist should recognize that labor is a resource to be protected and to be utilized.

Managing Creditors. The 1980s saw increasing complexity of capital structures along with the increasing use of debt instruments as opposed to equity to support growth and acquisitions. Debt-for-equity swaps will likely become more commonplace in the 1990s if the increased business failure rate proves to be linked to capital structures rather than to viability issues. As a result, management and turnaround specialists may be faced with the dual tasks of convincing bodies of creditors that debt-for-equity swaps are the most viable vehicle for creditors to recoup their investment or at least minimize apparent losses, and of convincing shareholders that a smaller portion of the company is preferable to no company at all.

Depending upon the level of distress, particularly if the company is insolvent, the creditors become active partners in the turnaround process. It is essential that management maintain open lines of communication, tell the truth, and not make promises that cannot reasonably be met. It's often difficult for management to understand that creditors would rather have straightforward bad news than a string of broken promises. Often by the time the turnaround specialist has been retained, credibility has become strained. Management often assumes that creditors will act harshly if told the truth, particularly when the truth is very bad news. Consequently, it is not uncommon for a turnaround specialist to discover that the previous management has made promises that have been broken, has not provided full information, and has generally tried to put its best foot forward by portraying the situation as being better than it really is, only to have created with the creditor constituencies expectations that have been unmet. In a crisis situation, management occasionally becomes a so-called plate spinner, the acrobat who can keep a dozen plates spinning on the top of a stick simultaneously . . . until one falls and the rest soon follow. Therefore, one of the most important aspects of the turnaround specialist's engagement is to renew credibility with creditor constituents and to convince management to face reality.

Furthermore, management must be made to understand that creditors, despite posturing, generally do not want a bankruptcy to occur. Creditors know that bankruptcy is advantageous to few and expensive to all, and that although the debtor writes the checks, the creditors, in fact, pay the fees through reduced dividends at the time of distribution. Creditors simply want the maximum recovery possible as soon as possible, fully understanding that liquidation of assets is generally not the preferred approach. The turnaround specialist must teach management to think like creditors.

Secured Lenders. Many factors related to the particular lender affect the workout process. Management needs to understand as much as possible about its lender's approach to impaired credits. Generally speaking, all banks establish various reserves based upon assessments of the collectibility of the loans in their portfolios. Knowledge of reserve policies in relation to the status of the impaired loan can enhance the troubled company's negotiation with its lender.

The secured lender's agenda is usually clear: it wants to obtain as much information and collect as much of its loan as possible, and as quickly as possible. It is said that small banks lend on the character of the company's owner; large banks lend on the company's financials. When the lending officer becomes the workout officer, usually unintentionally, he faces the dual objective of collecting the loan and protecting his own credibility and position within the bank. When the workout officer is not the lending officer (usually the case with larger lenders), the relationship is not clouded by his personal ego or history with the loan. Workout departments with professionals dedicated to managing impaired credits are becoming more commonplace as profit centers, particularly with larger banks. In some cases, workout officers receive incentives based upon collections in excess of the unreserved loan balance.

In the case of multiple lenders, intercreditor issues can severely impact the turnaround. When a negotiation involves a syndicated loan, it is important that a spokesman be identified to represent the lending group. This reduces the opportunity for miscommunication, and the responsibility for communication with the syndicated creditors shifts to their spokesman.

The liquidation analysis also assists in understanding the relationship of the creditors vis-à-vis one another. Collateralized loans should be examined to determine whether they have been properly secured and to determine whether or not the lender is fully secured. If the secured lender is fully secured, its initial desire is to protect the value of its collateral from deterioration or depletion. If the secured lender is not fully secured, at first blush, it would not appear that it would be as agreeable to a workout. However, no lender wants to incur the time and expense necessary to liquidate its collateral, particularly since liquidations tend to provide lower returns to the lender. Therefore, existing secured creditors are normally the best source of new funds for the turnaround if the business plan shows that keeping the business operating reasonably increases the value of the company.

Trade Creditors. Although secured lenders may appear to apply the most pressure in troubled situations, the company must carefully nurture the essential partnership that exists with its trade suppliers. That partnership can be used as leverage in negotiating with secured lenders because the cooperation of the trade is necessary to keep the doors open to preserve and enhance the company's going-concern value. Trade suppliers usually have the most to lose as well as the most to gain in a troubled situation. Being unsecured, they usually stand last in the creditors' line of recovery; however, they not only stand to lose their current investment, they also stand to lose an ongoing customer. Therefore, the trade must be kept fully informed of the plan, the projections, and the underlying assumptions. A plan of reorganization will probably need to provide incentives to the trade, despite its unsecured position, to encourage the trade to provide the necessary support.

Turnaround Financing. Financing is an integral part of a troubled company's plan of reorganization. An effective financing plan will stabilize the company's cash position during the crisis, provide the necessary capital base to allow the company to return to profitability, and restructure the balance sheet so that it can support the company into the future.

Financing strategies differ from situation to situation according to the liquidity and viability of the distressed business. Initially, turnaround specialists attempt to maximize the liquidity to provide sufficient time to evaluate the viability of the business. When necessary, the turnaround financing plan will involve a recapitalization or a restructuring of the right-hand side of the company's balance sheet. This involves changing the relationship between existing financial stakeholders through a combination of debt and equity conversions, exchange offers, stock rights offerings, and the addition of new financial stakeholders. Obviously, the more severe a company's situation is, the more difficult it is to work out an arrangement with existing trade creditors, lenders, subordinated debtholders, and equityholders, and the harder it is to attract new stakeholders.

Monitoring the Plan.   Turnaround plans should establish goals that are realistic, make sense, and identify specific completion dates. Timely comparison of actual results to projections is critical, however; given the many uncertainties in a distressed situation, the underlying assumptions must be reexamined regularly and any necessary changes should be implemented. Adherence to a plan that is growing more obsolete each day is a formula for failure.

Financial projections also serve as the measure against which performance is to be evaluated. It is often difficult to judge the effect that the distress will have upon meeting established targets. Management must be on the front line preparing the plan because it will ultimately be responsible for its execution.

Much can be learned about management in the planning process. Some managers will assume that business will return to normal with the arrival of the turnaround specialist and will make unreasonably optimistic assumptions, while others will assume the worst or even attempt to "sandbag" their projections for fear that their own performance will be measured against the standard they establish. Regardless of the psychological profile of different management personnel, the turnaround specialist may need to revise projections based upon what seems reasonable to him. Once the plan is in place, performance targets should be established quickly for key management personnel, providing for rewards upon reaching established goals within projected time frames. In addition, bonuses should be provided for exceeding established goals.

The turnaround plan often contains a management contingency reserve to bridge the gap between the plan's reasonably achievable goals and the possibility that all of the relevant assumptions may not fall into place as projected. Although the plan should not be overly aggressive, middle management must be encouraged to provide reasonable projections and discouraged from "sandbagging," or intentionally understating, their forecast. Underestimation establishes easy-to-reach goals that fail to add value to the turnaround process. The contingency reserve recognizes that the plan is close to a best-case analysis and serves as a buffer to cover shortfalls. Since the reserve is a management-provided contingency, the various divisions or segments contributing to the plan preparation must perform against their individual plans. As operations progress, top management must make the decision, when appropriate, to charge unanticipated but identified deviations from the plan against the reserve. This procedure provides an ongoing consistency for measurement of actual performance against projected performance.

Most important, the plan should make sense so that all constituents believe it is achievable. Regular reporting of progress against the plan with variance analyses included is necessary to foster cooperation. As mentioned previously, communication is the key to success. All constituents must be made a part of the recovery process.

Poststabilization: Transition and Strategies

Calling in a turnaround specialist is only a temporary fix. There may be some truth to the axiom that turnaround specialists do not make good permanent managers since they appear to thrive on the excitement of having to achieve very difficult goals in short periods of time with extremely limited resources.

Consequently, the turnaround specialist's final assignment is to assist the company in the transition to new permanent management after the company has achieved stabilization. The options available include "teaching" the old or remaining management how to properly manage the company; however, as was pointed out earlier, Bibeault found that successful turnarounds were almost always engineered by new management after the removal of the previous management. Alternatively and most commonly, the turnaround specialist assists the company in identifying, hiring, and putting into place the new management necessary to manage the company.

Once the post-crisis management team members have been hired, it is their job to develop a long-term strategy for the company. This plan should include a life cycle analysis of all products and services, new product introduction timetables, personnel requirements, marketing strategies, and a host of other factors that will be necessary for the company to be competitive and profitable in the future. A detailed discussion of the postcrisis business management process is beyond the scope of this chapter. Numerous books have been written on the subject of strategic planning. Although perhaps overlooked, the postcrisis long-range business plan should be considered the natural extension and conclusion of the turnaround process. It is significant to note that the efficacy of that plan will determine whether the company will progress down the road to long-term stability and growth or relapse into decline.

Conclusion

As markets change, businesses must evolve to meet these changes. Market economies continue to expand at unprecedented rates. Competition will shake out all but the fittest. Darwin's theory of evolution still applies. Unfortunately, capitalism breeds failure. However, through a turnaround process involving the integration of many business skills, the assistance of experienced professionals, and the cooperation of numerous stakeholders, companies can recover, jobs can be saved, and economic disruption can be minimized.

Turnaround professionals are emerging as specialists with the skills and with access to the resources necessary to guide companies through difficult times and to minimize the loss of value to all stakeholders involved.

Appendix*

Introduction

The authors have performed research for the last several years to identify publicly traded companies that have achieved successful turnarounds. Since 1988, TMA, a national nonprofit trade association of professionals engaged in the business of aiding distressed companies, has used that research to award its annual Turnaround of the Year Award.

The research examines companies that, over a period of five years or longer, have gone through a decline involving at least two years of net operating losses followed by recovery of two successive years of net operating income. The following case histories have been selected from that database to illustrate how five companies approached the turnaround process in the mid to late 1980s.

Although each company represents a unique industry or product that made its turnaround distinctive, it is believed that there are lessons to be learned from these examples. These are not shown as a prescriptive example of what to do when a company is in distress but rather to illustrate successful turnarounds.

In contrast to the majority of studies indicating that 80 to 90 percent of all business failures result from internal management-controllable factors, four of the five cases illustrated here involve distress caused by external factors that were ostensibly beyond management's control. What is remarkable about these turnarounds is that management had to adapt to circumstances it had not created, convince its creditors to provide continued support, and convince investors to put their money into declining situations.

*Mark J. Abrahams of KPMG Peat Marwick was primarily responsible for the research and the preparation of the case studies provided in this Appendix.

Two cases involve the retention of turnaround specialists to manage the recovery. Though only one case involves a chapter 11 filing, another involves a complete industry in turmoil with several competitors in bankruptcy. Two cases involve unforeseen legislative changes redefining and redirecting complete industries. Two cases involve overexpansion, and in one of those, the company eventually divested itself of one of its original businesses. In short, these cases paint a portrait of how creative management can be, especially in crisis.

The information contained in this analysis was obtained from public sources such as 10Ks and annual reports.

ADAC Laboratories

ADAC Laboratories designs, manufactures, markets, and services medical imaging devices and information systems for diagnostic and therapeutic use by hospitals and medical clinics. The company's products involve high-tech nuclear medicine applications, such as x-ray imaging systems used in radiation therapy for cancer treatment. Because of its ground-breaking advances in developing engineering systems and software, the company is regarded as one of the technological leaders in the industry.

In 1984, tax law changes in TEFRA (Tax Equity and Fiscal Responsibility Act) significantly impacted medical equipment manufacturers. Hospitals and medical clinics were required to provide economic justification, including detailed cost and benefit analysis, for all equipment purchases to qualify for Medicare reimbursement. As reasonable as the legislation appeared, it caught many equipment providers off guard by delaying the acquisition process of their customers. As a result, ADAC suffered a 64 percent decrease in sales, from $73 million in 1983 to $47 million in 1986. To be expected, losses were incurred, working capital decreased, and liquidity problems surfaced.

With the crisis becoming evident in 1984, the company sought the assistance of one of its existing investors, Hambrecht & Quist, a management and investor group specializing in high-technology companies. Q. T. Wiles, president of Hambrecht & Quist, was selected as ADAC's chairman, and with him came an additional capital infusion. Under Wiles's leadership in 1985 and 1986, the company's liquidity crisis was diffused through new issues of preferred stock, a renegotiated line of credit, and an exchange of debt for equity.

In addition, Wiles restructured both the senior management team and the organization of the company. Distinct operating profit centers were organized, each responsible for meeting specific quarterly revenue and expense budgets and goals, preparing business plans, and developing long-range strategies. This reorganization allowed greater control over both revenue growth and expense reductions.

As sales decreased from 1984 to 1986, the company reduced fixed costs at a corresponding rate, reduced staff size, deferred or dropped capital expenditure projects, and identified and closed unprofitable nonstrategic business units. As a result, variable product costs were reduced from 89 to 54 percent of revenues from 1984 to 1988. During the same period, operating expenses declined from 70 to 30 percent of revenues.

Despite its declining revenue base, the company maintained its commitment to research and development, recognizing how essential the continued development of new products and technologies was to its future. A market-driven research and development policy was implemented to ensure that new technologies met customer demand.

As hospitals and medical clinics adapted to the legislated changes in Medicare reimbursement policies, the company was well positioned for significant growth in sales and market share. The results: revenues grew 62 percent between 1987 and 1989. In 1989, the company paid its first-ever cash dividend to common stockholders and retired its long-term debt.

Although Wiles left the company in 1986, Hambrecht & Quest recognized ADAC's technological strengths and its potential for growth in a narrowly defined segment of the health care industry. ADAC's commitment to technology and to continued research and development provided the company with the products and the management structure to weather an extended industrywide crisis.

Bethlehem Steel

Bethlehem Steel is one of the largest steel producers in the United States. Although its core operations included the process of converting iron ore into raw steel and steel products, the company had also become involved in secondary steel-related operations such as marine, railroad, and construction products. Additionally, it had made several minor investments in companies outside the steel industry.

Between 1981 and 1985, Bethlehem Steel suffered annual losses totaling almost $2 billion. In 1985, its bond ratings were downgraded to a below-investment grade. The quarterly dividend on common stock was steadily reduced and was suspended in 1986 for the first time since the 1930s.

During the mid 1980s, the entire steel industry in the United States suffered because of a massive oversupply, reduced demand, poor quality, and severely depressed prices. Increased use of products as plastics, aluminum, ceramics, and glass not only reduced customer demand for steel, but also increased competition among steel producers. Further exacerbating the markets, foreign producers were dumping steel into the U.S. market at drastically reduced prices. In response to the foreign threat, President Reagan proposed the Comprehensive Fair Trade Program in an attempt to control and reduce foreign imports.

By 1986, steel companies representing 20 percent of the country's production capacity, including such industry leaders as LTV Corporation, had filed for protection under chapter 11 of the Bankruptcy Code. Given Bethlehem Steel's position in a mature, or perhaps declining, industry, a restructured management team decided to undertake a defensive strategy by reducing production capacity, creating more efficient operations, improving productivity, and eliminating noncore operations. Bethlehem Steel's plan was to pare down to its smaller, yet profitable core business so that when the industry downturn subsided, the company would be poised to grow while preserving margins.

Following traditional belt-tightening techniques, management increased working capital by implementing inventory control systems, revising receivable collection schedules, limiting capital expenditures, and eliminating dividends. Reserves for discontinued operations were established, and inventories were written down. Equity was issued to reduce debt and interest expense.

In addition, business segments and assets not related to its basic steelmaking operations were sold, including land, coal operations, marine operations, a limestone quarry, and a mineral wool plant, generating working capital to stabilize the company. Finally, unique approaches to converting available resources into working capital were utilized, such as the exchange of land for reductions in utility taxes and maintenance expenses for certain plant highways and bridges.

The cash generated from asset sales was partially allocated to plant modernization programs. Operational efficiencies measured by output per employee improved, thereby reducing costs and increasing production capacity. New products were introduced to respond to customer demand. The Comprehensive Fair Trade Program proved to be reasonably effective in controlling underpriced imports, thereby stabilizing both domestic and global markets by providing the industry with the time and resources to downsize, modernize, and restructure.

Renegotiated union contracts reduced labor costs in a spirit of cooperation between labor and management. The company implemented employee incentive and involvement programs including "Partners for Progress," a program designed to train employees to contribute new ideas for lowering costs, improving quality, and providing better customer service, and "Priority One Program," a plan in which hourly and salaried plant employees participated in establishing the production quality standards for the operating units.

From 1982 to 1987, steel production per employee increased 85 percent, cost per ton of steel decreased 24 percent, and sales per employee increased 70 percent, not only moving the company to profitability but also increasing the company's market share.

Current strategies at the end of 1989 suggest that Bethlehem Steel will continue to consider divesting nonsteel and other noncore businesses, consolidating or shutting down remaining inefficient facilities, and writing off obsolete inventories and operations. In an effort to increase the productivity of underutilized assets, the company is also considering the possibility of joint ventures, partnerships, facility-sharing arrangements, and mergers.

Midway Airlines

Midway Airlines is a regional airline serving commuter, business, and leisure travel out of Chicago's Midway Airport. It offers a convenient, less congested alternative to Chicago's O'Hare International Airport. With fewer flight delays, Midway Airport helps airlines cut expenses associated with aircraft holding and taxi delays.

The 1980s were a decade of change and substantial stress on the airline industry. The 1981–1984 air traffic controllers' strike severely curtailed industry growth. Deregulation initially led to the formation of new local and discount airlines, but by the end of the decade it resulted in the consolidation of airline companies into a mere handful of major carriers as price wars became common and profit margins declined. Furthermore, unstable fuel prices added significantly to the lack of stability in the airline industry.

In that environment, Midway suffered operating losses, rendering it incapable of expanding routes or increasing passenger seat miles. To gain market share, the company purchased additional aircraft from bankrupt Air Florida in 1984. The associated acquisition costs added to the company's operating losses. Midway suffered net losses in 1983, 1984, and 1985 with variable operating expenses running 111, 123, and 100 percent of revenues during those three years, respectively.

In 1984, the company implemented a series of measures to reduce operating expenses and to preserve cash. These efforts included eliminating service in nonprofitable low-volume markets, reducing staff, terminating certain capital expenditure programs including a helicopter venture, and disposing of nonessential assets. During this period, the company continued its policy of not paying cash dividends on common stock.

Marketing strategy was shifted from enhanced in-flight and business class services to a lower-cost, lower-frills strategy that included seating reconfigurations to increase capacity. To relieve the cash flow crisis, the company successfully negotiated a new line of credit, issued preferred stock, and executed a sale-leaseback of company aircraft in 1984.

A new subsidiary based in Florida was established to perform heavy aircraft maintenance and repairs. With Federal Aviation and Aeronautics repair certification, the subsidiary was not only able to provide contract maintenance services for Midway Airlines as a means of reducing maintenance costs, but it was also able to provide similar services to other airlines, thereby contributing to the earnings of the company.

By 1988, operating expenses had fallen from a high of 123 percent of revenues in 1984 to 96 percent. During those years, available seat miles tripled and the number of aircraft and the number of cities served more than doubled.

In 1989, on the crest of its turnaround and looking to expand into new markets, the company purchased Eastern Airlines' Philadelphia hub, venturing for the first time away from Chicago where all of its flights either originated or connected. The company again suffered operating losses in the face of expansion costs, increasing fuel costs, additional training expenses accompanying the introduction of new aircraft, and added interest and debt reduction obligations. Although financing for this expansion was well planned through the issuance of both preferred stock and long-term debt, in 1990 Midway abandoned the Philadelphia expansion strategy to refocus on its core business.

Storage Technology (StorageTek)

Storage Technology designs, develops and manufactures information storage and retrieval systems for the computer industry. Founded in 1969, StorageTek was one of the first companies to manufacture computer tape drives for data storage and output for original equipment manufacturers (OEMs) of computer systems and distributors. By emphasizing technologically innovative products and customer service, the company differentiated itself from its competitors and enjoyed early success fueled by the development of 79 domestic patents and 22 international patents.

Intense competition and a volatile OEM market caused many computer companies to falter in the mid-1980s. When IBM began competing in the data storage market in 1982, StorageTek was unable to match IBM's ability to offer an extensive product line at reduced prices. Foreign competition benefiting from inexpensive manufacturing capabilities also entered the market, further increasing the price competition. In 1984, the company lost $500 million on revenues of $800 million. These enormous losses caused severe liquidity problems, forcing the company to file for protection under chapter 11 of the Bankruptcy Code.

After the filing, Ryal Poppa, a turnaround specialist, was appointed chairman and CEO of the company. He immediately reorganized top management and filled 15 officer and director positions. He recognized that StorageTek's continued viability lay in its strong technological base and in its intellectual leadership. The company had to enhance its existing products while developing new, innovative product offerings and providing unparalleled customer service.

To generate needed working capital, the company sold weak divisions, certain nonstrategic assets, and its leasing company. One third of the employees were released, operations were consolidated, excess plant capacity was reduced, and inventory control systems were put into place. To cover possible losses from currency transactions, a foreign currency hedging program was initiated. With all of these changes and the promise of improvement, a new line of credit was successfully negotiated.

A more focused research and development strategy limited the company's risk and expense. Though reduced, the commitment to research and development remained substantial. Exploratory ventures into radically new products such as optical media technology were deferred with the plan to purchase the technology from others if that proved viable.

Customer service became the cornerstone of StorageTek's recovery plan. Domestic operations were restructured delegating profit and loss responsibility to the regional level, thereby shifting marketing and other services closer to the customer while decentralizing cost controls. Customer advisory boards were initiated to integrate the voice of the customer onto the design teams for new products. Not only did this strategy strengthen customer relationships, but it also helped management better understand customer requirements and shortened the response time to satisfy customer needs. Finally, the company formed a StorageTek users group.

Three years later, the plan of reorganization was confirmed. Chapter 11 had allowed the company the time to pare down its operations, reduce its costs, and enhance its cash flow through new debt and equity issues. From 1984 to 1989, cost of sales was reduced from 92 to 69 percent and operating expenses dropped from 34 to 25 percent of revenues. After the plan was confirmed, with the company focused on research and development, customer service, and increasing market share, revenues grew 63 percent from 1987 to 1989.

Recently, strategic alliances have resulted in the development and marketing of state-of-the-art products, further enhancing the company's technology and product lines. In 1989, the research and development budget was increased, reaching 9 percent of total revenues, an indication of StorageTek's reemergence as an industry innovator committed to the development of leading edge technologies.

Voit Corporation

Voit is a leading manufacturer of sporting goods and equipment and a leading operator of bowling alleys—both mature industries with relatively standard and competitively priced products and services. However, when Voit acquired certain product lines including inflatable balls, exercise equipment, racquet sports equipment, and underwater sports gear and equipment from AMF, Inc. in 1984, severe losses and liquidity problems followed. Although the leveraged purchase was intended to substantially expand the company's product lines, Voit was unable to handle the debt load. Within two years, operating losses, significantly increased interest expense, a negative working capital position, and a default under debt covenants led to a qualified auditor's opinion.

In April 1986, the largest secured creditor, Chemical Bank, demanded payment in full of Voit's obligations. The company immediately began negotiating with its other secured creditors to refrain from exercising their demand rights and to extend additional lines of credit.

Because of management's knowledge of the sporting goods industry, it was able to convince creditors that neither interim nor replacement management was necessary to lead a recovery. Although its bowling alley operations had been part of its original business, it was not considered one of Voit's strategically necessary core businesses since it was not generating sufficient cash flow. Instead, what once had been viewed as important leases and bowling alley operations were sold. Voit closed unprofitable plants and narrowed its product lines. Tighter inventory accounting methods were installed to improve the company's working capital position.

Voit then negotiated a new debt and equity structure with all secured creditors, including Chemical Bank. Recognizing that new product lines were the wave of the future, even in a mature industry, and with the support of its secured creditors, management adopted an offensive expansion strategy by allocating resources to research and development. As a result, the company introduced a line of home exercise equipment that significantly expanded Voit's share of the sporting goods equipment market and contributed to increased profits and cash flow.

After exiting the bowling alley business, which accounted for 30 percent of revenues in 1985, the company's new strategy was to build exclusively upon its sporting goods core business. Drastic reductions in staff and overhead expenses resulted in a decline of selling, general, and administrative expenses from 42 percent of revenues in 1985 to 19 percent in 1988. Manufacturing efficiencies reduced the cost of goods sold from 87 percent of revenues in 1985 to 72 percent of sales in 1988. As a result, Voit emerged from its crisis with increased margins, increased market share, and positive working capital and cash flow.

Notes

1. For the purposes of this chapter, no distinction is made between interim managers and turnaround consultants. Instead, the term "turnaround specialist" is used and refers to either profession interchangeably.
2. D & B's definition of a business failure, in substance, includes any situation in which loss to creditors or a compromise with creditors occurred. Therefore, a business ceasing operations for whatever reason but paying all creditors in full is not recorded as a failure. Furthermore, the statistical series was revised in 1984 to include all industries in the United States by adding three industry sectors to the coverage: agriculture, forestry, and fishing; finance, insurance, and real estate; and the service sector in its entirety.
3. Bibeault, Donald B. (1982). *Corporate Turnaround: How Managers Turn Losers Into Winners!* McGraw-Hill, New York. Bibeault's research found that "insider management" cited external factors as either the cause or a contributing factor of failure in 74 percent of the cases studied, whereas "outsider management" cited external factors as a contributing factor in only 25 percent of the cases studies.

"Outsider management" never identified external factors as the only cause of the failure.

4. Bibeault and Charles W. Hofer. (1980). "Turnaround Strategies," in William F. Glueck, ed., *Business Policy and Strategic Management*, McGraw Hill, New York, pp. 271–78.

5. A recent study by the United States Administrative Office of the Courts has shown that many companies, in fact, have used chapter 11 as a liquidation vehicle. The consensus among practicing professionals seems to be that recovery is maximized even in a so-called liquidating 11. Chapter 7 has become synonymous with fire-sale prices and can amount to an announcement seeking vultures. Although the result may appear to be the same, the psychological perception is different and assists the debtor in preserving maximum value for as long as possible.

6. See, for example Michael E. Porter, (1988), *Competitive Strategy: Techniques for Analyzing Industries and Competitors*, Free Press, New York; and Kathryn Rudi Harrigan, (1988), *Managing Mature Businesses: Restructuring Declining Industries and Revitalizing Troubled Operations*, Lexington Books, Lexington, MA.

7. It should be noted that this discussion is intended to serve as a checklist and not as a comprehensive discussion of the methodology for tweeking cash flow.

Tax Planning for Financially Troubled Company Restructuring

Paul F. Sheahen
Arthur Andersen & Co.

John R. O'Neill
Arthur Andersen & Co.

The restructuring or acquisition of a financially troubled company's debt or equity raises a variety of tax issues. Certain of these issues often arise in isolated commercial transactions outside the insolvency or bankruptcy context. In the case of a troubled company restructuring, these tax issues often seem to multiply and at times appear to be overwhelming.

This article will review the pertinent federal income tax issues in the area including the recognition or exclusion of discharge of indebtedness income to a debtor corporation, the taxation to creditors and shareholders in debt or stock exchanges, limitations imposed on the use of unused tax attributes in restructurings or acquisitions, and other relevant tax matters.

Discharge of Indebtedness—Taxable Income and Exclusions

Discharge of Indebtedness Income

Generally, a taxpayer must recognize income on discharge of indebtedness. Section 61(a)(12) of the Internal Revenue Code and Reg. Section 1.61-12(c)(3) (all "Section" references are to the Internal Revenue Code of 1986, as amended, and the regulations promulgated thereunder unless otherwise indicated). The statute does not specifically define "discharge of indebtedness." However, it is well settled that the repurchase of debt for less than its adjusted issue price constitutes income to the repurchasing debtor corporation. See *U.S. v. Kirby Lumber,* 284 U.S. 1 (1931). For this purpose, indebtedness includes any debt for which the taxpayer is liable

Note: The authors wish to thank William B. Boyle for his assistance in the development of this chapter.

or indebtedness subject to which the taxpayer holds property. Included in this definition are expenses accrued by a company, including accrued interest on debt, which it is relieved from paying. "Adjusted issue price" is generally the debt's original issue price, plus accrued original issue discount (OID), or less amortized bond premium.

Other Transactions Causing Debtor Corporation to Recognize Discharge of Indebtedness Income

A debtor corporation may recognize income from cancellation of indebtedness (COD) upon the purchase of its debt at a discount by a related party or the contribution of its debt to the capital of the debtor corporation by a shareholder.

Related party acquisitions of debt. Prior to the Bankruptcy Tax Act of 1980, an affiliate of a debtor corporation could purchase the debt of such corporation at a discount and income recognition could be deferred until the repayment of principal. Economically, the debtor corporation could effectively retire its debt at a discount and defer gain within the economic group. In response to this perceived abuse, Congress enacted Section 108(e)(4), which treats a debtor as repurchasing its debt, to the extent provided in Treasury regulations, when a related party acquires such debt from an unrelated creditor. This rule only applies for purposes of determining discharge of indebtedness and thus only to purchases of debt at a discount. Related parties are determined under the rules of Sections 267(b), 707(b)(1), and 414 and require a greater than 50 percent, direct or indirect, ownership.

Treasury has yet to issue regulations determining the amount of income the debtor must recognize. Although some argue that Section 108(e)(4) is not effective until regulations are issued, the Internal Revenue Service ("Service") has applied it in the absence of regulations. See Private Letter Rulings 8922080 and 8923021. The statute and legislative history provide that regulations will make adjustments on subsequent repayments or capital contributions of the debt. For example, assume a parent corporation purchases from an unrelated creditor for $900 debt of wholly owned subsidiary issued at par for $1,000. The subsidiary recognizes $100 of COD income under Section 108(e)(4). Subsequently, the subsidiary makes a $1,000 repayment of principal. Treasury regulations should provide that the subsidiary/debtor made a $100 dividend and $900 repayment of principal.

If the parent were to contribute the debt to the subsidiary after the subsidiary recognized the $100 of COD income, Treasury regulations are to provide that the amount of COD income recognized under the capital contribution rules of Section 108(e)(6) (discussed below) shall be reduced by the amount of COD income previously recognized by the debtor under the related party acquisition rules. Therefore, the debtor would not recognize COD income on this subsequent capital contribution. There would appear to be double recognition of income without appropriate adjustments.

In the majority of bankrupt/insolvent company situations, the creditors are the real owners of the company in an economic sense. An acquirer who intended to take over the company, practically, would need to acquire both the debt and the stock. If the debt and stock were acquired simultaneously, one could view the acquisition as triggering the rules of Section 108(e)(4). It is arguable that Section 108(e)(4) intends that the 50 percent relationship exist at the time of, or immediately before, the acquisition. Where the required relationship does not arise until the completion of the transaction, the acquiror could argue that Section 108(e)(4) does not apply to the simultaneous purchase of debt and stock by an unrelated purchaser. However, to the extent option attribution may apply or step transaction arguments may be raised, the transaction would not be without risk.

Capital contribution of debt. Prior to the Bankruptcy Tax Act of 1980, a shareholder could contribute debt of a corporation, acquired previously at a discount, to such corporation and Section 118 would preclude the debtor corporation from recognizing any income on the capital contribution. Congress enacted Section 108(e)(6) to preclude such treatment. Instead, Section 118 will not apply and such corporation shall be treated as having satisfied its debt with an amount of money equal to the shareholder's adjusted basis in such debt. Thus, if a shareholder acquires debt at a discount from an unrelated creditor and Section 108(e)(4) does not apply, the debtor corporation will recognize COD income upon the subsequent capital contribution. This rule also operates to generate COD income where a cash basis shareholder forgives an accrued expense of an accrual basis debtor corporation.

In order for the capital contribution rule to apply, the shareholder's canceling of the debt must be related to his status as a shareholder. If the shareholder/creditor cancels the debt as a creditor trying to maximize satisfaction of the claim, such as where the stock and bond are publicly held, then the rule should not apply. See related discussion under the Stock-for-Debt Exception.

Exclusions from Gross Income

As a matter of policy, Congress prefers that financially troubled companies continue to operate rather than liquidate. In order to provide a "fresh start" to these companies, Congress modified Section 108 in the Bankruptcy Tax Act of 1980 to allow deferral of tax liability from discharge of indebtedness. As will be discussed, this tax deferral results primarily from the tax attribute reduction requirements of Section 108(b). Thus, Section 108 provides an exception to the general rule that gross income includes income from discharge of indebtedness.

Section 108 exclusion. Section 108(a) excludes discharge of indebtedness from income if the discharge occurs in a Title 11 case or when the taxpayer is insolvent. A "Title 11 case" means a case under Title 11 of the

United States Code (relating to bankruptcy) where the discharge of indebtedness is granted by or pursuant to a plan approved by the court that has jurisdiction over the taxpayer. Section 108(d)(2). An insolvent taxpayer may exclude the amount of discharge of indebtedness from income only to the extent of the taxpayer's insolvency. Section 108(a)(3). Also, the Title 11 exclusion takes precedence over the insolvency exclusion. Section 108(a)(2)(A).

The amount of a taxpayer's insolvency is determined immediately before the discharge of indebtedness. Section 108(d)(3). The amount is based upon a balance sheet test, the excess of liabilities over the fair market value of assets. Although not expressly provided, this concept should include intangible assets (including goodwill or going-concern value). Contingent liabilities that would otherwise diminish the value of assets present a difficult valuation issue since the general tax bias is to exclude them until they become fixed and determinable. See Reg. Section 1.338(b) allocation rules. However, the correct answer should be to include a proper valuation of contingent liabilities, since the insolvency analysis is a fair market value analysis.

Reduction of tax attributes. As discussed earlier, Congress deferred the tax liability from discharge of indebtedness for bankrupt and insolvent taxpayers. In order to recoup its current loss in revenues, Congress requires a troubled company to reduce certain tax attributes that would otherwise be carried forward or would generate deductions to offset future income. The tax attribute reductions described below are made after the determination of tax for the taxable year of discharge. Section 108(b)(4)(A).

General rule—Taxpayers must reduce their tax attributes by the amount of COD income excluded from gross income under Section 108(a). Section 108(b)(1). The tax attributes are reduced in the following order under Section 108(b)(2):

1. Net operating loss for the current taxable year and then any net operating loss carryovers to such taxable year on a dollar-for-dollar basis.
2. General business credit carryovers to, and then such credits from, the taxable year of discharge are reduced in amounts equal to 33 1/3 cents for each dollar of excluded income.
3. Capital loss arising in the current year and then any capital loss carryover to such taxable year on a dollar-for-dollar basis.
4. Tax basis in property, on a dollar-for-dollar basis, on the first day of the tax year following the discharge of indebtedness. Section 1017(a). However, the tax basis cannot be reduced below the taxpayer's aggregate liabilities immediately after the discharge. Section 1017(b)(2).
5. Foreign tax credit carryovers to and, then such credits from, the taxable year of discharge are reduced in amounts equal to 33 1/3 cents for each dollar of excluded income.

Election to reduce tax basis in depreciable property—In lieu of reducing tax attributes in the order set forth in Section 108(b)(2), insolvent and Title 11 taxpayers may elect to first reduce the tax basis of depreciable property. Section 108(b)(5). The basis reduction may be made without regard to the aggregate liabilities limitation mentioned above.

Under certain circumstances, the taxpayer may elect to reduce tax basis in the following nondepreciable assets:

1. Any real property treated as inventory.
2. Stock of a subsidiary with which the debtor files a consolidated return, but only to the extent that the subsidiary reduces its tax basis in depreciable property, and
3. Basis in partnership interest to the extent of the partner's proportionate share of depreciable property in the partnership, but only to the extent the partnership reduces its basis in depreciable property

The taxpayer may apply any portion of the tax attribute reduction first to depreciable assets. Section 108(b)(5)(A). No requirement exists that taxpayer reduce its tax basis in depreciable property to zero before reducing other tax attributes through the ordinary rules of Section 108(b)(2).

In certain change of ownership situations it may be advantageous to the taxpayer to elect to reduce tax basis in depreciable property rather than net operating losses. For example, if tax basis in built-in loss assets were reduced to their fair market value, then depreciation taken during the recognition period would not be subject to the Section 382 limitations (discussed later).

Four primary distinctions exist between tax basis reduction under Sections 108(b)(2) and 108(b)(5). First, and most obvious, Section 108(b)(5) is elective and Section 108(b)(2) is not. Second, Section 108(b)(5) applies only to reduce the tax basis of depreciable property, whereas Section 108(b)(2) applies to all property other than cash. Third, as previously mentioned, tax basis reduction under Section 108(b)(2) is subject to an aggregate liabilities limitation and elective Section 108(b)(5) is not. Finally, there is no explicit requirement to apply Section 108(b)(2) tax basis reduction on a consolidated basis, unlike Section 108(b)(5). Accordingly, it might be possible to avoid or defer tax basis reduction under Section 108(b)(2) by transferring depreciable or amortizable assets (subject to creditor approval) to wholly owned subsidiaries prior to the discharge of indebtedness. The resulting tax basis reduction would occur with respect to the stock of the subsidiary, not the depreciable or amortizable assets of the subsidiary.

Discharge of indebtedness in excess of tax attributes—If the amount of discharge of indebtedness excluded from income exceeds the tax attributes of the Title 11 taxpayer, then the excess amount escapes taxation. Bankruptcy Tax Act of 1980, S. Rep. No. 1035, 96th Cong., 2d Sess. 13 (1980); H.R. Rep. No. 833, 96th Cong., 2d. Sess 11 (1980). This will also be true with respect to *insolvent* taxpayers except to the extent they become solvent in the restructuring.

Exceptions from Discharge of Indebtedness Income

Stock-for-debt exception. The stock-for-debt exception is a judicially created doctrine adopted in Service rulings and codified in the Bankruptcy Tax Act of 1980. The stock-for-debt exception provides that discharge of indebtedness income does not arise when a debtor corporation issues its stock in satisfaction of its own debt, even if the liability exceeded the fair market value of the stock received. See *Capento Securities Corp. v. Commissioner*, 47 BTA 691 (1942), aff'd 140 F. 2d 382 (1st Cir. 1944); *Commissioner v. Motor Mart Trust*, 156 F. 2d 122 (1st Cir. 1946). If applicable, operation of the stock-for-debt rule results in no tax attribute utilization or reduction since no income recognition has occurred.

The judicial doctrine was based upon two theories: (1) the substitution of liability theory and (2) subscription price theory. Under the "subscription price" theory, gain is not realized by a corporation in the receipt of the subscription price of its shares . . . the amount which has already been paid in as the principal of a bond loan. *Capento Securities Corp., V. Comm'r* 47 B.T.A. 691, 695 (1942). Subsequent case law and Service rulings appear to rely upon the substitution of liability theory to the exclusion of the subscription price theory, leaving the latter theory in doubt as to its current viability.

Neither the Bankruptcy Tax Act of 1980 nor any amendments thereto define the stock-for-debt exception. Instead, Congress relied on the definition as developed through case law. The rule is not conditioned on the debt constituting a "security" for tax purposes, a definition typically limited to long-term debt maturities. Bankruptcy Tax Act of 1980; S. Rep. No. 1035, 96th Cong., 2d Sess 17. (1980).

*Reduced effectiveness of exception—Nonapplication to solvent taxpayers—*As a result of significant discounted debt equity swaps in the early 1980s by solvent corporations without taxable income recognition, and in keeping with the spirit of the 1980 Act to provide flexibility to truly troubled companies, the Deficit Reduction Act of 1984 modified the stock-for-debt rule and narrowed its applicability. To the extent a debtor corporation is solvent immediately after a discharge and not in bankruptcy, the stock-for-debt exchange will be treated as if the debtor satisfied its indebtedness with an amount of money equal to the fair market value of the stock. Section 108(e)(10)(A). Where the value of the stock is less than the amount of debt retired in the exchange, taxable income will be triggered under Section 61(a)(12).

In light of this narrowed application of the rule, the stock-for-debt exception will be useful only to insolvent and Title 11 corporations. See Section 108(e)(10)(B).

Issuance of nominal or token shares—The statute states that the stock-for-debt exception does not apply to the issuance of "nominal or token" shares. Section 108(e)(8)(A). The legislative history enlightens only slightly, stating "nominal or token amount of stock is . . . to be determined according to all the facts and circumstances, so that the forgiveness rules may not be circumvented by the issuance of nominal or token shares to a creditor who has no real equity interest in the corporation." Bankruptcy Tax Act of 1980, S. Rep. No. 1035, 96th Cong., 2d Sess 17 (1980).

The Service addressed this nominal or "de minimis" issue in Technical Advice Memorandum 8837001 (May 10, 1988). Pursuant to a bankruptcy plan, the unsecured creditors received cash and new preferred stock in exchange for their debt. The preferred stock entitled the holder to preferential dividends, a 5 percent participation feature with the common stock, and the right to convert the preferred stock into common stock of the debtor's parent after a period of three years. The debtor could redeem the preferred stock after a period of five years. The Service theorized that Section 108(e)(8)(A) was intended to continue the general rule of the substitution of liability theory underlying the stock-for-debt rule and to limit the application of the rule to the case of a stock-for-debt exchange that was essentially a sham transaction. The Service applied a facts and circumstances approach focusing on elements that addressed the economic substance of the stock-for-debt exchange and the creation of a real equity interest. Accordingly, the Service gave weight to factors that indicate arms-length bargaining, including:

1. The existence of sufficiently adverse economic interests on each side of the exchange
2. The value of the stock exchanged in comparison to the face amount of the debt canceled
3. The value of the stock received in comparison to the total consideration received in the discharge of debt.

The stock received in the exchange amounted to 15 percent of the total consideration received and 10 percent of the amount of debt canceled in the exchange. The Service concluded that the stock received was not de minimis based upon the sufficient arms-length bargaining and the amount of stock received. Essentially, the stock would not be nominal or token if the issuance of stock was not part of a sham transaction.

The Service has not indicated any specific percentage or safe harbor amount that would establish the de minimis threshold. The lack of guidance in this area makes planning difficult.

Proportionality required among unsecured creditors—A second limitation to the stock-for-debt exception exists where unsecured creditors participate in a workout. Section 108(e)(8)(B). A "workout" includes a Title 11 case or other transaction or series of transactions involving a significant restructuring of the debt of a corporation in financial difficulty. In such a workout, the ratio of the value of stock received to the amount of indebtedness canceled or exchanged for such stock by any unsecured creditor must be at least 50 percent of the ratio for all unsecured creditors. The amount of unsecured claims includes secured claims to the extent the claim exceeds the fair market value of the security. Bankruptcy Tax Act of 1980, S. Rep. No. 1035, 96th Cong., 2d Sess 17 n. 19 (1980). For individual exchanges that do not meet the proportionality test, the excess of the unsecured debt that is canceled over the fair market value of stock received results in income from discharge of indebtedness.

Neither the statute nor legislative history addresses or recognizes certain distinctions among unsecured creditors. First, should unsecured creditors who received neither stock nor property be treated as participating in the workout? Second, no distinction is made between the different classes of unsecured creditors who have different priority with respect to their claims. Should the proportionality test be made for each class of claims, given the various priority of interests? In light of these currently unanswered issues, care should be exercised in structuring debt-for-stock exchanges with respect to unsecured creditors.

Use of preferred stock—The Service limited the application of the stock-for-debt exception with respect to certain preferred stock in Rev. Rul. 90-87, 1990-43 I.R.B. 1. In this ruling, a bankrupt debtor corporation owed a creditor $500,000. This debt was retired by the debtor in exchange for the debtor's preferred stock having a redemption price and limited and preferred liquidation preference of $300,000. Noting that the unlimited stock-for-debt relief from discharge of indebtedness income is available to bankrupt or insolvent corporations pursuant to Section 108(e)(10)(B) under the rationale that a capital stock liability is substituted for an indebtedness (i.e., equity appreciation potential is given away to creditors), the Service reasoned that complete stock-for-debt relief is not warranted when the redemption price/liquidation preference is limited to a set dollar amount. Subject to the Section 108(e)(8) exceptions discussed above, the stock-for-debt relief provision applies, under the facts of the ruling, to the extent of the preferred stock's redemption price/liquidation preference ($300,000). The remaining balance of debt forgiveness ($200,000) is subject to the general rules of Sections 108 and 1017.

The 1990 legislative proposals follow the lead of Rev. Rul. 90-87 in codifying its principle. Under the proposal, stock-for-debt relief to insolvent or Title 11 debtors will not be available with respect to "disqualified stock." Disqualified stock includes any stock with a stated redemption price if such stock has a fixed redemption date, is callable by the issuer, or is puttable by the holder. In addition, disqualified stock is treated as de minimis under Section 108(e)(8). Disqualified stock will presumably need to be valued at fair market value in measuring discharge of indebtedness.

Other considerations involving the stock-for-debt exception

Issuance of investment units—In many restructurings, a company issues to a particular class of creditors a combination of stock and cash or other property in satisfaction of the debt. The allocation of the discharged debt between the stock and cash affects the amount of COD income recognized by the company. The statute does not address such allocation. However, the committee reports to the Bankruptcy Tax Act of 1980 considered the issue.

The House Report proposed that the stock should be treated as satisfying "a proportion of the debt equal to its proportion of the value of the total consideration." Bankruptcy Tax Act of 1980, H.R. Rep. No. 833, 96th Cong., 2d Sess. 14 (1980).

The Senate Report adopted a different approach, providing that "cash and other property are to be treated as satisfying an amount of debt equal to the amount of cash and the value of other property, and the stock is to be treated as satisfying the remainder of the debt." Bankruptcy Tax Act of 1980, S. Rep. No. 1035, 96th Cong., 2d Sess 17 (1980).

The Senate approach results in a larger allocation of the debt discharge to the stock. Such allocation could potentially avoid greater tax attribute reductions under the stock-for-debt exception relative to a proportional allocation approach. Fortunately, the Conference Report adopted the Senate version.

Continuity of interest—As noted earlier, the stock-for-debt exception is premised on the substitution of liability theory. Discharge of indebtedness income is not recognized because the company is simply substituting one capital liability for another. This exchange may be a Section 368(a)(1)(E) tax-free recapitalization with respect to the creditor that does not possess a continuity of interest requirement. In Technical Advice Memoranda (TAMS) 8735006 and 8735007 (May 18, 1987), the Service allowed the stock-for-debt exception to apply to an exchange of stock-for-debt in which an underwriter tendered for the outstanding debt of the company with the express purpose of exchanging such debt for stock. Following the exchange, the underwriter resold the stock received in the exchange.

One could infer from these rulings that there is a somewhat liberal standard with respect to continuity of interest in the stock-for-debt exception. However, the TAMS state that an immediate redemption of such stock for cash by the issuing corporation would not qualify for the exception. Furthermore, the TAMS also dispel an "agency" argument on their facts in that the underwriter was not acting for the debtor in repurchasing debt at a discount since the underwriter was acting on its own behalf and not under the debtor's authority.

Furthermore, as discussed in greater detail below, the Service has implicitly acquiesced to a liberal continuity of interest standard in Rev. Rul. 59-222, 1959-1 C.B. 80.

Use of parent corporation stock—One might infer from applying Section 108(e)(4) that the use of stock of the debtor corporation's parent corporation should result in possible application of the stock-for-debt rule. In the absence of regulations in this area, it is unclear whether this is a proper interpretation, however.

Notwithstanding the lack of express statutory authority for the use of parent stock, one might find support for its use in Rev. Rul. 59-222. In this ruling, a bankrupt debtor corporation was acquired out of bankruptcy in an exchange where the creditors received voting stock of the acquiring corporation for their claims. The Service treated the transaction as a deemed stock-for-debt swap by the debtor corporation and the creditors (without income recognition under the stock-for-debt exception) followed by a Section 368(a)(1)(B) (Type B) tax-free reorganization in the exchange of the acquiring corporation's voting stock for the creditor/shareholder's stock. It is difficult to reconcile this ruling with the absence of a parent stock-for-debt exception. The same theory should apply irrespective of whether the "acquiring" corporation is related or unrelated prior to the exchange, since Type B reorganizations only require "control" immediately after the exchange. Literal application of Rev. Rul. 59-222 would limit the parent stock-for-debt exception to voting stock, however.

In addition, as noted below, the application of the Section 108(e)(7) recapture rules to creditors disposing of stock received in a stock-for-debt exchange, even where parent corporation stock is received, would seem to suggest that parent stock should be useable under the stock-for-debt exception.

The Service has recently ruled privately in favor of a parent stock-for-debt exception, albeit subject to some curious conditions. In Private Letter Rulings 8852039, 8914080, and 8933001, the Service has allowed stock-for-debt exception relief with the use of parent stock borrowing upon the principles of Rev. Rul. 59-222. However, the troublesome aspect of this series of rulings can be found in Private Letter Ruling 8933001. First, it states that its conclusion is predicated on the acquisitive exchange constituting a Type B reorganization even though this is not uniformly applied in all the aforementioned rulings. Second, it states that its conclusion assumes all the parties (the acquiring corporation and debtor corporation) are in bankruptcy even though this is an extension of the facts of Rev. Rul. 59-222. In the latter ruling, no reference to the acquiring corporation's bankruptcy is made. Moreover, stock-for-debt exception relief from Section 108(b) attribute reduction should equally be applicable to insolvent, but not bankrupt (under Title 11), taxpayers.

Recapture upon disposition of stock—Creditors participating in a stock-for-debt exchange who later dispose of such stock at a gain may have all or part of such gain characterized as Section 1245 ordinary income recapture. Section 108(e)(7) provides that this recapture potential will exist to the extent of prior Section 166(a) or (b) bad debt deductions or ordinary loss on the stock-for-debt exchange, reduced by gross income (if any) included in the creditor's gross income on such exchange. A special rule for cash basis creditors provides for comparable treatment notwithstanding differences in accounting methods. Section 108(e)(7)(B). As noted earlier, the recapture rule applies as well to stock of a corporation in "control" of the debtor corporation within the meaning of Section 368(c) (80 percent voting power and 80 percent of each other class of stock). Section 108(e)(7)(C). In addition, the rule applies to successor corporation stock. Section 108(e)(7)(D).

Other exceptions to discharge of indebtedness income

Purchase money debt reduction—Congress enacted this provision to eliminate disagreements between the Service and debtors as to whether a debt reduction should be treated as discharge income or a true price adjustment. If a reduction in the debt of a purchaser of property, out of which such debt arose, is made by the seller of such property, then the reduction should be treated as a purchase price adjustment rather than income from discharge of indebtedness. Section 108(e)(5). This adjustment only applies to solvent taxpayers and does not apply to taxpayers who are insolvent or in a Title 11 case. Also, the buyer and seller must have continuously owned the property and the debt, respectively, from the time the debt arose out of the sale of the property.

The application of Section 108(e)(5) is illustrated in Private Letter Ruling 9037033. In the ruling, buyers purchased stock from sellers for a series of notes. The buyers transferred the stock to a controlled corporation pursuant to Section 351, and the controlled corporation assumed the obligation to repay the note. The controlled corporation was insolvent when the debt was discharged in an amount greater than the corporation's insolvency. The Service ruled that Section 108(b) tax attribute reduction applied to the extent of the corporation's insolvency immediately before the discharge and that a Section 108(e)(5) purchase price adjustment applied to the balance of the debt discharge (since the seller became solvent in the discharge). Of equal significance is the fact that the Service allowed Section 108(e)(5) application even though the corporation was not the original obligor. This aspect of the ruling may limit the apparent extension of Section 108(e)(5) to the facts of the ruling.

Lost deductions—Discharge of indebtedness income will not be recognized to the extent that payment of the liability would have given rise to a deduction. Section 108(e)(2).

Debt Restructurings—Creditor and Debtor Tax Issues

Modifications of Existing Debt

In its initial stages of operating difficulty, a troubled company may modify its debt by amending the terms of the debt. If the changes made to the terms of the debt are significant, the modification of the debt may constitute an exchange of old debt for new debt. A significant body of case law and rulings exist interpreting Section 1001(a) to determine when a modification constitutes an exchange of old debt for new debt. An exchange under Section 1001(a) is a taxable transaction unless a nonrecognition provision applies (that is, tax-free recapitalization).

Section 1001(a) does not define what constitutes an "exchange" of property. Under Reg. Section 1001-1(a), a modification constitutes an exchange when the taxpayer has in substance received something "differing materially either in kind or in extent." A considerable body of law has developed in determining which modifications are material. In modifying a debt instrument, a myriad of terms may change, both alone and in combination. Following is a discussion of changes that may or may not be material under Section 1001(a):

Timing of payments.   Generally, a change in the maturity date does not in and of itself create an exchange. See Rev. Rul. 73-160, 1973-1 C.B. 365; *West Missouri Power Co. v. Commissioner*, 18 T.C. 105 (1952). However, one should consider debt subject to the original issue discount (OID) rules. Any lengthening or shortening of the maturity date on the timing of any payments may have a direct impact on the yield of the debt instrument. Furthermore, a significant extension of maturity dates could significantly increase risk to the holder and arguably could be viewed as an exchange.

Interest rate.   Generally, a material change in interest rate constitutes an exchange. Rev. Rul. 89-122, I.R.B. 1989-47. Changes in interest rates following a variable index that arises from the terms of the debt instrument should not be considered a change in the terms of the debt instrument. Rev. Rul. 87-19, 1987-1 C.B. 249. However, a waiver of the application of an interest rate adjustment was a material change in Rev. Rul. 87-19, since it had the effect of changing the yield.

Case law does not appear to indicate authority either way as to whether a change in interest rate alone is significantly material. However, the OID rules do provide examples where interest rate changes constitute a material change. Under Proposed Reg. Section 1.1274-1(c), a payment to or from the lender (or a successor) not provided for in the debt instrument shall be treated as a modification (under Section 1001(a)) of the debt instrument. A change in annual interest payments from 15 percent to 9 percent constitutes a Section 1001(a) exchange under this regulation's example. Under example 2 of Proposed Reg. Section 1.1274-7(a)(3), a change in interest rate from 10 to 11 percent also constitutes a modification.

Interest rate and timing of payments. The Service generally considers a change in interest rate combined with a change in maturity date as a material change. Rev. Rul. 81-169, 1981-1 C.B. 429. However, case law exists providing support that a material change has not occurred where the maturity date is extended and interest rate lowered. See *Truman H. Newberry*, 4 TCM 576 (1945) *Mutual Loan and Savings Co. v. Commissioner*, 184 F. 2d 16 (1950). These cases are difficult to reconcile with the views set forth in the proposed OID regulations.

Changes in obligor. Generally, the Service treats a change in the obligor as a material modification of the debt when accompanied by other modifications. Rev. Rul. 79-155, 1979-1 C.B. 153 and G.C.M. 39225, April 27, 1984. However, Section 1274(c)(4) and Proposed Reg. Section 1.1272-7 apply the standards of Reg. Section 1.1001-1(a) in treating an assumption of debt in a sale or exchange of property as not a material change.

Terms of original instrument. A change in the debt instrument according to the original terms of such instrument should not constitute an exchange. For example, conversion rights, Rev. Rul. 57-535, 1957-2 C.B. 513 or interest rates determined under a variable index, Rev. Rul. 87-19, 1987-1 C.B. 249, were not considered modifications constituting an exchange.

Exchanges of Debt for Debt

Debt restructurings may consist of exchanging an old note for a new note in form or in substance. The characterization of the transaction greatly affects the tax consequences. A debt-for-debt recapitalization may qualify for tax-free or taxable treatment to the creditor.

Tax-free debt recapitalizations. Generally, an exchange of an old debt "security" for a new debt "security" pursuant to a plan of reorganization qualifies as a tax-free recapitalization under Section 368(a)(1)(E). Unlike other reorganization provisions, continuity of interest and continuity of business enterprise are not required. See Rev. Rul. 77-415, 1977-2 C.B. 311 and Rev. Rul. 82-34, 1982-1 C.B. 59. The requirements of "plan of reorganization" appear easily met in an exchange of debt securities for debt securities. See Rev. Rul. 77-415.

"Security" defined—Tax-free treatment under Section 368(a)(1)(E) applies to exchanges of securities for securities. It does not apply if either debt instrument does not meet the definition of a "security." No specific statutory definition of a "security" exists. For purposes of determining a "security," the courts apply a facts-and-circumstances approach. Although not controlling, the maturity of a debt instrument is an important factor. "Though time is an important factor, the controlling consideration is an overall evaluation of the nature of the debt, degree of participation and continuing interest . . . compared with the similarity of the note to a cash payment." *Camp Wolters Enterprises, Inc. v. Commissioner*, 22 T.C. 737, 750 (1954).

Generally, a debt instrument with a maturity of 10 years or more will qualify as a "security", whereas a debt instrument with less than five years will not qualify as a debt instrument.

Treatment of creditor—Generally, the creditor recognizes no gain or loss on the exchange. Section 354(a)(1). Creditors generally recognize gain if "boot" is received in amount equal to the lesser of gain realized in the exchange or the fair market value of "boot" received. Section 356(a)(1). Boot is money or any property received by the creditor other than stock or a security of the debtor. In the case of troubled company debt restructuring, there will typically be no gain potential in the creditor's holdings. Losses are not allowed notwithstanding the receipt of boot. Section 356(c).

The excess of the principal amount of a new security received over the principal amount of the old security surrendered (if any) is treated as boot to a creditor. Section 354(a)(2)(A). Although not specifically stated in Section 354, the OID provisions should be applied to determine the principal amount of debt by substituting adjusted issue price (original issue price, plus accrued OID, less amortized bond premium) for the principal amount. In the debt restructurings of most troubled companies, the principal amount of the new securities will be less, rather than more, than the principal amount of the old securities.

Income recognition will result to a creditor to the extent of the receipt of stock, securities, or other property attributable to accrued interest not previously reported in taxable income. Section 354(a)(2)(B). In the absence of an agreement, it is unclear how this consideration is to be allocated between principal and current interest.

A creditor will generally take a substituted tax basis in a new debt instrument equal to the tax basis in the old debt instrument. Where boot is also received, the boot will take a fair market value tax basis and the new debt instrument's substituted tax basis will be decreased by such amount allocated to the boot and increased by any gain recognized by the creditor in the exchange. Section 358(a).

Treatment to debtor—To the extent the adjusted issue price of the old debt exceeds the adjusted issue price of the new debt, the debtor should recognize COD income. However, prior to the 1990 legislative changes, application of Section 1275(a)(4) limited full current recognition of gain to the debtor. The 1990 legislative changes repealed Section 1275(a)(4), resulting in current recognition of discharge of indebtedness income in more troubled company debt exchanges (subject to Section 108).

Section 1275(a)(4)—Congress enacted Section 1275(a)(4) to prevent the creation of additional OID on securities issued pursuant to a reorganization. Section 1275(a)(4) placed a floor on the determination of the issue price. If a debt instrument was issued for another debt instrument pursuant to a plan of reorganization (within the meaning of Section 368(a)(1)) and the issue price of the new debt instrument, determined without regard to Section 1275(a)(4), was less than the adjusted issue price of the old debt instrument, then the issue price of the new debt instrument was equal to the issue price of the old debt instrument.

This provision most clearly effectuated its intent when the principal amount of the old and new securities were the same. However, unintended consequences arose when both the issue price, without application of Section 1275(a)(4), and the principal amount of the new security were less than the adjusted issue price of the old security. Congress overlooked the potential impact of discharge of indebtedness upon the issue price as determined under Section 1275(a)(4). Generally, one would expect the debtor to realize income from discharge of indebtedness when the adjusted issue price of the old security exceeds both the issue price and the principal amount of the new security. Clearly, the debtor receives a benefit because he is released from a legal obligation to repay a portion of the principal. Literal application of Section 1275(a)(4) in this situation would not create COD income in the current period, but rather would create bond premium income that the debtor should be able to amortize over the remaining life of the new debt. See Reg. Section 1.61-12(c)(2). Note that this interpretation of Section 1275(a)(4) overrode the result in Rev. Rul. 77-437, 1977-2 C.B. 28, which would support the recognition of COD income in full in the year of exchange.

1990 legislative change: repeal of Section 1275(a)(4)—Section 1275(a)(4) was repealed under 1990 legislation and Section 108(e)(11) enacted. This latter provision requires that for purposes of determining discharge of indebtedness income in a debt-for-debt exchange, the debtor is treated as satisfying the old debt with an amount of money equal to the issue price of the new debt. Where either the old or new debt instrument is publicly traded, the issue price of the new obligation is the fair market value of the publicly traded obligation. Alternatively, where there is no publicly traded debt instrument, the issue price of the new debt will be its stated redemption amount, discounted by the applicable federal rate ("AFR") if the new debt does not have adequate stated interest. Thus, debt-for-debt exchanges involving an economic discharge of indebtedness must be accounted for under Sections 61(a)(12) or Section 108 and cannot be accounted for as bond premium income as under old Section 1275(a)(4).

To the extent the adjusted issue price of the new debt exceeds the adjusted issue price of the old debt (a rare case in a financially troubled company restructuring), the debtor would appear to have deductible bond premium in the year of exchange. Reg. Section 1.163-4(c)(1) and Proposed Reg. 1.163-7(f). However, case law has denied a current deduction where the new debt obligation is a substitute for the old debt obligation. *Great Western Power Co. v. Commissioner*, 297 U.S. 543 (1936); *South Carolina Continental Telephone Co. v. Commissioner*, 10 T.C. 164 (1948).

No bond premium deduction is allowed to a debtor corporation to the extent the premium is allocable to a conversion feature in the debt to exchange the debt for debtor's stock, or a corporation in control of, or controlled by, the debtor corporation. Section 249(a). "Control" for this purpose is at least 80 percent voting power of stock and at least 80 percent of each nonvoting class of stock. Sections 249(b)(2) and 368(c).

Taxable exchanges of old debt for new debt.   Debt swaps will be taxable in nature if neither the old nor the new debt instrument qualifies as a "security." In these situations the following rules are applicable.

Consequences to creditor—A creditor will recognize gain or loss on the exchange equal to the difference between the adjusted issue price of the new debt plus the fair market value of other property received and his adjusted basis in the old debt. In all likelihood, this amount will be a loss in the case of a financially troubled company restructuring. If the exchange did result in gain realization with respect to the old debt instrument, the gain would be deferred under Section 453 (assuming neither debt instrument was publicly traded nor otherwise excepted from installment reporting treatment).

Consequences to debtor—The same issues arise for the debtor corporation in a taxable recapitalization as with a tax-free recapitalization.

As noted earlier, the 1990 legislative proposals repealed Section 1275(a)(4) and require current income recognition (subject to Section 108) to be determined by the difference in the issue price of the new debt and the adjusted issue price of the old debt.

Exchanges of Stock for Debt

Tax-free recapitalizations.   The issuance of stock to a creditor in exchange for a debt security should qualify for tax-free treatment under Section 368(a)(1)(E). As discussed under tax-free debt recapitalizations, the debt instrument must be a "security" to receive tax-free treatment.

Creditor tax treatment—Tax treatment to the creditor would be similar to that described with respect to tax-free debt recapitalizations. Section 354(a)(1). The receipt of boot would be taxable to the creditor assuming a realized gain; otherwise, no loss is recognized on the exchange. Section 356.

Debtor tax consequences—The debtor should recognize neither gain nor loss on the issuance of its stock under Section 1032. However, Section 1032 does not provide protection against the recognition of discharge of indebtedness in the exchange. Therefore, if the fair market value of the stock issued is less than the adjusted issue price of the debt, the debtor might recognize COD income on the difference depending on the debtor's degree of solvency or insolvency and whether the debtor is under U.S.

bankruptcy jurisdiction. See earlier discussion on COD income, Section 108, and stock-for-debt exception.

In addition, the debtor will not be able to deduct stock issuance expenses because they are capital expenditures associated with issuing the stock. Conversely, any unamortized debt issuance costs should be treated as a deductible expense upon retirement of debt, assuming the debt retirement is not part of a debt exchange between issuer and holder.

Taxable recapitalizations. As discussed earlier, debt instruments that do not constitute a "security" cannot receive tax-free treatment under Section 368(a)(1)(E). Therefore, the issuance of stock in exchange for a debt instrument not qualifying as a security constitutes a taxable exchange under Section 1001(a).

Creditor tax consequences—A creditor recognizes gain or loss on the difference between the fair market value of the stock and its adjusted basis in the debt.

Debtor tax consequences—The debtor's tax treatment is unchanged from that described in stock-for-debt exchanges that are tax-free to creditors.

Time Value of Money Tax Principles

No discussion of debt restructurings would be complete without mention of prescribed tax rules designed to account for discount and premium inherent in debt instruments at the time of issuance or market purchase. Discussion of these rules in detail can be a treatise in itself. This section is intended to summarize relevant tax considerations with respect to original issue discount, market discount, and bond premium.

Original issue discount. OID is the excess (if any) of a debt instrument's stated redemption price at maturity over its issue price, subject to a one-quarter of one percent per annum de minimis rule. Section 1273(a). Stated redemption price at maturity generally includes all payments due at maturity including interest, unless such interest is required to be paid at least annually. Section 1273(a); Prop. Reg. Section 1.1273-1(b)(1)(ii).

A creditor holding an OID debt instrument and the issuer are required to include in income and expense, respectively, the economic accrual of OID on a yield to maturity basis.

As noted earlier, the application of OID rules to a debt exchange pursuant to a Section 368(a)(1) reorganization used to result in no new creation of OID with respect to the new debt instrument. Section 1275(a)(4) required that, in the case of a reorganization, the issue price of the new debt instrument equaled the greater of its issue price under general OID rules or the adjusted issue price of the old debt instrument. The resulting COD income and bond premium income issues of the debtor arising from the application of old Section 1275(a)(4) were discussed above.

However, as noted earlier, the repeal of Section 1275(a)(4) under the 1990 legislation now allows for the creation of OID in newly issued debt instruments in debt exchanges.

Market discount.　Market discount rules are generally applicable to debt instruments issued after July 18, 1984 that are not acquired at original issuance but rather in a secondary market. However, the rules can apply to new debt instruments received in exchange for market discount debt instruments in certain reorganizations and transferred basis transactions.

The significance of market discount arises in (1) the character of income upon disposition of the market discount debt instrument under Section 1276 and (2) the interest expense deferral rules with respect to a leveraged acquisition of market discount bonds under Section 1277.

Market discount is generally measured by the excess of stated redemption price at maturity over the basis of such bond immediately after its acquisition by the taxpayer. If the bond has OID, then market discount is measured by the excess (if any) of revised issue price (issue price plus accrued OID) over the taxpayer's basis in the bond immediately after acquisition.

Any gain recognized on disposition of a bond acquired with market discount will generally be ordinary income to the extent of accrued market discount. Section 1276(a). In addition, serial or partial principal repayments on a market discount bond will result in income recognition of accrued market discount. Section 1276(a)(3). Market discount is ratably accrued over the period held by the taxpayer, unless an election is made to accrue on the basis of a constant interest rate. However, if the election is made, the taxpayer must currently recognize in income the accrued market discount. If new debt or stock is received in a nonrecognition transaction such as tax-free recapitalization, market discount will generally carry over to the new instrument. Section 1276(c). Moreover, upon the initial acquisition of a market discount bond, interest expense incurred to carry such bonds in excess of interest income (including OID) with respect to such bonds is subject to deferral. Section 1277. An election to include accrued market discount in income will avoid this deferral of interest expense. Section 1276(b)(2).

Bond premium.　Bond premium is the excess of the basis in the debt instrument over its stated redemption price at maturity. Section 171. A holder of a debt instrument may generally amortize and deduct such bond premium on a yield to maturity basis. This treatment is elective. No premium may be deducted if attributable to a conversion feature of the debt instrument.

Limitations on the Utilization of Tax Attributes

Section 382—Net Operating Loss Limitation

Congress enacted new Section 382 in the Tax Reform Act of 1986 to limit a perceived abuse in loss corporation acquisitions. The theoretical underpinning for Section 382 is the "neutrality principle," the concept that a change in control of a loss corporation should not abrogate its ability to absorb its losses, nor should it offer the new owners the opportunity to use such losses to offset unrelated income. Presumably, a corporation will generate a rate of return on its assets and such return will offset accumulated losses. Section 382 arbitrarily posits that the return will generally be the long-term rate on tax-exempt obligations multiplied by the value of the loss corporation immediately before the ownership change. This product is the annual limitation of Section 382.

The following paragraphs will review the substantive nature of new Section 382. It must be noted that this area is exceptionally complex in practice and requires an extensive reading of the statute, regulations, and administrative interpretations. This article will attempt to summarize the relevant features of Section 382 as set forth in these various sources.

Prior law. Section 382 was substantially revised by the Tax Reform Act of 1986. Old Section 382 was a much narrower provision that distinguished taxable purchases and tax-free reorganizations. Net operating losses (NOLs) were completely disallowed if one or more of the loss corporation's 10 largest shareholders increased their aggregate stock ownership by at least 50 percent through taxable purchases within a two-taxable-year period *and* if the old trade or business of the loss corporation was not continued (a subjective and often manageable standard). A NOL following a tax-free reorganization was limited ratably based on how much the continuing interest of the loss corporation's shareholders in the acquiring corporation fell below a 20 percent minimum. Generally, new Section 382 eliminates this bifurcation by treating purchases (owner shifts) and reorganizations (equity structure shifts) equally. New Section 382 also imposes a less stringent continuity of business enterprise requirement, requiring only that the loss corporation retain a significant portion of the old corporation's historic business *or* assets, generally construed as one third of the historic operations, during the two-year period following the ownership change. These aspects of new Section 382 will be discussed in greater detail below.

Ownership change. Section 382 imposes its annual limitation on the utilization of NOLs after a corporation experiences an ownership change. An ownership change occurs if, immediately after any owner shift or equity structure shift, the percentage of stock in the loss corporation owned by one or more 5-percent shareholders has *increased* by more than 50 percentage points over the lowest percentage of stock in the loss corporation (or any predecessor) owned by such shareholder(s) at any time during the testing period. Section 382(g)(1). Thus, it is necessary to ascertain the identity of the loss corporation's shareholders to determine whether the requisite shift in ownership has occurred. The separate increases in percentage ownership of each 5-percent shareholder whose ownership in the corporation has increased over such shareholder's lowest percentage ownership interest at any time during the testing period are aggregated for purposes of the 50-percent test.

"Testing period" —The "testing period" is generally defined as the three-year period ending on the testing date. A testing date arises any time an "owner shift" or "equity structure shift" occurs. The testing period may be less than three years under certain circumstances. The testing period will not begin before the earlier of:

1. the first day of the first taxable year from which there is a loss carry-forward or an excess credit; or
2. the first day following the most recent change of ownership. Section 382(i).

"Owner shift" —An "owner shift" is defined as any change in the respective ownership of stock of a corporation that affects the percentage of stock held by a 5-percent shareholder before or after the change. Section 382(g)(2). Owner shifts are broad enough to cover all changes in equity ownership, including

1. A taxable purchase of loss corporation stock by a 5-percent shareholder
2. A disposition of stock by a 5-percent shareholder
3. A taxable purchase by a person who becomes a 5-percent shareholder as a result of the purchase
4. A Section 351 transfer that affects the percentage of stock ownership of a loss corporation by one or more shareholders
5. Conversion of debt to stock
6. Any other increase or decrease in the outstanding stock of a loss corporation that increases the percentage of stock ownership of the loss corporation by one or more 5-percent shareholders (for example, issuance of shares or redemption of shares)

"Equity structure shift" —An "equity structure shift" is generally defined as a Section 368 tax-free reorganization other than divisive Types D or G reorganizations or a Type F reorganization. It may include public offerings that do not include 5-percent shareholders or taxable reorganizations. Section 382(g)(3).

Stock—In general, all types of stock are counted in determining whether an ownership change occurs. An exception exists for "plain vanilla" preferred stock described in Section 1504(a)(4) (stock that is nonvoting, nonconvertible, nonparticipating, limited and preferred as to dividends, and not carrying an unreasonable redemption premium). Section 382(k)(6)(A).

Special rules provide that stock will be treated as not constituting stock and that interests not constituting stock will be treated as stock in certain situations. These rules are designed to avoid manipulation of Section 382 through creative capitalization strategies. Ownership interests otherwise constituting stock will be treated as nonstock if (1) at the time of its issuance or transfer to a 5-percent shareholder its likely participation in future corporate growth is disproportionately small, (2) treatment as nonstock results in an ownership change, and (3) the amount of the prechange loss is greater than two times the annual Section 382 limitation. Temporary Reg. Section 1.382-2T(f)(18)(ii). Conversely, nonstock interests are treated as stock if (1) such interests offer potential significant participation in corporate growth, (2) an ownership change would result under such treatment, and (3) the amount of the prechange loss is greater than two times the amount of the annual Section 382 limitation. Temporary Reg. Section 1.382-2T(f)(18)(iii). These rules are premised on subjective standards such as "likely" and "potentially significant" which undoubtedly make their administration difficult.

"Five-percent shareholder" — A "5-percent shareholder" is any person holding 5 percent or more of the stock of the corporation at any time during the testing period. In determining the ultimate ownership of a corporation, Section 382 generally applies the attribution rules of Section 318, on a modified basis, in order to take into account indirect ownership. These rules are designed to ensure that the determination of an ownership change occurs only at the ultimate level of stock ownership.

Generally, testing for a 5-percent shareholder is done at the immediate shareholder level. However, in certain cases it is necessary to view shareholders differently for purposes of Section 382 testing. For example, if an entity owns at least 5 percent of a loss corporation (first-tier entity), then shareholders of such entity are included in determining 5-percent shareholders, and so on (higher-tier entity). See Temporary Reg. Section 1.382-2T(g). Where the loss corporation (or first-tier entity or higher-tier entity as described above) has less than 5-percent shareholders, these public owners are aggregated under special rules and treated as one 5-percent shareholder. Section 382(g)(4)(A) and Temporary Reg. Section 1.382-2T(j).

Shareholders owning at least 5 percent of a loss corporation, directly or indirectly, at any time during the testing period are accounted for separately when testing. Temporary Reg. Section 1.382-2T(g)(1)(i). Shareholders of first-tier entities or higher-tier entities who are not 5-percent shareholders, directly or indirectly, are part of a public group. This public group will be considered a separate 5-percent shareholder if this group in the aggregate indirectly owns at least 5 percent of the loss corporation. Otherwise, such group is aggregated with a public group of the next lower entity, or loss corporation, if this is the next lower entity. Temporary Reg. Section 1.382-2T(g)(1)(ii). Any public group with direct interest in the loss corporation not included with any other higher-tier public group will constitute a separate 5-percent shareholder. Temporary Reg. Section 1.382-2T(g)(1)(iii).

Special segregation rules are also provided in the regulations. If a loss corporation has one or more direct public groups before and after a transaction and the transaction is specifically enumerated, then certain direct public groups in existence after the transaction will generally be segregated (and treated as a separate 5-percent shareholder) from direct public groups in existence before the transaction in order to account for each separately. Temporary Reg. Section 1.382-2T(j)(2). These segregation rules are presumptions that may be rebutted with actual knowledge to the contrary. Enumerated transactions include acquisitive tax-free reorganizations, issuances of shares by a loss corporation (including public offerings), redemptions of loss corporation stock, issuance of rights to acquire stock, and other transactions provided for by the IRS. These rules may also apply at first-tier entity or higher-tier entity levels. Temporary Reg. Section 1.382-2T(j)(3).

Options—Congress authorized the Treasury to prescribe regulations regarding the treatment of options under Section 382. Section 382(k)(6)(B)(i). Under these regulations, outstanding options will be treated as being exercised if such treatment results in an ownership change. Section 382(1)(3)(A) (iv) and Temporary Reg. Section 1.382-2T(h)(4). An option may be treated as exercised regardless of whether the option is currently exercisable or whether exercise of the option makes economic sense. The option rules cover not only options, but also contingent purchases, warrants, convertible debt, put options, call options, and so forth.

The option rule is inapplicable in certain situations. First, it will not apply when NOLs, built-in losses, or tax credit equivalents are de minimis (in other words, such items are less than two times the annual Section 382 limitation). Temporary Reg. Section 1.382-2T(h)(4)(ix). Second, certain options specified in Temporary Reg. Section 1.382-2T(h)(4)(x) are not subject to attribution. In addition, an election is available to have the actual exercise of the options be the ownership change date, rather than the issuance of the options. This election is referred to as the "120-day election." It is only available when the option is in fact exercised within 120 days of the granting of the option. Temporary Reg. Section 1.382-2T(h)(4)(vi)(B).

If an option that was deemed to have been exercised subsequently expires unexercised, it is treated as if it had never been issued. Amended tax returns may be filed, subject to the statute of limitations. Temporary Reg. Section 1.382-2T(h)(4)(viii). An option deemed exercised will generally not be counted again upon actual exercise. Temporary Reg. Section 1.382-2T(h)(4)(vi)(A).

Special option attribution rules are provided in certain special bankruptcy situations to ensure against tax avoidance. These rules are discussed later with respect to Section 382 and bankruptcy.

Convertible preferred stock—Preferred stock that is nonvoting and that offers little potential appreciation opportunity is closely analogous to debt. In the case of convertible preferred stock otherwise described in Section 1504(a)(4) (for example, nonvoting, limited participation in corporate growth, reasonable redemption premium), such an instrument could be viewed as stock (since the conversion feature takes it out of Section 1504(a)(4)) and, at the same time, an option to convert into common stock for Section 382 purposes. IRS Notice 88-67, 1988-1 C.B. 555, resolves this conflict by treating convertible "pure" preferred stock (stock otherwise described in Section 1504(a)(4) but for its conversion feature and disregarding potential participation in corporate growth through the conversion feature) like convertible debt and as an option for Section 382 purposes. Such stock is included for purposes of valuing a loss corporation, however. Other types of convertible preferred stock will generally be treated as stock.

Worthless stock—An owner shift will be triggered if any shareholder who held at least 50 percent of the stock of a loss corporation during any time during the last three-year period treats the stock as worthless and is entitled to a worthless stock deduction. Section 382(g)(4)(D). For purposes of determining an ownership change, the stock is deemed transferred on the first day of the first succeeding taxable year. The rule is designed to prevent worthless stock deductions without any risk of Section 382 ownership changes. At least one court granted an injunction enjoining certain parties from claiming a worthless stock deduction under the rationale that the creditors are automatically stayed against exercising control over property of a bankrupt's estate and that the NOL constituted an asset of the bankrupt. *In re Prudential Lines,* 107 Bankr, 832, further proceedings, 19 Bankr, Ct. Dec. (CRR) 1945.

Annual limitation. Section 382 limits a loss corporation's ability to offset postchange of ownership income with prechange of ownership losses. Prechange losses may offset postchange income in an amount equal to the value of the loss corporation immediately before the change of ownership multiplied by the "long-term tax-exempt" rate. The long-term tax-exempt rate is adjusted and published by the IRS on a monthly basis. The applicable rate is the highest such rate for the three-month period ending with the calendar month in which the ownership change occurred. Section 382(f).

The limitation applies more severely in a situation where the NOL is high in comparison to the corporation's value. For example, if a target corporation's NOL is $10 million, the long-term tax-exempt rate is 7 percent, and its stock is purchased for $100 million, then the annual limitation is $7 million. If the target's value was only $100,000, then only $7,000 of the NOL could be used annually. Because the Section 172 15-year carryforward period for NOLs remains in effect, some NOLs are not merely deferred, but permanently lost, as is readily apparent in this latter example.

Value—The "value" of a public company can easily be determined from the market value of the stock. However, if the company is private, determination of value becomes more difficult where an ownership change occurs other than by purchase of 100 percent of the stock. Items such as control premiums and minority interest discounts should be disregarded for purposes of determining value. Joint Committee on Taxation, General

Explanation of the Tax Reform Act of 1986, May 7, 1987 at 316. Also, the valuation of a loss corporation's stock does include "plain vanilla" nonvoting preferred stock as described in Section 1504(a)(4), which is not considered in testing for an ownership change. Temporary Reg. Section 1.382-2T(f)(18)(i).

Transactions affecting the measurement of value of loss corporation—As noted earlier, the general rule provides that the loss corporation's value for purposes of the Section 382 annual limitation is to be determined immediately before the ownership change. Section 382(e)(1). However, in certain situations, the rules are modified to produce a different valuation criteria.

1. *Redemption or corporate contractions*—If a redemption or corporate contraction occurs in connection with an ownership change, the value of the loss corporation is determined *after* taking the redemption or corporate contraction into account. Section 382(e)(2). This provision is targeted to leveraged buyouts, where acquisition indebtedness remains a direct or indirect obligation of the target company. There is no bright-line test. There is only a test of whether the target is a significant direct or indirect source of debt repayment. Joint Committee on Taxation, Description of the Technical Corrections Act of 1988 (H.R. 4333 and S. 2238) at 44 (March 31, 1988).

   For example, assume X corporation has a $20 million NOL, a 7 percent long-term tax-exempt rate exists, and X is acquired in a leveraged buyout for $100 million. The investors use $10 million equity and borrow the $90 million balance to acquire X. Assuming X is directly or indirectly the significant source of repayment of the acquisition indebtedness, the resulting value for purposes of Section 382 annual limitation is $10 million, not $100 million. The annual NOL limitation is $700,000, not $7 million. Thus, financial buyers are disadvantaged relative to strategic buyers with more equity resources.

2. *Nonbusiness assets*—Value is also reduced by "nonbusiness assets" in a situation where at least one third of a loss corporation's assets consist of assets held for investment, including cash, marketable stocks, and securities, immediately after the ownership change. Section 382(1)(4). If the loss corporation meets this threshold, its value is reduced by the value of the nonbusiness assets over the indebtedness attributable to those assets. Indebtedness is allocable to nonbusiness assets based on the ratio of nonbusiness assets to all assets on a fair market value basis. Section 382(1)(4)(D).

   For purposes of these rules, a "look-through" rule is provided with respect to at least 50 percent owned subsidiaries so that stock and securities of such subsidiaries are disregarded. Section 382(1)(4)(E). Investment entities such as regulated investment companies, real estate investment trusts, and REMICs are exempt from the nonbusiness asset rules. Section 382(1)(4)(B)(ii).

3. *Antistuffing rule*—Taxpayers might attempt to increase value by contributing assets prior to an ownership change. An "antistuffing" rule prevents this by providing that any capital contribution or transfer to a controlled corporation as part of a plan wherein the principal purpose is to avoid or increase its value for purposes of Section 382 is not taken into account in determining value. Section 382(1)(1)(A). An irrebuttable presumption exists that any capital contribution made during the two-year period ending on the change date will be treated as part of a prohibited plan, except as provided in future regulations. Section 382(1)(1)(B). Exceptions are intended to be provided for capital contributions made on formation, prior to the first year of a NOL, and to continue basic operations.

4. *Bankruptcy*—In Title 11 or similar cases where the general Section 382 annual limitation applies (and not the special bankruptcy exception of Section 382(1)(5) as described below), the value of the loss corporation is determined after the ownership change in certain situations. The purpose of this rule provided in Section 382(1)(6) is to allow the benefit for the increase in value of the loss corporation resulting from the surrender or cancellation of creditor's claims in the transaction. This rule is limited on its face to Type G reorganizations or debt-for-stock changes in a Title 11 or similar case.

Transactions increasing annual limitation—The annual Section 382 limitation is increased by any recognized built-in gains (discussed later) and certain gains recognized by making a deemed asset sale election under Section 338.

Excess limitation—If the annual limitation exceeds taxable income available for offset in any taxable year, the excess limitation not used may be carried forward indefinitely. In a subsequent year, such excess limitation plus that subsequent year's annual Section 382 limitation would be the maximum amount of preownership change NOL available for use. Section 382(b)(2).

Losses subject to Section 382 limitation—Prechange of ownership losses are subject to the Section 382 limitation. Prechange losses include

1. The portion of the loss corporation's NOL allocable to the period in the taxable year before the ownership change
2. NOL carryforwards that arose in a taxable year of the loss corporation preceding the taxable year of the ownership change
3. Certain recognized built-in losses and deductions, discussed subsequently. Sections 382(d)(1) and 382(h)(1)(B)(i).

Allocation of taxable income or loss in the year of change—If the ownership change occurs during the year and the tax year of the loss corporation does not close as a result of the ownership change, the income for that year must be allocated between the period before the ownership change (prechange period) and the period after the ownership change (postchange period). If there is a loss in the prechange period, that loss will be subject to the Section 382 limitation if it is used to offset income in the postchange period. The loss corporation must prorate the entire tax year's income or loss between the prechange period and the postchange period on a daily basis unless an advance ruling specifically allocating income or loss between the two periods (specific cutoff) is obtained from the IRS. Section 382(b)(3)(A) and IRS Notice 87-79, 1987-2 C.B. 387.

For example, if the ownership change occurs on June 30, 1990, and there is a $100 million net operating loss for 1990, approximately $50 million will be subject to Section 382 rules under the general daily proration rule. The other $50 million is generally not subject to limitation, although it could be subject to the built-in loss rules discussed below if it relates to losses accrued as of the change date. On the other hand, if an advance ruling was obtained demonstrating that no loss was accrued as of June 30, 1989, then the resulting $100 million loss accruing in the postchange period would not be subject to Section 382 (except for possible application of the built-in loss rule described below).

1. *Discharge of indebtedness*—In many restructuring transactions, the loss corporation will recognize COD income in the transaction. Under Notice 87-79, the taxpayer could request a private ruling to employ the cutoff method and allocate COD income, the recognition of which is integrally related to the change of ownership, to the prechange period. The allocation of COD income to the prechange period enables the taxpayer to offset the COD income with prechange losses unrestricted by Section 382. For example, see Private Letter Rulings 8834086, 8847067 and 9017020.

   As discussed below, this result would also follow by reason of the built-in gain rules of Section 382. Potential COD income should be construed as a built-in gain that can be offset by prechange NOLs if recognized within five taxable years of the ownership change. However, as indicated below, there is a de minimis rule that must be satisfied before application of the built-in gain rule will apply.

2. *Short taxable year following ownership change*—For a short taxable year following an ownership change, taxable income realized by a new loss corporation that may be offset by prechange losses is limited to a pro rata amount determined by multiplying the full Section 382 limitation by the ratio of the number of days in the postchange short taxable year to the total number of days in such year. Section 382(b)(3)(B).

Continuity of business enterprise—Unless a loss corporation's business enterprise is continued at all times during the two-year period following an ownership change, the NOL carryforwards of the loss corporation are completely disallowed. Section 382(c)(1). This requirement is generally met if the new owners either continue the acquired corporation's historic business or use a significant portion of its historic business assets in a business. This is the principle evidenced in Reg. Section 1.368-1(d)(2) with respect to tax-free reorganizations and made applicable to Section 382 in the Tax Reform Act of 1986. Tax Reform Act of 1986, H.R. Rep. No. 841, 99th Cong., 2d. Sess II-189. Notwithstanding the draconian result of failing this test, it is considered more liberal than old Section 382's change in trade or business standards.

Net unrealized built-in gains and losses. Section 382 contains rules regarding built-in gains and losses that increase the Section 382 annual limitation for certain built-in gains and subject certain built-in losses to the Section 382 limitation. Section 382(h). If the loss corporation has net unrealized built-in gains at the time of the change of ownership, the loss corporation increases its Section 382 annual limitation by the amount of recognized built-in gains. Section 382(h)(1)(A). If the loss corporation has net unrealized built-in losses, then recognized built-in losses are subject to the Section 382 limitation. Section 382(h)(1)(B). Net unrealized built-in gains or losses are determined by comparing the aggregate fair market value of the loss corporation's assets to the aggregate tax basis in the loss corporation's assets. Section 382(h)(3). If the aggregate fair market value of the assets exceeds the aggregate tax basis, the loss corporation has a net unrealized built-in gain. If the aggregate tax basis exceeds the aggregate fair market value of the assets, the loss corporation has a net unrealized built-in loss.

De minimis rule—Effective for ownership changes after October 2, 1989, if the net unrealized built-in gain or loss does not exceed the lesser of 15 percent of the aggregate fair market value of the assets or $10 million, then the de minimis rule applies and treats the net unrealized built-in gain or loss as zero. Section 382(h)(3)(B)(i). Prior to this date, the de minimis rule was the net unrealized built-in gain or loss relative to 25 percent of the fair market value of the assets.

Calculation—For purposes of computing the net unrealized built-in gain or loss, cash and cash items, account receivables, and marketable securities that do not have a value that differs from their adjusted basis are excluded from the computation. Currently, the regulations do not elaborate on what constitutes a cash item. Further regulations may clarify this matter and include account receivables in the net unrealized built-in gain or loss determination. Miscellaneous Revenue Act of 1988, H.R. Conf. Rep. No. 1104, 100th Cong., 2d Sess. 8 (1988).

A special rule limits the valuation of assets of a loss corporation for purposes of determining a net unrealized built-in loss. Where at least 80 percent (value) of the loss corporation's stock is acquired in one transaction (or a series of related transactions during any 12-month period), the fair market value of assets cannot exceed the purchase price grossed up for indebtedness and other relevant items of the corporation. Section 382(h)(8). Thus, assuming at least an 80 percent stock purchase, it will not be possible to argue a higher value of the net assets, or a "bargain" purchase, to avoid or reduce a net unrealized built-in loss. This argument will presumably be available in the relevant situation where 80 percent of the loss corporation stock has not been acquired in the prescribed 12-month period.

Recognized built-in gain—Recognized built-in gain means any gain recognized during the five-year period following the change of ownership to the extent of the tax appreciation in the asset at the time of the change of ownership. Sections 382(h)(2)(A) and (h)(7)(A). The total of potential recognized built-in gains cannot exceed the net unrealized built-in gain at the time of the ownership change. Section 382(h)(1)(A)(ii).

The built-in gain must be recognized within the five-year period following the ownership change in order to increase the annual Section 382 limitation. Moreover, the taxpayer must establish that the asset was on hand at the time of the ownership change and that the gain recognized (increasing the annual Section 382 limitation) existed at the time of the ownership change. Prudent planning would dictate an independent appraisal to verify and document the unrealized net built-in gain at the time of an ownership change.

Although the interplay of Section 382 and consolidated tax return rules have yet to be formally addressed by the Treasury, the IRS has expressed its view on the measurement of net unrealized built-in gains in a consolidated group. In Private Letter Rulings 8849061 and 8923021 the determination of net unrealized built-in gain of the consolidated group was made using the fair market value and tax basis of the underlying assets held by its subsidiaries. Measurement with respect to stock investments in subsidiaries was not considered appropriate. A condition of the "inside asset" measurement in each ruling is the reversal of any positive investment adjustment in the stock of any subsidiary disposed of where the positive adjustment is attributable to unutilized NOL or capital loss of the subsidiary.

Recognized built-in loss—Recognized built-in loss means any loss recognized during the five-year period following the change of ownership to the extent of the tax loss inherent in the asset at the time of the change of ownership. Sections 382(h)(2)(B) and (h)(7)(A). The term also includes depreciation, amortization, and depletion during the five-year recognition period to the extent of the inherent tax loss in those assets at the time of the ownership change. Similar to built-in gains, the total of potential recognized built-in losses cannot exceed the net unrealized built-in loss at the time of the ownership change. Section 382(h)(1)(B)(ii).

The bias in the law is that any loss recognized during the five-year period following the ownership change will be a recognized built-in loss unless the taxpayer can establish that the asset was not on hand at the time of the ownership change or the loss exceeds the asset's built-in loss at the time of the ownership change. Here again, an independent appraisal will be useful in verifying and documenting amounts of unrealized loss.

Built-in items of income and expense—Items of income and expense that are attributable to the prechange period but are recognized in income and expense during the five-year recognition period will be treated as recognized built-in gains and losses. Sections 382(h)(6)(A) and (B). Such items include the collection of cash basis accounts receivables that arose before the ownership change, the recognition of items of income arising from a change in accounting methods under Section 481, and the recognition of gain previously deferred under the completed contract method of accounting for long-term contracts.

It is arguable that the potential discharge of indebtedness income in outstanding debt of a loss corporation at the time of an ownership change represents an unrealized built-in income item. In fact, the IRS has ruled in favor of this treatment in Private Letter Rulings 8923021 and 8932049. Assuming net unrealized built-in gains in excess of the de minimis rule and recognition of the COD income within the five-year recognition period, the need for an advance ruling pursuant to Notice 87-79 regarding a specific cutoff of the loss corporation's taxable year at the ownership change date (where the year does not otherwise close) should be moot. This would not be the case if the built-in gain rule were inapplicable or if the loss corporation's taxable year end closed by reason of the ownership change transaction.

Built-in items of income and expense and the de minimis rule—Section 382(h)(6)(C) provides that the amount of net unrealized built-in gain or loss is to be adjusted for recognized built-in income or deduction items. The interplay between such items and calculation of the de minimis rule is uncertain. This uncertainty arises from the fact that the contingent items, such as contingent and potentially deductible items, may not be known with specificity as to existence, nature, and amount as of the date of the ownership change.

Notwithstanding this uncertainty, the IRS has ruled privately, in the case of COD income as a built-in income item, that such item be included in the amount of net unrealized built-in gain (i.e., the numerator in de minimis testing), but that the same item need not be included in fair market value of assets (the denominator in de minimis testing). See Private Letter Ruling 8923021. This will obviously be beneficial when applied in the context of built-in income items and detrimental if applied to built-in deduction items.

Coordination of recognized built-in gains or losses and proration rule during year of ownership change—Taxable income is determined by disregarding recognized built-in gains or losses where it is necessary to (1) prorate taxable income between the prechange period and the postchange period during a taxable year, the end of which does not close by reason of the ownership change, or (2) determine taxable income for such postchange period in order to apply the Section 382 annual limitation. Section 382(h)(5).

Section 382 and bankruptcy.   Bankrupt corporations are relieved from discharge of indebtedness income at the cost of a Section 108(b) reduction of the corporation's tax attributes including NOL carryforwards. Any NOLs that survive this reduction may be further reduced by the Section 382 annual limitation if an ownership change occurs in the debt restructuring (for example, stock-for-debt exchange).

The timing of the discharge of indebtedness income vis-à-vis the ownership change is critical in the Section 382 analysis when the taxable year does not close in the ownership change transaction. An ownership change occurring in the early part of the taxable year will result in the majority of the discharge income being subject to the Section 382 limitation using the daily proration rule of Section 382(b)(3)(A). Conversely, an ownership change occurring late in the taxable year will result in a large part of the discharge income being considered prechange income to which less limitation applies using the daily proration principles of Section 382(b)(3)(A). If the change and debt restructuring occur simultaneously during the year, the taxpayer may seek to use the Notice 87-79 advance ruling procedure in order to secure a specific cutoff and/or the 120-day option rule to structure the ownership change such that all the discharge income is treated as prechange income. The use of the built-in gain rule with respect to COD income may also be possible.

Value—Section 382(1)(6) provides for postdebt cancellation valuation of the loss corporation in calculating the annual Section 382 limitation in the case of Type G reorganizations or stock-for-debt exchanges involving bankrupt corporations.

Change date—In light of the broad potential application of the option rule, an issue arises in bankruptcy as to whether certain dates prior to the consummation of the plan of reorganization should be properly treated as the date of the ownership change. The IRS appears to have adopted the date on which the bankruptcy court confirms the plan of reorganization. See Private Letter Ruling 8902047.

Special Section 382 bankruptcy exception—A special exception to the Section 382 annual limitation is provided for certain Title 11 or similar cases under Section 382(1)(5). If the loss corporation's shareholders and qualified creditors own at least 50 percent (value and voting power) of the loss corporation stock (or stock of a controlling corporation also in bankruptcy) immediately after an ownership change and as a result of being shareholders or creditors immediately before the change, then in lieu of the annual Section 382 limitation, the loss corporation's NOL is scaled back for certain items. Creditors exchanging their debt for stock are included in this 50-percent test, but only if they held their indebtedness for at least 18 months prior to the date on which the bankruptcy petition was filed or the date on which the debt arose in the ordinary course of the debtor's trade or business and if the exchanging creditor has held the beneficial interest in the claim at all times. Section 382(1)(5)(E).

If this special rule applies, then the NOL is reduced for two items in lieu of the annual limitation. Accrued but unpaid interest expense arising in the prior three taxable years and in the year of the ownership change with respect to debt exchanged for stock is eliminated from the NOL. Section 382(1)(5)(B). In addition, 50 percent of debt canceled (after reduction for the aforementioned accrued but unpaid interest) in excess of the fair market value of stock exchanged for it will also reduce the NOL. Section 382(1)(5)(C). After reduction for these items, the NOL may be used without regard to the Section 382 annual limitation. However, if the loss corporation undergoes a second ownership change within two years of the Title 11 restructuring, then the NOL will be completely lost. Section 382(1)(5)(D).

Section 382(1)(5) takes precedence over the general Section 382 rules unless the loss corporation elects not to apply the special rules. Section 382(1)(5)(H). Depending on the particular facts and circumstances, the consequences of both general Section 382 and special Section 382(1)(5) should be evaluated. Assuming both are potentially available, certain important comparisons are noteworthy. First and most obvious, the annual Section 382 limitation is a limitation on rate of tax attribute utilization (assuming taxable income in the future) whereas the special bankruptcy rule reduces the NOL and does not limit the rate of NOL utilization. Second, the general corollary rules of the regular Section 382 limitation should be inapplicable to the special Section 382(1)(5) rule, in other words, the net unrealized built-in gain or loss rule, antistuffing rule, nonbusiness asset rule, and the continuity of business requirement. However, unlike the general Section 382 annual limitation, the special bankruptcy rule imposes a zero Section 382 limitation if there is a second ownership change within two years of the first ownership change. In addition, the reduction in NOL for 50 percent of debt canceled in exchange for stock and for certain accrued interest in effect abrogate part of the Section 108(e)(10)(B) stock-for-debt exception. This might not otherwise be the case under the general rules of Section 382.

It is often the case that the potential applicability of the special bankruptcy rule is an issue due to the uncertainty of whether creditors receiving stock in the plan of reorganization qualify under Section 382(1)(5)(E) as historic and continuous creditors (beginning 18 months prior to the petition date or credit date in the case of trade creditors). This concern will be most evident where the applicable debt trades publicly and arbitrageurs are prevalent and/or much public debt is held in street name by brokerage firms.

Because option attribution does not apply to Section 382(1)(5) restructurings, the Service is concerned that the 50 percent continuity requirement might be circumvented through the use of options in favor of new investors. New investors might then take advantage of an unrestricted NOL of the restructured corporation. Under proposed regulations issued on September 5, 1990, the option-attribution rules would apply for purposes of determining whether the Section 382(1)(5) continuing stock ownership requirements are satisfied. Options (and similar interests) would generally be deemed exercised if their exercise would cause the prechange shareholders and qualified creditors to own less than the requisite amount of stock. The proposed regulations would add a new rule to provide that the option-attribution rules do not apply to any option created by the confirmation of a plan of reorganization before such plan becomes effective. Thus, the proposed rule could not be circumvented by issuing options or similar interests to the historic shareholders and creditors; such options would be ignored and would not be treated as exercised if such exercise would meet the 50 percent test.

Section 382's interplay with other tax law provisions

SRLY, CRCO, and 269—The legislative history of Section 382 is clear that the consolidated return limitations, SRLY and CRCO, continue to apply despite the presence of Section 382. It is unclear, however, whether Section 382 should be applied on a consolidated basis to the group as a whole or separately to loss members of the group. Future regulations are to address this issue. The SRLY (separate return limitation year) rule limits the ability of a consolidated group to offset its income with NOL carryovers from members' separate return years. The CRCO (consolidated return change of ownership) rule prevents persons from buying control of a group that has been filing consolidated returns and causing the group to acquire new profitable members that can take advantage of the group's NOL carryovers. Because these doctrines still apply, presumably the simplest way to apply them in conjunction with Section 382 is to test each rule separately and apply the one that produces the most stringent limitation. These consolidated return limitations and others are discussed later.

Similar to the consolidated return regulation limitations, Section 269 remains as a viable limitation on tax attribute utilization. This section, among other applications, denies use of a loss corporation's NOL where the corporation was acquired with a principal purpose of using its tax benefits. Generally, a valid overriding business purpose will normally refute any Section 269 argument.

Section 269 generally grants IRS broad authority to disallow all or a portion of a corporate deduction, credit, or allowance if a person or persons acquire control (50 percent or more, vote or value) of a corporation, or a corporation acquires property in a carryover-basis transaction from another corporation not controlled by the acquiring corporation or its shareholders, *and* the principal purpose of the acquisition is the evasion or avoidance of federal tax by securing the benefit of a deduction, credit, or allowance not otherwise available. Consistent with the legislative history of Section 382, proposed regulations issued under Section 269 in August 1990 underscore the continuing application of Section 269 to deductions or credits limited or reduced under Sections 382 or 383. However, the degree and nature of application of these latter limitations is relevant in evaluating the principal-purpose test under Section 269. For instance, if the change in control of the corporation results in a severe limitation on the use of the corporation's NOLs, presumably the severity of the limitation would indicate the lack of a prohibited Section 269 principal purpose.

In bankruptcy situations to which Section 382(1)(5) applies, the general rules of Section 382 are inapplicable, including the annual percentage limitation and continuity-of-business standard. Since any NOLs or credits that survive the Section 382(1)(5)(B) and (C) reductions are not limited as to rate of use, the proposed regulations identify Section 382(1)(5) bankruptcies as potentially abusive situations from a Section 269 perspective. Accordingly, the proposed regulations provide that, absent strong evidence to the contrary, the Section 269 prohibited principal purpose is presumed present in such transactions unless the debtor corporation carries on more than an "insignificant amount of an active trade or business" during and subsequent to the bankruptcy proceeding.

Two additional matters are addressed in the proposed regulations. First, Section 269 "control" of a bankrupt corporation is treated as obtained by creditors no earlier than bankruptcy court confirmation of the plan of reorganization. Second, the Bankruptcy Code allows the government to request the bankruptcy court not to confirm a plan of reorganization if tax avoidance is the principal purpose of the plan (11 U.S.C. Section 1129(d)). The fact that the government does not seek a determination under 11 U.S.C. Section 1129(d) or a court under such statute determines that tax avoidance was not the principal purpose of the plan has no effect in the former case, and in the latter case is not controlling for Section 269 principal-purpose determinations.

Section 338—If a target corporation is acquired by a purchasing corporation in a transaction that constitutes a qualified stock purchase (80 percent acquired in a taxable purchase within a 12-month period), the purchaser may elect to treat the purchase as an asset acquisition under Section 338. The benefit of this election is the resulting step-up in tax basis of the assets of the target corporation in the case of a premium purchase price relative to the net assets of the target on a tax basis. This election causes the target to recognize gain as if it sold all its assets in a fully taxable transaction. This gain is treated as prechange income and thus is fully shelterable with NOLs not limited by Section 382. Section 382(h)(1)(C). However, certain tax costs may result under alternative minimum tax due to a limitation of 90 percent of alternative minimum taxable income on the use of NOLs.

Moreover, investment credit recapture and state tax consequences could add additional and possibly prohibitive tax costs.

Section 383—Limitation with Respect to Capital Losses and Certain Credits

The principles inherent in Section 382 with respect to NOL rate of utilization apply equally to capital loss carryforwards, general business credit carryforwards, minimum tax credit carryforwards, and foreign tax credit carryforwards. Temporary Reg. Section 1.383-1T provides rules on the application of the annual limitation to these items. In general, the Section 383 credit limitation is the excess (if any) of the loss corporation's regular tax liability (after NOL deduction and Section 382 limitation) for the postchange year over any tax liability computed after allowing a full NOL deduction for the Section 382 limitation.

Section 384—Restrictions on Utilizing Preacquisition Losses to Offset Built-in Gains

Congress enacted Section 384 in the Revenue Act of 1987 in a further attempt to prevent the trafficking in NOL companies. Section 384 prevents a loss corporation from offsetting recognized built-in gains of a gain corporation with preacquisition losses of the loss corporation. Section 384 applies to a corporation that acquires (either directly or indirectly) "control" of another corporation or the assets of another corporation in an acquisitive Section 368 tax-free reorganization (Types A, C, and D) *and* either corporation is a gain corporation. Section 384(a). Control for purpose of this rule means at least 80 percent voting power and 80 percent value of stock. Section 384(c)(5).

In its simplest context, Section 384 denies the use of a loss corporation as an acquisition vehicle to acquire built-in gain corporations and then sell off its pieces on a tax-advantaged basis. However, its application is broad enough to apply whenever a gain corporation and a loss corporation combine in one of the two prescribed manners, irrespective of which company technically acquires the other one.

Limitation of Section 384.   The Section 384 restrictions are triggered by the inclusion in income of recognized built-in gains during the five-year period following the acquisition. Generally, net unrealized built-in gains of the gain corporation need to be measured on the acquisition date. The same 15 percent/$10 million de minimis rule applicable to Section 382 also applies for Section 384 purposes. Gains recognized by the gain corporation during the five-year recognition period are presumed to be built-in gains subject to Section 384 unless it is demonstrated that the asset was not on hand at the acquisition date or the recognized gain exceeds the net unrealized built-in gain as of the acquisition date. Section 384(c)(1)(A). Built-in income items are also included as built-in gains. Section 384(c)(1)(B).

Recognized built-in gains are subject to Section 384 limitations only to the extent that the recognized built-in gains limited by Section 384 do not exceed the net unrealized built-in gains as of the acquisition date. Section 384(c)(1)(C). Preacquisition losses also include recognized built-in losses of the loss corporation when measuring the impermissible offset against recognized built-in gains. Section 384(c)(3).

Section 384 is applied on an affiliated group basis. Section 384(c)(6). Also, Section 384 limitations apply to any successor corporations. Section 384(c)(7). The statutory application of Section 384 on an affiliated basis is a welcome relief relative to the consolidated versus separate company application uncertainty of Section 382.

The IRS will not allow manipulation of the Section 384 rules through deferral of the recognized built-in gain beyond the five-year recognition period through use of Section 453 installment reporting. IRS Notice 90-27, I.R.B. 1990-15 (4/9/90). The notice indicates that the five-year recognition period will be extended as necessary to trap all Section 453 deferred gain as recognized beyond the normal five-year period.

Controlled corporation exception. The restrictive provisions of Section 384 will not apply where a corporation with preacquisition losses and a gain corporation were members of the same controlled group during the entire five-year period ending on the acquisition date. Section 384(b)(1). Section 384 adopts the definition of "controlled group" in Section 1563(a), but substitutes the phrase "more than 50 percent" for "at least 80 percent." The 50-percent "controlled group" test of common ownership is applied on the basis of both vote and value. Section 384(b)(2). Where either corporation has been in existence for less than five years, the controlled corporation test will be applied for the period that both corporations have been in existence. Section 384(b)(3).

Consolidated Return Issues

Numerous consolidated return issues arise in the context of financially troubled company restructurings where one or more corporations in the restructuring are members of a consolidated tax return for federal income tax purposes. All the tax attribute limitations described below have been in place much longer relative to Sections 382 and 383 as enacted in the Tax Reform Act of 1986 and Section 384 added by the Revenue Act of 1987. Many of the consolidated return limitations overlap in practice with the limitations set out in Sections 382 and 383. Until clarification, it must be assumed that these consolidated return limitations will also apply such that multiple limitations can possibly apply in tandem.

A discussion of these limitations follows. Thereafter, a discussion of other issues pertinent to restructurings of consolidated group members follows.

SRLY limitation. The SRLY (separate return limitation year) limitation limits the use of tax attributes including NOL carryovers from taxable years of a corporation for which it filed a separate return or for which it joined in the filing of a consolidated return by another group. Such tax attributes can be used only to the extent that the corporate member with the tax attribute generates taxable income and the consolidated group as a whole has sufficient taxable income. Reg. Section 1.1502-21(c).

Several aspects of the SRLY rule are noteworthy. The limitation applies on a company-by-company basis and not on a group basis. Therefore, acquisition of a parent company of a group will result in the SRLY limitation being applied to each acquired group member. In addition, the amount of consolidated NOL or other tax attributes must be apportioned to group members before carryback to consolidated or separate return years is permitted. Reg. Section 1.1502-79. Subject to Section 269, the SRLY rule can be somewhat managed through the combination, merger, or liquidation of SRLY members with profitable members.

Built-in deductions.   Similar to Section 382 and the concept of unrealized built-in losses, the SRLY rule has a comparable notion of built-in deductions, that is, deductions taken in a consolidated return year but economically accrued in a separate return limitation year. Reg. Section 1.1502-15. Such deductions or losses when recognized will be subject to the SRLY rule requirement that the member with the deduction or loss have taxable income sufficient to absorb such item (and the consolidated group as a whole have sufficient taxable income).

Two exceptions to this rule are provided. Built-in deduction limitations will not apply to assets acquired (directly or indirectly) more than 10 years ago or if the built-in loss was less than 15 percent of the fair market value of assets (excluding cash, certain marketable securities, and goodwill). Reg. Section 1.1502-15(a)(4).

CRCO limitation.   A CRCO (consolidated return change of ownership) triggers the application of yet another set of tax attribute limitation rules. Generally, a CRCO occurs if a common parent experiences more than a 50 percent (value) ownership change within the last two taxable years, measured by reference to ownership increases by the 10 largest shareholders, and the increases are attributable to taxable acquisitions or decreases in outstanding shares (other than redemption). Reg. Section 1.1502-1(g). If applicable, the CRCO rule limits the consolidated return NOL carryforward of the old group members in existence at the time of the CRCO from offsetting taxable income of any members other than the old group members. Reg. Section 1.1502-21(d). Unlike the SRLY rule, the CRCO rule applies in the aggregate to all old group members and it applies only to potentially limit carryforwards. Prior to Sections 382 and 384, the CRCO rule was intended to prevent the acquisition of loss groups and their use to add profitable business on a tax-advantaged basis.

Excess loss accounts.   Subsidiaries may be capitalized with a minimum amount of equity relative to debt (intercompany or third party). If such subsidiary generates substantial NOLs that are utilized by other members of the consolidated group, the consolidated group member owning stock in the subsidiary may have an "excess loss account" (ELA) with respect to that subsidiary. An ELA is an amount of net negative investment adjustments of an owning member with respect to subsidiary stock (in other words, net deficits in the subsidiary's earnings and profits and distributions) in excess of the tax basis of the stock of the subsidiary in the hands of the owning member.

Triggering of ELA—An ELA will be triggered into income upon the disposition of the subsidiary's stock. Reg. Section 1.1502-19(a). All the stock of a subsidiary will be deemed disposed of under the following situations:

1. The subsidiary or owning member ceases to be a member of the consolidated group
2. The stock is wholly worthless under Section 165(g) at any time during the tax year
3. The subsidiary has discharge of indebtedness that would have been COD income were it not for the insolvency of the subsidiary
4. On the last day of the tax year, 10 percent or less of the face amount of debt for which the subsidiary is primarily or secondarily liable would be recoverable at maturity by the creditors
5. The day a member transfers an obligation for which the subsidiary is primarily or secondarily liable to a nonmember for an amount that is 25 percent or less of the face amount of the obligation. Reg. Section 1.1502-19(b)(2).

Character of income—The general rule provides that an ELA will be treated as gain from the sale of stock that will normally be capital gain. Reg. Section 1.1502-19(a)(2)(i). However, an ELA will be considered ordinary income if (and to the extent) the subsidiary is insolvent at the time of the disposition of stock. Insolvency for this purpose is the excess of (1) liabilities, (2) discharged liabilities that would have generated COD income were it not for the insolvency of the subsidiary, and (3) limited and preferred stock over the fair market value of assets. Reg. Section 1.1502-19(a)(2)(ii). This insolvency rule will not apply to the extent that ELA was created by distributions in excess of earnings and profits of the subsidiary.

Investment adjustments and COD income.   Congress enacted Section 1503 (e)(1)(B) in the Revenue Act of 1987. This provision states that, solely for purposes of determining gain or loss of the disposition of intragroup stock and recognition in income of an ELA, the basis adjustments to stock for earnings and profits (investment adjustments) will not be increased by the amount of COD income excluded from gross income under Section 108 to the extent such amount did not result in attribute reduction (other than tax basis) under Section 108. This rule was intended to avoid the dual benefit of relief from COD income with a corresponding tax basis step-up to stock of a subsidiary through an earnings and profits adjustment.

Loss disallowance with respect to stock of a consolidated subsidiary.   The *General Utilities* doctrine allowed permanent elimination of corporate-level tax on the disposition of appreciated assets in certain circumstances. This was accomplished by giving the transferee a fair market value basis in the assets as they left the corporation, despite the fact that little or no corporate-level tax had been paid on the appreciation. Although the Tax Reform Act of 1986 repealed the *General Utilities* doctrine, the investment adjustment rules conflicted with this repeal, as illustrated by the following simple example.

Assume Corporation S has one asset with a basis of $0 and a fair market value of $100. Corporation P purchases all the stock of S for $100. P and S elect to file consolidated returns. S then sells the asset for $100 and recognizes a $100 gain. Under the investment adjustment rules, P's basis in the stock of S is increased to $200 because the asset sale generated $100 of earnings and profits to S. This basis increase allows P to recognize $100 of loss upon the sale of S stock for its fair market value of $100, offsetting the gain on the asset sale.

The IRS promulgated rules under Proposed Reg. Section 1.1502-20 on November 19, 1990 that retain the investment adjustment rules but that disallow any loss on the sale or other disposition by a member of the stock of a subsidiary. In lieu of tracing built-in gains, the new rules disallow all losses on the sale of stock of consolidated subsidiaries. The rule is broad enough to include worthless stock deductions under Section 165(g).

A special election allows NOL and capital losses allocated to the subsidiary disposed to be retained by the selling group to the extent a loss on disposition is subject to the loss disallowance rules. Other rules are also provided that adjust tax basis in remaining stock of loss subsidiaries downward to fair market value upon deconsolidation and that limit the "stuffing" or combination of built-in gain assets with loss subsidiaries otherwise subject to the loss disallowance rules. The latter rule applies where the combination and disposition occur within a two-year period.

Deconsolidation.   Where debt restructuring at a subsidiary level takes the form of a stock-for-debt exchange, the potential exists for deconsolidation by reason of the issuance of subsidiary stock to creditors outside the existing consolidated group. When a subsidiary of a consolidated group becomes deconsolidated, a number of potentially negative tax consequences can result. Deconsolidation will result when less than 80 percent (vote and value) of the stock of a corporation is owned by other consolidated group members. Nonvoting "plain vanilla" preferred stock owned by non–group members is not counted for this purpose. The resulting tax consequences include

a. Recognition of deferred intercompany transaction gains and losses under Reg. Section 1.1502-13(f)
b. Recognition of an excess loss account under Reg. Section 1.1502-19
c. Loss of tax basis in remaining shares of the subsidiary held within the consolidated group under Reg. Section 1.1502-20T

As noted earlier, the issuance of parent corporation stock would be a welcome relief in light of a deconsolidation concern. In Private Letter Ruling 8933001, cited earlier in the context of the parent stock-for-debt exception, the IRS ruled that the deemed exchange of debt-for-equity by subsidiary creditors would not result in a deconsolidation of the subsidiary from the group. However, the facts of the ruling are less than clear with respect to amounts and percentages, thereby making any generalization difficult.

Bankruptcy Reorganizations—Type "G" Reorganizations

Congress enacted the Type "G" reorganization provision, Section 368(a)(1)(G), in the Bankruptcy Tax Act of 1980 in order to "facilitate the rehabilitation of corporate debtors in bankruptcy." The provision was "designed to eliminate many requirements which have effectively precluded financially troubled companies from utilizing the generally applicable tax-free reorganization provisions of present law." Bankruptcy Tax Act of 1980 S. Rep. No. 1035, 96th Cong., 2d Sess. 35 (1980).

Requirements

Definition. A Type "G" reorganization is a transfer by a corporation of all or part of its assets to another corporation in a Title 11 or similar case, but only if, in pursuance of the plan, stock or securities of the corporation to which the assets are transferred are distributed under Sections 354, 355, or 356. The transfer of assets may be either to or from a party under the jurisdiction of the court and must be pursuant to a plan approved by the court. Section 368(a)(3)(B).

Mechanically, "G" reorganizations are similar to reorganizations under Section 368(a)(1)(D), with certain modifications intended to simplify the reorganization of financially troubled companies. One key difference between a "D" and a "G" is that the transferor corporation or its shareholders need not be in control of the transferee in a "G" reorganization. This modification is in recognition of the fact that creditors, rather than shareholders, have practical control of a corporation in a Chapter 11 or similar case. Furthermore, since a Type "G" reorganization requires a transfer of assets, it is inapplicable to an isolated readjustment of debt and equity in a recapitalization.

Title 11 or similar case.   Title 11 or similar case means a case under Title 11 of the U.S. Code or receivership, foreclosure, or similar proceedings in Federal or state court. Section 368(a)(3)(A).

Distribution under Sections 354, 355 or 356.   The distribution requirements of Section 354 or 355 dictate that the reorganization be an asset acquisition or a corporate separation, respectively. If only trade or short-term creditors (creditors holding debt not qualifying as a "security") receive stock of the reorganized corporation, the distribution will *not* qualify under Sections 354 or 355, and Type "G" reorganization treatment will arguably not apply. However, if even one former shareholder or security holder receives stock or securities, it would appear that the definitional threshold of at least Section 354 will be satisfied.

Section 354.   Under Section 354(a)(1), no gain or loss is recognized if stock or securities in a corporation that is a party to a reorganization are, pursuant to a plan of reorganization, exchanged solely for stock or securities in such corporation or in another corporation that is a party to the reorganization. Nonrecognition of gain or loss is accorded to a stockholder or security holder who exchanges stock or securities for new stock or securities. Short-term debt generally does not constitute a security. Thus, a trade creditor who receives stock or securities for a claim in a reorganization recognizes gain or loss.

Section 354(b) requires that the transferee corporation acquire "substantially all the assets" of the transferor. Generally, the IRS treats the test as satisfied in an acquisitive reorganization where the transferee receives at least 90 percent of the fair market value of the net assets of the transferor and at least 70 percent of the gross assets of the transferor. The application of the "substantially all test" may be problematic to a bankrupt company since it may be continuously streamlining its operations. However, Congress recognized the intention to facilitate the reorganization of bankrupt companies for rehabilitation purposes. Thus, asset dispositions to raise cash and pay creditors are to be liberally tolerated. Bankruptcy Tax Act of 1980, H. Rep. No. 96-833, 96th Cong., 2d Sess., 31 (1980); S. Rep. No. 96-1035, 96th Cong., 2d Sess., 35-36 (1980).

A transfer of assets of a debtor corporation that qualifies as a "G" reorganization by reason of satisfying Section 354 will result in the acquiring corporation inheriting the NOL carryforwards and other tax attributes of the transferor corporation as provided in Section 381(c). Section 381(a). However, the limitations to the use of such carryover attributes under Sections 382, 383, and 269 and the consolidated return regulations may also be applicable.

Section 355.   A "G" reorganization by reason of a distribution of stock or securities pursuant to Section 355 must have the following characteristics: (1) the transferor must be in control of the transferee immediately before the distribution, (2) the transaction may not be used principally as a device for the distribution of earnings and profits of the transferor or transferee or both, (3) stock or securities constituting control of the transferee must be distributed in the transaction, and (4) the transferor and transferee will both have carried on an active conduct of a trade or business for at least five years prior to the distribution.

A paramount consideration behind Section 355(a) is the preclusion of the "bailout" of earnings and profits to shareholders at capital gains rates. In addition to not having a preferential capital gains tax rate in our law at the present time, this "bailout" often is not a consideration in the case of an insolvent corporation because no earnings and profits exist. In any event, the fact that tax attributes do not carry over under Section 381 in the case of a drop down and subsequent Section 355 distribution and that the transferor may not "control" a bankrupt transferee may curtail the usefulness of Section 355 in "G" reorganizations.

Section 356. If a shareholder or creditor receives securities with a face amount in excess of those exchanged (if any), the fair market value of the excess is taxed. Section 356(d)(2). Note also that stock, securities, or other property received with respect to accrued interest may be taxable if such accrued interest has not been previously reported by the holder. See Section 354(a)(2)(B).

Exclusivity of "G" Reorganization

In general, if a Type "G" reorganization overlaps with other reorganizations or with Sections 332 (tax-free liquidations) or 351 (tax-free transfers to controlled corporations), "G" reorganization treatment will prevail. Section 368(a)(3)(C). However, the one exception to the "G" reorganization's priority over the other reorganization provisions, Section 332 or Section 351, is in the case of a transaction to which Section 357(c) applies. Section 357(c)(1), which applies to "D" reorganizations and Section 351 transactions, provides that a transferor recognizes gain to the extent that the sum of liabilities assumed by a transferee, plus the amount of liabilities to which property is subject, exceeds the total of the adjusted basis of property transferred. In the event a "G" reorganization overlaps a "D" reorganization or a Section 351 transaction, either of the latter two provisions will apply to the extent necessary to trigger gain to the transferor corporation under Section 357(c)(1) in the amount by which liabilities transferred exceed the adjusted basis of property transferred. In all other respects, the "G" reorganization provisions apply. However, Section 357(c)(1) does not apply in the case of a "G" reorganization where no former shareholders of the transferor corporation receive any consideration for their stock. Sec. 357(c)(2).

Continuity of Interest

The continuity-of-interest requirement in reorganizations has long been imposed by courts and the Treasury. *Pinellas Ice & Cold Storage Co. v.*

Comm., 287 U.S. 462 (1933); Reg. 1.368-1(b) and (c). The requirement operates to distinguish combinations of corporations in which equity interests are merged from mere sales of assets (or stock). The former is accorded tax-free treatment, whereas the latter is not. Generally, the continuity-of-interest requirement is satisfied if a substantial percentage of the consideration received by the shareholders of the acquired corporation consists of equity participation in the acquiring corporation. For advance ruling purposes, the continuity-of-interest requirement will be satisfied if stock of the acquiring corporation has a fair market value equal to or more than 50 percent of the fair market value of the acquired corporation's stock outstanding before the exchange.

In the context of a reorganization of an insolvent corporation, the continuity-of-interest principle can be difficult to apply. Shareholders of the insolvent corporation will often have zero equity in the corporation and may not be entitled to receive any consideration for their shares under the plan of reorganization. Creditors of the insolvent corporation often assume the position of equityholders of the corporation after a reorganization.

Before the Bankruptcy Tax Act of 1980, the courts and the Treasury recognized the conceptual difficulty of applying the continuity-of-interest doctrine to insolvency reorganizations. Thus, the interests of creditors were treated as the equivalent of a proprietary interest if the creditors had obtained effective command of the property of an insolvent corporation by appropriate legal steps. *Helvering v. Alabama Asphaltic Limestone Co.*, 315 U.S. 179 (1942); Reg. 1.371-1(a)(4). Effective command over the debtor's property was typically obtained by the creditors in initiating bankruptcy proceedings. In addition, to the extent assets of the debtor corporation were used to satisfy some senior classes of creditors, these classes of creditors would be ignored under the modified continuity-of-interest principle since they would have no continuing interest in the reorganized entity. In this case, continuity of interest would be tested by reference to the consideration received by the most senior class of creditor who could not be paid in full.

The Bankruptcy Tax Act generally follows the pre-Act law on the continuity-of-interest issue. This law is not codified, but committee reports advocate adherence to the former rule. For example, if an insolvent corporation's assets are transferred to a second corporation in a bankruptcy case, the most senior class of creditor to receive stock, together with all equal and junior classes (including shareholders who receive any consideration for their stock), should generally be considered the proprietors of the insolvent corporation for "continuity" purposes. However, if the creditors and shareholders receive consideration other than stock of the acquiring corporation, the transaction should be examined to determine if it represents a purchase rather than a reorganization.

Thus, short-term creditors who receive stock for their claims may be counted toward satisfying the continuity-of-interest rule, although any gain or loss realized by such creditors is recognized for income tax purposes under Section 354.

Triangular Reorganizations

The drafters of the Bankruptcy Tax Act of 1980 recognized that there was no justifiable policy for not providing reorganizations in bankruptcy with the same flexibility accorded to reorganizations of corporations outside of bankruptcy. Accordingly, several technical amendments to Section 368 provide for the merger of an acquired corporation directly into a subsidiary of the parent corporation in exchange for parent stock, and the merger of a subsidiary of a parent corporation into a target corporation by using stock of the parent corporation. In the broadest sense, these amendments parallel the preexisting forward triangular reorganization and reverse triangular reorganization, respectively. However, the use of parent corporation stock raises troublesome Section 108 stock-for-debt exception issues as discussed earlier.

The Act amended Section 368(a)(2)(D) to provide that a "G" reorganization could be accomplished by means of a forward triangular merger. As amended by the Act, Section 368(a)(2)(D) provides that a "G" reorganization may be accomplished by the direct transfer of the debtor corporation's assets to a subsidiary of the acquiring corporation in exchange for stock of the parent corporation. Section 368(a)(2)(D) requires that "substantially all of the properties" of the acquired corporation be transferred in the exchange. Although the Act is silent on this issue, there is no reason to believe that the liberal interpretation of the "substantially all of the assets" requirement in a straight "G" reorganization will not be extended to the "substantially all of the properties" requirement of a "G" reorganization by reason of Section 368(a)(2)(D).

A "G" reorganization by reason of a reverse triangular reorganization does not mirror its predecessor as closely as in the case of the forward triangular "G" reorganization and its predecessor. Two aspects of the reverse triangular "G" reorganization distinguish it from a Section 368(a)(2)(E) reverse triangular reorganization.

First, former shareholders of the surviving corporation need not receive any consideration in return for their stock. Section 368(a)(3)(E)(i). Second, the former creditors of the target corporation must exchange at least 80 percent of the fair market value of the debt of the target corporation solely for voting stock of the controlling (parent) corporation. Section 368(a)(3)(E)(ii). This latter requirement may be difficult to satisfy where secured or senior creditors have their claims satisfied with cash or other property. However, priority claims described in 11 USC Section 1129(a)(9) that are paid in cash may be excluded from this determination. Bankruptcy Tax Act of 1980, S. Rep. No. 96-1035, 96th Cong., 2d. Sess., 37, n. 7 (1980).

Miscellaneous

Alternative Minimum Tax

In spite of potential full utilization of tax attributes to shelter COD income and other items for regular tax purposes, corporate alternative minimum tax could represent a cash cost to a troubled company in a restructuring. Corporations are subject to the alternative minimum tax (AMT) to the extent that alternative minimum taxable income taxed at 20 percent (reduced by certain credits), or tentative minimum tax, exceeds regular taxable income taxed at 34 percent. The excess (if any) is AMT and is paid in addition to regular tax.

The alternative minimum taxable income base is regular taxable income before the NOL deduction adjusted for statutorily prescribed adjustments and preference items. For taxable years beginning before 1990, the *book income adjustment* was one such adjustment in arriving at alternative minimum taxable income. Thereafter, it is replaced with the *adjusted current earnings (ACE) adjustment*. In either case, AMT cannot be reduced through NOL deductions or foreign tax credits below 10 percent of the AMT tax before such tax benefit items.

Under the book income adjustment rule, 50 percent of adjusted net book income in excess of alternative minimum taxable income (before the AMT NOL deduction and the book income adjustment) is added to the AMT base. Since taxable income would not include COD income excluded under Section 108 or avoided by reason of the stock-for-debt exception, any financial accounting income inclusion in a debt restructuring could have a slight AMT cost of 1 percent (50 percent adjustment on 20 percent tax rate on the 10 percent amount of alternative minimum taxable income not shelterable by any combination of a NOL deduction or foreign tax credits).

Albeit a potentially small cost, this result was ironic in light of the spirit of the Bankruptcy Tax Act of 1980 and the exclusions and tax attribute reductions provided in Section 108. Fortunately, Congress also saw the irony and retroactively amended the book income adjustment in the Technical and Miscellaneous Revenue Act of 1988. Under Section 56(f)(2)(I), adjusted net book income disregards income arising from a stock-for-debt exchange in a Title 11 case or to the extent of the debtor's insolvency.

The ACE adjustment, applicable to tax years beginning after 1989, is 75 percent of the difference between a corporation's adjusted current earnings and its alternative minimum taxable income (determined before the ACE adjustment and the AMT NOL deduction). In keeping with prior AMT treatment, the Omnibus Budget Reconciliation Act of 1989 amended the AMT rules to provide that adjusted current earnings are not to include amounts excluded under Section 108. Section 56(g)(4)(B)(i). Likewise, adjusted current earnings do not include income amounts avoided under the stock-for-debt exception. Miscellaneous Revenue Act of 1988, H.R. Rep. No. 795, 100 Cong., 2d Sess. 90 (1988).

In calculating adjusted current earnings, the tax basis of assets may need to be redetermined (and stepped down in the aggregate) following a Section 382 ownership change if there is a net unrealized built-in loss under Section 382 principles. The tax basis is to be adjusted and reflected on a relative fair market value basis. Section 56(g)(4)(H). Presumably, the Section 382(h) de minimis rule will apply in determining this rule's potential application.

Earnings and Profits

Earnings and profits are a technical term used throughout the federal income tax law for various purposes. Its primary purpose is to measure the available source of funds from which a corporation's distribution to its shareholders will be treated as a dividend as opposed to a return of capital or capital gain. In the consolidated return area, it is the measure of investment adjustments to tax basis with respect to stock of subsidiaries.

Earnings and profits are not defined or measured by an all-inclusive test or definition, but rather it is the product of statutory inclusions, exclusions, and nonstatutory judgments whereby economic income or benefit is measured. Discharge of indebtedness (including income excluded under Section 108) will generally be included in earnings and profits since the relieved debtor benefits economically. However, earnings and profits do not include amounts for which tax basis of assets is reduced under Section 1017. Section 312(1). Reduced depreciation or increased gain on disposition of assets will increase earnings and profits in the current and future taxable years. No earnings and profits arise in the context of the stock-for-debt exception to COD income. Miscellaneous Revenue Act of 1988, H.R. Rep. No. 795, 100th Cong., 2nd Sess. 90 (1988).

Conclusion

As any serious reader can readily ascertain from a review of the aforementioned technical matters, the tax law's impact in many transactions affecting restructuring of financially troubled companies is both complex and uncertain in some areas. A clear understanding of available alternatives is critical to proper planning. Inevitably, different positions may develop with respect to similarly situated taxpayers, although each position is supportable in the "gray" of the tax law. Future legislative and administrative guidance will no doubt play a role in shaping the tax landscape. As a result, tax planning will continue to play a major role in troubled company restructurings, whether in or out of bankruptcy.

Acquisitions of Troubled Companies: Gearhart Industries, Inc. — A Case Study

Jeffrey Bagner
Fried, Frank, Harris, Shriver
& Jacobson

An increasing number of highly leveraged companies have been experiencing problems in satisfying their substantial debt service requirements. While there are various reasons for such companies to experience financial difficulties, those engaged in businesses in distressed industries are particularly vulnerable to these problems.

In the absence of the infusion of additional equity or the consummation of an internal restructuring acceptable to its various creditor and non–common equity constituencies (which may take various forms ranging from sales of assets in order to repay indebtedness to debt-for-equity exchanges), many of these troubled companies are ultimately forced to seek protection from their creditors under the United States bankruptcy laws. However, for a company engaged in a business that is highly competitive and in which continuing product maintenance and customer service are critical factors, the protections afforded by the bankruptcy laws may not provide the troubled company with an opportunity to reorganize itself and, thereafter, to operate in a profitable manner without the burden of unserviceable debt. Among other reasons, the customer base of a troubled company may be substantially eroded during the bankruptcy proceedings (with its customers utilizing alternative products or services—particularly if the companies providing these alternative sources have more stable financial conditions and more favorable prospects for continued business relationships). The troubled company may not be able to retain the services of essential personnel who decide, in light of an uncertain future, to find more stable employment elsewhere, or the troubled company may not have the working capital for research and development and other capital expenditures required for it to remain competitive.

Under the proper circumstances, troubled companies may be excellent acquisition candidates for companies that are seeking strategic acquisitions but do not want to pay the substantial acquisition premiums that have become prevalent in recent times. Obviously, the potential acquirer must assess the reasons for the troubled company's financial problems and then determine whether these problems are likely to be solved as a result of the acquisition. The risks associated with acquiring a troubled company are compounded if the troubled company's business is operated in an industry that is otherwise distressed. In this case, the potential acquirer must also determine the reasons for the industry's distressed conditions and whether these conditions are only cyclical in nature or are apt to be long-term or permanent. A potential acquirer that is engaged in business operations in the same distressed industry as the troubled company, but that enjoys a sounder financial condition than the troubled company (because it is engaged in profitable businesses in different industries or has better withstood the industry downturn), may find the troubled company's financial problems an excellent opportunity to increase its market share at a reasonable cost (subject, of course, to the restrictions imposed by the antitrust laws). A potential acquirer in the same business as the troubled company may also be able to realize economies of scale and other synergies that could make the acquisition more affordable to it than to other potential acquirers.

From a transaction perspective, the acquisition of a troubled company is often substantially more complex and time-consuming than the typical acquisition. For instance, when a financially sound company has entered into a definitive agreement with a proposed acquirer, there is a high probability that the transaction will be consummated with the proposed acquirer or, as sometimes is the case, with a third party willing to pay a higher acquisition price. On the other hand, there may be substantial uncertainty as to whether the proposed acquirer of a troubled company can successfully consummate the transaction even after it has entered into an acquisition agreement. The troubled company's indebtedness is likely to be in default (with scheduled principal and interest payments unpaid and principal amounts accelerated), its preferred stock dividend and/or sinking fund requirements (if any) are likely to be in arrears, and its other obligations (if any) to holders of equity securities may also be in default. Accordingly, unless the acquirer is prepared to repay in full all of these defaulted or accelerated payments or is able to reach satisfactory agreements with the various creditor and non–common equity constituencies to accept less than 100 percent of their claims against the troubled company, the acquirer must still negotiate satisfactory financial arrangements with these constituencies before completing the transaction. These negotiations are likely to present a formidable hurdle that is ordinarily not faced in the acquisition of a financially sound company, whereby the outstanding debt of the acquired company is typically assumed, redeemed in accordance with its terms, or refinanced at face or a premium above face. While the holders of a troubled company's indebtedness will often initially demand payment in full (including accrued interest) before any payments are made to the equity constituencies, if these creditors are convinced that the proposed acquisition is a better financial alternative to them than a bankruptcy proceeding, a determined acquirer may succeed in consummating the deal.

Before entering into a definitive agreement with a third party, the board of directors of the troubled company must assess whether the proposed transaction is more favorable to the shareholders of the company than the likely outcome of a bankruptcy proceeding and whether the proposed transaction is apt to receive the support of the holders of the troubled company's debt and other equity securities. The board of directors must be cognizant of the fact that, as a condition to their participation in the transaction, the creditors may insist upon reducing the amount of consideration to be received by the equityholders, which had theretofore been negotiated between the acquirer and the troubled company. Therefore, the board must factor this possibility into account when entering into a definitive acquisition agreement. Since the consideration being offered to the equityholders (particularly the holders of common stock) is often minimal, obtaining the requisite stockholder approval may also be problematic and should not be taken for granted, particularly if it is necessary to gain the approval of more than one class of equity securities.

In order to successfully acquire a troubled company, the acquirer and the troubled company must each assemble a team of professional advisors having restructuring, bankruptcy, and merger and acquisition expertise. The issues that arise during the acquisition process transgress the typical experience of professionals who specialize in the corporate, tax, employer benefit, and antitrust aspects of merger and acquisition transactions. As a general rule, the more complex the capital structure of the troubled company is, the more difficult and time-consuming the acquisition process is likely to be.

The following case study of the acquisition of Gearhart Industries, Inc. (Gearhart or the Company) by Halliburton Company, which was consummated in September 1988 (the Gearhart/Halliburton Transaction), illustrates a situation in which a publicly held, financially troubled company was compelled to seek a third-party acquirer to avoid what appeared to be an inevitable bankruptcy filing after it was unable, despite an extended negotiation process, to complete an internal restructuring with its creditors and holders of its non–common equity securities. In order to understand this process, one should know Gearhart's history of issuing various debt obligations and equity securities (including the terms of the instruments governing the rights of the holders of these securities), the economic environment to which Gearhart was subject, and various other factors. Gearhart's complex capital structure included several classes of unsecured senior debt, unsecured senior subordinated debt, unsecured subordinated debt (which was convertible into common stock), two classes of preferred stock (one of which was substantially a common-stock equivalent), common stock, warrants to purchase common stock, and a security referred to as "Rights." This security had unique terms but should not be confused with the securities that are issued in connection with stockholders' rights plans or "poison pills." In addition, a Gearhart subsidiary had obligations under an interest-rate swap agreement, and a foreign subsidiary had secured senior debt.

While all transactions are unique and a blueprint for the successful completion of an acquisition of a troubled company cannot be created, understanding the various issues involved in the Gearhart/Halliburton Transaction and the manner in which they were resolved may be useful when seeking to effect a comparable transaction.

Background

Gearhart, a Fort Worth, Texas–based company with its common stock (the Shares) listed on the New York Stock Exchange, was engaged in performing wireline and other well evaluation services for the oil and gas exploration, development, and production industry, and providing contract geophysical services to the oil and gas and mining industries. In addition, Gearhart manufactured wireline and other well evaluation and geophysical equipment and supplies for both its own use and sale to others. The Company's services and products were sold in highly competitive markets throughout the world. Gearhart was the third largest provider of wireline services (in a market dominated worldwide by Schlumberger Ltd.). It was also the fourth largest geophysical services company and the second largest provider of Measurement While Drilling services, a well evaluation service and process whereby measurements can be taken and information transmitted to the surface during the drilling process on a continuous basis.

Beginning in late 1981, weakened industry demand, declining oil and gas prices, depressed drilling activity, overcapacity, and price discounting caused a substantial erosion in the Company's profitability. During this period, Gearhart continued to increase substantially its capital and research and development expenditures and to enter new international markets in anticipation of future demand growth. The Company funded these increased expenditures, in part, with a $35 million private placement in December 1981 to a financial institution of 12 3/4 percent Convertible Subordinated Debentures due in 1993 (the Convertible Subordinated Debt), (having an initial conversion price of $35, subject to anti-dilution adjustments upon the occurrence of certain events) and a $30 million private placement in June 1983 to several financial institutions of 12 1/2 percent senior notes due June 15, 1988 (the 12 1/2% Senior Notes). In addition, in August 1983, the Company entered into a $60 million revolving credit agreement with a group of commercial banks, borrowings under which facility were convertible, at Gearhart's option, into senior notes having a five-year maturity. All of these financings were effected on an unsecured basis.

Demand for Gearhart's products continued to decrease and price competition in the wireline industry continued to escalate. The Company began to scale back capital and research expenditures dramatically at the end of 1983.

The Smith Takeover Attempt

In October 1983, Smith International, Inc., a major supplier of petroleum drilling and production services and products, purchased a block of 3,640,514 Shares at $31 per Share from a subsidiary of General Electric. This block represented approximately 22.7 percent of the then outstanding Shares. In addition, from December 1983 through April 16, 1984, Smith purchased an additional 1,669,500 Shares (or approximately 10.4 percent of the then outstanding Shares) in open market and privately negotiated transactions at prices ranging from $21 to $30 per Share, increasing its interest in the equity of Gearhart to approximately 33.1 percent of the then outstanding Shares. Under the rules adopted by the Securities and Exchange Commission, all of these purchases were publicly disclosed by Smith in Schedule 13D filings. In these filings, Smith stated that it was considering seeking to acquire control of Gearhart.

Commencing in November 1983, representatives of Smith and the Company met to discuss various alternative transactions, including a business combination of the two companies. However, they were unable to agree upon a satisfactory arrangement.

On April 30, 1984, Smith made an unsolicited tender offer (the Smith Offer) to acquire an additional 3.7 million Shares at $31 per Share. If consummated, this, together with the Shares that Smith already held, would result in Smith owning approximately 56.2 percent of the then outstanding Shares. The closing price of a Share on the date prior to the commencement of the Smith Offer was $28 1/8 per Share. The Shares had traded in the range of $19 1/8 to $30 per Share during the previous three months.

Gearhart's board of directors rejected the Smith Offers as inadequate and not in the best interests of Gearhart's shareholders for a number of reasons:

1. The opinion of Gearhart's financial advisor that the Smith Offer was inadequate from a financial point of view
2. The Smith Offer was for only approximately 23 percent of the out-

standing Shares (or approximately 35 percent of the outstanding Shares not then owned by Smith) and no plans were disclosed in the tender offer material or otherwise with respect to the acquisition of the remaining publicly held Shares

3. Smith's financial condition was inadequate and there was a material patent infringement litigation against Smith. The patent infringement litigation forced Smith's independent public accountants to render a qualified audit opinion in connection with Smith's latest year-end financial statements, thus raising, in the view of the Gearhart board of directors, concerns about Smith's financial condition, the financial viability of a combined Smith and Gearhart, and Smith's ability to acquire the remaining equity interest in the Company after it had consummated the Smith Offer. It should be noted that Smith filed for chapter 11 bankruptcy protection in March 1986, largely as a result of an adverse decision in the patent infringement litigation, as well as the substantial losses it incurred while attempting to acquire the Company.

Responding to the Smith Takeover Attempt

In response to this takeover attempt, the Company embarked on a financial restructuring program to increase shareholder value. In April 1984, prior to the Smith Offer, the Company retained Drexel Burnham Lambert.

On April 27, 1984, through a private placement arranged by Drexel Burnham, Gearhart sold to ten financial institutions units consisting of 8 ⅝ percent Senior Subordinated Debentures due April 30, 1994 in an aggregate principal amount of $98.7 million[1] (the Senior Subordinated Debt) and warrants (the warrants) to purchase an aggregate of 2.961 million shares, exercisable at any time during the succeeding five years at an initial exercise price of $33 per Share (subject to antidilution adjustments upon the occurrence of certain events). The total gross proceeds from the issuance of the units was approximately $73 million. Approximately $67 million was attributable to the Senior Subordinated Debt (since it was issued at a discount of approximately 68 percent of the principal amount thereof), and the remaining $6 million was attributable to the Warrants (or approximately $2 per Warrant). In the event of certain change-in-control transactions (which included a third party acquiring, without the Company's prior approval, ownership of at least 5.4 million Shares or a third party making an unsolicited offer to acquire Shares that would result in such party owning at least that number of Shares), the Senior Subordinated Debt could be used to pay the exercise price—with the exercising Warrant holder receiving credit based upon the principal face amount (as opposed to the discounted value) of the Senior Subordinated Debt being surrendered in connection with that exercise. As a result, upon the occurrence of a triggering event shortly after the Warrants were issued, the Warrants held by an initial purchaser of units would be exercisable at an effective exercise price of approximately $22.66 per Share instead of the stated exercise price of $33 per share[2], with the effective exercise price increasing as the original issue discount was amortized during the ten-year term of the Senior Subordinated Debt. Because of this provision, the Warrants were informally referred to as the "Springing Warrants." The Smith Offer constituted a change-in-control transaction that triggered the "springing" provision of the Warrants—whether or not any shares were actually purchased by Smith as a result. In addition, holders could put the Warrants to the Company for cash after the second year at varying prices (depending upon when the put right was exercised) ranging from $2.66 per Warrant at the end of the second year after issuance to $3.55 per Warrant at the end of the fourth year after issuance. The Company had various call options on the Warrants at higher cash prices. These ranged from $2.93 per Warrant at the end of the second year after issuance to $4.29 per Warrant at the end of the fourth year after issuance.

Furthermore, in July 1984, the Company purchased from Aetna Life & Casualty Company[3] all of the outstanding capital stock of Geosource Inc., then one of the largest geophysical services companies in the world. However, the geophysical services market had been stagnant and Geosource had incurred an aggregate of $68 million in losses during the previous five quarters. In consideration for the purchase of Geosource's capital stock, the Company

1. Issued to Aetna ten million Shares and 110,000 shares of preferred stock of a Gearhart subsidiary having an aggregate liquidation value of $110 million
2. Paid Aetna $30 million in cash
3. Guaranteed Aetna that it would receive at least $20 million upon the subsequent sale of the stock of a former Geosource subsidiary to either Gearhart or a third party (it being unlikely that the Company would be able to acquire the subsidiary's stock because of antitrust considerations)

Among Geosource's liabilities at the time of its acquisition was an approximately $14 million obligation under an interest-rate swap debt agreement with a commercial bank (the Interest-Rate Swap Debt).

After giving effect to the Shares issued to Aetna in the Geosource transaction, Aetna owned approximately 38 percent of the outstanding Shares[4]. Subsequently, Aetna exchanged the preferred stock of the Gearhart subsidiary for preferred stock of Gearhart (the "Series A Preferred Stock") having substantially the same terms and preferences as that of the subsidiary preferred stock. Among the other terms of the agreement relating to Geosource's acquisition was a provision entitling Aetna to designate four of the Company's ten directors (subject to decrease, under certain circumstances, if Aetna's equity interest in the Company decreased) and a commitment by Aetna not to purchase any additional Shares during the succeeding five years.

Although the Smith Offer remained in effect, Smith was preliminarily enjoined by a Federal district court in Fort Worth, Texas and subsequently by a federal court of appeals from purchasing any Shares pursuant to the Smith Offer. The preliminary injunction was imposed primarily as a result of Smith's failure to disclose in the soliciting materials relating to the Smith Offer all material information concerning the patent infringement litigation discussed above, in particular the effect an adverse determination in that litigation would have on the financial condition of Smith. On the other hand, the Company was enjoined from integrating its existing operations with those of Geosource pending the judicial outcome of Smith's attempts to have the Geosource transaction rescinded on the grounds that, in light of the pending Smith Offer, the board of directors of the Company breached its fiduciary duties to the Company's stockholders when it authorized the Geosource acquisition.

On March 27, 1985, after it became apparent to both Smith and Gearhart that a stalemate had been reached in connection with Smith's hostile takeover attempt (which by that time had been in progress for more than a year), Gearhart and Smith entered into an agreement providing for, among other things, the divestiture by Smith of its entire equity interest in Gearhart, the dismissal of all litigation between Smith and Gearhart, the termination of the Smith Offer, and an agreement by Smith not to acquire any Shares for a ten-year period. As part of this settlement agreement, if Smith did not receive at least $80 million from a secondary public offering of the Shares it held (an amount approximately 36 percent above the Shares' market value but only approximately 50 percent of Smith's cost basis), the Company agreed to pay Smith the difference between $80 million and the proceeds that Smith received in the contemplated secondary public offering.

In May 1985, the settlement agreement was consummated when units consisting of 6.9 million Shares and 6.9 million securities, referred to as "Rights," were sold in a registered public offering (the Public Offering) underwritten by Drexel Burnham Lambert & Co. for an aggregate consideration of $87 million, of which Smith received $80 million (with approximately $22.9 million of the $80 million being paid by Gearhart pursuant to the price guarantee provision described above). The Shares sold in the Public Offering consisted of 1,589,986 newly issued Shares and the 5,310,014 Shares that had been owned by Smith.

The Rights, which were all issued by Gearhart on a primary basis, were included in the Public Offering as a way to increase the proceeds received from the sale of Shares (thereby reducing Gearhart's obligation to Smith under the price guarantee provision). Because of the fact that the Public Offering consisted of approximately 26 percent of the then outstanding

Shares on a proforma basis, the underwriter did not believe that the Shares could be sold at or near the then market price of a Share on a stand-alone basis. However, when the Shares were combined with Rights, the underwriter was able to sell the Shares for $10.75, the closing market price of a Share on the day immediately preceding the effectiveness of the registration statement relating to the Public Offering. Each Right sold for $2.50.

The Rights, which had both equity and debt attributes, had a five-year term and were exercisable by the holder for a period of twenty consecutive business days each year, beginning in June 1986, subject to the Company's right not to honor, on a cumulative basis, more than 1,380,000 Rights during any one of these five exercise periods (that is, 20 percent of the number of Rights issued in the Public Offering). During each of these Rights exercise periods, Rights holders could exchange the Rights, together with an equivalent number of Shares (except when Shares were issued in exchange for Rights, in which case only a Right was required to be exchanged upon exercise), for cash, principal amount of five-year subordinated notes of Gearhart or Shares equal to a predetermined exercise price. (The value of these Shares would be based upon the average trading price for a specified period of time immediately preceding the commencement of the Rights exercise period.) The exercise price increased from $14.25 in respect of the first Rights exercise period to $21.68 in respect of the fifth and final Rights exercise period. The form of consideration to be paid in exchange for Rights was determined by the Company on an annual basis. However, if the Company elected Shares, holders of Rights could instead elect to receive shares of preferred stock of the Company. This preferred stock was essentially a common-stock equivalent having certain limited preferences over the Shares in respect of dividends and upon liquidation (the "Rights Preferred Shares").[5]

The purpose of the Rights was to provide those who purchased units with a "guaranteed" minimum 10 percent annual return on their investment.[6] Accordingly, the Rights were designed to have no value in the event the market value of the Shares increased at least 10 percent annually (or 35 percent in the case of the first Rights exercise period, since the initial exercise price was 10 percent over the combined price paid in the Public Offering for a Share and a Right). But these Rights would have value if the market value of the Shares did not achieve that target growth rate. However, since the Shares had a $0.50 par value and the Company received net proceeds of $2.35 for each Right issued in the Public Offering ($2.50 less a $0.15 underwriting commission), Texas corporation law prohibited more than 4.75 shares being issued in exchange for each Right surrendered during a rights exercise period ($2.35 divided by $.50).[7] After the first Rights exercise period, this limitation proved to be a significant factor in keeping the value of the rights from escalating even further since the maximum level of 4.75 Shares was reached in respect of the second Rights exercise period in June 1987 as a result of the substantial decrease in the market value of the Shares that had occurred by June 1987.[8] Due to restrictions contained in the Company's various loan agreements, it was contemplated, at least initially, that Gearhart would only be able to elect to issue Shares in exchange for the Rights (and, if the surrendering holders of Rights so elected, Rights Preferred Stock).

If the Company were to merge or consolidate with a third party (other than certain mergers that constituted an internal restructuring) or were to dissolve or liquidate, all of the outstanding Rights would become immediately exercisable into an amount of consideration based upon the then applicable exercise price for a Right (with the form of that consideration being the same as that paid in that transaction to the holders of Shares). However, unlike the 4.75 Share limitation existing under Texas corporation law with respect to the annual Rights exercise periods, no limitation on the consideration receivable by holders of Rights existed in the case of a merger, consolidation, dissolution, or liquidation. Thus, as a general rule, if the consideration paid in any extraordinary transaction was substantially less than the then applicable exercise price for a Right, the Rights holders would receive substantially more consideration upon the consummation of that transaction than the holders of Shares. Accordingly, when Gearhart began attempting to restructure its debt and non–common equity interests, the Rights holders held a very strong negotiation position over the holders of Shares in the event Gearhart sought to effect certain types of transactions to effect such restructuring. In fact, as discussed below, any Rights that were outstanding at the time of the consummation of the Gearhart/Halliburton Transaction were entitled to receive common stock of Halliburton having a market value of approximately $24 as compared to the consideration received by each holder of a Share in the Gearhart/Halliburton Transaction of Halliburton common stock having a market value of approximately $0.78 (a 30.77:1 ratio).

In July 1985, the Company issued $40 million in 10.55 percent senior notes due July 1990 (the 10.55 percent Senior Notes) to several financial institutions (many of whom had been the initial purchasers and remained holders of the 12.5 percent Senior Notes—although Aetna, which had been one of the initial purchasers of the 10.55 percent Senior Notes, did not purchase any of the 12.5 percent Senior Notes). In the same month, the Company converted its revolving credit facility into senior term notes (the Term Notes), also due in 1990, as permitted under the terms of the credit agreement relating to that facility. During its fiscal year ended January 31, 1986, Gearhart also issued an unsecured note to Aetna (the Aetna Note) in respect of the $20 million guarantee given in connection with the Geosource acquisition. This note ranked pari passu with the Company's other senior debt.

On April 29, 1985, when the Shares were trading in the range of $12 per Share, the Company paid what turned out to be its last dividend on the Shares. Accordingly, none of the Rights Preferred Stock to be issued during Rights exercise periods would accrue any dividends. By the end of calendar year 1985, the Shares had traded as low as $7 per Share.

Financial Trouble

By early 1986, primarily as a result of the continued decline in the oil services industry and the continued escalation of price competition, the Company's financial condition worsened. The Company was no longer in compliance with various financial covenants and restrictions contained in substantially all of its unsecured long-term loan agreements. The only material secured debt of the Company on a consolidated basis consisted of bank indetedness (the "Scottish Debt") of a Company subsidiary incorporated in Scotland. This debt was collateralized by assets of certain foreign subsidiaries of the Company.

As of April 30, 1986, the Company's capitalization was as follows (dollars in thousands):

Short-term debt:	
Scottish debt	$ 24,172
Current maturities of long-term debt	19,869
Reclassified long-term debt	227,034
Total short-term debt	271,075
Long-term debt:	
Term notes	54,000
10.55% Senior Notes	40,000
12 1/2% Senior Notes	30,000
Senior Subordinated Debt	70,034
Convertible Subordinated Debt	35,000
Aetna Note	15,000
Other	5,821
	$249,855
Less: current maturities	(19,869)
	229,986
Less: portion reclassified to current liabilities	(227,034)
Total long-term debt	2,952
Series A Preferred Stock	85,000
Stockholders' equity:	
Shares	13,908
Additional paid-in capital	265,202
Retained earnings (deficit)	(137,874)
Currency translation account	(11,600)
Total stockholders' equity	129,636
Total capitalization	$488,663

In response to its financial situation, the Company instituted various cost-reduction measures designed to keep costs in line with declining revenues. These measures included (1) reducing the Company's work force, wages, directors' fees, capital costs, and research and development expenditures and (2) closing unprofitable operations, including the Company's marine geophysical operations. Gearhart also hired a consulting firm to develop additional cost-reduction opportunities. Gearhart then began to (1) enter into joint venture agreements with well-positioned and well-financed international partners to reduce capital expenditures and other cash expenses, (2) redeploy assets into higher margin areas, and (3) increase marketing efforts.

In February 1986, holders of 2.76 million Warrants (of the 2.961 million Warrants outstanding), primarily Drexel Burnham, sought to surrender their Warrants to the Company for approximately $7.3 million ($2.66 per Warrant) in accordance with the terms of the Warrants. The Company was prohibited by its long-term loan agreements from satisfying this obligation and began negotiations with the holders to restructure the terms of the Warrants. As stated above, the surrender price increased on an annual basis for two years up to $3.55 per Warrant.

In the first quarter of fiscal 1987, the Company suspended interest payments on the Senior Subordinated Debt. In October 1986, Geosource failed to make a scheduled payment due on the Interest-Rate Swap Debt, causing the holder of that obligation to exercise its right to demand payment in full. In the third quarter of fiscal 1987, Gearhart suspended interest payments on the balance of its outstanding long-term indebtedness as a cash conservation measure. Furthermore, the Company suffered a loss of $337 million for the fiscal year ended January 31, 1987, and as of January 31, 1987, current liabilities exceeded current assets and total liabilities exceeded total assets. The Company's total shareholders' deficit was $224 million on that day.

As of July 31, 1986, circumstances existed which constituted a defined redemption event for the Series A Preferred Stock. The defined redemption event allowed Aetna to demand the redemption of the 110,000 shares of Series A Preferred Stock at $1,000 per Share or an aggregate of $110 million. In addition, the redemption event resulted in dividends accruing on the Series A Preferred Stock (previously dividends accrued only when the Company met certain defined earnings levels).[9] Under applicable Texas corporation law (since the Company had a deficit in unrestricted earned surplus), the Company was prohibited from either redeeming the Series A Preferred Stock or paying any dividends thereon.

Attempts At An Internal Restructuring

In April 1986, the Company began negotiating with holders of certain of its indebtedness and others to restructure the terms of its debt and other obligations. In May 1986, the Company hired Shearson Lehman as a financial advisor regarding a financial restructuring. Until the summer of 1987, Shearson's efforts on behalf of the Company focused primarily on an internal restructuring. From time to time, Gearhart met with its senior creditors and Aetna to discuss various restructuring proposals relating to all of the Company's debt, the Series A Preferred Stock, the Rights, the Warrants, and its other obligations. They discussed the possibility of rescheduling required principal payments, collateralizing the Company's assets, exchanging debt for equity, making alternative arrangements for the Warrants and the Series A Preferred Stock, reincorporating the Company from Texas to Delaware, and offering to exchange Shares for Rights. Gearhart also met with representatives of the holders of the Senior Subordinated Debt.

A review of all of the Company's assets was performed to decide which assets could be sold to fund an internal restructuring without adversely affecting the Company's ability to continue its core businesses in a competitive manner. As part of this process, the Company sold for approximately $2.5 million its 16 percent equity interest in Titan Services, Inc., a joint venture in which Gearhart had participated. The Company also sold, in private and public offerings, for approximately $43 million all but 5 percent of its equity interest in Computalog Gearhart Ltd. (Computalog), the Company's Canadian subsidiary through which the Company engaged in all of its operations in Canada. The minority shares of Computalog common stock had been publicly traded on various Canadian stock exchanges. The sale of the Computalog shares was effected shortly before the effectiveness of a change in Canadian tax law that would have adversely affected the attractiveness of the proposed sale to certain potential Canadian investors. The terms of various credit agreements relating to the senior debt prohibited the sale of the Company's interest in Computalog, and the debt holders' consent to the sale was not forthcoming within the time necessary to avoid the effectivenss of the new Canadian tax provisions. Nevertheless, Gearhart proceeded with the sale—but sought to minimize its legal exposure to claims by the senior creditors that it had violated certain negative covenants in the applicable credit agreements by depositing the proceeds of the sale in an escrow account (the Escrow Account). The Escrow Account was maintained for the benefit of certain of the Company's senior creditors pending consummation of an acceptable restructuring. (However, the terms of the escrow agreement were structured so that the funds could be withdrawn by the Company in the event a bankruptcy petition was filed. It was Gearhart's intention that these funds would be unencumbered assets of its estate in any bankruptcy proceeding and would be used as working capital during the pendency of any such proceeding.)

The Shares traded as low as $0.83 per Share in 1986.

In early 1987, the Company received unsolicited expressions of interest concerning possible business combination transactions from several parties, including Richard Rainwater, a Fort Worth–based investor who is a major shareholder of Energy Service Co., Inc. ("Ensco"), a Houston-based oil company. Gearhart also held discussions with Computalog regarding a possible joint venture with Gearhart or the purchase of selected assets from Gearhart. No firm offers were received.

The Company's financial difficulties continued into 1987, and the Company continued to operate at a loss. The Company's net loss for the fiscal year ended January 31, 1988 was approximately $3 million. In addition, as of January 31, 1988, current liabilities continued to exceed current assets and total liabilities continued to exceed total assets. The Company's total shareholders' deficit was $239.8 million as of January 31, 1988.

The senior creditors increased the pressure on the Company and its board of directors to agree to an internal restructuring having terms acceptable to them by accelerating principal payments and instituting legal proceedings against the Company. In March 1987, holders of the $54 million Term Notes called for acceleration of the amount due. In June 1987, a holder of the 10.55 percent and 12 ½ percent Senior Notes filed suit for collection of accrued and unpaid interest (but not principal) in the U.S. District Court for the Southern District of New York. In August 1987, holders of $10 million of the 12 ½ percent Senior Notes called for acceleration of the principal amount due plus accrued and unpaid interest.

Despite extensive negotiations throughout calendar years 1986 and 1987 and various proposals being considered by Gearhart and certain of its creditors and equity investors, no solution satisfactory to both the Company and these creditors and equity holders was reached. In an offering document, dated June 10, 1987, prepared by the Company in connection with the 1987 Rights exercise period, the Company stated: "If [a restructuring] is not consummated within a reasonable time, the Company may be forced to seek protection from creditors under title 11 of the United States Code. . . . In the event of the Company's bankruptcy, it is not likely that the value of the Company's assets would be sufficient to satisfy in full the claims of creditors upon liquidation."

The fact that none of the Senior Debt was secured by assets of Gearhart may have been a very important factor in the decision of the holders of the Senior Debt to continue seeking a negotiated settlement over an extended period rather than to force the Company into a bankruptcy proceeding. Furthermore, Aetna was concerned about a potential equitable subordination issue being raised in any bankruptcy proceeding since it held debt as well as a substantial portion of the equity of Gearhart (both 10 million Shares and all of the outstanding Series A Preferred Stock). It should also be noted that, under the terms of the agreement pursuant to which the Company had acquired Geosource, Aetna was entitled to have four of its designees serve as directors until June 4, 1986, when they all resigned because, as Aetna informed the Company, these directors wanted to avoid complicating the Company's efforts to restructure its long-term debt.

The Shares traded as low as $0.44 per Share in 1987.

Consideration of a Third-Party Transaction

Gearhart continued to pursue its internal restructuring (although it realized that an internal restructuring was unlikely to occur) and was faced with the prospects of its creditors escalating their pursuit of default remedies. In September 1987, the board of directors authorized Gearhart's management and its advisors to explore a possible transaction with a third party that could involve a change in control, whether by outright acquisition or through a restructuring involving an acquisition of all or a majority of the Company's outstanding equity. The Company also reviewed with its advisors the possibility of filing for chapter 11 protection under the U.S. bankruptcy laws.

A number of parties were contacted by Shearson, and proposals were received through November 1987 from Computalog, Halliburton, a competitor of Gearhart's in the wireline business, and a group of unaffiliated potential investors. The latter proposal was withdrawn after the October 19, 1987 stock market crash because of financing difficulties.

The Attempted Computalog Transaction

In October 1987, the board of directors heard a presentation from Richard Rainwater. This presentation did not, in the view of the Company, constitute an acquisition proposal. No specific terms of a restructuring or acquisition transaction were discussed except that Rainwater characterized any consideration that the holders of the Shares would receive in any such transaction as a "gift."

On November 11 and 16, 1987, the board considered proposals from both Halliburton and Computalog. Management also obtained expressions of interest from several other unaffiliated third parties. None of these expressions of interest, however, developed to the point at which such parties made a restructuring or acquisition proposal.

After considering the available options (including filing for a chapter 11 bankruptcy proceeding), the board selected the proposal from Computalog as being, at that time, the most favorable to the shareholders. On November 18, 1987, Gearhart entered into a letter of intent with Computalog (the Computalog Letter of Intent) pursuant to which each Share and Rights Preferred Share[10] would, as a result of a merger between Gearhart and either Computalog or a Computalog subsidiary, be converted into a fixed fraction of a share of Computalog common stock. This fraction of a share had a market value of $1.65 at that time. (As of the close of trading on November 17, 1987, the market price of a Share was $1.75.) The aggregate number of shares of Computalog common stock being proposed to be issued in exchange for Shares and Rights Preferred Shares represented on a pro forma basis approximately 25 percent of the Computalog common stock. The remaining equity interests on a pro forma basis were to be held as follows: existing Computalog shareholders (other than the Company, which then still owned approximately 5 percent of the outstanding Computalog shares), 50 percent; the financial institutions providing certain of the acquisition financing, 20 percent; and Computalog management, 5 percent. The Computalog Letter of Intent contemplated that consummation of the merger would be subject to a number of conditions, including the acquisition by Computalog of all the Term Notes, the 10.55 percent Senior Notes, the 12 1/2 percent Senior Notes, the Aetna Note, and the Interest-Rate Swap Debt (collectively, the Senior Debt), the Convertible Subordinated Debt, the Senior Subordinated Debt, the Series A Preferred Stock, and 95 percent of the Rights and Warrants. The Computalog Letter of Intent provided that the amount of consideration Computalog was required to pay in order to acquire such securities was subject to its negotiations with the various creditors, although Computalog did agree to consult with the Company during the course of these negotiations. While Computalog did discuss with the Gearhart board of directors its preliminary estimates of the amounts it was prepared to propose initially to the various creditors, Computalog told the board that it did not want to include these numbers in the terms of the Computalog Letter of Intent because it wanted to avoid establishing a floor price for its negotiations with Gearhart's debt and non–common equityholders. The source of the funds to be used by Computalog to satisfy the claims of these holders was to be cash then held by the Company and Computalog and external financing from third parties.

The Halliburton proposal presented at the November board meeting would have provided holders of Shares and Rights Preferred Shares with $0.50 in cash and a prorated number of shares of the outstanding common stock of Geosource (with Geosource becoming a publicly held company without any equity relationship with Halliburton and Gearhart). The Halliburton proposal also contemplated that Halliburton would acquire all of the Senior Debt, the Senior Subordinated Debt, the Convertible Subordinated Debt, the Series A Preferred Stock, the Warrants, and 95 percent of the Rights for cash in the aggregate amount up to approximately $196.45 million. The Board's strong reservations about the viability of Geosource on a stand-alone basis (particularly without a substantial cash infusion) was a key factor in the Board's decision to reject the Halliburton proposal. The Board was also in favor of having the holders of Shares and Rights Preferred Shares receive equity in exchange for their Gearhart securities in order to provide some upside potential to the holders thereof, particularly given the fact that many of these holders probably had a significantly higher cost basis than the value of the consideration being offered in the proposed transactions.

Shortly after entering into the Computalog Letter of Intent, with Gearhart's support, Computalog purchased the Convertible Subordinated Debt for $8 million in cash. This amount represented a substantial discount from the outstanding $35 million principal amount of the indebtedness plus accrued and unpaid interest. Both Gearhart and Computalog believed that this purchase made excellent business sense, particularly in view of the significant discount the holder was prepared to accept. Furthermore, the acquisition of the Convertible Subordinated Debt by Computalog would help facilitate the consummation of the proposed combination of Computalog and Gearhart. Obviously, the holder of the Convertible Subordinated Debt was concerned about the Company's continued viability and believed that, in light of the amount of debt having priority over the Convertible Subordinated Debt and the time delay for any amount to be paid to it by the Company whether in a bankruptcy proceeding or otherwise, $8 million in cash was a favorable price on a present value basis.[11] At the time of Computalog's purchase of the Convertible Subordinated Debt, the Company and Computalog entered into an agreement (the "Convertible Debt Agreement") that gave the Company the right, provided it had not breached its obligations under certain provisions of the Computalog Letter of Intent, to require Computalog to sell the Convertible Subordinated Debt to a nominee of the Company for $8 million (plus interest at the rate of 20 percent per annum from December 10, 1987). This right was exercisable during the 60-day period following the termination of the Computalog Letter of Intent. The sale commitment on the part of Computalog gave the Company the assurance that, if the Computalog transaction was not effected, the Convertible Subordinated Debt could be sold for $8 million plus interest to a party selected by the Company as a means of facilitating another transaction. At the same time, this commitment also minimized the potential for Computalog, if it ultimately became a rejected suitor, to block any other proposed transaction by demanding significantly more than the $8 million plus interest as consideration for its participation in that transaction.[12]

On December 17, 1987, having been unable to reach an accord on the terms of a definitive merger agreement with Computalog and faced with a December 20, 1987 termination date of the Computalog Letter of Intent, the Company and Computalog agreed to extend the termination date of the Computalog Letter of Intent until February 1, 1988. In consideration for this extension, Gearhart received an important concession from Computalog. Gearhart was permitted to solicit, initiate, or encourage initiation of inquiries or proposals from third parties regarding a business combination or other recapitalaization or reorganization and to participate in discussions or negotiations relating thereto during the pendency of the Computalog Letter of Intent (as extended) if prior thereto the third party provided an undertaking to the Company and Computalog that it would not, without the written consent of Computalog and the Company, make any approach to, or negotiate with, any of the holders of the Senior Debt, the Senior Subordinated Debt, the Series A Preferred Stock, the Rights, or the Warrants regarding any such business combination, recapitalization, or reorganization proposal. As is typically the case with the terms of letters of intent relating to acquisitions, the initial Computalog Letter of Intent had prohibited Gearhart from considering transactions with third parties, subject to the right of the board of directors to exercise its fiduciary duties to the Company stockholders.[13] As events transpired, Gearhart's ability to discuss alternative transactions with third parties during the pendency of the Computalog Letter of Intent proved to be an extremely valuable provision that probably prevented a Gearhart bankruptcy from being instituted.

After December 17, 1987, additional discussions were held between Computalog, Gearhart, and various Gearhart creditors, primarily the holders of the Senior Debt and Aetna. From these discussions, it became apparent that these security holders would not agree to accept the amounts proposed to be paid to them by Computalog, particularly in light of the amount contemplated by the Computalog Letter of Intent to be paid to holders of Shares and Rights Preferred Shares. An important point that became even more relevant later in the transaction is that the creditors viewed any proposed transaction on at least two bases: first, the settlement they would receive in connection with the transaction[14] as compared to their investment in Gearhart, and second, the settlement they would receive in connection with the transaction as compared to the settlement that would be received by the Company's equityholders and, in particular, the holders of Shares and Rights Preferred Shares.

As a result of the pressure being exerted by the creditors to increase the payments to them and decrease the payments to the equityholders, in late January Gearhart and Computalog agreed that the amount of funds to be paid to the holders of Senior Debt, Senior Subordinated Debt, and Series A Preferred Stock would be increased to $216 million from approximately the $190 million amount that Computalog had proposed during its discussions with the holders of the Senior Debt and Aetna, with a corresponding decrease in the amount to be paid to the holders of Shares and Rights Preferred Shares being made. Although the board was greatly concerned about the reduction in the consideration to be received by the holders of Shares and Rights Preferred Shares and spent many hours agonizing over the decision, the directors nevertheless authorized entering into a revised letter of intent on January 25, 1988 that would reflect this reduction. The board concluded that since the Company was not aware of any alternative proposals to pursue at that time (and any internal restructuring was not considered feasible), the proposed Computalog transaction—even at the reduced consideration to be paid to the holders of Shares and Rights Preferred Shares—was a more favorable alternative to these holders than a bankruptcy proceeding (which the board concluded was the most probable outcome if the Company did not agree to the revised terms, since it was the Board's assessment that a reduction in the consideration to be paid to holders of Shares and Rights Preferred Shares was a nonnegotiable prerequisite to obtaining an agreement with the creditors and, therefore, to consummating the proposed transaction). At the same time, however, the board of directors instructed Shearson to continue exploring alternatives to the Computalog proposal in accordance with the guidelines contained in the Computalog Letter of Intent, which expressly permitted the soliciting of alternative transactions. As was the case in all of its discussions concerning alternatives available to the Company during its financial crisis, the board explored the possibility of the Company filing a chapter 11 bankruptcy petition. The necessary documents to make the chapter 11 filing were prepared (and were kept current throughout the financial crisis).

On February 1, 1988, the Company and Computalog entered into the revised letter of intent (the February Letter of Intent) reflecting the reduced consideration to the holders of Shares and Rights Preferred Shares as described above. As was the case with the initial Computalog Letter of Intent, the February Letter of Intent contemplated the merger of the Company with either Computalog or a Computalog subsidiary and the acquisition prior thereto of all the Senior Debt, the Senior Subordinated Debt, the Series A Preferred Stock, the 10 million Shares held by Aetna, and substantially all the Rights and Warrants. In addition, the February Letter of Intent contemplated Computalog's acquisition of the Scottish Debt.[15] The February Letter of Intent contemplated the acquisition of the Senior Debt for $140.5 million in cash, of which $20 million was to be paid by the Company at the time that the Company and Computalog reached agreement with the holders of the Senior Debt. This "signing" payment was designed to provide these creditors with a significant immediate cash payment that was not conditioned upon the transaction being effected and that demonstrated the Company's seriousness in seeking to effect a transaction. It was contemplated that the Escrow Account would be the source of the $20 million payment. Furthermore, the February Letter of Intent contemplated the acquisition of the Scottish Debt for approximately $17.5 million; the acquisition of the Senior Subordinated Debt for $38.8 million in cash (of which $2.0 million was to be deferred for up to one year) and 2,033,334 shares of Computalog common stock; and the acquisition of the Series A Preferred Stock and the 10 million Shares owned by Aetna for $17.7 million in cash (of which $3.3 million was to be deferred for up to one year) and 2,833,334 shares of Computalog common stock. In addition, the February Letter of Intent contemplated the acquisition of all the Rights, Warrants, Rights Preferred Shares, and the remaining Shares for an aggregate of 9,345,812 shares of Computalog common stock (the acquisition of the Rights Preferred Shares and the remaining Shares to be effected pursuant to the merger). However, the February Letter of Intent did not seek to allocate these Computalog shares among these various securities, but merely provided that such allocation would be on terms satisfactory to Computalog and the Company. In other words, the negotiations of such allocation was deferred until the definitive acquisition agreement was negotiated. On January 29, 1988, the last trading day prior to entering into the February Letter of Intent, the closing price per share of Computalog common stock on the Toronto Stock Exchange was $4.20 Canadian (or $3.29 U.S. based on the then U.S. $/Canadian $ exchange ration of .7843/1). The February Letter of Intent contemplated that after the merger, on a fully diluted basis (but prior to giving effect to stock options), the following persons would own the indicated percentages of the outstanding shares of common stock of Computalog: the holders of Shares (other than Aetna), Rights Preferred Shares, Rights, and Warrants would own 20.87 percent; existing Computalog shareholders (other than the Company, which then still owned approximately 5 percent of the outstanding Computalog shares) would own 48.38 percent; the financial institutions providing certain of the acquisition financing would own 19.88 percent; Aetna would own 6.33 percent; and the holders of Senior Subordinated Debt would own 4.54 percent. The February Letter of Intent specified that the required cash payments would be funded from the existing cash balances of the Company and Computalog, the proceeds of the issuance by Computalog of up to $125 million of new securities, including senior debt, subordinated debt, and convertible preferred stock, and the proceeds (estimated at $5.3 million) from certain unspecified postclosing asset sales that would fund the deferred cash portion of the consideration. The February Letter of Intent provided that either party could terminate the letter of intent if the parties had not executed a definitive agreement regarding the proposed transaction by February 17, 1988.

By February 17, it was becoming increasingly apparent that Gearhart and Computalog would not reach an agreement. Although the terms of an agreement in principle with certain of the holders of the Senior Debt and Aetna had been reached on virtually all substantive issues, and the holders of the Senior Debt and Aetna had agreed upon an allocation of the proceeds amount themselves,[16] several important issues remained unresolved between Gearhart and Computalog. These included the allocation of the 9,345,812 shares of Computalog Common Stock to be issued to the holders of Shares, Rights Preferred Shares, Rights, and Warrants, certain conditions to Computalog's obligation to consummate the transaction, and the Company's potential liability to Computalog if the transaction was not consummated. Since the Rights were such a unique security and represented a "wild card" in terms of what amount of the equity "pot" they should receive, the Gearhart board was concerned that, without an allocation among the various equity constituencies, the holders of Shares (other than Aetna) and Rights Preferred Stock would probably receive little or no consideration if the proposed Computalog transaction were consummated (and with the potential that the holders of Shares would reject any such transaction when they were asked to approve it). Under the terms of the Rights, any Rights remaining outstanding at the time of the merger would have been entitled to receive all or substantially all of the shares of common stock of Computalog allocated to these equity constituencies unless some accommodation had been reached with substantially all of these holders beforehand. For this reason, the board reasoned that, at a certain point, a bankruptcy proceeding would be the more favorable alternative for the holders of equity securities, particularly the holders of Shares and Rights Preferred Shares. Furthermore, the board had become increasingly concerned, particularly after reviewing the terms of the Computalog's proposed financing arrangements and certain pro forma financial statements, that the combined Computalog/Gearhart would not be a viable entity and, in particular, would not have sufficient capital to provide for the necessary capital expenditures (including research and development) to compete effectively in the wireline industry. Of particular concern, especially given the problems that Gearhart had been experiencing, were the anticipated debt service requirements of the combined entity, the likely inability of the combined entity to obtain additional credit, the contemplated postclosing asset sales to repay a portion of the debt (and concerns about the consequences of the combined company not being able to effect such sales on reasonable terms or having to effect asset sales that, in the long run,, would not make good business sense), and the anticipated insufficient cash flow to fund the research and development expenditures required to maintain the combined entity's competitive position. It must be noted that the holders of Shares and Rights Preferred Shares were to become holders of common stock of Computalog, and therefore the consideration being received by these holders would be worthless unless the combined Computalog/Gearhart was itself a viable entity.

Subject to the constraints of the February Letter of Intent, representatives of Shearson contacted Halliburton, among others. After providing the undertaking required by the February Letter of Intent, Halliburton presented a new proposal to the Gearhart board of directors on February 17, 1988, which the Board of Directors took under advisement. The revised proposal, described in detail below, was a financially more favorable transaction to the Company's various debt and equity constituencies than the proposed Computalog transaction, and it differed substantially from Halliburton's initial proposal in November 1987. Subject to the constraints of the February Letter of Intent, representatives of Shearson and Gearhart had also contacted various other parties, but they received no indications of interest from such parties.

At the same time, Ensco representatives contacted management and other Gearhart representatives regarding a proposal to acquire the Company. Representatives informed Ensco that, while the Company would be amenable to considering such a proposal, the terms of the February Letter of Intent with Computalog did not permit Gearhart to furnish information or hold discussions or negotiations with Ensco (or, for that matter, with any other potential acquirer), unless Ensco would provide to Gearhart and Computalog a written guarantee that Ensco would not approach the holders of the Senior Debt, Senior Subordinated Debt, Series A Preferred Stock, Rights, or Warrants regarding any business combination, recapitalization, or reorganization proposal without the prior written consent of Gearhart and Computalog. (As noted above, Halliburton had executed an agreement to this effect prior to discussions being held between Halliburton and Gearhart.) Subsequently, in a letter dated February 17, 1988, Ensco informed Gearhart that it had acquired an interest in an undisclosed number of Shares and $29.5 million in principal amount of Senior Subordinated Debt (which Ensco would not have been permitted to acquire if it had complied with the Company's request to sign the written undertaking) and that, as a holder of Senior Subordinated Debt and an entity interested in acquiring Gearhart, it was willing to discuss a restructuring transaction. On February 24, 1988, Ensco finally agreed to comply with the terms of the February Letter of Intent, thereby permitting the board of directors to consider a proposal from Ensco.

The Halliburton Transaction

At its February 24, 1988 meeting, Gearhart's Board entertained proposals from Halliburton and Ensco and reviewed the status of the negotiations with Computalog and the holders of the Senior Debt and Aetna. While the February Letter of Intent could be terminated after February 17, 1988 by either Computalog or Gearhart (it did not automatically terminate but required an affirmative determination by either party to cause such termination), neither party had exercised this right of termination.

At the end of this meeting, the board of directors unanimously authorized management to terminate the February Letter of Intent with Computalog in accordance with the terms of that agreement and to enter into an agreement in principle with Halliburton (the Agreement in Principle). While the board was concerned with the reaction of the holders of the Senior Debt and Aetna to this decision (particularly since these creditors and Aetna had been assuming that Gearhart was very close to signing a definitive agreement with Computalog and, as stated above, were themselves close to signing a settlement agreement with Computalog and Gearhart), the board was prepared to be very candid with these holders in explaining the reasons for its decision. Halliburton's financial strength was considered an important element in trying to keep the creditors from reacting too negatively to the decision to abandon the proposed Computalog transaction. (However, Halliburton and Gearhart knew that they had to convince the Gearhart creditors that Halliburton did not bring a "deep pocket" to the table since if the demands by the creditors became unreasonable, the transaction would become too expensive for Halliburton to proceed.) The important message presented to the creditors and Aetna was that the termination of the Computalog transaction was not "another" means for the Company to stall a possible settlement. Instead, the decision to terminate was the result of the realization by the Company that the Computalog transaction had only a remote chance of success due to the reasons explained above—with it being in everyone's interest to expend their efforts in seeking to effect a transaction that had a higher probability

of success. Furthermore, the Halliburton proposal represented a more attractive transaction financially to the holders of debt and equity that, it
was estimated, could be consummated almost as soon as the Computalog
transaction could have been consummated (if such consummation were,
in fact, possible). Moreover, Halliburton was able to fund the acquisition
from its available cash resources and was not dependent upon a financial
institution for financing.

Had Gearhart not received the concession from Computalog in December 1987 that permitted Gearhart to solicit alternative acquirers, and had
Gearhart terminated the Computalog Letter of Intent without entering into
a definitive acquisition agreement, it is quite likely that the creditors would
have reacted more adversely to the termination of the proposed Computalog transaction and might even have forced Gearhart into bankruptcy. (One
could also speculate whether the Gearhart board of directors would have
been willing to terminate the proposed Computalog transaction without
having an alternative arrangement. However, the emergence of the revised
Halliburton proposal made that question moot.) In any event, from Computalog's perspective, giving Gearhart the right to actively solicit alternative
proposals proved to be a significant strategic mistake. The immediate sur-
facing of the Halliburton alternative upon the termination of the proposed
Computalog transaction offered "a ray of hope" for all parties concerned
and kept the negotiation process alive. Had Computalog not granted
Gearhart the right to solicit alternative acquisition proposals, it is extremely
unlikely that Halliburton would have approached the Company on an unsolicited basis with its more favorable proposal in the face of an agreement
in principle having been reached with Computalog. This is especially true
because Halliburton had not contacted Gearhart after the Computalog Letter of Intent was signed, but responded only to an inquiry from Gearhart's
financial advisors as to the possibility of Halliburton making a revised proposal that was expressly permitted by the terms of the Computalog Letter
of Intent. It should be noted that one reason that Halliburton submitted a
revised proposal was that after Halliburton had made its initial proposal in
November ($0.50 per Share plus the spin-off of Geosource to the Gearhart
shareholders), Halliburton had acquired a geophysical company whose potential combination with Geosource made the acquisition of Gearhart, as a
whole, more attractive to it.

The Halliburton proposal presented to the Company's board of directors in February 1988, as embodied in the Agreement in Principle, contemplated that each Share would be converted in a merger of Gearhart with
a Halliburton subsidiary (the Merger) into .03575 of one share of Halliburton common stock (approximately $1.10 based on the then current market
price of the Halliburton common stock). Halliburton's proposal was conditioned upon its acquisition of

- The Senior Debt, the Series A Preferred Stock, and the Senior Subordinated Debt for cash in the aggregate amount not exceeding $213.5 million

- Not less than 95 percent of the Rights and not less than 93 percent of the Warrants for an aggregate consideration of not more than $8.5 million in cash
- The Convertible Subordinated Debt in accordance with the terms of the agreement between the Company and Computalog (cash in the amount of $8 million plus interest)

Halliburton was prepared to assume the Scottish Debt since, unlike Computalog, Halliburton was not relying upon secured financing to fund the cash portion of the consideration being paid. The Agreement in Principle further contemplated that the definitive acquisition agreement would include a covenant by the Company to refrain, subject to the fiduciary obligations of its board of directors, from soliciting, initiating, or encouraging proposals of third parties concerning any recapitalization, reorganization, or business combination involving the Company (with an $850,000 liquidated damage plus out-of-pocket expenses provision applicable in the event of the breach of such covenant).

The Ensco proposal submitted at the February 24, 1988 meeting of the Company's board of directors (which, except as to certain financial terms, was based upon the February Letter of Intent with Computalog) contemplated the purchase by Ensco of

- The Senior Debt for $141.5 million in cash (of which $20 million would be paid by the Company at the time of execution of a definitive agreement out of the Escrow Account)
- The Senior Subordinated Debt not then held by Ensco for $31.4 million in cash
- The Series A Preferred Stock and the Shares owned by Aetna for $26.2 million in cash
- All of the Rights Preferred Stock, Shares (other than the Shares held by Aetna), Rights, and Warrants for 10 million shares of Ensco common stock (without any allocation among the securities being made in the proposal other than to state that such allocation would be on terms satisfactory to both the Company and Ensco)

The Ensco proposal further contemplated the purchase of the Convertible Subordinated Debt on terms to be negotiated. The acquisition of the Rights and Warrants was proposed to be effected by private purchase or tender offer, and the acquisition of the Rights Preferred Shares and Shares was proposed to be effected by a merger of the Company with Ensco or a subsidiary of Ensco. The proposal stated that a letter of intent resulting from the proposal could be terminated if the parties had not executed a definitive agreement by an unspecified date.

Based upon the terms and conditions of the two proposals and the status of the Computalog negotiations, the Gearhart board of directors concluded after considerable deliberations that the Halliburton proposal was clearly the most favorable alternative to both the Company's creditors and the equityholders. However, as compared to the Ensco proposal, the board of directors did realize that the Halliburton proposal had two major uncertainties in terms of the ability of Halliburton to consummate the Gearhart/Halliburton Transaction:

- The potential blocking position held by Ensco based on its acquisition of $29.5 million of the Senior Subordinated Debt (since Halliburton's obligation to consummate the Gearhart Halliburton Transaction was expressly conditioned upon Halliburton acquiring all of the Senior Subordinated Debt at a substantial discount)
- A possible antitrust concern relating the combination of the wireline businesses of Halliburton and the Company (which, as described below, would be subject to inquiry by federal regulators and by Texas and possibly other state regulators in the antitrust area).[17]

Notwithstanding these uncertainties (neither of which, the board concluded, were insurmountable), the board backed the Halliburton proposal. There were also many concerns expressed by board members and the Company's officers and advisors about the likelihood of Ensco being able to consummate its proposal, particularly since it required outside financing, as was the case with Computalog (which was not the case in respect of the Halliburton proposal). Also, in light of Ensco's assertion in October 1987 that the holders of Shares were not entitled to any payment as part of a restructuring, there was a concern as to the ultimate recovery (if any) the holders would receive pursuant to an Ensco transaction—particularly since the Ensco proposal had the same infirmity as the aborted Computalog transaction in providing a pool of shares of common stock in the post-transaction entity to satisfy the claims of holders of Shares (other than Aetna), Rights Preferred Shares, Warrants, and Rights without any allocation of such shares being made among these classes of securities.

On March 11, 1988, the Company exercised its right under the Convertible Debt Agreement to require Computalog to sell the Convertible Subordinated Debt to Halliburton as the Company's nominee. On March 14, 1988, Computalog advised the Company that it considered itself the absolute owner of the Convertible Subordinated Debt, free of any contractual restrictions, because the Company had breached its obligations under the Computalog Letter of Intent—a contention with which Gearhart strongly disagreed. Computalog also advised the Company that it had received an offer to purchase an interest in the Convertible Subordinated Debt and that it was preparing agreement to effect such purchase. Shortly thereafter, the Company obtained court orders in Texas and Alberta, Canada, restraining the disposition by Computalog of the Convertible Subordinated Debt. Gearhart was very concerned that Computalog would seek to sell the Convertible Debt to Ensco or would join forces with Ensco to make a joint acquisition proposal for the express purpose of preventing the consummation of the Gearhart/Halliburton Transaction.

In addition, on March 14, Halliburton and the Company made their initial filing with the Antitrust Division of the U.S. Department of Justice as well as with the Federal Trade Commission with respect to the Gearhart/Halliburton Transaction. This filing (which is known as a Hart-Scott-Rodino filing and which is required in nearly all acquisition transactions above certain minimum size thresholds) provides notice to the federal regulators of the proposed transaction and an opportunity before the transaction is legally permitted to proceed to consider what anticompetitive effects (if any) a proposed transaction would have on the industry or industries in which the parties compete. On April 13, 1988, the Company and Halliburton received from the Antitrust Division a request for additional information (commonly referred to as a "Second Request"). The making of a Second Request, which is an indication that the Antitrust Division has serious concern about the anticompetitive effects of a transaction, provides the federal regulators additional time and information to ascertain whether the transaction should be permitted to proceed. Complying with a Second Request often takes a substantial period of time because it typically requires the filing parties to provide a large amount of data. Gearhart and Halliburton were able to comply with the Second Request on May 23, 1988. Representatives of Gearhart and Halliburton also met several times with the Antitrust Division in Washington.

By mid-April it became apparent that the holders of the Senior Debt and Aetna would not participate in the Gearhart/Halliburton Transaction unless there was a reallocation to them of all or at least a substantial portion of the additional consideration proposed to be given to the holders of Shares and Rights Preferred Shares in the Halliburton proposal as compared to the consideration that these holders were to receive in the aborted Computalog transaction.[18] Thus, the fact that Halliburton had agreed to provide the holders of Senior Debt and Aetna with a more favorable settlement than they were prepared to accept as part of the Computalog transaction did not cause these creditors and Aetna to support the terms of the Halliburton proposal. Instead, these creditors and Aetna focused on the fact that the shareholders and other equityholders were also receiving a more favorable settlement. Since the total consideration that an acquirer of the Company was prepared to pay had increased, the holders of Senior Debt and Aetna reasoned that such increased consideration should be reserved exclusively for the benefit of Gearhart's creditors.

To demonstrate their displeasure with Halliburton's terms and to hasten negotiations, the holders of Senior Debt "turned up the heat." In March 1988, holders of the 10.55 percent Senior Notes and the 12 1/2 percent Senior Notes (collectively, the Senior Notes) accelerated the entire $70 million in principal amount plus accrued and unpaid interest, and they brought suit in New York Supreme Court in April 1988 seeking recovery of such amounts. (Previously, these holders had limited their claims to unpaid interest.) In the same month, one of the holders of the Senior Notes received a judgment in the approximate amount of $3.6 million for past interest and expenses associated with the collection of such interest and expenses associated with the collection of such interest in federal court in New York, and in connection with that judgment, received a restraining notice with respect to a portion of the funds held in the Escrow Account. In effect, this notice prevented the Company from reducing the Escrow Account below approximately $7.2 million (approximately twice the $3.6 million judgment), but did not require the Company to make any payments to such holder. In addition, two of the holders of the Term Loans instituted legal proceedings in state court in Texas, each seeking $18 million in principal plus past interest and expenses associated with the collection of such obligations. The following month, the other holder of the Term Loan instituted a similar proceeding. Aetna, as holder of 12 1/2 percent Senior Notes and the Aetna Note, also instituted litigation to recover the principal amount of such obligations and related interest and expenses. An additional lawsuit was commenced by the holder of the Interest-Rate Swap Debt. These actions, and in particular the restraining notice covering funds held in the Escrow Account, put enormous pressure on the Company to complete the Gearhart/Halliburton Transaction in a timely manner. Had any of the creditors reached the point in the litigations where they would have been able to obtain immediate access to Company funds (including funds in the Escrow Account), a bankruptcy proceeding would have been inevitable, since funds that the Company believed that it would need to operate its businesses during the bankruptcy process would have been diminished and the creditors not gaining such access to these funds would have been concerned about not receiving their fair allocation.

Meanwhile, in a letter dated March 7, 1988, Ensco reaffirmed its interest in restructuring the Company as set forth in its February 24, 1988 proposal or upon other terms acceptable to the Company, Ensco, and the other creditors of the Company. Ensco also stated that "substantial delays and material obstacles to a successful completion of the Halliburton proposal, apart from the current dissension among creditors, are unavoidable given the significant antitrust issues raised by Halliburton's proposed acquisition of [the Company]." In addition, Ensco stated that, based on its review of the criteria customarily used by the U.S. Department of Justice in analyzing horizontal mergers among competitors, it believed that Halliburton's acquisition of the Company failed to meet such criteria and that circumstances did not exist that would warrant an exception to such criteria.

In a letter dated April 11, 1988, Ensco reiterated its "willingness, ability, and commitment to immediately escalate our negotiations toward accomplishing a satisfactory restructuring of [the Company.]" Ensco further stated that its position in the Senior Subordinated Debt was "not for sale or satisfaction at a discount to the total amount due" and that it was aware that "various competing dynamics could lead to a precipitous bankruptcy proceeding for [the Company], but, based upon advice from [its] investment bankers, [it did] not believe that bankruptcy would have a serious impact upon the current operations of [the Company] so as to destroy the opportunity for a successful restructuring or bankruptcy reorganization which would be acceptable to all involved parties." In this same letter, Ensco stated that it was continuing discussions with Computalog "with a view to participating in a joint restructuring of [the Company.]" Ensco also stated that it still believed that consummation of the Gearhart/Halliburton Transaction faced the same legal and practical impediments previously described to the Company. On May 13, 1988, Ensco announced its acquisition of an additional $37.2 million in stated principal amount of Senior Subordinated Debt (increasing its interest to $66.7 million in stated principal amount of the $97.7 million stated principal amount outstanding, or 68.3 percent of the class) and thereby increased the pressure on the Board by once again threatening to be the "deal buster."[19] A senior officer of Ensco was quoted in the Dallas *Morning News* on May 13, 1988 as saying that the acquisition of the additional amount of Senior Subordinated Debt gave Ensco "a controlling position in that class of [the Company's] debt" and that there were "other alternatives for [the Company] other than the Halliburton restructuring or other than bankruptcy."

On May 17, 1988, the holder of 150,000 Warrants (not previously surrendered pursuant to the put provision) notified the Company of its intent to surrender these Warrants at $3.55 per Warrant in accordance with the terms of the Warrant. The Company did not accept the surrender of such Warrants. As noted above, most of the other outstanding Warrants had been surrendered pursuant to the put provision in February 1986 (although no payments had been made by the Company).

The Final Negotiations

By mid-April, it had become apparent to both Gearhart and Halliburton that the holders of the Senior Debt, the Senior Subordinated Debt (not including Ensco), and the Series A Preferred Stock would not participate under any circumstances in the Gearhart/Halliburton Transaction unless a portion of the value of the Halliburton common stock proposed to be paid to the holders of Shares and Rights Preferred Shares was reallocated to them. On the basis of this conclusion and the agreement that the consummation of the Gearhart/Halliburton Transaction was in the best interests of the holders of Shares and Rights Preferred Shares, Gearhart's board of directors agreed to a reduction in the fraction of a share of Halliburton common stock (or exchange ratio) to be received in the merger for each Share or Rights Preferred Share from .03575 to .02917. In connection with this reduction, Halliburton advised the holders of the Senior Debt, the Senior Subordinated Debt, and the Series A Preferred Stock that Halliburton would increase its offer to acquire these securities by an amount equal to at least the value of the shares of Halliburton common stock that had been taken away from the holders of the Shares and the Rights Preferred Stock by reason of this reduction in the exchange ratio. It should be noted that in agreeing to the revised exchange ratio, the Gearhart board of directors also considered the fact that from February 23, 1988 to May 5, 1988, the date prior to the meeting at which the Board approved the definitive acquisition agreement, the closing price of a share of Halliburton common stock as reported on the NYSE Composite Tape increased from $30.25 to $33.375.[20]

On May 11, 1988, Gearhart and Halliburton entered into a definitive agreement for the acquisition of Gearhart. Halliburton and Gearhart then focused their attention on reaching agreement with the various creditors. They decided to deal with one creditor constituency at a time. Acceptance by the holders of the Senior Debt and, given its diversified interest, Aetna (in its capacity as the holder of all of the Series A Preferred Stock and approximately one-third of the 30 million outstanding Shares), was critical to the success of the process.

By June 11, 1988, Halliburton, Gearhart, the holder of the Senior Debt, and Aetna had reached an understanding concerning the terms of a settlement agreement. However, as a prerequisite to signing any such agreement, the holders of the Senior Debt[21] insisted that Gearhart pay them approximately $30 million (plus costs and expenses up to an additional $1.5 million) from the Escrow Account. Not only would this payment provide the Senior Debt holders with an immediate cash return of part of their investment in Gearhart, but they would view such payment as an indication of Gearhart's commitment to consummate the Gearhart/Halliburton Transaction. After over two years of unsuccessfully pursuing various alternative resolutions to Gearhart's financial difficulties, there was a great deal of mistrust between the creditors and Gearhart, especially given the termination of the proposed Computalog transaction at the "eleventh" hour. It should be noted that the $30 million payment represented $10 million more than the signing payment which the holders of Senior Debt had been prepared to accept in connection with the aborted Computalog transaction. While Gearhart realized that the $30 million payment from the Escrow Account was a prerequisite to the consummation of the Gearhart/Halliburton transaction (although it had sought unsuccessfully in the negotiations to keep the signing payment at the $20 million level), Gearhart was not prepared to make the payment unless a favorable decision was made by the Antitrust Division (which up until that time had been expressing serious reservations concerning the anticompetitive effects of the transaction). Gearhart strongly believed that the payment of any substantial amount of funds from Escrow Account would be materially adverse to its interest and to the interests of the holders of Shares and Rights Preferred Shares in the event the Gearhart/Halliburton Transaction had to be aborted and the Company became subject to a bankruptcy proceeding. The Company was anticipating using the funds in the Escrow

Account to carry on its operations in the event of a bankruptcy proceeding. Until the antitrust issue was resolved, Gearhart believed that the consummation of the Gearhart/Halliburton Transaction remained questionable (particularly given the scope of the Antitrust Division's inquiry) and therefore wanted the potential of an antitrust "show stopper" removed before releasing any funds from the Escrow Account. On June 12, 1988 (and just before a deadline imposed upon the holders of the Senior Debt and Aetna for the execution of a settlement agreement), the Antitrust Division advised Halliburton and the Company that it would not challenge the Gearhart/Halliburton Transaction as a whole and would not seek to enjoin its consummation,[22] although it was continuing to review two relatively minor aspects of the transaction (which Halliburton could subsequently handle).

Shortly after learning of the Antitrust Division's favorable decision, Halliburton, Gearhart, the holders of Senior Debt, and Aetna entered into an agreement (the Debt and Equity Agreement) pursuant to which Halliburton agreed to acquire the Senior Debt for $123.6 million in cash, payable at the time of the consummation of the Gearhart/Halliburton Transaction. At that time, Gearhart paid the approximately $30 million cash "signing" payment from the Escrow Account (This amount was allocated among the holders of the Senior Debt on the basis of their outstanding claims against Gearhart other than costs and expenses and was paid in addition to the $123.6 million mentioned above.) The $30 million was treated as a payment of principal. As part of the Debt and Equity Agreement, Halliburton also agreed to acquire the Series A Preferred Stock (liquidation value $110 million) and 10 million Shares held by Aetna for $19.8 million in cash and 291,700 shares of Halliburton common stock (approximately $8.5 million based upon the market value of the Halliburton common stock) or, at Aetna's election, an equivalent cash payment. Upon signing the agreement, the Company also paid the holders of the Senior Debt an additional $1 million from the Escrow Account, representing costs and expenses incurred by the holders of Senior Debt in respect of which they were entitled to reimbursement under the various instruments governing their obligations. Upon the consummation of the Gearhart/Halliburton Transaction, Halliburton also agreed to pay the holders of the Senior Debt and Aetna (1) interest at the rate of 9 percent per annum on the amount of cash to be paid at the closing (but not the cash to be paid to Aetna for its Shares in lieu of Halliburton common stock) from May 1, 1988 through the date of closing, (2) interest at the rate of 9 percent per annum on the payments that were made from the escrow account from May 1, 1988 until the date the payment was made, and (3) any additional costs and expenses incurred by the holders of Senior Debt that were covered by the instruments governing their obligations, up to an additional $500,000 ($1.5 million less the $1 million paid upon signing). As part of the Debt and Equity Agreement, the Company agreed to comply with and to perform certain covenants relating to the operation of its businesses and to maintain, on a consolidated basis, not less than $70 million in cash or cash equivalents, less the payments made from the Escrow Account to the holders of Senior Debt. The Debt and Equity Agreement also contained provisions relating to amendments, some of which required 100 percent approval by the signatories and some of which required 60 percent approval of the signatories (the Required Creditors), determined on the basis of the aggregate consideration to be paid to each signatory. Unless the Gearhart/Halliburton Transaction had been consummated prior thereto, the Debt and Equity Agreement terminated by its terms on October 31, 1988—or on September 30, 1988 if Company stockholders had not approved the transaction by that date. In addition, the Debt and Equity Agreement was terminable by action of the Required Creditors on or after September 30, 1988 and also terminated by its terms if the definitive acquisition agreement between Gearhart and Halliburton was terminated. In connection with the Debt and Equity Agreement, the holders of the Senior Debt and Aetna also agreed that, until such termination date, they would not take any further action with respect to the pending litigations they had instituted against the Company nor would they seek to enforce any judgments obtained by them against the Company.

On June 15, 1988, Ensco once again informed the Company that it remained available to provide an alternative restructuring plan for Gearhart and that it expected to be paid in full with respect to the portion of the Senior Subordinated Debt that it held. It became very apparent to all concerned that the Ensco "piece to the puzzle" would more than likely remain the last stumbling block to a completion of the Gearhart/Halliburton Transaction.

On June 16, 1988, after completing its negotiations with the holders of the Senior Debt, Halliburton entered into an agreement with Computalog to purchase the Convertible Subordinated Debt for $12 million. This purchase, which was not conditioned upon the Gearhart/Halliburton Transaction being consummated (as was the case with the other classes of securities acquired by Halliburton), was consummated on June 20, 1988. While Halliburton had initially offered to purchase such debt for $8 million (plus 20 percent interest from December 10, 1987, amounting to an additional $825,000) in accordance with the terms of the Convertible Debt Agreement, Computalog contended that such obligation had been negated by Gearhart's alleged breach of certain provisions of the February Letter of Intent. (Gearhart strongly disagreed with the assertion that it had violated the terms of the February Letter of Intent). Since Computalog required certain products and services from Gearhart and Halliburton wanted to resolve the matter expenditiously (and prevent Ensco from purchasing the Convertible Subordinated Debt), the parties agreed to purchase the Convertible Subordinated Debt for $12 million after a face-to-face meeting between representatives of Halliburton and Computalog. After acquiring the Convertible Subordinated Debt, Halliburton set its sights on acquiring the Senior Subordinated Debt, the Rights, and the Warrants.

On June 30, 1988, the third annual Rights exchange period was consummated in accordance with the terms of the agreement governing the Rights. Pursuant to the 1986, 1987, and 1988 Rights exercise periods, the Company issued, in exchange for 4,140,000 Rights, an aggregate of approximately 19 million additional Shares and Rights Preferred Shares (representing approximately 40 percent of the aggregate outstanding Shares and Rights Preferred Shares). Each of the Rights exercise periods had been oversubscribed. Gearhart elected to issue Shares in exchange for Rights in connection with each of these Rights exercise periods, and relatively few surrendering holders of Rights exercised the option to receive Rights Preferred Shares.

The acquisition of the Rights was a complex strategic process given various factors. Their disproportionate value was realizable upon the effectiveness of the Merger. They were held in varying amounts by more than 50 recordholders (and an unknown number of beneficial owners, many of whom were not financial institutions or other sophisticated investors). The Rights were sporadically traded on the Pacific Stock Exchange, and, in particular, no one holder or group of holders purported to represent the class. Rights not acquired by Halliburton prior to the consummation would, in accordance with the terms of the agreement governing the Rights, be converted into Halliburton common stock valued at approximately $24 as a result of the Merger. Thus, there was tremendous incentive on the part of the holders of Rights not to sell these Rights to Halliburton but to have them converted pursuant to the Merger. However, Halliburton was not required to consummate the Gearhart/Halliburton Transaction unless almost all of the Rights were sold to Halliburton at a much lower price than $24. Furthermore, the value of the Rights in a bankruptcy proceeding was uncertain.[23]

In late June 1988, the office of the Attorney General of the State of Texas advised the Company that it was conducting an inquiry into the proposed Gearhart/Halliburton transaction under the antitrust laws of Texas and requested a meeting with Company representatives. At this July 5, 1988 meeting, the Company accepted service of a civil investigative demand and provided certain information relating to the proposed transaction. A similar civil investigative demand was served on Halliburton.

On July 22, 1988, Halliburton commenced a cash tender offer to acquire all of the Rights at $2.25 per Right, subject to the condition, among others, that at least 97 percent of the outstanding Rights were tendered. Less than 5 percent of the Rights tendered into this tender offer—obviously concluding that Halliburton would be prepare to increase the consideration to be paid to them. Halliburton soon increased its offer to $3.50 per right and, after meeting with holder representatives on August 31, again sweetened the cash price to be paid in the offer to $4 per Right. At the same time, however, Halliburton increased the minimum tender condition to 98 percent of the outstanding Rights. When Halliburton announced the price increase to $4 per Right, it expressly stated that such increase was to be its final increase. On September 23, 1988, the tender offer closed, with Halliburton acquiring approximately 2.7 million Rights of the 2.76 million Rights outstanding (approximately 98 percent) at $4 per Right. The increase from $2.25 to $4 per Right increased Halliburton's acquisition cost by approximately $5 million (although the additional 1 percent of the Rights that may have been acquired by Halliburton as a result of its increasing the minimum condition requirement from 97 percent to 98 percent of the outstanding Rights may have saved Halliburton approximately $552,000).[24] Obviously, the Rights holders realized that the significantly higher consideration which would have been available to them if they held onto their Rights until the merger was effected would not, as a practical matter, be available, since Halliburton would not consummate the Gearhart/Halliburton Transaction unless at least 98 percent of the Rights had been tendered at $4 per Right. Furthermore, as discussed above, the value of the Rights in a bankruptcy proceeding was uncertain. In order to prevent any holder from tendering only 98 percent of the Rights owned by it and realizing the higher consideration for the remaining 2 percent, a Rights holder was required to make a representation to Halliburton that the Rights tendered constituted all of the Rights beneficially owned by such holder as a condition to tendering Rights to Halliburton.

On August 10, 1988, Ensco filed a lawsuit against Halliburton and Gearhart seeking to enjoin consummation of the Gearhart/Halliburton transaction on the grounds that, in violation of the terms of the Senior Subordinated Debt, Halliburton intended to complete the Transaction without the consent of the holders of the Senior Subordinated Debt. However, since the definitive agreement between Gearhart and Halliburton expressly conditioned consummation of the Transaction upon Halliburton acquiring 100 percent of the Senior Subordinated Debt, both Halliburton and the Company believed that the litigation was without merit.

On August 16, 1988 the holders of approximately 68.5 percent of the outstanding Shares approved the terms of the Merger, which vote exceeded the 66 2/3 percent requirement. In addition, the requisite consent of the holders of the Series A Preferred Stock and the Rights Preferred Shares, voting separately and together with the Shares in various required combinations, was obtained. A proxy statement describing the terms of the Gearhart/Halliburton Transaction had been sent to the Gearhart stockholders on July 8, 1988.

After extensive negotiations, on September 6, 1988, Halliburton entered into an agreement to acquire the 2.76 million Warrants held by Drexel Burnham for $828,000 million, or $0.30 per Warrant, and the remaining 201,000 Warrants held by two financial institutions for $104,520, or $0.52 per Warrant.

On August 19, 1988, Halliburton improved its offer from $48 million to $60 million. On September 12, 1988, after intensive negotiations with the holder of the Senior Subordinated Debt—primarily Ensco—culminating with a "take it or leave it" ultimatum by Halliburton, Halliburton entered into an agreement to acquire all of the Senior Subordinated Debt for approximately $71 million ($66.7 million principal amount of Senior Subordinated Debt held by Ensco for approximately $46 million and the remaining $31 million principal amount of Subordinated Debt for approximately $21 million). Ensco had paid $33 million (primarily with nonrecourse debt) to acquire the Senior Subordinated Debt held by it.

However, the final chapter of the Gearhart/Halliburton Transaction had not yet been written. On September 16, 1988, literally at the time the parties were conducting a preclosing for the transaction, the Gearhart/Halliburton Transaction was temporarily restrained by a court order obtained in state court in Texas upon a motion made by the Attorney General of Texas to block the Gearhart Transaction on the ground that its consummation would violated the antitrust laws of the State of Texas. Halliburton settled the suit on September 22, 1988 by agreeing that it would not change Gearhart's practice of selling equipment to independent wireline operators.

On September 26, 1988 (just four days before the Required Creditors had the power to terminate the Debt and Equity Agreement), the final pieces to the restructuring puzzle were completed, and Halliburton and Gearhart consummated the merger. The total consideration paid in connection with Halliburton's acquisition of Gearhart is summarized in Table 18.1.

Column A represents the outstanding principal amount of the debt and the values, on the basis described above, attributable to certain equity securities of Gearhart.

Columns B and C represent the interest and penalties accrued on Gearhart's indebtness through April 30, 1988. The aggregate interest and penalties required to be paid on such indebtedness from May 1, 1988 to September 26, 1988 was approximately $13.0 million, but this amount has not been allocated among the various securities for purposes of the above table.

Column D represents the aggregate of Columns A, B, and C (the total amount owed to the holders of debt and equity securities of Gearhart (other than the Shares and Rights Preferred Shares) as of April 30, 1988).

Column E represents the amounts Halliburton agreed to pay to acquire the debt and equity securities of Gearhart, without giving effect to payments of interest on such amounts. The amounts do not include reimbursed costs and expenses of the holders of Senior Debt, including legal fees, aggregating $1.5 million.

Column F represents the interests paid by Halliburton to the holders of Senior Debt on the settlement amounts set forth under Column E in accordance with the terms of the Debt and Equity agreement.

Table 18.1 Halliburton's Acquisition of Gearhart

	(A) Principal	(B) Normal Interest	(C) Penalties	(D) Total Claims	(E) Agreed Settlement Amount	(F) Interest Paid on Settlement Amount of Senior Lender Claims	(G) Total Settlement Amount Paid	(H) Percentage Recovery
Senior Lender Claims[1]								
Term Notes	$54,000,000	$ 9,136,893	$2,306,245	$65,173,138	$53,236,138	$998,482	$54,234,620	83%(82%)
10.55% Senior Notes	40,000,000	7,560,833	2,738,912	50,299,745	40,356,982	756,845	41,113,827	82 (80)
12.5% Senior Notes	30,000,000	7,062,500	718,003	37,780,503	31,423,463	589,317	32,012,780	85 (83)
Aetna Note	15,000,000	2,616,803	1,613,756	19,230,559	14,582,080	273,465	14,855,545	77 (76)
Subordinated Lender Claims:								
Senior Subordinated Debt	75,034,253[2]	21,069,366	3,319,536	99,423,155	67,000,000		67,000,000	67 (67)
Convertible Subordinated Debt	35,000,000	10,511,667	1,372,916	46,884,583	12,000,000[3]		12,000,000[3]	26 (26)[3]
Other Claims:								
Interest-Rate Swap Debt		14,610,339	1,874,161	16,484,500	14,011,572	262,766	14,274,338	87 (85)
Warrants	10,511,550[4]			10,511,550	932,520		932,520	09 (09)[4]
Series A Preferred Stock	110,000,000[5]		28,875,000	138,875,000	19,800,000		19,800,000	14 (14)
Rights	66,240,000[6]			66,240,000	12,144,000[7]		12,144,000	18 (18)[7]
Total Claims	$435,785,803	$72,568,401	$42,548,529	550,902,733	265,486,755	$2,880,875	268,367,630	49 (48)
Shares held by Aetna					8,583,273[8]		8,583,273[8]	
Shares and Rights Preferred Shares[9]					29,116,967		29,116,967	
Total Consideration					303,186,995		306,067,870	
Payment from Gearhart's Escrow Fund					(30,000,050)		(30,000,050)	
Total Consideration Paid By Halliburton					$273,186,945		$276,067,820	

(1) Excludes the Scottish Debt (the secured debt of a Gearhart foreign subsidiary), which remained outstanding and unaffected by the Gearhart/Halliburton Transaction.

(2) Represents the amortized principal amount of the Senior Subordinated Debt. The Senior Subordinated Debt has a principal face amount of approximately $97.7 million (and was originally issued in April 1984 at a discount of 68 percent of such principal amount).

(3) The $12 million settlement represents payment received by Computalog from Halliburton. If the $8 million payment for Computalog to the initial holder was considered the more appropriate amount, the percentage recovery would be about 18 percent. (Since the sale to Computalog took place in December 1987, the interest and penalty amounts included in the above table were adjusted for purposes of determining the 18 percent recovery to take into account that these amounts represent balances as of April 30, 1988.)

(4) As of September 26, 1988, there were 2,961,000 Warrants outstanding. The holders of the Warrants had the right to put the Warrants to Gearhart at $3.55 per Warrant. Holders of 2,911,000 Warrants has previously notified Gearhart of their intention to surrender their Warrants to Gearhart. Gearhart did not accept the surrender of such Warrants. The recovery percentage is an average of the recoveries received. Drexel Burnham's recovery was approximately 8 percent, and the recovery of the other two holders was approximately 15 percent.

(5) Represents the liquidation value of the Series A Preferred Stock. Since Gearhart was in default under the terms of the Series A Preferred Stock, Aetna had the right to demand that Gearhart redeem the Series A Preferred Stock at $110 million in the aggregate plus accrued and unpaid dividends.

(6) As of September 26, 1988, there were 2,760,000 Rights outstanding. The Rights were converted in the Merger into shares of Halliburton common stock having a market value at that time of approximately $24 in accordance with the terms of the instrument governing the Rights.

(7) Ninety-eight percent of the Rights were tendered to Halliburton pursuant to the Rights tender offer at $4 per share for an aggregate cost of $10,819,200. The remaining 2 percent of the Rights outstanding were converted in the Merger into shares of Halliburton common stock having a market value at that time of approximately $24 in accordance with the terms of the instrument governing the Rights for an aggregate of $1,324,800. Thus, the recovery rate is an average of the recoveries received. The recovery rate for the holders accepting the tender was 17 percent and the recovery rate for the holders of the remaining 2 percent of the Rights was 100 percent.

(8) In accordance with the terms of the Debt and Equity Agreement, Aetna elected to receive cash in an amount of $8,583,273 in lieu of shares of Halliburton common stock in respect of the 10 million Shares held by Aetna, based on the market prices of the Shares and shares of Halliburton common stock on July 20, 1988, the date of such an election.

(9) Assumes a market value per share of Halliburton common stock on September 26, 1988, the price per share of Halliburton common stock on September 26, 1988. A total of 37,315,212 Shares and Rights Preferred Shares (excluding the 10 million Shares held by Aetna) were outstanding as of September 1, 1988. Each such Share and Rights Preferred Share was converted into .02917 of a share of Halliburton common stock. The market price per Share on September 23, 1988, the last trading day prior to the Merger, was $0.69 (with the market price of one Share on the basis of .02917 of a Share of Halliburton common stock being $0.78 as of the same day, or a 13 percent differential). No active trading market in the Rights Preferred Shares existed.

Column G represents the aggregate of Columns E and F (the total amount paid by Halliburton to the holders of debt and equity securities of Gearhart).

Column H represents the percentage calculated by dividing the amount in Column G by the amount in Column D (the percentage of recovery of total claims received by certain of the debt and equity holders of Gearhart, including the interests received, if any, on the settlement amounts). The percentage in the parenthetical represents the percentage calculated by dividing the amount in Column E by the amount in Column D (the percentage of recovery of total claims received by such debt and equity holders without regard to any interest received, if any, on the settlement amounts).

Epilogue

The acquisition of Gearhart by Halliburton succeeded for a number of reasons, although I am sure that each participant may allocate different weight to different factors. It is my view that among the principal reasons were (1) the reluctance of the Company and its creditors and non–common equity-holders, for varying reasons, to have the dispute resolved in a bankruptcy proceeding; (2) the efforts of the Gearhart board of directors to have the holders of Shares and Right Preferred Shares treated as fairly as possible in the process while realizing that the underlying equity value was minimal; (3) Halliburton's desire, perseverance, and use of financial resources to complete the transaction, although Halliburton was cognizant of the fiduciary duty of the Gearhart board of directors to its common shareholders and was flexible (but only within its own defined monetary limits) in its negotiations with the creditors and other non–common equity constituencies; and (4) the realization by the creditors and the holders of Rights and Warrants that it was unlikely that they could have received full recovery on their claims under any other scenario.

Notes

The author is a partner at Fried, Frank, Harris, Shriver & Jacobson. This firm acted as special counsel to Gearhart Industries, Inc. from February 1984 through September 1988 in connection with many of the matters discussed in this article. The author would like to acknowledge the invaluable assistance of Stuart H. Gelfond, an associate at Fried, Frank, Harris, Shriver & Jacobson, in preparing this article. Certain portions of the text, in particular the discussion of the acquisition proposals by Computalog Gearhart Ltd. and Halliburton Company, have been derived from the Gearhart Industries, Inc. Proxy Statement for the Special Shareholders

Meeting held on August 16, 1988 to consider the acquisition of Gearhart Industries, Inc. by Halliburton Company.

1. Shortly after the issuance of the Senior Subordinated Debt, the Company purchased 1 percent of the principal amount of the Senior Subordinated Debt from the initial purchasers at approximately the issue price plus accrued interest. Such purchase was in response to a request made by the New York Stock Exchange. Unless the Company retired at least 1 percent of the principal amount of the Senior Subordinated Debt, the issuance of the Shares upon the exercise of Warrants pursuant to the "springing" exercise provision would not have been in compliance with certain NYSE corporate governance provisions.
2. For example, debentures representing approximately $10,000 principal face amount of Senior Subordinated Debt (which had an actual cost to such initial purchaser of $6,797.60) could be used by the initial purchaser as the full consideration to purchase 300 Shares upon the surrender of an equal number of Warrants.
3. References to Aetna in this article will also refer to various subsidiaries of Aetna (when appropriate).
4. Shortly after the Geosource acquisition was consummated, the New York Stock Exchange instituted delisting proceedings in respect of the Shares on the grounds that the issuance of 10 million Shares to Aetna, without prior shareholder approval, violated certain of the exchange's existing corporate governance rules. The delisting proceedings were indefinitely delayed pending the exchange's review of certain of its corporate governance rules. In 1988, the exchange withdrew its delisting proceedings under a "grandfather" provision enacted by the exchange when it announced revised corporate governance rules.
5. The Company was under no obligation to establish a trading market for the Rights Preferred Shares, which were convertible, at the option of the holder at any time, into Shares on a one-for-one basis (subject to adjustment upon the occurrence of certain events). A different series of the Rights Preferred Shares was issued in respect of each Rights exercise period. Each series ranked pari passu with the other series with respect to the payment of dividends or upon liquidation. However, each series of Rights Preferred Shares had a different amount payable upon liquidation, since that amount was equal to the exercise price applicable with respect to each Rights exercise period. The amount of the quarterly dividends (if any) payable on the Rights Preferred stock could also vary from series to series since the amount of the dividend was equal to the highest quarterly dividend that had been paid on the Shares during the period from May 1985, the issuance date of the Rights, to the issuance date of that series of Rights Preferred Shares. (It should be noted that no dividends were paid on the Shares after the Rights were issued and, accordingly, none of the series of Rights Preferred Shares issued were required to pay any dividends.) In the case of certain mergers or other business combination transactions, holders of Rights Preferred Shares would receive the same consideration as the holders of Shares.
6. The initial exercise price was determined by increasing by approximately 10 percent, compounded on a semiannual basis, the combined price paid in the

Public Offering for a Share and a Right ($10.75 + $2.50, or $13.25). The exercise price for each succeeding Rights exercise period was determined by increasing the exercise price for the immediately preceding Rights exercise period by 10 percent compounded on a semiannual basis.

7. As is typical with state corporation laws, Texas law prohibits the issuance of shares of common stock by a domestic corporation for less than the par value attributed to those shares.

8. The drop in the market value of the Shares was probably caused not only by the Company's precarious financial condition but also, among other things, by the spiral effect resulting from the substantial number of Shares that were issued in exchange for Rights during the first Rights exercise period or that were anticipated to be issued in respect of future Rights exercise periods.

9. These earnings levels were never satisfied during the time the Series A Preferred Stock (and its predecessor security) had been outstanding.

10. Even though the Rights Preferred Shares had a priority over the Shares with respect to the payment of dividends and upon liquidation, the Board concluded that the Rights Preferred Shares should be treated as if they were Shares because the Rights Preferred Shares were generally intended to be the economic equivalent of Shares. In fact, the terms of the Rights Preferred Shares stated that in the case of a merger or other business combination transaction involving the Company, the Rights Preferred Shares were to be treated the same as Shares.

11. The holder of the Convertible Subordinated Debt had previously expressed a willingness to sell the debt for that amount and the Company had unsuccessfully sought to have the debt purchased by an unaffiliated third party from the holder as part of a commercial arrangement with that third party.

12. Because of its historical relationship with Gearhart and the fact that, even after Gearhart had sold nearly all of its equity interest in Computalog, Computalog still depended upon Gearhart for products as well as for a substantial amount of its research and development and other services, Computalog was viewed as likely to oppose attempts by certain parties to acquire control of Gearhart, particularly another wireline company such as Halliburton, unless it had assurances that these products and services would continue to be provided at rates it considered to be reasonable and that such proposed acquirer would not compete with it in Canada.

13. The fiduciary duties of a board director in such circumstance may include responding to unsolicited third-party proposals that have financial and/or other terms that are more favorable to the stockholders than the terms of the pending transaction.

14. This would include the dollar amount of the settlement, the form of consideration, the timing of the payments, and the certainty of the transaction being consummated.

15. No default existed with respect to the Scottish Debt. However, since the Scottish Debt was collateralized by assets of certain foreign subsidiaries of the Company and Computalog's proposed senior lenders required that they be granted a first security interest in substantially all of Gearhart's assets on a consolidated basis, the Scottish Debt had to be repaid upon Computalog's acquisition of Gearhart.

16. While the Interest-Rate Swap Debt was an obligation of Geosource and was to the limited extent of Geosource's assets structurally senior to the other classes of Senior Debt, the financial condition of Geosource was significantly worse than that of the Company. Notes payable to the Company represented a significant amount of Geosource's liabilities. The Interest-Rate Swap Debt was treated by both the Company and the other holders of Senior Debt as a senior debt of the Company for purposes of these negotiations.

17. The board of directors was also concerned that Ensco would seek to block the Gearhart/Halliburton Transaction by purchasing Rights in the open market. Because of the unique terms of the Rights and their increased value in the event of certain business combination transactions involving the Company, acquiring 5 percent or more of the outstanding Rights was a possible strategy a third party could take as a means to block Halliburton's acquisition of Gearhart, particularly given the relatively inexpensive investment that had to be made.

18. It should be noted that, based upon market prices at the time the applicable exchange ratios were negotiated, the original Computalog proposal accepted by the board of directors in November 1987 was $0.55 per Share (or 50 percent) higher than the Halliburton proposal accepted in February 1988.

19. Although Ensco appeared to be supporting its threat by expending additional funds to purchase Senior Subordinated Debt, the alternative view was that Ensco was making these purchase with the expectation of being able to exert pressure on the Company and the holders of the Senior Debt and Aetna in order to obtain a higher payment upon the consummation of the Gearhart/Halliburton Transaction. In fact, as a result of the consummation, Ensco made a profit of $13 million on a $33 million investment, which amounted to an annualized rate of return (without taking into account carrying costs and other out-of-pocket expenses) of close to 70 percent. It should be noted that Ensco reduced its downside risk by purchasing a substantial portion of the Senior Subordinated Debt with nonrecourse debt.

20. Thus, while the exchange ratio was reduced by an amount in excess of 18 percent, the market value of such reduction at the time was only 9 percent.

21. Aetna was not entitled to any of these funds in its capacity as a holder of Series A Preferred Stock or Shares.

22. It should be noted that while certain combinations that may be deemed to have anticompetitive effects are nevertheless permitted to proceed if the acquired company is considered to be a "distressed" or "failing" company, the Antitrust Division did not accept the "distressed" or "failing" company exception with respect to the Gearhart/Halliburton Transaction. One of the prerequisities of being able to rely upon the "distressed" or "failing" exception is that no viable alternatives are available to the target company other than the proposed transaction. Among the apparent reasons for the decision not to apply the "distressed" or "failing" company exception was the fact that Ensco held itself out as an alternative acquirer having no antitrust impediments.

23. In an exchange offer document prepared by the Company in connection with an exercise period for the Rights, the Company stated: "Moreover, it is not possible to predict what the consequences would be to a holder of Rights if the Company were to seek to restructure its obligations pursuant to a reorganization plan under chapter 11 of the Bankruptcy Code. The rights of a holder

of Rights in a bankruptcy proceeding are not entirely clear. Whether the Rights constitute equity securities or are a right to payment and therefore a claim will be a matter of judicial determination for which there is no clear precedent. In such event, it is likely that the Company's creditors will seek to have the Rights characterized in a way that will afford holders of Rights the lowest possible priority for purposes of distribution of the proceeds of liquidation of the Company's assets. The Company cannot predict with any precision how the Rights will be characterized in the event of the Company's bankruptcy."

24. The 98 percent condition was a minimum condition, not a maximum condition. Halliburton was prepared to accept all tendered Rights. If the condition had remained at 97 percent, it is possible that 98 percent of the Rights still would have been tendered.

Beker Industries Corp. Chapter 11 Reorganization, 1985–1988

William J. Rochelle, III
Fulbright Jaworski &
Reavis McGrath

Introduction

Beker Industries Corp., together with its subsidiary Beker Phosphate Corporation (collectively "Beker"), was one of the nation's largest producers and marketers of phosphate-based chemical fertilizers for the domestic and export market. Worldwide, the phosphate industry was in a cyclic decline. Beker had suffered more than many of its competitors because it was not diversified. Having already exhausted every method of raising cash to avoid bankruptcy, Beker retained bankruptcy counsel in October 1985.[1]

Hoping to avert bankruptcy, Beker's newly retained bankruptcy counsel arranged a meeting with the company's secured bank lenders. The banks evidenced little interest in working with the debtor outside of bankruptcy.

Beker's counsel concluded that some of the banks might be more willing to continue financing the company after it filed a chapter 11 petition, given the bulletproof protection that the bankruptcy court can provide a postpetition lender under Bankruptcy Code § 364.

With Beker nearing the point where it could no longer meet payroll, the company filed a chapter 11 petition in the Southern District of New York on October 25, 1985, after giving its counsel a substantial retainer paid with the knowledge and tacit consent of the bank lenders.

Principal Assets

At the filing date, Beker had four principal assets:

1. Florida Phosphate Mine. Beker Phosphate Corporation ("Phosphate"), one of the two debtor corporations, owned a 10,000-acre phosphate mine in Manatee County, Florida. Beker mined phosphate rock, using enormous dredges financed by MARAD. The phosphate mine also included a processing plant.
2. Louisiana Phosphate Plant. Beker owned a large phosphate plant on the Mississippi River near New Orleans. With a deep-water port, the plant historically shipped a substantial portion of its product into the world market. Phosphate rock mined in Florida was shipped to the Louisiana plant on the company's own oceangoing tug-barge, which was also financed by MARAD. Upon arrival in New Orleans, the phosphate rock was transformed into phosphate fertilizer.
3. Idaho Plant and Mine. Beker owned a second phosphate plant in a remote region of Idaho. Associated with the plant was a phosphate mine adequate to supply the raw material needs of the Idaho plant.
4. Connecticut Office Building. Beker owned a modern, four-story office building in Greenwich, Connecticut, where it maintained its corporate offices.

Principal Secured Debt at Filing Date

At the filing date, the principal secured claims against Beker were

1. $22 million working capital loan. The bank lenders had advanced approximately $22 million to Beker under a revolving loan agreement. The "revolver" was secured by a first lien on all accounts receivable.
2. $34 million term loan. The bank lenders had also advanced Beker approximately $34 million under several term loans. The principal collateral was a first lien on the Louisiana plant. The term loan was also secured by a second lien on accounts receivable and by a pledge of the stock of Phosphate, which owned the Florida mine. The Florida assets themselves were not subject to lien at the filing date.
3. $65 million in principal amount of secured subordinated debentures. Two years prior to filing, Beker had issued $65 million in principal amount of 15 7/8 percent secured subordinated sinking fund debentures (the "Debentures"). Although subordinated to borrow money, the Debentures were secured by a first lien on the Idaho plant and mine. Until a payment default occurred, the Debentures had been trading near par. After filing, the Debentures traded in the mid 60s, indicating the market's belief that the collateral would largely repay the principal owing on the Debentures.

4. The office building in Connecticut was also subject to a small, conventional mortgage. However, the office building was also subject to a contingent but otherwise valid lien to secure an insurance company that had issued standby letters of credit in connection with a sale of tax benefits from the tug-barge.

Problems at Filing

As a consequence of continuing losses and the erosion of working capital, Beker had exhausted its loan availability under the revolver. Having depleted working capital, Beker could not continue to purchase raw materials without additional financing.

As a consequence of the intercreditor agreement among the bank lenders, the banks did not have a pari passu interest in the collateral. Rather, the banks each had markedly different participations in the term loan and the revolver. More significantly, the banks had different priorities in the collateral. Consequently, the interests of the banks were not identical, and the banks had different strategies about how they could emerge from chapter 11 without a loss. The banks also had differing judgments concerning the values of the collateral.

At the filing date, it appeared that some of the banks were intent on terminating Beker's operations and liquidating the company. Later events confirmed the judgment that certain banks did not wish to see Beker continue operating because they believed their loans could be repaid through the sale of their collateral even in a liquidation.

Immediately after the filing of the chapter 11 petition, Baker could not make any agreement with its banks concerning the use of cash collateral. Having filed chapter 11, Beker was nonetheless out of business unless it could obtain the use of "cash collateral," that is, authorization under 11 U.S.C. § 363(c)(2) to use proceeds of its accounts receivable that were subject to the banks' liens.

Loan Agreements

Use of Cash Collateral over Banks' Objection

In the typical chapter 11 case, the banks will agree to allow the debtor to use "cash collateral" in return for a "cash collateral order" that gives the banks bulletproof protection for all postpetition loans. Through a fiction known as the rollover of prepetition debt, banks even obtain better collateral after the chapter 11 case than they enjoyed before bankruptcy.[2]

In the Beker case, however, the banks would not agree to advance any additional loans. Moreover, the banks would not even permit Beker to utilize proceeds from its accounts receivable. Under Bankruptcy Code

§ 363(c)(2), Beker could not use proceeds of accounts receivable without consent from the banks or the court's authorization.

Having failed to obtain the banks' consent, Beker arranged for a hearing on the second day of the case. It requested that the bankruptcy court authorize the use of cash collateral despite the banks' objections. At the hearing, Beker produced testimony from its officers and accountants establishing the likelihood of a successful reorganization and the need for the use of cash collateral. The bankruptcy court overruled the objection of the banks and authorized the debtor to use a limited amount of cash collateral for a few days pending a continued hearing on the "long-term" use of cash collateral.

The authority granted by the court gave the banks few protections other than permitting the banks' liens to attach to postpetition assets. Because the bankruptcy judge was reluctant to terminate operations of a major chapter 11 debtor at the outset of the case, the banks were placed in a position where they had little choice but to negotiate on the use of cash collateral.

If the banks had continued pressing for liquidation, they probably would not have succeeded, at least in the early weeks of the case. Likely as not, the bankruptcy court would have authorized the use of cash collateral, and the banks would have had substantially less in the way of protection than they would have received through negotiating a typical postpetition loan agreement. Consequently, the banks and the debtor initiated discussions on a postpetition lending arrangement.

Interim Loan Agreement—Months 1–3

Faced with a renewed hearing on the involuntary use of cash collateral, the banks agreed to an interim loan agreement that was intended to remain for approximately three months. Under the interim financing arrangement, the banks agreed to advance an additional $5 million in excess of the formula under the revolver. The postpetition loans were given superpriority status over administrative expenses under Bankruptcy Code §§ 503(b) and 507(b).

Although the interim loan agreement permitted operations to continue, the funding levels were not adequate because of the seasonal nature of the phosphate business. On the one hand, Beker needed additional availability. On the other, the banks needed even further protections than those granted under the interim loan agreement. As the interim loan agreement was expiring, the stage was set for negotiations on a long-term financing agreement.

Long-Term Financing Agreement

Beker needed substantially more financing than the additional $5 million granted under the interim loan agreement. The banks appeared willing to extend additional financing if they were adequately secured by new collateral. However, additional collateral was not readily available.

The debtor offered—and the banks accepted—a direct lien on the Florida plant and mine[3] as part of the collateral package to secure an additional $10 million of financing. However, the banks would not advance the additional $10 million based solely on the Florida collateral.

To break the logjam, the debtor offered to grant the banks a $10 million first lien on the Idaho plant and mine. Because the Debentures were already secured by a first lien on the plant and mine, the debtor's strategy required subordinating the debentureholders' lien to the new bank financing.

An official committee had been appointed to represent debentureholders.[4] The committee refused to agree to a subordination of the debentureholders' lien on the Idaho assets. Consequently, Beker initiated a proceeding in the bankruptcy court under Bankruptcy Code § 364(b)(1) to subordinate the debentureholders' lien to $10 million of new bank financing.

Financing Litigation

The effort by Beker to subordinate the debentureholders' lien led to approximately three months of nonstop litigation. Although successful, the litigation was costly to the debtor and its creditors in several respects.

Because of the seasonal nature of the phosphate business, a substantial portion of the new financing that the banks were willing to advance would have been required in the operation of the Idaho plant and mine. However, the banks held no collateral in Idaho. Thus, the banks advised the debentureholders that the banks were unwilling to finance assets on which they had no liens. The debentureholders were unable or unwilling to find any source of financing to operate their collateral in Idaho. In substance, the debentureholders were asking the banks to advance significant new monies for the benefit of the debentureholders. The result was a litigation that continued approximately three months.

Beker attempted to establish at trial in the bankruptcy court that the debentureholders' liens were adequately protected because new financing would permit the Idaho plant to remain in operation, thus preserving the going-concern value of the collateral. The bankruptcy court rejected the debtor's theory and required Beker to find replacement liens.

Meanwhile, the length of the litigation was damaging Beker's business. Beker needed new financing in the early winter to meet the seasonal demands of the Idaho plant. Because the litigation continued for months, Beker essentially "missed" the winter season. As a result, it later became necessary to terminate operations in Idaho and mothball the Idaho plant. If the debentureholders had not fought the subordination of their lien, the Idaho plant might have earned enough money in the winter season so that operations would not have been discontinued.

The financing litigation resulted in a lengthy opinion by Bankruptcy Judge Howard C. Buschman, which is also discussed in paragraph 3 below under "Reported Decisions." The Beker opinion is one of the few instances in which existing liens have been subordinated to new financing over the objection of the prepetition secured creditor. In addition, the Beker decision is apparently the only reported case in which public debt has been subordinated to new financing.

The bankruptcy court required, as a condition to the subordination of the debentureholders' lien, that the debentureholders be granted replacement liens. The bankruptcy court ruled that the debentureholders would have "adequate protection" by being granted a subordinate lien on the Connecticut office building and a subordinate lien on all collateral held by the banks.[5]

In the meantime, the banks finally obtained the watertight protections usually afforded in postpetition financing agreements. The new projections for the banks were

- Antipriming injunctions
- Precluding the debtor from obtaining any other financing without the banks' approval
- Precluding the debtor from substituting collateral held by the banks
- Prohibiting the debtor or any subsequent trustee from using cash collateral without the banks' agreement
- Prohibiting the debtor or any subsequent trustee from applying to use cash collateral in the event of a default under the bank loan agreement
- Requiring the debtor to confirm the validity of the prepetition liens
- Precluding the debtor and any subsequent trustee from challenging any of the banks' liens

The "long-term" financing agreement lasted one year. The banks, which had long sought a liquidation of Beker's assets, announced from the outset that they would not renew the loan upon its expiration. As it later turned out, the banks kept their word.

The "long-term" financing agreement permitted Beker to draw down an additional $10 million in an over-advance under the revolver. As security, the banks were given a direct lien on the Florida plant and mine together with a first lien for $10 million on the Idaho plant and mine.

The litigation over approval of the postpetition loan agreement was successful only in appearance. The litigation dragged on so long that fresh financing was not available until after the winter season in Idaho had closed. Consequently, Beker missed the best season of the year during which it could hope to make a profit. Having lost rather than made money in the winter, it soon became necessary for Beker to terminate operations in Idaho and move for authority to sell or abandon the facilities.[6]

In the meantime, the litigation was also costly for the debentureholders. After the Idaho plant was closed and mothballed, the Debentures fell to the low 20s. At the lowest point during the case, the Debentures traded in the low 10s. Anyone who bought Beker Debentures at the low point made one of the best investments in the 1980s. At the high when Beker was confirming its chapter 11 plan, the Debentures were trading at $140.

Complete Termination of Operations

The long-term financing agreement terminated one year after its commencement. From the outset, some but not all of the banks announced that they would not renew the loan agreement. They kept their promises.

The Idaho plant and mine already had been closed. With financing to be terminated, Beker's management and counsel concluded that continuing operations in Louisiana and Florida was impossible. Management and counsel also concluded that they could not establish "adequate protection" for the involuntary use of cash collateral under Bankruptcy Code § 363(c)(2)(B). More important, the financing agreement itself precluded the involuntary use of cash collateral. Further, utilizing proceeds of inventory and receivables would have not been adequate working capital to continue operations without fresh advances from the banks. Thus, management decided to discontinue operations at the plant in Louisiana and the mine in Florida. Discontinuing operations at a manufacturing plant destroys asset values. As a result of the termination of production at the Idaho plant and mine, the assets in Idaho were sold later in the case largely for paper consideration. Because the banks had a $10 million first lien on the Idaho assets, little was left for debentureholders.

The same fate befell the Louisiana plant. A major natural resources company offered to purchase the Louisiana plant for a substantial cash price. Some of the banks believed that the purchaser could be forced to raise its price. The purchaser, on the other hand, announced that the price would not increase, only drop if the sale were not completed on the schedule imposed by the purchaser. The debtor attempted to meet the purchaser's deadline, but secured creditors delayed, believing a higher price could be realized. As a consequence, the purchaser withdrew its offer and later renewed its bid at a fraction of the previous price. Ultimately, the sale closed at the substantially lower price, resulting in a loss to the estate and its creditors.

The Beker case demonstrated how delay can adversely affect a troubled company. Delay in the approval of the long-term financing agreement in the first months of the case caused the debtor to miss the most profitable season of the year and resulted in a termination of operations in Idaho. Unable to operate or even maintain the Idaho assets, the debtor was forced to sell its assets for a fraction of their replacement value.

Delay in the sale of the Louisiana plant led to another nightmare. The purchaser lived up to its threat and reduced the price when a sale could not be completed on schedule. Delay had other effects detrimental to the interest of creditors. The loss of sales resulted in the erosion of working capital, which caused the discontinuation of manufacturing operations. As it turned out, the market for phosphate fertilizer began to improve within weeks after the last of Beker's operations had been terminated. From the time that operations were discontinued until confirmation more than a year later, Beker's earnings (if it had been able to stay in business) as a result of increased world prices for phosphate fertilizers would have generated cash and created value sufficient to pay creditors nearly in full. Ultimately, the plan of reorganization paid debentureholders in full, resulted in a small loss to the secured bank creditors, but left the unsecured creditors recovering approximately 8 percent of their claims.

Appointment of a Reorganization Trustee and Confirmation of a Plan

The Beker case was an investor's nightmare. The infighting among the bank creditors damaged the business through inadequate financing in the early months and a complete termination of financing a year later. Using Beker as an example, investors should be wary of purchasing debt in a chapter 11 company when the secured bank creditors are at one another's throats.

Other unexpected heartaches befell creditors and investors. The slump in fertilizer prices continued longer than experts had predicted. Being forced to sell facilities at the bottom of a market is an unpleasant experience. The Beker case demonstrated how assets costing $250 million to duplicate may be sold for almost nothing in the midst of an industry recession. Taking Beker as an example, investors should not assume that hard asset values will survive an industry recession.

More than two years after the case began, confirmation remained elusive. A purchaser had come forward offering to buy Beker's remaining assets. The purchaser–plan sponsor was the same entity that had previously purchased the Idaho plant and mine. The proposal for a plan entailed purchasing the Florida mine, Beker's last remaining asset, issuing securities of the acquiror to the debentureholders, and cashing out the banks at a small loss.

Although a plan sponsor was available, the creditor constituencies were still in a stalemate, with certain of the banks fighting to avoid any loss. Unless the stalemate could be broken, the case would never confirm.

To break the logjam, the debtor's counsel embarked upon a bold strategy by moving to withdraw as attorneys for the debtor. The U.S. Trustee, recognizing the case's problems, responded by moving for the appointment of a reorganization trustee and threatening a conversion to chapter 7.

The strategy worked. The arsenal available to the bankruptcy judge gave the court leverage to bring the warring factions together on a plan.

After three years of torture, the case confirmed. By the last months, good fortune was finally smiling upon creditors. The phosphate fertilizer market had improved drastically, and so had the fate of the debentureholders. Under the plan of reorganization, the Beker debentureholders would own a substantial portion of the equity of a major phosphate fertilizer manufacturer. Where the Beker Debentures had traded in the 10s, the bonds traded in the 130s near the confirmation of the plan. The debentureholders' ultimate recovery was attributable to a substantial increase in the world price for phosphate fertilizers, not in the intrinsic value of hard assets.

A limited number of assets were carved out, and the proceeds from their liquidation were earmarked for general unsecured creditors. At confirmation, it was projected that unsecured creditors would recover 1 or 2 percent. Fortunately, the liquidator appointed by the unsecured creditors adroitly managed the sale of the earmarked assets and distributed 8 percent to his constituency.

Reported Decisions

The major constituencies in the Beker case were all represented by experienced and aggressive counsel. Given the staggering losses that were facing every creditor group, the result was continual litigation that led to several important, reported decisions. The following is a summary of the opinions[7] handed down in the Beker case:

1. *Appointment of Debentureholders' Committee*—55 B.R. 945 (1985). Some observers believe that the appointment of additional committees adds significant administrative expense or disrupts the chapter 11 process by providing equityholders or bondholders with counsel whose fees are paid by the estate. Consequently, some courts have avoided the appointment of additional committees, with the result that bondholders or their indenture trustees are found sitting on unsecured creditors' committees.

Although the debentures in the Beker case were secured, the bankruptcy court ordered the appointment under Section 1102(b) of an official debentureholders' committee. The bankruptcy court rejected the debtor's argument that secured creditors should not have the benefit of an official committee that would shift the cost of representing secured creditors to the estate. The bankruptcy court also rejected the argument that the well-represented indenture trustee obviated the need for a committee.

The *Beker* decision stands as leading authority for the appointment of an additional committee to represent bondholders. The *Beker* decision may also be used as authority for the appointment of an official committee to represent secured creditors when they are numerous.

2. *Injunction against Government Regulatory Action*—57 B.R. 611 and 57 B.R. 632 (1986). Beker sought to enjoin a state commission that had regulatory authority over the operation of trucking activities concerning the Florida phosphate mine. The bankruptcy court's decisions survey the authorities concerning the exception to the automatic stay for "police or regulatory power" under Section 362(b)(4). The opinions also examine the differing standards with respect to the granting of injunctions under Sections 105 and 362 and Rule 65 of the Federal Rule of Civil Procedure.

3. *Subordination of Prepetition Secured Claim to Postpetition Financing*—58 B.R. 725 (1986). The background for the court's 1986 financing opinion is contained in the sections of the case study entitled "Long-Term

Financing Agreement" and "Financing Litigation." The opinion is apparently the only reported case in which prepetition secured public debt was subordinated involuntarily to postpetition secured bank financing. The opinion is a magnificent example of how a court appraises a debtor's property. In addition, two legal conclusions stand out. First, the court ruled that Section 364(d) did not require that the proceeds of a secured loan be used for the benefit of collateral securing the loan. Second, the court held that granting additional collateral for a prepetition loan was not prohibited by the Bankruptcy Code under the doctrine of *Otte v. Manufacturers Hanover Credit Corp.*, 596 F.2d 1092 (2nd Cir. 1979), as long as the Code's requirement of "notice and a hearing" had been satisfied.

4. *Standards for Sale of Collateral for Less Than Secured Debt*—63 B.R. 474 (1986). Having closed the Idaho facility for lack of adequate working capital, the debtor proposed selling the plant for less than the amount of the secured encumbrances. The facility was subject to the banks' first lien for $10 million and the debentureholders' $65 million lien.

The debentureholders objected to a sale because the proceeds might not even have paid the banks in full. The resulting decision is a leading opinion on the power under Section 363(f) to sell collateral for less than the amount of the secured debt.

The bankruptcy court established a general rule that collateral ordinarily will not be sold unless the proceeds will produce an equity for the estate. Following a 1963 decision by a district court in the Southern District of New York, *In re Bernhard Altmann International Corp.*, 226 F. Supp. 201, the bankruptcy court held that collateral might be sold for less than the amount of the lien over the objection of a secured creditor when justified "by special circumstances to be developed at an evidentiary hearing" 63 B.R. at 477. Because of the "vagaries of the valuation process," the bankruptcy court further held that the proper exercise of discretion would require that the "special circumstances" be "compelling" and that the sale be "the best price attainable under the circumstances" *Idem.*

In the opinion, the court gave few examples of what might establish special circumstances. The court did indicate, however, that special circumstances might exist if the secured creditor chose not to take possession of the collateral but still refused to consent to a sale for less than the amount of its liens, thus "effectively insisting that others . . . continue to fund the property" 63 B.R. at 478. Other reported cases were more liberal in permitting the sale of property for less than the amount of a lien, but the bankruptcy court did not find the opinions compelling.

5. *Refusal to Permit Sale or Abandonment of Overcollateralized Property*—64 B.R. 900 (Bankr. S.D.N.Y. 1986), rev'd in part, 89 B.R. 336 (S.D.N.Y. 1988). The opinion by Bankruptcy Judge Buschman reported at 64 B.R. 900 was written after the trial that the court ordered in the opinion appearing at 63 B.R. 474. The vitality of the holding reported at 64 B.R. 900, and perhaps also that reported at 63 B.R. 474, is questionable in light of the reversal in part by District Judge Robert J. Ward reported at 89 B.R. 336.

In the opinion at 64 B.R. 900, the bankruptcy court examined whether there were "special circumstances" justifying a sale of collateral for less than the amount of the lien over the objection of the secured creditor. The court held that a sale was not justifiable under the *Lionel*[8] doctrine because the chapter 11 case was at a crucial stage. The court opined that the retention of the property "might serve as one of the vehicles attracting the investment capital that this Debtor needs" 64 B.R. at 906–7. The court also found that the apparently low price that the sale might bring offered no justification for a sale. The court found that Beker had adequate funds to maintain the nonoperating facility, although Beker itself chose not to utilize its limited cash resources in that matter.

Refusing to authorize the sale, the court then analyzed whether the debtor could abandon the property. In the eyes of the bankruptcy court, the legal issue was whether the *Lionel* test, which applies to preplan sales of property, should also apply to abandonment in chapter 11, even though the language of Section 554 apparently grants the debtor a nearly absolute right to abandon.

The bankruptcy court held that permitting abandonment could circumvent the plan process. Thus, the court held that the *Lionel* test, rather than the "business judgment test," applied to the abandonment of a significant asset in chapter 11.

In large part, the bankruptcy court based its decision not to abandon the property upon its holding that it was "perfectly clear" that the resulting cost of maintaining the property could be charged against secured creditors under Section 506(c). With respect to the liability of the secured bank creditors under Section 506(c), the court said it was "difficult to imagine a more clear case" 64 B.R. at 900. The district court, however, disagreed and reversed at 89 B.R. 336.

Based on undisputed evidence in the record, the district court found that the secured bank creditors had favored a prompt sale of the asset. The district court also found that there was insufficient evidence in the record to support the finding by the bankruptcy court that there was no bona fide offer to purchase the asset for a substantial amount. The district court suggested that the bankruptcy court should have attempted to sell the property in response to the substantial offer that had been made. Given these facts, the district court held that imposing costs on the banks under Section 506(c) was improper.

Strictly speaking, the district court reversed only that part of the opinion at 64 B.R. 900 that assessed maintenance expenses against the secured bank creditors under Section 505(c). The holding of the district court may actually have been broader. Some have read the opinion by District Judge Ward as ruling, after the fact, that the bankruptcy court was wrong both in refusing to sell the property and in refusing to abandon if a sale were not possible. One can only speculate as to whether the bankruptcy court would have refused to abandon had it known that the district court would not impose costs under Section 506(c).

6. *Assumption of Executory Contract*—64 B.R. 890 (1986). A party to the estate's largest executory contract had moved under Section 365 to compel an immediate assumption or rejection of the contract. The bankruptcy court, in the most significant aspect of its opinion, held that the relief it could grant was not limited to fixing a time for assumption or rejection. Consequently, the court conditioned an extension of time to assume or reject upon the assessment of the resulting costs against the secured creditors who sought more time. The holding by the bankruptcy court is possibly brought into question by the reversal of the district court on a related issue reported at 64 B.R. 900.

7. *Avoiding Unperfected Security Interest*—69 B.R. 937 (1987). The debtor was a party to a "lease" of telephone equipment at its executive office building. Because the telephone company had not filed a UCC financing statement, the bankruptcy court held that the telephone company was an unsecured creditor because its "lease" was actually a financing agreement, not a "true lease."

The opinion by Bankruptcy Judge Buschman surveys virtually all of the law with respect to a determination as to whether a lease is a "true lease" or a financing arrangement. For anyone litigating a similar issue, the opinion is a trial preparation checklist pointing out the significant facts of interest to the court.

Notes

1. Waiting so long to retain bankruptcy counsel is a mistake too often made by management. By the time counsel was retained, the debtor's working capital was exhausted. Most of the business problems in the case resulted from grossly inadequate working capital. Had counsel been retained earlier, the chapter 11 case could have been commenced when the company had greater cash availability, and the outcome likely would have been better.

2. Postpetition loan agreements usually provide that all proceeds from prepetition accounts receivable and inventory are applied first to repay prepetition debt. Soon after filing, the prepetition loans are fully repaid. All of the new advances under a revolver become postpetition loans that are often secured by greater assets than those that represented collateral for the prepetition debts. In addition, the typical postpetition financing order declares that the postpetition loans are valid and may not later be challenged. Thus postpetition lending often improves the bank's position.

3. Beker Phosphate Corporation was a separate debtor corporation with its own creditors. There was no readily apparent basis for substantive consolidation of the two debtors. Because there were no liens at the outset of the case on Phosphate's assets, the creditors of Phosphate stood to recover all of their debt. For whatever reason, Phosphate's creditors did not object to granting the banks a lien on the Florida plant and mine. The granting of the lien placed the Florida creditors in the same condition as the creditors of the parent corporation. Had the Phosphate creditors objected, it is not clear that the bankruptcy court would

have permitted the new financing over their objections or that the banks would have provided new financing without the Florida collateral. By not objecting, the unsecured creditors of Phosphate lost the chance to be repaid in full. Instead, they ended up recovering a few cents on the dollar just like all other creditors of Beker.

4. The opinion directing the appointment of a debentureholders' committee is discussed in paragraph 1 of the final section of this case study, entitled "Reported Decisions."

5. The Beker case demonstrated the unscientific nature of valuation hearings. Later in the case, it looked as though the replacement liens had no value and that the banks' first lien on the Idaho assets would wipe out the debentureholders. Fortunately, market conditions improved and allowed the debentureholders ultimately to recover all their debt.

6. The reported decisions on the resulting effort to sell or abandon the Idaho assets are discussed *infra* under paragraphs 4 and 5 of "Reported Decisions."

7. Unless otherwise noted, all opinions were by Bankruptcy Judge Howard C. Buschman, III.

8. See *Committee of Equity Security Holders v. Lionel Corp.*, 722 F.2d 1063 (2d Cir. 1983).

CHAPTER

20

Case Study: An Electric Utility Analysis

Martin J. Whitman
Whitman Hefferman Rhein Co., Inc.

This chapter has three purposes:

1. To explain how bankruptcy relief for troubled electric utilities under the Bankruptcy Reform Act of 1978, as amended, would be likely to operate
2. To explain how securities holders would be likely to fare (owners of first mortgage indebtedness, other secured obligations, debentures, preferred stocks, and common stocks)
3. To look at theoretical postbankruptcy scenarios that might be most helpful to reorganized electric utility businesses, in other words, making use of the favorable income tax attributes that could be created by asset write-downs in a chapter 11 reorganization.

Having troubled electric utilities seek relief under the Bankruptcy Code—despite its management burdens, uncertainties, and expenses— clearly ought to be helpful to the utilities themselves, their creditors, and their ratepayers. On the other hand, holders of equity securities—both preferred stocks and common stocks—probably will find their positions diluted materially. My firm, Whitman Heffernan Rhein Co., Inc., believes that the likely outcome of a reorganization is that the utility will be a leaner operation with a rational capitalization, creditors will emerge largely unscathed, and ratepayers will benefit by avoiding the burden of paying

Editor's note: This insightful case study of a utility bankruptcy attempts to show how an analysis made in 1985 by a sophisticated investor subsequently worked out. A summary of the reorganization plan filed in January 1990 is included, as well as the subsequent comments of the analyst.

electric rates derived from attempting to earn a return on grossly overvalued assets. Equityholders will be diluted, but much of their suffering will already have occurred through stock price drops that resulted when the nuclear problems became apparent.

The end result of a bankruptcy reorganization, pure and simple, is that assets are restated at realistic values, rather than at historic cost. Specifically, abandoned nuclear facilities are stated at zero, and nuclear facilities to be operated are stated at, say, a value of $2,000 per kilowatt rather than historic costs of, say, $4,000 to $6,000 per kilowatt. Rate-making decisions are based on earning a fair return on these reorganization values rather than historic costs. The reorganized company is recapitalized based on the new asset values. Debt securities are either reinstated or they participate in the reorganization. If there is reinstatement, the securities are deemed to be unimpaired.

Reinstatement, which would probably be the case for most first mortgages, entails curing defaults, paying back interest plus compensation for any damages incurred as a result of reliance by the mortgage holder on the contractual terms (perhaps equal to interest on interest?), and resuming payments on the reinstated securities. Debt securities, especially collateralized obligations, that participate in the reorganization are generally entitled to receive in value, but not in cash, their entire claim before payments are made to junior securities. Such claims are likely to be paid in cash, new mortgage securities, new debentures, new preferred stocks, and new common stocks. Reorganization plans are almost always consensual, growing out of negotiations among the participants in the reorganization: the company, known as the Debtor in Possession, or DIP, a secured creditors' committee, an unsecured creditors' committee, a preferred stockholders' committee, and a common stockholders' committee. A probable outcome of any electric utility bankruptcy reorganization would be that secured creditors would receive in value their entire claim, including postbankruptcy petition interest. This assumes that the reorganization value of the assets securing the debt equals or exceeds the face amount of the secured obligations, which was clearly the case for Consumers Power Company and Public Service Company of New Hampshire (PSNH). Unsecured creditors would receive almost all of their claim, but perhaps not all of the accrued, but unpaid, postpetition interest. Equity security holders would maintain their interest in the reorganized company, but on a highly diluted basis. For example, the common stockholders, who hold 100 percent of the common stock equity before reorganization, might hold anywhere between 2 and 20 percent of the common stock after reorganization.

It is probable that the write-off, or write-down, of overvalued nuclear facilities in a chapter 11 bankruptcy case would create for the electric utility favorable tax attributes in the form of net operating loss carrybacks and carryforwards; the NOL carryforwards would have a 1.5-year expiration. Given electric operations with a good earnings outlook and, in those cases where power requirements can be purchased for the indefinite future, good cash-flow outlooks, the reorganized companies can become attractive vehicles. Many probably will be unable to use up their NOLs in electric operations. For such reorganized companies, going to a holding company format and seeking diversified acquisitions may be very attractive; such reorganized companies could have the advantage over recently formed holding companies such as Dominion Resources and Florida Progress of having huge amounts of favorable tax attributes in the form of NOLs.

We do not believe that a chapter 11 reorganization for an electric utility need be, or ought to be, terribly complicated and protracted, even granting that many of the major reorganizations completed so far have been lengthy and have involved much struggle among the parties. First, unlike most chapter 11 reorganizations—Braniff Airways, White Motors, Itel, or Wickes—electric utilities have stable, predictable sources of operating income from their ongoing operations. Second, unlike Manville Corporation or UNR Corporation, the liabilities of, and claims against, an electric utility seem to be readily ascertainable and measurable. Insofar as earnings and cash flows can be predicted reliably, and insofar as the amount of claims can be determined, reorganization can be readily accomplished. The principal lack of predictability for electric utility earnings postreorganization are based on the rates and returns on investments that regulators are likely to allow. In the second section of this report, we speculate on simplified reorganization scenarios for Consumers Power and Public Service of New Hampshire based on two assumptions:

1. Normalized earning power is represented by operating income before federal income taxes for 1984—all as derived from existing facilities that are in operation and excluding all interest costs, other income, other expense, and AFUDC (Allowance for Funds Used During Construction).
2. Normalized earning power as above, increased by 50 percent.

I believe the calculations, while speculative, have enough elements of reality that they are useable for making investment decisions today, especially decisions by creditors.

My investment recommendation for troubled nuclear utilities is to acquire First Mortgage and General and Refunding Mortgage Obligations when available at yields to maturity of 17 percent or better. Within that parameter, the lower the dollar price of the obligation, the more attractive it is. If the issuers stay solvent, interest and principal repayment service will not be interrupted and the investors will enjoy an above-average yield based on either a "yield to maturity" or a "yield to the time of an improved credit rating." If chapter 11 relief is sought, there will be an interruption of debt service and probably a decline in the market price of the issue held. However, investment risk ought to be small to nil. Upon reorganization, the holder of secured obligations will receive full value (principal amount plus interest) in the securities of a company that will be stronger financially (and probably operationally) than it was prepetition. Investment judgments about junior securities, however, are harder to make.

How Seeking Bankruptcy Relief Would Be Likely to Affect Troubled Utilities

As far as we can tell, most people in the financial community, as well as in the electric utility industry, have little or no idea of what filing for bankruptcy reorganization will actually mean. Indeed, in many cases, it seems as if the common perceptions are the diametric opposite of reality. Many people seem to think there would be draconian consequences if there were to be a bankruptcy filing—to wit, the bankrupt utility would stop operating and/or the electric utility industry would be unable to raise new capital. This is just not so. Fundamentally, what will happen is that upon filing, the cost of capital for the filing utility will go down, not up. Day-to-day operations will be unaffected by the filing.

In order to understand what is likely to happen, we contrast below what we believe to be certain widely held beliefs of "conventional wisdom" with our own view of likely events. These views are based on our extensive experience with various chapter 11 cases. Many of the opinions that we think are popularly held and that contrast with our views appear to be contained in three articles:

1. *Report on Analysis of the Potential Effects of Bankruptcy—An Analysis of Strategic Options for Jersey Central Power & Light Company*

   A Study Prepared for New Jersey Board of Public Utilities by Arthur Young & Company. October 1980.

2. *The Effects of Bankruptcy—An Analysis of the Impact on Three Investor-owned Utilities*

   A. K. Rodgers Ratcliffe and Paula A. Tomasetti. Morgan Stanley & Co. May 1984.

3. "Public Utility Bankruptcy: Lessons for Management and Creditors," by Jacob J. Worenklein and Glenn S. Gerstell (both of Millbank, Tweed, Hadley & McCloy). *Public Utilities Fortnightly* (December 6, 1984).

The Morgan Stanley report is based in large part on the Arthur Young report. Thus, the two articles reflect similar views on most topics.

There is a common belief, as stated in the *Public Utilities Fortnightly* article that a bankruptcy filing would have adverse effects "on the state as a whole, including loss of tax revenues for state and local governments, loss of state pension fund investments in securities of the affected utility, higher levels of unemployment in the state, and loss of business confidence in the state."

These assertions seem to have no basis in fact. There is unlikely to be any loss of tax revenues for state and local governments resulting from a chapter 11 filing. Initially, there would be an "automatic stay" preventing payment of taxes that are due and payable but not yet paid. Governments would be a priority creditor, and there is no question that all taxes owed would be paid eventually. However, it is possible that tax payments could be stretched out for six years from the date of assessment. Postpetition tax debts would be paid as accrued by the utility operating under chapter 11. Insofar as state pension funds are invested in the debt securities of the affected utility, they are unlikely to suffer any loss from an investment point of view. There will be an interruption of debt service during the reorganization period, but eventual recovery should be at values that are well in excess of the current market prices for most of the debt securities of troubled utilities. If any one factor is likely to result in higher levels of unemployment in the state and loss of business confidence in the state, it would be ultrahigh electric rates caused by permitting utilities to earn a return on assets that, by any standard other than historic cost, are grossly overvalued.

The *Public Utilities Fortnightly* article also raises the specter of "uncertainty as to future levels of service by a bankrupt utility; possibly increased rates for customers of the bankrupt utility over the long term; and adverse impact on cost of capital to other utilities in the state" in the event that a utility files for bankruptcy.

The bankruptcy case will not have any material effect on future levels of electric service, whereas in bankruptcy reorganization, management would continue to operate the utility as DIP. Both Morgan Stanley and Arthur Young, in their analyses, seem to believe that a trustee will assume responsibility for the management of an electric utility seeking bankruptcy reorganization. This is unlikely to be the case. Theoretically, a trustee or, alternatively, an examiner could be appointed if there were suspicions of fraud, dishonesty, incompetence, or gross mismanagement. As far as we can tell, no such situation exists for any of the troubled utilities whose securities are publicly traded.

Throughout a bankruptcy case, management will be burdened by administrative problems of trying to devise and negotiate an acceptable plan of reorganization, and major (not day-to-day) operating and financial decisions will be subject to court hearings and scrutiny by various claimants and parties in interest. It is problematic, though, whether this would place greater burdens on management than does the present environment where intensive efforts have to be made to avoid filing. Rates to customers will be lower for those companies that file for relief compared with those that don't—both short-term and long-term. There is no evidence that a bankruptcy filing by one utility would impact the cost of capital for other utilities one way or the other, any more than the bankruptcies of Penn Central or Rock Island affected the cost of capital for the Union Pacific or CSX. Indeed, there are two separate electric utility industries today, largely unrelated insofar as the cost of capital for an individual company is concerned: troubled companies and untroubled companies.

One thing seems certain, however: the cost of capital postpetition for the troubled utility would be materially lower than it would be prepetition. Indeed, today the cost of capital for troubled utilities—either debt capital or equity capital—is prohibitive. Creditors, of course, would much rather lend to utilities postpetition than prepetition and would rather do so at lower rates based on the credit worthiness of either the postpetition securities while a company is in reorganization or the securities of the recapitalized company after reorganization. Soundly capitalized and with adequate interest coverage, the reorganized company's debt would probably sell on a Baa, or more likely, an A basis, even given the stigma of reorganization; this compares with current ratings in the B to Caa ranges for the debt of troubled utilities today. Equity investors, too, would make investments in the reorganized companies' securities based on how soundly financed the utility is, as well as the earnings and dividend outlooks. These outlooks would be far more certain postreorganization than they are now. The concept of bankruptcy reorganization embodies the idea of giving debtors a fresh start. We have no question that, postreorganization, the securities markets' evaluations of reorganized companies will look at the facts as they exist after the "fresh start."

In contrast to the above, the principal thrust of the Morgan Stanley and the Arthur Young analyses is that any electric utility filing for bankruptcy will be forever stuck with a materially higher cost of capital than if the utility did not file. We at Whitman Heffernan Rhein disagree. Neither Morgan Stanley nor Arthur Young provides any reasoning or statistical evidence to support this position.

It appears to us that the underlying rationale for the Arthur Young–Morgan Stanley positions that costs will go up if a utility seeks bankruptcy relief is based on a view that the emotional stigma attached to a firm that sought bankruptcy relief will cause investors to shun the securities of that issuer for the indefinite future, even though the problems leading to the filing revolved around nuclear cost overruns, something likely to be nonrecurring. In contrast, it is our view that investors, especially creditors, will examine the merits of particular securities in light of the economic and financial facts as they exist at the time. If, postreorganization, an electric utility is a healthy operator and soundly financed, we believe the market will appraise its securities to reflect the healthy, sound conditions that then exist. We, of course, believe we are right. We do not think it is a close call.

In one respect, we believe that the "conventional wisdom" about bankruptcy filings is absolutely correct. That revolves around the uncertainties created by seeking relief. A bankruptcy proceeding, like litigation, is an adversary proceeding. It gives rise to numerous uncertainties as to how protracted the reorganization proceedings will be and how any particular claimant or party will fare. This remains true even in the case of electric utilities where we think reorganization is fairly easy to accomplish because of the relatively high predictability of future earnings and future cash flows, as well as the relatively high ability to measure the amount and types of claims. As a matter of fact, while we think there is minimal investment risk for the holders of secured obligations of electric utilities, the principal risks that do exist for public holders of secured obligations arise out of the bankruptcy process itself. Representation of the publicly held secured debt on a creditors' committee may be less than vigorous, especially if the representatives on the committee are bank indenture trustees rather than bondholders with meaningful ownership positions. Because reorganization plans are consensual and basically the product of negotiations, public security holders tend to be less protected than in nonbankruptcy situations where aggrieved security holders may seek to obtain protection from the private bar and the SEC, both of whom have relatively unfettered access to our court systems. As a practical matter, such access does not exist in chapter 11 for passive security holders without direct representation on an official committee. The DIP, as a practical matter, usually has an almost indefinite period of exclusivity to propose a reorganization plan, during which time the DIP tries to reach a consensual agreement with the various committees (although, as a matter of law, the initial exclusivity period, without obtaining extensions, is only 180 days from the date of filing to the date when acceptances of a plan of reorganization are obtained). That plan is subject to veto by securities holders; in the case of debt instruments, the plan has to be approved by two thirds in dollar amount of an impaired class and more than half of the number of holders. However, in the case of public debtholders, it appears unlikely that there would be a vote against a plan of reorganization as long as that plan gave the security holder a meaningful premium above the market and unless there was a bondholder in a position to finance a proxy solicitation in opposition to a plan of reorganization. Acknowledging that this risk exists, we still think the odds favor the system working well enough so that, in the reorganization of a troubled electric utility, secured debtholders will either be reinstated (that is, unimpaired) or else receive in the reorganization a package of securities whose value will equal the face amount of the debt plus postpetition interest.

Based on our reorganization scenarios, acquiring unsecured debt securities at present prices has investment attraction. However, such instruments do have a special risk compared with Consumers Power and Public Service of New Hampshire mortgage debt in that, if both companies continue to seek to avoid filing, they can dilute a present unsecured holder's position by issuing more unsecured debt. Both companies are severely limited by indenture restrictions in issuing large amounts of new mortgage debt.

Morgan Stanley and Arthur Young believe that bankruptcy filings will raise operating costs for the operating utility. By and large, nothing could be farther from the truth. For example, Morgan Stanley and Arthur Young talk of "the need to obtain essential supplies and services (at prices probably far higher than those prior to bankruptcy) such as fuel or purchased power." Unless a vendor of supplies and services has taken leave of his senses, he would much rather ship postpetition than prepetition because of the reduced credit risk and the greater chance of receiving timely payments. Such costs would go down, not up.

Both Arthur Young and Morgan Stanley believe that the regulatory authorities would continue to set rates and otherwise regulate the electric utility during a reorganization, but that if a dispute arose between the court and a regulatory commission, the court's authority would prevail. We have no view. However, the practical probabilities are that courts would be passive and, unless there was a relatively clear showing of regulatory overreaching, the role of the state regulators would remain unchanged prepetition versus postpetition.

After filing, electric utilities' cash flows would improve dramatically because the "automatic stay" would stop cash payments to all unsecured prepetition creditors and dividends to shareholders. Some cash payments may well need to be made to secured creditors to avoid litigation on the issue of relief from the "automatic stay." On the other hand, a bankruptcy case is expensive; large fees, subject to court control, are paid to attorneys, investment bankers, experts, and accountants. In the case of a publicly owned troubled electric utility, however, such charges are unlikely to have a material adverse effect on either cash flow or reorganization values because these electric utilities are such large businesses. This, of course, would not necessarily be the case for small businesses.

Whether or not the nuclear facilities ought to be placed in operating service is, in the first instance, an engineering question. It most certainly is not a bankruptcy reorganization question. The bankruptcy case, in effect, addresses only the question of what is the appropriate value for nuclear facilities given the fact that historic cost is no longer an appropriate value. This report is a financial one, and we make no judgments as to whether any nuclear facility, be it Seabrook I or Midland 2, should be placed in operation. Rather, the conclusion we reach is that, as an integral part of the reorganization process, these facilities should be properly valued based on hard data about comparative costs for the efficient production of power. Such values, we suppose, could range from zero if a particular facility is to be abandoned to, say, $2,500 per kilowatt if the facility is properly placed in service and is to be used and useful.

A useful concept for determining a reorganization value for a nuclear plant that is to be used and useful might be the commonly accepted regulatory concept of "avoided cost" or "fully avoided cost." Under one "avoided cost" approach, the nuclear facility would be valued at that figure which would permit the plant, over its useful life, to generate electricity at the same price per kilowatt hour as would be allowed for a comparably sized modern coal-fired facility that is to be build *de novo* on time and within budget.

Insofar as it is appropriate from an engineering point of view to complete nuclear facilities and place them in service, lenders would prefer, by a wide margin, to finance completion of the plants postpetition rather than prebankruptcy petition. Postpetition credit risks ought to be minimal. This, however, does not mean that it would be easier for a utility to place a nuclear facility in service while a bankruptcy case is under way compared with prepetition. Since the financing of completion and construction expenditures would have to be approved by the bankruptcy court, this would introduce yet another arena in which antinuclear forces could oppose placing a facility in service. On the other hand, it may be possible that a particular bankruptcy court could be a catalyst to solve the regulatory morass companies now find themselves in by trying to complete, and place in service, facilities such as Midland and Seabrook. We doubt, however, that most bankruptcy courts would prove to be of any real help in this regard; most probably would not be much of a hindrance, either.

The fact of abandonment of nuclear facilities could give rise to a significant number of new claims against a utility by contractors, suppliers, and workers. These claims would have to be handled by the utility, whether or not it had filed for relief. If these claims are to arise postpetition for a filing company, the handling of these claims probably would not differ materially from what would happen in the case of a nonfiling company. Also, there probably would not be much difference between filing and nonfiling utilities in the treatment of claims against a utility that might arise out of allegations that the existence of nuclear facilities had created health and safety hazards for segments of the population.

Morgan Stanley and Arthur Young reiterate a commonly held belief that a utility seeking bankruptcy relief will lose the benefit of having outstanding low interest debt issued at times of lower general interest rates. It is reasoned, therefore, that postreorganization interest costs would have to be higher than would otherwise be the case. This is just not so for two reasons. First, when the business is recapitalized, one of the factors determined in the reorganization process itself is what the levels of debt service ought to be concerning periodic interest costs and debt amortization payments. There is a concerted effort to have the debt service payments meet a "feasibility" standard, that is, be conservative. (For example, in our reorganization scenarios below, we recapitalized the companies to have an indicated coverage-of-interest charge of not less than 2:1.) Second, there are many a priori reasons why, in the reorganization process, low interest debt will be found to be "unimpaired" (unaffected by the filing). In that event, the low interest debt would be reinstated with all terms of that debt instrument unchanged.

Simplified Reorganization Scenarios

It would be impossible today, before there has been any filing for bankruptcy relief, to state with any degree of precision what the capitalization of a reorganized electric utility would be. The specifics would be a function of the plan of reorganization that emerges from negotiations, as well as a determination of what reorganization value will be, which, in turn, will be determined at the bottom line by what normalized earning power is deemed to be, as well as the rate of return that results in that normalized earning power.

However, despite the lack of any precision, earning power for an electric utility company is relatively predictable (at least as compared with companies in other industries); and capitalization ratios, as well as allowed rates of returns, are so relatively uniform that preliminary calculations of simplified reorganizations can be made that are quite meaningful from an investment point of view. They become particularly meaningful from a secured creditors' point of view in measuring against the background of current bond prices the potential risks and rewards. However, risk reward judgments, by those interested in junior securities, become harder and harder to make as one moves down the scale of "juniority."

In each of our four simplified reorganization scenarios, holders of Consumers Power and PSNH First Mortgage Bonds and holders of PSNH General and Refunding (Second) Mortgage Bonds either are reinstated or receive full value, in other words, principal plus interest, regardless of how conservative our assumptions are. Holders of Consumers Power unsecured debt are also made whole under any of our scenarios, and holders of PSNH unsecured debt are made almost whole under any scenario. Holders of Consumers Power and PSNH preferred stock, preference stock, and common stock could conceivably face hugely dilutive "haircuts," using highly conservative assumptions. However, using less conservative, and probably more realistic, assumptions as to a normal earning power for reorganization purposes, all Consumers Power and PSNH securities holders would obtain meaningful participations in their reorganized companies.

Our simplified reorganization scenarios are based on the following assumptions.

Conservative Scenarios:

1. Normal annual earning power is deemed to be only actual 1984 results, equal to net operating income before income taxes (and excluding all interest costs, other income or expense, and AFUDC)—$600 million for Consumers Power and $140 million for Public Service of New Hampshire. Implicit in these figures is the concept of no return whatsoever on the Midland or Seabrook nuclear facilities, as well as no material amounts of future rate increases that would exceed increased expenses.

2. Asset value, which we also define as the rate base and as reorganization value, is to be that figure which results in the utility's net operating income before income taxes being equal to a 15 percent return on the rate base. Thus, the rate base or reorganization value for Consumers Power is $4 billion and for PSNH, $933,333,333. This compares with their actual total capitalizations at December 31, 1984 of approximately $7.2 billion for Consumers Power and $2.4 billion for PSNH.

3. As reorganized, the total capitalization will equal reorganization value, and capitalization ratios are to be as follows:

> Debt 50 percent
> Preferred stock 10 percent
> Common stock 40 percent

4. In no instance is net operating income before federal income taxes to provide coverage of interest charges of less than 2:1.

5. Insofar as new debt securities and preferred stocks are to be issued in the reorganization, they are to carry the following terms, which we estimate will cause the issues to sell at about their face amount given present market conditions:

Long-term unsecured debt
Coupon: 14 percent
Maturity: 15 Years
Callable: Three-year call protection then callable at 107; declining each year thereafter
Sinking fund: Modest after fifth year

Preferred stock
Dividend: 13 percent
Callable: Same as long-term unsecured debt
Sinking fund: Modest after seventh year
Redeemable: 20 Years

6. Postpetition interest plus penalties, if any, are to be paid in cash at the time of consummation of the plan of reorganization. Such cash would be readily available as it will accumulate during the period of reorganization. Other things being equal, reorganization value ought to increase during the pendency of the reorganization proceedings by approximately the amount of retained earnings created during the postpetition period prior to consummation of a plan, insofar as such retained earnings exceed postpetition interest, which is to be paid to creditors upon reorganization but which was not accrued for financial accounting purposes while the DIP was in reorganization. We have not taken these retained earnings figures into account in our scenarios.

Insofar as we would do so, increased values and participations ought to be attributed to junior securities.

7. The lowest coupon first mortgages of Consumers Power and all PSNH mortgage debt are deemed to be unimpaired and are reinstated. The amount of such debt to be reinstated is limited, in the case of Consumers Power, by the factor that overall indebtedness cannot exceed 50 percent of reorganization value.

8. The reorganization is to comport with a modified rule of absolute priority—senior securities are to have the value of their claims paid in full before anything of value is given to junior classes of securities, modified by the factor that all classes of securities are entitled to participate in the reorganization. As a practical matter, something like this modified rule of absolute priority is what will emerge from almost any plan of reorganization where the parties involved are reasonably competent, the parties try to obtain reasonable resolutions of conflict, and the law, as embodied in the Bankruptcy Reform Act of 1978, is complied with. For example, although holders of PSNH unsecured debt receive only 71 percent of their claims under our worst case, holders of PSNH common stock (who now own 100 percent of that issue) still receive 2.5 percent of the common stock to be issued by the reorganized Public Service Company of New Hampshire. On a "strict" rule of absolute priority basis, the old common stock would receive nothing.

Less Conservative Scenarios

Only assumptions 1 and 2 above are changed to reflect an increase in net operating income before taxes of 50 percent. Thus, annual normal earning power is deemed to be $900 million for Consumers Power and $210 million for PSNH. Consumers Power's rate base becomes $6 billion and PSNH's, $1.4 billion.

The Results

Details on how these assumptions work out are contained in Table 20.2 for Consumers Power and Table 20.3 for PSNH. Pertinent summaries of the data are shown in Table 20.1, as follows:

Table 20.1.

Consumers Power Company (000)

	Conservative Scenario	More Liberal Scenario
Total Capitalization 12/31/84		
(Actual)	$7,169,369	$7,169,369
Total Capitalization after Reorganization	4,000,000	6,000,000
% of Claims to be Paid in Reorganization by Reinstatement or in Reorganization Value:		
Old First Mortgage Debt	100.0%	100.0%
Old Unsecured Debt	100.0%	100.0%
Old Preferred-Preference Stock	13.7%	100.0%
Old Common Stock (vs. Book Value)	2.7%	13.7%
% of Reorganized Company's Common Stock to be Issued to:		
Old First Mortgage Debt	7.6%	0
Old Unsecured Debt	79.2%	11.8%
Old Preferred Stock	9.4%	68.6%
Old Common Stock	3.8%	19.6%
Interest Charges — Times Earned	2.5 times	2.6 times

Public Service Company of New Hampshire (000)

	Conservative Scenario	More Liberal Scenario
Total Capitalization 12/31/84		
(Actual)	$2,371,674	$2,371,674
Total Capitalization after Reorganization	933,333	1,400,000
% of Claims to be Paid in Reorganization by Reinstatement or in Reorganization Plan 2 Old Classes of Secured Debt		
First Mortgage and General and Refunding Debt	100.0%	100.0%
Old Unsecured Debt	70.6%	100.0%
Old Preferred Stock	2.9%	56.0%
Old Common Stock (vs. Book Value)	1.0%	9.2%
% of Reorganized Company's Common Stock to be Issued to:		
Old Unsecured Debt	95.0%	52.7%
Old Preferred Stock	2.5%	32.1%
Old Common Stock	2.5%	15.2%
Interest Charges — Times Earned	2.4 times	2.3 times

Table 20.1 Consumers Power Reorganization Plans 487

Table 20.2. Consumers Power Company Reorganization Plans (000)

A $600,000 Net Operating Income Before Income Taxes
Earnings

Rate Base (Earnings ÷ 15) $4,000,000

% of New Common Stock Issued

	% To:
Old 1st Mtg.	7.6%
Old Unsecured Debt	79.2
Old Pfd.-Preference	9.4
Old Common Stock	3.8
	100.0%

Capitalization at 12/31/84 (Actual)

1st Mortgage Debt	$2,521,743
Unsecured Debt and	
Capitalized Lease Obligations	1,266,671
Pfd. and Preference Stock	1,098,619
Common Stock	2,282,336
	$7,169,369

% of Claims Paid

Old 1st Mtg.	100.0%
Old Unsecured Debt	100.0%
Old Pfd.-Preference	13.7%
Old Common Stock	
(Claim Based on	
12/31/84 Book Value)	2.7%

Reorganization Capitalization

1st Mtg. Debt (Reinstated)	$2,000,000
New 13% Preferred Stock	400,000
New Common Stock	1,600,000
	$4,000,000

Reorganization Securities are
Issued as Follows:

Issue	Amount	To Whom Issued
1st Mtg. Debt Re- instated	$2,000,000	Old 1st Mtg.
New 13% Pfd. Stk.	400,000	Old 1st Mtg.
New Common Stock	121,743	Old 1st Mtg.
New Common Stock	1,266,671	Old Unsecured Debt
New Common Stock	150,000	Old Pfd.-Preference
New Common Stock	61,586	Old Common Stock

Reorganization Income Account

Net Operating Income	
Before Income	
Taxes	$600,000
Interest Charges	240,000
Income Before In- come Taxes	$360,000
GAAP Tax Accrual	
@ 50%	$180,000
Net Income	$180,000
Preferred Dividend	$ 52,000
Available for Common	$128,000
Interest Coverage	2.5 Times
Return on Common	
Equity Post Tax	8.0%

B $900,000 Net Operating Income Before Income Taxes
Earnings

Rate Base (Earnings ÷ 15) $6,000,000

% of Claims Paid

Old 1st Mtg.	100.0%
Old Unsecured Debt	100.0
Old Pfd.-Preference	100.0
Old Common Stock	13.7
(Claim Based on	
Book Value)	

Reorganization Capitalization

1st Mtg. Debt Reinstated	$2,521,743
New 14% Debentures	478,257
New Preferred Stock	600,000
New Common Stock	2,400,000
	$6,000,000

(continued)

Table 20.2.   (Cont.)

Reorganization Securities are Issued as Follows:

Issue	Amount	To Whom Issued
1st Mtg. Debt Reinstated	$2,521,743	Old 1st Mtg. Debt
New 14% Debentures	478,257	Old Unsecured Debt
New 13% Preferred Stock	600,000	Old Unsecured Debt
New Common Stock	188,414	Old Unsecured Debt
New Common Stock	1,098,619	Old Pfd.-Preference
New Common Stock	312,967	Old Common Stock

% of New Common Stock Issued To:

Old Unsecured Debt	11.8%
Old Preferred	68.6
Old Common Stock	19.6
	100.0%

Reorganization Income Account

Net Operating Income Before Income Taxes		$900,000
Interest Charges:		
1st Mtg.	$277,000	
14% Debentures	70,000	347,000
Income Before Income Taxes		$553,000
GAAP Tax Accrual @ 50%		$276,500
Net Income		$276,500
Preferred Dividend		$ 78,000
Available for Common		$198,500
Interest Coverage		2.6 Times
Return on Common Equity Post Tax		8.3%

Table 20.3.   Public Service Company of New Hampshire Reorganization Plans (000)

		A $140,000 Net Operating Income Before Income Taxes	
		Earnings	
Rate Base (Earnings ÷ 15)	$933,333	**% of New Common Stock Issued To:**	
		Old Unsecured Debt	95.0%
Capitalization at 12/31/84		Old Preferred Stock	2.5
		Old Common Stock	2.5
1st Mtg. Debt	$ 198,526		100.0%
Gen'l & Refunding Mtg. Debt	186,468		
Unsecured Obligations	750,000		
Preferred Stock	321,553	**% of Claims Paid**	
Common Stock	915,127		
	$2,371,674	2 Old Classes of Mtg. Debt	100.0%
		Old Unsecured Debt	70.6
Reorganization Capitalization		Old Preferred Stock	2.9
		Old Common Stock	1.0
1st Mtg. Debt Reinstated	$ 198,526	(Claim Based on Book Value)	
Gen'l & Refunding Mtg. Reinstated	186,848		
New 14% Debenture	81,292		
New 13% Preferred Stock	93,333		
New Common Stock	373,334		
	$ 933,333		

Table 20.3. (Cont.)

Reorganization Securities are As Follows:

Issue	Amount	To Whom Issued
1st Mtg. Debt Reinstated	$198,526	Old 1st Mtg.
Gen'l & Refunding Reinstated	186,848	Old Gen'l & Ref
New 14% Debentures	81,292	Old Unsecured Debt
New 13% Pfd. Stk.	93,333	Old Unsecured Debt
New Common Stock	354,667	Old Unsecured Debt
New Common Stock	9,334	Old Preference Stk.
New Common Stock	9,333	Old Common Stock
	$933,333	

% of New Common Stock Issued To: Reorganization Income Account

Net Operating Income Before Income Taxes	$140,000
Interest Charges on Reinstated Debt	47,000
Interest Charges on New Debentures	11,381
Income Before Income Taxes	$ 81,619
GAAP Tax Accrual @ 50%	$ 40,809
Net Income	$ 41,810
Preferred Dividend	$ 12,133
Available for Common	$ 29,676
Interest Coverage	2.4 Times
Return on Common Equity Post Tax	7.9%

% of New Common Stock Issued To:

Old Unsecured Debt	52.7%
Old Preferred Stock	32.1
Old Common Stock	15.2
	100.0%

% of Claims Paid

2 Old Classes of Mtg. Debt	100.0%
Old Unsecured Debt	100.0
Old Preferred Stock	56.0
Old Common Stock	9.2

B $210,000 Net Operating Income Before Income Taxes Earnings

Rate Base (Earn ÷ 15)	$1,400,000

Reorganization Capitalization

1st Mtg. Debt Reinstated	$198,526
Gen'l & Refunding Mtg. Reinstated	186,648
New 14% Debentures	314,626
New 13% Preferred Stock	140,000
New Common Stock	560,000
	$1,400,000

Reorganization Securities are Issued as Follows:

Issue	Amount	To Whom Issued
1st Mtg. Reinstated	$198,526	Old 1st Mtg.
Gen'l & Ref. Reinstated	186,848	Old Gen'l & Ref.
New 14% Debentures	314,626	Old Unsecured Debt
New 13% Debentures	140,000	Old Unsecured Debt
New Common Stock	295,374	Old Unsecured Debt
New Common Stock	180,000	Old Preferred Stock
New Common Stock	84,626	Old Common Stock
	$1,400,000	

Reorganization Income Account

Net Operating Income Before Income Taxes		$210,000
Interest Charges on Reinstated Debt	$47,000	
New 14% Debentures	44,048	91,048
Income Before Income Taxes		$118,952
GAAP Tax Accrual @ 50%		$ 59,476
Net Income		$ 59,476
Preferred Dividend		$ 18,200
Available for Common		$ 41,476
Interest Coverage		2.3 Times
Return on Equity Post Tax		7.4%

The Postbankruptcy Scenario

There has been a post–World War II trend for companies operating in regulated industries to become wholly owned subsidiaries of holding companies that frequently diversify outside of the original regulated business. This had occurred, *inter alia*, for airlines, independent telephone companies, natural gas transmission companies, fire and casualty insurance companies, and railroads. It seems to us that a good-sized number of such holding companies have been inordinately successful, at least from the point of view of their common stockholders, when competent managements were able to combine the excess cash flow from the operating subsidiaries with favorable tax attributes of the parent to engage in various "asset conversion" programs ranging from making aggressive acquisitions to reacquiring common stock.

Such a postbankruptcy scenario may be in the cards for one or more of the troubled electric utilities. It is probable that the write-off, or write-down, of nuclear facilities will result in the creation of huge net operating loss carryforwards—something especially likely to be the case under the provisions of the Bankruptcy Tax Act of 1980 insofar as the reorganization entails an exchange by debtholders of their credit instruments for voting equity securities.

Also, insofar as a reorganized utility has limited needs for, say, the next 10 or 15 years to build new power-generating capacity, that company probably will become a good-sized net cash generator.

Companies that distribute electricity (or gas) at retail are subject to regulation by the Securities and Exchange Commission under the Public Utility Holding Company Act of 1935. Such companies (for example, American Electric Power or Allegheny Power System) lack the flexibility to either diversify or use the holding company as a financing vehicle. It is possible for electric utilities to obtain exemptions from the Act. In the case of most utilities, though, there is an intrastate exemption from the Public Utility Holding Company Act for companies that distribute electricity in only one state (for example, Consumers Power Company).

It is highly speculative at this juncture to postulate that, postreorganization, a specific troubled utility could become a growth vehicle because its basic characteristics would include competent management, favorable cash flow, and good income tax attributes. Nonetheless, it seems productive to recognize the long-term possibility that such characteristics could exist.

Author's Subsequent Comments and Reflections
May 7, 1990

I recently reread my April 1985 article "Electric Utility Bankruptcy: Myths and Realities." Frankly, I am surprised at how prescient the article was. In January 1988, PSNH filed for relief under chapter 11 of the Bankruptcy Act.

That utility is expected to emerge as a reorganized company (and to be acquired by Northeast Utilities) before the spring of 1991. The New Hampshire bankruptcy provided an interesting laboratory in which to test out the propositions I was putting forward in the 1985 article.

I described in some detail how the bankruptcy process was likely to work. By and large, the article described quite accurately how the PSNH bankruptcy process actually did work. Further, the theories expounded there held up well as to how the various classes of securities holders would fare vis-á-vis each other—mortgage debt, unsecured debt, preferred stock, and common stock. The article also was correct in predicting that the bankruptcy case itself would enhance the financial viability of the Company from the date of filing forward. It was predicted in the article that the bankruptcy case itself would have little or no impact on whether or not the Seabrook Nuclear Station became operational; that was an engineering and political question, not a financial question. This, too, was right on the mark.

The article, however, proved to have been off-base in two key respects: to wit, the potential values of net operating loss carryforwards for income tax purposes, and the likely outcomes if the company sought rate increases and/or the appropriate regulatory authorities sought rate decreases or rate freezes.

The potential value attributable to tax losses was greatly diminished by the passage of the 1986 Tax Act. In particular, the 1986 Tax Act diminished the potential value of operating tax losses for chapter 11 companies in three ways: the basic corporate tax rate was reduced from 46 to 34 percent, making the cash savings from the use of tax losses less than before; rules on changes in ownership became more onerous; and in many cases the use of tax attributes in any given year became subject to extremely restrictive net worth limitations.

The biggest surprise to me, however, in the PSNH reorganization was the lack of resistance to large-scale rate increases by both the New Hampshire Public Utility Commission and the New Hampshire Consumer Advocate. It was reasoned in the article that (a) since a reorganized company is a new juridical unit, and (b) since historic cost was no longer the basis for financial accounting and therefore probably was not any basis for regulatory accounting, then the new retail rates set would be based on something other than historic cost. (For example, new rates could have been set at the average retail rates for New England utilities, something that would have resulted in drastic rate reductions in New Hampshire.) Instead, as part of the global reorganization package, PSNH is to be permitted annual rate increases that will ensure its rates will be either the highest, or among the highest, in the nation for the foreseeable future.

As far as I can tell, the legal basis for permitting such huge rate increases was that it was equitable to continue to place a large degree of weight on historic cost because, based on accepted utility standards, the Company had been, by and large, prudent in all its past actions, especially in regard to Seabrook. The practical basis for permitting such large rate increases was that it was popularly believed (though I disagree) that it prevented the bankruptcy case from being even more contentious and drawn-out than was actually the case.

In any event, the resolution of the rate-making problem in New Hampshire probably has set a precedent for what is likely to happen in future insolvencies of companies whose prices are regulated by the government authorities, especially public utilities. This means, of course, that junior securities will work out at far better prices than were assumed in the article because reorganization values will be larger. Based on the reasoning that was contained in the article, constituencies I represented acquired, between June 1987 and November 1987, for about $140 million cash, approximately $200 million principal amount of mortgage debt of PSNH. That debt, much of which received interest and principal payments while the bankruptcy case was in progress, now will be paid out at its principal amount plus interest (as well as interest on interest where interim interest payments were not received). While the returns on this investment in mortgage debt turned out to be highly satisfactory, the rewards would have been much greater had we invested in unsecured debt instead. Were I to do it all over again, however, I would still focus on mortgage debt. The risk/reward ratio is frequently much better in acquiring and holding unsecured debt. The risk/reward ratio in acquiring at a substantial discount and holding mortgage debt will still be good enough, though. In addition, there is no way to quantify the comfort factor that comes with being a large holder of debt that is adequately secured once the issuer of that debt has to seek chapter 11 relief.

Appendix: Reorganization of PSNH Public Service Company of New Hampshire*

On January 2, 1990, Northeast Utilities Service Company (NUSCO) filed a Third Amended Joint Plan of Reorganization. The Public Service Company of New Hampshire joined NUSCO, the Official Committee of Unsecured Creditors, the Official Committee of Equity Security Holders, Citicorp, Consolidated Utilities & Communications, Inc. and Shearson Lehman Hutton, Inc. as proponents of the Plan.

The Plan appears to contain no major differences from the Second Amended Joint Plan. The Disclosure Statement did, however, present a range of estimates for distributions to preferred and equity holders as a percentage of their respective claims under various scenarios and assumptions. Under the best case scenario, Preferred holders will receive a

*This appendix was submitted by George Putnam III of *The Bankruptcty Data Source.*

distribution equal to 69.75 percent of their claims. Under the worst case scenario, Preferred holders will receive a distribution equal only to 29.1 percent of their claims. When the same analysis is applied to Common shareholders, the distribution will be worth between $3.88 and $0.72.

The Third Amended Joint Plan of Reorganization Summary is reprinted here in its entirety for your information.

*Footnotes and Terms of Reorganization Securities**

1. During the Reorganization Case, PSNH has paid and continues to pay interest on its First Mortgage Bonds, its General and Refunding Bonds, the Nuclear Material Lease, and its Term Loan Agreements (Class 4). The estimates of claims assume that these interest payments will continue.
2. The Bankruptcy Court has authorized the Debtor to issue a new series of G & R Bonds and use the proceeds to retire the Series E G & R Bonds. If the new bonds are issued, they will be paid in full on the Effective Date.
3. Newco: A new corporation incorporated under New Hampshire law which shall be authorized to acquire and own PSNH's interest in Seabrook. The corporation's name shall be North Atlantic Energy Corporation or any name that NU may elect.
4. The Bankruptcy Court has authorized the Debtor to issue up to $112.5 million of new Pollution Control Revenue Bonds financing. This financing would be used to refinance the Nuclear Material Lease, the Domestic Term Loan, and the Enrodollar Term Loan. The financing would be secured by a new series of G & R Mortgage Bonds and the Series H G & R Bonds that currently secure these loans. If the refinancing takes place, NU may elect to either repay the financing in cash within 90 days after the Effective Date or keep such financing outstanding. Such financing would be secured by a new series of Reorganized PSNH First Mortgage Bonds.
5. Estimated principal plus pre- and post-petition interest and interest on interest through 7/1/90, the projected Effective Date of the Plan. If the Effective Date does not occur by July 1, 1990, the Plan provides that regularly scheduled current interest payments will resume with the first regularly scheduled interest payment after July 1, 1990.
6. Estimated principal plus pre- and post-petition interest and interest on interest through 7/1/90, the projected Effective Date of the Plan. If the Effective Date does not occur by July 1, 1990, the Plan provides that regularly scheduled current interest payments will resume with the first regularly scheduled interest payment after July 1, 1990.
7. If the new Reorganized PSNH first mortgage bonds are so substituted, they will be secured by a first lien on substantially all of the property of Reorganized PSNH other than the Seabrook assets.

*Footnotes refer to Table 20.4.

Table 20.4. Public Service Company of New Hampshire

Summary of Northeast Utilities Service Company's Third Amended Plan of Reorganization for PSNH (Jointly Proposed with the Public Service Company of New Hampshire, the Official Committee of Unsecured Creditors, the Official Committee of Equity Security Holders, Citicorp, Consolidated Utilities & Communications, Inc., and Shearson Lehman Hutton Inc. (All amounts in $millions except stock which is in shares)

	Estimated Allowed Claims	Will Receive Upon Reorganization
Class 1		
Secured Claims (First Mortgage Bonds, Series M through S, inclusive, and Series V)	131.585(1)	Unimpaired. Principal, post-petition interest, interest on interest, and fees and expenses under the indenture shall be paid in full in cash on the Effective Date or as soon as practical thereafter.
Class 2		
General and Refunding Mortgage Bonds, Series A through E, and any series issued to refinance Series E	195.7(1)	Unimpaired. Principal, post-petition interest, interest on interest, and fees and expenses under the indenture shall be paid in full in cash on the Effective Date or as soon as practical thereafter. (2) No distribution shall be made on account of the G & R Mortgage Bonds, Series H, which secure claims under the Nuclear Material Lease, the Eurodollar Term Loan Agreement, or the Domestic Term Loan Agreement. Distribution with respect to the Lease and the Agreements shall be limited to that provided in Classes 3 and 4.
Class 3		
Nuclear Material Lease	45.0(1)	Unimpaired. Principal, post-petition interest, interest on interest, and fees and expenses shall be paid in full in cash on the Effective Date or as soon as practical thereafter. On the Effective Date, the lease will be cancelled and the property subject to such lease shall be retained by Reorganized PSNH (or Newco (3) if the Merger occurs on the Effective Date).(4)
Class 4		
Term Loan Agreements (Eurodollar Term Loan and the Domestic Term Loan)	67.5(1)	Unimpaired. Principal plus post-petition interest, interest on interest, and fees and expenses paid in cash in full on the Effective Date or as soon as practical thereafter. (4)
Class 5		
Ser. A Third Mortgage Bonds	328.5(5)	Unimpaired. Principal, pre-petition, post-petition interest, and interest on interest at the rate specified in the bonds shall be paid in full in cash.

(continued)

494

Table 20.4. (Cont.)

	Estimated Allowed Claims	Will Receive Upon Reorganization
Class 6		
Secured Claims arising on account of the obligation of the Debtor under the 10.5% Pollution Control Bond Indenture which obligation is evidenced by $100 million in principal amount of Series B Third Mortgage Bonds.	134.5(est.)(6)	At the discretion of NU, Class 6 may be impaired or unimpaired. If Class 6 is impaired, the bonds will remain outstanding and claimants will receive cash equal to claims for pre-petition and post-petition interest, interest on interest at the rate specified in the bond and fees end expenses under the indenture. Under this alternative, most legal, equitable, or contractual rights will not be altered. However, if NU so elects, the indenture will be modified to provide for the substitution of $100 million in principal amount of Reorganized PSNH Mortgage Bonds for the $100 million in principal amount of Series B Third Mortgage Bonds. (7) Alternatively, NU may elect on or before July 1, 1990, to refund the 10.5% Pollution Control Bonds and pay all of the claims in cash in full.
Class 7		
Secured Claims for Taxes and other Secured Claims Not Included in Classes 1 through 6	undetermined	Unimpaired. Claimant will be treated under Option A or B at the election of Reorganized PSNH. Option A: the property securing the claim may be transferred to the claimant. Option B: defaults shall be cured and the maturity reinstated.
Class 8		
Priority Unsecured Claims	nominal	Unimpaired. Paid in full in cash.
Class 9		
Customer Deposits and Credits	2.00(est.)	Unimpaired. Paid or honored by Reorganized PSNH in cash or in the ordinary course of business.
Class 10		
General Unsecured Claims Not Included in Classes 8, 9, 10A or 11 through 13 (Including the existing PSNH Debentures)	857.4(8)	Impaired. Pro rata share of: a) $545 million in cash (less amount required to pay Class 10A); and b) an estimated 21,150,000 shares of Reorganized PSNH Common Stock which will be converted into $423 million in cash in the Merger. (9) (10) The total distribution is estimated to result in full payment of principal and pre-petition interest as well as $110.6 million of post-petition interest. If the Effective Date occurs after 7/1/90, the cash distribution will accrue interest from 7/1/90 to the Effective Date at the Contingent Bond Yield (11) to maturity less 175 basis points.

(continued)

495

Table 20.4. (Cont.)

	Estimated Allowed Claims	Will Receive Upon Reorganization
Class 10-A		
Unsecured Claims of $900 or less	2.0 (maximum allowed amount)	Unimpaired. Paid in full in cash. If the Effective Date occurs after July 1, 1990, the distribution will accrue interest from July 1, 1990, to the Effective Date at the Contingent Bond Yield (11) to maturity less 175 basis points.
Class 11		
Old Preferred Stock and Damage or Rescission Claims re Existing Preferred Stock	615,360 shares ($100 par value) as of 9/30/89, and 10,400,000 shares ($25 par value) as of 9/30/89	Impaired. Class 11 will receive the sum of the following: a) 82.2% of the first 8,555,000 shares of Reorganized PSNH Common Stock (10) distributable to claimants in Classes 11 and 12 (12); b) 44% of the next 1,335,000 shares of Reorganized PSNH Common Stock so distributable (12); c) 86.67% of the Series A Contingent Notes (14); d) 65% of the Series B Contingent Notes (14); e) 44% of the Series C Contingent Notes (14); and f) Contingent Warrant Certificates (15) evidencing the right to receive an aggregate of 65% of approximately 8,431,000 NU Warrants (16) that may be issued on the Merger. However, if a Seabrook Cancellation Event occurs prior to the Effective Date, no Contingent Notes will be issued and Class 11 shall receive a pro rata distribution of: a) 82.2% of the first 8,555,000 shares of Reorganized PSNH common stock distributable to Classes 11 and 12; b) 86.67% of all remaining shares so distributed; c) Contingent Warrant Certificates (17) evidencing the right to receive in the aggregate 86.67% of the NU Warrants (18) that will be issued on the Merger. Upon the Merger, holders of the common stock of Reorganized PSNH will be entitled to receive $20 per share and holders of Contingent Warrant Certificates will be entitled to receive the NU Warrants.
Class 12		
Old Common Stock and Damage or Rescission Claims re Existing Common Stock.	42,154,548 shares as of 11/8/89 (19)	The balance of the Reorganized PSNH Common Stock, the Contingent Notes, and the Contingent Warrant Certificates remaining after all distributions have been made to Class 11.
Class 13		
Warrants and Claims re Warrants	13,420,199 warrants as of 10/25/89 (19)	As of the Effective Date, all warrants shall be deemed to be void and of no further force or effect. However, claimants will receive an amount equal to $0.10 for each Warrant outstanding, immediately prior to the Effective Date.

496

8. Class 10 claims include: a) $813.7 million principal amount of unsecured debentures, notes, and other debt instruments less $62.7 million in unamortized original issue discount; b) $84.9 million of unpaid pre-petition interest on these instruments; and c) (NUSCO estimate) other claims of $21.5 million. This total assumes that all disputed claims are disallowed. It is possible that total allowed claims in Classes 10 and 10A will exceed $900 million. If this occurs, a condition to the Effective Date will not be satisfied.

9. Under the Plan, the number of shares of Reorganized PSNH Common Stock to be distributed to Class 10 shall be determined by the following formula: $A = (B - C)/20$; where A is the number of shares of Reorganized PSNH Common Stock to be issued to Class 10; B is the sum of the Petition Date Amount of Allowed Claims in Classes 10 and 10-A plus $110.6 million; and C is $545 million. The Plan provides that if the Debtor's cash on the balance sheet for the month immediately preceding the Effective Date is less than $60 million, then: a) the amount of cash distributed to Class 10 claimants will be decreased dollar for dollar by the amount of the shortfall; and b) the number of shares of Reorganized PSNH common stock distributed to Class 10 claimants will be increased at the rate of one share per $20 of shortfall provided that cash distributed to Classes 10 and 10-A will not be less than $525 million.

10. Reorganized PSNH Common Stock: Authorized: 100,000,000 shares. Par value: $1.00. Dividends may be declared and paid only from retained earnings accumulated after the Effective Date that exceed $75 million. However, prior to the Merger, Reorganized PSNH will be obligated to distribute a quarterly stock dividend at the rate of 2% per quarter during the period beginning on the earlier of 7/1/90 and the Effective Date and ending 12/31/90 and 3% per quarter thereafter until the merger or termination of the Merger. Upon the Merger Date, all shares shall be converted into the right to receive $20 per share in cash. After the shares have been converted, holders will have no continuing equity interest in Reorganized PSNH.

11. Contingent Bond Yield: (CBY) a percentage equal to 175 basis points in excess of the average yield to maturity as of the date which is 30 days prior to the Effective Date, of seven selected issues of electric utility first mortgage bonds or debentures. The CBY would have been 11.4% as of 10/25/89.

12. The number of shares of Reorganized PSNH Common Stock distributable to Classes 11 and 12 shall be determined by the following formula: $A = B/20$ where: A equals the number of shares distributable to Classes 11 and 12; and B equals the Residual Amount (13).

13. Residual Amount: By formula. The residual amount was projected to be $244 million as of July 1, 1989.

14. Contingent Notes: On the Effective Date or immediately thereafter, Reorganized PSNH will issue $82 million principal amount each of

Series A and Series B Contingent Notes and Reorganized PSNH (or Newco) will issue up to $41 million principal amount of Series C on the Contingency Termination Date. (15) Upon the transfer of Seabrook to Newco, the Notes will become the sole obligation of Newco. All notes will mature on July 1, 2000. The terms and conditions governing all series of Contingent Notes shall be identical. Interest shall be paid at a rate equal to the Investment Percentage (16) payable each January 1 and July 1 after the applicable Contingency Termination Date (16) and on and after 7/1/90 if the Contingency Termination dates have not occurred by that date. Until the respective Contingency Termination Dates occur, the notes will bear no interest and the obligors shall have no obligation with respect to the principal amount. Redeemable in whole or in part at the obligor's option at any time on or after July 1, 1995, at a redemption price equal to the principal amount, plus a premium equal to the applicable percentage outlined below of the Investment Percentage times the principal amount plus accrued interest to redemption.

If Redeemed	Percentage of Investment Percentage
After 6/30/95 and prior to	
7/1/96	102.1%
Thereafter and prior to	
7/1/97	71.8
7/1/98	43.7
7/1/99	22.2
On or after 7/1/99	0

If the respective Contingency Termination Dates have not occurred on or before five years after the Effective Date, the Notes, including accrued interest, shall be cancelled. The Contingent Note Agreement will prohibits the payment of cash dividends on Newco common stock during the first two years after the Effective Date.

15. Contingency Termination Dates: Each of the Contingent Notes have specific Contingency Termination Dates (the dates on which the Notes become obligations of Newco or Reorganized PSNH and begin to accrue interest.) In all cases, if the contingency termination date (CTD) occurs before the Effective Date, the Effective Date shall be deemed the CTD. The specifics of the CTD are as follows: Series A: the date upon which a) the NRC has issued an unrestricted full-power operating license for Seabrook Unit I and which license shall be in full force; and b) the operator of Seabrook shall have received permission from the NRC to proceed with power beyond 5% of the unit's rated

power. Series B: the earlier of a) the Series C CTD and b) the date upon which the following three conditions have been met: i) the NRC has issued a full power license for Seabrook and the license shall be in full force; ii) power ascension testing to an amount not less than 90% of rated power has been successfully completed; and iii) Seabrook Unit shall have been turned over to the New England Power Exchange for dispatch. Series C: the first date upon which the following two conditions are met and continue to be satisfied: i) the NRC shall have issued an unrestricted full-power operating license for Seabrook and the license shall be in full force; and ii) the warranty run shall have been successfully completed.

16. Investment Percentage: a percentage amount equal to the Contingent Bond Yield plus a Coupon Adder. The Coupon Adder would have been 400 basis points as of 10/25/89. The Coupon Adder will be adjusted up or down from 400 basis points on the Effective Date.

17. Contingent Warrant Certificates: (CWC) Issued on the Effective Date. Holders of the CWC will be entitled to receive NU Warrants at the time of the Merger. If the Merger Agreement terminates, the CWC will automatically be cancelled.

18. NU Warrants: The number of NU Warrants to be issued will be one-fifth of the number of shares of Existing PSNH Common Stock outstanding immediately prior to the Effective Date. (NU estimates the number of warrants to be 8,431,000). Each warrant entitles the holder to purchase one share of NU common at $24.00 per share in cash. The exercise for the NU Warrants will begin on the Merger Date.

19. According to the third quarter 10-Q of PSNH, the number of shares and warrants reflects all exchanges of warrants and 17.5% debentures for shares of existing PSNH common stock pursuant to the Spear, Leeds & Kellog Settlement.

SOURCE: Second Amended Joint Plan of Reorganization and Disclosure Statement by Northeast Utilities Service Company, the Public Service Company of New Hampshire, the Official Committee of Unsecured creditors, the Official Committee of Equity Security Holders, Citicorp, Consolidated Utilities & Communications, Inc. and Shearson Lehman Hutton, Inc., filed January 2, 1990.

Bond Ratings

Standard & Poor's modifies ratings with "+" designating a higher rating within a category and "−" designating a lower rating within a category.

Moody's applies numerical modifiers to ratings within a category, with 1 indicating rank's highest, 2 indicating midrange, and 3 indicating lowest (that is, B1 rates higher than B3).

Quality	Moody's	Standard & Poor's	Description
High grade	Aaa	AAA	Bonds that are judged to be of the best quality. They carry the smallest degree of investment risk and are generally referred to as "gilt edge." Interest payments are protected by a large or exceptionally stable margin, and principal is secure.
	Aa	AA	Bonds that are judged to be of high quality by all standards. Together with the first group, they comprise what are generally known as high-grade bonds. They are rated lower than the best bonds because margins of protection my not be as large.
Medium grade	A	A	Bonds that possess many favorable investment attributes and are to be considered as upper-medium-grade obligations. Factors giving security to principal and interest are considered adequate.
	Baa	BBB	Bonds that are considered as medium-grade obligations—they are neither highly protected nor poorly secured.
Speculative	Ba	BB	Bonds that are judged to have speculative elements, their future cannot be considered as well assured. Often the protection of interest and principal payments may be very moderate.
	B	B	Bonds that generally lack characteristics of the desirable investment. Assurance of interest and principal payments or of maintenance of other terms of the contact over any long period of time may be small.
Default	Caa	CCC	Bonds that are of poor standing. Such issues may be in default or there may be elements of danger present with respect to principal or interest.
	Ca	CC	Bonds that represent obligations which are speculative to a high degree. Such issues are often in default or have other marked shortcomings.
	C		The lowest-rated class in Moody's designation. These bonds can be regarded as having extremely poor prospects of attaining any real investment standing.
		C	Rating given to income bonds on which interest is not currently being paid.
		D	Issues in default withh arrears in interest and/or principal payments.

SOURCES: *Moody's Bond Record* (Moody's Investors Service, Inc., New York) and *Bond Guide* (Standard & Poor's).

B

Chapter 11 Filing Forms

The following are approved forms for filing a chapter 11 bankruptcy. As can be seen from perusing the forms, considerable information is on file concerning bankrupt companies. Chapter 11 filings are available to the public in the Bankruptcy Clerk's office at the Federal courts in the district where the case was filed.

Documents shown Below include the following:

Form 1: Voluntary Petition
Form 2: Schedule Of Assets And Liabilities
Form 3: Statement Of Financial Affairs For Debtor Engaged In Business
Form 4: List Of Creditors Holding 20 Largest Unsecured Claims

Form No. 1

VOLUNTARY PETITION

UNITED STATES BANKRUPTCY COURT FOR
THE ＿＿ DISTRICT OF ＿＿＿＿＿

In re

＿＿＿＿＿＿＿＿＿＿＿＿＿＿＿＿ ,

Debtor [set forth here all names including trade names used by Debtor within last 6 years].

Social Security No. ＿＿＿＿＿＿＿＿＿

and Debtor's Employer's Tax Identification No. ＿＿＿＿＿＿＿＿＿＿＿＿＿＿＿

Case No. ＿＿＿＿＿＿

VOLUNTARY PETITION

1. Petitioner's mailing address, including county, is ＿＿＿＿＿＿＿＿＿＿＿＿＿＿＿＿＿＿＿＿＿＿＿＿＿＿＿＿＿＿＿＿＿＿＿＿＿＿＿ .

2. Petitioner has resided [or has been domiciled or Petitioner's principal place of business has been or The principal assets of the petitioner have been] within this district for the preceding 180 days [or for a longer portion of the preceding 180 days than in any other district].

3. Petitioner is qualified to file this petition and is entitled to the benefits of title 11, United States Code as a voluntary debtor.

4. [If appropriate] A copy of petitioner's proposed plan, dated ＿＿＿＿ , is attached [or Petitioner intends to file a plan pursuant to chapter 11 or chapter 13] of title 11, United States Code.

5. [If petitioner is a corporation] Exhibit "A" is attached to and made part of this petition.

6. [If petitioner is an individual whose debts are primarily consumer debts] Petitioner is aware that [he or she] may proceed under chapter 7, 11, 12 or 13 of title 11, United States Code, understands the relief available under each such chapter, and chooses to proceed under chapter 7 of such title.

7. [If petitioner is an individual whose debts are primarily consumer debts and such petitioner is represented by an attorney.] A declaration or an affidavit in the form of Exhibit B is attached to and made a part of this petition.

WHEREFORE, petitioner prays for relief in accordance with chapter 7 [or chapter 11 or chapter 13] of title 11, United States Code.

Signed: ＿＿＿＿＿＿＿＿＿＿＿＿＿＿＿＿＿ ,

Attorney for Petitioner.

Address: ＿＿＿＿＿＿＿＿＿＿＿＿＿ ,

＿＿＿＿＿＿＿＿＿＿＿＿＿＿＿＿＿＿＿

OFFICIAL FORMS   **Form 1**

*[Petitioner signs if not represented
by attorney.]*

_____,
Petitioner.

I, _____, the petitioner named in the foregoing petition, declare under
penalty of perjury that the foregoing is true and correct.
Executed on _____.

Signature: _____
                    Petitioner.

Exhibit "A"

*[If petitioner is a corporation, this Exhibit "A" shall be completed and attached to the
petition pursuant to paragraph 5 thereof.]*

[Caption as in Form No. 1]

FOR COURT USE ONLY

_____

Date Petition Filed

_____

Case Number

_____

Bankruptcy Judge

1. Petitioner's employer identification number is_____.

2. If any of petitioner's securities are registered under section 12 of the Securities
and Exchange Act of 1934, SEC file number is_____.

3. The following financial data is the latest available information and refers to
petitioner's condition on_____.

a. Total assets:	$_____	
b. Total liabilities:	$_____	

		Approximate number of holders
Secured debt, excluding that listed below	$_____	_____
Debt securities held by more than 100 holders	$_____	_____
Secured	$_____	_____
Unsecured	$_____	_____
Other liabilities, excluding contingent or unliquidated claims	$_____	_____
Number of shares of common stock	$_____	_____

Form 1   OFFICIAL FORMS

Comments, if any: _____

_____

4.   Brief description of petitioner's business: _____

_____

5.   [*If presently available, supply the following information*]   The name of any person who directly or indirectly owns, controls, or holds, with power to vote, 20% or more of the voting securities of petitioner is _____

_____.

6.   [*If presently available, supply the following information*]   The names of all corporations 20% or more of the outstanding voting securities of which are directly or indirectly owned, controlled, or held, with power to vote, by petitioner are __

_____

_____.

Exhibit "B"

[*If the petitioner is an individual whose debts are primarily consumer debts, this Exhibit "B" shall be completed and attached to the petition pursuant to paragraph 7 thereof*].

[*Caption as in Form No. 1*]

FOR COURT USE ONLY

Date Petition Filed

Case Number

Bankruptcy Judge

OFFICIAL FORMS   **Form 2**

Form No. 2
SCHEDULES OF ASSETS AND LIABILITIES

[Caption as in Form No. 1]

Schedule A.—Statement of All Liabilities of Debtor

Schedules A–1, A–2, and A–3 must include all the claims against the debtor or the debtor's property as of the date of the filing of the petition by or against the debtor.

Schedule A–1.—Creditors having priority

(1)	(2)	(3)	(4)	(5)
Nature of claim	Name of creditor and complete mailing address including zip code	Specify when claim was incurred and the consideration therefore: when claim is subject to setoff, evidenced by a judgment, negotiable instrument, or other writing, or incurred as partner or joint contractor, so indicate; specify name of any partner or joint contractor on any debt	Indicate if claim is contigent, unliquidated, or disputed	Amount of claim

a. Wages, salary, and commissions, including vacation, severence and sick leave pay owing to employees not exceeding $2,000 to each, earned within 90 days before filing of petition or cessation of business (if earlier specify date). $_____

b. Contributions to employee benefit plans for services rendered within 180 days before filing of petition or cessation of business (if earlier specify date). $_____

c. Claims of farmers, not exceeding $2,000 for each individual, pursuant to 11 U.S.C. § 507(a)(5)(A). $_____

d. Claims of United States fishermen, not exceeding $2,000 for each individual, pursuant to 11 U.S.C. § 507(a)(5)(B). $_____

e. Deposits by individuals, not exceeding $900 for each for purchase, lease, or rental of property or services for personal, family, or household use that were not delivered or provided. $_____

f. Taxes owing [itemize by type of tax and taxing authority]

   (1) To the United States $_____

   (2) To any state $_____

   (3) To any other taxing authority $_____

      Total $_____

Form 2   OFFICIAL FORMS

Schedule A-2.—Creditors holding security

(1)	(2)	(3)	(4)	(5)	(6)
Name of creditor and complete mailing address including zip code	Description of security and date when obtained by creditor	Specify when claim was incurred and the consideration therefore; when claim is subject to setoff, evidenced by a judgment, negotiable instrument, or other writing, or incurred as partner or joint contractor, so indicate; specify name of any partner or joint contractor on any debt	Indicate if claim is contingent, unliquidated, or disputed	Market Value	Amount of claim without deduction of value of security
				Total	$_____

Schedule A-3.—Creditors holding unsecured claims without priority

(1)	(2)	(3)	(4)
Name of creditor [including last known holder of any negotiable instrument] and complete mailing address including zip code	Specify when claim was incurred and the consideration therefore; when claim is contingent, unliquidated, disputed, subject to setoff, evidenced by a judgment, negotiable instrument, or other writing, or incurred as partner or joint contractor, so indicate; specify name of any partner or joint contractor on any debt	Indicate if claim is contingent, unliquidated, or disputed	Amount of claim
		Total	$_____

Schedule B—Statement of All Property of Debtor

Schedules B–1, B–2, B–3, and B–4 must include all property of the debtor as of the date of the filing of the petition by or against the debtor.

Schedule B-1.—Real Property

Description and location of all real property in which debtor has an interest [including equitable and future interests, interests in estates by the entirety, community property, life estates, leaseholds, and rights and powers exercisable for the debtor's own benefit]	Nature of interest [specify all deeds and written instruments relating thereto]	Market value of debtor's interest without deduction for secured claims listed in Schedule A–2 or exemptions claimed in Schedule B–4
	Total $_____	

OFFICIAL FORMS **Form 2**

Schedule B–2. —Personal Property

Type of Property	Description and Location	Market value of debtor's interest without deduction for secured claims listed on Schedule A–2 or exemptions claimed in Schedule B–4 Total $_____
a.	Cash on hand	$_____
b.	Deposits of money with banking institutions, savings and loan associations, brokerage houses, credit unions, public utility companies, landlords and others	_____
c.	Household goods, supplies and furnishings	_____
d.	Books, pictures, and other art objects; stamp, coin and other collections	_____
e.	Wearing apparel, jewelry, firearms, sports equipment, and other personal possessions	_____
f.	Automobiles, trucks, trailers and other vehicles	_____
g.	Boats, motors and their accessories	_____
h.	Livestock, poultry and other animals	_____
i.	Farming equipment, supplies and implements	_____
j.	Office equipment, furnishings and supplies	_____
k.	Machinery, fixtures, equipment and supplies [other than those listed in Items j and l] used in business	_____
l.	Inventory	_____
m.	Tangible personal property of any other description	_____
n.	Patents, copyrights, licenses, franchises and other general intangibles [specify all documents and writings relating thereto]	_____
o.	Government and corporate bonds and other negotiable and nonnegotiable instruments	_____
p.	Other liquidated debts owing debtor	_____
q.	Contingent and unliquidated claims of every nature, including counterclaims of the debtor [give estimated value of each]	_____
r.	Interests in insurance policies [name insurance company of each policy and itemize surrender or refund value of each]	_____
s.	Annuities [itemize and name each issuer]	_____
t.	Stock and interests in incorporated and unincorporated companies [itemize separately]	_____
u.	Interests in partnerships	_____
v.	Equitable and future interests, life estates, and rights or powers exercisable for the benefit of the debtor (other than those listed in Schedule B–1) [specify all written instruments relating thereto] Total	$_____

Form 2   OFFICIAL FORMS

Schedule B–3. — Property not otherwise scheduled

Type of Property	Description and Location	Market value of Debtor's interest without deduction for secured claims listed in Schedule A–2 or exemption claimed in Schedule B-4
a. Property transferred under assignment for benefit of creditors, withing 120 days prior to filing of petition [specify date of assignment, name and address of assignee, amount realized therefrom by the assignee, and disposition of proceeds so far as known to debtor]		$_____
b. Property of any kind not otherwise scheduled		_____
	Total	$_____

Debtor selects the following property as exempt pursuant to 11 U.S.C. § 522(d) [*or* the laws of the State of _____ .]

Schedule B–4. — Property claimed as exempt

Type of Property	Location, description, and, so far as relevant to the claim of exemption, present use of property	Specify statute creating the exemption	Value claimed exempt
			$_____
		Total	$_____

Summary of debts and property.

[From the statments of the debtor in Schedules A and B]

Schedule		Total
	Debts	
A–1/ a,b	Wages, etc. having priority	$_____
A–1(c)	Deposits of money	_____
A–1/ d(1)	Taxes owing United States	_____
A–1/ d(2)	Taxes owing states	_____

OFFICIAL FORMS   **Form 2**

<u>Debts</u>

A–1/d(3)	Taxes owing other taxing authorities	$_____
A–2	Secured claims	_____
A–3	Unsecured claims without priority	_____
	Schedule A total	$_____

<u>Property</u>

B–1	Real property [total value]	$_____
B–2/a	Cash on hand	_____
B–2/b	Deposits	_____
B–2/c	Household goods	_____
B–2/d	Books, pictures, and collections	_____
B–2/e	Wearing apparel and personal possessions	_____
B–2/f	Automobiles and other vehicles	_____
B–2/g	Boats, motors, and accessories	_____
B–2/h	Livestock and other animals	_____
B–2/i	Farming supplies and implements	_____
B–2/j	Office equipment and supplies	_____
B–2/k	Machinery, equipment, and supplies used in business	_____
B–2/l	Inventory	_____
B–2/m	Other tangible personal property	_____
B–2/n	Patents and other general intangibles	_____
B–2/o	Bonds and other instruments	_____
B–2/p	Other liquidated debts	_____
B–2/q	Contingent and unliquidated claims	_____
B–2/r	Interests in insurance policies	_____
B–2/s	Annuities	_____
B–2/t	Interests in corporations and unincorporated companies	_____
B–2/u	Interests in partnerships	_____
B–2/v	Equitable and future interests, rights, and powers in personalty	_____
B–3/a	Property assigned for benefit of creditors	_____
B–3/b	Property not otherwise scheduled	_____
	Schedule B total	$_____

UNSWORN DECLARATION UNDER PENALTY
OF PERJURY OF INDIVIDUAL TO
SCHEDULES A AND B

I, _____, declare under penalty of perjury that I have read the foregoing schedules, consisting of __ sheets, and that they are true and correct to the best of my knowledge, information and belief.

Executed on _____.

Signature: _____

Form 2   OFFICIAL FORMS

UNSWORN DECLARATION UNDER PENALTY OF PERJURY ON BEHALF OF CORPORATION OR PARTNERSHIP TO SCHEDULES A AND B

I, _____, [the president *or other officer* or an authorized agent of the corporation] [*or* a member *or* an authorized agent of the partnership] named as debtor in this case, declare under penalty of perjury that I have read the foregoing schedules, consisting of ____ sheets, and that they are true and correct to the best of my knowledge, information, and belief.

Executed on _____.

Signature: _____

Amended eff. Sept. 19, 1986.

OFFICIAL FORMS   **Form 3**
Form No. 3
STATEMENT OF FINANCIAL AFFAIRS FOR
DEBTOR ENGAGED IN BUSINESS

[Each question shall be answered or the failure to answer explained. If the answer is "none" or "not applicable," so state. If additional space is needed for the answer to any question, a separate sheet properly identified and made a part hereof, should be used and attached.

If the debtor is a partnership or a corporation, the questions shall be deemed to be addressed to, and shall be answered on behalf of, the partnership or corporation; and the statement shall be certified by a member of the partnership or by a duly authorized officer of the corporation.

The term, "original petition," used in the following questions, shall mean the petition filed under Rule 1002 or 1004.]

1. **Nature, location, and name of business.**
    a. Under what name and where do you carry on your business?
    b. In what business are you engaged? (If business operations have been terminated, give the date of termination.)
    c. When did you commence the business?
    d. Where else, and under what other names, have you carried on business within the six years immediately preceding the filing of the original petition herein? (Give street addresses, the names of any partners, joint adventurers, or other associates, the nature of the business, and the periods for which it was carried on.)
2. **Books and records.**
    a. By whom, or under whose supervision, have your books of account and records been kept during the six years immediately preceding the filing of the original petition herein? (Give names, addresses, and periods of time.)
    b. By whom have your books of account and records been audited during the six years immediately preceding the filing of the original petition herein? (Give names, address, and dates of audits.)
    c. In whose possession are your books of account and records? (Give names and addresses.)
    d. If any of these books or records are not available, explain.
    e. Have any books of account or records relating to your affairs been destroyed, lost, or otherwise disposed of within the two years immediately preceding the filing of the original petition herein? (If so, give particulars, including date of destruction, loss, or disposition, and reason therefor.)

Form 3   OFFICIAL FORMS

3. Financial statements.
Have you issued any written financial statements within the two years immediately preceding the filing of the original petition herein? (Give dates, and the names and addresses of the persons to whom issued, including mercantile and trade agencies.)

4. Inventories.
   a. When was the last inventory of your property taken?
   b. By whom, or under whose supervision, was this inventory taken?
   c. What was the amount, in dollars, of the inventory? (State whether the inventory was taken at cost, market, or otherwise.)
   d. When was the next prior inventory of your property taken?
   e. By whom, or under whose supervision, was this inventory taken?
   f. What was the amount, in dollars, of the inventory? (State whether the inventory was taken at cost, market, or otherwise.)
   g. In whose possession are the records of the two inventories above referred to? (Give names and addresses.)

5. Income other than from operation of business.
What amount of income, other than from operation of your business, have you received during each of the two years immediately preceding the filing of the original petition herein? (Give particulars, including each source, and the amount received therefrom.)

6. Tax returns and refunds.
   a. In whose possession are copies of your federal, state and municipal income tax returns for the three years immediately preceding the filing of the original petition herein?
   b. What tax refunds (income or other) have you received during the two years immediately preceding the filing of the original petition herein?
   c. To what tax refunds (income or other), if any, are you, or may you be, entitled? (Give particulars, including information as to any refund payable jointly to you and your spouse or any other person.)

7. Financial accounts, certificates of deposit and safe deposit boxes.
   a. What accounts or certificates of deposit or shares in banks, savings and loan, thrift, building and loan and homestead associations, credit unions, brokerage houses, pension funds and the like have you maintained, alone or together with any other person, and in your own or any other name, within the two years immediately preceding the filing of the original petition herein? (Give the name and address of each institution, the name and number under which the account or certificate is maintained, and the name and address of every person authorized to make withdrawals from such account.)

OFFICIAL FORMS **Form 3**

b. What safe deposit box or boxes or other depository or depositories have you kept or used for your securities, cash, or other valuables within the two years immediately preceding the filing of the original petition herein? (Give the name and address of the bank or other depository, the name in which each box or other depository was kept, the name and address of every person who had the right of access thereto, a description of the contents thereof, and, if the box has been surrendered, state when surrendered or, if transferred, when transferred and the name and address of the transferee.)

8. **Property held for another person.**

What property do you hold for any other person? (Give name and address of each person, and describe the property, the amount or value thereof and all writings relating thereto.)

9. **Property held by another person.**

Is any other person holding anything of value in which you have an interest? (Give name and address, location and description of the property, and circumstances of the holding.)

10. **Prior bankruptcy proceedings.**

What cases under the Bankruptcy Act or title 11, United States Code have previously been brought by or against you? (State the location of the bankruptcy court, the nature and number of the case, and whether a discharge was granted or denied, the case was dismissed, or a composition, arrangement, or plan was confirmed.)

11. **Receiverships, general assignments, and other modes of liquidation.**

    a. Was any of your property, at the time of the filing of the original petition herein, in the hands of a receiver, trustee, or other liquidating agent? (If so, give a brief description of the property and the name and address of the receiver, trustee, or other agent, and, if the agent was appointed in a court proceeding, the name and location of the court, the title and number of the case, and the nature thereof.)

    b. Have you made any assignment of your property for the benefit of your creditors, or any general settlement with your creditors, within the two years immediately preceding the filing of the original petition herein? (If so, give dates, the name and address of the assignee, and a brief statement of the terms of assignment or settlement.)

12. **Suits, executions, and attachments.**

    a. Were you a party to any suit pending at the time of the filing of the original petition herein? (If so, give the name and location of the court and the title and nature of the proceeding.)

Form 3   OFFICIAL FORMS

    b. Were you a party to any suit terminated within the year imme-
diately preceding the filing of the original petition herein? (If so,
give the name and location of the court, the title and nature of the
proceeding, and the result.)

    c. Has any of your property been attached, garnished, or seized
under any legal or equitable process within the year immediately
preceding the filing of the original petition herein? (If so, describe
the property seized or person garnished, and at whose suit.)

13.   **a. Payments of loans, installment purchases and other debts.**
What payments in whole or in part have you made during the year
immediately preceding the filing of the original petition herein
on any of the following: (1) loans; (2) installment purchases of
goods and services; and (3) other debts? (Give the names and
addresses of the persons receiving payment, the amounts of the
loans or other debts and of the purchase price of the goods and
services, the dates of the original transactions, the amounts and
dates of payments, and, if any of the payees are your relatives or
insiders, the relationship; if the debtor is a partnership and any of
the payees is or was a partner or a relative of a partner, state the
relationship; if the debtor is a corporation and any of the payees
is or was an officer, director, or stockholder, or a relative of an
officer, director, or stockholder, state the relationship.)

    b. Setoffs.
What debts have you owed to any creditor, including any bank,
which were set off by that creditor against a debt or deposit owing by the creditor to you during the year immediately preceding
the filing of the original petition herein? (Give the names and addresses of the persons setting off such debts, the dates of the
setoffs, the amounts of the debts owing by you and to you and, if
any of the creditors are your relatives or insiders, the relationship.)

14. Transfers of property.
    a. Have you made any gifts, other than ordinary and usual presents
to family members and charitable donations during the year immediately preceding the filing of the original petition herein? (If
so, give names and addresses of donees and dates, description,
and value of gifts.)

    b. Have you made any other transfer, absolute or for the purpose
of security, or any other disposition which was not in the ordinary course of business during the year immediately preceding
the filing of the original petition herein? (Give a description of the
property, the date of the transfer or disposition, to whom transferred or how disposed of, and state whether the transferee is a

relative, partner, shareholder, officer, director, or insider, the consideration, if any, received for the property, and the disposition of such consideration.)

15. **Accounts and other receivables.**
   Have you assigned, either absolutely or as security, any of your accounts or other receivables during the year immediately preceding the filing of the original petition herein? (If so, give names and addresses of assignees.)

16. **Repossessions and returns.**
   Has any property been returned to, or repossessed by, the seller, lessor, or a secured party during the year immediately preceding the filing of the original petition herein? (If so, give particulars, including the name and address of the party getting the property and its description and value.)

17. **Business leases.**
   If you are a tenant of business property, what is the name and address of your landlord, the amount of your rental, the date to which rent had been paid at the time of the filing of the original petition herein, and the amount of security held by the landlord?

18. **Losses.**
   a. Have you suffered any losses from fire, theft, or gambling during the year immediately preceding the filing of the original petition herein? (If so, give particulars, including dates, names, and places, and the amounts of money or value and general description of property lost.)
   b. Was the loss covered in whole or part by insurance? (If so, give particulars.)

19. **Withdrawals.**
   a. If you are an individual proprietor of your business, what personal withdrawals of any kind have you made from the business during the year immediately preceding the filing of the original petition herein?
   b. If the debtor is a partnership or corporation, what withdrawals, in any form (including compensation, bonuses or loans), have been made or received by any member of the partnership, or by any officer, director, insider, managing executive, or shareholder of the corporation, during the year immediately preceding the filing of the original petition herein? (Give the name and designation or relationship to the debtor of each person, the dates and amounts of withdrawals, and the nature of purpose thereof.)

20. **Payments or transfers to attorneys and other persons.**
   a. Have you consulted an attorney during the year immediately

Form 3   OFFICIAL FORMS

preceding or since the filing of the original petition herein? (Give date, name, and address.)

b. Have you during the year immediately preceding or since the filing of the original petition herein paid any money or transferred any property to the attorney, to any other person on the attorney's behalf, or to any other person rendering services to you in connection with this case? (If so, give particulars, including amount paid or value of property transferred and date of payment or transfer.)

c. Have you, either during the year immediately preceding or since the filing of the original petition herein, agreed to pay any money or transfer any property to an attorney at law, to any other person on the attorney's behalf, or to any other person rendering services to you in connection with this case? (If so, give particulars, including amount and terms of obligation.)

(If the debtor is a partnership or corporation, the following additional questions should be answered.)

21. **Members of partnership; officers, directors, managers, and principal stockholders of corporation.**

a. What is the name and address of each member of the partnership, or the name, title, and address of each officer, director, insider, and managing executive, and of each stockholder holding 20 percent or more of the issued and outstanding stock, of the corporation?

b. During the year immediately preceding the filing of the original petition herein, has any member withdrawn from the partnership, or any officer, director, insider, or managing executive of the corporation terminated his relationship, or any stockholder holding 20 percent or more of the issued stock disposed of more than 50 percent of the stockholder's holdings? (If so, give name and address and reason for withdrawal, termination, or disposition, if known.)

c. Has any person acquired or disposed of 20 percent or more of the stock of the corporation during the year immediately preceding the filing of the petition? (If so, give name and address and particulars.)

I, _____, declare under penalty of perjury that I have read the answers contained in the foregoing statement of affairs and that they are true and correct to the best of my knowledge, information, and belief. Executed on _____.

Signature: _____

[Person declaring for partnership or corporation should indicate position or relationship to debtor.]

Amended eff. Sept. 19, 1986; eff. Aug. 1, 1987.

OFFICIAL FORMS **Form 4**

Form No. 4
LIST OF CREDITORS HOLDING 20 LARGEST UNSECURED CLAIMS

[Caption as in Form No. 2]

Following is the list of the Debtor's creditors holding the 20 largest unsecured claims which is prepared in accordance with Rule 1007(d) for filing in this chapter 11 [*or* chapter 9] case. The list does not include those (1) persons who come within the definition of insider set forth in 11 U.S.C. § 101(25), (2) secured creditors unless the value of the collateral is such that the unsecured deficiency places the creditor among the holders of the 20 largest unsecured claims, or (3) governmental units not within the definition of "person" in 11 U.S.C. § 101(35).

(1)	(2)	(3)	(4)	(5)
Name of creditor and complete mailing address including zip code	Name, telephone number and complete mailing address including zip code of employee, agent or department of creditor familiar with claim who may be contacted	Nature of claim (trade debt, bank loan, type of judgment, etc.)	Indicate if claim is contingent, unliquidated, disputed or subject to setoff	Amount of claim [if secured also state value of security]

Date: _____.

_____

Debtor.

Glossary

Automatic Stay: A court order that goes into effect when a bankruptcy petition is filed. An automatic stay prohibits collection action against a debtor. It effects a broad range of activities against the debtor, property of the debtor, and property of the bankruptcy estate. The automatic stay is lifted when a bankruptcy case is closed or the debtor is discharged.

Bankruptcy: A term implying that a firm has been admitted to a legal proceeding under the Bankruptcy Reform Act of 1978, its assets are under the control of the bankruptcy court, and it will be either liquidated or reorganized. Bankruptcy may be initiated by the debtor (voluntary) or by creditors (involuntary).

Bar Date: The last date on which a creditor may make a claim against a debtor by filing it with the clerk of the bankruptcy court; claims not filed by the bar date are not enforceable.

Bond Covenants: Restrictions contained in the bond indenture limiting the actions of the issuer.

Bond Indenture: That portion of a bond describing the rights of the bondholder and the obligations of the issuer.

Composition: A settlement under which the creditors of a firm that cannot meet its obligations agree to accept a reduced percentage payment and absolve the debtor of the remaining debt.

Confirmation: A court order implementing the conditions and terms of a chapter 11 plan. It usually results in the discharge of the debtor.

Cramdown: The confirmation of a plan to reorganize over the objection of a creditor or class of creditors.

Debtors in Possession (DIP): A chapter 11 debtor that remains in possession of its property and continues to operate its business.

Defaulted Bond Index: (Altman-Merrill Index): The index measures the investment performance of the defaulted bond sector and includes all public non-convertible issues of corporations which have defaulted on interest or principal or which have filed for bankruptcy. The index is constructed by weighing the bond prices, as a percent of par, by the face amount of the issue outstanding. Prices are obtained from the S & P *Bond Guide*. The index for December 1986 is taken as 100. The index is compiled by Merrill Lynch.

Discharge: The relief of all dischargeable debt incurred prior to filing for bankruptcy.

Exclusive Period: The first 120-day period during which the chapter 11 debtor has the exclusive right to file a plan of reorganization.

Extension: An arrangement under which the creditors of a firm that cannot meet its financial obligations agree to a postponement or extension of maturity of debt obligations.

Fallen Angels: Investment-grade bonds that have become junk or defaulted bonds.

Flat: A bond that trades without accrued interest added to the price. Generally bonds in default trade flat.

Foreclosure: Sale of real property in order to collect a debt.

Fraudulent Transfer: A transfer (conveyance) of property where the object is to defraud a creditor or put a property beyond the reach of the creditor. If intent cannot be shown, the following may suffice if within one year before the date of filing.

- The debtor was or became insolvent because of the transfer
- The debtor received unreasonably small value for the exchange
- As a result of the transfer, the debtor had unreasonably small capital for the conduct of the business

Such transfers may be invalidated by the trustees.

Funded Debt: The long-term debt obligations of a company, including bonds and bank loans.

Index of Bankrupt Stocks (Quintero Index): This index measures the aggregate daily price fluctuations of all actively traded common stock of US bankrupt companies. This index is composed by forming the price ratios for each stock (obtained by dividing the closing price by the previous day's closing price) and then taking the geometric mean of the price ratios so obtained. The index is compiled by R.G. Quintero & Co.

Leverage: Pertaining to the use of debt.

Lien: A claim on property providing the right to seize and sell the property if a default occurs in an obligation, such as the repayment of a debt.

Leveraged Buyout (LBO): A purchase of a company's stock with borrowed money secured by the assets of the firm being acquired. Often a leveraged buyout is consummated by managers of the firm or a small group of investors.

Net Worth (Book Value): Assets of a firm less liabilities and preferred stock.

Paid-in-Kind Bonds (PIK): Bonds that pay interest in the form of more bonds (or other debt) instead of cash. They become convertible into cash at a specified date.

Poison pill: An arrangement under which the current shareholders can purchase additional shares of a corporation's stock at an extremely low price.

This device may be used in an effort to fend off a hostile takeover attempt because it dilutes the value and voting power of shares held by or tendered to the acquiring firm.

Preferences: Transfer of assets to creditors that may be invalidated under the Bankruptcy Code, provided that

- There is a larger payment than would be due in a liquidation.
- The debtor is insolvent.
- It occurs within 90 days of bankruptcy or within one year if involving an insider.
- It is a secured claim not based on a loan or trade credit made within 90 days of bankruptcy filing. Such preferences can be downgraded to an unsecured claim.

Reset Bonds: Bonds for which the issuer promises to reset the interest rate by a specified date so that the bonds trade at or near par.

Reverse split: When a company is reorganized, shareholders often are asked to accept a reverse stock split in which they receive fewer shares in the reorganized firm than they held in the old firm. They may be asked, for example, to give up 50 old shares for 10 new ones.

Trustee: A person having no previous connection with a debtor who is appointed to administer the debtor's assets.

U.S. Trustee: An employee of the U.S. government who has the responsibility of holding the initial meeting of the creditors and appointing members of the various creditors' committees. The U.S. Trustee should not be confused with the trustee defined above.

Voidable Transfer: Invalid transfer of assets that may be nullified under the Bankruptcy Code; for example, fraudulent transfers or preferences.

Zero Coupon Bonds: Bonds that do not pay semiannual interest but that do provide investors with a return when the bonds mature.

INDEX